토익
한번에
끝내기
RC

토익 한 번에 끝내기 RC 신토익 개정판

지은이 플랜티 어학연구소
펴낸이 임상진
펴낸곳 (주)넥서스

초판 1쇄 발행 2015년 1월 15일
초판 3쇄 발행 2016년 1월 10일

2판 1쇄 발행 2016년 7월 20일
2판 8쇄 발행 2019년 8월 22일

출판신고 1992년 4월 3일 제311-2002-2호
10880 경기도 파주시 지목로 5
Tel (02)330-5500 Fax (02)330-5555

ISBN 979-11-5752-884-4 13740

저자와 출판사의 허락 없이 내용의 일부를
인용하거나 발췌하는 것을 금합니다.

가격은 뒤표지에 있습니다.
잘못 만들어진 책은 구입처에서 바꾸어 드립니다.

www.nexusbook.com

TOEIC 신유형 개정판

20일 만에 끝내는
가장 빠른
토익 솔루션

플랜티 어학연구소 지음

토익 한번에 끝내기 RC

넥서스

PREFACE | 머리말

토익! 지금도 너무나 많은 교재가 매월 출간되고 잊혀집니다.

토익 시험을 분석하고 대비하는 교재라고는 하지만, 준비하는 수험생에 맞추기보다는 저자나 강사의 일방적인 이론과 검증되지 않는 비법과 전략을 강요하고 있는 게 현실입니다. 토익 교재의 콘텐츠도 이를 공부하는 수험생의 상황과 그때의 경향에 따라 변해야 합니다. 시간이 지나도 내 것이 되지 않는 백과사전식의 나열식 구성보다는 단기간에 토익 공부를 끝내길 원하는 수험생들의 요구에 맞추어 중도에 포기하지 않도록 20일 안에 각 파트별로 문제에 접근하는 최소한의 전략과 비법을 숙지하고 바로 문제에 적용하는 훈련을 통해 불필요한 이론 학습에 들이는 시간을 줄이며 원하는 점수 달성에 최종 목표를 두었습니다.

본 교재는 20일, 700점 이상 점수 달성을 위한 이론과 내용만 담았습니다.
700점 이상이 목표라면 매월 80% 정도 중복으로 출제되는 부분만 확실히 숙지해도 중급 이상의 점수 획득이 가능합니다. 그동안 초중급자임에도 모든 내용을 숙지하기 위해 불필요한 시간을 소비하고 있었다면 이 책이 당신에게 최적의 교재입니다.

매일매일 제시된 이론을 학습한 후 바로 복습하고 실전 활용하는 3단계로 구성했습니다.
교재를 완전히 습득하기 위한 전체 20일 구성으로, 하루하루 정해진 시간과 절차에 맞추어 학습하면 중도에 포기하지 않고 하루 4~5시간, 월 80시간 정도의 학습량만으로 700점 이상을 달성할 수 있도록 구성되어 있습니다.

최근 3년간 토익 출제 경향을 완벽히 분석하여 반영했습니다.
교재의 출간을 위해 매월 시험을 분석하였고, 이런 과정을 통해 개발한 문제를 1,000명이 넘는 학생들이 직접 풀어보고 피드백에 참여하였습니다. 무조건적으로 암기하지 마세요. 이론은 시험에 꼭 나오는 유형과 경향만 최소한으로 파악하면 되고 직접 문제로 들어가는 것이 장기 학습자가 되지 않는 비결입니다.

이제 토익을 시작하는 초보자부터 매월 중도에 학습을 포기하는 학습자, 토익 시험을 목전에 두어 당장 실전 문제를 여러 차례 풀어 봐야 하는 수험생까지 단 20일 만에 이 모든 과정을 끝내기를 원하는 모두에게 최고의 교재라고 자부할 수 있습니다.

CONTENTS | 목차

머리말	5
구성과 특징	10
신토익 구성과 핵심 정보	12

SECTION 1
영역별 집중 분석

Grammar

Day 01	주어 • 동사	16
Day 02	목적어 • 보어 • 수식어	20
Day 03	명사	24
Day 04	대명사	29
Day 05	형용사	34
Day 06	부사	40
Day 07	전치사	45
Day 08	동사의 종류와 형태	50
Day 09	수 일치	55
Day 10	태	60
Day 11	시제	65
Day 12	부정사	69
Day 13	동명사	74
Day 14	분사	79
Day 15	접속사	83
Day 16	관계사	87
Day 17	명사절 접속사	92
Day 18	부사절 접속사	97
Day 19	비교급과 최상급	101
Day 20	가정법과 도치	105

Reading

Day 01	주제 · 목적 문제	110
Day 02	육하원칙 문제	113
Day 03	일치 · 불일치 문제	116
Day 04	추론 문제	119
Day 05	동의어 문제	122

Day 06	편지/이메일	125
Day 07	제품 광고	128
Day 08	구인 공고	131
Day 09	공지, 안내, 정보	134
Day 10	기사	137
Day 11	양식 및 기타 지문	140
Day 12	연계 문제	143
Day 13	문장 삽입	148
Day 14	의도 파악	150
Day 15	삼중 지문	153
Day 16	독해 유형 연습 1	158
Day 17	독해 유형 연습 2	161
Day 18	독해 유형 연습 3	163
Day 19	독해 유형 연습 4	167
Day 20	독해 유형 연습 5	169

SECTION 2 영역별 실전 연습

Part 5·6 유형 연습

Day 01	연습 문제 1	176
Day 02	연습 문제 2	178
Day 03	연습 문제 3	180
Day 04	연습 문제 4	182
Day 05	연습 문제 5	184
Day 06	연습 문제 6	186
Day 07	연습 문제 7	188
Day 08	연습 문제 8	190
Day 09	연습 문제 9	192
Day 10	연습 문제 10	194
Day 11	연습 문제 11	196
Day 12	연습 문제 12	198
Day 13	연습 문제 13	200
Day 14	연습 문제 14	202
Day 15	연습 문제 15	204
Day 16	연습 문제 16	206
Day 17	연습 문제 17	208
Day 18	연습 문제 18	210
Day 19	연습 문제 19	212
Day 20	연습 문제 20	214

CONTENTS | 목차

실전 랜덤 연습

Day 01	연습 문제 1	218
Day 02	연습 문제 2	220
Day 03	연습 문제 3	222
Day 04	연습 문제 4	224
Day 05	연습 문제 5	226
Day 06	연습 문제 6	228
Day 07	연습 문제 7	230
Day 08	연습 문제 8	232
Day 09	연습 문제 9	234
Day 10	연습 문제 10	236
Day 11	연습 문제 11	238
Day 12	연습 문제 12	240
Day 13	연습 문제 13	242
Day 14	연습 문제 14	244
Day 15	연습 문제 15	246
Day 16	연습 문제 16	248
Day 17	연습 문제 17	250
Day 18	연습 문제 18	252
Day 19	연습 문제 19	254
Day 20	연습 문제 20	256

어휘 집중 연습

Day 01	연습 문제 1	260
Day 02	연습 문제 2	262
Day 03	연습 문제 3	264
Day 04	연습 문제 4	266
Day 05	연습 문제 5	268
Day 06	연습 문제 6	270
Day 07	연습 문제 7	272
Day 08	연습 문제 8	274
Day 09	연습 문제 9	276
Day 10	연습 문제 10	278
Day 11	연습 문제 11	280
Day 12	연습 문제 12	282
Day 13	연습 문제 13	284
Day 14	연습 문제 14	286

Day 15	연습 문제 15	288
Day 16	연습 문제 16	290
Day 17	연습 문제 17	292
Day 18	연습 문제 18	294
Day 19	연습 문제 19	296
Day 20	연습 문제 20	298

독해 집중 연습

Day 01	연습 문제 1	302
Day 02	연습 문제 2	304
Day 03	연습 문제 3	306
Day 04	연습 문제 4	308
Day 05	연습 문제 5	310
Day 06	연습 문제 6	312
Day 07	연습 문제 7	314
Day 08	연습 문제 8	316
Day 09	연습 문제 9	318
Day 10	연습 문제 10	320
Day 11	연습 문제 11	322
Day 12	연습 문제 12	324
Day 13	연습 문제 13	326
Day 14	연습 문제 14	328
Day 15	연습 문제 15	330
Day 16	연습 문제 16	332
Day 17	연습 문제 17	334
Day 18	연습 문제 18	336
Day 19	연습 문제 19	338
Day 20	연습 문제 20	340

SECTION 3
Actual Test

Actual Test 342

별책부록_ 정답 + 해석 + 해설

FEATURES | 구성과 특징

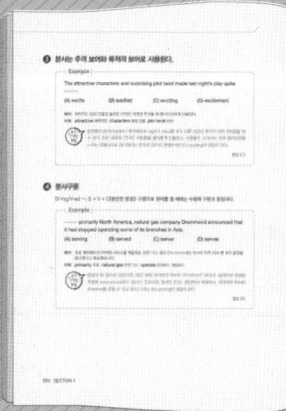
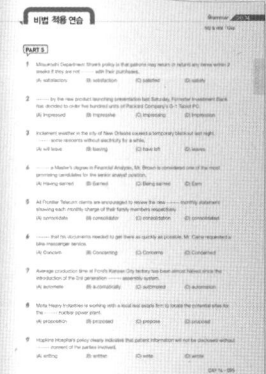

단 20일 만에 유형과 전략을 완벽하게 파악하는 토익 RC 비법

문법 및 독해 영역의 핵심 포인트를 예제와 함께 짚어 가며 분석하여 철저한 전략 학습이 가능하다.

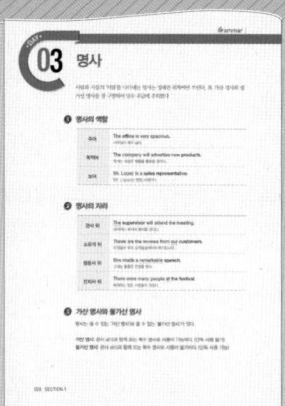
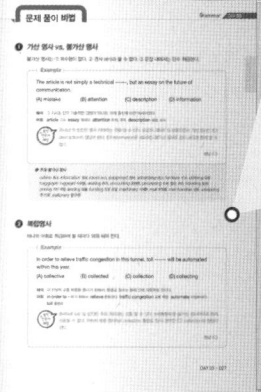

현장의 노하우가 생생하게 살아 있는 토익 전문가 해설

각 파트의 문제 풀이 핵심과 오답 함정을 피하는 노하우만을 정확하게 분석한 토익 전문가의 해설로 꼼꼼하게 오답에 대비한다.

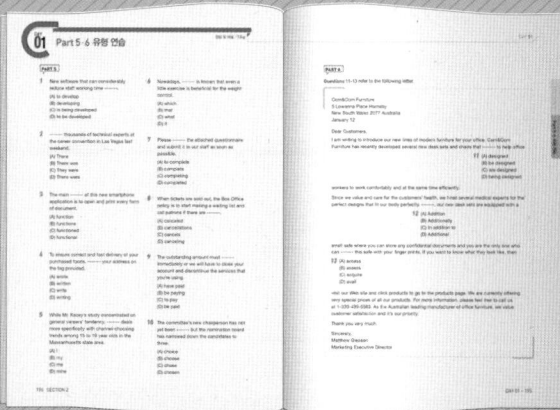

단 20일 동안의 실전 감각 집중 훈련 4종

실제 토익 시험을 보지 않고도 영역별 실전 감각을 극대화할 수 있는 문법, 어휘, 독해 집중 훈련 4종 세트

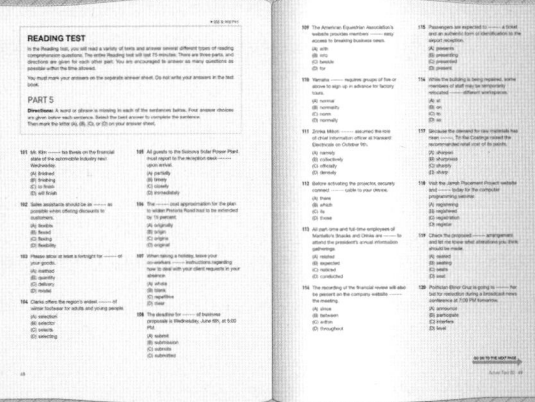

실제 정기 시험과 가장 가까운 Actual Test

최신 출제 경향을 정확하게 반영한 Actual Test로 시험 직전 실전 대비 자신감을 키운다.

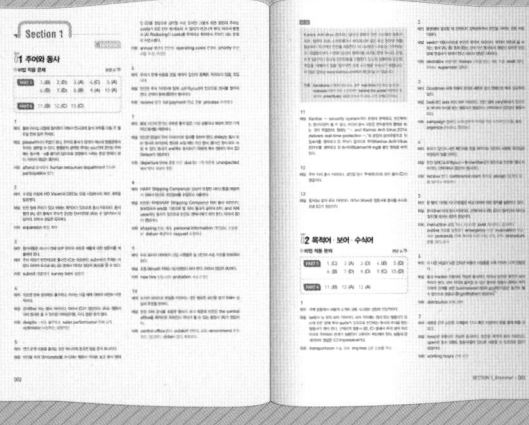

모든 문제의 상세한 정답+번역+해설+어휘

모든 문제에 대한 상세하고 친절한 해석+해설+어휘 정리를 통해 이 책만으로 완벽하게 마무리한다.

신토익 구성과 핵심 정보

TOEIC®은 Test of English for International Communication의 약자로 영어가 모국어가 아닌 사람들을 대상으로 언어 본래의 기능인 '커뮤니케이션' 능력에 중점을 두고 일상생활 또는 국제 업무 등에 필요한 실용영어 능력을 평가하는 시험이다.

» 출제 분야

TOEIC은 일상생활과 비즈니스 현장에서 필요한 영어 능력을 측정하는 실용영어 평가 시험이다. 따라서 일상생활과 비즈니스 현장에서 자주 사용되는 말들이 TOEIC 문제로 출제된다. 이외 전 세계 모든 응시자에 대한 타당한 시험이 될 수 있도록 다음과 같은 기준을 적용하고 있다.

1. 어휘, 문법, 관용어 중에서 미국 영어에만 쓰이는 특정한 것은 피한다.
2. 특정 문화에만 해당되거나 일부 문화권의 응시자에게 생소할 수 있는 상황은 피한다.
3. 여러 나라 사람의 이름을 고르게 등장시킨다.
4. 특정 직업 분야에만 해당되는 상황은 피한다.
5. 다양한 문화와 성에 대한 편견이 없도록 유의한다.
6. 듣기 평가에서는 다양한 국가(주로 미국, 영국, 호주)의 발음 및 악센트가 출제된다.

» 신토익 시험의 구성

구성	Part	Part별 내용	문항 수	시간	배점
Listening Comprehension	1	사진 묘사	6	45분	495점
	2	질의 응답	25		
	3	짧은 대화	39		
	4	설명문	30		
Reading Comprehension	5	단문 공란 채우기	30	75분	495점
	6	장문 공란 채우기	16		
	7	단일 지문	29		
		이중 지문	10		
		삼중 지문	15		
Total	7 Parts		200문제	120분	990점

» 신토익 핵심 정보

Part 3	화자의 의도 파악 문제	2~3문항	• 대화문에서 화자가 한 말의 의도를 묻는 유형
	시각 정보 연계 문제	2~3문항	• 대화문과 시각 정보(도표, 그래픽 등)간 연관 관계를 파악하는 유형
	3인 대화	대화 지문 1~2개	• 일부 대화문에서 세 명 이상의 화자가 등장함
	5턴 이상의 대화		• 주고 받는 대화가 5턴 이상으로 늘어난 대화 유형 추가

Part 4	화자의 의도 파악 문제	2~3문항	• 담화문에서 화자가 한 말의 의도를 묻는 유형
	시각 정보 연계 문제	2~3문항	• 담화문과 시각 정보(도표, 그래픽 등)간 연관 관계를 파악하는 유형

Part 6	알맞은 문장 고르기	4문항 (지문당 1문항)	• 지문의 흐름상 빈칸에 들어갈 알맞은 문장 고르기 • 선택지가 모두 문장으로 제시되며 문맥 파악이 필수

Part 7	문장 삽입 문제	2문항 (지문당 1문항)	• 지문 흐름상 주어진 문장을 삽입할 수 있는 적절한 위치 고르기
	문자 메시지·온라인 채팅	각각 지문 1개	• 2명이 대화하는 문자 메시지, 다수가 참여하는 온라인 채팅
	의도 파악 문제	2문항 (지문당 1문항)	• 화자가 말한 말의 의도를 묻는 문제 • 문자 메시지, 온라인 채팅 지문에서 출제
	삼중 지문	지문 3개	• 세 개의 연계 지문에 대한 이해도를 묻는 문제

SECTION 1
영역별 집중 분석

Grammar

Day 01	주어·동사	16
Day 02	목적어·보어·수식어	20
Day 03	명사	24
Day 04	대명사	29
Day 05	형용사	34
Day 06	부사	40
Day 07	전치사	45
Day 08	동사의 종류와 형태	50
Day 09	수 일치	55
Day 10	태	60
Day 11	시제	65
Day 12	부정사	69
Day 13	동명사	74
Day 14	분사	79
Day 15	접속사	83
Day 16	관계사	87
Day 17	명사절 접속사	92
Day 18	부사절 접속사	97
Day 19	비교급과 최상급	101
Day 20	가정법과 도치	105

주어 · 동사

❶ 문장이란?

- 문장은 주어와 동사로 이루어져 있다.
- 영어는 위치가 중요한 언어로 반드시 〈주어+동사〉의 순서를 지킨다.
- 주어·동사를 구성할 때, 주어의 수에 따른 동사의 수를 반드시 일치시킨다.

주어가 될 수 있는 것은 다음과 같다.

명사	**James** will attend the meeting. James는/ 참석할 것이다/ 회의에
대명사	**He** is my coworker. 그는/ 나의 직장 동료다
동명사	**Achieving goals** is our priority. 목표를 달성하는 것은/ 우리의 최우선이다
to부정사	**To get enough sleep** is very important. 잠을 충분히 자는 것은/ 매우/ 중요하다
명사절	**That we need more staff** is true. 우리가 직원이 더 필요하다는 것은/ 사실이다

❷ 동사의 종류

(1) be동사

be동사(am/are/is, was/were)는 주어의 '상태'를 설명하며, 형용사나 명사를 보어로 취한다.

> Kevin is an accountant. Kevin은 회계사이다.
> They are competitive. 그것들은 경쟁력이 있다.

(2) 일반 동사

be동사와 조동사를 제외한 나머지 동사로, 보통 주어의 '행위'를 설명한다.

> The company runs several branches. 그 회사는 몇 개의 지사를 운영하고 있다.

(3) 조동사

'동사원형'과 함께 사용되며, can(~할 수 있다; ~일 수도 있다), may(~해도 된다; ~일지도 모른다), must (~해야 한다; ~임에 틀림없다), will (~할 것이다; ~일 것이다), should(~해야 한다) 등이 있다.

> Mr. Thompson can get a raise. Thompson 씨는 급여 인상을 받을 수 있다.
> He should attend the 4-day seminar. 그는 4일간의 세미나에 참석해야 한다.

문제 풀이 비법

❶ 주어와 동사의 자리 파악

한 문장은 하나의 주어와 하나의 동사로 이루어진다.
주어는 주로 문장의 맨 앞에 위치하며, 주어 다음에는 반드시 동사가 온다.

Example

------ innovative training programs for new employees is needed.

(A) Development   (B) Developing   (C) Developed   (D) Develop

해석 신입사원들을 위한 혁신적인 연수 프로그램을 개발하는 것이 필요하다.
어휘 innovative 혁신적인 training program 연수 프로그램 new employee 신입사원

 빈칸은 문장의 맨 앞, 주어 자리이므로 명사가 들어가야 한다. (A) Development의 경우 명사이기는 하나 영어는 복합명사를 제외하고는 명사를 두 번 연이어 쓰지 않는다. 따라서 training programs를 목적어로 취하면서 명사 역할을 할 수 있는 동명사 (B) Developing이 정답이 된다.

정답 (B)

❷ 주어와 동사의 수/태 파악

- 단수 주어인 경우 '단수 동사'로, 복수 주어인 경우 '복수 동사'로 수 일치를 해야 한다.

  She **has[have]** to make a presentation at the board meeting.
  그녀는 이사회 회의에서 발표를 해야 한다.

  All the members of the library **are[is]** invited to the annual event.
  도서관의 모든 회원들은 연례 행사에 초대된다.

- 동사 뒤 명사는 보어나 목적어이다. 수동태는 보통 목적어가 없다.

  The company **will hold** the award ceremony at TCC Hotel.
  　　　　　　　　능동태　　　　　목적어
  회사는 TCC 호텔에서 시상식을 열 것이다.

  The concert **will be held** outdoors this year.
  　　　　　　　수동태　　　　부사
  올해의 콘서트는 야외에서 열릴 것이다.

| Example |

Recreational facilities 100 meters away from the city hall ------ a swimming pool and a park with a running track and tennis courts.

(A) include   (B) including   (C) are included   (D) includes

해석 시청에서 100미터 떨어져 있는 휴양 시설은 수영장과 육상 트랙이 딸린 공원, 테니스 코트를 포함하고 있다.
어휘 recreational facility 휴양 시설, 오락 시설 swimming pool 수영장

 동사 앞에 있는 명사라고 해서 무조건 주어가 아니다. 동사 앞 '100 meters away from the city hall'이 모두 주어(Recreational facilities)를 꾸며주는 수식어구이다. 따라서 동사인 (A) include가 정답이 된다. (C) are included는 수동태로 뒤에 목적어(a swimming pool ~)를 취할 수 없기 때문에 오답이 된다.

정답 (A)

❸ 주어가 숨어 있는 명령문

명령문은 '동사원형'으로 시작된다.

| Example |

Please ------- an apron with you to the cooking class.

(A) brought   (B) bring   (C) bringing   (D) brings

해석 요리 수업에 앞치마를 가져오시기 바랍니다.
어휘 apron 앞치마 cooking class 요리 강좌

 동사 자리 문제의 경우 〈-ing〉와 〈to부정사〉는 동사가 아니므로 선택지에서 우선 지워내야 한다. 따라서 (C) bringing은 오답이 된다. 문장은 주어 없이 동사원형으로 시작할 수 있는 명령문이므로 (B) bring이 정답이 된다.

정답 (B)

비법 적용 연습

Grammar DAY 01

정답 및 해설 / 2p

PART 5

1. To attend the leadership course this year, please ------- the human resources department of your participation before next Monday.
   (A) to inform   (B) inform   (C) informs   (D) informed

2. On the morning of Wednesday, HD Vision's CEO ------- the expansion plan in the European market.
   (A) announce   (B) to announce   (C) announcement   (D) announced

3. ------- should submit their survey form of the new line of skin-care products before leaving.
   (A) Participants   (B) Participation   (C) Participate   (D) Participating

4. Despite the poor sales performance, the ------- is still optimistic about the next season.
   (A) directive   (B) direct   (C) director   (D) directed

5. ------- annual operating costs is one of the manager's priorities.
   (A) Reducing   (B) Reduce   (C) Reduction   (D) Reduced

6. Until we receive full payment, your ------- will not be processed.
   (A) registered   (B) registration   (C) registers   (D) to register

7. ------- in departure time are largely due to bad weather conditions or unexpected mechanical problems.
   (A) Delaying   (B) Delayed   (C) Delay   (D) Delays

8. HAAY Shipping Company ------- and uses your personal information to deliver the services you have requested.
   (A) to collect   (B) collects   (C) collection   (D) collected

9. Most new hires in our company must ------- one year of probation.
   (A) complete   (B) completes   (C) completion   (D) completed

10. ------- the central office to the outskirts of the city is highly recommended to obtain needed space.
    (A) Relocating   (B) Relocation   (C) Relocate   (D) Relocated

목적어 · 보어 · 수식어

목적어와 보어는 동사 다음에 오는 내용으로 동사의 대상이 되는 말을 '목적어', 주어나 목적어를 보충해 주는 말을 '보어'라고 한다.
또 '수식어'는 꾸며 주는 역할을 하며, 보통 형용사와 부사로 이루어져 있다.

❶ 목적어

목적어는 타동사(동작)의 대상이 되며, 보통 '~을, ~를'로 해석된다.

> The manager will <u>meet</u> **the clients** as soon as possible.
> 매니저는 최대한 빨리 고객들을 만날 것이다.
> Mr. Park <u>deals with</u> **the customers' complaints** effectively.
> Park 씨는 고객의 불만을 효과적으로 다룬다.

❷ 보어

보어는 주어를 보충 설명해 주는 주격 보어와 목적어를 보충 설명해 주는 목적격 보어가 있다. 문장에 부족한 정보를 보충해 주는 역할을 하며 보통 형용사나 명사가 보어가 된다.

> <u>The company leave policy</u> will remain **unchanged**.
> 회사의 휴가 정책은 변경이 없을 것입니다.
> The employees found it **difficult** <u>to finish the report on time</u>.
> 직원들은 보고서를 제시간에 끝내는 것이 어렵다는 것을 알게 되었다.

❸ 수식어

수식어는 꾸며 주는 역할을 하며 영어는 우리말과 달리 뒤에서 앞에 있는 내용을 꾸미는 '후치 수식'이 발달해 있다.

형용사류 수식어: 형용사, 분사(-ing/-ed), 전치사+명사, to부정사, 관계사절
부사류 수식어: 부사, 전치사+명사, to부정사

> One **of the most popular tourist attractions** will be closed **for 2 weeks**.
> 가장 유명한 관광 명소 중 한 곳이 2주간 폐쇄될 것이다.
> Employees are going to gather **in the lobby to have a survey form**.
> 직원들은 설문조사서를 받기 위해 로비에 모일 것이다.

문제 풀이 비법

❶ 타동사의 목적어

타동사 뒤에는 목적어가 온다. 동사 뒤에 오는 명사는 대부분 목적어이다.

> **Example**
>
> Unfortunately, our company cannot accept ------ for belongings unattended.
>
> (A) responsible　　(B) responsibility　　(C) respond　　(D) responsive
>
> 해석　불행히도, 우리 회사는 방치된 소지품에 대해서는 책임을 질 수 없습니다.
> 어휘　unfortunately 불행히도　belongings 소지품　unattended 지켜보는 사람이 없는, 방치된
>
>  accept는 목적어를 취하는 타동사이다. 따라서 명사인 (B) responsibility가 정답이 된다.
>
> 정답 (B)

❷ 주격 보어

'2형식 불완전 자동사' 뒤에는 형용사나 명사와 같은 주격 보어가 온다.

> **Example**
>
> Because of the limited budgets, the renovation of the training center will not be ------ as planned.
>
> (A) completing　　(B) complete　　(C) completely　　(D) completion
>
> 해석　한정된 예산으로 인해, 교육 센터의 개보수 공사는 계획대로 마무리되지 않을 것이다.
> 어휘　limited 한정된, 제한을 받는　budget 예산　renovation 개조, 보수　as planned 계획대로
>
> be동사 뒤 '보어 자리'이다. 명사 보어의 경우 주어인 the renovation과 같은 개념이 되어야 하므로 (D) completion은 오답이다. 따라서 형용사인 (B) complete가 정답이다. complete는 동사와 형용사의 형태가 같다는 것을 기억해야 한다.
>
> 정답 (B)

○ 대표적인 2형식 동사

be ~이다	become ~이 되다	remain/stay ~인 상태로 남아 있다	look ~하게 보이다
sound ~하게 들리다	taste ~한 맛이 나다	smell ~한 냄새가 나다	feel ~하게 느껴지다

❸ 목적격 보어

'5형식 불완전 타동사' 뒤에는 형용사나 명사와 같은 목적격 보어가 올 수 있다.

┤ **Example** ├

The marketing team found the project ------- than they expected because of the unfavorable market condition.

(A) differ (B) difficult (C) difficulty (D) more difficult

해석 마케팅팀은 불리한 시장 여건으로 인해, 기대했던 것보다 프로젝트가 더 어렵다는 것을 알았다.
어휘 unfavorable 호의적이 아닌, 불리한 expect 기대하다, 예상하다 market condition 시장 여건

find의 과거형인 found는 목적격 보어를 취할 수 있는 5형식 동사이다. 선택지 중 형용사인 (B) difficult나 (D) more difficult 중에서 정답을 골라야 한다. 빈칸 뒤 than이 등장하는 것을 근거로 비교급 형태인 (D) more difficult를 정답으로 한다. 항상 빈칸 앞뒤를 모두 보는 것이 중요하다.

정답 (D)

○ 대표적인 5형식 동사

동사	목적어	목적격 보어
make(~하게 만들다), keep(~하게 유지하다), find(~라는 것을 알다), consider/deem(~라고 간주하다), think (of)(~라고 생각하다)	명사	형용사, 명사
name(~라고 명명하다), appoint(~로 임명하다), call(~라고 부르다)	명사	명사

❹ 수식어

'명사 수식 형용사, 부사(구/절), 전치사구, 관계사절, 분사구문'과 같은 수식어들은 문법 계산 시에는 지워 낸다.

┤ **Example** ├

People who want to have Mr. Jackson's autograph ------- his new book.

(A) having (B) is having (C) must have (D) has been

해석 Jackson 씨의 사인을 원하는 사람들은 그의 새 책을 가지고 있어야 한다.
어휘 autograph (유명인의) 사인

빈칸 앞 관계대명사절(who want ~ autograph)은 주어 people을 꾸며 주는 수식어이므로 빈칸은 동사 자리이다. (A) having을 제외한 나머지는 모두 동사이지만 주어(people)가 복수이므로 단수 동사인 (B) is having이나 (D) has been은 모두 오답이 된다. 따라서 (C) must have가 정답이다.

정답 (C)

비법 적용 연습

PART 5

1 The newly introduced transportation system at the international airport is quite -------.
(A) impress (B) impressed (C) impressive (D) impression

2 It is desirable that a trainee seek ------- from a supervisor whenever needed.
(A) advice (B) advisor (C) advisory (D) advisable

3 The new advertising campaign organized by Mr. Goodman was very -------.
(A) successfully (B) success (C) succeed (D) successful

4 Until we receive your written ------- the conference room will not be assigned for your use.
(A) confirm (B) confirmation (C) confirmed (D) confirming

5 Instructions posted next to the door outline the ------- for emergency evacuation.
(A) proceed (B) proceeds (C) procedural (D) procedures

6 Better distribution and lower web costs made businesses more -------.
(A) profit (B) profitable (C) profiting (D) profitability

7 The new working hours will keep stores ------- until 11 or midnight.
(A) opening (B) opens (C) to open (D) open

8 Managers at the manufacturing facilities must continue to keep work procedures -------.
(A) produce (B) product (C) production (D) productive

9 Joint research teams are considered more ------- in reducing the time and effort needed.
(A) effect (B) effects (C) effective (D) effectiveness

10 King Brothers, the biggest American fast food brand, plans ------- the GBS Inc. as part of its expansion.
(A) acquire (B) acquisition (C) acquiring (D) to acquire

Grammar

DAY 03 명사

사람과 사물의 '이름'을 나타내는 명사는 정해진 위치에만 쓰인다. 또 가산 명사와 불가산 명사를 잘 구별해야 한다.

❶ 명사의 역할

주어	The **office** is very spacious. 사무실이 매우 넓다.
목적어	The company will advertise new **products**. 회사는 새로운 제품을 홍보할 것이다.
보어	Mr. Lopez is a **sales representative**. Lopez 씨는 영업 사원이다.

❷ 명사의 자리

관사 뒤	The **supervisor** will attend the meeting. 관리자는 회의에 참석할 것이다.
소유격 뒤	These are the reviews from our **customers**. 이것들은 우리 고객들로부터의 후기입니다.
형용사 뒤	She made a remarkable **speech**. 그녀는 훌륭한 연설을 했다.
전치사 뒤	There were many people at the **festival**. 축제에는 많은 사람들이 있었다.

❸ 가산 명사와 불가산 명사

명사는 셀 수 있는 '가산 명사'와 셀 수 없는 '불가산 명사'가 있다.

가산 명사: 관사 a(n)와 함께 또는 복수 명사로 사용이 가능하다. (단독 사용 불가)
불가산 명사: 관사 a(n)와 함께 또는 복수 명사로 사용이 불가하다. (단독 사용 가능)

024 SECTION 1

문제 풀이 비법

❶ 가산 명사 vs. 불가산 명사

불가산 명사는 ① 복수형이 없다. ② 관사 a(n)와 쓸 수 없다. ③ 문장 내에서는 단수 취급한다.

> **Example**
>
> The article is not simply a technical ------, but an essay on the future of communication.
>
> (A) mistake　　(B) attention　　(C) description　　(D) information
>
> **해석** 그 기사는 단지 기술적인 설명이 아니라, 미래 통신에 대한 에세이였다.
> **어휘** article 기사　essay 에세이　attention 주의, 주목　description 설명, 묘사
>
>  관사(a) 뒤 빈칸은 명사 자리라는 것을 알 수 있다. 문장의 의미와 잘 어울리면서 가산 명사인 (C) description이 정답이 된다. (D) information은 대표적인 불가산 명사로 관사 a(n)과 함께 쓸 수 없다.
>
> 정답 (C)

○ 주요 불가산 명사

advice 충고, information 정보, news 뉴스, equipment 장비, advertising 광고, furniture 가구, clothing 의류, baggage(= luggage) 수화물, seating 좌석, accounting 회계학, processing 수속, 절차, 처리, ticketing 발권, pricing 가격 책정, lending 대출, funding 자금 조달, machinery 기계류, mail 우편물, merchandise 상품, weaponry 무기류, stationery 문구류

❷ 복합명사

하나의 어휘로 취급하며 볼 때마다 외워 둬야 한다.

> **Example**
>
> In order to relieve traffic congestion in this tunnel, toll ------ will be automated within this year.
>
> (A) collective　　(B) collected　　(C) collection　　(D) collecting
>
> **해석** 이 터널의 교통 체증을 줄이기 위해서, 통행료 징수는 올해 안에 자동화될 것이다.
> **어휘** in order to ~하기 위해서　relieve 완화하다　traffic congestion 교통 체증　automate 자동화하다　toll 통행료
>
> 동사(will be) 앞 빈칸은 주어 자리라는 것을 알 수 있다. toll(통행료)은 불가산 명사이므로 혼자 사용될 수 없다. 따라서 복합명사(toll collection 통행료 징수) 형태인 (C) collection이 정답이 된다.
>
> 정답 (C)

자주 출제되는 복합명사

account number 계좌 번호	application form 신청서
arrival date 도착 일자	assembly line 조립 라인
attendance record 출석(출근) 기록	customer satisfaction 고객 만족
customs office 세관	confirmation number 주문 번호
earnings growth 수익 성장	exchange rate 환율
expansion project 확장 계획	expiration date 만기일
feasibility study 타당성 조사	growth rate 성장률
housing department 주택 개발부	interest rate 이자율
investment advice 투자 조언	keynote speaker 기조 연설자
living expenses 생활비	performance appraisal/evaluations 업무 평가
public relations department 홍보부	product information 제품 정보
quality requirement 품질 요구 사항	reception desk 접수처
reference letter 추천서	registration form 등록 서류
retail sales 소매 판매	retirement celebration 퇴직 기념 축하연
retirement luncheon 퇴직 기념 오찬	return policy 반환 정책
safety inspection 안전 검사	sales representative 영업직 직원
sales division/promotion 영업 부서/판촉	savings account/plan 예금 계좌/상품
security card 보안 카드	weather forecast 일기 예보

❸ 비슷한 형태의 명사 구분

반드시 암기하고, [어법/논리]를 따져서 문장 내에서 [가산/불가산] 명사로 쓰였는지를 살펴야 한다.

> **Example**
>
> Mr. Kim worked as a chief mechanical ------- at Cisco Manufacturing before joining our firm.
>
> (A) engineer　　　(B) engineering　　　(C) engineered　　　(D) engineers
>
> **해석**　Kim 씨는 우리 회사에 합류하기 전, Cisco 제조업체에서 수석 기계 엔지니어로 일했었다.
> **어휘**　mechanical 기계적인, 기계와 관련된　manufacturing 제조업
>
>  관사(a) 뒤 빈칸은 명사 자리이다. 관사 a와 잘 어울리는 단수 명사인 (A) engineer가 정답이다.
> (B) engineering(공학)은 불가산 명사이므로 관사 a(n)과 같이 쓸 수 없다.
>
> 　　　　　　　　　　　　　　　　　　　　　　　　　　　　　　　　　　　정답 (A)

○ 주의해야 할 비슷한 형태의 명사

가산 명사(사람)	불가산 명사(행위)
engineer 기술자, 공학도	engineering 공학
applicant 지원자, 신청자	application 지원, 신청
author 작가	authorization 허가, 인가
prosecutor 검사, 고발자	prosecution 기소, 고소
manufacturer 제조업자	manufacture 제조
competitor 경쟁자	competition 경쟁(불가산), 시합(가산)
collector 수집가, 징수원	collection 수집, 징수 (요금)
attendant 참석자(= attendee)	attendance 참석
consultant 상담원, 자문역	consultation 상담, 자문
resident 거주자, 주민	residence 주거, 주택, 거주
recipient 수혜자, 받는 사람	receipt 수령(불가산), 영수증(가산)
translator 번역가, 통역가	translation 번역, 통역
subscriber 구독자	subscription 구독
contributor 기부자	contribution 기여, 기부
supervisor 감독, 관리자	supervision 관리, 감독
performer 공연자	performance 수행, 성과

비법 적용 연습

PART 5

1. All visitors are required to present at least one form of ------- before entering the facility.
   (A) identify   (B) identification   (C) identifiable   (D) identifying

2. Every ------- for the quality control managerial position will receive a response via e-mail within the next 2 weeks.
   (A) apply   (B) applied   (C) application   (D) applicant

3. Employees have been informed that business hours will be in effect for the ------- of the month.
   (A) remain   (B) remained   (C) remaining   (D) remainder

4. Following each program, course ------- should be completed and submitted to instructors for review.
   (A) evaluative   (B) evaluations   (C) evaluator   (D) evaluate

5. Ever since new equipment was installed, ------- has been significantly increased.
   (A) producer   (B) production   (C) produced   (D) producing

6. Dr. Koon's own findings were different from the other researchers' ------- of the test results.
   (A) interprets   (B) interpretation   (C) interpreter   (D) interpreted

7. Those who maintain exemplary ------- records will be eligible for the bonus this year.
   (A) attend   (B) attended   (C) attendant   (D) attendance

8. The upcoming promotional events will focus only on items currently under -------.
   (A) develop   (B) developing   (C) development   (D) developer

9. Smart Life has created an effective advertising ------- for its new wearable devices.
   (A) strategic   (B) strategically   (C) strategize   (D) strategy

10. We spent an extra $2,300 on a new copy machine since there was really no -------.
    (A) alternate   (B) alternately   (C) alternative   (D) alternating

Grammar

DAY 04 대명사

대명사는 명사를 대신한다. 같은 명사의 반복을 피하기 위해 사용되며 대신하는 명사의 수에 따라 형태가 달라진다.

❶ 인칭 대명사

- **대명사는 '위치'가 중요하다.**
  대명사는 위치(주어 또는 목적어 자리, 명사 앞)에 따라 '격'을 맞춰야 한다.
- **대명사는 '수'를 맞춰야 한다.**
  대신하는 명사가 단수인지 복수인지를 확인해서 그에 맞춰 사용한다.
- **대명사는 '성'을 맞춰야 한다.**
  대신하는 명사가 남자인지 여자인지, 아니면 단순히 사물인지를 확인해 사용한다.
- **재귀대명사는 주어와 목적어가 같을 때 목적어 자리에 사용한다.**
  재귀대명사(-self)는 목적어 자리에 사용되는 명사 역할과 강조의 부사 역할로 사용된다.

❷ 지시 대명사

비교급에서의 지시 대명사 **that/those**는 비교 대상의 수에 맞춰 결정한다.

> Our price is more competitive than **that** of other stores.
> 우리 가격은 다른 가게의 가격보다 더 경쟁력이 있다.

❸ 부정 대명사

● one ● the other	● one ● another ● the other
"둘"이라는 범위가 정해진 경우 둘 중 하나: **one**, 나머지 다른 하나: **the other**	"셋"이라는 범위가 정해진 경우 셋 중 하나: **one**, 또 다른 하나: **another**, 나머지 다른 하나: **the other**
●●●● some ●●●● others ●●…	● one ● another ●●●● the others
범위가 불특정할 경우 몇몇: **some**, 다른 것(사람)들: **others**	범위가 특정할 경우 '여섯 개' 중 하나: **one**, 또 다른 하나: **another**, 나머지 전부: **the others**

> We have two qualified candidates. **One** is from Canada and **the other** is from Australia.
> 자격이 있는 후보자 두 명이 있다. 한 명은 캐나다 출신이며 나머지 한 명은 호주 출신이다.
> There are a lot of performances scheduled this year. **Some** are for kids and **others** are for families.
> 올해 많은 공연들이 잡혀 있다. 몇몇은 아이들을 위한 공연이고, 다른 것들은 가족을 위한 공연이다.

문제 풀이 비법

❶ 대명사의 이해

대명사 문제는 앞에 나온 명사와 〈단수/복수〉의 일치를 묻는 형태로 출제된다.

> **Example**
>
> The two companies announced that ------- decided to reduce their production costs.
>
> (A) it　　　　　　(B) they　　　　　　(C) its　　　　　　(D) their
>
> **해석**　두 회사는 생산비를 줄이기로 결정했다고 발표했다.
> **어휘**　announce 발표하다, 알리다　reduce 줄이다, 낮추다　production costs 생산비
>
>  빈칸은 that절 동사(decided) 앞 주어 자리이다. 소유격인 (C) its와 (D) their은 주어 자리에 들어갈 수 없고, (A) it은 단수이므로 오답이 된다. 복수 주어(two companies)를 대신하는 주어 자리이므로 정답은 (B) they이다.
>
> 정답 (B)

❷ 인칭 대명사의 일치

소유격은 뒤에 명사를 취하고, 소유 대명사(소유격+명사)는 명사를 포함하므로 뒤에 명사가 올 수 없다.

> **Example**
>
> Because Mr. Park had finished his business report ahead of time, he offered to help Ms. Hasebe finish -------.
>
> (A) hers　　　　　　(B) her　　　　　　(C) she　　　　　　(D) herself
>
> **해석**　Park 씨는 업무 보고서를 미리 끝냈기 때문에, Hasebe 씨가 보고서를 끝낼 수 있도록 도와주겠다고 제안했다.
> **어휘**　finish (완성하여) 끝내다　ahead of time 예정보다 빨리　offer 제안하다, 제공하다
>
> 동사(finish) 뒤 빈칸은 목적어 자리이므로, 주어 자리에 들어가야 하는 (C) she는 오답이 된다. 문맥상 끝내는 대상이 사람인 (B) her나 (D) herself는 올 수 없다. 빈칸은 her business report가 되어야 하므로 소유 대명사인 (A) hers가 정답이다.
>
> 정답 (A)

❸ 지시 대명사 that vs. those

한 문장 내에서 명사가 중복될 때, 단수 명사가 중복되면 that, 복수 명사가 중복되면 those를 사용한다.

> **Example**
>
> The views written in this article are ------- of the writer and are not necessarily the opinions of the newspaper.
>
> (A) this   (B) that   (C) these   (D) those
>
> **해석**   그 기사에 쓰여진 견해는 작가의 견해이며, 신문사의 의견은 아닐 수 있습니다.
> **어휘**   view 관점, 견해   article 기사   necessarily 필연적으로   opinion 의견
>
>  빈칸은 be동사 뒤 전명구(of the writer)의 수식을 받는 명사 자리이다. 앞 명사 views를 대신하는 지시 대명사 (D) those가 정답이 된다. 비교나 대조의 의미로 사용될 경우 (C) these는 사용할 수 없다.
>
> 정답 (D)

❹ 부정 대명사 some vs. any

some은 '몇몇의'라는 뜻으로 주로 긍정문에서, any는 주로 부정문, 의문문, 조건문에서 쓰인다.
any가 긍정문에서 쓰일 때는, '그 어떤 (것/사람이라도)'으로 해석한다.
some과 any는 가산·불가산 명사를 모두 수식할 수 있다. (형용사 역할)

> **Example**
>
> Seminar participants may choose ------- seat except those in the first two rows, which are reserved for the speakers.
>
> (A) some   (B) both   (C) any   (D) all
>
> **해석**   세미나 참석자들은, 발표자들을 위해 따로 마련된 맨 앞 두 줄을 제외하고는, 어느 자리든 선택할 수 있습니다.
> **어휘**   participant 참가자   reserve 예약하다, 따로 잡아 두다
>
>  빈칸 뒤에 seat라는 가산 명사 단수가 왔으므로 복수 명사를 취해야 하는 (A), (B), (D)는 오답이 된다. 따라서 정답은 (C) any이다.
>
> 정답 (C)

❺ 부정 대명사 one, another, other(s), the other(s)

각각의 수에 따라 쓰임이 다르며 특히 자체가 대명사인 것(others)과 형용사(other)인 단어에 주의한다.

단수	복수
one another the other	others the others

* the other, the others에서 정관사 the는 범위가 정해져 있어야만 사용 가능하다.
* others는 자체가 대명사다. 바로 뒤에 어떤 명사도 같이 올 수 없다.

Example

The weekly or monthly train rail pass is the cheapest option for travelers, but ------- are available.

(A) other　　　　(B) others　　　　(C) the other　　　　(D) another

해석　주간 또는 월간 열차권은 여행자들을 위해서 가장 저렴한 선택 사항이지만 다른 것도 이용 가능합니다.
어휘　rail pass 승차권 available 이용 가능한

 빈칸 뒤 동사(are)가 복수이므로 단수인 (C) the other과 (D) another은 오답이 되고 (A) other(다른)은 형용사이므로 단독 사용이 불가능하다. 따라서 정답은 (B) others이다.

정답 (B)

비법 적용 연습

PART 5

1. After Rhodora's promotion, ------- will be responsible for operations of all regional branches.
   (A) her (B) hers (C) herself (D) she

2. All the part-time employees must inform their immediate supervisors of the hours ------- worked.
   (A) them (B) their (C) those (D) they

3. Inspired by the success of ------- first movie, Mr. Shin started planning a sequel immediately.
   (A) he (B) his (C) him (D) himself

4. As soon as Dr. Beck finishes the research paper, ------- will be forwarded to his assistant researcher to be copied.
   (A) it (B) itself (C) other (D) them

5. Directors of each department will decide -------- who will make a presentation at the seminar.
   (A) themselves (B) itself (C) they (D) yourself

6. When inspecting the equipment, please record ------- technical failures in the checklist attached to the equipment.
   (A) some (B) where (C) every (D) any

7. The business model has both benefits and risks involved, so those interested in this business should weigh each factor carefully against -------.
   (A) other (B) the other (C) another's (D) the one

8. Gloria will receive a lifetime achievement award at the retirement banquet for ------- 32 years of service to the company.
   (A) hers (B) her (C) herself (D) she

9. Please let ------- know when you will arrive, so I can arrange for someone to pick you up.
   (A) I (B) me (C) my (D) mine

10. Mr. Gonzales will return from the conference the day after tomorrow but Mr. Delgado, director of the human resources department, will not meet with ------- until next week.
    (A) him (B) he (C) his (D) himself

형용사

형용사는 명사의 '상태나 성질'을 구체적으로 설명하는데 명사 앞에서 명사를 직접 수식하거나 be동사류 뒤에서 주어를 수식하는 역할을 한다.

• 형용사는 '명사'를 수식한다.

명사 앞	The **negative** feedback from users should be included in the report. 사용자들이 준 부정적인 피드백이 보고서에 포함되어야 한다.
보어 자리	Our company is putting lots of efforts to keep customers **satisfied**. 우리 회사는 고객 만족을 유지하기 위해서 많은 노력을 기울이고 있다. It is very **important** to ask for advice when you make an investment decision. 투자 결정을 할 때 조언을 구하는 것은 매우 중요하다.

• 형용사는 '부사'의 수식을 받는다.

> The finalized contract between the two companies will be **mutually beneficial**.
> 두 회사 사이에 성사된 계약은 서로에게 이익이 될 것이다.

• 가산 명사와 불가산 명사에 따라 앞에 오는 '수량 형용사'가 다를 수 있다.

> **Many** young college graduates have difficulty finding a job.
> 많은 젊은 대학 졸업생들이 직업을 구하는 데 어려움을 겪고 있다.
> You've never paid that **much** attention to his opinions.
> 너는 그의 의견에 그렇게 주의를 기울인 적이 없다.

• 비슷한 형태의 형용사는 '의미'에 따라서 정답이 결정된다.

> Mr. Lee will receive an award for his **impressive** contributions to the company.
> Lee 씨는 회사에 대한 인상적인 공헌으로 상을 받을 것이다. (impressive 인상적인)
> I was very **impressed** by your company's work principles.
> 나는 당신 회사의 경영 방침에 매우 **감명받았다**. (impressed 감명받은)

문제 풀이 비법

Grammar DAY 05

❶ 형용사의 서술적 용법

2형식, 5형식 동사 뒤에서 보어로 사용되며, 명사를 서술해 준다.

┤ Example ├

In order to meet the customer's needs, our ferry service rate will remain ------- at $2.75 per trip for the next 12 months.

(A) unchange   (B) unchanging   (C) unchanged   (D) unchangeability

해석 고객의 요구를 충족시키기 위해서, 우리 여객 서비스의 요금은 앞으로 12개월간 회당 2달러 75센트로 동결될 것입니다.

어휘 meet one's need 요구를 충족시키다 ferry 나룻배, 여객선 rate 요금 per ~당, ~마다

 동사(remain) 뒤 보어 자리이므로 동사인 (A) unchange는 오답이며 명사 보어는 주어와 같아야 하므로 (D) unchangeability 역시 오답이 된다. 명사 rate(요금)와 잘 어울리는 형용사 (C) unchanged(변경되지 않은)가 정답이다. 형용사는 항상 명사와 관련이 있기 때문에 수식을 받는 명사를 찾는 것이 중요하다.

정답 (C)

❷ 형용사의 제한적 용법

형용사는 명사 앞에서 명사를 수식하며, 명사를 한정해 줄 수 있다.

┤ Example ├

Kelly's Cleaners provides linen cleaning and delivery service to many hospitality businesses near you at ------- prices.

(A) reason   (B) reasons   (C) reasoning   (D) reasonable

해석 Kelly's Cleaners는 합리적인 가격으로 침구 세탁 및 배송 서비스를 여러분 주변의 많은 숙박 업체에 제공합니다.

어휘 linen 리넨 제품(셔츠, 시트, 테이블보 등) delivery service 배송 서비스 hospitality 환대, 접대; 숙박 시설

 전치사(at)와 명사(prices) 사이 형용사 자리이다. 따라서 형용사가 아닌 (A)와 (B)는 오답이다. '추론, 추리'의 의미인 (C)도 오답이다. '합리적인'이란 의미의 (D) reasonable이 정답이다.

정답 (D)

❸ 수량 형용사

'수'를 나타내는 형용사 뒤에는 가산 명사(단수/복수)가, '양'을 나타내는 형용사 뒤에는 불가산 명사가 오는 등 동사의 수 일치와도 관련이 있다.

> **Example**
>
> ------- chief directors are invited to participate in the seminar in the conference room.
>
> (A) Each   (B) Every   (C) All   (D) Some of
>
> **해석** 모든 이사장들은 회의실에서 있는 세미나에 참석해야만 한다.
> **어휘** chief director 이사장   participate in ~에 참가하다   conference room 회의실
>
>  빈칸 뒤 주어가 복수 명사(directors)이다. 따라서 단수 명사와 함께 쓰이는 (A) Each와 (B) Every는 오답이다. 복수 명사와 함께 쓰이는 (C) All이 정답이다.
> *some of/one of/any of/several of 등의 표현은 반드시 뒤에 'the(소유격)+명사'와 같이 써야 한다.
>
> 정답 (C)

○ 수량 형용사

가산 명사 단수 앞	가산 명사 복수 앞	불가산 명사 앞	복수 가산 · 불가산 명사 앞
one each every another	many several various both one of each of (a) few/fewer numerous a couple of a number of	much (a) little/less a great deal of a large amount of	all some/any a lot of/lots of plenty of more/most

❹ 특이한 형태의 형용사

형용사는 보통 '-al, -ive, -ful, -ous, -ic, -able, -ate, -ing/-ed' 등의 모양을 갖지만 특이한 형태의 형용사도 있으므로 기억해 두어야 한다.

┤ Example ├

Applications for research grants should be submitted to the board of trustees in a ------- manner.

(A) time (B) timer (C) timely (D) timing

해석 연구 지원비 신청서는 시기에 맞춰 이사회로 제출되어야 합니다.

어휘 application 지원서 research grant 연구 보조금 submit 제출하다 the board of trustees 평의원회, 이사회 in a timely manner 시기에 맞춰

 빈칸은 관사(a)와 명사(manner) 사이 형용사 자리이다. 선택지 중 형용사는 부사처럼 생긴 (C) timely 뿐이다.

정답 (C)

○ '명사 + ly' 형태의 형용사

| timely 시기적절한 | hourly 매시간의 | daily 매일의 | weekly 주간의 | monthly 매달의 |
| quarterly 분기별의 | yearly 매년의 | friendly 친절한 | costly 비싼 | likely ~할 것 같은 |

❺ 주의해야 할 형용사

형태가 비슷하여 의미를 정확히 기억해야 한다.

┤ Example ├

Shoppers depend on *Customers' Right Magazine* for ------- product testing results and related information.

(A) rely (B) relies (C) reliant (D) reliable

해석 쇼핑객들은 믿을 수 있는 제품 테스트 결과와 관련 정보에 대해서 〈Customers' Right〉 잡지에 의존하고 있다.

어휘 depend on ~에 의존하다 result 결과 related 관련된

 빈칸은 명사(results) 앞 형용사 자리이므로 동사 (A) rely와 (B) relies는 오답이 된다. (C) reliant는 '의존적인'이란 의미로 주로 서술적으로 사용된다. 문맥상 '믿을 수 있는'이란 뜻의 (D) reliable 이 정답이 된다.

정답 (D)

주의해야 할 형용사

advisable 바람직한	advisory 자문의
considerable 상당한	considerate 사려 깊은
comparable 필적할 만한	comparative 비교의
comprehensible 이해할 수 있는	comprehensive 종합적인
dependent 의존하는	dependable 믿을 만한, 신뢰할 만한
distinguished 저명한	distinguishable 구별할 수 있는
economic 경제의	economical 경제적인, 돈이 덜 드는
favorable 호의적인	favorite 가장 좋아하는
impressive 인상적인	impressed 감명받은
industrial 산업의	industrious 근면한
informed 정보에 입각한, 신중한	informative 유익한
moderate 적절한, 온건한	modest 겸손한
persuasive 설득력이 있는	persuadable 설득될 만한
profitable 수익이 되는, 이익이 많은(= lucrative)	proficient 능숙한
reliable 믿을 수 있는	reliant 의존적인
responsible ~에 책임이 있는	responsive ~에 민감한
respectful 존경스러운	respective 각각의
seasonal 계절의	seasoned 경험이 많은
satisfied 만족감을 느끼는	satisfactory 만족스러운
sensitive 민감한	sensible 분별력 있는
successful 성공한, 성공적인	successive 연속적인, 상속의

비법 적용 연습

PART 5

1. Our team is ------- about our projected revenues for this quarter because of our successful expansion into the East Asian market.
   (A) visionary   (B) willing   (C) optimistic   (D) assertive

2. Beginning next week, ------- staff members must wear their IDs when on the company premises.
   (A) every   (B) all   (C) each   (D) either

3. Mr. Burke made a keynote speech at the international green energy conference and I found it very -------.
   (A) inform   (B) informed   (C) information   (D) informative

4. All the personal information gathered on the Web site should remain -------.
   (A) confidential   (B) confident   (C) confidence   (D) confidentially

5. KMP Airlines, which was established almost 20 years ago, offers a(n) ------- range of excellent services especially for business travelers.
   (A) open   (B) wide   (C) high   (D) round

6. The vice president of Jump High made the announcement that a few branches will be ------- for annual inspections during the summer season.
   (A) close   (B) closer   (C) closed   (D) closure

7. All computer components and other ------- office supplies have to be stored in a designated cabinet in each office.
   (A) achievable   (B) alike   (C) interested   (D) related

8. All the information regarding the most visited attractions in London is ------- in *London Life*'s latest issue.
   (A) possible   (B) capable   (C) available   (D) able

9. The office managers are ------- for purchasing items needed for daily tasks.
   (A) responsive   (B) responsible   (C) response   (D) respond

10. Please reschedule our 3:15 P.M. meeting for a ------- time because Mr. Smith has an urgent meeting with a client from Japan at 3:30 P.M.
    (A) recent   (B) later   (C) further   (D) following

부사

부사는 명사를 제외한 나머지(형용사, 동사, 부사, 문장, 구 등)를 수식한다. 부사는 말 그대로 '부가 정보'이기 때문에 없어도 문법적으로 완전한 문장이 된다. 따라서 위치는 비교적 자유로운 편이다.

- **대부분의 부사는 '형용사 + ly'의 형태를 취한다.**

clearly, properly, significantly, promptly 등과 같이 '형용사+ly'의 형태가 일반적이지만 well, hard 등의 특이한 형태의 부사들은 주의해야 한다.

> The manager **clearly** explained the rule.
> 그 부장은 명확하게 규칙을 설명했다.
> The application was not **properly** filled out.
> 신청서가 제대로 작성되지 않았다.

또한, 'fast, late, early' 등 형용사와 부사의 모양이 같은 부사도 있기 때문에 따로 숙지해 두어야 한다.

> I'm going to the airport now, just in case my flight boards **early**.
> 나는 비행기가 탑승을 일찍 시작하는 경우에 대비해 지금 공항으로 가고 있다.
> I stayed **late** at the office the other day to wait for my friend.
> 나는 얼마 전에 친구를 기다리며 사무실에서 늦게까지 남아 있었다.

- **부사는 특정 시간을 나타내기도 한다.**

'~ ago, yesterday, recently' 등과 같이 시간을 나타내는 부사는 시제 문제의 힌트가 되기도 한다.

> He didn't take the bus to work **yesterday**.
> 어제 그는 버스를 타고 출근하지 않았다.
> She has **recently** returned from a trip to Japan.
> 그녀는 최근 일본 여행으로부터 돌아왔다.

- **부사 어휘 문제는 무엇을 수식하느냐가 관건이다.**

부사는 수식어이기 때문에 이 부사가 '무엇을 수식하느냐'를 파악하는 것이 가장 중요하다.

> The bank is **really** crowded today.
> 오늘따라 은행이 정말 붐빈다.
> **Finally** having finished the homework, he went to bed.
> 마침내 숙제를 마치고 그는 잠자리에 들었다.

문제 풀이 비법

Grammar DAY 06

❶ 부사의 수식과 위치

부사는 동사의 앞 또는 뒤에서 동사를 수식한다.

Example

The financial challenges facing the town must be addressed ------- by its elected leaders.

(A) urgency   (B) urgencies   (C) urgently   (D) urgent

해석 지역이 직면한 재정적인 어려움은 선출된 리더에 의해 긴급하게 해결되어야 한다.
어휘 financial 재정적인 challenge 도전, 어려움 face 직면하다 address 연설하다; 해결하다 elected 선출된 urgent 긴급한

 주어와 동사가 모두 있고 완전한 문장이므로 빈칸은 부사 자리가 된다. 따라서 부사가 아닌 (A), (B), (D)는 오답이다. 선택지 중 유일한 부사인 (C) urgently가 정답이 된다.

정답 (C)

❷ 시간 부사

부사는 특정한 시간을 나타내어 문장의 시제를 결정한다.

Example

Mr. Lim joined our company two years ------- as a Chief Financial Officer.

(A) then   (B) than   (C) ago   (D) lately

해석 Lim 씨는 재무 이사로 2년 전에 우리 회사에 입사했습니다.
어휘 Chief Financial Officer 재무 이사

 명사 our company 뒤에 two years라는 명사가 있다. 이를 부사로 만들어 줘야 한다. 따라서, 시간 표현과 함께 쓰이는 (C) ago가 정답이 된다. (ago를 고르는 경우 반드시 시제가 과거임을 확인)

정답 (C)

○ 시간을 나타내는 부사

two days ago 이틀 전에 yesterday 어제 once 한때 recently, lately 최근에 just 막, 방금	→ 보통 '과거 시제'와 함께 사용된다. * recently, lately, just는 '현재완료 시제'와도 사용 가능 * just의 경우 only(오직, 유일한)의 의미로도 사용 가능
soon, shortly 곧	→ 보통 '미래 시제'와 함께 사용된다.

문제 풀이 비법

○ **빈도를 나타내는 부사**

always 항상 typically 전형적으로 often 종종 routinely 일상적으로	usually 대개, 보통 customarily 통상적으로 frequently 자주 regularly 규칙적으로	→ 보통 '현재 시제'와 자주 사용된다.
hardly/ seldom/ rarely/ scarcely/ barely 거의 ~하지 않다		문두에 사용될 경우 도치가 일어난다. (Day 12 도치편 참고)

❸ 부사 어휘

특수한 의미를 가진 부사가 자주 출제된다.

Example

Although the task force team solved a lot of problems, there are ------- issues to be handled.

(A) already   (B) still   (C) yet   (D) once

해석 비록 특별 업무 전담 팀이 많은 문제를 해결했지만, 여전히 다루어야 할 문제들이 있다.
어휘 task force (특정 문제를 해결하기 위한) 대책 위원회 issue 문제 handle 다루다, 해결하다

선택지를 보고 부사 어휘 문제임을 파악한다. 부사절(Although the task force ~ problems,) 문장에서 '해결했음에도 불구하고'의 의미와 어울리는 (B) still이 정답이 된다. although는 부사 어휘를 고르는 데 단서가 되는 접속사로 많이 등장한다.

정답 (B)

○ **꼭 알아 두어야 할 부사**

already	긍정문: 이미, 벌써 – 위치 중요 be + already + p.p. / have + already + p.p.
yet	부정문: 아직 ~ 않다 ex) I haven't finished it **yet**. ★관용구: have yet to v 아직 ~해야만 한다 = 아직 ~하지 않았다
still	긍정문/의문문/부정문: 아직도, 여전히 (동작, 상태의 계속) – 반드시 해석 ex) I **still** didn't finish it. (부정문일 때, not보다 앞에 온다.)

○ 어휘 문제로 자주 출제되는 기타 부사

efficiently perform 효율적으로 수행하다	efficiently complete 효율적으로 마무리하다
carefully[closely] examine 신중하게[면밀히] 살펴보다	carefully[closely] review 신중하게[면밀히] 검토하다
thoroughly inspect 철저하게 점검하다	easily communicate 쉽게 의사소통하다
directly report 직접 보고하다	adequately wrap 적절하게 포장하다
remarkably reduce 눈에 띄게 줄어들다	rapidly change 빠르게 변화하다
significantly increase 상당히 증가하다	dramatically improve 극적으로 개선되다
consistently provide 지속적으로 제공하다	rely heavily on ~에 크게 의존하다
be currently renovated 현재 리모델링 중이다	

❹ 비슷한 모양이지만 다른 의미의 부사

모양이 비슷해서 혼동이 되는 부사들도 알아 두어야 한다.

┤ **Example** ├

Workers are requested to remove all the branches that hang ------- to the ground to ensure safety on the road.

(A) low　　　　　(B) lowly　　　　　(C) lowest　　　　　(D) lower

해석 인부들은 도로의 안전을 확보하기 위해서 바닥으로 낮게 늘어져 있는 나뭇가지들을 제거할 것을 요청 받았습니다.
어휘 request 요청(하다)　branch 나뭇가지　ensure 보장하다, 확실하게 하다　safety 안전

'바닥으로 낮게 늘어져 있는'이란 의미로 빈칸은 '낮게'를 의미하는 부사 자리이다. 선택지 중 부사는 (A) low뿐이다. (B) lowly는 '지위 등이 낮은, 하찮은'이란 의미의 형용사이다. 이 문제의 경우 low가 형용사와 부사 모양이 같다는 것을 알고 있는지 물어보는 문제이다.

정답 (A)

○ 형태가 비슷해서 주의해야 할 부사

hard 어려운/열심히	hardly 거의 ~하지 않다
high 높은/(물리적) 높이, 높게	highly (정도·수준) 높이, 매우
late 늦은/늦게	lately 최근에
most 매우/가장 많이	mostly 대체로, 주로
near 가까운/가까이	nearly 거의

비법 적용 연습

Grammar DAY 06

정답 및 해설 / 6p

PART 5

1. Mr. Jefferson is ------- responsible for on-time delivery of GRN products.
   (A) slowly
   (B) nearly
   (C) primarily
   (D) variously

2. Mr. Lukas has been asked to complete the annual sales report ------- since it is due tomorrow.
   (A) quickly
   (B) quicken
   (C) quickened
   (D) quickness

3. The new research study suggests that the number of people working part-time has risen ------- over the last 5 years.
   (A) efficiently
   (B) dramatically
   (C) openly
   (D) hastily

4. World Bank's employee benefits policies proposed during the seminar last year have ------- been implemented.
   (A) already
   (B) a great deal
   (C) soon
   (D) by far

5. At a press conference yesterday, Ms. Chang ------- announced the company she founded had been acquired by Jin Education.
   (A) customarily
   (B) externally
   (C) observantly
   (D) formally

6. Mr. David Lindarton, the CEO of the company, is confident that the quarter's poor sales will not ------- affect the company's stock price.
   (A) adversary
   (B) adverse
   (C) adversely
   (D) adversity

7. After all the machinery is repaired, Crimpsons manufacturing facilities are expected to reopen -------.
   (A) initially
   (B) equally
   (C) shortly
   (D) nearly

8. The Grand Hotel branches are all ------- located, and they provide guests with easy access to major tourist attractions.
   (A) center
   (B) central
   (C) centrally
   (D) centered

9. The company specializing in organizing events such as an award ceremony and a company banquet ------- arranges to hire temporary staff, especially for large events.
   (A) occasionally
   (B) occasional
   (C) occasion
   (D) occasions

10. Fans of successful movie director Charles Pearson ------- await the sequel to his previous movie.
    (A) eagerly
    (B) eager
    (C) eagerness
    (D) more eager

044 SECTION 1

전치사

전치사는 명사 앞에 위치해서 문장을 이어주거나 더 풍성하게 만드는 역할을 한다.

• **명사 앞에 위치하는 전치사**
전치사는 명사 앞에 위치하여 수식어(형용사, 부사)가 된다. 전치사 뒤에는 명사나 동명사가 목적어로 나온다.

> I took an accounting course **during** my vacation.
> 나는 휴가 동안 회계 강좌를 수강했다.
> She is known for her skill **in** selecting the freshest ingredients.
> 그녀는 가장 신선한 재료를 고르는 능력으로 유명하다.

• **전치사 뒤에는 '주어+동사, 즉 절'이 올 수 없다.**
비슷한 의미의 전치사와 접속사를 구별하는 문제가 등장한다. 이때에는 비슷한 의미이더라도 접속사인지 전치사인지 구별하는 것이 중요하다.

> She likes ABC athletic wear **because of** its durability.
> 그녀는 내구성 때문에 ABC 운동복을 좋아한다.

• **숙어로 등장하는 전치사**
전치사에 따라서 뒤에 올 수 있는 명사는 어느 정도 정해져 있다. 하지만 전치사 앞에 등장하는 어휘(동사, 명사, 형용사)와 관련된 표현을 체크하는 것도 매우 중요하다.

> We should **concentrate on** our core business.
> 우리는 핵심 사업에 주력해야 한다.
> His **attention to** detail was remarkable.
> 세부 사항에 대한 그의 관심은 놀라웠다.

• **전치사는 어휘처럼 관련 표현들을 기억해야 한다.**
전치사의 경우 시간, 장소, 이유, 양보 등과 같이 분류해서 기억하는 것이 도움이 된다.

> I was bored **throughout** the negotiation process.
> 나는 협상 과정 내내 지루했다.
> **In spite of** his talent, he had to work hard to achieve success.
> 그의 재능에도 불구하고 그는 성공하기 위해서 열심히 일해야 했다.

문제 풀이 비법

❶ 전치사 vs. 접속사

'문장을 연결'하는 접속사와 뒤에 '목적어인 명사를 취하는' 전치사를 구분하는 문제가 자주 출제된다.

| Example |

-------- the inclement weather, the renovation of the employee dormitory was completed on schedule.

(A) Despite   (B) Although   (C) Even though   (D) Nonetheless

해석 좋지 않은 날씨에도 불구하고, 직원 기숙사 보수가 일정대로 완료되었다.
어휘 inclement weather 좋지 않은 날씨 renovation 개조, 보수 employee dormitory 직원 기숙사 on schedule 일정대로

 선택지에 비슷한 의미의 전치사, 접속사가 등장하면, 빈칸 뒤에 명사가 오는지, 문장이 오는지를 확인한다. 빈칸 뒤에 명사어구(the inclement weather)가 있으므로 빈칸은 전치사 자리이다. 선택지 중 전치사는 (A) Despite뿐이다.

정답 (A)

○ 양보의 전치사
in spite of(= despite) + 명사(구): ~에도 불구하고

❷ 앞에 등장하는 표현을 보고 푸는 전치사 문제

보통 전치사 문제는 전치사 뒤 명사를 보고 푸는 경우가 많다. 하지만 전치사 앞에 나오는 표현이 결정적인 힌트가 되는 경우도 있다.

| Example |

The regular meeting usually begins at 2 P.M. and lasts ------- 3 P.M. every Monday.

(A) at   (B) on   (C) from   (D) until

해석 정기 회의는 보통 매주 월요일 오후 2시에 시작해 3시까지 계속된다.
어휘 regular meeting 정기 회의 last 계속하다, 지속하다

 명사 앞 전치사 자리이다. 빈칸 앞에 last(계속되다)를 힌트로 (D) until을 정답으로 고른다. 절대 빈칸 뒤만 보고 전치사 문제의 정답을 고르지 않는다.

정답 (D)

❸ 이유·목적·부가 등의 전치사

'두 단어 이상'으로 구성되어 있는 표현은 꼭 같이 암기해 두어야 한다.

> **Example**
>
> Though Barden Publishers will send orders anywhere in the world, due --------- company policy, all payments must be made in U.S. dollars.
>
> (A) by (B) to (C) on (D) for
>
> 해석   Barden Publishers는 전 세계 어디로든 주문품들을 배송할 것이지만, 회사의 정책 때문에 모든 요금은 미국 달러로 지불되어야만 한다.
> 어휘   publisher 출판사 company policy 회사 정책
>
>  빈칸은 명사(company policy) 앞 전치사 자리이다. 빈칸 앞의 due와 함께 '~때문에'라는 의미를 갖는 (B) to가 정답이 된다.
>
> 정답 (B)

○ 이유·제외·부가의 전치사

이유	due to = because of = owing to = thanks to = on account of ~때문에, ~덕택에 for ~때문에, ~을 위해서
제외	except (for) = aside from = apart from ~을 제외하고
부가	on top of = in addition to = besides ~뿐만 아니라, ~와 더불어

❹ 시간의 전치사의 구별

시간의 전치사가 '시점'을 나타내는 명사를 취하는지, '시간, 기간'을 나타내는 명사를 취하는지를 구분해서 알아 두어야 한다.

> **Example**
>
> The renovation of Montauk is expected to continue ------- the remainder of this month.
>
> (A) for (B) at (C) than (D) which
>
> 해석   Montauk의 개조 작업은 이달 남은 기간 동안 계속될 것으로 보인다
> 어휘   renovation 개조, 수리 remainder 나머지
>
>  빈칸 뒤에 '기간 명사(the remainder of this month)'가 있으므로 빈칸은 전치사 자리이다. 따라서 동사 continue(계속되다)와 어울리는 (A) for가 정답이 된다. (B) at은 '정확한 시점이나 장소' 앞에 쓰인다.
>
> 정답 (A)

○ 시간의 전치사

시점을 나타내는 전치사	at + 시각 ~시에 until + 시점 ~까지 from + 시점 ~부터	on + 날짜/요일 ~일/요일에 by + 시점 ~까지 before/prior to + 시점 ~전에	in + 연도/달 ~년도/월에 since + 시점 ~이래로
기간을 나타내는 전치사	in + 기간 ~후에 over + 기간 ~동안, ~이상 within + 기간 ~이내로	for + 기간 ~동안	during + 기간 명사 ~동안 throughout + 기간 ~내내

❺ 위치의 전치사

위치에 관련된 전치사의 의미와 각각의 특성을 알고 있어야 한다. 또한 물리적인 위치를 나타내는 말과 추상적인 의미를 모두 기억하고 있어야 한다.

| Example |

The company CEO commended the managers' effort to improve at-work productivity ------- employees.

(A) between   (B) among   (C) beside   (D) about

해석 회사의 대표 이사는 직원들 사이의 현장 생산성을 개선하기 위한 관리자들의 노력을 칭찬했다.
어휘 commend 칭찬하다, 추천하다   at-work 현장의, 일하고 있는   productivity 생산성

 빈칸은 명사 앞 전치사 자리이다. '직원들 사이의 생산성'이라는 의미로 복수 명사(employees) 앞이기 때문에 (B) among이 정답이다. 같은 의미인 (A) between은 '둘 사이의'라는 의미로 오답이다.

정답 (B)

○ 위치의 전치사

above/over ~ 위에   below/under ~ 아래에   between/among ~ 사이에   behind ~ 뒤에   within ~ 내에
near ~ 근처에   around ~의 주변에   beside/next to ~ 옆에   adjacent to ~의 가까이에

비법 적용 연습

PART 5

1. All the employees of Wyoming Communications are invited to attend a March 7 seminar ------- stress management.
   (A) at   (B) with   (C) on   (D) as

2. Betty is responsible for approving all expense reports ------- those for international travel.
   (A) aside   (B) even if   (C) additionally   (D) except

3. ------- the extra hours Ms. Hale spent on her project, she was unable to finish her paper by the deadline.
   (A) During   (B) Even though   (C) In spite of   (D) As if

4. The agenda for the series of meetings was distributed to everyone ------- the first meeting.
   (A) prior to   (B) in favor of   (C) owing   (D) in case of

5. Wage increase ------- T&T Advertising is based on the annual employee evaluations.
   (A) as   (B) to   (C) at   (D) on

6. When the management consultants arrive ------- London, they will be given access to confidential information such as financial data.
   (A) on   (B) from   (C) around   (D) into

7. ------- days of negotiations, Rousch Drinks and H&H Chemicals reached an agreement regarding new research initiatives.
   (A) Unlike   (B) After   (C) Expect   (D) About

8. Sales of the wearable devices from Cerabo Electronics have doubled ------- the last 5 years.
   (A) on   (B) of   (C) at   (D) in

9. As soon as you complete your first assignment, you should contact Mr. Cager ------- further instructions.
   (A) along   (B) onto   (C) within   (D) for

10. Mr. Lindstein posted a notice on the board requesting all employees to register ------- one of the four career development sessions.
    (A) for   (B) as   (C) about   (D) near

동사의 종류와 형태

동사는 종류에 따라 쓰임과 문장 구조가 달라지는데 이를 이용한 출제 비중이 높은 편이다.

- **조동사 뒤에는 반드시 동사원형이 와야 한다.**

동사원형이 쓰이는 구조와 함께 다양한 형태의 동사 모양을 기억해야 한다.

> You **must** <u>get</u> permission from the owner.
> 반드시 소유자에게 허락을 받아야 한다.
> Jim and I **might** not <u>get</u> along socially, but we **can** <u>work</u> together.
> Jim과 나는 친하게 잘 지내지는 못하지만 우리는 같이 일을 할 수 있다.

- **자동사와 타동사를 구별할 수 있어야 한다.**

'자동사'는 목적어를 취하지 않는 동사이고, '타동사'는 목적어를 취해야 하는 동사이다. 얼핏 보면 어휘 문제처럼 보이지만 자·타동사 구별 문제도 상당히 많다.

> They refused to **comply** with the guideline. (자동사)
> 그들은 지침서에 따르기를 거부했다.
> They will **provide** a free buffet to celebrate the final day of the program. (타동사)
> 그들은 프로그램의 마지막 날을 기념하여 무료 뷔페를 제공할 것이다.

- **동사의 이후 구조에 초점을 맞춘다.**

동사 뒤에 '형용사'를 취하는지 아니면 '목적어와 목적격 보어'를 취하는지 등 이후 구조에서 정답이 나오는 경우도 상당하기 때문에 꼭 같이 기억해 둔다.

> You were lucky to **remain** <u>unharmed</u>.
> 네가 다치지 않아서 다행이다.
> She **offered** <u>me the report</u>.
> 그녀는 내게 보고서를 주었다.

문제 풀이 비법

Grammar DAY 08

❶ 동사원형이 답이 되는 구조

- 조동사 + 동사원형
- 명령문에서, Please/Simply/Just + 동사원형
- to + 동사원형

Example

Although the cosmetic samples were sent by overnight delivery, they did not ------- until the following Monday.

(A) arriving   (B) arrived   (C) arrives   (D) arrive

해석 화장품 샘플이 익일 배송으로 보내졌지만, 제품은 그 다음 주 월요일까지도 도착하지 않았다.
어휘 although 비록 ~이지만 cosmetic 화장품 overnight delivery 익일 배송 following 그 다음의

did not 뒤에 본동사가 없다. did는 부정문이나 의문문을 만들기 위한 조동사이므로 동사원형인 (D)가 정답이 된다. (C) arrives와 같은 3인칭 단수 형태는 동사원형이 될 수 없다.

정답 (D)

❷ 〈자동사 + 전치사 + 목적어〉 vs. 〈타동사 + 목적어〉

Example

Patrons who need technical advice are advised to ------- with our service representatives.

(A) call   (B) contact   (C) speak   (D) touch

해석 기술적인 조언이 필요한 단골 고객들은 저희 서비스 직원들과 이야기를 나누어 주세요.
어휘 patron 단골 고객 technical 기술적인 representative 직원 contact 연락하다

선택지가 의미가 다른 동사들로 이루어져 있다. 빈칸 뒤에 전치사(with)가 있으므로 자동사가 와야 한다. 선택지 중 자동사는 (C) speak뿐이다. 나머지 동사들은 전치사 없이 목적어를 바로 취하는 타동사들이다.

정답 (C)

○ 자주 출제되는 자동사

단독으로	appear 나타나다 exist 존재하다	disappear 사라지다 emerge 드러나다	rise 오르다
숙어로	contend with 대처하다 proceed in 진행하다 interfere with 방해하다 account for 설명하다 object to 반대하다	specialize in ~를 전문으로 하다 contribute to ~에 기여하다 communicate with 의사소통 하다 work on 일하다, 작업하다 deal with 다루다, 처리하다	apologize for 사과하다 depend on 의지하다 graduate from 졸업하다 comply with 준수하다 respond to 응답하다

❸ 자동사로 오해하기 쉬운 타동사

우리말과 해석의 차이로 어렵게 느껴지는 타동사들은 따로 암기해야 한다.

┤ **Example** ├

The office assistant is responsible for ------- the phone calls for the supervisor.

(A) answering   (B) talking   (C) responding   (D) replying

해석 사무 보조는 상사에게 오는 전화를 응대해야 할 책임이 있다.
어휘 assistant 보조, 비서 be responsible for ~을 책임지다, 담당하다 supervisor 감독관, 상사

빈칸 뒤에 명사(the phone calls)가 있으므로 목적어를 취할 수 있는 타동사가 와야 한다. 선택지 중 명사를 전치사 없이 바로 목적어로 취할 수 있는 동명사 형태의 (A) answering이 정답이다.

정답 (A)

○ 뒤에 '목적어만' 오는 타동사 → 전치사를 쓰면 틀린다.

discuss ~~about~~ 논의하다	reach ~~to~~ 도달하다	attend ~~to/at~~ 참석하다
resemble ~~like~~ 닮다	enter ~~in~~ 들어가다	approach ~~to~~ 접근하다
mention ~~about~~ 언급하다	explain ~~about~~ 설명하다	regret ~~for~~ 유감이다
answer ~~to~~ 대답하다	join ~~in~~ 가입하다	exceed ~~at~~ 초과하다
check ~~of~~ 확인·점검·조사하다	disclose ~~about~~ 폭로하다	emphasize ~~on~~ 강조하다

❹ 〈동사 + 목적어 + of + 목적어〉 / 〈동사 + 목적어 + that 주어 + 동사〉

구조만으로 풀 수 있는 어법 문제가 자주 등장한다. 해석만으로 풀다가 오답을 고를 수 있다.

Example

The tour guide should ----- all the tourists that they have to be at the parking lot by 4 P.M. in order not to delay the tour.

(A) recall　　　　(B) memorize　　　　(C) remind　　　　(D) identify

해석　투어를 지체하지 않기 위해서 관광 가이드는 모든 관광객들에게 오후 4시까지 주차장으로 올 것을 상기시켜야 한다.

어휘　parking lot 주차장　recall 상기하다　memorize 암기하다　remind 상기시키다　identify 신원을 확인하다

 선택지가 의미가 다른 동사로 이루어져 있다. 문장의 구조를 보니 '빈칸+사람+that절'이 등장한다. 이와 같은 구조를 취하는 동사는 선택지 중 (C) remind뿐이다.

정답 (C)

○ 〈동사 + 사람 목적어 + that절〉 구조의 동사

구조만 잘 알아도 문제를 쉽게 풀 수 있는 내용으로 반드시 암기한다.

tell advise	사람 목적어 that **주어+동사** 사람 목적어 **to부정사**
remind inform notify	사람 목적어 that 주어+동사 또는 사람 목적어 **of 명사** 사람 목적어 **to부정사**

비법 적용 연습

Grammar DAY 08

정답 및 해설 / 8p

PART 5

1. Although Bruce is a good manager, his inability to speak foreign languages ------- him from moving up in a company.
   (A) threatens (B) steals (C) distributes (D) prevents

2. Cogin's Business Consulting Corporation ------- in offering customized staffing solutions for small businesses.
   (A) increases (B) specializes (C) facilitates (D) utilizes

3. Supervisors have to make sure that all construction workers ------- with the new safety regulations on site.
   (A) perform (B) fulfill (C) comply (D) observe

4. Normal business hours will ------- as soon as the renovation of the building is completed.
   (A) assemble (B) repair (C) supply (D) resume

5. Torrex agent called to ------- Ms. Pam that a promising new lot came up for sale.
   (A) recommend (B) inform (C) invite (D) persuade

6. All the contracts must be reviewed by the legal department to ------- that the company is in compliance with local laws and regulations.
   (A) search (B) correct (C) reprint (D) ensure

7. The role of a commercial bank ------- primarily of accepting deposits from the general public and investing some of those deposits.
   (A) spreads (B) consists (C) includes (D) cooperates

8. Technical Director Kelvin ------- the next training session on the new teleconferencing system for October 2.
   (A) scheduled (B) served (C) invited (D) presented

9. Customers have ------- concern about the measures SA Telecom took after its service breakdown last February.
   (A) focused (B) appeared (C) applied (D) expressed

10. Since Mr. Cook has a urgent meeting, we ------- that Victoria fill in for him.
    (A) recommend (B) compel (C) recall (D) invent

054 SECTION 1

수 일치

주어가 단수인지 복수인지에 따라 동사를 맞춰야 한다. 주어는 대부분 −(e)s가 붙으면 복수형이지만, 동사는 반대로 단수 동사일 경우 −(e)s가 붙는다.

• '-s로 끝나는 단수형'과 '-s가 붙지 않는 복수형'을 혼동하지 말자.
-s로 끝나는 단수 명사: 학문명(politics, economics …), 회사명(SA electronics …)
-s로 끝나지 않는 복수 명사: people, personnel …

> **Economics** is a field of social science.
> 경제학은 사회 과학의 한 분야이다.

• 행위나 문장은 단수로 취급한다.
행위를 나타내는 '동명사(-ing)'나 'to부정사(to+동사원형)', '명사절'은 복수가 없으므로 단수로 취급한다.

> **Achieving goals** is our priority. 목표를 달성하는 것이 최우선이다.
> **That we need more staff** is true. 우리가 직원이 더 필요하다는 것은 사실이다.

• be동사를 제외한 나머지 동사는 '현재 시제'일 경우에만 수 일치를 따진다.
be동사의 경우 현재 시제(am/are/is), 과거 시제(was/were)에서 모두 따지지만 나머지 동사들은 현재 시제일 경우에만 수 일치를 따진다.

> **Smith Housewares** opened a new store in downtown last Monday.
> Smith Housewares는 지난 월요일에 시내에 새로운 가게를 오픈했다.
> **Smith Housewares** opens at 10 A.M.
> Smith Housewares는 아침 10시에 문을 연다.

• 부분을 나타내는 수량 표현은 of 이후 명사의 가산/불가산의 구별로 정답을 고른다.
부분을 나타내는 말은 '여러 개 중에 일부'를 나타낼 수도, '하나에서 일부분'을 나타낼 수도 있으므로 반드시 of 이후의 명사를 확인한다.

• 수식어를 걸러낼 수 있어야 한다.
주어 명사 뒤 수식어로 인해서 단/복수가 혼동이 되도록 출제가 된다. 따라서 전명구, 형용사절, 분사 등 '후치 수식어'를 걸러낼 수 있어야 제대로 수 일치를 파악할 수 있다.

문제 풀이 비법

❶ 주어가 단수면 '동사+(e)s'를, 복수면 '동사원형' 형태로 사용한다.

단수 주어에는 단수 동사가 붙는다.
부정사 주어/동명사 주어/절 주어는 반드시 동사를 단수로 한다.

Example

Delivering products on time ------- critical to getting clients' trust.

(A) is (B) are (C) be (D) have

해석 제품을 정시에 배송하는 것은 고객의 신뢰를 얻는 데 매우 중요하다.
어휘 on time 정시에 critical 대단히 중요한; 비판적인

 동명사 주어 뒤의 빈칸은 동사 자리이다. 동명사는 단수 취급하므로 복수인 (B) are와 (D) have는 오답이 된다. 따라서 be동사의 단수형인 (A) is가 정답이다.

정답 (A)

❷ 부분을 나타내는 수량 표현은 'of 뒤 명사'에 맞춘다.

복수의 일부분은 복수, 단수의 일부분은 단수로 본다.
→ of 뒤를 보고 전체가 복수인지 단수인지를 본다.

some/ any/ all/ most/ a lot/ lots/ plenty/ half/ part/ the rest/ 분수/ percent	of + 단수 ex) some of **the wine**
	of + 복수 ex) some of **my friends**

Example

------- of the three financial reports were submitted to the Chief Financial Officer two days ago.

(A) Much (B) All (C) One (D) Every

해석 세 가지 모든 재정 보고서는 이틀 전에 재무 이사에게 제출되었다.
어휘 submit 제출하다 Chief Financial Officer 재무 이사

 빈칸은 명사 주어 자리이고, 동사는 복수 형태인 were이다. 따라서 복수 동사와 함께 사용될 수 있는 (B) All이 정답이 된다. every(모두)는 복수 의미지만 단수 취급되며 형용사로만 사용되기 때문에 every of the라는 표현은 없다.

정답 (B)

❸ 수식어를 이용한 수 일치 문제

수식어구인 '전치사구, 관계사절, 분사구문'은 지워내고 문제를 본다.

Example

The quarterly operating costs at the ASJ manufacturing plant ------- steady compared with those of previous quarters.

(A) is remaining (B) to remain (C) have remained (D) were remained

해석 ASJ 제조 공장의 분기별 운영 비용은 이전 분기와 비교했을 때 꾸준하게 유지되어 오고 있다.
어휘 quarterly 분기별의 manufacturing plant 제조 공장 compared with ~와 비교하여 previous 이전의

빈칸은 동사 자리이므로 주어를 찾아야 한다. 전명구 수식어구(at the ASJ manufacturing plant)를 지워내면 주어가 costs라는 것을 알 수 있다. 따라서 복수 동사인 (C) have remained 가 정답이 된다. remain은 자동사로 수동태가 불가능하므로 (D) were remained는 오답이다.

정답 (C)

---

❹ 수 일치를 무시하는 경우

'요구, 주장, 제안, 명령'의 의미를 갖는 '형용사/명사/동사+that+주어+(should)+동사원형'

Example

We ask that everyone ------- their cellphones on mute during the regular meeting.

(A) put (B) puts (C) putting (D) to put

해석 정기 회의 중에는 모두 휴대폰을 무음으로 해 놓을 것을 부탁드립니다.
어휘 cellphone 휴대폰 regular meeting 정기 회의

빈칸은 that절의 주어(everyone) 뒤 동사 자리이다. 앞에 '요청'을 의미하는 본동사 ask를 보고 동사원형을 고른다. everyone은 '단수 취급'하기 때문에 (B) puts가 답이 될 것 같지만 everyone 뒤에 should가 생략되어 있기 때문에 오답이 된다.

정답 (A)

○ 요구, 주장, 제안, 요청의 의미를 갖는 어휘

형용사	important 중요한 essential/necessary/imperative 필수적인 critical 중요한
동사	suggest/propose 제안하다 recommend 추천하다, 권고하다 ask/request 요청하다 require 요구하다 insist 주장하다 command/order 명령하다
명사	advice 조언

❺ 주격 관계대명사의 수 일치

단수 명사(선행사)+that/who/which + 단수 동사
복수 명사(선행사)+that/who/which + 복수 동사

Example

Our Web site provides you with information which ------- very useful for your future career.

(A) is   (B) are   (C) has   (D) have

해석 저희 웹 사이트는 미래의 진로를 위한 매우 유용한 정보를 제공하고 있습니다.
어휘 provide 제공하다 information 정보 useful 유용한 career 경력, 직업

 빈칸은 주격 관계대명사(which) 뒤 동사 자리이다. 선행사(information)가 불가산 명사이므로 단수인 (A) is가 정답이다. 명사 목적어를 취하는 (C) has와 (D) have는 정답이 될 수 없다.

정답 (A)

비법 적용 연습

PART 5

1. A high-contrast projector ------- a picture with clearly-defined shadows and details.
   (A) produce (B) produces (C) product (D) producing

2. The new e-accounting solution significantly ------- the number of errors in the financial records of Duway corporations.
   (A) having reduced (B) reduce (C) reduced (D) reducing

3. Only half of the workers at the construction site ------- to work by bus.
   (A) commute (B) commuting (C) has commuted (D) commutes

4. ------- who is interested in joining the data analysis forum should contact Glenn before the end of this month.
   (A) Anyone (B) Yourself (C) Oneself (D) Those

5. Our new ------- was developed in Canada with off-site support provided by skilled engineers in India.
   (A) technology (B) technologies (C) technological (D) technologists

6. Researchers at the Hopkins Medical Center ------- the effect on human brains of using electronic devices.
   (A) researches (B) researching (C) have researched (D) will be researched

7. Mr. Andrew Sato, Director of Technical Support, ------- responsibility for all training seminars on the proper use of office equipment.
   (A) assuming (B) to assume (C) assume (D) will assume

8. Recent ------- in technology have made it possible for regional branches to communicate with each other much easier and faster.
   (A) advancement (B) advanced (C) advances (D) advancing

9. A number of employees at Bowden Energy ------- stairs instead of an elevator in an effort to save electricity and to stay fit.
   (A) use (B) uses (C) using (D) to use

10. ------- for the annual company banquet scheduled for December 23 have been sent to all staff members.
    (A) Invite (B) Invitation (C) To invite (D) Invitations

Grammar

DAY 10 태

주어가 행위의 주체가 되면 능동태가 되고 주어가 수동적으로 행위를 당할 때 그 문장을 수동태라 한다.

기본형	be p.p.	The company **was built** in 1992.
진행형	be being p.p.	The new technology **is being developed**.
완료형	have/has/had been p.p.	The computer **has been fixed**.

- **수동태의 주어는 능동태의 목적어다.**

수동태는 행위를 당하는 입장, 즉 능동태의 목적어 입장에서 쓴 것이기 때문에 목적어가 있는 능동태 문장만이 수동태 문장으로 사용 가능하다. 따라서 수동태 문장에서는 be p.p. 뒤에 보통 목적어가 없다.

- **자동사는 be p.p.가 없고 전치사구와 함께 쓰여 타동사로 쓰는 경우만 가능하다.**

자동사는 목적어가 없기 때문에 수동태 문형인 be p.p. 형태로 사용할 수 없다.

> Most of the inventory has **been accounted for**.
> 재고가 거의 파악되었다.

- **수동태이지만 목적어를 취하는 경우가 있다.**

4형식 동사(give, offer, send, grant 등)의 경우 '목적어가 두 개'이므로 be p.p. 뒤에 목적어가 올 수 있다.

> All the staff members <u>were sent</u> the invitation to the company outing.
> 모든 직원들이 회사 야유회 초대장을 받았다.

- **수동태(be p.p.) 이후에 명사나 형용사를 취하는 경우**

5형식 동사(make, keep, find, consider, deem 등)는 be p.p. 이후에 형용사나 명사를 취할 수 있다.

> The meeting <u>was found</u> very useful.
> 그 회의는 매우 유용하다고 알려졌다.

- **be p.p. 이후 'by 행위자' 외에 다양한 전치사들이 사용될 수 있다.**

by 행위자는 수식에 불과하기 때문에 의미에 따라 다양하게 사용될 수 있다.

> Customers <u>were satisfied</u> with the products.
> 소비자들은 그 상품에 만족했다.
> This training session <u>was aimed</u> at developing your skills.
> 이 교육 과정은 당신의 기술 개발에 목표를 두었다.

문제 풀이 비법

Grammar DAY 10

❶ 목적어가 있으면 능동태, 목적어가 없으면 수동태이거나 자동사이다.

| Example |

Teaching materials are ------- for the school teachers from our state's charitable organizations.

(A) provide (B) providing (C) being provided (D) have provided

해석 교육 자료는 주 자선 단체들로부터 학교 선생님들에게 제공되고 있다.
어휘 material 자료; 재료 charitable organization 자선 단체

be동사 뒤 빈칸 자리에는 분사(-ing/-ed) 형태만 올 수 있다. 동사원형이나 또 다른 동사는 올 수 없으므로 (A) provide나 (D) have provided는 오답이 된다. 또 provide(제공하다)는 목적어를 취하는 타동사인데 빈칸 뒤에 목적어가 없다. 따라서 수동태인 (C) being provided가 정답이 된다.

정답 (C)

❷ 자동사는 수동태가 될 수 없다.

수동태를 만들기 위해서는 목적어가 반드시 필요하므로, 목적어를 취할 수 없는 자동사는 수동태, 즉 'be + p.p.' 형태로 쓸 수 없다.

| Example |

The reception will ------- promptly at 5:00 P.M. at the Lincoln Ballroom.

(A) take place (B) took place (C) taking place (D) be taken place

해석 연회는 Lincoln 연회장에서 정확히 오후 5시에 열릴 것입니다.
어휘 reception 연회 promptly 정확히 제시간에; 즉시 ballroom 연회장 take place 개최되다, 일어나다

조동사 뒤 빈칸은 동사원형이 와야 하므로 (B) took place와 (C) taking place는 오답이다. take place(개최되다, 일어나다)는 목적어를 취하지 않는 자동사이므로 수동태가 불가능하다. 따라서 정답은 (A) take place가 된다.

정답 (A)

○ **자동사**: arrive 도착하다, rise 오르다, remain 남다, exist 존재하다, appear 나타나다, disappear 사라지다, happen 발행하다, occur 일어나다, take place 개최되다, function 기능하다, work 작동하다, speak 말하다, proceed 진행되다, deteriorate 악화되다

❸ 4형식의 수동태

4형식 동사들은 목적어를 두 개(간접 목적어, 직접 목적어)를 취할 수 있기 때문에 'be p.p. + 직접 목적어'가 가능하다.

> **Example**
>
> All sales representatives ------- a bonus for the remarkable increase in market share last year.
>
> (A) to give　　　(B) to be giving　　　(C) will be given　　　(D) have given
>
> 해석　모든 영업 사원들은 작년 시장 점유율의 눈에 띄는 증가로 상여금을 받을 것입니다.
> 어휘　sales representative 영업 사원　remarkable 눈에 띄는, 주목할 만한　increase 증가(하다)
>
>  빈칸은 동사 자리이므로 동사가 아닌 (A) to give와 (B) to be giving은 오답이 된다. 4형식 동사는 'be p.p.+직접 목적어'가 있는 형태가 가능하므로 정답은 (C) will be given이 된다.
>
> 정답 (C)
>
> ● 4형식 동사: give 주다, send 보내다, grant 수여하다, offer 제안하다, award 수상하다, win 안겨주다, owe 빚지다, lend 빌려 주다, show 보여 주다, pay 지불하다

❹ 5형식의 수동태

> **Example**
>
> To protect personal information, only authorized personnel are ------- to enter the document archive.
>
> (A) allow　　　(B) allowing　　　(C) allowed　　　(D) allowance
>
> 해석　개인 정보를 보호하기 위해서는, 관계자만이 문서실에 들어갈 수 있다.
> 어휘　protect 보호하다　authorized 권한을 부여받은　archive 기록 보관소
>
> be동사와 to부정사 사이 빈칸에 들어갈 수 있는 p.p. 형태인 (C) allowed가 정답이 된다. be동사와 함께 쓰일 수 없는 동사원형 (A)는 오답이 된다. be -ing는 능동이기 때문에 목적어가 없는 위 문장에서 (B) allowing은 정답이 될 수 없다.
> *[S + allow + O + to V] → [S + be allowed + to V]
>
> 정답 (C)

○ 〈be p.p.+to V〉로 사용되는 동사

능동태 (5형식) S+V+O+to V	주어+	allow/ advise/ encourage/ require/ request + 목적어 + to V force/ cause/ remind/ invite/ urge + 목적어 + to V

↓

수동태 (2형식) S+be p.p.+to V	주어+be	advised/ encouraged/ required/ requested + to V forced/ allowed/ urged/ reminded/ invited + to V

The company president **allowed** employees **to wear** casual dress on Friday. (능동태)
    주어   동사   목적어   목적격 보어
회사 사장은 금요일에 직원들이 평상복을 입을 수 있도록 허락했다.

↓

Employees **were allowed to wear** casual dress on Friday. (수동태)
 주어   동사   주격 보어
직원들은 금요일에 평상복을 입는 것이 허용되었다.

❺ 감정 동사의 능동태와 수동태

감정은 수동으로 느끼는 것이기 때문에 수동태를 쓰고, 감정의 원인이 되는 것은 능동의 형태로 사용한다.

Example

According to the business research, customers who ------- with products have a tendency to pay late.

(A) dissatisfied   (B) dissatisfying   (C) are dissatisfied   (D) has dissatisfied

해석 비즈니스 연구에 의하면, 제품에 만족을 못하는 고객은 늦게 지불하는 경향이 있습니다.
어휘 according to ~에 따르면 tendency 경향

관계사 이후 동사 자리 빈칸이다. 따라서 동사가 아닌 (B) dissatisfying은 오답이 된다. dissatisfy라는 단어는 감정 유발 타동사이기 때문에 감정을 느끼는 주어(customers)와는 수동의 의미로 써야 한다. 따라서 정답은 (C) are dissatisfied이다.

정답 (C)

○ 감정 유발 타동사

interest 흥미를 불러일으키다	excite 흥분시키다	please 기쁘게 하다
fascinate 매료시키다	satisfy 만족시키다	dissatisfy 불만을 갖게 하다
tire 피곤하게 하다	discourage 낙담시키다	encourage 용기를 주다
depress 낙담시키다	frustrate 좌절시키다	surprise[amaze] 놀라게 하다
bewilder 당황하게 하다	embarrass 황당하게 하다	shock 충격을 주다

비법 적용 연습

PART 5

1. Visitors to the P&G Chemical Lab must ------- by our public relations representative at all times.
   (A) be accompanied (B) accompany (C) to accompany (D) accompanying

2. The Deutsche Motor Imports employee handbook ------- a list of work-related company phone numbers.
   (A) contain (B) containing (C) is contained (D) contains

3. The Pierson subway station is ------- for repairs until the end of May.
   (A) close (B) closes (C) closed (D) closings

4. The manufacturer ------- the warranty period on its camera lens line by 6 months.
   (A) extend (B) was extended (C) extending (D) has extended

5. Applicants for transfer to other branches must ------- their paperwork by the end of this week.
   (A) submitted (B) submitting (C) submit (D) be submitted

6. A Lutz Mobile spokesperson guaranteed that all their smartphones would be properly ------- if there are any mechanical problems.
   (A) repair (B) repairs (C) repaired (D) repairing

7. The purpose of this meeting is to confirm the details and budget of your team's trip to Copenhagen for the trade fair to ------- on August 15.
   (A) be holding (B) be held (C) hold (D) holds

8. Those with previous experience in the field of sales or customer relations will ------- the better chance to be hired for the vacant positions.
   (A) give (B) be given (C) be giving (D) have given

9. The Dunham Titan 2000 XG is a reliable truck, but some car experts argue that the seats of the vehicle are poorly -------.
   (A) design (B) designed (C) designer (D) designing

10. Employees interested in contributing to the company charity activities ------- to sign up to the volunteer list posted in front of Gregory Moreland's office.
    (A) will invite (B) are inviting (C) can invite (D) are invited

Grammar

DAY 11 시제

시제는 동작이 일어나는 시간을 의미하며 영어에는 현재, 과거, 미래 세 가지 기본 시제가 있고 이외에 완료 및 진행 시제가 있다.

❶ 기본 시제

현재	항상 그런 것, 정해진 것을 표현한다. The company **sends** out a monthly newsletter to all members. 회사는 모든 고객에게 월간 소식지를 보낸다.
과거	명백한 과거의 행위나 상태를 표현한다. The package **was delivered** to Mr. Pam two days ago. 소포는 Pam 씨에게 2일 전에 배송되었다.
미래	현재와 관련 없는 미래의 행위나 상태를 표현한다. TJ Tech **will hold** an end-of-the-year award ceremony this December. TJ Tech는 올 12월에 연말 시상식을 열 것이다.

❷ 완료 시제

현재완료	have/has + p.p. 형태로 과거 행위나 상태가 지금까지 이어진 경우 Sean **has served** as a company lawyer <u>for 15 years</u>. Sean은 회사의 변호사로 15년간 근무했다.
과거완료	had + p.p. 형태로 특정 과거 시점보다 먼저 일어난 경우 By the time Jack <u>found</u> the computer problem, some of the important data **had** already **disappeared**. Jack이 컴퓨터의 문제를 발견했을 때는 이미 중요한 데이터 일부가 사라진 상태였다.
미래완료	will have + p.p. 형태로 미래 특정 시점까지 과거의 일이 영향을 미친 경우 **By tomorrow**, the annual financial report **will have been completed**. 내일이면 연례 재정 보고서가 마무리될 것이다.

❸ 진행 시제

특정 시점에 진행이 되고 있는 동작을 의미할 때 사용된다.

Demian **was printing** out some documents when I called him.
Demian은 내가 전화를 걸었을 당시에, 몇 가지 서류를 인쇄하고 있었다.

*현재 진행의 경우 미래를 의미할 때도 있다.

문제 풀이 비법

❶ 각각의 시제와 함께 쓰이는 시간 부사 표현

시제 문제를 해결할 때 문장에 등장하는 시간의 부사 표현이 힌트가 되는 경우가 많다.

> **Example**
>
> Most of the directors at SJ Holdings ------- the expansion plan at the meeting last week.
>
> (A) welcome (B) welcomed (C) will welcome (D) has welcomed
>
> **해석** SJ Holdings의 임원 대부분은 지난주 회의에서 확장 계획을 환영했다.
> **어휘** director 임원; (부서 등의) 책임자 expansion 확장
>
>  빈칸은 동사 자리로 동사의 알맞은 형태를 고르는 문제이다. 문장 맨 뒤에 시간 부사인 'last week(지난주)'가 보이기 때문에 과거형인 (B) welcomed가 정답이다. has welcomed는 주어가 Most of the directors이기 때문에 단·복수 수 일치에서 오답으로 지워진다.
>
> 정답 (B)

○ 시제의 힌트가 되는 부사 표현

과거	yesterday, ~ ago, last + 명사(week/weekend/month/year 등) recently, lately
현재	usually, always, often, generally, typically, periodically, regularly, routinely, customarily, ordinarily every, each + 명사(week/weekend/month/year 등)
현재완료	since + 주어 + 과거 동사, since + 과거 시점 명사 in/for/during the past[last] + 숫자 + 기간 명사 over the past[last] + 숫자 + 기간 명사 recently, lately
미래/미래완료	tomorrow, next + 명사(week/weekend/month/year 등) by/until + 미래 표현 as of + 미래 starting/beginning + 미래 표현 by the time 주어 + 현재 동사 when 주어 + 현재 동사

❷ 현재완료의 계속적인 용법 (since의 올바른 사용법)

주어 + 현재완료 동사 + [since + 과거 시점]
① since 뒤에는 반드시 과거 시점 + ② 주절의 시제는 현재완료
③ 위와 같은 시제 조건에 맞지 않으면 since는 '~ 때문에'로 해석한다.

Example

Since last month's pay raises, employee productivity ------- a lot more than anticipated.

(A) improves (B) improving (C) has improved (D) to be improved

해석 지난달 급여 인상 후로, 직원 생산성은 예상했던 것보다 훨씬 더 많이 향상되었다.
어휘 pay raise 임금 인상 employee productivity 직원 생산성 anticipate 예상하다
improve 개선하다, 향상시키다

빈칸은 주어 뒤 동사 자리이므로 동사가 아닌 (B) improving과 (D) to be improved는 오답이 된다. Since last month's pay raise(과거 사건)를 단서로 현재완료가 정답이 된다.

정답 (C)

❸ 시간/조건의 부사절에서는 현재가 미래를 대신한다.

⟨When/If 주어 + 현재/현재완료 동사, 주어 + 조동사 + 동사원형(or 명령문)⟩의 구조를 취한다.

Example

If you ------- today, you will get an additional 15 percent discount from the registration fee.

(A) join (B) joined (C) has joined (D) joins

해석 오늘 가입하신다면 등록비에서 15% 추가 할인을 받을 것입니다.
어휘 additional 추가적인 registration fee 등록비

빈칸은 조건 부사절 안의 동사 자리이다. 주절의 동사 will get(미래 시제)을 근거로 현재 시제인 (A) join이 정답이 된다.

정답 (A)

○ 시간·조건 부사절 접속사

시간	when ~할 때 after ~ 이후에	until ~까지 before ~ 전에	as soon as ~하자 마자 by the time ~할 때 즈음에
조건	if ~한다면	unless ~하지 않는다면	as long as ~하는 한 once 일단 ~하면

비법 적용 연습

Grammar DAY 11

정답 및 해설 / 11p

PART 5

1. The school shuttle bus ------- every 30 minutes from the school's main gate.
   (A) depart   (B) was departed   (C) are departing   (D) departs

2. Guitarist Carlos Santana ------- his hit songs with young musicians at a charity concert in Los Angeles last Sunday.
   (A) performed   (B) performs   (C) performing   (D) will perform

3. By the time Dr. Cassel retires as chief researcher of Zurich Physics Laboratory, he ------- to increase the lab's reputation significantly.
   (A) manages   (B) will have managed   (C) managed   (D) has been managing

4. The product development team began a scramble for innovative ideas after a new competitor's product ------- their working prototype obsolete.
   (A) rendering   (B) rendered   (C) renders   (D) will render

5. Library members who don't return borrowed items by the due date ------- late fees.
   (A) charges   (B) will be charged   (C) having charged   (D) charged

6. By the time Demon's Lair from Winex Japan goes online as a role-playing game, its engineers ------- all of the errors reported in its beta testing.
   (A) will have corrected   (B) had been correcting   (C) are correcting   (D) to be corrected

7. Trey Jones ------- Columbia University 34 years ago, making him the longest serving faculty member in the Burrows School of Engineering and Applied Science.
   (A) join   (B) joins   (C) joined   (D) joining

8. If the company ------- union members to work extra hours on the weekends, it must give the workers meals and beverages.
   (A) asks   (B) were to ask   (C) will ask   (D) will have asked

9. We ------- countless inquiries since the advertisement aired on TV last weekend.
   (A) receive   (B) have received   (C) will receive   (D) receiving

10. When Malcolm Merchant Marine ------- its Vehicle Carrier department, considerable numbers of employees were assigned to other departments in the company.
    (A) was restructured   (B) restructures   (C) was restructuring   (D) to restructure

부정사

동사를 다른 품사로 사용하기 위한 준동사의 하나로, 문장에서 명사, 형용사, 부사로 사용되며 위치나 역할에 따라 품사가 결정된다.

❶ 부정사의 형태

기본형	to 동사원형(능동)	to give
수동형	to be p.p.	to be given
완료형	to have p.p.	to have given
진행형	to be -ing	to be giving

❷ 부정사의 기능

- to부정사는 명사 자리에 사용할 수 있다.

주어	**To finish the editing work on time** is very important. 편집 작업을 제시간에 끝내는 것은 매우 중요하다. = **It**(가짜 주어) is very important **to finish the editing work on time**(진짜 주어).
보어	The purpose of this meeting is **to discuss the ways to improve our brand awareness**. 이 회의의 목적은 우리의 브랜드 인지도를 개선할 수 있는 방법을 논의하는 것이다.
목적어	The company CFO decided **to cut the operating costs**. 회사의 재무 이사는 운영 비용을 삭감하기로 결정했다.

- to부정사는 형용사 역할을 할 수 있다. (명사+to부정사)

> There are several new products **to demonstrate**.
> 시연할 몇 가지 새로운 제품이 있다.

- to부정사는 부사 역할을 할 수 있다. (보통 완전한 문장에 들어간다.)

> **To ensure that it is clean and safe**, we should check the equipment regularly.
> 장비가 깨끗하고 안전하다는 것을 확실히 하기 위해서, 우리는 장비를 정기적으로 점검해야 한다.

- to부정사의 의미상의 주어는 to 앞에 'for+명사(또는 대명사의 목적격)'를 사용한다.

> In order **for you to arrive** on time, you should leave a little earlier.
> 당신이 제시간에 도착하기 위해서는 조금 더 일찍 출발해야 한다.

문제 풀이 비법

❶ 가주어/진주어 구문

부정사의 명사적인 용법인 [It + is + 형용사 + (for 사람) + to V]
　　　　　　　　　　　　가주어　　　　　　　　　　　　　　진주어

| Example |

To turn all our customers into loyal customers, it is important ------- to their requests as quickly as we can.

(A) response　　　(B) respond　　　(C) responding　　　(D) to respond

해석　모든 우리 고객들을 단골 고객으로 만들기 위해서는, 고객의 요청에 최대한 빨리 대응하는 것이 중요합니다.
어휘　turn A into B A를 B로 바꾸다　loyal customer 단골 고객, 우량 고객

콤마 뒤 it은 가짜 주어이기 때문에 빈칸에는 진짜 주어가 필요하다. 따라서 주어가 될 수 있는 (D) to respond가 정답이 된다.

정답 (D)

❷ 부정사의 부사적인 용법

'~를 위하여(목적)'의 의미로 주로 사용되는데 특히, 문장의 맨 앞이나 맨 뒤에 나오는 부정사를 주의한다.

| Example |

------- its 100th anniversary, the National Theatre will feature a brand new musical next month.

(A) Celebrated　　　(B) Celebrates　　　(C) Celebration　　　(D) To celebrate

해석　100주년을 축하하기 위해서, 국립 극장은 다음 달에 새로운 뮤지컬 공연을 선보일 것이다.
어휘　anniversary 기념일　feature 특징으로 삼다　brand new 완전히 새로운

문장에 동사(will feature)가 있기 때문에 빈칸은 동사 자리가 아니다. 따라서 동사인 (B) Celebrates는 오답이 된다. 빈칸 바로 뒤에 명사 its 100th anniversary가 있기 때문에 역시 명사인 (C) Celebration도 오답이다. '축하하기 위하여'의 의미로 to부정사인 (D) To celebrate가 정답이 된다.

정답 (D)

❸ 부정사를 이용한 어휘 문제

Example

Only those who are able ------- the deadline will be invited to the wine party sponsored by the company.

(A) meet　　　　　(B) meeting　　　　(C) met　　　　(D) to meet

해석 마감 기한을 맞출 수 있는 사람만이 회사에서 후원하는 와인 파티에 초대될 것이다.
어휘 deadline 기한, 마감 시간[일자]　sponsor 후원자, 후원하다

 be able 이후 빈칸으로 (D) to meet가 정답이 된다. 빈칸 앞에 이미 be동사가 존재하므로 동사인 (A) meet나 (C) met은 정답이 될 수 없다.

정답 (D)

○ 동사 + to부정사

want 원하다	need 필요하다	wish 바라다	hope 희망하다
expect 기대하다	plan 계획하다	decide 결정하다	choose 선택하다
aim 겨냥하다	fail 실패하다	promise 약속하다	manage 간신히 해내다
pretend ~인 척하다	afford 여유가 있다		

○ 동사 + 목적어 + to부정사(목적격 보어)

want 원하다	need 필요하다	expect 기대하다	invite 초대하다, 요청하다
ask 요청하다, 부탁하다	encourage 장려하다	persuade 설득하다	cause 야기하다
force 강요하다	require 요구하다	compel 강요하다	tell 말하다
forbid 금지하다	enable 가능하게 하다	permit 허가하다	allow 허락하다
remind 상기시키다	warn 경고하다	advise 조언하다	inform 안내하다

○ 명사 + to부정사

ability 능력	time 시간	place 장소	purpose/goal/objective 목적
plan 계획	way 방법	effort 노력	decision 결정
right 권리	authority 권한	capacity 능력	chance/opportunity 기회

○ 형용사 + to부정사

be able to V ~가 가능하다	be unable to V ~가 불가능하다
be willing to V 기꺼이 ~하다	be unwilling to V ~가 내키지 않다
be reluctant to V ~하기 싫다	be ready to V ~할 준비가 되다
be likely to V ~할 것 같다	be unlikely to V ~할 것 같지 않다
be important to V ~하는 게 중요하다	be necessary to V ~하는 게 필요하다
be essential to V ~하는 게 필수적이다	be advisable to V ~가 권장된다
be difficult[hard] to V ~하기 어렵다	be easy to V ~하기 쉽다

❹ 부정사의 의미상 주어

to부정사의 의미상 주어로 'for+명사(대명사의 목적격)'를 사용한다.

> **Example**
>
> It is very necessary ------- entry-level employees to receive a detailed pay slip every month.
>
> (A) from (B) to (C) for (D) in
>
> **해석** 신입사원이 매월 상세한 급여 명세서를 받는 것은 매우 필수적이다.
> **어휘** entry-level 초보자용의; 말단인 detailed 상세한 pay slip 급여 명세서
>
>  가주어/진주어 구문이라는 것을 파악한다. 가주어 It과 진주어 to receive를 보고 앞에 entry-level employees는 의미상의 주어라는 것을 알 수 있다. to부정사의 의미상 주어 앞에는 전치사 for를 사용하므로 정답은 (C)가 된다.
>
> 정답 (C)

비법 적용 연습

Grammar DAY 12

정답 및 해설 / 12p

PART 5

1. The Boston Tourism Office invites tourists and visitors ------- the hotels and restaurants located in the city's historic area.
   (A) patronize   (B) patronized   (C) to patronize   (D) be patronizing

2. Even with increasing competition from various new restaurants in the area, Romano's Bistro is still attracting many customers ------- in business.
   (A) stay   (B) to stay   (C) stayed   (D) staying

3. Mr. Miller has requested permission ------- the company's auditorium for the annual technology seminar that will be held next month.
   (A) will use   (B) have used   (C) using   (D) to use

4. In an effort ------- staff morale, the board of directors is planning to implement a new incentive program.
   (A) enhancement   (B) enhancing   (C) to enhance   (D) enhanced

5. Mobile phone companies often depend on discounts and various incentives ------- new customers.
   (A) attraction   (B) attracted   (C) attracts   (D) to attract

6. Our product development team is doing everything they can ------- the deadline for the official product launching press conference.
   (A) to meet   (B) meeting   (C) met   (D) be met

7. Please visit our Web site ------- designs, features and prices of all the appliances on the market.
   (A) to compare   (B) comparing   (C) compared   (D) will compare

8. Union executives are requested ------- early on June 1 in order to welcome the new employees.
   (A) arriving   (B) arrived   (C) to arrive   (D) have arrived

9. ------- the process, please include your item's model name and serial number on all the paperwork.
   (A) To be expedited   (B) Expedite   (C) Expedited   (D) To expedite

10. In order to cope with the seasonal demand increase, the personnel department intends ------- some new employees.
    (A) recruited   (B) recruitment   (C) recruiting   (D) to recruit

DAY 12 » 073

Grammar

DAY 13 동명사

동명사는 동사가 명사로 된 형태로 '~하는 것'의 의미를 갖고 명사의 역할을 하지만 동사의 성격과 기능도 그대로 가지고 있다.

❶ 동명사의 형태

기본형	동사+ing	giving
수동형	being p.p.	being given
완료형	having p.p.	having given

❷ 동명사의 기능

• 동명사는 문장 내에서 명사의 역할을 한다.

주어	**Carrying a valid ID card** is required. 유효한 신분증을 지니고 다니는 것이 요구된다.
타동사의 목적어	The theater has discontinued **offering accommodations to performers**. 극장은 공연자들에게 숙박 제공을 중단했다.
전치사의 목적어	Customers can renew their services without **visiting our Web site**. 고객은 홈페이지 방문 없이도 서비스를 갱신할 수 있다.
보어	Tian's hobby is **listening to music**. Tian의 취미는 음악을 듣는 것이다.

• 동명사의 의미상 주어는 '소유격'을 사용한다.

> I appreciate **your** participating in the event.
> 당신이 행사에 참여해 준 것에 대해 감사드립니다.

• 동명사는 동사에서 온 명사 형태(행위 명사)이기 때문에 동사의 성질은 그대로 가지고 있다. 따라서 타동사의 동명사는 목적어를 갖는다.

> SNS advertising became another way of <u>attracting</u> **customers**.
> SNS 광고는 고객을 끌어 모으는 또 하나의 방법이 되었다.

• 동명사는 부사의 수식을 받는다.

> After **carefully** <u>interviewing</u> qualified applicants, we offered Mr. Kim a position.
> 자격이 되는 지원자들을 신중하게 인터뷰한 후 우리는 Kim 씨에게 자리를 제안했다.

문제 풀이 비법

Grammar DAY 13

❶ 동명사는 전치사의 목적어로 쓰인다.

〈전치사 + 동명사 + 동명사의 목적어〉의 순서에 주의한다.
　　　　　(-ing)　　　명사

Example

Our vice president Mr. Anderson is good at ------- unique solutions to our clients.

(A) offer　　　　(B) offers　　　　(C) offering　　　　(D) offered

해석　우리 부사장인 Anderson 씨는 의뢰인들에게 독창적인 솔루션을 제공하는 데 능하다.
어휘　vice president 부사장　be good at ~에 능숙하다　solution 해법, 해결책

 be동사가 이미 있기 때문에 빈칸은 동사 자리가 아니다. 또한 빈칸 이후 명사가 있기 때문에 명사 역시 정답이 될 수 없다. 빈칸 이후 목적어 unique solutions를 목적어로 취하면서 전치사의 목적어 역할을 할 수 있는 동명사 (C) offering이 정답이 된다.

정답 (C)

❷ 전치사 to vs. 부정사 to

Example

The charity organization has been dedicated to ------- the well-being of poor children in the world.

(A) promote　　　(B) promoting　　　(C) promotion　　　(D) promotes

해석　그 자선 단체는 전 세계의 불쌍한 어린이들의 복지 활성화에 기여해 왔습니다.
어휘　charity organization 자선 단체　well-being 복지, 행복　be dedicated to ~에 전념하다, 헌신하다

 동사(has been dedicated)가 있으므로 빈칸은 동사 자리가 아니다. 따라서 (A) promote와 (D) promotes는 오답이 된다. dedicated 이후 to는 명사나 동명사를 취하는 전치사이므로 동명사 (B) promoting이 정답이 된다. (C)는 빈칸 뒤 명사(the well-being)와 품사가 중복되므로 오답이다.

정답 (B)

○ 전치사 to + 동명사(-ing)

- object to -ing ~을 반대하다
- lead to -ing ~을 초래하다
- contribute to -ing ~에 기여[공헌]하다
- when it comes to -ing ~에 관해 말하자면
- apply to -ing 적용하다
- respond to -ing ~에 응답하다
- be devoted[dedicated/committed] to -ing ~에 전념하다, 헌신하다
- be used[accustomed] to -ing: ~하는 데 익숙하다 cf. be used to do: ~하는 데 사용되다
- be opposed to -ing ~을 반대하다
- look forward to -ing ~을 바라다, 고대하다
- attribute A to -ing A를 ~탓으로 돌리다
- be subject to -ing ~하기 쉽다; ~하기로 되어 있다
- refer to -ing 참고하다, 언급하다

❸ 동명사를 목적어로 취하는 동사

┤ **Example** ├

To avoid ------- the audience, we decided to omit some of the pictures and charts.

(A) distract　　　(B) distracts　　　(C) distracting　　　(D) distracted

해석　청중들의 주의가 분산되는 것을 피하기 위해서, 우리는 그림이나 차트를 생략하기로 결정했다.
어휘　audience 청중　omit 생략하다　distract 산만하게 하다

 빈칸은 동사(avoid) 뒤 목적어 자리이다. avoid는 목적어로 명사 또는 동명사를 취하므로, 선택지 중 동명사인 (C) distracting이 정답이 된다.

정답 (C)

○ 〈동명사〉를 목적어로 취하는 동사

admit 받아들이다	advise 조언하다	avoid 피하다	evade 피하다
consider 고려하다	delay 늦추다, 연기하다	deny 부인하다	reject 거절하다
enjoy 즐기다	finish 끝내다	quit 그만두다	postpone 연기하다, 늦추다
suggest 제안하다	include 포함하다	discontinue 중단하다	recommend 추천하다

○ 〈동명사〉와 〈to부정사〉 모두를 목적어로 취하는 동사

| like 좋아하다 | love 좋아하다, 사랑하다 | prefer 선호하다 | hate 싫어하다, 증오하다 |
| begin/start 시작하다 | attempt 시도하다 | continue 계속하다 | intend 의도하다, 작정하다 |

❹ 동명사 vs. 명사[-ing형 명사]

동명사는 '부사'의 수식을 받지만, 명사는 '형용사'의 수식을 받는다.
동명사는 관사와 함께 쓰일 수 없지만 명사는 관사와 함께 쓰일 수 있다.
타동사의 동명사는 목적어를 취할 수 있지만, 명사는 그렇지 못하다.

Example

The ------- opening of the third branch will take place next Monday with a number of guests.

(A) official　　　(B) officially　　　(C) officials　　　(D) officialize

해석 세 번째 지점의 공식적인 개소식이 많은 게스트들과 함께 다음 주 월요일에 열릴 것이다.
어휘 branch 지사, 분점　take place 개최되다, 일어나다　a number of 많은

 빈칸은 -ing형 명사(opening) 앞 형용사 자리이다. 따라서 정답은 (A) official(공식적인)이 된다.

정답 (A)

○ -ing형 명사

training 교육, 훈련	seating 좌석	advertising 광고	founding 설립
processing 처리, 가공	funding 자금 지원	clothing 의류	ticketing 발권
heating 난방	banking 은행 업무	planning 기획	accounting 회계
spending 지출	housing 주택	keeping 보관	manufacturing 제조
purchasing 구매	understanding 이해	pricing 가격 책정	shipping 선적
budgeting 예산 책정	testing 검사	staffing 직원 충원, 배치	meaning 의미
gathering 모임	beginning 시작	offering 제공(물)	meeting 회의
opening 공석, 개관			

비법 적용 연습

PART 5

1. Mr. Gleason looks forward to ------- potential alternative investment options at the July business meeting.
   (A) explore   (B) exploring   (C) exploratory   (D) exploration

2. To avoid ------- your prospective clients during your business presentation, please refrain from using complicated layouts.
   (A) distraction   (B) distracts   (C) distracted   (D) distracting

3. Our senior consultant Anthony Dinozo is responsible for ------- customized advertising strategies to small-sized client companies.
   (A) offer   (B) offered   (C) offering   (D) offers

4. Please be aware that all the programs held outside the university premises are subject to ------- without prior notice.
   (A) cancellation   (B) canceling   (C) canceled   (D) cancel

5. ------- us of defect rate increases on our newly introduced assembly line made it possible for us to examine the entire machinery in our factory.
   (A) Warned   (B) Warn   (C) Warning   (D) Warns

6. The Tokyo branch spends plenty of time ------- its existing staff members and new recruits.
   (A) training   (B) trains   (C) trained   (D) trainer

7. It is crucial for government tourism officials to consistently find new ways of ------- international tourists.
   (A) attracts   (B) attracting   (C) attraction   (D) attractive

8. ------- an international rock festival for over 100,000 was the most challenging project of this year.
   (A) Preparation   (B) Preparing   (C) Prepared   (D) Being prepared

9. The magazine company's circulation division is dedicated to ------- responsive and excellent service.
   (A) provision   (B) provided   (C) providing   (D) provides

10. Francis Taylor creates the interesting patterns and textures in his work by ------- the amount of paint on his palette knife and brush.
    (A) varying   (B) varies   (C) varied   (D) vary

DAY 14 분사

동사에서 온 형태로 현재분사와 과거분사가 있다. 능동형인 현재분사는 보통 '~하는', 수동형인 과거분사는 '~된'으로 해석한다.

❶ 분사의 형태

현재분사	V+ing	giving
과거분사	V+ed(p.p.)	given

❷ 분사의 기능

- **분사는 명사를 수식하거나 보충한다.**
분사는 동사에서 온 형용사 수식어이기 때문에 명사를 수식하거나 보어가 된다. 따라서 분사가 문장에 등장하면 반드시 명사와 관련이 있다. 이때 수식을 받는 명사와 분사의 관계가 능동이면 -ing, 수동이면 p.p.를 사용한다.

> The **revised** paper recycling policy will be posted on the company bulletin board.
> 수정된 종이 재활용 정책이 회사 게시판에 게시될 것이다.

- **자동사는 p.p. 형태로 명사 수식이 불가하다.**
자동사의 경우 현재분사로만 명사를 수식할 수 있다.

> The **existing** equipment should be checked regularly.
> 기존 장비는 정기적으로 점검되어야 한다.

- **분사구문은 '주절의 주어'와의 관계에 따라 현재분사 또는 과거분사를 써 준다.**
기본적으로 분사구문에서 현재분사냐 과거분사냐의 문제 역시 능동태, 수동태 문제 풀이와 같다. (수동태 참고)

> **Achieving** the sales target, Mr. Ling will be promoted.
> = If Mr. Ling achieves the sales target, Mr. Ling will be promoted.
> 판매 목표를 달성하면 Ling 씨는 승진할 것이다.

- **'Having p.p. ~/ Having been p.p.'와 같이 완료 분사구문의 경우, 주절의 시제보다 한 시제 앞선다.**

> **Having finished** the report, Kenneth forwarded it to Mr. Carter for review.
> = After he had finished the report, Kenneth forwarded it to Mr. Carter for review.
> Kenneth가 보고서를 끝낸 후에 검토를 위해 Carter 씨에게 보냈다.

- **해석으로 풀기 어려운 '분사형 형용사'를 기억해 두자.**
모양은 분사 모양이지만 태생 자체가 형용사인 어휘들은 따로 기억해 두어야 한다.

문제 풀이 비법

❶ 분사는 명사를 수식하는 형용사로 사용된다.

| Example |

Factory workers were asked to work overtime due to the ------- demands from European markets.

(A) increase　　(B) to increase　　(C) increasing　　(D) increasingly

해석　유럽 시장의 증가하는 수요로 인해 공장 직원들은 초과 근무를 요청 받았다.
어휘　work overtime 초과 근무를 하다, 야근하다　due to ~때문에　demand 수요

빈칸은 관사(the)와 명사(demands) 사이 형용사 자리이다. 선택지 중 형용사 역할을 할 수 있는 (C) increasing이 정답이 된다. to부정사인 (B) to increase도 형용사 역할을 할 수 있지만 명사를 뒤에서 수식해야 하므로 오답이 된다.

정답 (C)

❷ '감정/기분 동사'의 분사 활용

다른 것(사람)에 의해 감정이나 기분을 느끼게 되면 과거분사 (-ed)
다른 사람의 감정이나 기분 변화에 영향을 미치면 현재분사 (-ing)
감정은 어떤 원인에 의해 수동적으로 느끼는 것으로 과거분사를 사용하게 된다.

| Example |

Those ------ in the computer music workshop are advised to register for it in advance because of its popularity.

(A) interest　　(B) interested　　(C) interesting　　(D) interests

해석　컴퓨터 음악 워크숍에 관심 있는 사람들은 이 행사의 인기 때문에 사전에 등록하는 것이 바람직합니다.
어휘　register for ~에 등록하다　in advance 미리　popularity 인기

문장에 동사(are advised)가 있으므로 빈칸은 동사 자리가 아니다. 따라서 Those를 수식할 수 있는 분사가 필요한데 '관심 있는'은 다른 것에 의해 감정을 느끼게 된 것이므로 과거분사 형태인 (B) interested가 정답이 된다.

정답 (B)

○ 감정/기분 관련 동사: excite, interest, bore, satisfy, tire, disappoint, surprise, shock, confuse, convince, exhaust, embarrass, frustrate, encourage, discourage, fascinate

❸ 분사는 주격 보어와 목적격 보어로 사용된다.

| Example |

The attractive characters and surprising plot twist made last night's play quite
-------.

(A) excite (B) excited (C) exciting (D) excitement

해석 매력적인 등장 인물과 놀라운 반전은 어젯밤 연극을 꽤 흥미진진하게 만들었다.
어휘 attractive 매력적인 character 등장 인물 plot twist 반전

문장에서 동사(made)나 목적어(last night's play)를 보고 이후 빈칸이 목적격 보어 자리임을 알 수 있다. 반전 때문에 연극은 사람들을 흥미롭게 만들었고, 사람들은 그것으로 인해 흥미로움을 느끼는 상황이므로 여기에서는 전자의 경우라 현재분사인 (C) exciting이 정답이 된다.

정답 (C)

❹ 분사구문

〈-ing/-ed ~, S + V + O[완전한 문장]〉 구문으로 문제를 풀 때에는 수동태 구문과 동일하다.

| Example |

------- primarily North America, natural gas company Drummond announced that it had stopped operating some of its branches in Asia.

(A) Serving (B) Served (C) Server (D) Serves

해석 주로 북아메리카 지역에 서비스를 제공하는 천연 가스 회사 Drummond는 아시아 지역 지사 몇 곳의 운영을 중단했다고 발표했습니다.
어휘 primarily 주로 natural gas 천연 가스 operate 운영하다, 영업하다

문장의 맨 앞자리 빈칸이며, 빈칸 뒤에 목적어인 North America가 보인다. 콤마로만 연결된 주절에 announced라는 동사가 있으므로 동사인 (D)는 정답에서 제외된다. 목적어인 North America를 받을 수 있고 동사가 아닌 (A) Serving이 정답이 된다.

정답 (A)

비법 적용 연습

PART 5

1. Mitsukoshi Department Store's policy is that patrons may return or refund any items within 2 weeks if they are not ------- with their purchases.
   (A) satisfactory   (B) satisfaction   (C) satisfied   (D) satisfy

2. ------- by the new product launching presentation last Saturday, Forrester Investment Bank has decided to order five hundred units of Packard Company's G-1 Tablet PC.
   (A) Impressed   (B) Impressive   (C) Impressing   (D) Impression

3. Inclement weather caused a blackout last night, ------- some residents without electricity.
   (A) will leave   (B) leaving   (C) have left   (D) leaves

4. ------- a Master's degree in Financial Analysis, Mr. Brown is considered one of the most promising candidates for the senior analyst position.
   (A) Having earned   (B) Earned   (C) Being earned   (D) Earn

5. All Frontier Telecom clients are encouraged to review the new ------- monthly statement showing each monthly charge of their family members respectively.
   (A) consolidate   (B) consolidator   (C) consolidation   (D) consolidated

6. ------- that his documents needed to get there quickly, Tom requested a bike messenger service.
   (A) Concern   (B) Concerning   (C) Concerns   (D) Concerned

7. Average production time at Ford's Kansas City factory has been almost halved since the introduction of the 3rd generation ------- assembly system.
   (A) automate   (B) automatically   (C) automated   (D) automation

8. MOTA Heavy Industries is working with a local real estate firm to locate the potential sites for the ------- nuclear power plant.
   (A) proposition   (B) proposed   (C) propose   (D) proposal

9. Hopkins Hospital's policy clearly indicates that patient information will not be disclosed without ------- consent of the parties involved.
   (A) writing   (B) written   (C) write   (D) wrote

10. There are some ------- signs that public views of international marriage are changing in Korea.
    (A) encourage   (B) encouraged   (C) encouraging   (D) encouragement

DAY 15 접속사

❶ 접속사의 종류

등위접속사와 상관접속사는 서로 대등한 절, 구, 단어를 연결한다.
등위접속사: and, but, or, nor, so, for, yet 등
상관접속사: both A and B, either A or B, neither A nor B,
　　　　　　 not only A but also B, not A but B

❷ 등위접속사

• 등위접속사는 문맥에 적절하게 써야 한다.
－ and는 긍정적이면 긍정적인 내용끼리, 부정적이면 부정적인 내용끼리 연결해 주어야 한다.
－ but은 긍정적인 내용이 앞에 왔다면 이후는 부정적인 내용을 연결한다.
－ or의 경우 선택의 개념에서 많이 쓰인다.

> The instruction should be clear **and** easy.
> 지시 사항은 명확하고 쉬워야 한다.
> She is not available on Tuesday **but** she is free on Friday.
> 그녀는 화요일에는 시간이 나지 않지만 금요일에는 시간이 있다.
> Mr. Kim should choose to take a vacation **or** take it as money.
> Kim 씨는 휴가를 갈 것인지 아니면 휴가 대신 돈으로 받을 것인지를 선택해야 한다.

• 등위접속사는 '같은 형태'의 다른 의미를 연결한다.
〈문장 and 문장〉, 〈명사 and 명사〉, 〈형용사 and 형용사〉와 같이 동일한 형태의 다른 의미를 연결한다. 이를 이용한 품사 문제도 간혹 출제된다.

> You need dedication **and** patience to survive there.
> 당신이 거기에서 살아남으려면 헌신과 인내심이 필요하다.
> He needs to complete this form **and** return it to our office by tomorrow.
> 그는 이 서류를 작성하고 내일까지 우리 사무실에 제출해야 한다.

❸ 상관접속사

• 상관접속사는 '서로 짝인 것'끼리 사용하며 수 일치에도 주의한다.
or이 들어가 있는 상관접속사는 or 뒤에 있는 명사에 수 일치를 맞춘다. 나머지는 해석상 중요한 정보에 수 일치를 맞춘다.

> Either the employer or **the employees** are responsible for the accident.
> 고용주나 직원들 둘 중 하나가 그 사고에 대해 책임이 있다.
> Not only you but also **your friend** has to make an extra effort.
> 너뿐만 아니라 네 친구도 더 노력을 해야 한다.

문제 풀이 비법

❶ 등위접속사는 병렬 구조를 취한다. → 생략되는 부분에 주의

Example

Your opinions are very important ------- will help us serve you better in the future.

(A) because   (B) and   (C) therefore   (D) either

해석 당신의 의견은 매우 중요하며 향후 당신에게 더 나은 서비스를 제공하는 데 저희에게 큰 도움이 될 것입니다.
어휘 opinion 의견 serve (손님을) 응대하다 in the future 향후에

 빈칸 앞에 문장이 있고 빈칸 뒤에는 동사가 있다. 따라서 이 둘을 연결하는 접속사를 고르는 문제이므로 동사와 동사를 연결할 수 있는 (B) and가 정답이 된다. (A) because는 부사절 접속사로 완전한 두 문장을 연결해야 한다.

정답 (B)

---

❷ 상관접속사 → 숙어와 병렬 구조 문제로 출제

Example

Employees are requested to use either the southern gate ------- the rear exit of the building during the period of renovation.

(A) into   (B) with   (C) not   (D) or

해석 직원들은 개조 공사 중에는 남문이나 건물의 뒷문을 이용하라는 요청을 받았다.
어휘 southern 남쪽의 rear exit 뒤쪽 출구 renovation 개조, 수리

 〈either+명사+빈칸+명사〉의 문장 구조로 either과 어울리는 접속사 (D) or이 정답이 된다.

정답 (D)

● 상관접속사

both A and B A, B 둘 다   either A or B A, B 둘 중 하나   neither A nor B A도 B도 아니다
not A but B A가 아니라 B   not only A but also B (= B as well as A) A뿐만 아니라 B도

❸ 상관접속사의 수 일치

Example

Not only you but also your supervisor ------- attend the marketing strategy meeting for the new product.

(A) have to   (B) had to   (C) has to   (D) only to

해석 당신뿐만 아니라 당신의 상관도 신제품을 위한 마케팅 전략 회의에 참석해야 한다.
어휘 supervisor 관리자, 감독자 new product 신제품, 신상품

 위 문장에서 중요 정보는 당신이 아닌, 당신의 '상사'이다. 따라서 단수 동사인 (C) has to가 정답이 된다.

정답 (C)

◯ 상관접속사의 수 일치

① both A and B + 복수 동사
Both Ms. Park and Mr. Marx **are attending** the marketing seminar next week.
Park 씨와 Marx 씨는 다음 주 마케팅 세미나에 참석할 것이다.

② not   A   but   B
   not only A   but also   B
   either   A   or   B
   neither A   nor   B
   동사를 전부 B에 일치시킨다.
Neither she nor I **am** in charge of the department.
그녀도 나도 부서 책임자가 아니다.

③ B as well as A
해석의 순서 때문에 동사를 B에 일치시킨다.
Ms. Kim, as well as the male colleagues, **has** learned how to use the new intranet one more time.
남자 동료들뿐만 아니라 Kim 씨도 한번 더 인트라넷 사용법을 배웠다.

비법 적용 연습

Grammar DAY 15

정답 및 해설 / 14p

PART 5

1. The office automation training sessions are open to both full-time ------- part-time employees of Colors United Corp.
   (A) and (B) or (C) not (D) to

2. Participants in the MOMA Art History classes must pay a nominal fee before the first class begins in order to defray the expenses of materials and -------.
   (A) to supply (B) supplied (C) supplier (D) supplies

3. We are pleased to inform you that Jones & Brown Shopping Mall will lower prices ------- raise membership discount rates effective as of July 1.
   (A) and (B) again (C) too (D) still

4. Mr. Nishimoto has recommended that ------- Ms. Wiseman or Mr. Yoon attend the trade conference next week.
   (A) both (B) neither (C) as (D) either

5. To get promoted to a regional sales manager, employees should possess an outstanding sales record in previous years ------- a willingness to take on more responsibility.
   (A) in addition (B) as well as (C) further (D) along

6. Our on-line catalog is comprehensive, ------- certain items may not be available in every shop.
   (A) but (B) nor (C) how (D) then

7. Our interior designers can help you decide whether to use projector ------- large screen TVs when decorating your rooms.
   (A) so (B) but (C) nor (D) or

8. The Central Disaster Safety Task Force was made up of directors from ten private firms ------- twelve government agencies.
   (A) in (B) both (C) by (D) and

9. The company's renewed workplace improvement proposal included neither a salary increase ------- expanded staff welfare facilities.
   (A) or (B) and (C) nor (D) even

10. Autobahn Car Rental offers a wide range of rate plans that make a car rental affordable and easy, whether for pleasure ------- business.
    (A) or (B) and (C) if (D) either

086 SECTION 1

관계사

앞과 뒤의 단어나 문장과의 관계를 설명하는 것이 관계사이다.

The headquarters is located in Tokyo, Japan.
본사는 일본 도쿄에 위치해 있다.
↓
the headquarters [which is located in Tokyo, Japan]
[일본 도쿄에 위치해 있는] 본사
↓
We visited the headquarters [which is located in Tokyo, Japan].
우리는 [일본 도쿄에 위치해 있는] 본사를 방문했다.

- 선행사에 맞추어 관계대명사를 고른다.

선행사	주격	소유격	목적격
사람	who	whose	whom
사물	which	whose	which
사람 or/and 사물	that	–	that

- 관계대명사 이후 '불완전한 문장'이 온다.

관계대명사는 '대명사'이기 때문에 이후 문장에서 명사 자리 하나가 빠진 불완전한 문장이 나온다.

The guests who (주어) want to use the laundry service should tell one of our maids.
세탁 서비스를 이용하고자 하는 투숙객께서는 청소 직원에게 말씀해 주세요.
These are the documents that applicants should submit (목적어) tomorrow.
이것이 지원자가 내일 제출해야 하는 서류들입니다.

- 관계부사는 이후 '완전한 문장'이 온다.

관계부사(when, where, why, how)는 '부사'이기 때문에 완전한 문장이 이어진다.

Ms. Kat stayed at the Gifford Hotel where she had stayed a year ago.
Kat 씨는 그녀가 1년 전에 묵었던 Gifford 호텔에서 머물렀다.

- 전치사 + 관계대명사 = 관계부사

관계부사의 경우 '전치사 + 관계대명사'로 바꿀 수 있다.

Multinational companies should respect the different cultures where(= in which) they do business.
다국적 기업들은 그들이 사업을 하는 곳의 다른 문화를 존중해야 한다.

- 부분 명사 + of + 관계대명사

We have 12 applicants, most of whom are women.
우리는 12명의 지원자들이 있는데 그들 중 대부분은 여성이다.

문제 풀이 비법

Grammar DAY 16

❶ 관계대명사 who/which

Example

The orientation has been designed for the new employees ------- are unfamiliar with the company policies.

(A) they   (B) where   (C) whose   (D) who

해석 오리엔테이션은 회사 정책에 익숙하지 않은 신입 직원들을 위해 고안되었다.
어휘 orientation 오리엔테이션   be unfamiliar with ~에 익숙하지 않다

 빈칸은 동사 has been designed와 are를 연결해 줄 수 있는 접속사이면서 동사 are의 주어 역할을 할 수 있는 관계대명사 자리이다. 선행사(employees)가 사람이기 때문에 주격 관계대명사 (D) who가 정답이 된다. 소유대명사 (C) whose는 반드시 명사와 함께 와야 하므로 오답이다.

정답 (D)

❷ 관계대명사 that

• 사람/사물에 관계없이 사용 가능하다.
• 주격/목적격에 다 사용 가능하다.
• 콤마(,) 또는 전치사 뒤에서는 사용할 수 없다.

Example

The subway station, ------- is located near the museum, is under construction.

(A) it   (B) that   (C) which   (D) whose

해석 박물관 근처에 있는 지하철역은 현재 공사 중입니다.
어휘 be located ~에 위치하다   be under construction 공사 중이다

 명사 뒤 빈칸이며, 빈칸 뒤 '불완전한 문장'이 왔다. 동사 is located와 is under construction을 연결해 줄 수 있는 접속사이면서 대명사 역할을 하는 관계대명사 자리이다. 따라서 정답은 (C) which가 된다. that 역시 관계대명사의 기능이 있지만 콤마(,) 뒤에는 오지 못하므로 오답이다. 소유격 관계사 (D) whose 뒤에는 명사가 함께 와야 한다.

정답 (C)

❸ 관계대명사 whose

소유격 관계대명사인 whose의 정답 조건: ① 명사와 명사 사이 빈칸 + ② 빈칸 뒤 완전한 문장

| Example |

When hiring new office assistants, employers tend to prefer applicants --------- résumés are well-written and clearly organized.

(A) who　　　　(B) whose　　　　(C) that　　　　(D) than

해석　새로운 사무 보조를 고용할 때, 고용주들은 잘 쓴 구성이 좋은 이력서의 지원자들을 선호하는 경향이 있다.
어휘　hire 고용하다　assistant 조수, 비서　tend to ~하는 경향이 있다　prefer 선호하다　applicant 지원자
　　　résumé 이력서

빈칸은 명사(applicants)와 명사(résumés) 사이이며, 빈칸 뒤에 완전한 문장이 온다. 따라서 소유격 관계대명사인 (B) whose가 정답이 된다. (A) who의 경우 사람을 선행사로 하는 관계대명사이지만 빈칸 뒤에 주어 자리가 비어 있는 불완전한 문장이 와야 한다.

정답 (B)

❹ 전치사 + 관계대명사

전치사 뒤에 관계대명사 that은 올 수 없다.
전치사는 선행사와 관계사절 내 문장과 잘 어울려야 한다.

| Example |

The favorable tax rate introduced recently has made Karratha a city ------- which people can start a new business.

(A) for　　　　(B) on　　　　(C) during　　　　(D) in

해석　최근에 소개된 유리한 세율은 Karratha를 사람들이 새로운 사업을 시작하기에 좋은 도시로 만들었다.
어휘　favorable 유리한, 호의적인　tax rate 세율　recently 최근에

관계대명사 which 앞의 올바른 전치사를 고르는 문제이다. 선행사 a city와 잘 어울리는 전치사는 '그 도시에서'라는 장소적 의미를 만드는 (D) in이 된다. which 이후 문장과 잘 어울리는지를 확인하는 것이 실수를 줄일 수 있는 방법이라는 것도 기억하자.

정답 (D)

❺ 수량 표현 + of + 목적격 관계대명사

문제가 두 문장으로 분리되는지 반드시 확인한다.

Example

Mr. Shinichi has four accounts at our bank, all of ------- have considerable amount of funds.

(A) them   (B) their   (C) which   (D) whom

해석 Shinichi 씨는 우리 은행에 4개의 계좌를 가지고 있는데, 그 계좌 모두에는 상당한 금액의 자금이 있다.
어휘 account 계좌, 예금(액) considerable 상당한 fund 자금

 has와 빈칸 이후 have 동사를 연결하는 접속사의 역할을 하면서 전치사(of) 뒤 명사 자리에 들어갈 수 있는 관계대명사를 고르는 문제다. 선행사(accounts)가 사람이 아닌 '사물'이므로 (D) whom이 아닌 (C) which가 정답이다.

정답 (C)

○ 수량 표현 + of + 관계대명사

one/each some/any many/much/most all/both several/(a) few half/the rest/~%	of + 관계대명사(which, whom, whose + 명사)

비법 적용 연습

PART 5

1. The fact-checking process will be revised due to the increasing number of correction applications ------- reported.
   (A) is (B) are (C) were (D) being

2. The weather specialist ------- spoke at last week's conference on Yellow Dust awareness has been nominated for this year's Asian Environment Journalism Award.
   (A) whoever (B) when (C) wherever (D) who

3. Please be aware that applicants ------- résumés and cover letter are postmarked on or after May 11 will not be considered for the hiring process.
   (A) who (B) whose (C) their (D) they

4. Customers can receive full refund on any merchandise with ------- they are not satisfied if they have the original receipt.
   (A) who (B) what (C) which (D) whose

5. Those employees ------- in our laboratories are required to wear protective clothing at all times.
   (A) are working (B) have worked (C) working (D) work

6. The new subway line, ------- has been operating since September, serves the city's twenty two stations.
   (A) who (B) what (C) where (D) which

7. The general affairs department has announced a revised incentive policy ------- will take into effect on May 3 for all employees.
   (A) that (B) such (C) when (D) until

8. Most of the people ------- were interviewed during the research said that they did not need an additional car.
   (A) which (B) where (C) what (D) who

9. Quality Control Managers ------- to transfer to our New Jersey branch will receive full relocation assistance at the company's expense.
   (A) agree (B) were agreed (C) agreeing (D) agreement

10. Agostino Audio is owned by Daniel Agostino, a genius audio developer ------- sells hand-made system as well as mass-produced products.
    (A) who (B) whom (C) whose (D) which

명사절 접속사

명사절 접속사는 일반적인 절을 명사화시키는 접속사로 문장 내에서 주어, 목적어, 보어 역할을 한다.

○ 명사절 접속사의 종류

- **that**

that은 **완전한 문장**을 이끌며, '~라는 것(사실)'의 의미를 갖는다.

> We are pleased to announce **that free home delivery will be available starting next month**.
> 저희는 자택 무료 배송이 다음 달을 시작으로 이용 가능하다는 것을 알리게 되어 기쁩니다.

- **whether/if**

whether과 if는 **완전한 문장**을 이끌며, '~인지 (아닌지)'의 의미를 갖는다.

> We are considering **whether we should buy new computers or fix the existing ones**.
> 우리는 새로운 컴퓨터를 사야 할지 아니면 기존 컴퓨터를 고쳐 써야 할지를 고민하고 있다.

- **의문사 what, which, who[m]**

what, which, who[m]은 명사 자리가 하나 비워져 있는 **불완전한 문장**을 이끈다.

> We don't know yet **who will give a presentation at the seminar**.
> 우리는 누가 세미나에서 발표를 할지 아직 모른다.

- **의문사 when, where, why, how**

when, where, why, how는 이후 **완전한 문장**을 이끈다.
단, how의 경우 'how 형용사/부사 S+V'의 형태로 '얼마나 ~한지'의 의미를 갖기도 한다.

> The visitors are invited to see **how the TV shows are made**.
> 방문객들은 TV 쇼가 어떻게 제작되는지를 보기 위해 초대된다.

- **what/which/whose + 명사**

위 접속사는 형용사 역할을 하면서 명사절을 이끈다.

> It is very hard to decide **which option is more suitable for our needs**.
> 어떤 옵션이 우리의 요구에 더 적합한지를 결정하는 것은 매우 어렵다.

- **복합 관계대명사 whoever, whomever, whichever, whatever**

whichever/whatever는 'anything', whoever/whomever는 'anyone'의 의미를 가지고 있으며 **불완전한 문장**을 이끈다. whichever/whatever의 경우, 바로 뒤에 명사를 취해서 형용사와 명사절 역할을 동시에 하기도 한다. (*위 접속사들은 부사절을 이끌기도 한다-부사절 참조)

> Unless it is on the list of prohibited items, participants are allowed to bring **whatever they want to the class**.
> 금지 품목 리스트에 있지만 않다면, 참가자들은 수업에 무엇이든지 원하는 것을 가져올 수 있다.

문제 풀이 비법

❶ 명사절을 이끄는 접속사

① that   ② whether/if   ③ what
④ 의문사(who, which, when, where, how, why) → 관계사와 헷갈리면 안 됨
⑤ 복합 관계대명사(whoever, whomever, whichever, whatever, whosever)

Example

The selection committee decided ------- B. J. Parker was the employee of the year.

(A) since   (B) because   (C) that   (D) whoever

해석   선발 위원회는 B.J. Parker를 올해의 직원으로 결정했다.
어휘   selection committee 선발 위원회   employee of the year 올해의 직원(상)

빈칸은 동사(decided) 뒤 목적어 자리이다. 빈칸 뒤 '완전한 문장'이 왔으므로 문장 전체를 명사절로 만들어 줄 수 있는 명사절 접속사를 고른다. 따라서 (C) that이 정답이 된다. (D) whoever는 '불완전한 문장'이 와야 하므로 오답이다.

정답 (C)

❷ that 명사절 관용 표현

Example

Please be aware ------- all the documents must arrive by the end of this month.

(A) unless   (B) that   (C) on   (D) concerning

해석   모든 서류는 이번 달 말까지 도착해야 한다는 것을 알아 두시기 바랍니다.
어휘   be aware of[that절] ~을 알다

빈칸은 동사(be aware)의 목적어가 되는 명사절을 이끄는 접속사 자리이다. 따라서 정답은 (B) that이 된다. 〈be aware of+명사〉의 형태로 사용되나 명사절 접속사 that은 전치사와 함께 쓸 수 없기 때문에 'of'가 없어진 경우이다.

정답 (B)

○ that 명사절 관용 표현
① 사람 주어+be+[aware/afraid/sure, certain, convinced]+that S+V
   ~를 알다/ 두려워하다/ 확신하다
② It+is+[sure, certain/likely/impossible]+that S+V
   ~은 확실하다/ ~일 것 같다/ 불가능하다

❸ 명사절 접속사 whether vs. if

whether는 주어, 목적어, 보어 자리에 모두 올 수 있지만, if는 주어 자리에 오지 못한다.
whether는 "whether to V", "whether or not"처럼 사용 가능하지만 이 자리에 if는 사용할 수 없다.

Example

Designers at Kioko Smart Office can decide ------- to work in the office or at home.

(A) whether (B) what (C) that (D) if

해석 Kioko Smart Office의 디자이너들은 사무실에서 일할지 재택 근무를 할지 결정할 수 있다.
어휘 whether ~인지 if ~인지; 만약에

 빈칸은 동사(decide) 뒤 목적어 자리이다. 빈칸 뒤 'to부정사'와 함께 명사절을 이끌 수 있는 (A) whether가 정답이다. if도 '~인지 아닌지'의 의미로 사용될 수 있으나 빈칸 뒤 to부정사를 바로 취할 수는 없다.

정답 (A)

---

❹ 복합 관계대명사

Example

------- has met the sales quota first will have a higher chance of promotion to the sales manager position.

(A) Who (B) Whoever (C) Whatever (D) Whenever

해석 누구든지 영업 할당량을 먼저 채운 사람이 영업 관리직으로 승진할 확률이 더 높다.
어휘 sales quota 영업 할당량 promotion 승진

 본동사 will have의 주어 역할을 하면서 명사절 역할을 같이 할 수 있는 명사절 접속사를 고르는 문제이다. 따라서, '누구든지'의 의미가 있는 (B) Whoever가 정답이다. (C) Whatever의 경우 구조적으로는 무리가 없지만 what은 보통 '사물'을 이야기하므로 오답이 된다. (D) Whenever의 경우, 이후 '완전한 문장'을 취하므로 역시 오답이다.

정답 (B)

❺ what/which/whose + 명사

what, which, whose의 경우 명사를 수식하는 형용사 역할을 하면서 동시에 명사절을 이끌 수 있다.

| Example |

Although Mr. Ralph examined all the details, he was still not able to determine ------- proposal would be better for the new product.

(A) who　　　　　(B) whose　　　　　(C) whoever　　　　　(D) whom

해석　Ralph 씨가 모든 세부 사항들을 검토했음에도 불구하고, 그는 여전히 누구의 제안서가 신제품에 더 좋을지 결정할 수가 없었다.

어휘　examine 조사하다, 검토하다　details 세부 사항　determine 알아내다, 결정하다　proposal 제안(서)

빈칸은 동사(determine) 뒤 목적어 자리이며 빈칸 뒤에 '완전한 문장'이 나온다. 따라서 proposal을 수식할 수 있는 형용사 역할을 하면서 명사절을 이끌 수 있는 (B) whose가 정답이 된다. 나머지 선택지들은 명사로 사용되기 때문에 빈칸 이후 문장에서 명사 자리 하나가 빠져 있어야 한다.

정답 (B)

비법 적용 연습

Grammar / DAY 17

정답 및 해설 / 16p

PART 5

1. Teachers are reminded to print only ------- is necessary in order to reduce wasted paper.
   (A) what (B) there (C) as much as (D) as though

2. ------- achieves the highest sales figure by the end of the second week of December will receive the Contributor of the Year Award with $10,000 cash prize.
   (A) Whose (B) Someone (C) Whoever (D) Nobody

3. ------- pleased the customers most was the responsiveness of the servers at the restaurant.
   (A) Who (B) That (C) What (D) This

4. ------- the majority of the residents involved agree with the redevelopment is a critical matter.
   (A) Where (B) However (C) Whether (D) While

5. One recent study sponsored by the International Association of Athletics Federations suggests ------- left-handed players are more likely to achieve better performance in most events of sports.
   (A) that (B) which (C) when (D) as to

6. ------- needs help is welcome to come to the Adolescent Counseling Center for whatever problems they may have.
   (A) Whoever (B) What (C) If (D) Since

7. Choosing ------- marketing strategies best suit your company needs a wide range of research.
   (A) which (B) that (C) whoever (D) there

8. It is not easy to determine ------- Ms. Vasquez is the best candidate to lead the new initiative.
   (A) whether (B) what (C) so that (D) for

9. When asked ------- he will resign from his position, Mr. Engle said that he intends to continue his work as long as he can.
   (A) while (B) whereas (C) whenever (D) whether

10. ------- is given the research fund will be able to begin the necessary work immediately.
    (A) Whatever (B) Whenever (C) Whoever (D) Whichever

096 SECTION 1

부사절 접속사

부사절 접속사는 절을 시간, 조건, 이유, 양보 등의 부사로 만들어 주는 역할을 하며, 보통 완전한 두 문장을 연결한다. 부사는 부가적인 정보로서 완전한 문장에 들어간다는 기본 문법의 적용을 그대로 받는다.

❶ 부사절 접속사의 종류

시간	when, after, before, as soon as, until	I will call you **as soon as** we arrive at the airport. 공항에 도착하자마자 전화드리겠습니다.
조건	if, as long as, unless, once, providing[provided] that, assuming that, in case that	You will get a discount **if** you are a Gold card holder. 골드 카드 소지자라면 할인 혜택을 받으실 겁니다.
양보	although, (even) though, whereas/while	**Although** the meeting started late, we were able to cover almost every item on the agenda. 회의가 늦게 시작되었음에도 불구하고, 안건의 거의 모든 내용을 다룰 수 있었다.
이유·목적	because/as/since, now that, in that, so that, in order that, so[such] ~ that	Mr. Kim had to fill in for the marketing director, **since** he had another urgent meeting. 마케팅 부장은 또 다른 급한 회의가 있었기 때문에, Kim 씨가 마케팅 부장을 대신해야 했다. **Now that** the trial period of the new product is over, it will be installed in every office. 이제 신제품의 시험 기간이 종료되었기 때문에, 이 제품은 모든 사무실에 설치될 것이다.
복합 관계부사	whenever, wherever, however	You can access the data **wherever** you are. 당신이 어디에 있든, 데이터에 접근할 수 있습니다.

❷ 비슷한 의미의 부사절 접속사와 전치사

전치사는 '명사나 동명사'를 취하며, 접속사는 '문장'을 취한다.

Most flights have been canceled due to(~~because~~) the inclement weather.
좋지 않은 날씨 때문에 대부분의 비행편이 취소되었다.

문제 풀이 비법

Grammar DAY 18

❶ 부사절을 이끄는 접속사 vs. 부사구를 이끄는 전치사 → 의미는 같지만 품사가 다름

│ Example │

The New York University Central Library will be closed ------- the air conditioning system is renovated.

(A) however　　(B) while　　(C) during　　(D) along

해석 New York 대학의 중앙 도서관은 냉난방기 보수 작업이 진행되는 동안 폐쇄될 것입니다
어휘 air conditioning system 공기 정화기, 냉난방 장치　renovate 개조하다, 보수하다

 빈칸은 완전한 두 문장을 연결하는 접속사 자리이다. 따라서 (B) while이 정답이 된다. (A) however는 문장을 연결하지 못하고, (C) during(~하는 동안)은 의미는 같지만 전치사이기 때문에 문장을 이끌 수 없다.

정답 (B)

○ 접속사 vs. 전치사

전치사 (뒤에 목적어 온다)	의미	종속접속사 (두 문장을 연결)
despite, in spite of, notwithstanding	~에도 불구하고	although, though, even though
because of, owing to	~ 때문에	because, since, as
during	~ 동안에	while
without	~이 아니라면	unless
in case of	~인 경우에, ~이면	if, in case (that)
except for	~을 제외하면, ~ 없이는	except that, unless

❷ 양보의 접속사/부사/전치사 구분

│ Example │

------- minor defects were continuously reported, Fontenz fourth quarter sales figures have slightly increased.

(A) Although　　(B) Despite　　(C) Nonetheless　　(D) Regardless of

해석 사소한 결함이 지속적으로 보고되었음에도 불구하고, Fontenz의 4분기 영업 실적은 약간 증가했다.
어휘 minor defect 사소한 결함　sales figures 매출액　slightly 약간　increase 증가하다

 빈칸은 완전한 두 문장을 연결하는 부사절 접속사 자리이므로 정답은 (A) Although이다. 비슷한 의미의 전치사인 (B) Despite의 경우 명사를 취해야 하므로 오답이 된다.

정답 (A)

098 SECTION 1

○ 접속사 vs. 부사 vs. 전치사

접속사	although = (even) though	[문장 두 개]를 연결
전치사	in spite of = despite = notwithstanding	뒤에 목적어인 [명사/동명사]
부사	nonetheless = nevertheless	[문장 한 개]를 한정 [Nonetheless, S+V ~]의 형태

❸ 부사절의 〈주어 + be동사〉 생략 → 1년에 10번 이상 출제

| Example |

------- not required, it is very helpful to get a computer-related license to get entry-level jobs.

(A) Though　　　　(B) Despite　　　　(C) Without　　　　(D) Since

해석 필수적이지는 않지만, 컴퓨터 관련 자격증을 따는 것은 신입사원으로 직업을 구하는 데 도움이 된다.
어휘 required 필수적인　license 자격증　entry-level 초급용의; 말단의

 빈칸 뒤 과거분사(required)가 왔으므로, 명사나 동명사를 취해야 하는 전치사 (B) Despite와 (C) Without은 오답이 된다. (D) Since(~ 이래로)는 해석상 어울리지 않기 때문에 오답이고, 주절의 의미와 잘 어울리는 (A) Though가 정답이다.

정답 (A)

○ 능동형 vs. 수동형

① 능동형
When they interview students, the professors will meet to decide the scholarship recipients.
그들이 학생들을 인터뷰할 때, 교수들이 장학금 수령인을 결정하기 위해 만날 것이다.
→ When **interviewing** students, ~
　　목적어가 있으면 '능동형' 사용

② 수동형
Once it is confirmed, your airline ticket reservation cannot be refunded.
일단 확정되면, 당신의 비행기 티켓 예약은 환불될 수 없다.
→ Once **confirmed**, ~
　　목적어가 없으면 '수동형' 사용

비법 적용 연습

Grammar DAY 18

정답 및 해설 / 17p

PART 5

1. ------- this quarter's sales are as high as projected, Hoshiro Designs anticipates emerging as one of the leading graphic design companies in Japan.
   (A) In case of
   (B) After all
   (C) Provided that
   (D) Subsequent to

2. Visitors are asked to turn off their electronic devices when ------- the laboratory.
   (A) enters
   (B) entering
   (C) enter
   (D) entered

3. ------- the band has finally confirmed its availability, the outdoor concert will be scheduled for Sunday, June 11.
   (A) In order for
   (B) Now that
   (C) So that
   (D) Regarding

4. ------- the Kendal Company has been in business for only nine months, it has very quickly become profitable.
   (A) Although
   (B) Unless
   (C) Before
   (D) During

5. ------- or not Dr. Danawala accepts the position, we will need to hire at least two more physicians.
   (A) Whether
   (B) So
   (C) Either
   (D) If

6. Ms. Hagger is planning to attend the regional seminar ------- it is not absolutely necessary that she be there.
   (A) where
   (B) or
   (C) due to
   (D) although

7. Employees currently working in Ridge Manufacturing's branch offices will move into the new headquarters ------- the building is finished.
   (A) once
   (B) even
   (C) besides
   (D) moreover

8. ------- the initial application form has been received in our office, you will not be required to provide any further documentation.
   (A) Whether
   (B) Once
   (C) As if
   (D) Yet

9. Business Notes reported that ViStar's stock prices plummeted ------- the merger announcement.
   (A) after
   (B) soon
   (C) since
   (D) because

10. When ------- your payment, please be sure to include the top portion of your invoice.
    (A) mail
    (B) mails
    (C) mailing
    (D) mailed

100 SECTION 1

비교급과 최상급

비교급이나 최상급은 대상의 성질이나 상태를 서로 비교하는 구문으로 형용사와 부사로 표현한다.

❶ 원급 비교

'as 형용사/부사의 원급 as' 의 형태로 '~만큼 …한'의 의미를 갖는다.

> The replaced system runs **as efficiently as** the previous one.
> 교체된 시스템은 이전 것만큼이나 효율적으로 작동한다.

원급 비교 표현을 수식하는 부사로 just, nearly, twice, almost 등이 있다.

> The number of Chinese-owned businesses has grown **twice** <u>as fast as</u> others in the U.S.
> 중국인 소유의 사업체 수는 미국의 다른 업체들보다 2배만큼 빠르게 증가하고 있다.

❷ 비교급

'형용사/부사+-er than' 또는 'more 형용사/부사의 원급 than'의 형태로 '~보다 더 …한'의 의미를 갖는다. **둘 사이**의 비교에서 주로 사용된다.

> Those who work at home proved to be **more productive than** those in the office.
> 재택 근무하는 사람들이 사무실에서 일하는 사람들보다 더 생산적인 것으로 증명되었다.

비교급을 수식할 수 있는 부사로는 even, much, far, a little, a lot, still 등이 있다.

> A-Tech's new smart watch looks **even** <u>more beautiful</u> than that of its competitor.
> A-Tech의 새로운 스마트 워치는 경쟁사의 것보다 훨씬 더 아름다워 보였다.

❸ 최상급

'the 형용사/부사+-est' 또는 'the most 형용사/부사의 원급'의 형태로 '가장 ~한'의 의미를 갖는다. **셋 이상**의 비교 대상에서 하나를 콕! 집어서 이야기할 때 주로 사용된다.
*부사의 경우 the가 생략되기도 한다.

> This bonus recognizes Mr. Louis for having worked **the hardest** of all.
> 이 보너스는 전 직원 중에서 가장 열심히 일한 Louis 씨의 공로를 인정하는 것이다.

문제 풀이 비법

❶ 원급 비교

'as 형용사/부사 원급 as'의 형태이다.
원급 비교를 이용한 '형용사 보어'를 찾는 품사 문제가 많이 출제된다.

Example

Our researcher, Dr. Morgan developed a new material which is as ------- as diamond.

(A) strong　　　(B) strongly　　　(C) strength　　　(D) strengthen

해석 우리 연구원인 Morgan 박사는 다이아몬드만큼 강한 새로운 물질을 개발했다.
어휘 researcher 연구원　material 재료; 자료

 as ~ as 사이 빈칸은 비교급을 물어보는 문제로 형용사와 부사 중 정답을 고른다. 따라서 형용사나 부사가 아닌 명사 (C) strength와 동사 (D) strengthen은 오답이다. 비교급에서 형용사와 부사의 구별 문제는 보통 앞에 동사를 보고 판단한다. 비교 표현 앞에 be동사가 있으므로 형용사 보어인 (A) strong이 정답이 된다.

정답 (A)

---

❷ 비교급 수식어구

오직 비교급만을 수식한다.
very와 too 등이 함정 선택지로 많이 출제된다.

Example

Gryphon System's philosophy is that retaining loyal clients is ------- more important than trying to draw new ones.

(A) very　　　(B) such　　　(C) too　　　(D) a lot

해석 Gryphon System의 철학은 단골 고객을 유지하는 것이 새로운 고객을 끌어 모으기 위해 노력하는 것보다 훨씬 더 중요하다는 것이다.
어휘 philosophy 철학　retain 보유하다, 유지하다　loyal client 단골 고객　draw 끌다; 뽑다; 그리다

 비교급(more important) 앞의 빈칸은 비교급을 수식할 수 있는 부사 자리이다. 따라서 (D) a lot이 정답이다. (A) very나 (C) too는 형용사/부사의 원급만을 수식하고 비교급은 수식할 수 없다.

정답 (D)

○ 비교급을 수식하는 부사

| much, still, even, far, a lot, a little + 형용사/부사의 비교급(-er, more) | so, too, very, relatively, quite, extremely + 형용사/부사의 원급 |

❸ 최상급 공식

최상급은 반드시 '범위 설정' 표현과 함께 써야 한다.

> **Example**
>
> Of all the people the personnel director has interviewed, he considered Derrick Rhode the ------- qualified candidate.
>
> (A) much　　　　(B) such　　　　(C) very　　　　(D) most
>
> **해석** 인사부장은 자신이 면접을 본 사람들 중에서, Derrick Rhode가 가장 적임자라고 생각했다.
> **어휘** personnel director 인사부장　consider A (as) B A를 B로 여기다　qualified candidate 적임자
>
>  관사(the)와 명사(qualified candidate) 사이 빈칸으로 앞에 'of all the people'이라는 범위 설정 표현이 나온다. 따라서 Derrick이라는 특정 사람을 이야기하는 구조로 최상급을 만드는 (D) most가 정답이 된다.
>
> 정답 (D)

○ 범위 설정 표현

the 최상급	in+범위 ~에서 of/among+복수명사 ~ 중에서 ever 이제껏 ~ 중에서 주어+have (ever) p.p. 주어가 ~했던 중에서

비법 적용 연습

PART 5

1. The research findings showed that the survey participants responded even ------- to the design of the new Nautilus 1000 Diamond Speakers than expected.
   (A) favorably   (B) most favorable   (C) more favorably   (D) favorable

2. Car Sales dropped by 5.8 percent in June, showing a somewhat ------- demand than anticipated.
   (A) weaker   (B) weakly   (C) weakened   (D) more weakly

3. Mahin Motors' newly launched cars are considered more ------- than those of its competitors.
   (A) impressively   (B) impressive   (C) impression   (D) impress

4. The new LZ3 smartphone has the same camera features ------- many other models in the current market.
   (A) as   (B) than   (C) most   (D) more

5. Once a wine cork is removed from a bottle, we should drink all the wine in it as ------- as possible.
   (A) quicken   (B) quicker   (C) quickest   (D) quickly

6. Among all the delivery options available, Langston Bike Messenger Service is the ------- way to send things to someone in the city.
   (A) more quickly   (B) quickly   (C) quickest   (D) quick

7. Rising fuel expenses have made it ------- than ever for our company to stay profitable.
   (A) hard   (B) harden   (C) harder   (D) hardly

8. Eurolink Telecom's Board of Directors decided yesterday on Aming's proposal over that of Sopa, admitting that it would be ------- to introduce and operate.
   (A) ease   (B) easily   (C) more easily   (D) easier

9. More and more companies and public institutions are switching to recycled toner cartridges since it is much less ------- than new ones.
   (A) expensiveness   (B) expense   (C) expensive   (D) expensively

10. Our Executive Marketing Director always stresses that creating a royal customer base is a lot ------- essential than developing a new one.
    (A) most   (B) more   (C) very   (D) much

Grammar

가정법과 도치

가정법이란 '현재나 과거 사실을 반대'로 가정하여 표현하는 문장이다.
도치는 〈주어+동사〉의 어순을 취하지 않고, 〈동사+주어〉의 의문문 어순을 취하는 문장으로 구조 파악을 다소 까다롭게 만든다.

❶ 가정법

가정법 과거	If + 주어 + 동사의 과거형, 주어 + would[could, might] + 동사원형 *be동사의 경우 주어에 관계없이 were를 쓴다. If the raw material prices **were** low, we **could earn** more than $13 million. 원자재 가격이 낮았다면 우리는 1,300만 달러 이상을 벌어들일 수 있다.
가정법 과거완료	If + 주어 + had p.p., 주어 + would[could, might] have + p.p. If the company **had had** more funds, it **would have invested** in R&D. 회사가 더 많은 자금이 있었다면, 연구 개발에 투자했을 것이다.
혼합 가정법	If + 주어 + had p.p., 주어 would[could, might] + 동사원형 *if절과 주절의 시제가 다르다. If Mr. Kim **had listened** to his supervisor, he **wouldn't have** any problem now. Kim 씨가 상사의 말을 들었었다면, 그는 지금 아무 문제가 없을 것이다.
가정법 미래	[If + 주어 + should + 동사원형, 주어 ┌ + will[can, may] + 동사원형 └ + 명령문 If you **should have** any problem with the product, please **contact** our service center. 혹시라도 제품에 문제가 있다면, 저희 서비스 센터에 연락 주시기 바랍니다.

❷ 도치

• 가정법 도치
가정법에서 if가 생략되면, 주어와 동사는 도치된다.

> **Should** you **have** any questions, feel free to call me.
> 혹시라도 질문이 있으시다면 주저하지 마시고 저에게 전화 주시기 바랍니다.

• 부정어 또는 시간/장소 부사(구) 도치
부정어나 시간, 장소 또는 기타 부사가 문장의 맨 앞에 위치하면, 주어와 동사는 도치된다.

> Only recently **did the manager** find out what the problem was.
> 최근에서야 관리자는 문제가 무엇인지 파악했다.

문제 풀이 비법

Grammar DAY 20

❶ 가정법 과거

If + 주어 + 동사의 과거형, 주어 + would[could, might] + 동사원형 ~

Example

If the total price of the orders ------- over ₩100,000, they could be delivered free of charge.

(A) is　　　　　(B) are　　　　　(C) were　　　　　(D) was

해석 주문 물품의 총액이 10만 원이 넘으면, 제품은 무료로 배송될 것이다.
어휘 order 주문(하다)　free of charge 무료로

접속사 if와 주절의 〈could+동사원형〉의 구조를 보고 〈가정법 과거〉의 문장 형태라는 것을 파악한다. 따라서 정답은 (C) were가 된다. 주어(price)가 단수이기 때문에 was를 써야 할 것 같지만 가정법 과거에서 be동사는 주어에 관계없이 were를 사용한다는 것을 기억해야 한다.

정답 (C)

❷ 가정법 과거완료

If + 주어 + had + p.p., 주어 + would[could, might] + have + p.p. ~

Example

If we had finished the initial design earlier, we ------- enough time to improve it following the latest trend.

(A) could had　　(B) could have　　(C) could have had　　(D) could have been

해석 초기 디자인이 좀 더 빨리 완성되었다면, 우리는 최근 트렌드를 따라 디자인을 개선할 충분한 시간을 가질 수 있었을 것이다.
어휘 initial 처음의, 초기의　improve 개선하다, 향상시키다　latest trend 최신 트렌드

if절의 시제가 'had p.p.'임을 확인하고 주절의 시제는 〈가정법 과거완료〉에 맞는 '조동사의 과거형 + have p.p.'의 형태를 골라야 한다. 따라서 정답은 (C) could have had이다. (D) could have been도 시제는 맞지만 내용상 enough time을 목적어로 받을 수 있는 능동형이 나와야 하므로 오답이 된다.

정답 (C)

❸ if 대신 전치사 without을 사용하는 가정법

Without + 명사, 주어 + would[could/might] + 동사원형
Without + 명사, 주어 + would[could/might] + have p.p.

---| Example |---

------ our marketing team's cooperation, we would not have succeeded in launching our new product.

(A) If (B) Until (C) Without (D) For

해석 우리 마케팅 팀의 협력이 없었다면, 우리는 신제품 출시에 성공하지 못했을 것이다.
어휘 cooperation 협력 succeed in ~에 성공하다 launch 시작하다, 출시하다

 빈칸 이후 명사가 등장했고, 주절에 가정법 과거완료의 동사 형태를 보이고 있다. 따라서 가정법과 함께 사용될 수 있는 전치사 (C) Without이 정답이 된다. (A) If의 경우 가정법과 함께 사용될 수 있지만 주어+동사를 취해야 하는 접속사이기 때문에 위 문장에는 어울리지 않는다.

정답 (C)

❹ if가 생략된 가정법 도치

'가정법 미래'와 '가정법 과거완료'는 if가 생략되어 도치된 형식으로 자주 출제된다.
Should가 문두에 있으면 '가정법 미래', Had가 문두에 있으면 '가정법 과거완료'

---| Example |---

------ you need any help with the new copy machine, please don't hesitate to contact me.

(A) Had (B) Should (C) Having (D) Have

해석 혹시라도 새 복사기 관련 도움이 필요하시면, 주저하지 마시고 저한테 연락 주시기 바랍니다.
어휘 copy machine 복사기 hesitate to ~하는 것을 망설이다, 주저하다 contact 연락하다

 동사가 need와 don't hesitate 두 개가 나왔는데 접속사가 선택지에 없을 때에는 가정법 도치를 생각한다. 따라서 위 문장의 정답은 (B)가 된다. 주절의 문장이 명령문인 것을 보고 가정법 미래의 형태를 고르는 것 또한 포인트이다.

정답 (B)

○ 자주 출제되는 가정법 도치

① **Should** you need the wake-up call service, please call the receptionist.
→ If you should need the wake-up call service, please call the receptionist.
② **Had** the parts arrived earlier, we would have finished the repairing work on time.
→ If the parts had arrived earlier, we would have finished the repairing work on time.

비법 적용 연습

PART 5

1. Mr. Vasquez would not ------- with such bitter opposition if he had made his intentions clear to the board members.
   (A) having confronted   (B) have been confronted   (C) have confronted   (D) had been confronted

2. If you had bought the new smartphone, you ------- enjoying it by now.
   (A) would be   (B) will be   (C) would have been   (D) are

3. If you ------- the package including all the legal documents, please let us know that the paperwork has been forwarded to you.
   (A) had received   (B) received   (C) receive   (D) receiving

4. ------- any participant have a problem during the seminar, please come to the help desk in the lobby.
   (A) Will   (B) Should   (C) Because   (D) If

5. Had it not been for his devotion, they ------- awarded the additional funding for their Parthenon project.
   (A) could not have been   (B) are able could not   (C) had not been   (D) are not

6. Only after all the board members reached the unanimous decision did the firm ------- to reorganize its whisky manufacturing division.
   (A) begin   (B) began   (C) beginning   (D) begun

7. If the client ------- about the card's discount's at major department stores in the city, he would have made the decision to sign up for the membership even sooner.
   (A) had known   (B) knew   (C) should know   (D) knows

8. If the train accident had not been reported so quickly, all the passengers ------- the timely medical treatment.
   (A) are not receiving   (B) will not receive   (C) would not have received   (D) cannot receive

9. If the company's proposal ------- a little bit more detailed, Kawasaki Steel Corporation would be our sole supplier of steel parts by now.
   (A) has been   (B) had been   (C) was being   (D) were being

10. ------- have the market atmosphere been worse for investing your money in the stock market.
    (A) Seldom   (B) Ever   (C) Appropriately   (D) Because

Reading

Day 01	주제 · 목적 문제	110
Day 02	육하원칙 문제	113
Day 03	일치 · 불일치 문제	116
Day 04	추론 문제	119
Day 05	동의어 문제	122
Day 06	편지/이메일	125
Day 07	제품 광고	128
Day 08	구인 공고	131
Day 09	공지, 안내, 정보	134
Day 10	기사	137
Day 11	양식 및 기타 지문	140
Day 12	연계 문제	143
Day 13	문장 삽입	148
Day 14	의도 파악	150
Day 15	삼중 지문	153
Day 16	독해 유형 연습 1	158
Day 17	독해 유형 연습 2	161
Day 18	독해 유형 연습 3	163
Day 19	독해 유형 연습 4	167
Day 20	독해 유형 연습 5	169

Reading

주제·목적 문제

주제나 목적을 묻는 문제는 보통 "mainly about, discuss, why ~ written, purpose" 등의 표현이 등장한다.

> **질문 유형**
>
> 주제
> - What is the article **mainly about**?
> - What does the letter **discuss**?
>
> 목적
> - **Why** was this e-mail **written**?
> - What is the **purpose** of this memo?

비법 1 '제목'을 반드시 확인하자.

'기사나 편지·이메일' 등 제목이 있는 글은 반드시 제목을 확인하고, 머릿속에 전체적인 그림을 그려 보는 것이 중요하다.

비법 2 글의 '전반부'에 주목하자.

영어는 '두괄식' 글을 좋아하기 때문에 주제나 목적은 대부분 글의 초반에 등장한다.

비법 3 '연결어'에 주의하자.

초반부의 글을 읽고 섣불리 정답을 골라서는 안 된다. '앞의 내용을 뒤집는 어구(But, However 등)'가 등장하면, 이후 내용에 집중한다.

비법 4 '패러프레이징(paraphrasing)'된 선택지를 고르자.

지문의 내용이 그대로 선택지에 등장한 경우에는 정답이 아닐 확률이 높다. 대체로 같은 의미의 다른 말로 바꿔 쓴 내용이 정답인 경우가 많다.

비법 5 목적을 묻는 문제는 다음 표현에 집중하자.

I would like to V ~을 하고 싶다
I am writing to V ~하기 위해 이 글을 씁니다
This is to V 이 글은 ~하기 위함이다
I regret to V ~하게 되어 유감이다
announce 발표하다 inform 알려 주다 remind 상기시키다
But/However 하지만 So/Therefore 그러므로

비법 적용 연습

Questions 1-3 refer to the following article.

Electric power interruptions

Starting Tuesday, October 20, at 10:00 A.M. there will be a series of power interruptions in the Broadway area up to the Marina Bay area. These power interruptions will last approximately one hour but in some cases may stretch longer. The project is expected to last approximately five working days with no interruptions on weekends.

The reason for these power interruptions is to upgrade the existing power lines which are estimated to be over 30 years old. The upgrade is to avoid any future problems caused by aging power lines as well as the safety of our citizens. Please bear with us while work is in progress and we promise to provide a steady uninterrupted flow of electricity when this maintenance project is completed.

The public is encouraged to complete their electricity-related duties before the interruption or wait until power is restored. We apologize for this inconvenience and we hope for your consideration and understanding.

---

1 What is the purpose of this article?

(A) To schedule the maintenance
(B) To explain the current problem
(C) To apologize for an inconvenience
(D) To inform the public of a project

2 When will the project be completed?

(A) On Monday
(B) On Tuesday
(C) On Friday
(D) On Saturday

3 What is NOT suggested in the article?

(A) Citizens are currently experiencing interruptions.
(B) Some of the areas might have an interruption of more than one hour.
(C) Workers must turn off their electronic gadgets during the project.
(D) Power interruptions do not affect Saturday and Sunday.

Questions 4-6 refer to the following e-mail.

---

e-mail

To: Oscar Wilde Literary Guild <oscarwildliteraryguild@wea.com>
From: James Takahashi <jtakash@smail.com>
Subject: 75th Oscar Wilde commemorative anniversary
Date: July 17

Dear Oscar Wilde collectors and fans,

The Oscar Wilde foundation has opened its doors to collectors and fans of Oscar Wilde and has announced a series of auctions of Oscar Wilde memorabilia. The auction will be held on Wednesday from 10:00 A.M. to 2:00 P.M. and on Thursday from 10:00 A.M. to 12:00 noon. There will be a very limited amount of items on auction and the minimum price for each personal item on sale will be decided by the surviving relatives of Oscar Wilde. There will be a pre-screening of the items and personal memorabilia may be for bidding but handwritten manuscripts are off limits for public bidding.

Please reply to this e-mail for a spot at the auction since only a few attendees will be allowed at this very exclusive event.

---

4 Why was this e-mail sent?

(A) To show their admiration for Oscar Wilde
(B) To schedule a literary club meeting
(C) To provide information on items for sale
(D) To announce a special holiday

5 Who most likely are the members?

(A) Freelance artists
(B) Gallery owners
(C) Literature buffs
(D) Auctioneers

6 Which items are NOT for sale?

(A) Clothing
(B) Manuscripts
(C) Household items
(D) Typewritten notes

Reading

육하원칙 문제

육하원칙 문제는 '언제, 어디서, 누가, 어떻게, 무엇을, 왜'와 같은 의문사로 된 질문이다. what을 제외한 who, when, where, why, how로 시작되는 문제는 대체로 세부 사항을 물어본다.

> **질문 유형**
> - **Who** can participate in the seminar?
> - **When** does the offer end?
> - **From where** can Mr. Yun get the application form?
> - **Why** did the company hire additional caterers?
> - **How much** is Mr. Lin charged in total?

비법 1) 질문의 '키워드' 파악이 우선이다.

키워드(key word)를 파악하고 지문에서 키워드가 변형된 부분을 찾게 되면 그 문장의 주변 표현에서 정답이 도출된다.

비법 2) '의문사'가 곧 선택지이다.

what을 제외한 나머지 의문사는 의문사가 곧 선택지이기 때문에 세부적인 내용을 물어본다. 예를 들어, who로 시작되는 질문의 선택지는 사람이나 단체이기 때문에 문제의 키워드만 제대로 잡으면 쉽게 해결할 수 있다.

비법 3) '시간, 숫자'와 관련된 정보를 묻는 문제는 지문에서 정답을 직접적으로 주지 않는다.

'시간'을 물어보는 when, what time, '숫자'와 관련된 정보를 물어보는 how much 등은 지문에서 정답을 직접적으로 주지 않는다. 예를 들어, '지불 금액'을 물어보는 경우 할인이나 어떠한 혜택으로 인해 변경된 금액이 정답이며, 그 정답은 지문에 등장하지 않는 경우가 대부분이다. 또 '시간'을 물어보는 문제에서 지문에 등장한 내용이 그대로 선택지에 등장하면 오답일 확률이 높다.

비법 적용 연습

Questions 1-3 refer to the following information.

Downsizing Workshops, 5 March 2014

How do I downsize efficiently and where do I start? How and when should I prepare my home for sale? What are my lifestyle options in retirement?

The Downsizing Workshop financially supported by property sales professionals will feature current local area real estate trends, effective home selling strategies, and how to create an action plan for living your ideal retirement lifestyle.

Venue: Constitution Hill
Address: 1 Centenary Avenue, Northmead NSW 2152
Date: Wednesday, 5th of March 2014
Time: 11:00 A.M. – 1:00 P.M.
Registration cut-off: Tuesday 4th of March 2014

1 What does the event NOT feature?

(A) Housing trends
(B) Techniques in home selling
(C) Senior citizen lifestyle plans
(D) Remodeling ideas

2 By when should potential clients register?

(A) A day before the event
(B) A few days before the event
(C) On the day of the event
(D) There is no registration date.

3 According to the information, who will be sponsoring the event?

(A) Real estate agents
(B) Lifestyle experts
(C) Retirees
(D) Homebuyers

Questions 4-5 refer to the following advertisement.

A Retirement That Is Well Connected

Imagine living within walking distance from shops and amenities at Pittwater Palms.

Don't be misled. Retirement living doesn't mean cutting yourself off from the world. In fact, at Pittwater Palms, you can get better connected than you've ever been before. Enjoy a life of independence and friendship, right from the heart of Avalon. With a selection of living options available, and a range of social and recreational activities on offer, it's time to start planning for tomorrow, today.

Call us to arrange an inspection and find out how Pittwater Palms can enrich your retirement lifestyle.

Pittwater Palms
82 Avalon Parade, Avalon, NSW 2107
13 AVEO (13 28 36) www.avewo.com.au

4 For whom is this advertisement intended?

(A) Those desiring independence from others.
(B) Those who want to leave Avalon.
(C) Those who like recreational activities.
(D) Those working at local companies.

5 How can potential clients arrange a visit to the facility?

(A) By making a call
(B) By visiting a Web site
(C) By personally asking an employee
(D) By enriching themselves

일치·불일치 문제

일치·불일치 문제는 보통 문제에 'NOT 또는 true'의 단어가 포함되어 등장한다.
(일치 문제의 경우 true가 없는 경우도 있다.)

질문 유형

- What is **NOT** mentioned in the article?
- What is **NOT** suggested about Mr. Kim?
- Which of the following is **NOT** true?
- What is **true** about the PAP Restaurant?
- What is mentioned about the café?
- What does the letter say about the Mr. Dufree?

비법 1 선택지를 보면서 키워드를 체크한다. 키워드는 주로 지문 내 '희소성'이 있는 내용이다.

포괄적인 내용보다는 '지엽적'인 내용이 키워드일 확률이 높다. 따라서 지문에서 잠깐 등장하는 내용 위주로 파악한다. 예를 들어, 제품 광고에서 "What is NOT mentioned as a **payment method**?(지불 방법으로 언급되지 않은 것은?)"라는 질문에서 payment method(지불 방법)는 지문 전반에 걸쳐 등장하는 내용인 아닌 구체적인 내용이기 때문에 바로 키워드가 된다.

비법 2 일치 문제는 '정답'을, 불일치 문제는 '오답'을 고른다.

일치 문제의 경우, 지문에 등장하는 내용이 정답이다. 그러나 불일치 문제의 경우, 지문에 등장하는 어휘들을 가지고 오답을 만들기 때문에 오답 역시 지문에 등장하는 내용이 부분적으로 포함된다. 따라서 확인할 수 있는 내용을 먼저 찾는 데 집중해야 한다.

비법 적용 연습

Questions 1-2 refer to the following e-mail.

---

e-mail

From: Anytime & Anywhere Service Team <service@anytimeanywhere.co.de>
To: Kenneth Schneider <Schneider79@smail.co.de>
Date: 10 August
Subject: Your New Plan

Dear Mr. Schneider,

We at Anytime & Anywhere, are introducing new service plans to better reflect the needs of our customers. We are separating unlimited DVDs by mail and unlimited streaming into two separate plans. Now our members have a choice:

- **Plan 1:** Unlimited Streaming (no DVDs) for $6.99 a month
- **Plan 2:** Unlimited DVDs, 2 out at-a-time (no streaming) for $6.99 a month

Your price for getting both of these plans will be $13.98 a month ($6.99+$6.99). If you want to continue with your current service plan (unlimited streaming and DVDs), you don't need to do anything since it will be continued with the new charge mentioned above. These prices will start for charges on or after September 1, 2014.

However, you can easily change or cancel your unlimited streaming plan, unlimited DVD plan, or both, by going to the Plan Change page in Your Account.

We realize you have many choices for home entertainment, and we thank you for your business. As always, if you have questions, please feel free to call us at 1-888-436-5453.

The Anytime & Anywhere Team

---

1 What is the purpose of this e-mail?

(A) To promote new streaming services
(B) To apologize for an overcharge
(C) To inform customers of a price change
(D) To encourage members to renew their subscription

2 What is suggested about Mr. Schneider?

(A) He is currently paying $13.98 a month.
(B) He is a new customer.
(C) He may keep the current service at no extra charge.
(D) He can change his plan on the Web site.

Questions 3-5 refer to the following article.

World of Hobbits

World of Hobbits is the creation of Hubert Abernathy, a prolific online gamer who launched this game on the Blizzard gaming platform barely a year ago and has so far garnered 56,000 gamers worldwide. Teens who mostly are fans of *the Lord of the Rings* series of books written by JRR Tolkien are generally its mainstay.

The story is loosely adapted from the fourth book of the Fellowship of the Ring series. This online game is very appealing to young people whose intellectual ability are generally higher than the average adolescent.

The Web site where the game is played on a massive scale is extremely important for companies wanting to advertise their teen-oriented products to a larger target market.

So far, companies advertising their products have been very satisfied with the exposure this game has garnered. And, since this game has been proven to be very successful in advertising, Mr. Abernathy will be creating a new online game which he promises to be more successful and popular for teens and most especially for advertisers whose target is within that age bracket.

3 What is the main topic of the article?
(A) Advertisers are satisfied.
(B) The book series has many followers.
(C) Teens who play this game buy more products.
(D) Tolkien will release a new novel.

4 The word "mainstay" in paragraph 1, line 4, is closest in meaning to
(A) base
(B) audience
(C) contradictors
(D) adult

5 What is NOT mentioned about the game?
(A) Adolescents love the game.
(B) Adults often play the game.
(C) The game was very successful around the country.
(D) Mr. Abernathy will create a new game.

추론 문제

| Reading |

추론 문제는 지문의 사실을 바탕으로 한다. 문제를 풀 때에는 반드시 지문에 등장한 내용에서 추론할 수 있는 '또 다른 사실'이어야 한다. 근거 없이 막연히 '그럴 수도 있겠다'라고 미루어 짐작만 하는 것은 대개 오답이다.

질문 유형

- Where would this advertisement **most likely** be found?
- What can be **inferred** from this notice?
- What does Mr. Durst **suggest** about the delivery of the product?
- For whom is this article **intended**?

비법 1 구체적인 문제인가 아닌가를 먼저 파악한다.

구체적인 문제냐 아니냐에 따라서 지문에 힌트가 한 곳에만 있는지 아니면 고르게 분포되어 있는지를 예측할 수 있다. 그것에 따라 난이도가 확연히 차이가 난다.

비법 2 패러프레이징이 가장 많이 되는 문제 유형이다.

추론 문제에서는 패러프레이징 방법, 즉 '재진술(같은 의도의 말을 완전히 바꾸어 하는 것)'을 많이 활용한다. 따라서 지문에서 나온 단어가 선택지에서 그대로 나왔다면 오답으로 이어질 확률이 높다.

비법 적용 연습

Questions 1-3 refer to the following announcement.

Are you feeling down lately?

- Our registered psychologists provide highly skilled, individualized services in a compassionate and supportive environment.
- Assistance for concerns such as adjustment to life changes, anxiety, depression, stress, relationship problems, substance abuse & trauma.
- Immediate support provided if you are in crisis.
- Working together to alleviate distress, improve your coping skills, move toward effective resolutions and ultimately regain stability in your life.
- State-run health insurance reimbursements available.

Balanced Psychological Services
Telephone: 9877-4998 or 0416-884-0394
www.balancedps.com

1 For whom is this announcement intended?

(A) Psychologists
(B) Mentally handicapped people
(C) Medical experts
(D) Emotionally troubled people

2 What is NOT implied about the psychologists?

(A) They are very efficient and quick-working.
(B) They provide one-on-one consultation.
(C) They care about their patients' well-being.
(D) They can support the patients' lifestyles.

3 What is stated in the article regarding payment methods?

(A) The government can pay for treatment.
(B) The patient can pay at a later date.
(C) The facility can provide low cost financing.
(D) Some patients are entitled to free treatment.

Questions 4-5 refer to the following advertisement.

Attention all carpet buyers!

Australia's leading carpet manufacturer, Carpet Right, has chosen to urgently clear another 50,000m² of top quality carpets. 100% NZ wool twist piles, textured loops, sisals, plush piles and solution dyed nylons. All extra heavy duty and first quality premium grade.

At prices never seen before!
*Save up to 40%!

All carpets are in stock now and can be stored and laid at your convenience. Hurry up! Offers available at all stores while stocks last.

*On selected lines only.

BELROSE
Warehouse
56 Clide St. Niangala Cl (Next to Homemakers Supa Centre)
2354

4 Where most likely would this passage appear?

(A) In a carpet catalogue
(B) In a newspaper
(C) In a business textbook
(D) In a carpet instructions

5 What is implied about this advertisement?

(A) Value added tax is included.
(B) All items are 40% off.
(C) Carpet Right wants to clear their stock of carpets.
(D) This sale is happening in only one area.

Reading

DAY 05 동의어 문제

지문에 나온 '특정 단어나 구'의 의미를 물어보는 문제 유형이다. 제시되는 어휘의 난이도는 대체로 높지 않지만 우리가 흔히 알고 있거나 더 잘 알려진 동의어를 오답으로 제시하는 경우가 많다. 따라서 반드시 "문맥상" 가장 어울리는 의미를 정답으로 골라야 한다.

질문 유형

The <u>rest</u> of the conference, including the schedule indicated in my July 16 memo, remains the same.
7월 16일자 메모에 나와 있는 일정을 포함한 컨퍼런스의 나머지 일정은 변경이 없을 것입니다.

The word "rest" in paragraph 2, line 1, is closest in meaning to
(A) break	(B) basis	(C) action	(D) remainder

 rest는 명사로 '휴식' 또는 '나머지', 동사로 '휴식을 취하다'의 의미이다. 따라서 지문 속에서 어떤 품사로 어떤 내용과 함께 쓰였는지를 확인하고서, 선택지에서 문맥상 가장 자연스러운 동의어를 고르면 된다.

정답 (D)

비법 1 지문 내 해당 어휘를 체크해 둔다.

동의어 문제가 등장하면, 가장 먼저 해당 지문의 어휘를 체크해 놓는다. '문맥상' 가장 가까운 의미를 고르는 문제이기 때문에, 문맥 속에서 의미를 파악하는 것이 중요하다. 따라서 지문을 읽으며 다른 문제를 해결하면서 동의어 문제를 해결하는 것이 실수를 줄일 수 있는 방법이다.

비법 2 그 단어의 주변 표현들을 같이 이해한다.

예를 들어, 동사 어휘가 나왔을 경우에는 그 동사의 주어나 목적어가 무엇인지, 또는 그 동사를 꾸미는 부사가 무엇인지를 함께 이해하면 문제 풀이에 많은 도움이 된다.

비법 적용 연습

Questions 1-4 refer to the following advertisement.

Office Solutions
Convenient and comfortable offices shouldn't come at a high price.

Most businesses spend a large part of their budget on office furniture and equipment that will later become obsolete in their businesses. Aware of this large amount of money spent unnecessarily in furnishing their offices, the owners of Office Solutions created a company with the purpose of introducing a cost-efficient way of furnishing workplaces. Open for the past 20 years, Office Solution now has 18 branches located throughout the country, with plans to open two new stores in Los Angeles.

Office Solutions buys and repairs used furniture and equipment and leases them to clients. Besides offering affordable rates, Office Solutions assists clients in saving money by recommending the most suitable equipment and furniture for their day-to-day needs. Office Solutions leases computers, printers, copiers, and fax machines as well as desks and filing cabinets. It also maintains a team of experienced and skilled technicians who ensure that all leased electronic equipment is in good working condition.

So if you are starting a new business, or simply need additional equipment, you can skip spending a large percentage of your budget on office equipment and furniture. Call us now at (619) 285-2923.

---

1 What does the advertisement say about new business owners?

(A) They have problems with interior decorating.
(B) They spend the majority of their expenses on office equipment.
(C) They buy used equipment from other offices.
(D) They do not know to how to manage their employees wisely.

2 The word "obsolete" in paragraph 1, line 2, is closest in meaning to

(A) old
(B) not usable
(C) observed
(D) expensive

3 How does Office Solutions help businesses save money?

(A) By selling off the furniture of an office
(B) By introducing direct suppliers
(C) By giving discounts on large orders
(D) By giving advice on what is proper equipment

4 What is NOT stated about Office Solutions?

(A) It has been in operation for 2 decades.
(B) It has technicians to maintain their equipment.
(C) It purchases used equipment.
(D) It provides free delivery services.

Questions 5-7 refer to the following article.

Local Business Legend Retires

Frank Plimpton is a rare businessman: he knows many of his customers by name and he offers generous salaries, stock options, and vacation pay to each of the employees at his five Mary's Supermarket stores. He is a legend in this area, and his success is deserved and respected. Yesterday was his final day on the job, and after more than forty years and five satellite stores, he will finally take a vacation.

Plimpton came to Yorktown with a vision of opening his own general food store, named Mary's, after his mother, who taught him the values of kindness and generosity which he still cherishes today. His friendly demeanor and hard-working approach helped his business flourish, and in 1960 he opened a store in the neighboring town of Springfield.

Even with all that success, he still stressed the importance of small, welcoming stores. Since then, he has opened four more stores in the area, creating one of the only chains in the country that does not advertise. Plimpton says he would rather spend the money on his employees, and word-of-mouth is most effective for him, since his customers value his business enough to tell their friends to go there.

5 What is indicated about Mr. Plimpton?

(A) He wanted his stores to be small and friendly.
(B) He wanted to make money to give to his mother.
(C) He wanted to have the most popular store in the area.
(D) He wanted to achieve fame as a businessman.

6 The word "demeanor" in paragraph 2, line 3, is closest in meaning to

(A) reasoning skills
(B) attitude
(C) generosity
(D) intentions

7 How do most people find about Mary's Supermarket stores?

(A) By television advertising
(B) Because of the prominent locations
(C) From customer recommendations
(D) Through newspaper articles about Mr. Plimpton

Reading

편지 / 이메일

편지나 이메일 지문에서는 편지를 쓴 이유나 목적을 묻거나 수신자와 발신자에 관한 문제가 출제된다. 따라서 메일의 수신자와 발신자 항목을 잘 파악하고 보통 지문 초반에 등장하는 목적을 정확히 파악해 둔다.

❶ '발신자'와 '수신자'를 확인한다.

우리가 이메일(e-mail)을 확인하거나 편지(letter)를 받았을 때 가장 먼저 보는 곳을 떠올려 보자. 바로 발신자이다. '누가 보낸' 것인가에 따라 대략 무슨 내용일지를 예상할 수 있을 것이다. 하지만 토익 지문에서는 '수신자'도 중요하다. 따라서 '누가 누구에게' 보냈는지를 함께 확인한다.

● 발신자와 수신자의 관계

발신자	수신자	내용
개인	회사 or 단체	고객의 불만, 고객의 정보 문의, 채용 지원 등
회사 or 단체	개인	문의한 정보에 대한 안내, 신제품 정보, 공지사항 등
개인	개인	직장 동료 사이에 주고받는 이메일
회사	회사	프로젝트 관련 내용, 구매 부서에서 다른 업체에 연락을 취하는 내용 등

❷ '자주 등장하는 내용'들을 미리 알아 둔다.

- 불만 또는 그에 대한 답신
- 칭찬, 감사를 전하는 이메일
- 인사 이동 (ex. 승진, 퇴임), 고용에 관한 내용
- 기념식, 우수사원 포상에 관한 내용
- 가격 문의, 견적서와 이에 대한 답신
- 주문, 선적 관련, 사업 제안
- 여행 또는 출장 일정표 관련 내용
- 변경 사항 전달 (ex. 회의 날짜/시간/장소 등)

비법 적용 연습

Questions 1-2 refer to the following e-mail.

---

e-mail

From: Caren Doles <carend@hatmail.com>
To: Doy Chanders <doychanders@superfurniture.com>
Date: Wednesday, January 1, 14:24
Subject: Order No. 255671

Dear Ms. Chanders,

I recently purchased one DIY bed, two computer desks, and two chairs. However, a kitchen table, which I had not ordered was delivered along with the bed and chairs. So upon receipt, I called one of your customer service representatives and he informed me that the items delivered are correctly corresponding to what was itemized on the delivery order.

I will drop the kitchen table at one of your stores here in town. It will be very much appreciated if you settle this up and send me the desks I ordered. Just in case, I have attached a copy of the purchase order.

Thank you for your cooperation.

Sincerely,
Caren Doles

---

1. What is the purpose of this e-mail?
   (A) To order some office furniture
   (B) To request for a full refund
   (C) To inquire about the products
   (D) To correct a problem

2. What is included in the e-mail?
   (A) An order form
   (B) A receipt
   (C) An invoice
   (D) A brochure

3. What is Ms. Doles planning to do next?
   (A) Return an item
   (B) Call the customer service department
   (C) Order new furniture
   (D) Visit the Web site

Questions 4-5 refer to the following letter.

August 10

Chris Allen
6325 Brownsville Avenue
Pittsburgh, PA 14739

Dear Mr. Allen:

I am in receipt of your e-mail of July 23 in which you inquired about the facility. I started this business almost two decades ago and have had only the very best reviews from my guests. My staff members and I take great pride in the quality of our services and the facilities. With everything you need provided for, I am confident that you will have a pleasant stay here.

As you requested, I have attached a brochure with our prices. Between September 15 and November 14, we offer a 30% discount for weekday accommodation. To reserve a room, please contact our supervisor, Mr. Andy Smith, at 335-3293 or visit our Web site at www.thebestinn.com where you can book by just clicking a few times. We suggest that you book a room at least two weeks in advance of your actual stay.

Feel free to contact us with any other questions you might have.

Best regards,

Robin Hober
Robin Hober

4 Who is Mr. Hober?

(A) An employee of the hotel
(B) A supervisor
(C) A hotel owner
(D) A hotel guest

5 How long does the special offer apply?

(A) For 3 months
(B) For 2 months
(C) For 30 days
(D) For 2 weeks

제품 광고

광고문에서는 누구를 대상으로 무엇을 광고하는지가 자주 출제된다. 보통 제품이나 서비스 광고가 많으며 구인·구직 공고, 관광 상품 홍보 등의 지문도 출제된다.

> **질문 유형**
> - What is being **advertised**?
> - What is NOT mentioned as **a feature** of the computer?
> - How can customers get **a coupon**?
> - What is required for customers to get **a discount**?
> - What is NOT mentioned as **a way to purchase** the product?
> - What is NOT mentioned as **a payment method**?

❶ '무엇'을 파는 광고인지에 초점을 맞춰 읽는다.

제품을 파는 것 자체가 목적이기 때문에 보통 목적 문제는 나오지 않는다. 글에서 설명하는 제품의 특징들을 종합하여 무엇을 광고하는 것인지를 파악하는 것이 중요하다.

❷ 제품의 '특징'은 무엇인가?

제품을 홍보하는 것이기 때문에 제품의 상세한 특징을 자세히 파악해야 한다.
제품의 특징들이 등장하는 경우, 번호를 매겨 놓는 것도 하나의 방법이 될 수 있다.

❸ 제공하는 '혜택'은 무엇인가?

제품 구매 시 제공되는 혜택이 빠지지 않고 등장하는데 이때 중요한 것은 혜택을 받을 수 있는 '조건'이다.

❹ '구매 방법'을 확인하자!

어떻게 제품을 구매할 수 있는지, 즉 온라인/오프라인 구매가 가능한지, 정상 또는 할인 가격이 얼마인지를 체크해 둔다.

❺ '배송'은 어떻게 되는가?

배송과 관련된 질문인 경우, 비용이 드는지 여부와 '무료 배송' 조건 등을 구분해서 기억해 둔다.

비법 적용 연습

Questions 1-3 refer to the following advertisement.

Don't Give Up Any Of These: Spacious Room & Style

List price: $150.00
Sale Price: $100.00 & Free Shipping

Size: 17 inch
Color: Black, Brown, Gray
*All three colors in stock

Please note that this item will be shipped in its own packaging and cannot be gift-wrapped.

- 100% polyester
- 18" high
- 12" wide

- Perfect fit adjustable laptop system provides custom fit for 13-15.6" laptops
- Front pocket organization with tablet pocket for all your business needs
- Cool-flow padding on the back provides comfort and heat regulation
- Smart-strap slides over upright handles for easy mobility
- Two secure, zipped quick stash pockets

Special offers and product promotions
- If you purchase the item with a credit card, you will get $20 off.
- Free 3-dial lock will be given to all buyers from August 10 to 23.

---

1 What is being advertised?

(A) A laptop computer
(B) A 3-dial lock
(C) A backpack
(D) A suitcase

2 How much will one have to pay when paying by credit card?

(A) $150.00
(B) $100.00
(C) $80.00
(D) $20.00

3 What is NOT mentioned in the advertisement?

(A) The product comes in three different colors.
(B) The product can accommodate any size of laptop computers.
(C) A present will be given for a certain period of time.
(D) The item has several pockets.

Questions 4-5 refer to the following advertisement.

For sale

Bungalow (currently being occupied)

Location: 2378 Clairemont Avenue
San Diego, California

Lot Area: 1,050 square feet

Price: $130,000 (negotiable)

This pre-owned and pre-loved home has 2 bedrooms, 1 bathroom and a spacious sunroom. It also has a comfortable backyard ideal for weekend barbecues and a parking area good for 2 small cars. Perfect for a small family just starting their new lives.

For more information, do not hesitate to give Ericka Matthews (the broker) a call at (619) 286-9934.

Serious and direct buyers only. No real estate agents.

---

4 What is NOT a feature of this property?

(A) Sunroom
(B) Parking lot
(C) Backyard
(D) Balcony

5 What is indicated in this advertisement?

(A) Real estate agents will be given priority.
(B) There will be a discount.
(C) Ms. Matthews resides in the property.
(D) This house can be rented.

Reading

DAY 08 구인 공고

질문 유형

- **What position** is being advertised?
- What is NOT mentioned as **a requirement** for the position?
- **How** can people interested in the position **apply**?
- What is NOT listed as **a job benefit** offered by the company?
- **What** should be **submitted** for the managerial position?

❶ 모집하고 있는 '직책'에 초점을 맞춰 읽는다.
구인 공고는 직원을 뽑는 것이 목적이기 때문에 목적 문제는 나오지 않는다.

❷ '담당 업무'는 무엇인가?
구인 공고에 빠지지 않고 나오는 질문 중 하나가 바로 '직무 설명'에 관련된 내용이다. 번호를 매기면서 읽는 것이 중요하다.

❸ 지원자의 '자격 요건'은 무엇인가?
지원을 위해 필요한 자격 요건들이 있다. 이러한 자격 요건이 나올 때에도 반드시 번호를 매기면서 읽어야 참고 시 혼란스럽지 않다.

❹ '지원 방법'은 무엇인가?
지원 방법은 '온라인 지원(회사의 홈페이지, 이메일)'이 가장 많다.

❺ '제출 서류'는 무엇인가?
"다음 중 제출 서류로 언급되지 않은 것은 무엇인가?"라는 질문 역시 자주 등장한다.

❻ 입사 후 '복지 혜택'은 무엇인가?
보통 구인 공고에는 직원들을 위한 복지 혜택들이 소개된다. 자주 등장하는 관련 어휘들을 기억해 두는 것이 좋다.

benefits package 복지 혜택	medical insurance 의료 보험
paid leave 유급 휴가	considerable bonus 상당한 보너스
incentive pay 장려금	pension 연금
retirement plan 퇴직금 연금 제도	
comprehensive training program 종합적인 교육 프로그램	

비법 적용 연습

Questions 1-2 refer to the following job advertisement.

Job Openings for MS Publications Inc.

COPY EDITOR (SYDNEY OFFICE)

- College graduate, major in journalism or other related course
- With 2 years or more editing experience in a news media agency
- Above average skill in written English
- Preferably with knowledge in layout and page design
- Willing to work in the evenings and holidays and thrives under the pressure of daily deadlines

ACCOUNTING ASSISTANT (CANBERRA OFFICE)

- Accounting or accountancy graduate with a minimum of 3 years experience in audit or general accounting
- Well-organized, mature and with a very high sense of responsibility
- Can work with minimum supervision, hardworking, results-oriented
- Willing to work overtime if required

Interested applicants may send their résumés to
wagnerronaldo@mspublications.com
or bring their résumés,
transcript of records, and any valid I.D.
to our office located at
the 2nd floor, Louie R. Prieto press building,
9 Pirie St, Fyshwick Act 2609

---

1 What is NOT mentioned as a requirement for the copy editor position?

(A) Previous experience in a related field
(B) A bachelor's degree
(C) Writing proficiency
(D) Knowledge in layout and page design

2 How can people interested apply for the accounting assistant position?

(A) Fax a résumé to the office
(B) Email required documents
(C) Visit the company's Web site
(D) Call the Canberra Office

Questions 3-5 refer to the following job advertisement.

J&P Design
James and Pett Design Company

We have recently opened a New York branch in order to meet the growing demand for our unique and expressive design expertise. So we are in need of an Administrative Aide who is able to process inter-departmental and external correspondence, deal with a wide range of documents, mail, and phone calls for managers, and is also responsible for routine maintenance of computers and software. Ordering office supplies and making travel arrangements for the supervisor and other managers is also involved. Applicants interested should have at least 3 years of administrative work and be highly familiar with computers and other office equipment. Good verbal and written communication skills are also required. An associate's degree is a prerequisite. A bachelor's degree, however, is preferred. This challenging position would suit a candidate with a can-do attitude and an eye for detail. The company offers an excellent base salary with bonuses.

If you are interested in the position, please visit www.jpdesign.com, fill out an online application and click "submit" with your résumé and one recommendation letter attached.

3 What type of position is being advertised?

(A) Office assistant
(B) Web designer
(C) Department manager
(D) Manager's secretary

4 What is NOT indicated in the advertisement?

(A) The expected salary range
(B) The location of the company
(C) The way to apply for the position
(D) The specific title of the position

5 What responsibility of the position is mentioned?

(A) Scheduling meetings
(B) Meeting with clients
(C) Giving a tour
(D) Purchasing items for the office

Reading

공지, 안내, 정보

공지(notice), 안내(announcement), 정보(information) 글은 모두 '다수의 특정 대상'을 가지고 있다. 따라서 '누구를 위한 글'인지를 파악하면 한결 편하게 지문을 이해할 수 있다. 누구를 위한 내용인지를 물어보는 문제도 자주 출제된다.

질문 유형

- What is **the purpose** of this notice?
- **Why** was this notice **written**?
- **For whom** is the information most likely intended?
- **Where** is this notice most likely **found**?
- What are the readers **asked to do**?

❶ 공지나 안내문에는 주제에 대한 서술, 목록, 표가 등장하는 경우가 많다.

공지는 철저하게 정보를 알리기 위한 기능적인 글이기 때문에, 주제에 대한 이야기를 서술하는 경우도 있지만 '목록'이나 '표'로 제시하는 경우가 많다. 목록의 경우 첫 줄을 읽게 되면 전반적인 단락의 주제를 알 수 있다.

❷ 공지는 대부분 "~해 주세요"라는 부탁으로 마무리한다.

다른 종류의 글도 그렇지만 주제를 알려 주고 세부 내용을 알려준 뒤 "~해 주세요"라는 부탁이나 지시로 글을 마무리 하는 경우가 많다. 따라서 대부분 이러한 내용은 글의 후반부에 등장한다.

비법 적용 연습

Questions 1-3 refer to the following notice.

As you know, we have recently expanded our facility. We have added a pool, increased the size of our workout room, and begun offering free day care. To help offset the cost of construction, we must increase our family membership fees by $25, effective February 1. Slim Gym now offers swimming, weight lifting, ice skating, and aerobic conditioning for the entire family. And even with the higher price, we offer one of the lowest prices in the state. Those who have already renewed their membership will not be assessed the additional $25 fee until your next renewal date. If you want to use the facility at the current membership fee, please renew your membership before the end of this month. We appreciate your support and hope that you will continue to choose Slim Gym as the place for your family's fitness.

1 Why was this notice written?

(A) To announce the reopening of a fitness center
(B) To advertise added services
(C) To inform members of an increase in fees
(D) To thank patrons for their continued support

2 For whom is this notice most likely intended?

(A) New members
(B) Aerobics instructors
(C) Existing gym users
(D) Non-paying members

3 What should customers do if they want to use the facility without paying the increased fees?

(A) Renew their membership on February 1
(B) Register for the Aerobic class
(C) Contact the instructor
(D) Renew in the current month

Questions 4-5 refer to the following memo.

From: Jimmy Clint, management
To: All employees
Subject: Absence policy and procedures

As winter approaches, we want to remind you of our policy regarding absence due to severe weather conditions. Now is a good time to prepare your car for safe travel in winter weather; our employees' safety is our greatest concern. We have rarely found it necessary to close our offices completely; however, we have done so when road conditions are too hazardous for travel.

If you are unsure about whether to report to work, you may call our employee hotline at 555-5555. We will provide information concerning company hours in the case of severe weather or any other emergency. Employees are expected to be at work when the office is officially open; if you are unable to be at work, you must notify your supervisor that you are taking a personal day off.

4 What is the memo mainly about?
   (A) Preparing your car for safe travel
   (B) Severe weather conditions
   (C) Policies regarding absences
   (D) Employee safety

5 What should employees do if they are unable to come to work?
   (A) Call the employee hotline
   (B) Contact their manager
   (C) Prepare their cars for safe travel
   (D) Get information regarding road conditions

Reading

DAY 10 기사

기사(article)는 기업 소식이나 지역 행사 등 다양한 소재를 다루지만 대부분 비즈니스에 한정되어 있다. 다양하고 높은 수준의 어휘를 필요로 하기 때문에 학습자가 가장 까다롭게 느끼는 지문 유형이기도 하다.

❶ 자주 등장하는 주제들을 알아 둔다.

Policy change, Salary Increase, new line of products, Employment, Expansion, M&A, New CEO, Retirement, Financial reports, Business trends, Local tourist attractions, Wine, Weight Loss, Exercise, Taking a nap, Festival, Seminar, Conference, Exposition, Announcement, Company's decision, Company's contribution to the environment, Electronic cars, Solar panel, Transportation, Renovation, Historic attractions, Weather forecasts, Book or Show review, Restaurant and Hotel review

❷ 기사는 재진술(paraphrasing)이 가장 많이 적용된다.

● 재진술의 유형

① '동의어'를 이용하는 방법
- free = complimentary (무료의)
- individualized = personalized = customized (고객 맞춤의)

② '반의어'를 이용하는 방법
- during weekdays = except weekends
- Our office has not that big. = Employees use a small office.

③ '상위 범주의 단어'를 이용하는 방법
- conference, company banquet, ceremony, concert = event
- résumé, contract, form, slip, report = document

④ 문장을 새롭게 쓰는 방법
- He felt disappointed. = He was unhappy.
- Early registration is required because of the limited seats.
  = The event will be completely full.

비법 적용 연습

Questions 1-3 refer to the following article.

Mona Vale Business Fair

City Council of Mona Vale is committed to creating a city where people want to live, work, play and shop. A growing local economy is critical to building a vibrant community. The Mona Vale Business Fair is an exciting opportunity for businesses and citizens to work together to accomplish this goal.

When: Friday, 19 September
Where: Bay View Golf Club
Time: 8:30 A.M. to 5:00 P.M.

This one-day business fair will showcase Mona Vale locally and regionally and include a series of panel talks on place making, tourism and craft industries from expert presenters, as well as providing a great opportunity for business to network and promote their products and services. Take a look at this exciting program booklet which introduces the biographies of the panel speakers.

For more information about the Fair, please visit:
www.pittwater.nsw.gov.au

---

1 What does the article imply?

(A) A new community will be inaugurated.
(B) A local government will hold an official event.
(C) A number of councilors will have a speech.
(D) The detailed schedule will be posted.

2 Who will NOT attend this event?

(A) Expert presenters
(B) Businessmen
(C) Golfers
(D) Panel members

3 The word "showcase" in paragraph 3, line 1, is closest in meaning to

(A) open
(B) imitate
(C) display
(D) design

Questions 4-6 refer to the following article.

Everglades Amphibian Preserve

The Everglades Amphibian Preserve has launched a new attraction for amphibian lovers yesterday. In addition to more than 30 exhibits of amphibians from around the world, the preserve's newest facility is an alligator farm that will educate visitors on how alligators live, breed, and survive. The farm, which stands on the zoo's former man-made mini lake, houses more than 50 freshwater crocodiles.

Furthermore, guests will have a chance to watch the animals up close through windows in the underwater observatory area. The new area also has a research facility used for captive amphibian breeding. This was made possible through a partnership between the preserve management and professors from the Durban Biological Institute. The farm is envisioned to highlight the importance of protecting wildlife in danger of extinction, which is overlooked by many people nowadays. It is essential that adults and children know the importance of caring for our wildlife since animals, no matter how they look or how they are portrayed in movies, are necessary for our environment.

In order for our guests to have a deeper appreciation for our wildlife, the facility has opened an incubation area where they can personally care for baby alligators. The preserve will also show a documentary movie this weekend featuring alligators and other reptiles that are close to extinction. Those interested in learning about wildlife preservation, or the hours and fees of the preserve, can visit www.evergladesmarine.org.

4 In which part of a newspaper can this be article be found?

(A) Sports
(B) Opinion
(C) Local news
(D) Science and technology

5 Who helped the Preserve build the new facility?

(A) Reporters
(B) The government
(C) Farmers
(D) Scientists

6 What is stated about the alligator farm?

(A) It will breed animals for commercial sale.
(B) It will provide animals for documentaries.
(C) It will be used only by scientists.
(D) It will help conserve endangered species.

양식 및 기타 지문

Reading

질문 유형

- What are the new employees scheduled to do?
- When will the visitors go to the lobby?
- Why did Mr. Kang send the fax?
- In which of the following situations should Mr. Allen call the company?
- What is implied about the security deposit?
- What will Mr. Baek probably do on Thursday?

❶ 설문지(survey), 신청서 (application form) 또는 대여 관련 서류

무엇에 관한 양식인지만 빠르게 파악되면 문제의 정답이 쉽게 보이는 경향이 있다. 기타 '**고객의 의견(comments)**'란에 내용이 적혀 있는 경우 보통 그 부분에서 한 문제 정도 출제된다.

❷ 설명서나 규정 등의 지문

'설명서는 제품이나 서비스의 이용 방법'에 관한 지문으로 '**시간이나 장소**'와 같은 정보가 가장 중요하다. 규정의 지문이 나오게 되면 고객이나 이용자가 반드시 숙지해야 할 '변경 사항이나 취소' 등이 서술된 부분을 잘 읽어 두어야 한다.

❸ 스케줄이나 영수증 관련 지문

여행 일정표(itinerary)나 회의 일정표(schedule)가 나오는 경우, 공통적으로 '**시간과 장소**'에 관해서 꼼꼼히 읽어둔다. 변경이 가능한 경우, 따로 체크해 둔다. 회의 일정표는 회의나 발표를 진행하는 사람이 누구인지 이름이나 직책을 주의 깊게 봐둘 필요가 있다. 영수증(receipt)의 경우 어떤 물건을 샀는지, 총액이 얼마인지, 세금(tax) 관련 내용 또는 혜택이 주어지는지에 대해 살펴두는 것이 필요하다.

*특이한 종류의 지문들은 각각 항목별 내용이 길지 않다. 따라서 시간이 부족한 경우 첫 문장만 읽어도 주제가 드러나므로 필요한 정보를 쉽게 찾을 수 있다.

비법 적용 연습

Reading DAY 11

정답 및 해설 / 32p

Questions 1-2 refer to the following information on the Web page.

Traveler	
Patty Hearst	

Flight-Worldspan Airlines	Monday, May 19, 2014

Flight Number:	2227	Confirmation Number: YIE88G
Class:	Economy	
Depart:	Gatwick Airport London United Kingdom Terminal N	12:00 P.M. Monday, May 19
Arrive:	Atlanta Hartsfield-Jackson Intl Airport Atlanta, GA USA	02:15 A.M. Tuesday, May 20
Seat:	Not Assigned	Stopovers: 0
Meal:	Meal Service	Mileage: 4213
Aircraft:	MD10	Travel Time: 09:15

*Fragile or perishable items, cash, valuables, business documents, personal medicine, laptop, camera, mobile phone and etc. cannot be transported as checked baggage and should be carried with you on the plane. Worldspan Airlines shall not be liable for any loss or damages caused by violation of this regulation.

Flight Status	Maps / Driving Directions	Add To Calendar	Online Check in

1 What is NOT stated in this itinerary?

(A) Travel distance
(B) Seat number
(C) Terminal
(D) Type of aircraft

2 What is indicated about the checked luggage?

(A) Fragile items must be wrapped.
(B) Personal medicine can be checked in.
(C) Electronic gadgets must not be checked in.
(D) 20 kilograms per person is allowed.

Questions 3-4 refer to the following form.

Runner's world Magazine	We regret to hear that you wish to cancel your subscription. To formally cancel your subscription, please fill out this card and e-mail it back to us. Thank you.
	Name: Fred Durst **Address:** 478 Elm street, Oakland, CA **E-mail:** fredurst@aol.com **Tel:** (692) 647-3377
Irvine Blvd. Mission Viejo California www.runnersworld.com	**Reasons for the cancellation:** ☐ Price ■ content ☐ service **Comments:** *I received this subscription for free and I wish to cancel it because this is not my hobby.*

3 Why does Mr. Durst want to cancel his subscription?

(A) He finds the magazine to be too expensive.
(B) He doesn't enjoy running.
(C) He is moving to another city.
(D) He has another subscription.

4 What must Mr. Durst do to cancel his subscription?

(A) Call the magazine office
(B) Answer a phone survey
(C) Send the information through regular mail
(D) Complete the form and send it to *Runner's world*

Reading

DAY 12 연계 문제

이중 지문(Double Passages)은 두 개의 연계된 지문을 보고 5문제를 푸는 유형으로, 181번부터 200번까지 총 4세트가 출제된다.

비법 1 연계 문제는 보통 한 문제뿐이다.

연계 문제는 각각의 내용을 이해하고 종합적인 사고를 통해 푸는 문제 유형이다. 보통 5문제 중 1문제가 출제되므로, 나머지 4문제는 기존의 Single Passage를 푸는 방식 그대로 해결하면 된다. 모든 문제를 두 지문 모두 신경 쓰면서 풀지 않도록 하자.

비법 2 둘 중 어느 지문을 볼지는 '질문'에서 결정 난다.

간혹 첫 번째 지문에서 풀어야 할 문제를 두 번째 지문에서 찾아 헤매는 경우가 있다. 하지만 어느 지문을 보고 풀지는 질문에서 결정이 난다.

ex) · According to the **e-mail**, what should employees do when parking on the street?
· Based on the **article**, which of the followings is NOT true?
· What is NOT indicated in the **advertisement**?

비법 3 연계 문제는 공통적으로 언급하는 부분에서 정답을 찾는다.

- 두 지문을 모두 보고 풀어야 하는 문제는 종합적인 사고를 원한다. 따라서 두 지문 모두에서 언급한 내용이어야 출제가 가능하다. 예를 들어, 첫 번째 지문에서 표가 등장했다면 두 번째 이메일에서는 그 표에 관해, 첫 번째 지문에서 스케줄이 나왔다면 두 번째 지문에서는 그 스케줄에 관련된 내용이 반드시 나올 것이다. 표현 방법이나 의도가 다를 뿐 실제 언급하는 내용은 같다.

- 키워드를 찾아 지문을 읽다가 정답이 나올 것 같은 부분을 찾았지만 정작 정확하게 언급되지 않은 경우, 다른 지문에서 관련 내용이 언급된 부분을 찾는다.

비법 적용 연습

Questions 1-5 refer to the following announcement and e-mail.

Community Event

September 9th
Ceremony – 10:00 A.M.
Guided Hikes – 11:30 A.M.

293th Street. Just west of La Union Rd.

*Honored guest speakers and city officials will partake to celebrate the prairie restoration that has been achieved by a collaboration of agencies and community volunteers as the restoration baton passes from the Army Corps back to the RSCP.

*Rain: All the scheduled ceremonies, displays and treats will move to the Bronton Public Library.

*Free guided hikes: First hike at 11:30 led by the honored guest, Hubo Gatton; others thereafter by Dui, Pinn, and Alkan. Last hike leaves at 1:30 P.M.

*Good for families, students and all those who want to experience prairie wilderness.

*More than a hike: You will see displays, get informational maps and literature, and refreshments.

*Dress for Success: Enjoy your experience by dressing for hiking in natural terrain. Flip flops, shorts and tank tops not recommended.

---

e-mail

From: Tylor Watson <tylorwatson889@unimail.com>
To: Daniel Graham <danielgraham@brontontown.org>
Date: September 13
Subject: Upcoming event

Dear Mr. Graham,

Recently, my family and I participated in your prairie hiking event organized by the Bronton Community Center and I had so much fun there during the hiking and it was too great to forget. By the way, I suggested to my company CEO that we go hiking with our employees to repeat the great experience I had with your guide Mr. Hubo Gatton and he said yes to my suggestion. So I would like to ask for Mr. Gatton's contact number or an e-mail address to see if he is able to guide us as he did for me and my family. The company hiking will take place October 2 at the same location. Travel and hotel expenses will be covered by the company and we will also provide an extra payment for his participation.

Please e-mail me his contact information or confirm his availability no later than September 19.

Regards,

Tylor Watson

Reading　DAY 12

1. According to the announcement, for whom is this information most likely intended?
   (A) City officials
   (B) Local residents
   (C) Foreign students
   (D) Tour guides

2. Based on the announcement, which of the followings is true?
   (A) There will be more than two group of hikers.
   (B) Slippers and tank tops are prohibited.
   (C) Hiking will start from the Bronton Public Library.
   (D) The event will take place regularly.

3. What time did Mr. Watson's hiking take place?
   (A) 10:00 A.M.
   (B) 11:00 A.M.
   (C) 11:30 A.M.
   (D) 1:30 P.M.

4. What is the purpose of Tylor Watson's e-mail?
   (A) To register for the hiking program
   (B) To arrange for the community event
   (C) To ask for some information
   (D) To inform his CEO of a previous event

5. What can be inferred from the e-mail?
   (A) Tylor Watson sent Hubo Gatton an e-mail before.
   (B) Tylor Watson already visited the venue of the proposed hike.
   (C) The company had an outdoor activity.
   (D) Employees and their family can attend the event.

Questions 6-10 refer to the following warranty and e-mail.

Warranty

NTGX Laptop computer warranty applicable to all models
(100% Care program operated by seasoned technicians at any New Tech store)

Basic Care Plan: If your computer and accessories are damaged or lost during a one-year period after purchase, you are eligible for a repair or product replacement. Whenever you have problems mentioned above, you can visit any of our New Tech service center and file a claim by filling out a simple form. In compliance with the policy, a repair or replacement will be completed within two working days and free delivery will be made to your home address.

Premium Care Plan: With only additional $40, you can purchase New Tech's Premium Care Plan and this plan extends your coverage for an additional 12 months. It can be purchased at any time within the first 6 months of your Basic Care Plan. For more information, visit www.newtech.com/warranty/premiumcare or call us at 229-4854-0039.

e-mail

From: Kuger Smith <ks1122@eskbroadcasting.com>
To: servicedepartment@newtech.com
Date: December 12
Subject: Case No. (223GE1224)

To whom it may concern:

A couple of weeks ago, I experienced a problem with the Internet connection of my computer so I filed the claim at the New Tech service center near my office on December 2. The following day, I received a call from one of your service representatives and he told me that it will be repaired soon and that it will be covered by my Premium Care Plan. However, I haven't received any other news regarding my claim. It will be very much appreciated if you reply to this e-mail as soon as you can and let me know when I can get my laptop back.

Thank you.

Kuger Smith

6 For whom is this warranty intended?

(A) Technicians at the New Tech service center
(B) Owners of the recently purchased computer
(C) Sales representatives of the IT company
(D) Those who want to upgrade their computer

7 What service is NOT available at the service center?

(A) Premium Care Plan purchase
(B) Free delivery service
(C) Same-day repairs of damaged products
(D) Product replacement

8 What are customers asked to do if they are experiencing problems?

(A) Visit the Web site
(B) Call the service center
(C) Bring their computer to the service center
(D) Fill out a form online

9 Why does Mr. Smith send the e-mail?

(A) To request for a refund
(B) To request an estimate on some items
(C) To describe a faulty product
(D) To inquire about the status of his claim

10 What is most likely true about Mr. Smith?

(A) He was an employee of New Tech.
(B) The original warranty of his computer has expired.
(C) He had his computer fixed before.
(D) He has used his computer for less than 6 months.

문장 삽입

Reading

지문에 상관없이 어떤 유형에서도 출제될 수 있는 문제이다. 주어진 하나의 문장을 문맥상 적절한 곳에 삽입하는 유형으로 해당 번호 앞뒤에 힌트가 될 만한 내용들을 찾고 이를 이용하여 문제를 푼다.

질문 유형

- In which of the positions marked [1], [2], [3] and [4] does the following sentence best belong?

비법 1 대명사, 시간, 순서, 숫자 등의 연관성을 유추한다.

전체 글과 연관성이 있는 '힌트'를 바탕으로 앞뒤 관계를 파악하여 문제를 해결한다.

비법 2 접속사, 연결구 등을 통해 파악한다.

접속부사(therefore, furthermore, moreover, however, thus 등) 또는 접속사가 있다면 이를 토대로 적절한 곳을 찾아 해결한다.

비법 적용 연습

Questions 1-4 refer to the following letter.

Noa Engineering & Construction

22 October
The Monolith Constructions
39-43 Sands Street, Kennedy Town,
Hong Kong

Dear Mr. Theodor Yi,

I am writing this letter to recommend my former employee James Chun, who has been under my guidance here at Noa Engineering & Construction for the past five years. As a prospective graduate, Mr. Chun first joined our company as an intern. Knowing his potential, we were quick to offer him a full-time position at our head office in Singapore right after he graduated from Linden University. – [1] –.

With a strong sense of responsibility, Mr. Chun has proven himself a resourceful individual, attracting some of our major clients to our company. This is something noteworthy as his efforts contributed to making our company more recognized than ever before. He oversaw operations inside and outside the country, primarily in tourist regions in southeast Asia. – [2] –. Not only that, thanks to his meticulousness, Mr. Chun was most impressive when he planned and organized the budgets and schedules for one of our major construction projects last summer. – [3] –.

I have to say that it truly pains me to see Mr. Chun leave our company, but we root for him in his new start in Hong Kong. His service at Noa was remarkable, and he will be missed. I have no doubt in my mind that he will be noted as a great asset wherever he works. – [4] –. His work ethic is beyond comparison, so it will be a wise decision to take him as one of your own. For any additional information about Mr. Chun, I will be more than happy to give you my sincerest replies.

Regards,

Anes Kim
Management Director

1   Why is Ms. Kim contacting Mr. Yi?

   (A) To ask for a recommendation letter
   (B) To comment on an ex-worker
   (C) To announce a job opening
   (D) To discuss the results of an internship program

2   What is suggested about Mr. Chun?

   (A) He started his career in Hong Kong.
   (B) He attracted tourism business to his company.
   (C) He served as a project manager for a decade.
   (D) He started working before his graduation.

3   What is NOT suggested about Noa Engineering & Construction?

   (A) It specializes in road construction.
   (B) It is now better known in the industry than before.
   (C) Its headquarters is located in Singapore.
   (D) It sometimes offers a permanent job opportunity to interns.

4   In which of the positions marked [1], [2], [3] and [4] does the following sentence best belong?

   "Ever since, in just five years, he has been promoted to the project manager and is currently doing a superb job."

   (A) [1]
   (B) [2]
   (C) [3]
   (D) [4]

DAY 14 의도 파악

LC의 part 3, 4와 더불어 part 7에서도 "화자의 의도를 파악"하는 문제가 출제된다. 문장의 기본 의미 그대로를 묻는 것이 아니라 문맥 속에서 어떠한 의미인지를 묻는 유형이다.

질문 유형

- At 12:09 P.M., what does Mr. Anderson mean when he writes, "I'm not used to it"?

비법 1 주어진 문장 앞뒤로 힌트가 반드시 제시될 것이다.

직역을 해서 풀 수 있는 문제는 출제되지 않는다. 반드시 주어진 문장 주변에 그 말을 한 이유가 제시될 것이다. 따라서 앞뒤로 살펴봐야 한다.

비법 2 항상 Paraphrasing 표현을 주의하자.

아무리 해당 문장을 잘 해석하고 문맥 속에서 그 의미 파악을 잘했다고 하더라도 정답을 쉽게 고를 수 있는 것은 아니다. 선택지를 보면 본문의 내용과 관련해서 혼동을 주는 표현이 많이 출제될 것이다. 정답도 그대로 주어지지 않고 paraphrasing된 표현이 출제될 것이다. 본문에서 주어진 단어를 그대로 단어를 사용했다면 오답일 가능성이 높다.

비법 적용 연습

Questions 1-2 refer to the following text message chain.

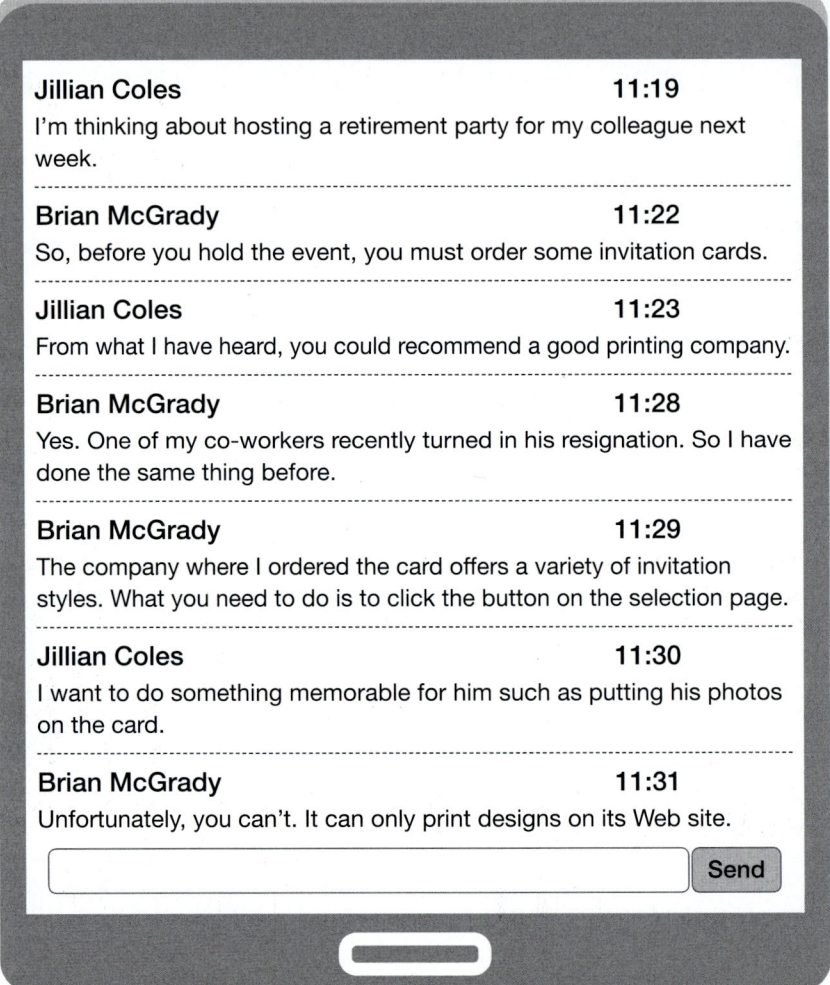

Jillian Coles   11:19
I'm thinking about hosting a retirement party for my colleague next week.

Brian McGrady   11:22
So, before you hold the event, you must order some invitation cards.

Jillian Coles   11:23
From what I have heard, you could recommend a good printing company.

Brian McGrady   11:28
Yes. One of my co-workers recently turned in his resignation. So I have done the same thing before.

Brian McGrady   11:29
The company where I ordered the card offers a variety of invitation styles. What you need to do is to click the button on the selection page.

Jillian Coles   11:30
I want to do something memorable for him such as putting his photos on the card.

Brian McGrady   11:31
Unfortunately, you can't. It can only print designs on its Web site.

---

1 What is suggested about Ms. Coles?

(A) She threw a party for her co-worker.
(B) She will retire from her company.
(C) She currently works in a printing company.
(D) She wants to put a photo on the invitation.

2 At 11:31, what does Mr. McGrady mean when he writes, "Unfortunately, you can't"?

(A) Customized cards are not available in this printing company.
(B) A retirement party will not be held due to other arrangements.
(C) The Web site is under construction.
(D) An order can't be placed because the printing company went out of business.

삼중 지문

삼중 지문은 3개의 지문이 나오고 5문제를 풀어야 하는 유형이다. 186번에서 200번까지 총 3세트가 출제된다. 이중 지문과 거의 비슷한 난이도로 출제되기 때문에 생각보다 어렵지는 않다. 다만 익숙하지 않기 때문에 처음에는 고전할 수 있다. 지문을 연계해서 풀어야 하는 것은 세트마다 1~2문제 정도 출제된다. 지문은 웹 페이지, 이메일, 공고문, 편지, 일정표, 양식, 기사, 평론, 정보문, 온라인 서평 등 모든 유형이 나올 수 있다. 읽어야 하는 텍스트 양이 상대적으로 많아졌으므로 시간이 부족할 수밖에 없다. 빠른 독해 속도가 관건이다.

비법 1 문제를 먼저 파악하자.

지문을 읽는 것은 결국 문제를 풀기 위해서이다. 따라서 문제를 먼저 읽고 파악한 후 지문을 읽는 것이 시간을 줄이는 방법 중 하나이다.

비법 2 미리 표시해야 하는 것들은 지문을 읽기 전에 표시하자.

주제, 목적 묻는 문제, 동의어 문제들은 미리 체크했다가 지문을 읽으면서 푸는 것이 좋다. 주제, 목적 문제는 글의 처음과 마지막에 나올 확률이 높고, 토익에서는 글이 미괄식보다 두괄식이 더 많이 나오기 때문에 주제, 목적은 첫 문단에, 동의어 문제는 미리 언급된 위치에 체크를 하고 글을 읽어야 한다.

비법 3 숫자, 고유명사, 명사 등 이정표가 될 수 있는 것을 체크하면서 읽자.

사실 여부 확인, 암시, 추론, 세부 사항 등의 유형은 어쩔 수 없이 문제를 읽으면서 지문으로 다시 가서 확인을 해야 하는 유형이다. 그렇기 때문에 얼마나 빨리 찾을 수 있는지가 관건이다. 미리 체크를 해 두는 것이 시간이 점점 부족해지는 토익에서 큰 역할을 할 것이다.

비법 적용 연습

Questions 1-5 refer to the following advertisement, brochure and e-mail.

Jessica's Catering Service

Jessica's Catering Service specializes in offering premier catering services in Lombard, Jacksonville and Divisadero in San Francisco. We could help various events prepare perfectly, such as business gatherings, personal or corporate events, birthdays, weddings as well as anniversary celebrations. If you decide to host such events, any of our four rooms would make your event a sincerely memorable and special one. Our top event coordinator would be happy to assist you to make a unique dining experience tailored to your needs.

If you need further information or inquiries, feel free to contact 724-266-8001 or email events@jessicas_cateringservice.com. We advise you to make reservations at least two weeks in advance.

Welcome to Jessica's Catering Service

Thank you for choosing Jessica's Special Room in San Francisco. Jessica's caters for a wide range of functions. We also have fully-customized catering menus. Four room types are available: Rockhopper Suite, Gentoo Hall, Emperor Hall and Royal Garden.

Room	Features	Total Capacity
Rockhopper Suite	Auditorium style Fully equipped with two flat-screen TVs and LED projector	15 people
Gentoo Hall	Banquet style Full bar set-up and special linens are available	40 people
Emperor Hall	A state-of-the-art integrated audiovisual system with adjustable lighting	100 people
Royal Garden	Exotic dining experience on the open-air patio	150 people

e-mail

From: shinohara@yakuruwringle.com
To: events@jessicas_cateringservice.com
Date: November 15
Subject: Retirement ceremony

Dear Staff at Jessica's Catering Service,

I am planning to host a retirement ceremony for one of my colleagues and considering Jessica's Catering Service as a possible location. My colleague, Ms. Johansson, already did a business with your company to hold a business gathering last September. She was very satisfied with your staff. So, she strongly recommended Jessica's.

The ceremony is scheduled to be held on December 12 and should begin around 7 P.M. We expect approximately 80 to 100 people will attend. We need a big monitor and sound system that could show a memorable speech.

Please inform us immediately if you can give us discounted prices on the recommendation of Mr. Johansson. That should help us decide how to proceed.

Best regards,

Takeuchi Shinohara
Creative Director, Yakuru Wringle

---

1. What is the purpose of the advertisement?
   (A) To announce a discount on its service fee
   (B) To promote its service
   (C) To introduce its new types of catering service
   (D) To report on the merger of two companies

2. What is mentioned about all of the dining rooms?
   (A) They have audio systems.
   (B) They are designed to use for various events.
   (C) They are indoors.
   (D) They offer complimentary valet service.

3. What room best meets Shinohara's needs?
   (A) Rockhopper Suite
   (B) Gentoo Hall
   (C) Emperor Hall
   (D) Royal Garden

4. What is stated about Ms. Johansson?
   (A) She hosts events every month.
   (B) She is working for Jessica's Catering Service.
   (C) She used catering service.
   (D) Her co-worker retired last year.

5. What does Mr. Shinohara ask for?
   (A) A room rate negotiation
   (B) An extra television
   (C) An extension of time
   (D) A special menu

Questions 6-10 refer to the following Web page, online review and e-mail.

http://www.microearbuds.com

MICRO EARBUDS Series are NOW RELEASED!

No cables. No wires. No distractions.

Better sound is just the beginning. Our goal is to create a new premium earphone, headphone as well as speaker segment and help customers to enjoy their music for the extended period of time without experiencing any discomfort. More than a decade of research has resulted in an incredibly detailed and excellent sound.

Enjoy Free Shipping When You Order Today!

MICRO EARBUDS Wireless Headphone	MICRO EARBUDS Wireless Earphone
In stock	In stock
$279.95	$147.95
Available to ship: 1-3 business days	Available to ship: 5-7 business days
MICRO EARBUDS Wireless Speaker	MICRO EARBUDS Noise Cancelling Headphone
Out of stock	In stock
$200.00	$300.00
Unavailable to ship	Available to ship: 1-3 business days

---

http://www.microearbuds.com

| HOME | FEATURED | PRODUCTS | FAQs | **REVIEW** |

This could be the best product in all wireless headphones.

I have been searching several types of wireless headphones for months. In my endless search for wireless perfection, MICRO EARBUDS wireless headphone is just what I'm looking for. I would recommend this to anyone who wants to enjoy their music without being disrupted by background noise. Sound quality is remarkably good, just as described on the Web site. As a matter of fact, it seems to be more expensive compared to those in the same categories in the market. The wireless headphone, however, is worth the price. As advertised, the battery life lasts almost 10 hours or more. The headphone absolutely delivers you the sound as it was recorded.

e-mail

From: Jenny Brown <jennybrown@smail.com>
To: Customer Service <customerservice@microearbuds.com>
Subject: Hard to find elsewhere
Date: Tuesday, September 15

I recently purchased a set of MICRO EARBUDS wireless headphones for my daughter's birthday present. She liked it a lot. After she listened to music with the headphones, she was interested in buying another type of product. She has been considering MICRO EARBUDS noise cancelling headphones.

However, I don't understand your products are so hard for us to find stores to experience them firsthand. Even if I searched your Web site to find locations nearest my place, I couldn't get any information. Please let me know where to find the one.

Regards,

Jenny

---

6 Which item cannot be purchased on the Web site?

(A) MICRO EARBUDS Wireless Headphone
(B) MICRO EARBUDS Wireless Earphone
(C) MICRO EARBUDS Wireless Speaker
(D) MICRO EARBUDS Noise Cancelling Headphone

7 In the online review, why would the reviewer recommend to buy the product?

(A) Because of its affordable price
(B) Because of its performance
(C) Because of its shipping policy
(D) Because of its design

8 According to the e-mail, how much did the birthday gift cost?

(A) $147.95
(B) $200.00
(C) $279.95
(D) $300.00

9 What does Ms. Brown request Customer Service to do?

(A) Check on location
(B) Change shipping method
(C) Update Web site product line
(D) Return a product

10 In the e-mail, the word "firsthand" in paragraph 2, line 2, is closest in meaning to

(A) reasonably
(B) accordingly
(C) directly
(D) nearly

Reading

DAY 16 독해 유형 연습 1

지금까지 학습한 토익 '질문 유형'과 '지문 유형'을 잘 숙지한 후, 각 유형에 맞는 문제 풀이 전략으로 많은 문제를 더욱 빠르고 효과적으로 풀어보는 연습을 합니다.

Questions 1-3 refer to the following information.

West Coast Home Opportunities Credit Union

We're working to help people stay in their homes, not just buy their homes.

We're taking the lead to change how the lending industry works with borrowers. For customers in need, we're offering to modify over 100 billion dollars in mortgages to help keep up to 630,000 borrowers in their homes.

For those who are ready to buy, we're taking steps to make sure people are getting loans that enable them to be successful homeowners. And we're going to do that by lending responsibly—which means no hidden fees, no surprises, and full confidence in every borrower's ability to repay their mortgage.

As you see, we care as much about keeping customers in their homes as we do about putting them there. If they don't succeed, neither do we.

We're ready today as always to help people finance their homes in ways that are right for them. If you're ready, call us at 1-888-995-6745.

---

1 What kind of company is this?

(A) A real estate company
(B) A government housing subsidizer
(C) A mortgage foreclosure company
(D) A bank

2 What is stated about this company?

(A) It wants people to have homes.
(B) It is popular with small shop owners.
(C) It prefers people who can pay their mortgages.
(D) It is lending 100 billion dollars to potential homebuyers.

3 According to the information, why does West Coast Opportunities want to change the lending industry?

(A) It wants to lend more money to people.
(B) It wants people to be successful homeowners.
(C) It wants to be the biggest lending company.
(D) It wants no surprises.

Questions 4-8 refer to the following information.

Event Details
Local musicians supporting women in their healing journey

What is Muse Fest? It is an exciting evening which celebrates talented local female musicians. Last year, we raised over ten thousand dollars to support the programs at the Women's Centre.

> The Women's Centre offers support groups, counseling services, peer support, and assistance in gaining and maintaining employment. Last year 307 women walked through our doors and we responded to 3,273 calls from local women seeking information, support and referrals. The feedback from clients invariably reflects the positive impact of our services:
> "The Women's Centre was my haven. You opened your arms and accepted me as I was. You believed in me when I didn't...and now I do. Keep doing what you're doing and don't stop caring".

Over 200 people attended our inaugural Muse Fest last year and were wowed by the amazing talent in our community. DJ Donna Lovejoy, Marra Koren, Lori Yates & Buckshot Bebee, Melissa Marchese (Weekend Riot Club) and Gillian Nicola are only a few of this year's musicians who are excited to perform. The event will be held Friday November 7th, at the new Braddocks Arts Theatre located at 951 East King Street.

For any questions or inquiries, please contact Annie Horton at develop@intervalhousehamilton.org. Have questions about Muse Fest? Contact Interval House of Hamilton/Women's Centre.

4 What is mainly stated about this event?

(A) It is a concert given by abuse survivors.
(B) It is for a charitable cause.
(C) It promotes public safety.
(D) It has healing power for listeners.

5 Who will be playing at this event?

(A) Artists and musicians from around the country
(B) Rock bands
(C) Internationally famous female singers
(D) Talent from the region

6 What does the Women's Centre not do?

(A) It provides counseling service.
(B) It sponsors support groups.
(C) It helps women gain employment.
(D) It gives shelter to women.

7 How many times has this festival taken place before?

(A) Every year
(B) Twice
(C) Once
(D) Never

8 Who should be contacted for more information?

(A) Ms. Horton
(B) Ms. Koren
(C) Ms. Yates
(D) Ms. Nicola

DAY 17 독해 유형 연습 2

지금까지 학습한 토익 '질문 유형'과 '지문 유형'을 잘 숙지한 후, 각 유형에 맞는 문제 풀이 전략으로 많은 문제를 더욱 빠르고 효과적으로 풀어보는 연습을 합니다.

Questions 1-3 refer to the following advertisement.

Choy's Chinese Chow

Having a tight schedule? No time to prepare your meals? Too tired to cook or even go to the supermarket with all those long line just for one meal?

Choy's Chinese Chow, the largest oriental restaurant in San Francisco, is now offering free delivery right to your doorstep, whether it's your office, school, dormitory or home.

In business for more than 40 years in the Bay area, we can deliver day or night, any day of the week.

Please note that actual delivery time may vary depending on the size of your order or the location of your address. A minimum order of 3 menu items is required to avail of this service.

For more information about our menu and special requests, call toll free 1-800-976-CHOW.

---

1 For whom is this advertisement especially intended?

(A) Customers planning a party
(B) People residing in far places
(C) Office workers
(D) Busy people

2 What is NOT a feature of Choy's?

(A) 24 hour delivery
(B) Online ordering
(C) Meal preparation
(D) Phone ordering

3 What is said about Choy's Chinese Chow?

(A) It opened a new branch in San Francisco.
(B) Food is delivered in 30 minutes or less.
(C) Delivery time depends on the distance and amount.
(D) It cannot accommodate special requests.

Questions 4-5 refer to the following receipt.

Big Green World
158 Huánuco St
Uluru NSW 5445
Online dealer of literary or educational materials

Customer: Hannah Gasik
Shipping address: 53 Stingray Street, Cucamonga CA 5609
Order number: 11245 (placed 9 July, 09:43 A.M.)

Quantity	Item	Price
1	*Dog Days: short story collections* by Angel Lassick	$22.00
1	*Piano Basics: Volume 1* by Glenda Owynne-Johnson	$31.00
1	*Baseball Skills and Drills* by American Baseball Coaches Association	$20.00

Subtotal	$73.00
Tax	$5.30
Express Shipping (overnight delivery)	$7.00
Order total	$85.30
Payment status	(paid)

Order Shipped: 12 July, 3:45 P.M.

Thank you for using our company. You can return any item that is not used within 30 days and please include an original receipt or proof of payment when returning your item. For more information on our return policy, visit our Web site at www.biggreenworld.com.au/returns.

4 What kind of items does Big Green World sell?

(A) Pet supplies
(B) Management Textbooks
(C) Musical instruments
(D) Sports goods

5 What is indicated about Ms. Gasik?

(A) She received a package on July 12.
(B) She is a regular customer of Big Green World.
(C) She wants to return an item.
(D) She paid for fast delivery.

독해 유형 연습 3

Reading

지금까지 학습한 토익 '질문 유형'과 '지문 유형'을 잘 숙지한 후, 각 유형에 맞는 문제 풀이 전략으로 많은 문제를 더욱 빠르고 효과적으로 풀어보는 연습을 합니다.

Questions 1-3 refer to the following advertisement.

Chula Vista Credit Union
Quick n' Eazy car loans

Owning your first car is easy with Chula Vista Credit Union's "Quick n' Eazy" car loans. This winter, why suffer the cold while waiting for the bus? That's why we are giving you the chance to own your dream car through our first time buyer's program.

We have available loan packages that can suit your budget for brand-new cars for as low as 3.95% a year. No down payment is required. This program can also avail you of loans for used cars that are less than 7 years old.

To get your car, all you need are three easy steps. First, visit our Web site, click on the loans icon and download the loan application form. Fill this out and submit it. Next, wait three days for the loan approval and credit investigation results. And finally after your loan has been approved by our credit investigators, come to the dealership and claim the car that suits your taste.

You may also come to our office personally at any of our branches citywide and fill out a form with any of our staff members who can assist you.

*This promotion is good until December 20 only.
*Interest rates may vary based on your current credit standings.

1. What is a fact about the interest rates?
   (A) It can be below 3 percent.
   (B) It depends on the borrower's credit history.
   (C) It may increase depending on the national economy.
   (D) It is higher than other banks.

2. According to the advertisement, what is NOT required from the borrower?
   (A) Opening an account in one of their branches
   (B) Completing a form
   (C) Visiting a Web site
   (D) Waiting for a credit assessment

3. What is said about the promotion?
   (A) It requires a down payment.
   (B) There is a time limit.
   (C) It is not available at all branches.
   (D) It can be applied at the car dealership.

Questions 4-7 refer to the following letter.

Double Wishbone publishers Inc.
125 Bath Road, Trafalgar, London N1 0RW

Olga Kuzminski
453 Merrion Square, Dublin
Ireland

Dear Ms. Kuzminski,

Much gratitude to you for taking the time to travel to London to confer with us last week. We are very glad to offer you the position of column editor. I feel certain that your experience and education will be of great benefit for us. We were also very impressed with your references. After meeting with our Human Resources Chief, we have decided to offer you the following employment package:

Salary: £42,000 per year
Benefits: relocation allowance of £6,000. Two weeks paid holiday. Full retirement plan.
Bonuses: Two annual bonuses based on performance from £1,000 to £5,000
Included with this letter is a contract with all the necessary information and details you may need. If you need more information, please send me an e-mail at annhath@doublewishpub.co.uk.

Once you have read and agreed to the attached contract, please sign it on all the indicated areas and mail it to me. Please make a copy for yourself for future reference. After we have received the contract, you will be scheduled for a one-week training period.

Much gratitude and I do look forward to working with you in the future.

Sincerely yours,

Ann Hathaway

Ann Hathaway
Chief Copy Editor, Double Wishbone Publishers Inc.

4 Why did Ms. Hathaway write Ms. Kuzminski?

(A) To offer her an employment package
(B) To tell her that she is impressed with her references
(C) To fill a position
(D) To ask for more information

5 What is NOT included in the contract?

(A) Moving expenses
(B) Half month paid vacation
(C) Two yearly bonuses
(D) Supplemental education

6 What will Ms. Kuzminski probably do after reading the letter?

(A) Fly to Ireland immediately
(B) Travel to London to give more information
(C) Wait for her allowance
(D) Send a document

7 Who most likely is Ms. Hathaway?

(A) An employment agent in London
(B) A department head in a company
(C) An owner of a publishing company
(D) A human resources manager

Reading

독해 유형 연습 4

지금까지 학습한 토익 '질문 유형'과 '지문 유형'을 잘 숙지한 후, 각 유형에 맞는 문제 풀이 전략으로 많은 문제를 더욱 빠르고 효과적으로 풀어보는 연습을 합니다.

Questions 1-2 refer to the following letter.

April 29, 2014

Dear Mr. Siva,

Welcome! Your application to Woculus has been approved. We are proud to have you as one of our editors.

As I have said before, our vision at Woculus is to be the one-stop site where business owners, marketers and sales personnel can learn how to use technology profitably for their businesses. Our posts are well-researched, practical and rich. As an up and coming blog, we constantly strive to provide the highest quality posts to our readers. If there is a better post about any of our areas of interest on the Internet, we are not doing our job well.

Find your login details below:

• Username: Don Siva

• Password: siVA2013

The entire Woculus team looks forward to a very professional working relationship with you; and we are ready to support you in any way possible to serve our audience better.

Yours very truly,

Donald Warchowsky

Donald Warchowsky
Chief Editor

1. What is the purpose of this letter?
   (A) To promote the business
   (B) To recruit an editor
   (C) To welcome a new business
   (D) To accept a new employee

2. What is NOT indicated about the company?
   (A) Its posts are well-researched.
   (B) It claims to be the best in that field.
   (C) It is not doing its job well.
   (D) Its blogs are useful and popular.

Questions 3-4 refer to the following letter.

To customer service department
Sears home appliances
Duluth, Michigan

Two weeks ago I received the enclosed pruning shears, ordered from your spring catalog. One of my friends told me that your products are far better and more durable than those of other companies. However, it turns out that it was not true in my case. I was trimming a lilac bush, a relatively simple task for a pair of shears, when the handle split in two. The terms of the warranty indicate that if I am not satisfied, I am entitled to receive a full refund. So I am sending the faulty shears back and I want my money refunded, including my shipping costs. I have enclosed receipts for the shears and for the shipping. Please send the check to my home address shown on both the check and this letter.

Mary White
Mary White

3. Why was this letter written?
   (A) To report a faulty product
   (B) To cancel an order
   (C) To receive a full refund
   (D) To request an estimate

4. What might Sears do upon receiving the letter?
   (A) Send her payment back
   (B) Ask for a receipt
   (C) Visit a company
   (D) Cancel the warranty

독해 유형 연습 5

지금까지 학습한 토익 '질문 유형'과 '지문 유형'을 잘 숙지한 후, 각 유형에 맞는 문제 풀이 전략으로 많은 문제를 더욱 빠르고 효과적으로 풀어보는 연습을 합니다.

Questions 1-3 refer to the following memo.

To: Department/Purchasing Manager
From: Kent Feldstein
Date: Jan 7
Re: Request for Recycled Paper
Note: please pass this memo around after reading

I am writing to request that our department adopt the use of recycled chlorine-free paper as the standard for our company. Buying recycled paper is a simple and convenient way our organization can help the environment and join the many major corporations worldwide that are adopting environmentally sound procurement practices.

More than 90 percent of the printing and writing paper made in this country is still made from new trees. Every ton of recycled paper substituted for non-recycled paper saves 17 trees, uses fewer chemicals and natural resources, and reduces air and water pollution. High quality recycled paper is widely available. In fact, recycled paper is made by the best paper mills in the world. Recycled paper performs as competitively as non-recycled sheets in printing presses, copiers, laser printers, computers, inserters, and other office equipment. Recycled paper is much more reasonably priced than paper without recycled content.

1   Why was this letter written?
    (A) To encourage employees to use recycled paper
    (B) To request his department use recycled paper
    (C) To state the pros and cons of recycled paper
    (D) To compare recycled paper with non-recycled paper

2   According to the memo, what benefits does recycled paper have over non-recycled paper?
    (A) It is simpler and more convenient.
    (B) Major corporations prefer to use it.
    (C) It saves a lot of natural resources.
    (D) It performs much better than non-recycled paper.

3   What is NOT stated about the use of recycled paper?
    (A) It can save the company some money.
    (B) It can be ecologically friendly.
    (C) It is widely practiced.
    (D) It is more convenient.

Questions 4-6 refer to the following advertisement.

DISPLAY KITCHENS WANTED!

70% of normal prices

Kitchener's Kitchens

has an impressive range of brand-new kitchen finishes and designs. We need clients with homes in your area to "show them off." We'll need to take photos of your new kitchen for our brochure when it's installed. (It's cheaper than building a set and it looks better in a real home). We may also need your testimonial when completed.

PLUS INTEREST FREE FINANCING AVAILABLE.
HURRY, ORDER NOW FOR PRE-XMAS DELIVERY.

Call 1-800-826-1446 now (24hrs) for a free design and quote or visit www.kitcheners.com.

4 What is the main purpose of this advertisement?

(A) To show a finished product in a brochure
(B) To give potential customers a big discount
(C) To find a home to be featured in an advertisement
(D) To inform clients about interest free financing

5 The word "quote" in paragraph 2, line 3, is closest in meaning to

(A) say
(B) estimate
(C) repeat
(D) mention

6 What can be inferred from the advertisement?

(A) Free delivery is available.
(B) Customers must provide a product review.
(C) Customers' kitchens will appear on TV commercials.
(D) Payment should be made before Christmas.

SECTION 2
영역별 실전 연습
(Day 01~20)

Part 5·6 유형 연습	174
실전 랜덤 연습	216
어휘 집중 연습	258
독해 집중 연습	300

Part 5·6 유형 연습

Day 01	연습 문제 1	**176**
Day 02	연습 문제 2	**178**
Day 03	연습 문제 3	**180**
Day 04	연습 문제 4	**182**
Day 05	연습 문제 5	**184**
Day 06	연습 문제 6	**186**
Day 07	연습 문제 7	**188**
Day 08	연습 문제 8	**190**
Day 09	연습 문제 9	**192**
Day 10	연습 문제 10	**194**
Day 11	연습 문제 11	**196**
Day 12	연습 문제 12	**198**
Day 13	연습 문제 13	**200**
Day 14	연습 문제 14	**202**
Day 15	연습 문제 15	**204**
Day 16	연습 문제 16	**206**
Day 17	연습 문제 17	**208**
Day 18	연습 문제 18	**210**
Day 19	연습 문제 19	**212**
Day 20	연습 문제 20	**214**

DAY 01 Part 5·6 유형 연습

PART 5

1. New software that can considerably reduce staff working time -------.
   (A) to develop
   (B) developing
   (C) is being developed
   (D) to be developed

2. ------- thousands of technical experts at the career convention in Las Vegas last weekend.
   (A) There
   (B) There was
   (C) They were
   (D) There were

3. The main ------- of this new smartphone application is to open and print every form of document.
   (A) function
   (B) functions
   (C) functioned
   (D) functional

4. To ensure correct and fast delivery of your purchased foods, ------- your address on the tag provided.
   (A) wrote
   (B) written
   (C) write
   (D) writing

5. While Mr. Kacey's study concentrated on general viewers' tendency, ------- deals more specifically with channel-choosing trends among 15 to 19 year olds in the Massachusetts state area.
   (A) I
   (B) my
   (C) me
   (D) mine

6. Nowadays, ------- is known that even a little exercise is beneficial for the weight control.
   (A) which
   (B) that
   (C) what
   (D) it

7. Please ------- the attached questionnaire and submit it to our staff as soon as possible.
   (A) to complete
   (B) complete
   (C) completing
   (D) completed

8. When tickets are sold out, the Box Office policy is to start making a waiting list and call patrons if there are -------.
   (A) canceled
   (B) cancellations
   (C) cancels
   (D) canceling

9. The outstanding amount must ------- immediately or we will have to close your account and discontinue the services that you're using.
   (A) have paid
   (B) be paying
   (C) to pay
   (D) be paid

10. The committee's new chairperson has not yet been ------- but the nomination board has narrowed down the candidates to three.
    (A) choice
    (B) choose
    (C) chose
    (D) chosen

176 SECTION 2

PART 6

Questions 11-14 refer to the following e-mail.

From: donotreply@wmusic.com
To: paulcarter@exmail.com
Subject: Confirmation, Wire Music
Date: September 10

Dear Mr. Carter,

Thank you for using Wire Music, your number one music streaming service. This is a confirmation e-mail of your ------- to Wire Music. You have selected the Premium Package.
11.
Your transaction has been completed, and now you can enjoy unlimited music downloads each month. And of course, music videos and interviews are ------- available to all our
12.
members. These all services are only $ 5.99 per month. -------. If you wish to ------- your
13. **14.**
service, please send us your un-subscription request via e-mail at customersupport@wmusic.com.

Regards,
Wire Music

11. (A) application
    (B) complication
    (C) cancellation
    (D) subscription

12. (A) exclusive
    (B) exclusively
    (C) exclusivity
    (D) exclusion

13. (A) This package also includes a subscription to our weekly newsletter.
    (B) Unfortunately, we are not able to process your payment at this time.
    (C) We will charge your credit card this amount on the fifth of every month.
    (D) You may enroll in our streaming service by emailing a sales specialist.

14. (A) terminate
    (B) refinance
    (C) upgrade
    (D) install

DAY 02 Part 5·6 유형 연습

정답 및 해설 / 47p

PART 5

1. Ms. Elliot has mentioned ------- to retire from her current position in August, but a successor has not yet been found so far.
   (A) planned
   (B) plans
   (C) planner
   (D) was planning

2. Mr. Koh from Arthur D. Stowa Consulting was ------- in making everyone understand how to use our new intranet system.
   (A) help
   (B) helper
   (C) helpful
   (D) helpfully

3. The Historical Museum's tenth exhibition of human anatomy will be ------- to the public starting from next month.
   (A) open
   (B) opens
   (C) openly
   (D) opener

4. The producers of the new musical, *Till Dawn After Dusk*, decided to perform one more month ------- the overwhelming demands for the show.
   (A) because of
   (B) while
   (C) in fact
   (D) as soon as

5. The majority of Cook County residents have expressed ------- to the construction of a new sports complex right by the historic Shackenberg Mansion.
   (A) oppose
   (B) opposing
   (C) opposes
   (D) opposition

6. The National Highway Maintenance Service advises motorists to be ------- on wet roads.
   (A) caution
   (B) cautiously
   (C) cautious
   (D) cautions

7. Our company offers outstanding ------- as a method of keeping its valued employees.
   (A) benefits
   (B) benefitting
   (C) benefitted
   (D) beneficial

8. Despite having experienced decreases in revenue over the last half year, the Lockhart & Gardner firm has the ------- to hire three new attorneys next year.
   (A) intend
   (B) intention
   (C) intentional
   (D) intentionally

9. Tony Borelli's flagship shop in Ginza has still maintained its popularity with customers ------- the increasing competition from other stores that have relocated into the area.
   (A) until
   (B) even though
   (C) in case
   (D) despite

10. To build better customer relations, we need to keep our sales representatives ------- of product developments in greater detail.
    (A) informed
    (B) information
    (C) inform
    (D) informant

178 SECTION 2

PART 6

Questions 11-14 refer to the following article.

Cameron's Thai restaurant

------- Mr. Cameron completed his studies in North Sydney College, his professor had recommended him for a general manager at Sri Thai Kitchen in Pam Plaza. Sri Thai Kitchen carries various Thai dishes such as Tom Yum Goong (Spicy Shrimp Soup), Som Tum (Spicy Green Papaya Salad), Tom Kha Kai (Chicken in Coconut Soup) and other traditional Thai foods. Many Thai restaurant ------- in the area have been concerned with how to boost their sales and how they could find a qualified manager who speaks both English and Thai. -------. As soon as Mr. Cameron is hired as a general manager, he will ------- the current working environment to a more Western one, and try to attract more local as well as international customers.

11. (A) Since
    (B) By the time
    (C) When
    (D) While

12. (A) owner
    (B) own
    (C) owned
    (D) owners

13. (A) They have decided that their restaurant will be closed on weekends.
    (B) The price of their menus will increase by 10 percent.
    (C) Customers should book a reservation three days in advance.
    (D) They ran an advertisement to seek a bilingual manager in the local newspapers.

14. (A) change
    (B) exceed
    (C) request
    (D) announce

DAY 03 Part 5·6 유형 연습

PART 5

1. After completing your order placement, please print the order ------- for keeping a record of your purchase.
   (A) confirm
   (B) confirming
   (C) confirmation
   (D) confirmed

2. A nominal processing fee will be added to ------- received after June 6th.
   (A) order
   (B) have ordered
   (C) ordered
   (D) orders

3. For clients seeking effective product awareness campaigns, BBDO Media provides a reasonable -------.
   (A) alternated
   (B) alternating
   (C) alternatively
   (D) alternative

4. Ms. Sawamura's promotion to the position of regional ------- was announced at today's team meeting.
   (A) manage
   (B) manager
   (C) managed
   (D) manageable

5. Current job ------- at Phariva Insurance have been announced on the company's own Web site and on some Internet job-search sites.
   (A) open
   (B) openings
   (C) opened
   (D) opens

6. Ms. Shuster expressed her ------- for the hard work and dedication of the attendants during the recent exhibition.
   (A) appreciate
   (B) appreciates
   (C) appreciation
   (D) appreciated

7. The ------- fee for every advanced accounting course is 250 USD per person.
   (A) enrollment
   (B) enroll
   (C) enrolled
   (D) enrolls

8. This signed agreement indicates the contractor's ------- of all stated terms and conditions.
   (A) accept
   (B) accepts
   (C) accepted
   (D) acceptance

9. Please keep in mind that any changes to your reservation must be made at least two days before your ------- at the resort.
   (A) arrive
   (B) arrival
   (C) arrives
   (D) arrived

10. Shoppico's Web site provides customers with reviews and price ------- of audio products currently on the market.
    (A) compare
    (B) comparisons
    (C) have compared
    (D) compares

180 SECTION 2

PART 6

Questions 11-14 refer to the following memo.

To: All staff members
From: Dennis Baird
Subject: New Phone System training
Date: 21 November

The company has decided to employ an Internet-based phone solution starting next month, the tech assistants will begin ------- required equipment in every meeting room first and the other offices will be done by the end of the month.
11.

To ensure a smooth transition to the new system, staff training sessions led by the tech department will be scheduled for Monday at 2:00 P.M. and Wednesday at 11:00 A.M. ------- will take place in Room 301. During these one-hour sessions, the new equipment demonstrations will be given; -------, it is mandatory for all employees to attend one of
12.   13.
these sessions. -------. If you have any important appointments with clients then please
14.
inform one of your supervisors by the end of the week. Detailed information on these sessions will be posted on the company bulletin board.

11 (A) holding on
    (B) setting up
    (C) calling back
    (D) searching for

12 (A) Many
    (B) Another
    (C) Some
    (D) Both

13 (A) namely
    (B) still
    (C) thus
    (D) initially

14 (A) Their participation will be considered in the annual performance appraisals.
    (B) The company will hire more employees related to the sessions.
    (C) Its schedule is subject to change without any prior notice.
    (D) The tech department manager will be appointed as the new vice president.

DAY 04 Part 5·6 유형 연습

PART 5

1. Ms. Johansson has an outstanding career in the news broadcasting field, so ------- is highly qualified for the position.
   (A) he
   (B) they
   (C) it
   (D) she

2. Before leaving the office, please print out the business report for Ms. Patel and forward it to -------.
   (A) her
   (B) herself
   (C) she
   (D) hers

3. The new CEO of the company has earned praise internationally for ------- innovative strategy planning.
   (A) herself
   (B) her
   (C) hers
   (D) she

4. When you purchase your new batteries, show this voucher to the cashier for an additional 20% discount on new -------.
   (A) some
   (B) others
   (C) ones
   (D) any

5. If your pickup truck is not ready until tomorrow, you can use ------- to move your stuff to the new apartment.
   (A) us
   (B) our
   (C) we
   (D) ours

6. Ms. Cahill compiled the business report by ------- to meet the submission deadline.
   (A) she
   (B) her
   (C) herself
   (D) hers

7. ------- of the newly recruited employees was invited to show up to the welcoming party hosted by the CEO.
   (A) Most
   (B) All
   (C) Every
   (D) Each

8. The residents of the apartment complex decided to create flyers to promote their recycling policies -------.
   (A) themselves
   (B) them
   (C) their
   (D) theirs

9. This year's figures for purchasing building materials are quite similar to ------- of the preceding three years.
   (A) them
   (B) that
   (C) this
   (D) those

10. Although a monthly subway pass is the most economical option for commuters, ------- are available.
    (A) some
    (B) others
    (C) ones
    (D) any

PART 6

Questions 11-14 refer to the following e-mail.

Date: January 11
To: Eugene Landy
From: Cam Dunkan
Re: Your stay

Dear Mr. Landy,

I would like to thank you for staying at the Minetta Inn on January 7. We hope you ------- your visit with us.
　　　　　　　　　　　　　　　　　　　　　　　　　　　　　　　　　11.

Since we value customer satisfaction, it will be very much appreciated if you take a few minutes to fill out this survey form attached to let us know ------- well we met your needs. -------.
　　　　　　　　　　　　　　　　　　　　　　　　　　　　　　　　　　　12.　　　　　　　　　　　　　　　13.

Please do not hesitate to contact us ------- should you have any questions. If you plan to
　　　　　　　　　　　　　　　　　　　　14.
visit here next time, we would be very happy to serve you again.

Sincerely,
Cam Dunkan, General Manager
Minetta Inn
1-223-342-0101

---

11 (A) are enjoying
　　 (B) will enjoy
　　 (C) enjoy
　　 (D) enjoyed

12 (A) too
　　 (B) how
　　 (C) that
　　 (D) so

13 (A) Then, we will give you a discount coupon saving up to 10 percent off the regular price.
　　 (B) We are going to conduct a customer survey.
　　 (C) After that, you may enroll in our latest promotions at the front desk.
　　 (D) If so, you will receive a voucher good for a one-year subscription.

14 (A) evenly
　　 (B) strongly
　　 (C) directly
　　 (D) formerly

DAY 05 Part 5·6 유형 연습

PART 5

1. Political columnist Folly Byun has published a ------- new book about opposition parties.
   (A) controversy
   (B) controversial
   (C) controversies
   (D) controversially

2. As there were ------- people signed up for the computerized accounting training session, it was postponed until the following month.
   (A) few
   (B) barely
   (C) less
   (D) hardly

3. There will be time for the general public to debate ------- issue presented in the public hearing.
   (A) most of
   (B) all
   (C) entire
   (D) each

4. Former president Ms. Patel's newly published autobiography is the subject of ------- debate.
   (A) mostly
   (B) almost
   (C) much
   (D) many

5. The Peninsula Resort, which recently opened on the Iomantu island, features many activities designed to be ------- to families with children.
   (A) attraction
   (B) attracting
   (C) attract
   (D) attractive

6. Grayson Global is seeking to employ a ------- sales representative who can introduce our merchandise to a wider customer base.
   (A) motivate
   (B) motivated
   (C) motivation
   (D) motivations

7. Bethiad Apparel is a family-owned firm providing high-quality children's clothing at ------- prices.
   (A) affordably
   (B) affordable
   (C) afford
   (D) afforded

8. After days of discussion on the global mining industry, the board members of TS Holdings decided to invest a ------- sum of money in the market.
   (A) consider
   (B) considerable
   (C) considerate
   (D) considered

9. Applications for Smithson International Scholarship should be submitted to the selection board in a ------- fashion.
   (A) time
   (B) timer
   (C) timely
   (D) timing

10. Kaneko Imports distributes Gallo sunglasses to a ------- section of the greater Tokyo and Osaka areas.
    (A) broadly
    (B) broadness
    (C) broaden
    (D) broad

PART 6

Questions 11-14 refer to the following article.

The newly-renovated Melbourne library will officially reopen its door to the public on December 23 at 7 A.M. The ribbon-cutting ceremony celebrating its new birth will be held with a number of ------- dignitaries.
    11.

Menitez Brown, the chief librarian, told us that a new multimedia section was the major focus of this project and it ------- tens of thousands of audio-visual materials for library
                                                12.
patrons to use.

In order to educate library users to effectively utilize the new section, a series of workshops have been scheduled, the first of which ------- the ways patrons can use the new facilities
                                                          13.
for academic research. -------.
                         14.

11 (A) industrious
    (B) prominent
    (C) expert
    (D) formal

12 (A) accommodates
    (B) distributes
    (C) encase
    (D) consists

13 (A) feature
    (B) featuring
    (C) featured
    (D) will feature

14 (A) We will learn about the trends on the library renovation.
    (B) The rest of which will focus on taking advantage of new gadgets for accessing digital materials.
    (C) The subject on complying with the library regulations will be discussed.
    (D) Participants should know the importance of keeping voices down.

DAY 06 Part 5·6 유형 연습

PART 5

1. Please put the volume down ------- so as not to disturb the other tenants in the apartment.
   (A) slight
   (B) slighter
   (C) slightly
   (D) to slight

2. The financial crises our city is experiencing have to be addressed ------- by its newly elected mayor and his staff.
   (A) urgency
   (B) urgencies
   (C) urgently
   (D) urgent

3. To be a new member of our club, ------- complete the application form on our Web site.
   (A) simple
   (B) simply
   (C) simplify
   (D) simplicity

4. Project works have been distributed ------- among all the city council members.
   (A) even
   (B) evened
   (C) evenly
   (D) evenness

5. The Stafford County Planning Council will ------- place recycling bins at all gates of the Wilshire Park before the concert begins.
   (A) strategy
   (B) strategically
   (C) strategic
   (D) strategize

6. The Stanford Consulting Group will give you the strategies in ------- promoting your products to the most desirable potential customers.
   (A) creatively
   (B) create
   (C) creative
   (D) created

7. Our Chief Personnel Director Jason Park understands that recruiting dedicated employees and retaining them are ------- critical to the company's future.
   (A) equal
   (B) equally
   (C) equality
   (D) equalize

8. After remaining high for almost two weeks, temperatures eventually dropped ------- today.
   (A) slight
   (B) slighter
   (C) slightly
   (D) slightest

9. Once the receipts are forwarded from business travelers, they must be processed ------- so that we can precisely keep the spending records.
   (A) prompt
   (B) promptly
   (C) promptness
   (D) more prompt

10. The board of directors has not ------- decided which logo design to use for the new company product lines.
    (A) still
    (B) yet
    (C) already
    (D) soon

PART 6

Questions 11-14 refer to the following letter.

Dear Ms. Lopez,

We received the rain coat that you sent to us as a merchandise return. Since you didn't include the original receipt with the item, we weren't able to ------- whether the coat was
11.
purchased from one of our stores.

Please contact one of our customer service representatives by calling 1-800-982-1096 as soon as possible. We'd like to ask you a couple of questions to process your return. Additionally, please note that our policy regarding returns requires a receipt for a full refund. ------- proof of purchase, we can only offer you a store credit in exchange for your returned
12.
product. Store credit ------- for the most recent sale price of the item either online or in
13.
stores.

We are looking forward to hearing from you. -------. Please give us a call.
14.

Regards,
E&C Customer Service Team

11. (A) determine
    (B) coordinate
    (C) arrange
    (D) settle

12. (A) Above
    (B) Against
    (C) Without
    (D) Despite

13. (A) was issued
    (B) has been issued
    (C) were issued
    (D) is issued

14. (A) We hope to help you make your merchandise return smoothly.
    (B) You are entitled to get a benefit of free shipping.
    (C) We will extend your warranty expired in August this year.
    (D) Due to our promotional event, you will get a gift certificate.

DAY 07 Part 5·6 유형 연습

PART 5

1. The Willard University Theater will raise ticket prices next year ------- the cost of installing the state-of-the-art sound and lighting equipment.
   (A) out of
   (B) when
   (C) because
   (D) due to

2. All of the Howrett-Packard employees must fill out the employee satisfaction survey ------- Thursday at 5:00 P.M.
   (A) as
   (B) of
   (C) by
   (D) in

3. The ticket counter stops selling tickets twenty minutes ------- the start of the show.
   (A) between
   (B) before
   (C) up
   (D) for

4. The Freedom Trail Committee leads tours of historical sites of the Boston area every day ------- Sunday and Monday.
   (A) other
   (B) except
   (C) than
   (D) some

5. To guarantee your reservation at the Inter-Continental Hotel Taipei, please reply to this e-mail ------- twenty-four hours.
   (A) within
   (B) about
   (C) since
   (D) into

6. Office supplies are stored in the storage closet, ------- the mail room.
   (A) next to
   (B) down
   (C) throughout
   (D) onto

7. Discounted prices for sale items not on the list can be obtained ------- the sales operating department.
   (A) to
   (B) except
   (C) from
   (D) under

8. Detailed information of the advertising campaign will be provided ------- the Assistant Commercial Director.
   (A) of
   (B) on
   (C) by
   (D) alone

9. Ms. Deshields tried to let the management know that they could benefit ------- her extensive experience in international marketing.
   (A) from
   (B) concerning
   (C) within
   (D) about

10. Notices ------- any room or time changes will be posted on the bulletin board set up at the lobby of the Convention Center.
    (A) concern
    (B) concerns
    (C) concerned
    (D) concerning

PART 6

Questions 11-14 refer to the following letter.

Ashley Winston
630 W. 5th Street
Los Angeles, CA 90071

Dear Ms. Winston,

I am pleased to inform you that Jillian Mitchell ------- the Los Angeles branch of our firm on July 1.
                                                    11.

She comes to us from Henderson & Carney, where she has been a junior corporate law attorney for the last five years. Ms. Mitchell is ------- knowledgeable in the fields of domestic and international copyright law, and I think it is very good for us to have her.
                                              12.
Should you wish ------- a meeting with her, Ms. Mitchell can be contacted at 962-235-2580.
              13.

She is a very dedicated and talented lawyer. Her former employer Mr. Carney said he felt really sorry to lose her. -------. She will be a great helper in the litigation case against the
                                            14.
Chinese cell phone company. I hope you like her.

Sincerely,

William Simmons
Sonberg & Simmons

---

11 (A) designated
   (B) spoke
   (C) joined
   (D) arrived

12 (A) vaguely
   (B) extremely
   (C) wishfully
   (D) carefully

13 (A) to arrange
   (B) have arranged
   (C) be arranged
   (D) arranging

14 (A) She has little experience in Mergers and Acquisitions deals.
   (B) She would be your greatest asset in the near future.
   (C) Starting her service as a lawyer, she will be assigned to the copyright law division.
   (D) Recently she moved to a different area.

DAY 08 Part 5·6 유형 연습

PART 5

1. For the past decade, SSC Motors has consistently ------- among the North American top three supercar manufacturers.
   (A) rank
   (B) ranked
   (C) ranking
   (D) ranks

2. All the staff should ------- the floor manager if a production process is interrupted by machinery malfunction.
   (A) inform
   (B) speak
   (C) respond
   (D) inquire

3. The government-sponsored international marathon event will be held on September 20, and all the citizens ------- to participate.
   (A) to invite
   (B) invite
   (C) inviting
   (D) are invited

4. Please ------- your room card key at the front desk when you're heading outside of the hotel.
   (A) to leave
   (B) leaving
   (C) leaves
   (D) leave

5. Patrons having difficulties using our Web site are advised to ------- with our Customer Support officers at our toll-free phone number.
   (A) call
   (B) contact
   (C) speak
   (D) touch

6. Lots of companies and law firms have strongly ------- the three provisions in the government's latest tax revision plan.
   (A) critical
   (B) criticism
   (C) criticizing
   (D) criticized

7. The President of Cote Pharmaceutical did not let the recent international sales problems ------- the firm's long-term global expansion plans.
   (A) have affected
   (B) to affect
   (C) affect
   (D) affecting

8. Most of the test engine parts provided by our contractors failed to ------- with the quality standards we currently apply.
   (A) adhere
   (B) comply
   (C) belong
   (D) approach

9. The CEO is confident that professional development and training seminars held every year help the entire staff to ------- the knowledge and expertise in a number of areas.
   (A) broaden
   (B) broader
   (C) broadly
   (D) broad

10. The Chief Financial Director and the Director of General Affairs ------- quite differently to the suggestion about budget increases next year.
    (A) reacted
    (B) was reacted
    (C) reacts
    (D) reacting

190 SECTION 2

나혼자 끝내는 첫걸음 시리즈

혼자 공부해도 문제없어!

외국어 첫걸음도 나혼자 편한다!
동영상 강의 등 8~10가지 학습자료 무료 제공

- 독학 일본어 첫걸음 13,000원
- 독학 중국어 첫걸음 12,500원
- 독학 영어 첫걸음 15,500원
- 독학 러시아어 첫걸음 16,000원
- 독학 프랑스어 첫걸음 17,000원
- 독학 독일어 첫걸음 16,500원
- 독학 스페인어 첫걸음 15,000원
- 독학 베트남어 첫걸음 15,000원

외국어 단어도 나혼자 끝낸다!

〈나혼자 끝내는 독학 일본어 첫걸음〉
무료 동영상강의를 들어 보세요.

각 권 11,200원

ENJOY 여행 외국어 시리즈

해외여행 처음 갈 때 이 책!

여행지에서 하고 싶었던 바로 그 말!
왕초보 맞춤형 표현 엄선

- ENJOY 여행영어 9,000원
- ENJOY 여행일본어 9,000원
- ENJOY 여행중국어 7,000원
- ENJOY 여행프랑스어 6,500원
- ENJOY 여행스페인어 6,500원
- ENJOY 여행독일어 6,500원
- ENJOY 여행러시아어 6,500원

〈ENJOY 여행일본어〉
MP3 파일을 들어 보세요.

필기노트 시리즈

쓰면서 외우는 초간단 학습법!

듣고 → 쓰고 → 말하기의 3단계 자동암기 훈련
생활회화 300문장 통암기

- 영어회화 필기노트 9,500원
- 영어패턴 필기노트 9,500원
- 여행영어 필기노트 9,500원
- 영어성경 필기노트 9,500원
- 왕초보영어 필기노트 9,500원
- 일본어 필기노트 일상회화 8,000원
- 일본어 필기노트 여행회화 8,000원
- 중국어 필기노트 기초회화 9,500원
- 중국어 필기노트 일상회화 9,500원
- 중국어 필기노트 여행회화 9,500원

써서 외워진다!
필기노트 시리즈의 듣기 MP3와
회화연습 MP3를 들어 보세요.

미래를 준비하는 고품격 어학 길잡이

NEXUS

어학

- 100일의 기적 시리즈
- 패턴 플러스 시리즈
- 필기노트 시리즈
- ENJOY 여행 외국어 시리즈
- 나혼자 끝내는 첫걸음 시리즈
- 나혼자 끝내는 신토익 시리즈
- 시울대 텝스 최신기출 1200제 시리즈
- THIS IS 시리즈
- 공감 시리즈

넥서스

이것이 This is 시리즈다!

강남인강 강의 교재
5백만부 돌파

THIS IS GRAMMAR 시리즈
넥서스영어교육연구소 지음 | 각 12,000원

초급자부터 중·고급 학습자들을 위한 필독서

THIS IS VOCABULARY 시리즈
권기하, 넥서스영어교육연구소 지음 | 각 12,000원 내외

강남인강 강의 교재

THIS IS READING 시리즈
넥서스영어교육연구소 지음 | 각 10,000원

공부감각 업그레이드 프로젝트!

강남인강 강의 교재

주니몰생구문독해BASIC 시리즈
김성근 지음 | 각 14,000원

강남인강 강의 교재

READING 공감 시리즈
넥서스영어교육연구소 지음 | 각 10,000원

특단 시리즈
김상근, 정상운 지음
각 10,000원

구문독해204 시리즈
김상근 지음 | 각 15,000원

LISTENING 공감 시리즈
넥서스영어교육연구소 지음
각 12,000원

GRAMMAR 공감 시리즈
넥서스영어교육연구소 지음
각 12,000원

패턴 플러스 시리즈

말문이 터지는 회화 공식!

왕초보도 쉽고 간단하게 패턴으로 영어 실력 업그레이드
8~107가지 학습자료 무료 제공

- 영어패턴 500+ 13,000원
- 왕초보 영어패턴 200+ 13,800원
- 실전회화 영어패턴 500+ 13,000원
- 미드 영어패턴 500+ 13,000원
- 비즈니스 영어패턴 500+ 13,800원

- 이메일 영어패턴 500+ 13,800원
- 인터뷰 영어패턴 500+ 13,800원
- 초급 번역패턴 500+ 13,800원
- 리스닝 영어패턴 200+ 13,800원

영어회화 베스트셀러!
《영어패턴 500 플러스》
이수정 저자의 해설강의를 들어 보세요.

100일의 기적 시리즈

100일 만에 외국어 초보 탈출!

책 + 강의 + MP3 학습자료로 3D 입체 학습
저자 해설강의 무료 제공

외국어 분야 1위

- 영어회화 100일의 기적 13,500원
- 왕초보 영어회화 100일의 기적 12,000원
- 여행영어 100일의 기적 12,000원
- 영문법 100일의 기적 13,000원
- 비즈니스영어 100일의 기적 13,500원
- 이메일영어 100일의 기적 12,500원

- 기초영작 100일의 기적 12,500원
- 초등영어 100일의 기적 12,000원
- 중국어회화 100일의 기적 13,000원
- 일본어회화 100일의 기적 13,000원
- 여행일본어 100일의 기적 11,200원
- 스페인어회화 100일의 기적 13,800원

외국어 분야 1위 베스트셀러!
《영어회화 100일의 기적》
문성현 저자의 해설강의를 들어 보세요.

PART 6

Questions 11-14 refer to the following e-mail.

From: Benjamin Willis
To: Yoon-sung Kim
Sent: February 28, 2:45 P.M.
Subject: Your inquiry

Dear Mr. Kim,

Thank you for inquiring about the matchmaking services provided by our consultants at Evermates Agency. We specialize in creating satisfying matchmaking events both for ladies and gentlemen. We have plenty of experience and our consultants have vast data for fine gentlemen and ladies with good looks and financial stability. -------, we think Evermates agency is best-suited to meet your dating needs.
                                                                                                    11.

We would like to meet with you to let us know of your personal taste, then we will arrange the first dating event. Our know-how and ------- are guaranteed for dealing personal information
                                                                      12.
and keeping confidentiality for all the events. Clients are also guaranteed to have a first event ------- one week of consulting with a matchmaking specialist of our agency.
        13.

-------. Please let us know if we can be of any further assistance.
14.

Sincerely,

Benjamin Willis
Senior Matchmaking Consultant

---

11 (A) Otherwise
(B) For instance
(C) Nonetheless
(D) In short

12 (A) profession
(B) professional
(C) professionalism
(D) professionally

13 (A) within
(B) amid
(C) until
(D) between

14 (A) Evermates Agency is the leading company in the field.
(B) It shouldn't take more than 30 minutes.
(C) Our experts will help you develop a relationship that can make you satisfied.
(D) It is imperative for you to fill out the following application.

DAY 09 Part 5·6 유형 연습

PART 5

1. Our latest research on rechargeable batteries indicates that the newly invented battery in our new flagship smart phone ------- better than others in the same class.
   (A) perform
   (B) performing
   (C) performs
   (D) performance

2. Last Friday, New York City ------- were forced to take alternate routes, because of a flipped truck on 42nd Street.
   (A) commuters
   (B) commutes
   (C) to commute
   (D) commuting

3. Rainy season and unexpected legal problems ------- the greatest challenges to the construction of the 2nd Illinois State Science Center.
   (A) have posed
   (B) is posing
   (C) does pose
   (D) will have been posed

4. High-speed trains for Paris ------- only at 10:00 A.M. from Platform D during weekdays.
   (A) depart
   (B) is departed
   (C) departs
   (D) is departing

5. Thorpe Industrial Design Co. offers all kinds of design ------- that match the individual client's needs.
   (A) to service
   (B) service
   (C) serviced
   (D) services

6. The details of this business proposal ------- a result of the strategy discussion at last Thursday's meeting.
   (A) was
   (B) being
   (C) is
   (D) are

7. The ------- provided by the productivity specialist are supposed to improve overall production rates.
   (A) suggestion
   (B) suggest
   (C) suggestions
   (D) suggesting

8. For the past three years, the number of customers requesting refunds ------- steadily because of our constant effort to meet the strict quality standards.
   (A) declined
   (B) has declined
   (C) decline
   (D) have declined

9. Nearly half of the employees at Packard-Dewitt ------- to work by subway.
   (A) commutes
   (B) commute
   (C) is commuting
   (D) has commuted

10. The freshness of the vegetables served at this food court ------- a lot depending on the supplier.
    (A) vary
    (B) varies
    (C) varying
    (D) to vary

192 SECTION 2

PART 6

Questions 11-14 refer to the following e-mail.

From: Paul Mitchell
To: Delilah Simpson
Date: Thursday, October 15
Re: Your inquiry

Dear Ms. Simpson,

Thanks for your e-mail inquiry about constructing a new Web site for your company. We are a Web design company specializing in ------- customized Web sites for clients with various needs.
                                                    11.

We offer customized Web sites, paying special attention to each site's unique concepts. In addition, we also carefully focus on content to meet all customer requests. At CCD, we strongly believe ------- well-made Web sites do contribute to attracting customers. In order
                      12.
for us to help you achieve your objective, our highly ------- specialists provide beautiful and
                                                         13.
functional designs with our original graphics and custom programming.

-------. Thank you for considering us for your Web site. I look forward to doing business
14.
with you soon.

Paul Mitchell
Chief Commercial Producer
Chicago Commercial Design Ltd.

---

11 (A) provides
(B) providing
(C) provided
(D) provision

12 (A) by
(B) that
(C) for
(D) what

13 (A) qualified
(B) qualification
(C) qualify
(D) qualifies

14 (A) If you were not satisfied with our service, you will be issued a refund.
(B) I've attached some samples and the initial complimentary estimate you requested.
(C) The application deadline is November 15.
(D) Please upload the presentation file on our Web site.

DAY 10 Part 5·6 유형 연습

PART 5

1. Our company ------- as one of the top ten employers to work for in the country, according to the latest survey by the magazine *Healthcare Today*.
   (A) will know
   (B) to know
   (C) has known
   (D) is known

2. Our shipment of light bulbs ------- this week due to storms and weather on the East Coast, which is currently in the middle of a hurricane season.
   (A) interrupts
   (B) was interrupted
   (C) to interrupt
   (D) be interrupted

3. Our new company magazine will ------- on the first of each month and distributed at all company locations, including overseas.
   (A) publish
   (B) be published
   (C) published
   (D) publishing

4. Reimbursement for employee expenses will ------- after the submission of the appropriate forms available from the HR division.
   (A) made
   (B) makes
   (C) make
   (D) be made

5. The safety demonstration by flight attendants ------- by an announcement from the captain.
   (A) be preceded
   (B) will be preceded
   (C) would precede
   (D) were to precede

6. With the passage of the FTA, agricultural trade from the United States is ------- to increase by 100% in the first year and 200% in the second year.
   (A) expected
   (B) expecting
   (C) expects
   (D) expect

7. No employees will be ------- to enter the main office building, without first showing their ID card to the security officer.
   (A) permit
   (B) permitting
   (C) permission
   (D) permitted

8. The HR division will be ------- all candidates who will receive interviews by the end of next month, due to the large amount of applicants.
   (A) notification
   (B) notifying
   (C) notified
   (D) notifies

9. Our research and development lab in Austin, Texas, has been ------- new ultra capacitors that will replace batteries and can be recharged over one million times.
   (A) developing
   (B) develop
   (C) development
   (D) developed

10. We will be ------- our newest solar and mechanically-powered flashlights, which has two forms of power.
    (A) promotes
    (B) promote
    (C) promoting
    (D) promoted

194 SECTION 2

PART 6

Questions 11-14 refer to the following advertisement.

NOS Chemicals, one of the leading chemical companies in the world, has several vacancies in China for ambitious, recent university graduates who are ready to make a difference. No previous ------- is required.
                    11.

All necessary training will be provided by the company. Successful candidates should possess excellent communication skills and problem-solving abilities. ------- coursework in
                                                                                                12.
economics and marketing is not necessary, it can be advantageous.

-------. To apply for one of these positions, you must send your résumé to our human
  13.
resources department at www.noschemicals.com. Then you ------- an application to
                                                              14.
complete and return.

For further details, please visit our Web site.

11 (A) extension
    (B) assistance
    (C) attempt
    (D) experience

12 (A) In spite of
    (B) In case
    (C) However
    (D) Even though

13 (A) We expect many ambitious individuals to take advantage of this opportunity.
    (B) Applicants must have a minimum of five years of professional experience.
    (C) Applications will be retained in our database for one year.
    (D) Interns are expected to meet the deadline for their interviews.

14 (A) are sending
    (B) will be sent
    (C) are being sent
    (D) will have been sent

DAY 11 Part 5·6 유형 연습

PART 5

1. The sales division ------- a new training manual for the training of all our marketing and sales employees.
   (A) write
   (B) writing
   (C) wrote
   (D) written

2. The planning commission ------- on Tuesday night at 7 P.M., to vote on the approval of the building permit.
   (A) to convene
   (B) convening
   (C) will convene
   (D) have convened

3. Once the conference -------, the speaker is going to talk on the new direction for the entire company.
   (A) have started
   (B) start
   (C) starts
   (D) started

4. Ever since the company was founded 20 years ago, it ------- continued growth fueled by its creative marketing strategies.
   (A) is experiencing
   (B) had experienced
   (C) experience
   (D) has experienced

5. After the new CEO ------- the company, he began promoting the importance of research and development of innovative products.
   (A) join
   (B) joins
   (C) joined
   (D) to join

6. The company board of directors ------- last night and elected to spend an additional $800,000 on advertising.
   (A) met
   (B) meet
   (C) meets
   (D) meeting

7. By the time we received the building contracts from the manager, some important documents -------.
   (A) are disappearing
   (B) will have disappeared
   (C) disappear
   (D) had disappeared

8. The company board of directors ------- on Friday to discuss the possible construction of a new manufacturing facility in Seattle, Washington.
   (A) assembled
   (B) assembles
   (C) assembling
   (D) assemble

9. The company ------- a new vender for the procurement of semiconductors for our rechargeable smartphones, which should provide more efficient service.
   (A) selecting
   (B) selected
   (C) select
   (D) to select

10. Mr. Jones ------- as vice president of sales, assuming a new position at a different company.
    (A) is being resigned
    (B) would have resigned
    (C) has been resigning
    (D) will resign

PART 6

Questions 11-14 refer to the following letter.

Com&Com Furniture
5 Lowanna Place Hornsby
New South Wales 2077 Australia
January 12

Dear Customers,

I am writing to introduce our new lines of modern furniture for your office. Com&Com Furniture has recently developed several new desk sets and chairs that ------- to help office workers to work comfortably and at the same time efficiently.
              11.

Since we value and care for the customers' health, we hired several medical experts for the perfect designs that fit our body perfectly. -------, our new desk sets are equipped with
                                                                                  12.
a small safe where you can store any confidential documents and you are the only one who can ------- this safe with your finger prints. If you want to know what they look like,
           13.
then visit our Web site and click products to go to the products page. -------. For more
                                                                          14.
information, please feel free to call us at 1-330-499-5583.

Sincerely,

Matthew Gleason
Marketing Executive Director

---

11 (A) designed
 (B) be designed
 (C) are designed
 (D) being designed

12 (A) Addition
 (B) Additionally
 (C) In addition to
 (D) Additional

13 (A) access
 (B) assess
 (C) acquire
 (D) avail

14 (A) Please fill out the form enclosed in an e-mail.
 (B) We are currently offering very special prices for all our products.
 (C) The website is temporarily unavailable due to max connection number.
 (D) Please read the attached letter with this application.

DAY 12 Part 5·6 유형 연습

정답 및 해설 / 60p

PART 5

1. As an effort ------- ticket sales, the airline is announcing a lower fare structure, where passengers can save 50% on advance ticket sales.
   (A) to improve
   (B) improved
   (C) has improved
   (D) improving

2. We have hired an energy management company to ------- our overall utility costs by at least 25%.
   (A) reduced
   (B) reduction
   (C) reduce
   (D) reduces

3. Each employee that has been named an employee of the month is ------- honored at the annual New Year's Eve party.
   (A) to be
   (B) to
   (C) been
   (D) has

4. Managers are advised to ------- due diligence when dealing with a customer's complaint, as our company's number one priority is customer service.
   (A) exercise
   (B) exercises
   (C) exercising
   (D) exercised

5. The two top American automakers have recently signed an agreement ------- together to develop a new hybrid vehicle.
   (A) to work
   (B) works
   (C) to works
   (D) have worked

6. The airline needs ------- a survey on the viability of service between New York and Seattle; the results will be released on May 1.
   (A) conductor
   (B) conducts
   (C) to conduct
   (D) be conducting

7. Our company has decided ------- with Consolidated Container for the design and sales of our packaging materials starting next month.
   (A) to partner
   (B) be partnering
   (C) is partnered
   (D) will partner

8. The airline wants ------- service between Orange County and Lake Tahoe on the first of December.
   (A) restoring
   (B) to restore
   (C) restored
   (d) is restored

9. The purpose of this training session is ------- the employees to better serve the customers in this demanding industry.
   (A) to enable
   (B) enables
   (C) enabling
   (D) enabled

10. Any employees that have questions regarding company policy on interstate transfers should contact HR and ask ------- with Karen White.
    (A) speaking
    (B) to speak
    (C) spoke
    (D) has spoken

198 SECTION 2

PART 6

Questions 11-14 refer to the following article.

Mr. Raymond, CEO of the Your Diners, has announced that his 20-year-old chain restaurant that was established as his first satellite diner is scheduled to reopen its door after three months in Chicago. Its ------- project consists of a restaurant itself and a parking lot.
            11.

In order to celebrate its reopening, Mr. Raymond is planning to ------- a cooking contest
                                                                    12.
whose winner will have a chance to add his or her cuisine to the new menu. -------.
                                                                             13.
Mr. Raymond said, ------- asked for some advice, that the most important factor that
                    14.
contestants have to remember is that his restaurant cherishes nutritional factors very much. The first prize winner will not only be awarded $5,000 and but also have a chance to be a chef here at Yours Diners.

11. (A) renovate
    (B) renovations
    (C) renovation
    (D) renovated

12. (A) manage
    (B) view
    (C) hold
    (D) reward

13. (A) The winner will also receive three days of culinary instruction by Mr. Raymond.
    (B) Many restaurants want to update their menus.
    (C) Mr. Raymond will create his menu with local favorite dishes.
    (D) The restaurant will keep the popular menu while introducing some exotic menu.

14. (A) why
    (B) that
    (C) when
    (D) which

DAY 13 Part 5·6 유형 연습

정답 및 해설 / 61p

PART 5

1. Our company has saved money in building maintenance costs by ------- temperatures in buildings using programmable thermostats.
   (A) regulate
   (B) regulation
   (C) regulating
   (D) regulator

2. The company will begin ------- applications for the hiring of 150 new flight attendants beginning on June 1.
   (A) accept
   (B) accepts
   (C) accepting
   (D) accepted

3. Upon ------- the massive order for LED units, we decided to employ a second and third shift to increase overall production.
   (A) to receive
   (B) has received
   (C) received
   (D) receiving

4. The company is considering ------- some of the franchise stores in the downtown area.
   (A) remodel
   (B) remodeling
   (C) to remodel
   (D) remodels

5. We want to express our thanks for ------- Best Value Guided Tours for your travel.
   (A) choose
   (B) chooses
   (C) choice
   (D) choosing

6. We are really interested in your new product and look forward to ------- out more about it.
   (A) find
   (B) found
   (C) finding
   (D) be found

7. By ------- a new company logo, MAC Electronics will be able to raise public awareness of the company and its products.
   (A) development
   (B) developing
   (C) develops
   (D) developed

8. In addition to ------- instructions in managerial procedures, the redesigned training module should give encouragement to the new recruits.
   (A) provision
   (B) providing
   (C) provide
   (D) provides

9. The director of public relations is responsible for ------- the company's image through ongoing publicity.
   (A) promotion
   (B) promote
   (C) promoting
   (D) promoted

10. Sherwood reserves the right to change its free gift items without ------- customers in advance.
    (A) notifying
    (B) notifies
    (C) notified
    (D) notification

200 SECTION 2

PART 6

Questions 11-14 refer to the following e-mail.

From: Revera Computer <sales@reveracomputer.com>
To: All Our Loyal Customers
Date: November 12
Subject: Keep your money in the pocket

Our ------- has expanded! Revera Computer now offers our valued customers all kinds
    11.
of brand computer products. We would like to celebrate this change by giving even

more benefits to our loyal customers who hold an RCR Card! ------- free shipping on all
                                                                12.
orders, card bearers will get 10 percent off the total amount when ordering $300 or more

on computer products from our stores by November 30. Just visit our Web site at www.

reveracom.com and click Members to apply for a membership card.

This e-mail is generated automatically since we haven't heard from ------- yet. -------.
                                                                       13.   14.

Regards,

Revera Computer

---

11 (A) management
  (B) expiration
  (C) profit
  (D) inventory

12 (A) In case of
  (B) In response to
  (C) In addition to
  (D) In order to

13 (A) yourselves
  (B) you
  (C) your own
  (D) yours

14 (A) This is the first e-mail that is sent to you.
  (B) This is to verify the availability of information requests.
  (C) If you want to cancel your e-mail newsletter subscription, click here.
  (D) You may subscribe to our monthly newsletter for free.

DAY 14 Part 5·6 유형 연습

PART 5

1. It is important that employees keep their current phone numbers and addresses -------.
   (A) updating
   (B) update
   (C) updated
   (D) are updated

2. Our computers are unable to run the newly ------- corporate software until the technicians update the memory.
   (A) develop
   (B) developing
   (C) developed
   (D) develops

3. Our company made a contract with the Energy Star Foundation, an internationally ------- firm that has the best energy conservation devices.
   (A) recognizing
   (B) recognized
   (C) recognize
   (D) was recognized

4. The ------- memo is somewhat ambiguous in its meaning, so please resubmit it with the objectives more clearly outlined.
   (A) attaching
   (B) attached
   (C) attach
   (D) attachment

5. We are proud to announce that our company employees have ------- over one million dollars this year to charity.
   (A) contributions
   (B) contribute
   (C) contributed
   (D) contributor

6. Mr. Allen found it cost-effective to replace the ------- printers with new ones.
   (a) exist
   (B) existing
   (C) existed
   (D) exists

7. We are ------- to announce that David Shaffer has been awarded as employee of the month with his outstanding customer service.
   (A) pleasure
   (B) pleasing
   (C) pleased
   (D) pleasant

8. Please read the ------- letter regarding the introduction of our new solar-powered 'Old Time Lantern,' which is will be sold in stores starting next week.
   (A) enclosed
   (B) opposite
   (C) absent
   (D) innocent

9. The management was very ------- to hear that its proposal was rejected by the city council.
   (A) disappointing
   (B) disappointed
   (C) disappoint
   (D) disappointment

10. Almost all the movie critics found the new thriller movie ------- in a preview.
    (A) interest
    (B) interests
    (C) interesting
    (D) interested

PART 6

Questions 11-14 refer to the following letter.

Mathew Smith
1519 Walnut Ave
Antioch, CA 94883

Joanna Evens
Personnel Director
Oasis Health Club
Las Vegas, NV 89154

Dear Evens,

I am submitting my résumé for ------- 11. at Oasis Health Club for the position of personal trainer. I have 5 years' experience as a personal trainer at the Tropics Health Club in Manhattan. While there, I wrote two books on exercises, and both of my works received ------- 12. responses from readers. I also appeared in a TV show on the Heath channel several times and recommended exercise routines to a number of celebrities. After a few months later, they all thanked me through e-mail saying they now have body shapes they've always dreamed of. I believe my expertise will be of great help to your health club. Please let me know when you ------- 13. interviewing for the position. I have many ideas that will attract new customers to your gym. ------- 14.. I hope I can hear from you soon.

Sincerely,

Mathew Smith

11 (A) staff
    (B) personnel
    (C) profession
    (D) employment

12 (A) favorite
    (B) favor
    (C) favorable
    (D) favorably

13 (A) will have been
    (B) will be
    (C) have been
    (D) had to be

14 (A) I spent so much time on preparing my presentation.
    (B) I would like to share those ideas with you as soon as possible.
    (C) I took part in the Las Vegas competition.
    (D) I had an experience of hosting an exercise program.

DAY 15 Part 5·6 유형 연습

정답 및 해설 / 64p

PART 5

1. Employees may sign up for the company sponsored annuity ------- the employee shareholding programs.
   (A) except
   (B) but
   (C) or
   (D) so

2. The CEO is seriously considering selling off his company and ------- a new business.
   (A) starting
   (B) to start
   (C) start
   (D) starts

3. UPC Deliveries has minimized shipping delays with its effective scheduling and ------- system.
   (A) distribute
   (B) distributor
   (C) distributed
   (D) distribution

4. There were over one hundred employee requests for transfers to the LA office, ------- there were only ten openings in that office.
   (A) or
   (B) but
   (C) which
   (D) both

5. Employees can sign up for the Gold Star Medical plan ------- the Silver Star Medical plan, but keep in mind the employer contribution cap is $887 a month.
   (A) also
   (B) but
   (C) yet
   (D) or

6. ------- the marketing and sales divisions will be working on the new advertising program on the 'Old Time Lantern.'
   (A) Neither
   (B) As
   (C) Either
   (D) Both

7. Employees at Sear Electronics are allowed to have longer vacation by taking their days off ------- right before or right after national holidays.
   (A) neither
   (B) and
   (C) either
   (D) both

8. Neither the Detroit ------- the Boston plant does not need additional employees, but the one in LA is planning to hire 20 workers.
   (A) but
   (B) nor
   (C) or
   (D) and

9. A pilot applicant must have ------- a certificate, but also extensive experience in the aviation industry.
   (A) not only
   (B) in addition
   (C) over
   (D) nevertheless

10. Employees being hired for union positions must either join the employee union ------- decline membership within 30 days from the date of hire.
    (A) or
    (B) as
    (C) nor
    (D) and

204 SECTION 2

PART 6

Questions 11-14 refer to the following memo.

To: All Employees
From: John C Charter, VP Personnel
Date: September 21
Subject: Employee flight benefits

Please note the attached revisions to SOP Personnel Policy 21-340, employee flight benefits. The company is liberalizing the employee flight benefit program to include extended family members. Effective immediately, all immediate and extended family members are eligible for air passes. Please note, these benefits are effective ------- the **11.** employee's tenure of full-time employment.

The tickets will expire ------- when the employee terminates employment with the company.
12.
Employees are required to submit HR-21-340 at least two weeks prior to the relatives travel. The form should be signed by the director of the department. -------. Once it is
13.
approved, employees will receive passes that must be ------- with valid passports at an
14.
airport. If you have any questions, please call us at extension 8766.

11 (A) after
   (B) since
   (C) during
   (D) except

12 (A) immediately
   (B) previously
   (C) occasionally
   (D) accidentally

13 (A) It should be submitted to the personnel department for the final approval.
   (B) It verifies the eligibility for the new position.
   (C) Any requests for adjustments to reflect travel expenses should be notified.
   (D) The way to improve flight benefit programs should be reported.

14 (A) donated
   (B) presented
   (C) directed
   (D) sponsored

DAY 16 Part 5·6 유형 연습

정답 및 해설 / 65p

PART 5

1. All employees ------- wish to participate in the upcoming New Year's Eve party should RSVP at least by December 15 to insure reservations.
   (A) who
   (B) whose
   (C) when
   (D) what

2. The employees are questioning about the memo ------- was posted in the lobby by the human resources division.
   (A) there
   (B) any
   (C) where
   (D) that

3. Many employees at Vector Design avoid taking their vacation at the peak of the holiday season ------- flight ticket and hotel rates are high.
   (A) which
   (B) why
   (C) when
   (D) where

4. The company's new Web site, ------- was updated last month, will allow customers to create their own product designs and post them online.
   (A) and
   (B) which
   (C) though
   (D) when

5. BTS IT Solutions has recently developed new software, ------- any deleted files can be restored perfectly.
   (A) when
   (B) most of which
   (C) which
   (D) with which

6. The quarterly meeting of departmental managers and supervisors will be at the Hilton, ------- we will discuss how to improve employee morale.
   (A) what
   (B) where
   (C) which
   (D) who

7. Jenna Harrison, ------- is in charge of market analysis, wants to meet with the research team to discuss the allocation of tasks.
   (A) who
   (B) when
   (C) what
   (D) he

8. PIC Communications Ltd. recently recruited five graphic artists, all of ------- are women.
   (A) their
   (B) which
   (C) they
   (D) whom

9. Michael Stevens, ------- paintings are currently at the NY Fine Art Center, is considered one of the most influential painters.
   (A) who
   (B) their
   (C) them
   (D) whose

10. Any agreement ------- is not signed within 10 days will be automatically discarded and need to be negotiated again.
    (A) who
    (B) which
    (C) whose
    (D) what

206 SECTION 2

PART 6

Questions 11-14 refer to the following article.

Due to the recent global increase in the use of wind power, Apex Wind Energy Systems of Fremont, California ------- to merge with Beta Alternative Energy Company of Charlotte, North Dakota. The merger will be advantageous to Apex, as it will enable the company to serve the entire North American continent ------- Canada. Beta Alternative Energy Company has been licensed to operate its windmill systems in Canada, and is fulfilling a procurement contract with the Canadian Department of Energy. Apex is an officially recognized vendor by the United States Department of Energy. After the merger is completed, the two companies will ------- duplication of effort and streamline their operations. -------.
11. 12. 13. 14.

11 (A) decide
(B) to decide
(C) has decided
(D) were decided

12 (A) encouraging
(B) revising
(C) including
(D) concerning

13 (A) eliminate
(B) boast
(C) demonstrate
(D) specify

14 (A) It will weaken their competitiveness.
(B) Their businesses will have a negative influence on nature.
(C) Apex will suffer from a heavy workload.
(D) This merger is expected to advance wind power technology to a new level.

DAY 17 Part 5·6 유형 연습

PART 5

1. ------- wishes to attend the business writing seminar must register by the end of the month.
   (A) Them
   (B) Anyone
   (C) Whoever
   (D) Whomever

2. A recently published study indicates ------- most of the skincare products have almost the same quality in protecting skin.
   (A) that
   (B) but
   (C) what
   (D) like

3. The research participants were asked to say ------- came to their mind, regardless of how minor it may seem.
   (A) whatever
   (B) anywhere
   (C) whenever
   (D) everything

4. The Redmond Foundation review committee is going to meet on Tuesday to decide ------- educational organization to fund.
   (A) which
   (B) who
   (C) where
   (D) when

5. Due to the recent economic downturn, the CEO announced ------- the company's manufacturing plants should implement the new cost-cutting plan.
   (A) about
   (B) what
   (C) that
   (D) if

6. GSEM Energy has to decide ------- to open new offices in Osaka during the board of directors meeting.
   (A) whether
   (B) since
   (C) whereas
   (D) if

7. We are not sure yet ------- our 3rd branch office will be located since the management is still discussing this matter with the local governments.
   (A) when
   (B) what
   (C) where
   (D) that

8. To make sure to have enough seats, we have to determine ------- will be using the free shuttle service to the airport.
   (A) what
   (B) who
   (C) which
   (D) that

9. ------- pleased the clients most was the quality dishes and services provided by the restaurant.
   (A) Who
   (B) That
   (C) What
   (D) This

10. The employee handbook explains ------- new employees have to know regarding the company policies.
    (A) that
    (B) whether
    (C) what
    (D) who

PART 6

Questions 11-14 refer to the following notice.

Amtrak's See America Pass

We are very pleased to introduce our new travel program named "The See America Pass" that ------- travelers to use Amtrak to travel anywhere in North America over a ninety day period. There is no limit on using the See America Pass and its use is only limited by the travelers' imagination. This new promotion is ------- in the history of the United States. Also, we are offering military, student, and senior citizen discounts of 20% off the price of the pass. The ninety-day See America Pass is only $150! -------. This is a money saving investment! The one caveat is time. We will only be offering the pass for one week ------- on May 1. After that, they will not be available for sale. Please note, the See America Pass cannot be combined with any other offer or promotion.

11. (A) was allowing
    (B) allowed
    (C) will allow
    (D) would have allowed

12. (A) unprecedented
    (B) attended
    (C) outnumbered
    (D) distinctive

13. (A) You can invest in travel package program.
    (B) You can introduce it to your family members or friends.
    (C) The program is created with the government aid.
    (D) This value is unheard of in the travel industry today.

14. (A) following
    (B) beginning
    (C) including
    (D) regarding

DAY 18 Part 5·6 유형 연습

PART 5

1. The computer technician can install the new software, even ------- other users are using the computer system.
   (A) altogether
   (B) while
   (C) despite
   (D) initially

2. ------- the soccer final was interrupted by a heavy shower, the most of the audience didn't leave the stadium until the game ended.
   (A) In spite of
   (B) So as
   (C) Despite
   (D) Though

3. ------- we have received approval for the acquisition of Consolidated Container, we will combine facilities from both companies to make operations more efficient.
   (A) Soon
   (B) Ever
   (C) Ago
   (D) Once

4. ------- we have received the confirmation, the orders will be shipped to the address right away.
   (A) As soon as
   (B) Unless
   (C) Therefore
   (D) Before

5. ------- our products may cost a lot initially, they pay for themselves over time due to energy savings.
   (A) In spite of
   (B) However
   (C) Even though
   (D) Moreover

6. ------- Ms. Karen returns to the office from her business trip as planned, there will be no change to the meeting schedule.
   (A) Provided that
   (B) Because
   (C) Otherwise
   (D) However

7. All the employees are asked to turn off lights of the meeting rooms ------- they are not in use.
   (A) unless
   (B) when
   (C) that
   (D) which

8. ------- all the employees have transferred to the new London office, we can now focus on improving training and procedures.
   (A) Regarding
   (B) Usually
   (C) Instead of
   (D) Now that

9. ------- the company saved considerable money last year, we are able to offer all employees ten percent across the board raise.
   (A) Despite
   (B) Since
   (C) Unless
   (D) So

10. Our store's policy is that we do not process any exchange or refund ------- the product is defective.
    (A) if
    (B) in case
    (C) unless
    (D) once

210 SECTION 2

PART 6

Questions 11-14 refer to the following notice.

The annual employee picnic ------- at Riverside Park in Newark, New Jersey. This annual
                                11.
picnic will be ------- to the wonderful efforts our employees put last year. As you all know,
                12.
last year was the most profitable ever for our company. Moreover, it was all due to the
hard work and dedication of our employees in making quality products and providing great
customer service. This is why we invest large sums of money on recruitment, pay and
benefits ------- the best people for our company. We are pleased to sponsor this employee
         13.
picnic. -------.
        14.

11 (A) has been held
    (B) will be held
    (C) will hold
    (D) would be held

12 (A) dedicated
    (B) capable
    (C) certain
    (D) valid

13 (A) find
    (B) found
    (C) finding
    (D) to find

14 (A) Instead, training session will be delayed until Saturday.
    (B) Company's profit has been increased over the last five years.
    (C) The company will provide all the food, drinks, and entertainment.
    (D) The job interview is the core of a successful recruitment process.

DAY 19 Part 5·6 유형 연습

PART 5

1. Being a flight attendant is a ------- and rigorous job than many recruits anticipate it would be.
   (A) difficult
   (B) difficulty
   (C) more difficult
   (D) much difficulty

2. Before opening the Austin, Texas's plant, we must decide if cooling with conventional air conditioning is cheaper ------- using a high pump.
   (A) as
   (B) while
   (C) than
   (D) whether

3. The newly redesigned Sadler LED camping lantern has a ------- construction than before to be durable and waterproof.
   (A) stronger
   (B) strengthen
   (C) strengths
   (D) strong

4. A recent study indicates that more crime is committed in major cities ------- in rural areas.
   (A) better
   (B) as
   (C) than
   (D) most

5. The Sydney Opera House is the ------- impressive building I have ever seen.
   (A) more
   (B) very
   (C) most
   (D) well

6. Our company is committed to providing the ------- level of customer service in the entire airline industry, along with the best on-time arrivals.
   (A) highly
   (B) high
   (C) highest
   (D) higher

7. Our new advertising sign is the ------- of all displays in the downtown area and this was proven by a helicopter flight of a news crew last week.
   (A) bright
   (B) brightens
   (C) brightest
   (D) brightness

8. This new shelf is just as durable as the old one even though it is ------- cheaper.
   (A) very
   (B) such
   (C) so
   (D) much

9. The committee chose Mr. Raven's plan over the alternative, stating his idea is the ------- to materialize of the two.
   (A) easy
   (B) easier
   (C) easily
   (D) easiest

10. Employees are encouraged to become more ------- with the company's standard operations procedure manual, also known as SOP.
    (A) familiar
    (B) familiarity
    (C) familiarly
    (D) familiarize

212 SECTION 2

PART 6

Questions 11-14 refer to the following advertisement.

About Moody's Business.com

Moody's Business.com is a leading independent provider of economics, financial, country and industry research, ------- to meet the diverse planning and information needs of
11.
business, governments and experts.

Our services include financial, industrial, and regional market analyses. Moody's Business.com information and services are used in a variety of ways, such as strategic planning, risk management and investment research. We have ------- 3,000 clients worldwide, including
12.
banks and many companies.

-------. We also ------- offices in London, New York and Hong Kong. To find more
13.   14.
information, please visit our Web site www.moodysbiz.com.

11 (A) design
(B) designed
(C) designs
(D) designing

12 (A) beyond
(B) between
(C) over
(D) along with

13 (A) The business is designed to help you find data management platform.
(B) Its headquarters is located in Canberra, the capital of Australia.
(C) The company is a fruitful resource for the new entrepreneurs.
(D) We provide customers with marketing solutions.

14 (A) assert
(B) prolong
(C) maintain
(D) compile

DAY 20 Part 5·6 유형 연습

PART 5

1. ------- is the budget report you have to review and approve before the next business meeting.
   (A) Attach
   (B) Attachment
   (C) Attaching
   (D) Attached

2. ------- your presentation been more specific, you would have won the contract with our company.
   (A) If
   (B) Have
   (C) Had
   (D) If had

3. If the production team ------- able to finish their job on schedule, we could meet the delivery deadline.
   (A) was
   (B) were
   (C) is
   (D) be

4. If we ------- more money on education, we would have prevented many juvenile crimes taking place at school.
   (A) spent
   (B) spend
   (C) had spent
   (D) spending

5. If he had passed the bar exam, he ------- become a lawyer to help the poor.
   (A) will
   (B) should
   (C) could have
   (D) could

6. If our new product ------- earlier, it would be more favorably received by consumers by now.
   (A) will be introduced
   (B) was introduced
   (C) were introduced
   (D) had been introduced

7. ------- you need any additional information on your ticket, please consult a ticket agent at an airline counter.
   (A) Had
   (B) Should
   (C) For
   (D) That

8. ------- did the company exceed this year's sales target but it set a new record for revenue.
   (A) When
   (B) If
   (C) Not only
   (D) So

9. ------- is a copy of the minutes from the last strategic planning meeting you requested.
   (A) Enclosing
   (B) Enclose
   (C) Enclosed
   (D) Enclosure

10. ------- you have any questions or concerns about the revised tax law, please feel free to contact the accounting department at your convenience.
    (A) Could
    (B) May
    (C) Can
    (D) Should

PART 6

Questions 11-14 refer to the following notice.

The company is ------- to announce the creation of a new sales lead incentive program.
11.
Starting on May 1, all employees who submit leads to the sales division will be given a one hundred dollar stipend. The lead must result in the actual opening of a commercial trading account. Moreover, the employee with the ------- leads by the end of the fiscal year will be
12.
awarded an all-expense paid vacation to Hawaii for two weeks. -------.
13.

We are very ------- with our employees' service to our company and we truly believe that
14.
this is the key to our company's sustainable growth.

11. (A) pleasing
    (B) pleasure
    (C) please
    (D) pleased

12. (A) more
    (B) most
    (C) very
    (D) better

13. (A) This program will play a pivotal role in promotion.
    (B) The annual performance review will be conducted.
    (C) The company will announce the relocation of its headquarters.
    (D) Employees will maintain a level of knowledge and understanding of current status.

14. (A) satisfaction
    (B) satisfactory
    (C) satisfied
    (D) satisfying

실전 랜덤 연습

Day 01	연습 문제 1	218
Day 02	연습 문제 2	220
Day 03	연습 문제 3	222
Day 04	연습 문제 4	224
Day 05	연습 문제 5	226
Day 06	연습 문제 6	228
Day 07	연습 문제 7	230
Day 08	연습 문제 8	232
Day 09	연습 문제 9	234
Day 10	연습 문제 10	236
Day 11	연습 문제 11	238
Day 12	연습 문제 12	240
Day 13	연습 문제 13	242
Day 14	연습 문제 14	244
Day 15	연습 문제 15	246
Day 16	연습 문제 16	248
Day 17	연습 문제 17	250
Day 18	연습 문제 18	252
Day 19	연습 문제 19	254
Day 20	연습 문제 20	256

DAY 01 실전 랜덤 연습

PART 5

1. Andy Garcia stated that he had set ------- apart from other singers by trying to elevate rap music to new heights.
(A) he
(B) himself
(C) his
(D) him

2. We would never have succeeded in winning the Texco account without your ------- effort and expertise.
(A) whole
(B) multiple
(C) exceptional
(D) inclusive

3. We recommend that you check ------- to see if new videos have been added.
(A) periodically
(B) incidentally
(C) indefinitely
(D) considerably

4. ------- is involved in the CNA Project is requested to submit an outline of their plans by the end of the month.
(A) No one
(B) Some
(C) Whoever
(D) Everyone

5. Due to an unexpected rise in oil prices, many local companies ------- budget cuts.
(A) are faced
(B) faces
(C) have been faced
(D) have been facing

6. The newspaper's circulation department is committed ------- providing excellent service.
(A) that
(B) of
(C) to
(D) so

7. The upcoming media campaign will focus on products currently under -------.
(A) development
(B) developing
(C) developed
(D) develops

8. ------- we requested that the replacement parts be sent immediately, we were informed that they could not arrive before the end of the week.
(A) However
(B) Although
(C) Otherwise
(D) Yet

9. Many software firms that began several years ago with a relatively small amount of capital are extremely ------- today.
(A) succeed
(B) success
(C) successfully
(D) successful

10. A pamphlet containing product ------- will be included in the packaging.
(A) informative
(B) information
(C) informed
(D) informatively

218 SECTION 2

11 The longer we wait to make this decision, the ------- it will be to announce it to the public.
    (A) most difficult
    (B) difficult
    (C) difficulty
    (D) more difficult

12 ------- her husband was being transferred to Tokyo, she requested a transfer, too.
    (A) Whether
    (B) For
    (C) Since
    (D) Which

13 If you attempt to repair this machine, please follow basic safety -------.
    (A) precautions
    (B) preparations
    (C) predictions
    (D) prescriptions

14 Mr. Yamamoto said he was ------- to call me when I met him in the hallway.
    (A) about
    (B) nearly
    (C) close
    (D) off

15 The workshop, ------- scheduled to begin at 2 P.M., was called off because of a scheduling conflict.
    (A) origin
    (B) originated
    (C) original
    (D) originally

16 Due to ------- rents in the downtown area, our company has decided to move to the suburbs.
    (A) rising
    (B) rose
    (C) arisen
    (D) rise

17 He cannot realistically expect to finish the revised project specifications before the ------- deadline.
    (A) proposes
    (B) proposing
    (C) proposed
    (D) propose

18 ------- the fact that a great deal of money had been invested in the project, it was a failure.
    (A) Although
    (B) However
    (C) Despite
    (D) Yet

19 The outdoor music festival scheduled for this weekend has been ------- until next Wednesday.
    (A) abbreviated
    (B) terminated
    (C) postponed
    (D) scheduled

20 Due to complaints from its customers, Hong Kong Airlines changed its -------, and now allows two suitcases per passenger.
    (A) accommodation
    (B) policy
    (C) handling
    (D) measure

DAY 02 실전 랜덤 연습

PART 5

1. Before you ------- the aircraft, check the overhead compartments for your personal effects and belongings.
   (A) leaving
   (B) to leave
   (C) leave
   (D) will leave

2. AHJ Comtech has won an award for the third ------- year from a local business magazine.
   (A) consecutive
   (B) constant
   (C) following
   (D) consequent

3. Should you need secretarial services during ------- stay, please contact the hotel receptionist.
   (A) you
   (B) your
   (C) yours
   (D) yourselves

4. Shoppers are encouraged to describe the nature of their complaint to the Customer Service Department as ------- as possible.
   (A) specifically
   (B) specific
   (C) specify
   (D) specification

5. The company has invested money not for improving the training procedures, ------- for adopting and installing the latest technology.
   (A) but
   (B) or
   (C) unless
   (D) so

6. As a result of extensive renovations over the last month, we can now ------- our customers much better service.
   (A) provide
   (B) regain
   (C) offer
   (D) make

7. There are no two-bedroom apartments available ------- lease at the present time.
   (A) as
   (B) into
   (C) for
   (D) with

8. The Autoland Company recently introduced a labor-saving device that automatically sweeps and ------- the floor.
   (A) polishes
   (B) pours
   (C) flows
   (D) presses

9. The Southern Hill department store's longstanding ------- to top-quality service has earned the company a distinguished reputation.
   (A) committable
   (B) committed
   (C) committing
   (D) commitment

10. Next time, make sure to write the report much more ------- to avoid costly misunderstanding.
    (A) clear
    (B) clearly
    (C) clearing
    (D) clearness

11 ------- will soon be mailed for a formal dinner honoring Dr. Lee.
(A) Invite
(B) Inviting
(C) Invitation
(D) Invitations

12 Members can renew their membership ------- they have outstanding payments, in which case their renewal will be denied.
(A) without
(B) otherwise
(C) unless
(D) although

13 The type of exercise recommended varies ------- depending on the age and health condition of the individual.
(A) willingly
(B) agreeably
(C) cordially
(D) considerably

14 The marketing manager cannot continue the work until he receives a definite answer about the changes ------- proposed.
(A) that
(B) he
(C) were
(D) until

15 The sales director asked his team members to make sure that none of the recommendations made by the consultant are -------.
(A) behaved
(B) attended
(C) operated
(D) ignored

16 The security system for our latest invention has reached the final -------.
(A) paths
(B) scenes
(C) drafts
(D) stages

17 In order to ------- the diverse needs of its consumers, Twin's Market offers a wide variety of products.
(A) meet
(B) encounter
(C) contend
(D) form

18 Since all of the furniture in our store has been handcrafted with great care, we guarantee that ------- you choose will bring you the utmost satisfaction.
(A) whenever
(B) wherever
(C) whatever
(D) however

19 The pioneering research project has received an award ------- $20,000 in its first year.
(A) worth
(B) costly
(C) valued
(D) prized

20 The local telephone company will cancel any account for which payment is three months -------.
(A) expensive
(B) permanent
(C) overdue
(D) insignificant

DAY 03 실전 랜덤 연습

PART 5

1. The director expects research proposals to be turned in ------- the end of the month.
   (A) on
   (B) by
   (C) between
   (D) except

2. Janet's shop will officially open on January 28 when she will unveil ------- own brand.
   (A) she
   (B) her
   (C) hers
   (D) herself

3. The young pianist's performance at the Carter Center tonight demonstrated the kind of talent that make up for the ------- he made last night.
   (A) mistake
   (B) attention
   (C) description
   (D) information

4. It ------- that the merger of two renowned manufacturers into a larger one will draw sharp criticism.
   (A) expects
   (B) has expected
   (C) expecting
   (D) is expected

5. Overseas travelers should be aware of ------- government regulations about using cameras in restricted areas.
   (A) various
   (B) variety
   (C) variably
   (D) variation

6. As of next Monday, the National Health Association will publish the results of surveys conducted by healthcare ------- at the Richmond Clinic.
   (A) professionally
   (B) professionals
   (C) profession
   (D) professional

7. Our office has ------- moved, so contact us at our new mailing address printed above.
   (A) usually
   (B) relatively
   (C) recently
   (D) vaguely

8. An anonymous donation enabled the local orphanage to purchase a ------- number of things that are indispensable to the children.
   (A) great
   (B) numerous
   (C) many
   (D) little

9. ------- local farmers have been unable to supply enough corn and wheat, bakeries in northern Texas areas have had to buy ingredients from other sources.
   (A) Owing
   (B) Although
   (C) For
   (D) Because

10. ------- to comment further on the case, the president left the press conference.
    (A) Refused
    (B) Refuses
    (C) Refusing
    (D) Refusal

11 Our company spent more than a month enhancing product quality, and -------, the contractors are now satisfied.
    (A) fortunately
    (B) fortunate
    (C) fortunes
    (D) fortune

12 Harper Pharmaceutical is pleased to ------- that all of its workers are eligible for membership at the nearby health club.
    (A) maintain
    (B) announce
    (C) involve
    (D) tell

13 As our charity event had such high attendance, we have reached our donation -------.
    (A) destination
    (B) opinion
    (C) organization
    (D) goal

14 Japan's annual trade surplus is in excess ------- $200 billion and is expected to get bigger next year.
    (A) of
    (B) over
    (C) by
    (D) than

15 After reviewing proposals for the road construction project, the president decided that Dr. Kim's was the most ------- choice.
    (A) appropriateness
    (B) appropriate
    (C) appropriation
    (D) appropriately

16 This month only, Heavenly Gym is offering new members the full use of its facilities, including the swimming pool, for as ------- as $30 a month.
    (A) little
    (B) much
    (C) far
    (D) less

17 Those ------- wish to attend the international education conference in Seoul should register this month.
    (A) when
    (B) what
    (C) whom
    (D) who

18 Because Ms. Baker ------- disappointment with the service, the floor manager has been keeping his eyes on the staff's behavior for the last few days.
    (A) shows
    (B) is showing
    (C) will be showing
    (D) showed

19 If you want to get a job quickly, it is critical that you are ------- in all job interviews.
    (A) promptly
    (B) promptness
    (C) prompt
    (D) prompter

20 ------- my dismay, Ms. Saito made a dismal presentation even though her ideas were not that bad.
    (A) About
    (B) To
    (C) On
    (D) For

DAY 04 실전 랜덤 연습

PART 5

1. The new car has both excellent handling ------- a great deal of power to cope with almost any kind of terrain.
   (A) but
   (B) and
   (C) or
   (D) either

2. If you want to park your car on company property, you must ------- a parking permit to the windshield.
   (A) enclose
   (B) push
   (C) attach
   (D) give

3. To avoid possible breakdowns, you should purchase machines that are highly -------.
   (A) rely
   (B) relying
   (C) relied
   (D) reliable

4. Early tomorrow, the Labor Minister will be ------- a press conference to publicize the launch of his innovative job creation plan.
   (A) holding
   (B) opening
   (C) attending
   (D) taking

5. After the thorough medical examination, the doctor made a ------- of lung cancer.
   (A) diagnose
   (B) diagnosis
   (C) diagnostic
   (D) diagnostically

6. Considering our financial situation, we do not have any ------- choices but to close down the factory.
   (A) another
   (B) other
   (C) the other
   (D) others

7. Health experts ------- control the fast food industry to protect consumers.
   (A) close
   (B) closely
   (C) closing
   (D) closed

8. ------- had only twenty minutes to prepare for the speech, Peter made a considerable number of mistakes.
   (A) Having
   (B) Had
   (C) Have
   (D) Has

9. Any attempt to falsify any document may result in ------- in a very short period of time.
   (A) prosecutes
   (B) prosecutor
   (C) prosecuted
   (D) prosecution

10. Ms. Brown was absent ------- the staff meeting because of the urgent meeting with her client.
    (A) to
    (B) of
    (C) about
    (D) from

224 SECTION 2

11 The conclusion of the report was ------- the government should lower taxes in order to stimulate consumption.
(A) whom
(B) which
(C) what
(D) that

12 Staff ------- overtime are requested to turn off all the computers when leaving the office.
(A) work
(B) working
(C) may work
(D) have worked

13 Due to time -------, the committee members were not able to reach a fruitful conclusion.
(A) obstacles
(B) constraints
(C) inhibitions
(D) prohibitions

14 Many workers try to break the monotony of their jobs by ------- the tasks that they undertake.
(A) varying
(B) variety
(C) varied
(D) vary

15 In spite of the dismal expectations on the economic situation, the volume of the Korea Stock Exchange was ------- higher yesterday.
(A) respectively
(B) lately
(C) previously
(D) slightly

16 ------- you have any questions concerning the products, please contact the customer service department.
(A) Should
(B) Would
(C) Might
(D) Unless

17 To prevent illegal fishing, the government has decided to hire additional coast guards for the ------- fishing season.
(A) arising
(B) upcoming
(C) resulting
(D) forwarding

18 Mr. Washington will not be able to attend the conference, and ------- will Ms. Monroe.
(A) however
(B) also
(C) neither
(D) now

19 Since taking office last year, the government has made ------- changes in employment policy that concerns the public.
(A) a lot
(B) several
(C) much
(D) little

20 Since Office Box is ------- under construction, try the drugstore down the street.
(A) readily
(B) assuredly
(C) currently
(D) extremely

DAY 05 실전 랜덤 연습

정답 및 해설 / 78p

PART 5

1. A majority of students ------- were interviewed said that breaks between terms were too short.
   (A) which
   (B) whom
   (C) whose
   (D) who

2. Due to cold weather and recent snow, the ski season will ------- until the end of March.
   (A) expire
   (B) finish
   (C) last
   (D) endure

3. In New York, whether you want to eat western or eastern food, your choices are -------.
   (A) vary
   (B) varied
   (C) variety
   (D) variously

4. Evaluating workers in ------- with other workers must be based on the individual circumstances.
   (A) compare
   (B) comparative
   (C) comparison
   (D) compared

5. Customers must get specific approval from the bank manager when ------- money in excess of $10,000 abroad.
   (A) sending
   (B) send
   (C) to send
   (D) sent

6. In our factory, supervisors spend ------- time on making sure workers come on time, and the assembly line runs smoothly.
   (A) consider
   (B) considerate
   (C) considerable
   (D) consideration

7. Reading good books is like having ------- balanced meals that bring harmony to your body.
   (A) nutritional
   (B) nutritionally
   (C) nutrition
   (D) nutritionist

8. In countries where malnutrition is prevalent, the Peace Corps frequently distributes vitamins to ------- people's meager diets.
   (A) supplement
   (B) impose
   (C) pursue
   (D) add

9. The clinic decided not to hire her as a nurse when they discovered her ------- to the suffering of patients.
   (A) indecision
   (B) discouragement
   (C) unwillingness
   (D) indifference

10. If holders of New Zealand citizenship do not register in time, they may not be ------- to vote.
    (A) accessible
    (B) capable
    (C) eligible
    (D) applicable

226 SECTION 2

11 When dealing with anxious customers in the store, salespeople must ------- reassure them that they will be served as soon as the urgent matters are addressed.

(A) potentially
(B) politely
(C) possibly
(D) progressively

12 This year's government campaign to prevent people from smoking has proved to be -------.

(A) successive
(B) successful
(C) sumptuous
(D) submissive

13 Despite many financial worries, many ------- that the company will put more emphasis on the foreign market rather than on the domestic market.

(A) expect
(B) expects
(C) are expected
(D) has expected

14 Please submit the ------- of this year's annual sales report to Mr. Jackson by the end of this week.

(A) copy
(B) issue
(C) edition
(D) mark

15 Technology experts have predicted that software enhancement will continue well in the ------- future.

(A) ongoing
(B) prevalent
(C) foreseeable
(D) appreciable

16 Although the company's employees ------- requested a pay raise, it has not been granted to them for over three years.

(A) repeatedly
(B) exactly
(C) incredibly
(D) briefly

17 The police have found three bodies believed to be crew members of the ------- missing boat.

(A) mystery
(B) mysterious
(C) mysteriously
(D) mysteriousness

18 Twilight Charity is an organization ------- mission is to educate and support the local children who are in poverty.

(A) what
(B) that
(C) which
(D) whose

19 The president reminded workers that all the computers at work are ------- official use only.

(A) about
(B) from
(C) for
(D) above

20 All of the questions were answered ------- before the interviewer left the room.

(A) others
(B) another
(C) each other
(D) one after another

DAY 06 실전 랜덤 연습

PART 5

1. Every year since he -------, the president has recommended rebuilding the public transportation system.
   (A) had elected
   (B) elected
   (C) was elected
   (D) elects

2. Dr. Robert's previous experience as a therapist will greatly help ------- in her volunteer work.
   (A) hers
   (B) her
   (C) she
   (D) herself

3. Because of a record amount of rain last winter, there is a low ------- of a water shortage this year.
   (A) likable
   (B) likeness
   (C) liken
   (D) likelihood

4. ------- Jeff thinks we should go with a small advertising firm, Jessica thinks a big one will be better.
   (A) As soon as
   (B) And
   (C) However
   (D) While

5. Make sure your helmet is ------- fastened before riding on a bike.
   (A) complete
   (B) completely
   (C) completed
   (D) completion

6. ------- Mr. Brown be elected, it is expected that this project will undergo a thorough review.
   (A) Would
   (B) Might
   (C) Should
   (D) Will

7. Any misleading information ------- in your resume may result in automatic disqualification.
   (A) give
   (B) gave
   (C) was given
   (D) given

8. David Collins entered our company only six months ago, but he has ------- become the top salesperson.
   (A) once
   (B) already
   (C) still
   (D) yet

9. Because of his previous successes, the director did not have ------- reason to doubt that he could do the job well.
   (A) its
   (B) ones
   (C) any
   (D) few

10. Michael White who worked ------- for the company was selected as the Employee of the Year.
    (A) hard
    (B) hardly
    (C) later
    (D) lately

228 SECTION 2

11 All applications for the position must be in by seven o'clock Friday ------- the very latest.
(A) at
(B) before
(C) until
(D) up to

12 Any passenger who does not have a landing card may obtain ------- from a flight attendant.
(A) other
(B) the other
(C) one
(D) any

13 All the computer rooms on the second floor are closed for renovations until further -------.
(A) notice
(B) conversation
(C) mark
(D) information

14 Rescue workers will conduct an ------- search for survivors of the shipwreck, but it is feared that no one survived.
(A) extensive
(B) inclusive
(C) exclusive
(D) apprehensive

15 Again last year, tens of thousands of tourists were ------- by the breathtaking views of Yellowstone National Park.
(A) allocated
(B) announced
(C) annoyed
(D) attracted

16 ------- way you look at it, an Olympics bronze medal is a remarkable achievement for one so young.
(A) Whichever
(B) However
(C) Whenever
(D) Whoever

17 There is no doubt that the company will benefit ------- Ms. Parker's experience in international trade.
(A) from
(B) concerning
(C) within
(D) about

18 The soldiers were commended for the very ------- way they dealt with the situation.
(A) impressively
(B) impression
(C) impressed
(D) impressive

19 If the accident occurs during the ------- of your regular duties, you will be covered by disability insurance.
(A) performer
(B) perform
(C) performing
(D) performance

20 Honeycutt can finally afford to move its headquarters to the most ------- piece of land in New York City.
(A) extinguishable
(B) considerable
(C) desirable
(D) erectable

DAY 07 실전 랜덤 연습

PART 5

1. The company policy makes it possible ------- workers to use the staff lounge whenever they want.
   (A) with
   (B) in
   (C) for
   (D) of

2. Professor Jackson ------- that a new preservation plan will double the number of wild animals in this region.
   (A) anticipating
   (B) to anticipate
   (C) is anticipated
   (D) anticipates

3. Anyone who chooses to consume alcohol in a bar must be a ------- of 18 years of age.
   (A) minimize
   (B) minimizing
   (C) minimal
   (D) minimum

4. Sign in before starting each shift; -------, time worked may not be accurately reflected in your paychecks.
   (A) otherwise
   (B) however
   (C) nevertheless
   (D) whereas

5. -------, management cannot accept responsibility for belongings left behind in rooms.
   (A) Regret
   (B) Regretless
   (C) Regretful
   (D) Regrettably

6. We do not intend to employ new staff now ------- the economy is forecast to grow significantly next year.
   (A) regardless of
   (B) despite
   (C) whether
   (D) even if

7. Many economists blamed rising taxes ------- the increase in the prices of consumer goods.
   (A) for
   (B) of
   (C) because
   (D) during

8. As his retirement day approached, the Human Resources manager experienced a ------- array of emotions.
   (A) bewilderment
   (B) bewildering
   (C) bewildered
   (D) bewilders

9. In an effort to establish the potential ------- of its environmentally friendly solar energy, we are conducting a nationwide survey.
   (A) appeal
   (B) appealable
   (C) appealing
   (D) appealingly

10. Some of the items designed by Stephen Covey are more popular overseas than they are -------.
    (A) local
    (B) locals
    (C) locally
    (D) locale

230 SECTION 2

11. The Local Plan has made ------- for an additional 2,000 new dwellings between 2007 and 2008.
    (A) omission
    (B) allowance
    (C) impression
    (D) elimination

12. The union members ------- agreed to the new labor contracts but in the end rejected them.
    (A) newly
    (B) already
    (C) initially
    (D) strictly

13. We would like to thank you for being so ------- during such a difficult negotiation.
    (A) cooperatively
    (B) cooperation
    (C) cooperative
    (D) cooperativeness

14. ------- it has been 10 years since you first came to this country is unbelievable.
    (A) What
    (B) That
    (C) After
    (D) Whatever

15. Please consult the hotel directly for more detailed information as room rates vary ------- a regular basis.
    (A) in
    (B) with
    (C) by
    (D) on

16. Prospective game-show contestants are asked to ------- out the attached questionnaire.
    (A) fill
    (B) filling
    (C) filled
    (D) be filled

17. When I returned to work after a long vacation, I realized that one of my colleagues -------.
    (A) was resigned
    (B) had been resigned
    (C) had resigned
    (D) will have resigned

18. ------- payment must be sent by the end of this month; otherwise, further action will be taken.
    (A) Partly
    (B) Parted
    (C) Partial
    (D) Parting

19. Ten days before the contract expires, tenants should submit written ------- of the renewal or non-renewal of their lease.
    (A) contraction
    (B) leave
    (C) declaration
    (D) notification

20. The management team announced that interviews will be ------- in the board room.
    (A) alerted
    (B) conducted
    (C) engaged
    (D) protected

DAY 08 실전 랜덤 연습

정답 및 해설 / 82p

PART 5

1. Many customers ------- furniture through this Web site which offers a wide range of products.
   (A) purchase
   (B) purchasing
   (C) are purchased
   (D) to purchase

2. Upon ------- examination, we discovered many flaws in the contract that were not initially detected.
   (A) closer
   (B) closed
   (C) closing
   (D) closure

3. The airline will ------- daily service between New York and San Francisco early next month.
   (A) depart
   (B) resume
   (C) cause
   (D) drive

4. Both sides are waiting for the results of the independent ------- which was conducted only a few days ago.
   (A) arbitrate
   (B) arbitrated
   (C) arbitration
   (D) arbitrator

5. Home heating prices in the Northeast, a region that relies heavily on oil to heat homes, ------- doubled over the past year.
   (A) has
   (B) have
   (C) is
   (D) are

6. The two CEOs met to sign a formal contract to complete a ------- of the companies.
   (A) incorporation
   (B) merger
   (C) fusion
   (D) annexation

7. To maximize our profit, we need to pursue our potential clients more -------.
   (A) aggressive
   (B) aggressively
   (C) aggression
   (D) aggress

8. ------- of the tenants in this apartment building are billed exclusively by Brenda Housing, the biggest real estate developer in town.
   (A) The most
   (B) All
   (C) Each
   (D) Anyone

9. Sections of the minutes of the April meeting do not seem to make ------- in light of the agenda for the meeting.
   (A) reason
   (B) sense
   (C) cause
   (D) basis

10. Initial reports from the third quarter show that our store sales have increased by 20 percent since the ------- year.
    (A) consecutive
    (B) previous
    (C) following
    (D) subsequent

232 SECTION 2

11 According to the itinerary, the tourists are scheduled to leave ------- Coosa Bay where they will enjoy a boat trip to Pimentel Island.

(A) towards
(B) for
(C) between
(D) to

12 If the new marketing strategy had not been so successful, they ------- such a huge financial support from the banks.

(A) will not be receiving
(B) will not receive
(C) would not have received
(D) cannot receive

13 Many local shop owners will be closing their shops tomorrow in ------- of a public holiday.

(A) observance
(B) observant
(C) observable
(D) observation

14 Purustan's painting, Olympia, is admired as one of the most ------- pieces in recent years.

(A) impression
(B) impressive
(C) impress
(D) impressively

15 For over 30 years, First National Bank has brought their customers the ------- and advice necessary to manage investments.

(A) expertise
(B) reimbursement
(C) request
(D) conversion

16 Our hotel offers full housekeeping services every day and replenishes your refrigerator ------- day.

(A) each other
(B) one another
(C) every another
(D) every other

17 The post office is open from 8 A.M. to 6 P.M. every day ------- national holidays.

(A) except
(B) for
(C) during
(D) even if

18 None of the candidates have been ------- yet, but those who majored in economics have the best chance.

(A) choice
(B) choosing
(C) chose
(D) chosen

19 One of the most attractive ------- of using telecommunications is the ability to work from the comfort of one's own home.

(A) helps
(B) advantages
(C) favors
(D) profits

20 ------- for the opening early does not guarantee anything but it does give a positive impression.

(A) Apply
(B) Applicants
(C) Applicable
(D) To apply

DAY 09 실전 랜덤 연습

PART 5

1. ------- the accounting department and the marketing department should cooperate to handle this task together.
   (A) Both
   (B) Either
   (C) Neither
   (D) Not only

2. Scott Bond ------- A&C Inc. thirty years ago, making him the longest-serving employee in the company.
   (A) join
   (B) has joined
   (C) joined
   (D) was joined

3. Management is expected to agree ------- on the union's suggestion to decrease working hours.
   (A) unanimous
   (B) unanimously
   (C) unanimity
   (D) untimely

4. We would like to ------- a free camera to any customer spending more than two hundred dollars in one of our stores.
   (A) make
   (B) control
   (C) offer
   (D) restore

5. As the market leader, we are confident that you will be ------- with our service.
   (A) patient
   (B) potential
   (C) content
   (D) constant

6. Of the ruins in Rome, the most well-preserved and the most impressive ------- is the Colosseum.
   (A) structural
   (B) structure
   (C) structurally
   (D) structuring

7. We make sure that all of our rooms stay as ------- as possible for our guests.
   (A) clean
   (B) cleanly
   (C) cleaner
   (D) cleanness

8. It still remains ------- whether the new employment policy will actually reduce the rate of unemployment.
   (A) seeing
   (B) seen
   (C) to see
   (D) to be seen

9. An emergency meeting is held to survey the extent of the ------- caused by the hurricane.
   (A) damage
   (B) damaged
   (C) damaging
   (D) damagingly

10. Factory workers are getting used to ------- the new regulations that just took effect last week.
    (A) follow
    (B) following
    (C) followed
    (D) being followed

11 The legislators unanimously ------- the proposed policy on agricultural subsidies.
   (A) rejected
   (B) rejecting
   (C) to reject
   (D) were rejected

12 Please note ------- the union membership fees vary, depending on the industry.
   (A) concerning
   (B) about
   (C) which
   (D) that

13 Advances ------- technology have brought entrepreneurs more profits than expected.
   (A) on
   (B) in
   (C) by
   (D) to

14 This system will deliver quality service to the user ------- maintenance checks are performed regularly.
   (A) whereas
   (B) although
   (C) as long as
   (D) unless

15 Our company needs to ------- new management skills in the next few years.
   (A) register
   (B) adopt
   (C) adapt
   (D) replace

16 The oriental beauty of this temple has ------- a lot of tourists from all over the world.
   (A) attracted
   (B) contracted
   (C) retracted
   (D) protracted

17 Only after Mr. Telicka has finished looking ------- the documents will approval be given.
   (A) out
   (B) after
   (C) into
   (D) back

18 Prosecutors will act ------- against any government official who has proven links to corruption.
   (A) firm
   (B) firms
   (C) firmly
   (D) firming

19 Both sides have finally found the common ground ------- to the terms of the contract.
   (A) agree
   (B) agreeing
   (C) to agree
   (D) agreed

20 The sales manager is going to outline the long-term ------- to increase sales at the board meeting this afternoon.
   (A) strategy
   (B) strategic
   (C) strategist
   (D) strategically

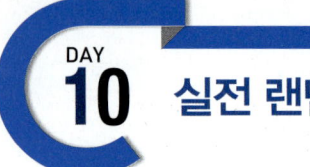

DAY 10 실전 랜덤 연습

PART 5

1. The primary objective of the marketing department is to keep customers ------- about the company.
   (A) inform
   (B) information
   (C) informing
   (D) informed

2. Fishermen who catch fish without a permit should neither sell them for commercial gain ------- consume them for pleasure.
   (A) nor
   (B) yet
   (C) and
   (D) or

3. The newly appointed manager was instructed to report all the policy changes ------- to his supervisors.
   (A) direction
   (B) directing
   (C) directly
   (D) directive

4. Without considerable expertise, it is not possible to fully ------- what customers want.
   (A) satisfaction
   (B) satisfy
   (C) satisfactory
   (D) satisfying

5. The latest vehicle ------- and distributed by Norton Motors is very well designed.
   (A) manufacture
   (B) manufacturer
   (C) manufacturing
   (D) manufactured

6. Consumers who are unsatisfied with the quality of the products should ------- the manager at once.
   (A) tell
   (B) speak
   (C) give
   (D) offer

7. Once Mr. Lewis's ------- had been received, the personnel manager started his search for a new advertising executive.
   (A) resignation
   (B) resignedly
   (C) resigned
   (D) resign

8. She made a request that he ------- the books he borrowed from her two month ago.
   (A) returns
   (B) returned
   (C) be returned
   (D) return

9. The nationwide ------- of these products largely depends on how good the transportation network is.
   (A) contribution
   (B) attribution
   (C) tribute
   (D) distribution

10. Of the places we visited on our holiday, Niagara Falls were the ------- interesting.
    (A) much
    (B) such
    (C) so
    (D) most

11 According to the latest medical research, the number of people who die of cancer ------- rapidly increased for the past ten years.
    (A) have
    (B) has
    (C) was
    (D) were

12 The police could not ------- a single clue from the crime scene.
    (A) defect
    (B) detect
    (C) interact
    (D) contact

13 We are very pleased ------- that Mr. Lennox will be in charge of the accounting department from next week.
    (A) announcement
    (B) announced
    (C) to announce
    (D) announcing

14 The cheerleaders supported their team with such ------- that the players started to play better and eventually won the game.
    (A) enthusiast
    (B) enthusiasm
    (C) enthusiastic
    (D) enthusiastically

15 My ------- concern is how we can finance this costly project.
    (A) prestigious
    (B) prominent
    (C) primary
    (D) preliminary

16 ------- the children before they went to bed, Mr. Cohen cancelled all his evening appointments.
    (A) By seeing
    (B) As seen
    (C) To be seen
    (D) In order to see

17 All airport security staff get special training in ------- to deal with terrorist attacks.
    (A) how
    (B) way
    (C) often
    (D) calmly

18 We would not have finished this on time without your help, so you deserve a lot of -------.
    (A) complements
    (B) compliments
    (C) implements
    (D) implementation

19 You have to ------- this stamp on the right upper corner of the envelope.
    (A) affix
    (B) afflict
    (C) conflict
    (D) reflect

20 This is a list of ------- asked questions by clients who are interested in product safety.
    (A) frequent
    (B) frequented
    (C) frequently
    (D) frequency

DAY 11 실전 랜덤 연습

PART 5

1. The special sale at Two Hearts Bakery ------- next Saturday.
   (A) begin
   (B) began
   (C) will begin
   (D) has begun

2. The editor of Great Golf Courses' Magazine invited a famous player to write about ------- favorite golf courses.
   (A) he
   (B) him
   (C) his
   (D) himself

3. Please forward the following message ------- the Washington branch to Mr. Smith's office.
   (A) of
   (B) out
   (C) as
   (D) from

4. The manager asks crews to take a rest at least once every two hours while working, no matter ------- busy they are.
   (A) where
   (B) how
   (C) if
   (D) so

5. Please ------- the customer satisfaction form before you check out of the hotel.
   (A) complete
   (B) completion
   (C) completely
   (D) completed

6. Our newly renovated convention center is ------- suited for your next event such as meetings, conferences, and banquets.
   (A) slowly
   (B) gradually
   (C) perfectly
   (D) heavily

7. Ms. Smith ------- to use public transportation instead of private vehicles because of the limited travel budget and for efficiency.
   (A) like
   (B) is liking
   (C) was liking
   (D) would like

8. We want you to give a demonstration ------- the next season's products at the weekly staff meeting.
   (A) of
   (B) along
   (C) during
   (D) into

9. Mr. Johnson solved a problem with the newly installed hardware unit ------- after consulting with the computer technician.
   (A) easily
   (B) ease
   (C) eased
   (D) easy

10. Kayan Chemicals signed a three-million-dollar ------- with Geneva Inc. last week.
    (A) contracting
    (B) contracted
    (C) contracts
    (D) contract

11 We ordered the desktop computer last Tuesday, but it was not shipped until the ------- Friday.
(A) available
(B) future
(C) following
(D) frequent

12 ------- Ms. Krause had a good evaluation, she has a chance to be promoted as general manager.
(A) So that
(B) Since
(C) Besides
(D) Because of

13 Children sixteen and under must be accompanied by ------- a parent or a guardian when visiting the Benson Museum of Art.
(A) and
(B) either
(C) both
(D) neither

14 The Oliver Sports Injury Clinic ------- awards for outstanding technical and professional achievements over the past ten years.
(A) is receiving
(B) receives
(C) would receive
(D) has received

15 Hess Corporation's third-quarter net income ------- increased to $50 million in 2012.
(A) sharp
(B) sharpen
(C) sharply
(D) sharpness

16 In order to achieve their sales target, the employees have to work effectively on -------.
(A) their own
(B) they
(C) themselves
(D) their

17 The company chose fundraising to Community Health Projects as its highest ------- of this year.
(A) change
(B) adjustment
(C) provision
(D) priority

18 Owing to the ------- of the existing facility, we were able to produce more products.
(A) expand
(B) expansive
(C) expansion
(D) expandable

19 For safety reasons, factory employees must wear steel-toed shoes and helmets at ------- times.
(A) every
(B) all
(C) much
(D) any

20 In a rapidly growing city like Las Vegas, ------- use of office space has been increasing over the last five years.
(A) economical
(B) economy
(C) economist
(D) economize

DAY 12 실전 랜덤 연습

PART 5

1. The local factory recently issued its ------- regulations for all their employees.
   (A) safely
   (B) safety
   (C) safe
   (D) safeties

2. ------- process a refund, you need to submit all information and receipts.
   (A) Even as
   (B) Since
   (C) In order to
   (D) Unless

3. At Benson Inc., we believe that we have a ------- to promote health and happiness among our employees.
   (A) responsibility
   (B) responsibly
   (C) responsible
   (D) responsibilities

4. Green Technology has made a successful ------- to next-generation technology.
   (A) suspension
   (B) cooperation
   (C) location
   (D) transition

5. The assistant manager will explain the ------- paper-recycling policy at the staff meeting.
   (A) revising
   (B) revised
   (C) revision
   (D) revise

6. The most generous ------- to the university's fundraising campaign was made by Mr. David Johnson of PedEx Inc.
   (A) donation
   (B) donate
   (C) donor
   (D) donated

7. Ms. Wilson reminded her teammates to read the updated report ------- Wednesday afternoon.
   (A) by
   (B) with
   (C) toward
   (D) among

8. Larry Miller Automobiles will ------- an intense advertising campaign to improve sales.
   (A) strike
   (B) pass
   (C) spend
   (D) launch

9. Business analysts are ------- predicting a merger between Grand Tech and Albertson Works Inc., based on recent news of top level negotiations.
   (A) cautiously
   (B) accidentally
   (C) equally
   (D) tightly

10. As a result of ------- problems with the construction site, the local company introduced new safety measures.
    (A) controlled
    (B) dissolved
    (C) ongoing
    (D) thoughtful

11 The merchandise delivered last week did not match the color of the ones ------- in the catalog.
(A) informed
(B) pictured
(C) sampled
(D) exposed

12 We will discuss ways to enhance ------- among staff members.
(A) cooperation
(B) cooperative
(C) cooperate
(D) cooperated

13 Now that the deadline for submitting the budget report is rapidly -------, we have to work extra hours to finish it on time.
(A) approaching
(B) assigning
(C) setting
(D) declaring

14 Company regulations state that safety goggles and a helmet must ------- be worn on the factory floor.
(A) always
(B) nearly
(C) closely
(D) strongly

15 Compared to the previous version, the new software places ------- emphasis on speed and quality.
(A) greatly
(B) greater
(C) more greatly
(D) as great as

16 The following information must be completed for the agreement to be -------.
(A) validate
(B) validity
(C) valid
(D) validates

17 In order to build customer -------, we must meet or exceed our customers' rising expectations.
(A) brands
(B) honesty
(C) locations
(D) loyalty

18 The company was able to make huge profits at the very beginning ------- it had high start-up costs.
(A) in spite of
(B) on the contrary
(C) consequently
(D) even though

19 The new computer equipment is supposed to be ------- at the end of the month.
(A) set up
(B) taken to
(C) given in
(D) put down

20 The medical equipment should be handled with caution ------- most other high-tech equipment.
(A) despite
(B) aside
(C) unlike
(D) except

DAY 13 실전 랜덤 연습

PART 5

1. The real estate company ------- next month to make an estimate of the property.
   (A) is coming
   (B) came
   (C) had come
   (D) coming

2. The recently hired chef has received a lot of positive feedback for ------- innovative recipe.
   (A) he
   (B) his
   (C) him
   (D) himself

3. The company will conduct mandatory seminars in safety procedures and equipment handling for all shifts at 3 P. M. ------- Monday afternoon.
   (A) on
   (B) to
   (C) of
   (D) at

4. Although the two models of smart phones feature different options, they look ------- identical.
   (A) near
   (B) nearness
   (C) nearly
   (D) nearing

5. After performing an ------- review of Dr. David's proposal on renewable energy, the budget committee has decided to provide full funding for his project.
   (A) extensive
   (B) extent
   (C) extensively
   (D) extensiveness

6. Our printed catalog contains only a partial listing of the ------- that are available to clients in the computer industry.
   (A) customers
   (B) products
   (C) employees
   (D) deposits

7. Company managers have been praised by the ------- of the marketing division.
   (A) perform
   (B) performer
   (C) performing
   (D) performance

8. No one should be allowed to enter the concert hall ------- the musical performance.
   (A) between
   (B) concerning
   (C) during
   (D) inside

9. According to the manager, we should begin by addressing our sales revenue, ------- has fallen 20 percent since last year.
   (A) which
   (B) what
   (C) who
   (D) when

10. The company policy ------- states that each department is responsible for ordering its own office supplies.
    (A) very
    (B) clearly
    (C) slowly
    (D) variably

242 SECTION 2

11 Over 200 radio and television announcers have gathered at the Benson conference center ------- the annual convention.
(A) to attend
(B) attend
(C) attended
(D) attending

12 A formal ------- will be held on Friday evening to honor the winners of the drawing contest.
(A) completion
(B) reception
(C) establishment
(D) accomplishment

13 The ------- brochure details the services provided by Green Thumb Landscaping Service clearly.
(A) enclosure
(B) enclosing
(C) enclosed
(D) enclose

14 Market analysts ------- an increase in sales of smart phones in the forthcoming year.
(A) earn
(B) inspect
(C) hold
(D) predict

15 Mr. Hendrickson regrets that he must decline the invitation to the president dinner party due to a scheduling -------.
(A) conflicts
(B) conflicting
(C) conflict
(D) conflicted

16 International travelers are ------- to check that their passports are valid before traveling abroad.
(A) advanced
(B) registered
(C) advised
(D) praised

17 Ace Trading Inc. has hired a financial consultant John Anderson to ensure a fair ------- of funding across all departments.
(A) distribute
(B) distributional
(C) distribution
(D) distributed

18 Northwest Air reported that all flights out of Las Vegas would be delayed due to ------- weather conditions.
(A) estimated
(B) departed
(C) frequent
(D) severe

19 Of the 300 applicants who applied for the manager position, ------- had more impressive qualifications than Mr. Graham.
(A) few
(B) both
(C) only
(D) each

20 U-Hall Transport handles ------- items with extreme care to prevent any possible shipping damage.
(A) fragile
(B) deliberate
(C) cautious
(D) industrious

DAY 14 실전 랜덤 연습

PART 5

1. Employees should call the local office to ------- ground transportation as soon as their plane arrives at the airport.
   (A) arrive
   (B) proceed
   (C) communicate
   (D) arrange

2. After ------- reviewing the plans for the new manufacturing facility, the safety inspectors made some recommendations.
   (A) faithfully
   (B) seriously
   (C) carefully
   (D) extremely

3. The financial analysts emphasized that the available data must be interpreted -------, until further studies have been completed.
   (A) cautious
   (B) cautiously
   (C) caution
   (D) cautionary

4. During recent job interviews, interviewers were surprised by the candidates' ------- technical experience.
   (A) lack of
   (B) so few
   (C) hardly any
   (D) least

5. ------- the film *Harpy's Journey* received such a positive review, HJ Studios is planning a sequel.
   (A) Owing to
   (B) When
   (C) Although
   (D) Because

6. The company achieved an increase in earnings, but its profits did not ------- executives' expectations.
   (A) meet
   (B) surface
   (C) apply
   (D) seem

7. The World Handy I-6 mobile phone is one of the most ------- models on the market because it has many useful features.
   (A) competitor
   (B) competitive
   (C) competitively
   (D) competition

8. Outgoing vice president Peter Smith celebrated his retirement at a private dinner held ------- for his closest colleagues.
   (A) gradually
   (B) nearly
   (C) exclusively
   (D) precisely

9. Mr. Brown explained the proposed project while he ------- a lunch meeting with the new clients.
   (A) has
   (B) was having
   (C) will have
   (D) having

10. Over the past ten years, Detroit Motors has developed a ------- for providing the best customer service in the automotive industry.
    (A) destination
    (B) reputation
    (C) renewal
    (D) transfer

244 SECTION 2

11 ------- hiring a well-known athlete to endorse athletic shoes, Trend Lead Group is expecting a sales growth of 3 percent.

(A) By
(B) Up
(C) About
(D) To

12 Mr. Smith believes that it will be ------- for KCU Finance to consider expanding into the European countries before its rivals do.

(A) advantage
(B) advantages
(C) advantaged
(D) advantageous

13 Due to unforeseen -------, the Provo Dance Company was forced to cancel its performance tonight at the Varsity theater.

(A) circumstances
(B) qualifications
(C) classifications
(D) instances

14 Mr. Manning dealt with his clients' last-minute requests efficiently and with great -------.

(A) profession
(B) professional
(C) professionally
(D) professionalism

15 New safety regulations approved last month ------- all workers wear hard hats and safety gears in construction areas.

(A) assemble
(B) mandate
(C) investigate
(D) organize

16 Since most employees in the human resources department will be attending conferences in April, they prefer that the company's picnic ------- until May.

(A) postponed
(B) be postponed
(C) to postpone
(D) postponing

17 Five more customer service representatives were hired last month so that customer requests can be handled more -------.

(A) efficiently
(B) nearly
(C) largely
(D) particularly

18 Researchers at Morgan Inc., gather ------- information from international sources in order to forecast economic trends for the next year.

(A) utmost
(B) comprehensive
(C) eventual
(D) industrious

19 Unless otherwise stated, all content posted on this Web site is the ------- property of the Breeden Pharmacy.

(A) limiting
(B) observant
(C) considerate
(D) exclusive

20 This machine is programmed to run from 8 A.M. to 5 P.M., ------- staff members are present.

(A) during
(B) while
(C) whereas
(D) through

DAY 15 실전 랜덤 연습

PART 5

1. After John's promotion, ------- is going to be responsible for human resources management.
   (A) him
   (B) his
   (C) himself
   (D) he

2. Mr. Anderson, the retiring head chef, has a reputation for ------- efficiency and creativity in his recipes.
   (A) and
   (B) both
   (C) either
   (D) rather

3. Baek Electronic's latest TV model ------- a clearer display than previous models did.
   (A) produce
   (B) produces
   (C) product
   (D) producing

4. ------- further information, you can visit our Web site at www.bestshopping.com.
   (A) From
   (B) Of
   (C) For
   (D) By

5. ------- for the K-pop music competition must be submitted by October 20.
   (A) Enter
   (B) Entries
   (C) Being entered
   (D) Entering

6. Clients of Dunning Bank can ------- access account information from their workplace at anytime.
   (A) easily
   (B) easy
   (C) easing
   (D) ease

7. The chief executive officer of Simpson Electronics congratulated the sales staff members on the ------- work they had done.
   (A) excellent
   (B) interested
   (C) grateful
   (D) absolute

8. Regrettably, Ms. Han cannot attend the trade conference, but Mr. Johnson will represent the firm -------.
   (A) where
   (B) this
   (C) there
   (D) when

9. Street Art Exhibition will be delayed ------- bad weather conditions.
   (A) even though
   (B) due to
   (C) since
   (D) besides

10. The human resources department's delay in dealing with Mr. Charlton's paperwork may ------- him from launching his new business.
    (A) begin
    (B) hurry
    (C) prevent
    (D) enhance

11 Ms. Joan ------- finds time to mentor accounting students, even after an outstanding 20-year career in the field.
(A) once
(B) far
(C) yet
(D) still

12 Mr. Choi's Fitness Center requests that all staff members participating in Neo Fitness Trend Seminar make ------- for their trip.
(A) arranges
(B) arranged
(C) arranging
(D) arrangements

13 All the applicants for the position were very experienced, but Mr. Ruben's interview was the most -------.
(A) impressive
(B) impressing
(C) impressed
(D) impressively

14 Prior to applying for a ------- or permit, please visit our Web site to check the requirements we set.
(A) license
(B) licensor
(C) licensing
(D) licensed

15 Mrs. Lee is ------- in charge of quality assurance processes for Blue Peel goods.
(A) slowly
(B) nearly
(C) primarily
(D) variously

16 All the employees of DMC Corporation have to keep record of hours ------- work.
(A) them
(B) their
(C) those
(D) they

17 Because the deadline is coming around the corner, Ms. Harry has been asked to edit the second-quarter sales report -------.
(A) quickly
(B) quicken
(C) quickened
(D) quickness

18 All of the employees of KS Telecommunications are invited to take part in a May 18 workshop ------- maintaining both their physical and mental health.
(A) at
(B) with
(C) on
(D) over

19 The marketing team at Dong-Pyo Electronics initially had problems with the advertising campaigns for the new product, but now everything -------.
(A) is correcting
(B) was correcting
(C) will be correcting
(D) has been corrected

20 If you plan to attend the TIC band concert tonight, you are advised to buy tickets today because seating is -------.
(A) guided
(B) timely
(C) early
(D) limited

DAY 16 실전 랜덤 연습

PART 5

1. The new company policy is expected to give more flexibility to accounting staff members in selecting ------- to work in the office or from home.
   (A) which
   (B) while
   (C) what
   (D) whether

2. Your signature implies that you agree to call BSW's Automobile Company's service center if your car -------.
   (A) picks up
   (B) hangs up
   (C) turns down
   (D) breaks down

3. All the members in attendance will have an opportunity to ask questions ------- after the presentation on the research.
   (A) immediacy
   (B) immediate
   (C) immediateness
   (D) immediately

4. Mrs. Simpson advises customers about the new modern home decor styles at her interior-design ------- in New York.
   (A) sketch
   (B) solution
   (C) stylist
   (D) studio

5. The local council is planning to invite to the public hearing all residents that are ------- about the proposed landfill on Dennis Avenue.
   (A) concern
   (B) concerns
   (C) concerned
   (D) concerning

6. Most of the pictures ------- the book aid readers in understanding the text.
   (A) among
   (B) throughout
   (C) during
   (D) toward

7. The ideal applicant for the marketing representative position at ABC Supplies should be creative and have a sociable -------.
   (A) personal
   (B) personality
   (C) personally
   (D) personalize

8. Employees at the Smart Box company have ------- new packaging ideas for the smartphone.
   (A) thought
   (B) based
   (C) resulted
   (D) developed

9. The research team staff members suggested some highly ------- measures to decrease the production costs at BOB Cosmetics.
   (A) effective
   (B) total
   (C) raised
   (D) complete

10. The summer schedules for subways commuters in Washington D.C. ------- on June 13.
    (A) will be published
    (B) will publish
    (C) are publishing
    (D) publishes

11 Ms. Anderson was recently promoted to the regional manager for her ------- remarkable contributions toward the success of Max Finance.

(A) exactly
(B) jointly
(C) hardly
(D) consistently

12 While the design of the new football stadium is -------, the location is not very accessible to people living in suburban areas.

(A) attraction
(B) attractive
(C) attracted
(D) attractively

13 Bear Technologies is maintaining the highest ------- of workplace safety in every manufacturing unit.

(A) standards
(B) guides
(C) documents
(D) precautions

14 Perris Inc. is going to have a special stockholder's meeting to discuss Zebra Auto's ------- needs to widen the appeal of its sports utility vehicles.

(A) urgent
(B) urgency
(C) urgently
(D) urgencies

15 Employees of the research team were not ------- expecting the good responses that their presentations received from the sales division.

(A) full
(B) fully
(C) fuller
(D) fullness

16 Since the city library will be ------- its hours, citizens will have increased access to the facility.

(A) reaching
(B) submitting
(C) extending
(D) offering

17 City leaders agreed that the installation will be ------- to the community, even though the expense of setting up a water drainage system seemed relatively high.

(A) conclusive
(B) financial
(C) beneficial
(D) regulated

18 Hello Food's coffee bags are wrapped separately in foil ------- to keep the product fresh as to add to its appearance.

(A) so far
(B) so that
(C) as much
(D) as long as

19 Sun Publication Company delivered 130,000 books to local bookstores on September 6, fulfilling its contractual ------- two months early.

(A) surplus
(B) indication
(C) forecast
(D) obligation

20 Mango Travel ------- plans activities to ensure trouble-free tours as well as provides the best flights and accommodations.

(A) meticulously
(B) considerably
(C) enormously
(D) compatibly

DAY 17 실전 랜덤 연습

PART 5

1. The newly developed data system considerably ------- the number of errors in MEGA Corporation's digital documents.
   (A) having reduced
   (B) reduce
   (C) reduced
   (D) reducing

2. Mr. Simpson visits the plant ------- in Detroit on a regular basis to check that its safety rules are well observed.
   (A) locate
   (B) located
   (C) locating
   (D) to locate

3. AZ Supermarket will be the fourth business to open in the building ------- the Seeley apartment complex.
   (A) between
   (B) among
   (C) near
   (D) onto

4. We are now looking for people who can willingly work 12-hour -------.
   (A) orders
   (B) permits
   (C) shifts
   (D) entries

5. Manchester-based Bobby's Hamburger has ------- good relationships with local food suppliers.
   (A) led to
   (B) developed
   (C) practiced
   (D) reserved

6. Some shoppers complained that SAC Electronics' catalogue did not include enough detail in its product -------.
   (A) describe
   (B) descriptions
   (C) descriptive
   (D) describable

7. One of the articles in this week's Good Morning Today paper showed that the number of employees working from home has risen ------- since about ten years ago.
   (A) efficiently
   (B) dramatically
   (C) openly
   (D) hastily

8. Having equipment malfunction that needs -------, you can submit a request directly to the maintenance team.
   (A) concerning
   (B) repairing
   (C) establishing
   (D) determining

9. Most of the changes suggested to our customer service center have ------- been implemented.
   (A) already
   (B) a great deal
   (C) soon
   (D) by far

10. Customers can explore the beach in front of Family Hotel with a surfboard ------- take a guided tour riding on a luxury yacht.
    (A) as
    (B) so
    (C) if
    (D) or

11 Thanks to a recently installed high-speed rail system, business trips to distant cities is easily -------.
   (A) managing
   (B) manage
   (C) manageable
   (D) manageability

12 Dr. Paul is not always able to meet with ------- himself, since so many medical representatives ask him to bring samples to the laboratory.
   (A) they
   (B) their
   (C) theirs
   (D) them

13 The new GAD Inc. water pump system will be available for both lease and purchase in response to customer ------.
   (A) demands
   (B) payments
   (C) conventions
   (D) designs

14 The ------- growth of sales astonished a lot of industry analysts who had predicted a slow retail season.
   (A) short
   (B) poor
   (C) virtual
   (D) steady

15 Mr. Watson, as a chief manager of Men's clothing shop, ------- responsibility for all sales events.
   (A) assuming
   (B) to assume
   (C) assume
   (D) will assume

16 To generate more business during evening hours, VRP Restaurant is going to move to Ruby Street, ------- the Swan Department Store.
   (A) among
   (B) opposite
   (C) throughout
   (D) upon

17 The fence that ------- Eastern Zoo will be installed using recycled materials.
   (A) was enclosing
   (B) will enclosed
   (C) enclosed
   (D) will enclose

18 Customers of Town Bank have been ------- unaffected by the new computer system recently installed in the customer service department.
   (A) larger
   (B) large
   (C) largely
   (D) largeness

19 Members of the David Institute's committee ------- for an hour upon suggested changes to the budget for additional lectures.
   (A) mediated
   (B) deliberated
   (C) regarded
   (D) supposed

20 The Ministry of Environment allows ------- access to greenbelt districts for the sake of national interest.
   (A) restrict
   (B) restrictedly
   (C) restricted
   (D) restriction

DAY 18 실전 랜덤 연습

PART 5

1. The merger of two major eyeglass makers will make the country's largest ------- of customizable eyewear.
   (A) produce
   (B) producer
   (C) product
   (D) productive

2. Mr. Dennis ------- announced at a news conference this afternoon that the company had been acquired by Son Tech.
   (A) customarily
   (B) externally
   (C) observantly
   (D) formally

3. Mr. Nelson has only been working as a magazine editor for a short time, ------- he has been writing magazine essays for many years.
   (A) even though
   (B) despite
   (C) when
   (D) for

4. Prospective students should weigh each option carefully against -------, because both full-time and part-time business programs have lots of benefits.
   (A) other
   (B) the other
   (C) another's
   (D) the one

5. Ms. Allen was pleased to find the revised version of the song ------- more competitive than the original draft.
   (A) considerable
   (B) considering
   (C) considerably
   (D) consider

6. Mr. Simon announced that MIS Company will move ------- with plans to enlarge its oil refinery at the press conference.
   (A) around
   (B) forward
   (C) altogether
   (D) never

7. Some Olive Photography customers say that they are ------- to buy the new Jenssen camera model because it is not considered user-friendly.
   (A) suspicious
   (B) uncertain
   (C) reluctant
   (D) worrisome

8. Merci Hotel in Korea is usually fully booked, owing to its ------- to main tourist attractions.
   (A) exclusion
   (B) proximity
   (C) efficiency
   (D) availability

9. Entertainment agent, Mr. Long is famous for skillful ------- for the artists he represents.
   (A) cooperation
   (B) conducts
   (C) negotiations
   (D) remarks

10. Sera is responsible for approving all expense reports ------- those for overseas travel.
    (A) aside
    (B) even if
    (C) additionally
    (D) except

11 The position of sales manager requires ------- in the face of obstacles and willingness to take on unexpected responsibilities and challenges.
    (A) attendance
    (B) abundance
    (C) persistence
    (D) frequency

12 Tony Financial recommends long-term investments that are ------- against fluctuations to maximize the value of its customer's portfolios.
    (A) secure
    (B) security
    (C) secures
    (D) securing

13 The survey suggests that the city board did not ------- address problems local business owners have regarding revised zoning laws.
    (A) adequately
    (B) objectionably
    (C) approximately
    (D) mutually

14 Expanding the London storehouse should result in a 30 percent ------- in storage capacity.
    (A) to increase
    (B) increase
    (C) increased
    (D) increasingly

15 The president of Ohio Industries is confident that the decrease in recent profits will not ------- affect the company's stock price.
    (A) adversary
    (B) adverse
    (C) adversely
    (D) adversity

16 Over the last six years, the Harry Wilson Foundation has made ------- donations to the Dawson Institute of Pharmaceutical Research in Bradford.
    (A) substantial
    (B) contented
    (C) generating
    (D) acquired

17 ------- the additional hours Dr. Park contributed to his project, he was not able to finish his study before the deadline.
    (A) During
    (B) In spite of
    (C) Even though
    (D) As if

18 Since it has a lot of loyal customers, Blue Gift shop ------- the fierce competition against new stores in the area until now.
    (A) withstanding
    (B) to withstand
    (C) is withstood
    (D) has withstood

19 Dr. King explained in her presentation how both scientists and farmers are ------- to the success of local preservation efforts.
    (A) diligent
    (B) prepared
    (C) displayed
    (D) integral

20 The agenda was distributed to each member ------- the first conference in order to help committee members prepare for the series of upcoming conferences.
    (A) in favor of
    (B) prior to
    (C) owing to
    (D) in case of

DAY 19 실전 랜덤 연습

PART 5

1. The Seoul Fair's most famous event is the cooking ------.
   (A) competing
   (B) competitive
   (C) competes
   (D) competition

2. Buyers of this product are advised ------- the contents of the package in a cool, dry place.
   (A) storing
   (B) store
   (C) stores
   (D) to store

3. Ministry of National Defense has ------- the launch of a new warship in the West Sea.
   (A) informed
   (B) joined
   (C) announced
   (D) applied

4. After Ms. Lee finishes the report, ------- will be submitted to Mr. Newton.
   (A) it
   (B) itself
   (C) other
   (D) them

5. Our supervisor, Mr. Rogers, was ------- invited to visit the prospective client's office in Tokyo.
   (A) closely
   (B) perfectly
   (C) recently
   (D) highly

6. A salary increase ------- ACE Shipping Company is based on performance evaluation.
   (A) as
   (B) to
   (C) on
   (D) at

7. The information technology department suggests that all staff members back up their computer data on a ------- basis.
   (A) regular
   (B) regularly
   (C) regularity
   (D) regulating

8. Mason's work on recent fashion trends has made his travel -------.
   (A) extensive
   (B) extensively
   (C) extension
   (D) extending

9. Ms. Miller must decide ------- or not to submit the private data to the Federal Bureau of Investigation.
   (A) neither
   (B) whether
   (C) either
   (D) unless

10. As a reminder, all travel expenses must be reviewed by Ms. Moore or one of ------- colleagues in the accounting department.
    (A) her
    (B) hers
    (C) she
    (D) herself

11. Bella's Sweet now offers some delicious new candy flavors, in ------- to customer's demands.
    (A) respond
    (B) response
    (C) responsive
    (D) responded

12. All food products must be ------- by a hygienic manager before being approved for distribution.
    (A) inspection
    (B) inspected
    (C) inspect
    (D) inspecting

13. Because Mr. Baek has served here at Nice Insurance for ten years, he is one of our most ------- employees now.
    (A) previous
    (B) included
    (C) experienced
    (D) actual

14. Ms. Sanders can successfully finish his work this Wednesday ------- the computer software arrives on time.
    (A) if
    (B) or
    (C) even
    (D) both

15. Because of unexpected repair work, electricity cutoff notices were posted early ------- morning throughout the company building.
    (A) those
    (B) this
    (C) which
    (D) whose

16. When arriving ------- Ipswich Town, the engineering technician will be given access to the laboratory.
    (A) on
    (B) around
    (C) from
    (D) into

17. While the landing is under construction, travelers are advised to use ------- when riding in Lucky Ferry.
    (A) cautious
    (B) cautiously
    (C) caution
    (D) cautiousness

18. Workers who have not ------- handed in their time records must do so by 7:30 P.M. today.
    (A) only
    (B) earlier
    (C) yet
    (D) rather

19. All workers are required to wear protective work clothing and eyewear before ------- the factory.
    (A) stepping
    (B) entering
    (C) processing
    (D) producing

20. Murrell Labs is expected to reopen -------, because all the damaged machinery has already been repaired.
    (A) initially
    (B) equally
    (C) shortly
    (D) nearly

DAY 20 실전 랜덤 연습

PART 5

1. Timon Corporation is interested in exploring new business opportunities as part of an ongoing ------- to enlarge its production lines.
   (A) growth
   (B) effort
   (C) rise
   (D) strength

2. Ms. Adams ------- her firm two years ago while she was studying in Berlin University.
   (A) started
   (B) had started
   (C) would start
   (D) will be started

3. ------- extended negotiations, the president of Emson Hospital and his counterpart from Jason Medical Center reached an agreement about new medical treatments.
   (A) Expect
   (B) After
   (C) Unlike
   (D) About

4. Bicycles are the ------- means of transportation for many people commuting to their workplace.
   (A) prefer
   (B) preferred
   (C) preference
   (D) preferring

5. KS Corporation will open new manufacturing plants in ------- that are more convenient to operations currently under construction.
   (A) locate
   (B) location
   (C) located
   (D) locations

6. ------- you pay for the product on time, we will be able to ship your package as scheduled.
   (A) As long as
   (B) Prior to
   (C) Despite
   (D) In order to

7. Expecting a higher ------- for organic fruits next season, local farmers want to raise their yield by 20 percent.
   (A) efficiency
   (B) demand
   (C) influx
   (D) benefit

8. Invitations to the monthly charity event were sent to all 40 board members, but ------- will be able to attend.
   (A) little
   (B) whoever
   (C) few
   (D) so

9. Main Corporation's annual report showed that the volume of its export to China had risen by 3.5 percent compared to the ------- year.
   (A) precede
   (B) precedes
   (C) preceded
   (D) preceding

10. Mr. Ahn has been promoted to director of NLLP Education's Singapore branch ------- he can focus on all the instructors' attitude toward students.
    (A) nor
    (B) instead of
    (C) so that
    (D) before

256 SECTION 2

11. Flights in and out of Incheon International Airport are frequently postponed because of ------- on the runways.
    (A) congested
    (B) congestion
    (C) congestive
    (D) congests

12. At the previous company banquet, 31 workers were ------- with special awards for having served the company for 30 years.
    (A) advocated
    (B) assumed
    (C) administered
    (D) recognized

13. During his business trip to France, Mr. Dickens ------- visited some of the fabric suppliers there.
    (A) brief
    (B) briefer
    (C) briefly
    (D) briefness

14. DBC Renovation may charge more than the original estimate ------- additional time be required to set up cabinets.
    (A) in fact
    (B) through
    (C) should
    (D) when

15. New customers who open an account today at the new DX regional branch will be ------- from paying service charges for two months.
    (A) complimentary
    (B) exempt
    (C) privileged
    (D) offered

16. Each of the participants in the Space safety course will be ------- with a flotation device.
    (A) accustomed
    (B) donated
    (C) distributed
    (D) outfitted

17. Rexter's DS340 cutting machine is ------- of all the company's industrial products.
    (A) represent
    (B) representation
    (C) represented
    (D) representative

18. New workers ------- themselves with the workplace safety guidelines prior to attending next week's training session.
    (A) are familiar to
    (B) will be familiar with
    (C) been familiarized
    (D) should familiarize

19. The e-mail explained why the present procedures were ------- and how proposed alternative strategies would be able to conserve the company's resources.
    (A) vacant
    (B) scattered
    (C) deserted
    (D) wasteful

20. ------- the November newsletter is published, the final decision on whether or not to sign the maintenance contract will be made.
    (A) in order for
    (B) By the time
    (C) As much as
    (D) Now that

어휘 집중 연습

Day 01	연습 문제 1	260
Day 02	연습 문제 2	262
Day 03	연습 문제 3	264
Day 04	연습 문제 4	266
Day 05	연습 문제 5	268
Day 06	연습 문제 6	270
Day 07	연습 문제 7	272
Day 08	연습 문제 8	274
Day 09	연습 문제 9	276
Day 10	연습 문제 10	278
Day 11	연습 문제 11	280
Day 12	연습 문제 12	282
Day 13	연습 문제 13	284
Day 14	연습 문제 14	286
Day 15	연습 문제 15	288
Day 16	연습 문제 16	290
Day 17	연습 문제 17	292
Day 18	연습 문제 18	294
Day 19	연습 문제 19	296
Day 20	연습 문제 20	298

DAY 01 어휘 집중 연습

PART 5

1. The ATP grocery store is very famous for a wide ------- of products for its customers.
   (A) group
   (B) variety
   (C) kind
   (D) plenty

2. Please refrain ------- using your cell phones while in the theater in order not to disturb others.
   (A) from
   (B) to
   (C) over
   (D) by

3. You are not ------- for a refund if you don't bring your receipt with you.
   (A) available
   (B) dependable
   (C) entitled
   (D) eligible

4. -------, the Jason Manufacturing is expected to hire additional employees to meet the increasing demand.
   (A) Roughly
   (B) Differently
   (C) Strangely
   (D) Fortunately

5. The flight to Los Angeles takes ------- one hour, unless there are air traffic control delays or weather problems.
   (A) ultimately
   (B) closely
   (C) approximately
   (D) neatly

6. Some industry analysts talked about the ------- of rising oil prices on the global economy.
   (A) methods
   (B) effects
   (C) suggestions
   (D) recommendations

7. That large corporation is not considered ------- because it has always continued on a conservative course.
   (A) profound
   (B) progressive
   (C) proficient
   (D) prohibitive

8. In order to maintain the freshness of produce, all the products should be delivered -------.
   (A) recently
   (B) previously
   (C) promptly
   (D) approximately

9 According to the company policy, ------- to approve of any legal documents will be given only to department heads.
   (A) enrollment
   (B) admission
   (C) certificate
   (D) authority

10 After the 3-month renovation period, TERA Fitness has ------- its original schedule for customers.
   (A) resumed
   (B) recovered
   (C) responded
   (D) replied

11 Our store policy says that all the orders are delivered to clients safely ------- three working days.
   (A) at
   (B) from
   (C) for
   (D) within

12 The applicants' résumés for a full-time office assistant position should list their experience in ------- order.
   (A) chronological
   (B) regular
   (C) recent
   (D) simultaneous

13 Unless your order is ------- large, we will have it delivered in one box.
   (A) respectively
   (B) efficiently
   (C) particularly
   (D) randomly

14 When hiring security personnel, the personnel department will take into ------- all the valid information on candidates.
   (A) perspective
   (B) consideration
   (C) effect
   (D) speculation

15 ------- pressure from the public eventually forced the president to resign from the office.
   (A) Mounting
   (B) Climbing
   (C) Straightening
   (D) Intimidating

DAY 02 어휘 집중 연습

PART 5

1. Over one million dollars' ------- of TV commercials will be aired across the country soon.
   (A) expense
   (B) worth
   (C) cost
   (D) estimation

2. Texon Play decided to reduce the prices of its new games for the first two days in ------- countries.
   (A) much
   (B) affluent
   (C) several
   (D) affordable

3. You are not able to ------- files bigger than 50 megabytes through this system for security reasons.
   (A) allocate
   (B) attach
   (C) alternate
   (D) allow

4. Medical school graduates ------- to pursue a career at one of the major hospitals are facing the toughest job market in 15 years.
   (A) declining
   (B) looking
   (C) considering
   (D) accessing

5. Despite several last-minute changes made to the -------, Bostic CEO John Malcolm agreed to accept it.
   (A) proposal
   (B) intent
   (C) expression
   (D) recommendation

6. Our new line of products will be ------- at reasonable prices in over 300 stores nationwide.
   (A) accessible
   (B) considerate
   (C) available
   (D) reliable

7. Mr. Durek, director of the planning department, suggested that a few of the ------- be changed in light of the company's financial situation.
   (A) causes
   (B) proofs
   (C) aims
   (D) answers

8. The government agency did not ------- understand how serious the current problem could be in a month.
   (A) fully
   (B) approximately
   (C) frequently
   (D) annually

9. Due to the company downsizing its personnel in response to a poor economy, we will no longer be able to ------- our clients high quality consulting service.
   (A) suggest
   (B) offer
   (C) maintain
   (D) provide

10. Mica will ------- be chosen for the employee of the year award because of her great contributions she demonstrated during the project last quarter.
    (A) regularly
    (B) slightly
    (C) undoubtedly
    (D) infirmly

11. You should send this ------- of this memo on policy changes to all the managers yourself.
    (A) dot
    (B) number
    (C) copy
    (D) sign

12. The final sales figures set by the management for next year at the annual planning meeting have been -------.
    (A) overflowed
    (B) exceeded
    (C) overcome
    (D) overestimated

13. Mr. Wallen will be held responsible for the ------- of all the on-site workers during the period of construction.
    (A) promotion
    (B) distribution
    (C) coordination
    (D) activation

14. When complaining about a problem, you make sure to be as ------- as possible in order not to have any misunderstanding.
    (A) long
    (B) soon
    (C) outstanding
    (D) specific

15. Nagle Research conducted the poll and it ------- that almost 60 percent of the respondents want the president to step down.
    (A) predicts
    (B) provides
    (C) indicates
    (D) assumes

DAY 03 어휘 집중 연습

PART 5

1. The small local businesses around major tourist attractions ------- to hire additional temporary staff during the peak season.
   (A) intend
   (B) suggest
   (C) introduce
   (D) alleviate

2. The proposed relocation of the company headquarters from Russia to Germany is still ------- on the final authorization of the board of directors.
   (A) ultimate
   (B) thoughtful
   (C) contingent
   (D) voluntary

3. After the last training session on the financial planning and analysis, all the trainees were invited to attend the light -------.
   (A) admissions
   (B) refreshments
   (C) expansions
   (D) entrances

4. H&P Computers will ------- you for computers and other accessories that you purchase from our online stores after you receive them.
   (A) bill
   (B) estimate
   (C) assess
   (D) write

5. With the discount coupon you download from our Web site, you can renew your service plan for as ------- as $40 per month.
   (A) small
   (B) little
   (C) petty
   (D) few

6. Josh has asked for ------- to the annual sales data so that he can complete the sales projection report.
   (A) enrollment
   (B) agreement
   (C) approach
   (D) access

7. The president had to cancel all the ------- schedules because there was an urgent meeting with the important client from Japan.
   (A) subsequent
   (B) sustainable
   (C) successful
   (D) suspending

8. Fueled by the increasing demand, the Malaysia's cocoa industry has grown ------- over the last ten years.
   (A) relatively
   (B) rapidly
   (C) roughly
   (D) recently

9 Those experts provided us with a thorough ------- of the latest food market trends after putting together all the sales data.

(A) foundation
(B) affirmation
(C) analysis
(D) deployment

10 All the construction workers are required to wear protective gears which ------- them properly.

(A) resemble
(B) hold
(C) place
(D) fit

11 The newly elected president has once more confirmed his ------- pledge to resolve the current economic problems.

(A) irrelevant
(B) disinterested
(C) unwavering
(D) improper

12 Before vacating your apartment, you must give the management office written ------- at least 30 days in advance.

(A) distribution
(B) addition
(C) completion
(D) notification

13 The agenda for the annual financial meeting ------- the analysis of operations, the meeting attendees, and the detailed meeting schedules.

(A) includes
(B) encloses
(C) devotes
(D) registers

14 The company has decided to outsource the safety control company which will ------- with increasing workplace accidents.

(A) effect
(B) deal
(C) affect
(D) support

15 Hotel accommodation and rental cars will be covered by the organizing committee, but additional stay is the participants' -------.

(A) response
(B) negotiation
(C) responsibility
(D) cooperation

DAY 04 어휘 집중 연습

PART 5

1. Though not required, a little bit of experience in network solution will be an -------.
   (A) adoption
   (B) alleviation
   (C) advantage
   (D) accumulation

2. Tickets to Master G's special concert will be given to those who use our online VOD streaming services and winners will be ------- chosen at the end of the month.
   (A) randomly
   (B) ambiguously
   (C) unclearly
   (D) carelessly

3. The trade center is ------- under construction and is expected to be completed in about two months.
   (A) deliberately
   (B) exclusively
   (C) presently
   (D) reluctantly

4. Applicants are asked to ------- their job preference by checking the box on the online application form.
   (A) indicate
   (B) develop
   (C) generate
   (D) allocate

5. The documents must be reviewed by the government inspector ------- in order to avoid any possible mistakes.
   (A) closely
   (B) narrowly
   (C) generally
   (D) highly

6. SHS Electronics ------- as a strong competitor in the semiconductor industry after its merger with GM Tech.
   (A) collapsed
   (B) emerged
   (C) revolutionized
   (D) translated

7. You are required to get a parking ------- at the gate before you enter the facility.
   (A) warrant
   (B) permit
   (C) authority
   (D) allowance

8. Effective March 1st, the new leave policy will be ------- to resolve the problems that occurred last year.
   (A) realized
   (B) implemented
   (C) solicited
   (D) designed

9 Passengers are reminded that any luggage that is ------- after two months will be sent to the Lost & Found center.

(A) unclaimed
(B) redeemed
(C) nominated
(D) detected

10 For detailed information on the new savings plans you can switch to, you can ------- with one of our financial consultants.

(A) tell
(B) attend
(C) speak
(D) telephone

11 Our experienced advisers can ------- you in managing your accounts.

(A) tell
(B) lend
(C) assist
(D) explain

12 It is widely believed that the politician under prosecution is closely ------- with industry insiders.

(A) associated
(B) disappointed
(C) mixed
(D) satisfied

13 If the class you registered for is full or not available, your name will ------- be placed on a waiting list.

(A) considerably
(B) intermittently
(C) progressively
(D) automatically

14 The unemployment rate for the last 2 years has risen ------- due to the long-term economic recession.

(A) finally
(B) significantly
(C) fundamentally
(D) impartially

15 Please remit ------- online if you want to renew your service.

(A) mail
(B) payment
(C) pay
(D) check

어휘 집중 연습

PART 5

1. Kroll Accounting will offer some monetary ------- to those who have volunteered to transfer to the new branch office in Texas.
   (A) formats
   (B) measures
   (C) incentives
   (D) types

2. In response to growing demands for the online shopping, the company is looking for those who ------- in web design and developments.
   (A) considers
   (B) measures
   (C) specializes
   (D) receives

3. Headquartered in Los Angeles, Saint Electronics is an ------- company which has operations in 12 countries worldwide.
   (A) accomplished
   (B) encouraged
   (C) increased
   (D) implemented

4. The fragrant ------- of this lotion has gained unprecedented popularity among many young customers in the country.
   (A) gas
   (B) blaze
   (C) stench
   (D) scent

5. Some reviews indicate that the newly released film depends heavily on ------- effects.
   (A) foreseeable
   (B) optical
   (C) unforeseen
   (D) visual

6. If you want some ------- of our lines of products, please visit our newly updated Web site.
   (A) expectations
   (B) samples
   (C) shapes
   (D) frames

7. Customers seeking help with a technical problem should ------- it in detail.
   (A) dispose
   (B) denounce
   (C) describe
   (D) derive

8. Please make sure that all the delivery personnel deliver the ------- ingredients to restaurants promptly.
   (A) breakable
   (B) rotten
   (C) rusted
   (D) perishable

9 The company is seeking a few suitable candidates for the position of plant ------- who will be in charge of supervising the production process.
   (A) investor
   (B) manager
   (C) consumer
   (D) arbitrator

10 You will see all the technological ------- in automobile production at the Science and Technology Museum.
   (A) advances
   (B) communications
   (C) excavations
   (D) limitations

11 The research conducted by Krieger Informatics ------- that consumer preferences has changed significantly over the last ten years.
   (A) amplifies
   (B) constitutes
   (C) illustrates
   (D) jeopardizes

12 With an additional ------- of $50, you can upgrade your room to the premium suite.
   (A) charge
   (B) claim
   (C) number
   (D) worth

13 Job applicants are requested to ------- the other required documents to the personnel office no later than March 27.
   (A) submit
   (B) revise
   (C) apply
   (D) collect

14 Steve Marl has been ------- to director of public relations at Astella Pharmaceuticals.
   (A) tried
   (B) applied
   (C) promoted
   (D) agreed

15 Due to the lawsuit filed by a number of customers, industry analysts ------- that MS Foods' restaurant chains will go out of business.
   (A) expand
   (B) expect
   (C) excuse
   (D) exchange

DAY 06 어휘 집중 연습

PART 5

1. The experiment for the last six months turns out to be meaningless because it was ------- conducted.
   (A) carelessly
   (B) neutrally
   (C) objectively
   (D) reluctantly

2. We are currently looking for a ------- supplier who can consistently provide us with high quality dry wood.
   (A) accessible
   (B) applicable
   (C) sustainable
   (D) reliable

3. ------- 80 percent of the respondents told us that the quality of the new products improved a lot.
   (A) Absolutely
   (B) Generally
   (C) Nearly
   (D) Well

4. Those who want to participate in the company stress management seminar have to ------- up for it before this Friday.
   (A) mark
   (B) write
   (C) forward
   (D) sign

5. Starting February 1, the manufacturing plant of Copen Ltd. will be shut down for ------- which will take around two months.
   (A) explanation
   (B) fabrication
   (C) renovation
   (D) salvation

6. The patent for the cell phone design established 20 years ago will ------- this December.
   (A) expire
   (B) intimidate
   (C) specialize
   (D) volunteer

7. User's reviews on the company's new service were mostly favorable except for some ------- about the high price.
   (A) complaint
   (B) praise
   (C) objection
   (D) view

8. Any parcel including fragile items requires ------- handling to avoid any possible damage to contents inside.
   (A) typical
   (B) casual
   (C) careful
   (D) grateful

9 The firm has ------- established a strategic partnership with a fast-growing distribution company to expand its business into a new area.

(A) continually
(B) frequently
(C) recently
(D) urgently

10 W&T Dental Clinic will offer a wide ------- of dental-care services to local residents.

(A) sense
(B) condition
(C) variety
(D) placement

11 Wastler, the company's CEO, has expressed his ------- to push forward the factory expansion plan at the inauguration ceremony.

(A) comfort
(B) increase
(C) importance
(D) willingness

12 The company will launch a series of advertising campaigns to ------- its new image as an innovative player in the market.

(A) compete
(B) complicate
(C) match
(D) memorize

13 It is a bit challenging to complete the large project within our limited -------.

(A) budget
(B) cost
(C) economy
(D) purse

14 Guests of the Vinobeach Hotel are asked to store their belongings ------- in the in-room safe.

(A) securely
(B) broadly
(C) vastly
(D) severely

15 The price of Super Com's new computers will be lower than ------- due to the decrease in the cost of materials.

(A) experimented
(B) organized
(C) anticipated
(D) inclined

DAY 07 어휘 집중 연습

PART 5

1. Turnover rate reduction was one of the most ------- topics at the annual meeting last month.
   (A) abundant
   (B) constant
   (C) important
   (D) potent

2. The Wednesday seminar was clearly ------- to help the staff members understand different aspects of the business.
   (A) compiled
   (B) designed
   (C) eliminated
   (D) hesitated

3. Efforts to ------- the manufacturing process in our Osaka plant should lead us to lower operating costs.
   (A) contact
   (B) simplify
   (C) overweigh
   (D) progress

4. Saito Ginjo's ------- cost-cutting measures resulted in the increased profits in the second quarter this year.
   (A) innovative
   (B) potential
   (C) uncertain
   (D) billable

5. The price of raw materials rose ------- again last month, but industry analysts expect a dramatic decrease in the coming months.
   (A) highly
   (B) slightly
   (C) rarely
   (D) previously

6. Beginning next month, we need to ------- the monthly order of paper from 10 to 15 boxes.
   (A) combine
   (B) invite
   (C) maintain
   (D) increase

7. Ayaka's Bakery offers a ------- of gift items to those who purchase products worth more than $50.
   (A) selection
   (B) pleasure
   (C) compound
   (D) preference

8. A recent survey indicates that workers ------- up to forty-five minutes each day discussing personal matters.
   (A) throw over
   (B) hang on
   (C) buy out
   (D) spend

9 Because of the repeated delay of shipments, the contract with the Japanese shipping company has been -------.
(A) affected
(B) observed
(C) pretended
(D) terminated

10 Since the economy has been recovering from the recession, many companies are expecting increased ------- this year.
(A) costs
(B) amounts
(C) profits
(D) discounts

11 During the ------- five years, the level of on-site workers' safety has been enhanced significantly.
(A) coming
(B) advancing
(C) past
(D) upcoming

12 Additional funds from the government body have been ------- for buying new books for the public library.
(A) announced
(B) allocated
(C) suggested
(D) testified

13 All the speakers for today's committee meeting are asked to ------- presentations to 15 minutes.
(A) attend
(B) vote
(C) follow
(D) limit

14 The site for the new semiconductor plant was chosen because of its ------- location.
(A) excessive
(B) accessible
(C) accommodating
(D) accustomed

15 We have recently hired a very ------- individual who has a strong background in sales.
(A) talented
(B) protected
(C) annoyed
(D) majestic

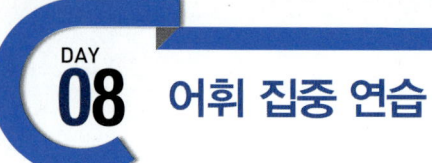

PART 5

1. Exercise is ------- for good health, and walking as little as ten minutes a day may be all you need.
   (A) regional
   (B) grateful
   (C) essential
   (D) final

2. Regular dish-washing soaps and other ------- can contain harsh chemicals that may harm a car's finish.
   (A) detergents
   (B) insights
   (C) detonators
   (D) inspectors

3. Ace Scientific is pleased to ------- a new 1.5 million dollar contract with Associated Aircraft for the sales and installation of a new radar guidance system.
   (A) enclose
   (B) announce
   (C) measure
   (D) bargain

4. The city council has decided to increase the budget for the city renovation project -------.
   (A) substantially
   (B) spontaneously
   (C) unbiasedly
   (D) voluntarily

5. The National Park Ranger Award was presented to Mr. Frigs Cameron by the Governor during a ------- at City Hall.
   (A) ceremony
   (B) solution
   (C) pleasure
   (D) constant

6. Our annual employee retreat will be ------- at Bear Creek Lodge at Yellowstone National Park.
   (A) sustained
   (B) held
   (C) supported
   (D) met

7. The State Fair this year ------- an all-star lineup of bands and singers, including Grammy Award Winner Maria Cypress.
   (A) observes
   (B) transmits
   (C) features
   (d) secures

8. We cannot ------- our products against any external damage caused by misuse or negligence on the part of the user.
   (A) expand
   (B) notice
   (C) afford
   (D) guarantee

9 Employees are required to attend two ------- per year on customer service and sign-up sheets for the next training series will be posted on the employee bulletin board.

(A) conferences
(B) contributions
(C) agendas
(D) prescriptions

10 The construction of the new factory in Ohio is a 100 million dollar -------, which will take over two years to build.

(A) approval
(B) method
(C) format
(D) project

11 One of the maintenance staff members was sent to the sales department office to find out why the printer didn't work -------.

(A) eloquently
(B) finitely
(C) properly
(D) steadily

12 The recent decline in worldwide oil prices is ------- due to the ease in demand and more sources of oil.

(A) nearly
(B) usefully
(C) safely
(D) probably

13 We will merge with a business partner ------- this year, which will increase our market share by 25 percent.

(A) past
(B) next
(C) later
(D) afterwards

14 The funds from the sale of the property will be used ------- the construction of a new factory in Georgia, which will build the semiconductor boards for our products.

(A) along
(B) to
(C) for
(D) while

15 We require a safety inspection of all of our products, before they are considered ------- for use.

(A) total
(B) ready
(C) actual
(D) absolute

DAY 09 어휘 집중 연습

PART 5

1. JJ Capital's market researchers indicate that IT companies are ------- to grow at a rapid rate for many years to come.
   (A) likely
   (B) meaningful
   (C) observant
   (D) pertinent

2. Our company is the ------- producer of LED bulbs for use in the home and in automobiles, supplying 75 percent of market share.
   (A) originated
   (B) leading
   (C) incident
   (D) anticipated

3. I ------- received permission from my department director for a three week vacation to India, which had to be approved by the Assistant Vice President of Marketing since it was over two weeks.
   (A) soon
   (B) finally
   (C) yet
   (D) closely

4. The job advertisement clearly stated that only those with two or more years of work-related experience will be considered -------.
   (A) delicate
   (B) emotional
   (C) qualified
   (D) strengthened

5. The university is expected to ------- all students to be equipped with a tablet PC upon entrance.
   (A) promote
   (B) allow
   (C) accept
   (D) give

6. We will ------- an additional 100 workers for employment in our new Ohio factory, which is scheduled for completion in June of next year.
   (A) recruit
   (B) expand
   (C) revise
   (D) converse

7. Our company should have at least 500 employees working at the Laos plant ------- the end of the year and all positions require membership in the local machinist union.
   (A) against
   (B) between
   (C) by
   (D) under

8. The computer technicians have ------- a virus on the servers, which will require installation and update of new antivirus software.
   (A) diagnosed
   (B) shifted
   (C) collapsed
   (D) responded

9 ------- the company saved considerable money last year, we are able to offer all employees a ten percent across-the-board raise.

(A) Despite
(B) Since
(C) Unless
(D) So

10 All employees must now wear identification badges as a ------- measure in building security, which will be checked upon entry by security guards.

(A) continuous
(B) settled
(C) protective
(D) rival

11 The guys from tech support determined the cause of the downed ------- was a server failure.

(A) relevance
(B) connection
(C) acquaintance
(D) mixture

12 The employee training for the new computer system, including software installation, will take three weeks ------- start to finish.

(A) of
(B) from
(C) by
(D) during

13 Please read the ------- letter regarding our new electric 'Old Time Lantern,' which is will be sold in stores starting next week.

(A) enclosed
(B) opposite
(C) absent
(D) innocent

14 Sales of our ultra-thin line of laptops should reach ------- 50 million dollars this year, due to a rigorous advertising campaign by the marketing division.

(A) farther
(B) aside from
(C) over
(D) in addition to

15 If you wish to receive the magazine mailed to your home, please submit your address to the marketing department ------- the 25th of this month.

(A) at
(B) before
(C) in
(D) upon

DAY 10 어휘 집중 연습

PART 5

1. Our company's profit sharing plan will increase by ------- 10 percent beginning on the first of next year.
   (A) firmly
   (B) almost
   (C) strongly
   (D) completely

2. All employees are required to take the fastest ------- when using a company car on official business, to save money on expenses and gas.
   (A) total
   (B) place
   (C) route
   (D) point

3. Our company has ------- exceeded its sales projections for this year by 38 percent of the goal.
   (A) straight
   (B) yet
   (C) already
   (D) even

4. You should be careful when ------- an insurance plan, while keeping in mind the size of your family and its needs.
   (A) directing
   (B) supporting
   (C) requiring
   (D) choosing

5. A successful leader must be ------- to the ideas of all his/her employees, by having an open door policy where everyone feels welcome.
   (A) convinced
   (B) receptive
   (C) probable
   (D) plausible

6. Our complete product lineup is ------- low in comparison to other competitors in our own country and overseas.
   (A) audibly
   (B) relatively
   (C) plentifully
   (D) anonymously

7. If an employee wishes to transfer to a different department in the company, he must ------- permission from the department supervisor and manager.
   (A) join
   (B) learn
   (C) protect
   (D) obtain

8. Mr. Thompson has decided to rent a car for the ------- of his visit to Paris.
   (A) duration
   (B) circumstance
   (C) education
   (D) vacation

9 A study by our company's human resources division confirms that our pay increases each year is more than -------.
   (A) adequate
   (B) numerous
   (C) thankful
   (D) adjacent

10 All shipments overseas must have full documentation and paperwork required for ------- with all international regulations.
   (A) diagnosis
   (B) compliance
   (C) settlement
   (D) criticism

11 The escalators to the 5th floor of the building will be ------- shut down for safety inspections tomorrow.
   (A) formerly
   (B) annually
   (C) temporarily
   (D) cautiously

12 The sales ------- last December because of a surge in holiday retail sales.
   (A) peaked
   (B) divided
   (C) collected
   (D) recorded

13 ------- the marketing division, there will be a 10 percent cut in personnel, which will take effect at the first of next month.
   (A) Even if
   (B) Rather than
   (C) Apart from
   (D) If it were not for

14 The new employee schedule will be from 9 to 5 each day, with a paid lunch period ------- the work time.
   (A) during
   (B) among
   (C) aboard
   (D) inside

15 All employees must ------- the standard operating procedures when dealing with any customer complaint.
   (A) take
   (B) follow
   (C) lead
   (D) carry

DAY 11 어휘 집중 연습

PART 5

1. Our company will have a booth at the World Green Expo in London to ------- our renewable energy products.
   (A) achieve
   (B) demonstrate
   (C) encourage
   (D) distinguish

2. No employees are allowed to visit the research facilities, ------- those specifically assigned to the lab projects.
   (A) as
   (B) while
   (C) so
   (D) except

3. The fuselages of our new planes are a ------- of carbon fibers and titanium which reduces the overall weight.
   (A) plan
   (B) team
   (C) blend
   (D) shade

4. All questions ------- the research and development of our new products should be addressed to the public relations division.
   (A) assuming
   (B) versus
   (C) rather
   (D) concerning

5. The corporate headquarters had to be evacuated yesterday ------- a power blackout that affected the entire downtown area.
   (A) because of
   (B) prior to
   (C) pertaining to
   (D) past

6. All employees must wear ------- earmuffs when working on the tarmac with airplanes flying past.
   (A) absolute
   (B) savory
   (C) protective
   (D) expired

7. It is considered unacceptable and ------- for employees to be absent from work without notice.
   (A) concise
   (B) equivalent
   (C) submissive
   (D) improper

8. Please note that the vacation eligibility period is posted on the bulletin board; employees are asked to plan their vacations ------- .
   (A) accordingly
   (B) subsequently
   (C) conversely
   (D) assuredly

9 The new employee protective gear is ------- for use of all employees and have been certified by OSHA.

(A) similar
(B) suitable
(C) consistent
(D) accurate

10 The ------- of our agency's new Pan-Europe Tour is printed in the new brochures we just received from production.

(A) summary
(B) total
(C) product
(D) registration

11 An investigation of the product defects showed continued violations of standards, -------company policy.

(A) contrary to
(B) even though
(C) except for
(D) in place of

12 Employees that wish to take a floating holiday must notify their supervisor and HR division of a minimum of thirty days -------.

(A) ahead of
(B) initially
(C) behind
(D) in advance

13 Our new solar-powered batteries are very eco-friendly, as ------- to the regular batteries in the world landfills.

(A) supposed
(B) opposed
(C) evidenced
(D) agreed

14 It was announced today the company ------- to buy Koontz for 1.4 billion dollars by the end of the fiscal year.

(A) intends
(B) pursues
(C) appoints
(D) explains

15 Our quality control division ------- performs quality checks on products throughout the year to insure compliance.

(A) essentially
(B) regularly
(C) primarily
(D) accessibly

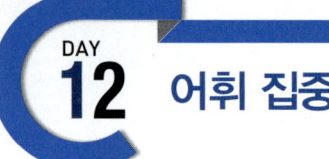

DAY 12 어휘 집중 연습

PART 5

1. The company board of directors will be ------- a new five-year plan that calls for further diversification of our product lines.
   (a) distributing
   (B) achieving
   (C) developing
   (D) contributing

2. Employees are reminded that all records used and viewed by employees are -------, and must never be disclosed to outside parties.
   (A) confidential
   (B) limited
   (C) former
   (D) mandatory

3. All employees should ------- an employee savings account, which the company will match up to 6 percent each year in contributions.
   (A) place
   (B) offer
   (C) create
   (D) enter

4. Every New Year's Eve, our company ------- a companywide party for all employees and their families, to celebrate the successes of the previous year.
   (A) holds
   (B) closes
   (C) waits
   (D) meets

5. Our company's warranty on our products is considered the best ------- the entire consumer electronics industry.
   (A) throughout
   (B) ahead of
   (C) except
   (D) between

6. Customer complaints are a very ------- issue, and must be investigated and dealt with immediately.
   (A) courteous
   (B) sensitive
   (C) affordable
   (D) competitive

7. Our company's training division sponsors workshops throughout the year, using a ------- structured program, which requires employees to have at least 25 hours of training per year.
   (A) highly
   (B) hopefully
   (C) probably
   (D) rarely

8. The company will build an ------- employee cafeteria to relieve the overcrowding occurring in our headquarters cafeteria.
   (A) infrequent
   (B) additional
   (C) ongoing
   (D) incidental

282 SECTION 2

9 Our sales have fallen by 14 percent due to lower demand and ------- market conditions.

   (A) unfavorable
   (B) unwilling
   (C) opposing
   (D) reluctant

10 I appreciate the president's candor whenever he gives an address; he is direct and to the ------- without beating around the bush.

   (A) grade
   (B) point
   (C) feet
   (D) spot

11 The maintenance division ------- vacuums out the HVAC system to provide clean and pure air for our employees.

   (A) prematurely
   (B) marginally
   (C) occasionally
   (D) uncommonly

12 The new solar-powered LED lamp will be available for sale ------- July 17, with limited quantities available for participating retailers.

   (A) by
   (B) with
   (C) until
   (D) in

13 We will ------- be moving into our new offices located in downtown Stockholm.

   (A) shortly
   (B) previously
   (C) overly
   (D) rarely

14 We discovered a water leak that damaged some computers in the personnel office; the maintenance division is trying to ascertain what is ------- for the leak.

   (A) transparent
   (B) possible
   (C) probable
   (D) responsible

15 The latest feedback surveys ------- the employees would like to have more benefits working for the company.

   (A) indicate
   (B) transfer
   (C) advise
   (D) designate

DAY 13 어휘 집중 연습

PART 5

1. All customers will be ------- with a coupon that will allow them to purchase any of our renewable energy products with a 30 percent discount.
   (A) equipped
   (B) filled
   (C) provided
   (D) requested

2. We will be providing free ------- software updates for all of our products so customers will not have to pay for expensive software upgrades.
   (A) promising
   (B) numerous
   (C) frequent
   (D) repetitious

3. All new employees will be trained in the use of the copy machines ------- one of the technicians in the support department.
   (A) over
   (B) behind
   (C) out of
   (D) from

4. Our company must be in ------- with all union labor contract provisions, including working conditions, pay and benefits.
   (A) combination
   (B) competence
   (C) compliance
   (D) fulfillment

5. Employees on business travel must receive permission from their department manager for expenditures that ------- $250 per transaction.
   (A) exceed
   (B) excel
   (C) promote
   (D) interrupt

6. In order to receive the lowest rate on airline travel, tickets must be purchased at least 60 days ------- the flight.
   (A) within
   (B) between
   (C) before
   (D) below

7. Our new CEO will ------- a meeting of all employees on Friday, July 17 at the Civic Center Auditorium in the downtown area.
   (A) address
   (B) stand
   (C) arrive
   (D) inform

8. All employees with over five years' experience with the company will be given ------- in company promotions.
   (A) preference
   (B) treatment
   (C) relocation
   (D) amount

9. Our company is ------- the leader in skin-care products for consumers, with over 3 billion dollars in worldwide sales.
   (A) rarely
   (B) currently
   (C) eagerly
   (D) quickly

10. All applicants applying for management positions or higher are ------- to have at least a bachelor's degree.
    (A) submitted
    (B) interviewed
    (C) applied
    (D) required

11. The company has just appointed John Brenan as the new vice president ------- Labor Relations, to deal directly with union contract negotiations.
    (A) by
    (B) to
    (C) of
    (D) on

12. Our company's Spring Clearance sale will be selling merchandise with a 35 percent discount ------- the end of this month.
    (A) until
    (B) since
    (C) for
    (D) in

13. John Davis announced the company has ------- its lawsuit out of court.
    (A) defeated
    (B) arrived
    (C) approached
    (D) settled

14. Our company's ------- of its product line is predicted to increase sales of our green products by 250 percent.
    (A) action
    (B) process
    (C) downsizing
    (D) expansion

15. The State Department of Consumer Affairs ------- that the batteries found in our competitors' products could catch on fire.
    (A) differed
    (B) reported
    (C) canceled
    (D) sustained

DAY 14 어휘 집중 연습

PART 5

1. It has become ------- that new marketing program promoting our furniture is working, with over 12 million units sold this month.
   (A) bright
   (B) busy
   (C) adequate
   (D) apparent

2. Our client was very ------- with the hotel room and customer service he received as a guest at The Oasis Hotel.
   (A) impulsive
   (B) uncommon
   (C) overstated
   (D) dissatisfied

3. Our Eastern European stores have reported a ------- in overall sales, due to the Eurozone economic crisis.
   (A) rejection
   (B) denial
   (C) decline
   (D) negation

4. Due to its tropical climate, South America is the largest ------- of coffee for our coffee franchises in the United States.
   (A) ability
   (B) practice
   (C) source
   (D) group

5. The customer privacy policy requires that customers' names be ------- from all mailing lists if they request it.
   (A) removed
   (B) replaced
   (C) sent
   (D) stored

6. Employees are requested to read memo, which ------- the procedures required in reporting discrepancies in the system.
   (A) creates
   (B) notices
   (C) differs
   (D) instructs

7. Our new vice president of Labor Relations has a ------- familiarity with labor relations law, with 25 years of experience as a labor negotiator.
   (A) clear
   (B) broad
   (C) whole
   (D) round

8. Our flashlights are ------- designed for everyday use, although we also recommend them for emergency use as well.
   (A) frequently
   (B) originally
   (C) numerically
   (D) independently

9 Our company is seeking a mechanical engineer, with a comprehensive ------- of renewable energy and ultra-capacitors.
   (A) opinion
   (B) ability
   (C) knowledge
   (D) collector

10 Our company will be holding a no reserve auction in order to sell off ------- equipment that is no longer being used.
   (A) surplus
   (B) lengthy
   (C) opportune
   (D) brief

11 Employees are required to clean the rollers and drums of the copy machines every week, as this will ------- the life of the machines.
   (A) persist
   (B) endure
   (C) enlarge
   (D) prolong

12 Our company's compensation package is one of the best in the entire industry, with very high pay and ------- paid to our employees.
   (A) interests
   (B) benefits
   (C) controls
   (D) forces

13 Our digital cameras have been developed using a new state-of-the-art ------- that does not require as many mechanical parts in its production.
   (A) response
   (B) technique
   (C) combination
   (D) goal

14 The vice president of logistics ------- the supply chain plan for our new plant in Texas and approved it.
   (A) searched
   (B) advised
   (C) reached
   (D) reviewed

15 The vice president of sales ------- had a reservation to San Francisco so it didn't matter that the flight was booked solid.
   (A) already
   (B) well
   (C) soon
   (D) never

DAY 15 어휘 집중 연습

PART 5

1. Our company ------- has not reached its sales goals for this year of LED one million units in the North American market.
   (A) always
   (B) still
   (C) usually
   (D) yet

2. We will be ------- our newly hired employees on Friday morning at 8 A.M. in the employee lounge.
   (A) wishing
   (B) welcoming
   (C) giving
   (D) looking

3. We are requiring all employees to enroll in the professional development seminar on sales; advance ------- is required.
   (A) registration
   (B) influence
   (C) operation
   (D) significance

4. The vice president of the marketing division is very ------- regarding company sales of our home appliances for this year.
   (A) willing
   (B) optimistic
   (C) visionary
   (D) assertive

5. Our company has been a leader in energy saving consumer products ------- over twenty years.
   (A) in
   (B) for
   (C) up
   (D) form

6. All customers receiving complimentary samples of our new perfume are asked to ------- a brief survey about our product.
   (A) answer
   (B) talk
   (C) respond
   (D) reply

7. All employees are required to check and respond to all e-mail messages ------- to insure the best customer service.
   (A) exactly
   (B) regularly
   (C) officially
   (D) evenly

8. All new recruits will be required to ------- a one-week training class on the standard operating procedures of our company.
   (A) occur
   (B) attend
   (C) contain
   (D) arrive

9 The proper ratio of airline agents to passengers is ------- 1 agent per 200 passengers.

(A) approximately
(B) briefly
(C) rapidly
(D) unpredictably

10 Due to the ------- demand of air traffic at the main airport, the city has elected to build an additional runway.

(A) increased
(B) resolved
(C) approached
(D) involved

11 All employees are required to submit their daily sales ------- to the accounts receivable department.

(A) procedures
(B) journeys
(C) directions
(D) receipts

12 The airport has undergone ------- renovations including a new restaurant, terminal, ticket counters and baggage claim area.

(A) mature
(B) producing
(C) substantial
(D) consumable

13 We are inviting interested employees who want to come ------- with the commercial sales division to Los Angeles for a seminar.

(A) into
(B) among
(C) without
(D) along

14 Our company headquarters have been located in New York ------- its initial founding in May of 1976.

(A) before
(B) since
(C) on
(D) by

15 We will go ------- a trip to Tokyo, Japan to attend the International Alternative Energy Conference on August 12.

(A) over
(B) on
(C) about
(D) out

DAY 16 어휘 집중 연습

PART 5

1. Our company believes in offering promotional ------- to employees within the company first before hiring from the outside.
   (A) occurrences
   (B) occasions
   (C) actions
   (D) opportunities

2. We will be ------- transfer requests from our European sales offices through the end of June, when all transfer forms will be reviewed.
   (A) advising
   (B) renovating
   (C) accepting
   (D) running

3. Our customers are very satisfied with our products and customer service, which is reflected ------- the latest consumer surveys.
   (A) up
   (B) by
   (C) of
   (D) among

4. The ------- news from the air conditioning contractor is that the installation of the cooling system in the Austin plant will be completed by May 21.
   (A) latest
   (B) immediate
   (C) shortest
   (D) constant

5. The delay in delivery of the shipment to Albers was ------- a shortage of equipment and personnel.
   (A) in that
   (B) as for
   (C) due to
   (D) even so

6. The shipping department places a high ------- on shipments by sending all outbound packages via overnight express.
   (A) resolve
   (B) priority
   (C) credit
   (D) standard

7. With the construction of our two new plants, we will ensure the highest rate of ------- in filling orders from around America.
   (A) discrepancy
   (B) obligation
   (C) determination
   (D) reliability

8. Our company will be hosting the Green Energy Fair in Seattle, which will be ------- at the Seahawks stadium.
   (A) stayed
   (B) referred
   (C) held
   (D) went

9 Sales of our solar-powered emergency road lights have ------- increased due to the new advertising and market campaigns on television.

(A) accidentally
(B) expressively
(C) dramatically
(D) eagerly

10 A new financial ------- program for students who want to enter medicine is now available, if they agree to work in rural areas for ten years.

(A) division
(B) association
(C) assistance
(D) statement

11 The company will be arranging ------- transportation for all employees who need rides from the airport to the convention center.

(A) by
(B) about
(C) for
(D) in

12 In compliance with federal regulations, only certified flight crew members are ------- to enter the cockpit of the aircraft.

(A) permitted
(B) associated
(C) decided
(D) written

13 The vice president of logistics has announced the creation of a greatly improved ------- network for our products.

(A) exception
(B) distribution
(C) repetition
(D) solution

14 The CEO of our company announced that a total of 1.5 million dollars has been ------- to charity.

(A) become
(B) made
(C) bought
(D) given

15 Due to the tight visa requirements, the embassy ------- at least 30 percent of our applicants for working in its country.

(A) rejected
(B) escaped
(C) objected
(D) accepted

DAY 17 어휘 집중 연습

정답 및 해설 / 122p

PART 5

1. The shipping and receiving department has discovered that damage claims are lower when the components are ------- wrapped in bubble packaging.
   (A) jointly
   (B) diversely
   (C) separately
   (D) partially

2. The monthly meeting has been ------- one week due to the upcoming holidays.
   (A) postponed
   (B) expected
   (C) scheduled
   (D) continued

3. The general contractor in charge of expanding the employee lounge has issued an ------- for 1.5 million dollars for the project.
   (A) expectation
   (B) emphasis
   (C) estimate
   (D) elimination

4. Our corporation will have a ------- of its 25th anniversary of founding, with a party for all employees held at the Oakland Convention Center.
   (A) progress
   (B) preparation
   (C) celebration
   (D) memorization

5. Our products are very ------- as they are solidly constructed and are housed in high impact plastics.
   (A) skilled
   (B) earnest
   (C) tactful
   (D) reliable

6. Many ------- celebrities have expressed their high satisfaction with our services.
   (A) definite
   (B) customary
   (C) elaborate
   (D) notable

7. Despite low economic growth, investment in research and development will continue in ------- years.
   (A) subsequent
   (B) late
   (C) next
   (D) followed

8. The CEO appreciates the importance of good communications ------- logistics, marketing, and research divisions.
   (A) under
   (B) past
   (C) among
   (D) out of

9. All employees are expected to ------- their employee identification cards visibly at all times when on company property.

   (A) decrease
   (B) shape
   (C) limit
   (D) wear

10. The Web site announces our goal is to secure the highest ------- in the world market in our field.

    (A) order
    (B) schedule
    (C) position
    (D) record

11. Presently, our company is the leader in Bluetooth technology in North America, ------- Mexico and the Caribbean states.

    (A) somewhat
    (B) including
    (C) regarding
    (D) everywhere

12. Executive pay package is worth 25 million dollars per year; however, it is deemed ------- the investment.

    (A) worth
    (B) expensive
    (C) valued
    (D) prized

13. Any employee with over thirty days of continuous employment ------- to join the new company savings plan.

    (A) equips
    (B) supplies
    (C) qualifies
    (D) arrange

14. In order to promote the good ------- of our employees, the company is providing free gym membership to all employees and their families.

    (A) health
    (B) measure
    (C) dimension
    (D) substance

15. The company will ------- each employee via e-mail when it makes matching payments into the employee savings plan.

    (A) accept
    (B) notify
    (C) deliver
    (D) present

DAY 18 어휘 집중 연습

PART 5

1. Company policy forbids the employment of ------- employees in the same division; this policy is in the employee manual.
   (A) achievable
   (B) alike
   (C) interested
   (D) related

2. We are offering all customers that pay cash rather than a credit card a five percent ------- on all future purchases, as we must pay a commission to credit card companies.
   (A) delivery
   (B) restraint
   (C) discount
   (D) renewal

3. All employees should ------- in the company sponsored employee stock options program, where employees will receive yearly stock bonuses.
   (A) admit
   (B) apply
   (C) subscribe
   (D) enroll

4. When the fire alarm rings, all employees are required to leave the building ------- sixty seconds.
   (A) within
   (B) onto
   (C) so that
   (D) much as

5. The company is ------- new retail outlets in France and our local staff is drawing up a strategy.
   (A) looking
   (B) seeking
   (C) entering
   (D) inquiring

6. The sales ------- have been printed and are in the hands of the sales team visiting French department stores at this time.
   (A) resource
   (B) reforms
   (C) reports
   (D) views

7. The vice president of public relations is the only person in the company authorized to ------- to any questions regarding our merger proposal.
   (A) promise
   (B) advise
   (C) explain
   (D) respond

8. All managers are expected to be able to pass a test on the presentation, which is required ------- certification.
   (A) for
   (B) at
   (C) than
   (D) which

294 SECTION 2

9 The ------- for the position of internal auditor are very well qualified, which is a real benefit for our company.
(A) applicants
(B) jobs
(C) offers
(D) accounts

10 The vice president of human resources ------- all managers to attend an anti-discrimination workshop on Monday.
(A) agreed
(B) demanded
(C) instructed
(D) intended

11 All employees must have their passports ------- approaching the boarding gate at the airport.
(A) since
(B) when
(C) enough
(D) afterward

12 Since we have a large group of employees attending the seminar in London, we will ------- fill up the first class section of the aircraft.
(A) deeply
(B) easily
(C) softly
(D) slowly

13 The vice president of cargo sales will give a ------- on the benefits of cargo sales.
(A) administration
(B) presentation
(C) assistance
(D) profession

14 ------- copies of the bloodborne pathogens informational chart can be obtained by contacting the safety committee.
(A) Obtained
(B) Additional
(C) Decided
(D) Approximate

15 The head of cargo listed the ------- advantages in promoting cargo as much passenger business.
(A) supportive
(B) spoiled
(C) voluntary
(D) numerous

DAY 19 어휘 집중 연습

PART 5

1. All employees are required to follow the emergency exit plan ------- as outlined to insure the safe and prompt evacuation of the building.
   (A) doubly
   (B) only
   (C) exactly
   (D) nearly

2. Given his many years of experience in the field, Mr. Chae is the right person to ------- demanding customers' complaints.
   (A) disperse
   (B) handle
   (C) prolong
   (D) tailor

3. All employees that do not evacuate the building immediately will be ------- responsible for any injuries to themselves.
   (A) relevantly
   (B) realistically
   (C) prosperously
   (D) personally

4. All employees are required to ------- the bloodborne pathogens training, which insures employee safety in the event of blood contamination.
   (A) present
   (B) make
   (C) complete
   (D) retire

5. After the completion of the bloodborne pathogens workshop, all employees will be given a ------- of a reference chart of the correct emergency procedures.
   (A) procedure
   (B) copy
   (C) subject
   (D) indication

6. ------- 60 percent of the staff members turned out to be opposed to the new work schedule which was established by the department managers.
   (A) Coincidently
   (B) Desperately
   (C) Genuinely
   (D) Roughly

7. The manager ------- the early flight from Los Angeles to San Francisco and should be arriving soon.
   (A) spent
   (B) had
   (C) took
   (D) went

8. All new employees are expected to arrive ------- at 9 A.M. in the Sierra Room for an orientation session.
   (A) soon
   (B) sometimes
   (C) presently
   (D) promptly

9 The airline was ------- with the fact that the route application between San Diego and Lake Tahoe had been declined.

(A) indebted
(B) eliminated
(C) disappointed
(D) complicated

10 Dr. Choi, one of the highly regarded stress management experts, will visit our company to give a series of ------- on how to deal with workplace stress.

(A) behaviors
(B) lectures
(C) operations
(D) points

11 Employees must ------- a valid parking permit in their vehicle at all times.

(A) print
(B) state
(C) display
(D) commit

12 The company's safety record is ------- the highest in the airline industry and it has received safety awards from various government bodies.

(A) between
(B) among
(C) beside
(D) about

13 Mr. Chae, one of the local government officials ------- us that our application for the grants this year was finally approved by the city council.

(A) assimilated
(B) equalized
(C) notified
(D) retaliated

14 All the ------- in the sporting event are required to sign a waiver absolving the organizers from any liability.

(A) actors
(B) interviewees
(C) owners
(D) participants

15 The board of directors will have a meeting this Saturday to work a plan to ------- the serious problem of increasing debts.

(A) alleviate
(B) annihilate
(C) domesticate
(D) refurbish

DAY 20 어휘 집중 연습

PART 5

1. Cultural differences should be considered when a new product is ------- to a foreign market.
   (A) detonated
   (B) introduced
   (C) positioned
   (D) reiterated

2. After 12 months of employment, every employee is ------- to receive a year-end bonus.
   (A) encouraged
   (B) engaged
   (C) ensured
   (D) entitled

3. Mr. Lee was hired only a few months ago and he already became one of the most ------- employees in the company.
   (A) abnormal
   (B) expensive
   (C) loyal
   (D) valuable

4. In spite of its high quality, Brill's latest model was not considered ------- to customers.
   (A) affordable
   (B) believable
   (C) correctable
   (D) expendable

5. Vohex Energy is expected to experience rapid growth after the new refinery construction is -------.
   (A) absolute
   (B) complete
   (C) elusive
   (D) factual

6. To offset the worsening profit margin, D&P Electronics has decided to attempt to reduce operating ------- by 20 percent for the next 2 years.
   (A) commissions
   (B) expenses
   (C) pay
   (D) taxes

7. Ms. Choi received a ------- promotion after she finalized the contract with the company's largest client.
   (A) frequent
   (B) significant
   (C) capable
   (D) proficient

8. Sales revenues nearly ------- over the last six months after SJ Communications revamped its services.
   (A) doubled
   (B) invested
   (C) released
   (D) upgraded

9 The production of new monitors has been ------- due to the technical problems with factory equipment.

(A) delayed
(B) fallen
(C) replied
(D) provided

10 The company's new manufacturing plants in the Philippines will be operational once the facilities passes the ------- safety inspection.

(A) damaged
(B) final
(C) confident
(D) numerous

11 With all the employees' hard work, the small company could ------- from the severe economic downturn.

(A) come
(B) refrain
(C) recover
(D) stem

12 The recently released movie directed by Fahey is ------- on the true story that happened in Korea.

(A) based
(B) taken
(C) heard
(D) read

13 The articles on national health care programs were written by experts who have worked in the medical ------- for more than 20 years.

(A) description
(B) course
(C) industry
(D) direction

14 Even though Lomax Tech has a ------- excellent sales records over the years, it is still struggling to increase the market share.

(A) barely
(B) rarely
(C) relatively
(D) slightly

15 The new medicine proved it could reduce the ------- of breast cancer during the clinical testing.

(A) reaction
(B) return
(C) risk
(D) residue

독해 집중 연습

Day 01	연습 문제 1		302
Day 02	연습 문제 2		304
Day 03	연습 문제 3		306
Day 04	연습 문제 4		308
Day 05	연습 문제 5		310
Day 06	연습 문제 6		312
Day 07	연습 문제 7		314
Day 08	연습 문제 8		316
Day 09	연습 문제 9		318
Day 10	연습 문제 10		320
Day 11	연습 문제 11		322
Day 12	연습 문제 12		324
Day 13	연습 문제 13		326
Day 14	연습 문제 14		328
Day 15	연습 문제 15		330
Day 16	연습 문제 16		332
Day 17	연습 문제 17		334
Day 18	연습 문제 18		336
Day 19	연습 문제 19		338
Day 20	연습 문제 20		340

PART 7

Questions 1-2 refer to the following advertisement.

Citrus Uptown Villas

Citrus Uptown Villas is now renting out one and two-bedroom condominium units. Situated in the midst of downtown Oceanside, this new 20 unit residential condominium is designed by professionals. Within the complex are a complete business center, a swimming pool, a gym, and indoor parking, and all of these are included with the monthly rent. The condominium is also perfectly situated, with a beautiful view of the Pendleton Bridge and a few minutes walk to theaters, fine diners and a beautiful park. Come and see for yourself our model units and see what we can give you. Our rental staff is available every day to take you on a tour of the condominium complex and model units.

Citrus Uptown Villas
17 Basilone Way, Oceanside
818-555-1123
www.citrusuptown.com

1. What does the advertisement describe?
   (A) Vacation residences for sale
   (B) Apartments for rent
   (C) Office relocation service
   (D) Local tourist areas

2. What are readers asked to do?
   (A) Close a contract
   (B) Make a payment
   (C) Visit the area
   (D) Make a lease agreement

Questions 3-5 refer to the following information.

All-in-One Office Printers

All-in-one office printers can be very convenient for small or home offices. They are an excellent choice for use in small offices or the home. This is due to the small footprint they require. All-in-one printers are a combination of a printer and scanner. Therefore, less shelf space is required, freeing up valuable office space. We have tested several different brands of all-in-one printers and found them all very capable and convenient. However, we did find the WGB Printer superior in overall functions. We are listing the test results in order of favorability.

WGB-145 All-in-One Printer retails for $149 and is sold in leading retailers nationwide. The scanning processor was excellent, revealing very detailed copies. The printing of pages in black and white and color were vivid and crisp.

NAV 12-1 All-in-One Printer retails for $179 and is mostly sold online. While we were impressed with the overall functions of this printer, we were disappointed in the scanner as it produced somewhat blurry copies with small print.

HTR 12-4 All-in-One Printer retails for $99 and is sold at retailers nationwide. Although most of the functions are acceptable, we were taken aback by the cost of ink refills and the slowness of the printing. We rate this third in overall quality.

Therefore, we suggest the WGB All-in-One Printer for its overall quality and ratings.

3 What is the topic of this information?
(A) The best computers
(B) The cheapest printers
(C) Review of all-in-one printers
(D) New computer technology

4 What model is recommended by the author?
(A) WGB-145
(B) NAV 12-1
(C) HTR 12-4
(D) BTV-126

5 What is NOT mentioned in the article?
(A) Cost per page
(B) Printer quality
(C) Scanning quality
(D) Cost of ink refills

DAY 02 독해 집중 연습

PART 7

Questions 1-3 refer to the following e-mail.

---

e-mail

To: Victoria Beck, HR Director <victoriabeck@blackandwhite.com>
From: Stuart Barney, CEO <stuartbarney@blackandwhite.com>
Subject: Plans for structural reorganization

I have just approved, in collaboration with the board of directors, a plan to reorganize the entire company structure. Last month, our company underwent an audit by Strategic Business Consultants of New York. In the study, the consultants recommended restructuring of the management pyramid of the company. They stated the company is too top heavy in upper management positions, with layers of unneeded bureaucracy that creates inefficiencies in management and decision-making. Therefore, we are cutting five assistant vice president positions and transferring their duties to the vice president of the respective divisions. This change will take place on June 15. This will make our company more streamlined and profitable.

---

1. What does this e-mail mainly discuss?

   (A) Company restructuring
   (B) Negotiations with labor unions
   (C) New employee benefits
   (D) Transferring employees to New York

2. What positions are going to be cut?

   (A) Consultants
   (B) Assistant vice presidents
   (C) Clerical positions
   (D) Directors

3. Who recommended these changes?

   (A) Stuart Barney
   (B) An internal auditor
   (C) Victoria Beck
   (D) Strategic Business Consultants

Questions 4-6 refer to the following notice.

Thank you for the purchase of a Brother B-112 printer. One free ink cartridge is included in the box. As this is only a sample, it is not designed for full use, and therefore it is advised that you replace it with a proper cartridge some time soon. You can easily buy replacement cartridges online at www.brotherprinterink.com. We guarantee that you will have your ink cartridges within 5 working days or you pay nothing. As a special customer, you are entitled to a 30 percent discount off your first purchase of ink. Simply enter the code 2213 when ordering. If you find buying ink at a retail outlet is more convenient, they are available at all leading computer supply outlets. Please be aware that most retailers do not use our corporate discount.

If you have any questions or comments on your new printer, please call 799-334-8897 24 hours a day for technical aids, or 799-334-8899 Monday through Friday 8 A.M. to 8 P.M. for sales and accounts.

4. For whom was the notice written?
   (A) Employees of the technical support department
   (B) Computer technicians
   (C) Purchasers of new printers
   (D) Sales personnel

5. What promise is made about placing orders for ink?
   (A) The item is free if delivery is delayed.
   (B) Ink cartridges will last for a full year.
   (C) Sales representatives are available all the time.
   (D) Technicians will return calls promptly.

6. How can shoppers receive a discount?
   (A) By making a phone call
   (B) By typing in a number on a Web site
   (C) By buying from any computer supply store
   (D) By present a coupon

PART 7

Questions 1-3 refer to the following article.

In old town St. Pierre, one can find a large variety of activities and experiences that will please even the most demanding consumer. St. Pierre was founded in 1725, with the Pilgrims being the original inhabitants. Most of the old buildings that were built in the 1700's still remain in the old town business district today. We recommend that tourists first visit the old Mill Creek Grainery. The Mill Creek Grainery goes back to the founding of St. Pierre. The mill operates using waterpower to grind grains into flour. It is truly amazing that the mill still operates today, using the same system and technology that was built hundreds of years ago. This does prove the notion that things were made much better in the past than the present. Tools and implements were made to last in those days, as people's lives and survival depended on them. All visitors at the Mill Creek Grainery will be given a free sample of our freshly ground whole wheat flour that tastes delicious in any bread recipe. The mill also has freshly baked bread products produced from the freshly milled wheat.

1 What is mainly discussed in the article?

(A) Introducing new technology
(B) Purchasing some bread
(C) Sightseeing in St. Pierre
(D) Operating waterpower

2 What is the most famous at the Mill Creek Grainery?

(A) The bakery
(B) The buildings
(C) The mill
(D) The musical instruments

3 What does the Mill Creek Grainery do?

(A) It serves food to tourists.
(B) It offers bread baking classes.
(C) It generates electric power.
(D) It sells cookies and drinks.

Questions 4-7 refer to the following newsletter.

Dear Subscriber,

Thank you for subscribing to *Omega Holistic Health Newsletter*. This month, we will be discussing the use of natural herbs to promote health. The first herb in our article is Echinacea. The American Indians first discovered Echinacea's medicinal properties. Echinacea is known for its ability to fight colds and infections. Studies have shown that Echinacea has natural antiseptic, antibiotic and immunity building compounds. It is typically taken in capsule form in what are known as 'double O' capsules. It may also be used as a tea or tincture. Herbal tinctures are derived by soaking the raw herb in alcohol or vinegar. This process extracts the medicinal qualities of the herbs in a liquid.

The second herb we will discuss today is called goldenseal. It is also considered to be a natural antibiotic and blood purifier that is often prescribed by Naturopathic physicians for colds, flu or infections. It is usually consumed as a powdered form using double O gelatin capsules. Due to its bitterness, it is usually not consumed as a tea.

4 What does this newsletter mainly discuss?

(A) Choosing a doctor
(B) Benefits of exercise
(C) Naturopathic doctors
(D) Medicinal uses of herbs

5 What are double O capsules?

(A) Capsules used for taking herbs
(B) A multiple vitamin
(C) A blend of herbs
(D) Prescribed medicine

6 What are herbal tinctures?

(A) Soaking herbs in water
(B) Concentrated liquid form of herbs
(C) A powdered form of herbs
(D) Standardized form of herbs

7 Why is goldenseal not usually consumed as a tea?

(A) It is very bitter.
(B) It is not effective.
(C) It loses its potency.
(D) It is too expensive.

PART 7

Questions 1-2 refer to the following information.

Congratulations on the purchase of your new Acer Mattress set. Only the finest of materials and workmanship have been used in the manufacture of our mattresses. All of our mattresses, including all the components are manufactured in the United States. Our mattresses carry a 100% warranty for a twenty-year period for any defects in materials or workmanship. For service of this warranty, the consumer must return the mattress to any of our sales outlets nationwide, where any repairs, replacements or refunds will be made. Our mattresses carry the strongest warranty in the entire industry. Most competitors only have a three-year warranty that is prorated. That is, they only pay for a portion of the cost to repair or replace the mattress based upon the amount of time the consumer has owned it. For example, if the mattress has a three-year warranty and the consumer returns it after two years, then only a 33% credit would be given for replacement or repairs. We find this unacceptable and this is why we have a 100% non-prorated warranty on all our mattresses.

1 What does the information mainly discuss?

(A) Components of mattress
(B) Mattress warranties
(C) Manufacturing processes
(D) Bedroom sections

2 According to the information, what type of warranty does Acer offer on mattresses?

(A) 100% for 20 years
(B) 50% for 10 years
(C) Prorated for 20 years
(D) Prorated for 3 years

Questions 3-5 refer to the following advertisement.

Secondhand Book Sale

Sponsored by the Liverpool literary guild volunteers of Liverpool library
Three days only, July 8 to 10!

Choose from thousands of books, the majority in almost mint condition! There will be books for readers of all ages.

Thursday: Pre-Sale
7:00 P.M.-8:00 P.M.
$10 admission fee

Friday: General Sale
7:00 A.M.-4:00 P.M.
*Renowned authors will give special lectures.

Saturday: Last Day Sale
10:00 A.M.-3:00 P.M.
All books 40% off

All profits will go towards the renovation and refurbishing of the Liverpool Community Library at Hartford Lane.

Location: Liverpool recreation Center, Main Hall, 42 Grendel Street

Questions? Contact Seymour Butts, Chairman of the Liverpool Literary Guild Volunteer Association, at 564-7778.
Note: We have stopped accepting donated books for this sale.

3 Where will the sale happen?

   (A) At the Liverpool Library
   (B) At a local bookshop
   (C) At Mr. Butts' residence
   (D) At a recreation center

4 What is stated about the Thursday sale?

   (A) It is open only to possessors of library cards.
   (B) There will be an admission fee.
   (C) Only cash will be accepted as payment.
   (D) It will happen in the morning.

5 What is suggested about the books being sold?

   (A) Some books are good for children.
   (B) Many of them are not in good condition.
   (C) All of them were donated by association members.
   (D) Some will be offered at a reduced price on Saturday.

PART 7

Questions 1-3 refer to the following article.

New Facilities at the University of San Francisco

Following the 2014 fundraising drive organized by the USF Alumni Association, the University of San Francisco's board of directors, in coordination with the student council, has researched and decided upon ways in which to spend the money.

A new library to replace the old Memorial Library is planned to be constructed during the summer of 2015. This new library will increase the number of books, journals, and magazines available to USF students. It will provide students with more study desks. In addition, the new library will include several expanded computer labs with online equipment.

Secondly, a state-of-the-art sports complex will be built next to the auditorium. This new complex will contain an indoor track, Olympic-sized pool, work-out facilities, and a large gymnasium.

1. What is the purpose of this article?
   (A) To raise funds for the Alumni Association
   (B) To discuss the renovation of a gymnasium
   (C) To inform readers of a construction project
   (D) To inform the foundation of the USF Alumni Association

2. What is NOT mentioned about the new library?
   (A) Updated access cards
   (B) Computer labs
   (C) More books, journals and magazines
   (D) Study desks

3. Where did the funds for the new facilities come from?
   (A) A loan from the state government
   (B) Donations from the USF Alumni Association
   (C) The former school president
   (D) The 2014 fundraising campaign

Questions 4-6 refer to the following note.

From the Editor

This March issue of *Northern Culinary* marks the magazine's first year in publication. Just one year ago we sold our first copies, and since then, we have developed into one of the region's most popularly read magazines on regional culinary arts. Our customer base has reached 20,000, and that number of subscribers continues to increase. Local foodies have raved about our articles, and at the Northern Food Festival in January, we were awarded "Best Culinary Magazine." As editor-in-chief, I am deeply grateful to our dedicated staff, our columnists and our advertisers, and especially to our expanding community of readers, all of whom have contributed greatly to our success.

Erik Bourdain

4. What is the purpose of the note?

   (A) To express gratitude
   (B) To extend an offer
   (C) To honor a contributor
   (D) To solicit donations

5. What is stated about *Northern Culinary*?

   (A) It is in need of more writers.
   (B) It will have an international edition.
   (C) It is growing in popularity.
   (D) It has increased its advertising rates.

6. What is Northern Food Festival?

   (A) Mr. Bourdain presented his cuisine there.
   (B) Mr. Bourdain was awarded the editor of the year there.
   (C) The magazine funded the event.
   (D) The magazine was honored at the event.

PART 7

Questions 1-3 refer to the following memo.

To: All Salaried Employees
From: William Stevens, HR Director
Date: April 17
Re: Overtime pay

Up to now, salaried employees have not been paid overtime pay. However, the board of directors has just approved an overtime compensation plan for salaried, nonunion employees. Salaried employees that work over 40 hours per week shall be given compensatory time off. In other words, if an employee works eight hours overtime in a one-month period, they will be given eight hours of time off that can be added to their vacations or holidays. Employees with questions are urged to read the official policy on the company Web page under the heading Personnel.

1 What is this memo about?
(A) New employee salaries
(B) Overtime for union employees
(C) Compensatory time off for overtime
(D) Complaints from the customers

2 Whom does the new overtime policy apply to?
(A) Salaried employees
(B) Union employees
(C) Hourly workers
(D) Executives

3 What does the new overtime policy offer?
(A) Extra money for overtime
(B) Time and a half on the basic pay
(C) Extended sick leave
(D) Time off for overtime

Questions 4-5 refer to the following memo.

From: Dan McCormick HR Director
To: Quidel Maintenance Staff
Re: Costa Rica R&R
Date: December 20

Starting this January 10 to the 20th, we are inviting you to this rare opportunity to buy our popular Costa Rica vacation package at deeply discounted rates. Included in this package are airfare to Costa Rica and hotel accommodations for $410 per person or $750 per couple. A discount of $200 and $400 respectively. (Get in touch with the travel office for family discounts.)

This R&R includes a 3-night stay in the luxurious El Verga Rainforest Hotel. Also, employees who avail themselves of this package will get 3 gift vouchers, cash worth $20 (convertible to Costa Rican Pesos) which can be used for meals at the exotic El Hombre Restaurant.

For purchases and reservations, please visit the travel office on the first floor on or before the 20th of January.

4 Why was this memo written?
(A) To inform employees of an opportunity
(B) To advertise a new travel destination
(C) To announce the grand opening of a hotel
(D) To report a change in airfares

5 What is indicated about the Costa Rica Package?
(A) It can be gotten through the Internet.
(B) It includes free meals.
(C) The indicated price will not be the same after January 20.
(D) It is limited to 2 persons or less.

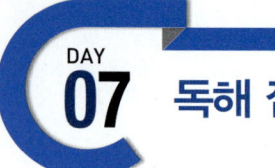# DAY 07 독해 집중 연습

Questions 1-2 refer to the following advertisement.

NORMA JEAN'S COFFEE SHOP

Office worker Specials for April 1-14

Large espresso	$2.25 (regularly $2.75)
A cup of lentil soup	$2.95 (regularly $3.75)
Soup and Subway Combo	$6.25 (regularly $7.00)
Small Cold Drink	$1.25 (regularly $1.85)

These discounted prices are applicable at all three branches.
Special items can be bought at no limit.
Cannot be used with other coupons or discounts.
Company identification card must be presented at time of purchase to avail of yourselves discount.

We accept cash, debit cards or credit cards.
We're open every day from 6:00 A.M. to 10:00 P.M.

---

1 What is being advertised?

(A) An expanded drink menu
(B) A recently established coffee shop for office workers
(C) Lower prices for certain customers
(D) New hours of operation

2 What is said about Norma Jean's Coffee Shop?

(A) It accepts variety of payment.
(B) It offers discounted prices for a month.
(C) It serves only one kind of soup each day.
(D) It has branches internationally.

Questions 3-5 refer to the following letter.

Dear Mr. Giuliani,

We are pleased to announce the opening of our new Pacific Cascade Dental Clinic in downtown Portland, Oregon. This new state of the art building cost over twenty-five million dollars to construct. It will have day care facilities for parents. The new facilities will have the latest in dental technology. This includes the new blue light xenon laser drill. The advantages to using the new laser drills are immense. Dental procedures can be performed without requiring anesthesia or medication. Laser drills are painless and do not emit any sound. The recovery time with laser drills are much faster than traditional drilling and anesthesia. Under traditional care, patients would often have to take a day or two off to recover from the procedures. However, laser technology changes this paradigm where patients can return to work or everyday activities immediately. We look forward to serving you soon in our new facility. I am inviting you to our open house, which is scheduled for Friday, May 19 at 5 P.M. We will have free tours, entertainment and pizza for all of our guests.

Dr. Bonnie Dickenson, D.D.S.

3 What is the main topic of this letter?

(A) To announce a new drilling procedure
(B) To describe the advantages of lasers
(C) To announce the opening of a new dental office
(D) To compare traditional with laser drills

4 What type of business is describe in the letter?

(A) Family medical practice
(B) Orthopedics practices
(C) Cardiology practice
(D) Dental practice

5 According to the letter, what is one of the advantages of using a laser drill?

(A) It offers shorter recovery time
(B) It is cheaper to use
(C) It can destroy tooth decay
(D) It can be used for gum disease

DAY 08 독해 집중 연습

PART 7

Questions 1-3 refer to the following memo.

Air California

To: All Air California Employees
From: John Roberts, CEO
Date: July 14

Dear Employees,

You may have read in the media that Air California is negotiating with Horizon Airways for a proposed merger. Many Air California employees have contacted me expressing their deep concerns about job losses because of the merger. I can assure all of the employees of Air California that no job will be cut or eliminated. In fact, we anticipate hiring additional employees. This is because Horizon Air has not hired any employees for over two years due to a hiring freeze. Consequently, the company has serious personnel shortages. The merger will increase the business overall for Air California due to the expansion of the route structure. Horizon Air will now become part of the Air California family and will be known only as Air California. We look forward to this exciting time in our company's history.

Thank you,

John Roberts, CEO
Air California
Newport Beach, CA

---

1. What is the main topic of the memo?
   (A) A plan for layoffs
   (B) Airline merger
   (C) New aircraft
   (D) Appointment of a new CEO

2. What will the new company be called?
   (A) Air California
   (B) Horizon Airlines
   (C) NorCal Airlines
   (D) Air America

3. Why did many employees contact the CEO?
   (A) They wanted to transfer.
   (B) They wanted a raise.
   (C) They were worried about job losses.
   (D) They wanted a promotion.

Questions 4-5 refer to the following survey.

CENTER PLACE HOTEL

Name: Jonathon Smith
Address: 1556 North First Street, Anaheim, California
Phone number: 714-555-1212
Date of stay: April 12   **Room number:** 567
Main purpose of visit:
☑ Pleasure   ☐ Business   ☐ Convention/Group meeting

Guest room:	Excellent	Good	Fair	Poor
Cleanliness	☑	☐	☐	☐
Design	☐	☑	☐	☐
Comfort	☐	☑	☐	☐

Comments: *Noisy neighbors. Not enough sound insulation between rooms.*

Restaurant:	Excellent	Good	Fair	Poor
Menu selection	☐	☐	☑	☐
Quality of food	☑	☐	☐	☐
Quality of service	☑	☐	☐	☐

Comments: *An unusually wide selection of fish dishes!*

Would you stay with us again? Yes ☑   No ☐

Other comments:
I really appreciate the warm customer service I received from your personnel. One thing I was not happy about was the long check-in time once I arrived by cab from the airport. I had to wait in line for 35 minutes just to check in and get my room. This is the last thing I wanted to do when arriving after a long flight. Please hire more people to work at your front desk.

Please leave this card at the front desk. Thank you!

---

4 What is stated about Center Place Hotel?

(A) It is used mostly by tourists.
(B) Its soundproofing is excellent.
(C) It provides complimentary shuttle services.
(D) It serves seafood to guests.

5 Why was the customer unhappy?

(A) The hotel personnel were not friendly.
(B) They had to wait a long time to check in.
(C) The food at the restaurants was poor.
(D) The hotel rooms were not clean.

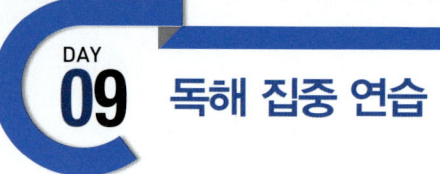

PART 7

Questions 1-2 refer to the following survey.

Global Airways Customer Satisfaction Survey

	Yes	No
Did the flight depart and arrive on time?	×	
Were the ticket agents courteous?	×	
Did you have to wait long in the ticket line?	×	
Was the inflight service satisfactory?		×
Was the food on the flight satisfactory?	×	
Did you receive your luggage within 15 minutes after landing?	×	
Were you satisfied with your legroom during the flight?		×

Additional Comments: *I think the legroom is ridiculous on the flights. I am 6 feet 3 inches tall and cannot even cross my legs due to the lack of legroom. I feel extremely cramped. I wished Global Airways gives its passengers more legroom instead of trying to crowd more people on the flights.*

1. What is the survey mainly about?
   (A) Service at a hotel
   (B) Service on an airline
   (C) Service at a service station
   (D) Service at a spa

2. What did this passenger like the least about the Global Airways?
   (A) Inflight meals
   (B) The long ticket lines
   (C) The delay of the flight
   (D) The legroom on the flight

Questions 3-5 refer to the following e-mail.

From: Beth Anne George <generalmanager@hillahotel.com>
To: Dr. James Peterson <jamespeterson09@straforduniversity.edu.au>
Date: April 20
Subject: Response

Dear Dr. Petterson,

Thank you for your e-mail yesterday requesting the Presidential Suite Penthouse room on the 35th floor of the Hilla Hotel.

Unfortunately, all of the penthouse suites have been reserved for the entire week, as there will be an electronics convention at the hotel. However, we would like to offer you our Senator's Suite, which is on the 34th floor at the standard room rate. You will find the Senator's Suite also has unparalleled luxury compared to any other hotel in the city. The only difference between the Presidential and Senator's Suite is the overall size of the room, which is slightly smaller. We are confident you will enjoy the Senator's Suite and look forward to having you as a guest. If you would like to reserve the suite, please call me A.S.A.P. as the rooms are quickly selling out. Thank you again for your continued patronage.

Sincerely,

Beth Anne George
General Manager, Hilla Hotels

---

3 What is the main purpose of this e-mail?
(A) To reserve the Senator's Suite
(B) To inquire about room rates
(C) To explain the room situation at the Hilla
(D) To book a convention

4 What is the stated problem in the e-mail?
(A) The Senator's Suite is sold out.
(B) There are not many restaurants in town.
(C) It is the holiday season.
(D) The Presidential Suite is sold out.

5 What solution is proposed by Ms. George?
(A) To reserve the Senator's Suite
(B) To find a room in another hotel
(C) To offer a refund
(D) To reserve the same room on another date

PART 7

Questions 1-5 refer to the following article.

Clint's Travels:
24 hours in El Paso
By Clint Smith, Staff Writer

APRIL 9—This week, I am setting aside my usual account of exotic places and far lands. Instead, I am writing this column about what our beloved El Paso has to offer. This is my personal idea of making the most of a nice day in our hometown.

8:00 A.M.—To start your day right, you might want to visit Big Mike's, where an oversized breakfast awaits you. Although this diner is one of El Paso's newest, long lines of customers patiently queue outside its doors. Being a regular customer there myself, I would like to suggest the breakfast burrito. This dish alone makes the visit and the long wait worth it.

10:00 A.M.—For the next stop, I recommend a leisurely stroll or a bike ride around the old Spanish park. The sights and scenery of the old Spanish homes and tropical trees will surely amaze you.

12:00 P.M.—When lunch hunger sets in; the Old Opry Restaurant just might be the place to be. The family owned restaurant is popular for its delicious home-cooked meals. Their menu can be viewed online at www.oldopry.com. If you plan to dine there on the weekend, better make a reservation, or you will be in for a long wait since the place is often packed. Another way is, you can have your meal to go and then bring it to the old Spanish Park, which is a short distance from the Old Opry.

2:30 P.M.—End your tour of El Paso with a side trip to the Torquemada exhibition at the El Paso Civic Center (EPCC), featuring prose and poetry by the El Paso Writers Guild. The poems range from the funny and ridiculous to thought provoking and inspiring. If you can't make it to the exhibitions, which ends April 19, no worries, they have something new every month.

If you have better ideas about how to spend 24 hours in El Paso, please e-mail your suggestions to clintsmith@texsun.com. Write "24 hours in El Paso" in the subject line.

1 What is mentioned about Big Mike's?

(A) It is an exotic place in El Paso.
(B) It is a recently opened restaurant.
(C) It is not very popular in the region.
(D) It doesn't serve breakfast.

2 The word "account" in paragraph 1, line 1 is closest in meaning to

(A) description
(B) fund
(C) guests
(D) concern

3 What is suggested about Mr. Smith's articles?

(A) It is focused on local destinations.
(B) It ordinarily involves funny anecdotes.
(C) It is published monthly.
(D) It is the newspaper's most read column.

4 According to the article, what is true about Old Opry?

(A) It has a several branches.
(B) It only opens for lunch.
(C) It is owned by a corporation.
(D) It is very busy on Saturdays and Sundays.

5 What is NOT a suggestion made by Mr. Smith?

(A) Ordering a specific dish for breakfast
(B) Taking a walk in Spanish Park
(C) Visiting the EPCC Web site for exhibition details
(D) Suggesting other interesting El Paso activities

Questions 6-7 refer to the following advertisement.

Introducing the new MP3 Solar Player from Whimmy Electronics!

How many times have you been listening to your favorite songs on your MP3 player and how many times have the batteries gone out in the middle? How many times have you accidently left your MP3 player on and how many times have the batteries run out? Most people will have these experiences and it can be very frustrating when you have to replace the batteries on these units.

Our new solar-powered MP3 player never needs batteries! Instead, it is powered by the light in your room or by the sun. Never get caught without your favorite music again. Buy the Whimmy MP3 player now! It's on sale until this Friday! For more information, please contact Ms. Susan Robinson, our product sales manager, via e-mail (s.robinson@whimmy.com) or phone (1-452-3684).

6 According to the passage, what is true about the Whimmy MP3 player?

(A) It is currently on sale.
(B) It is more expensive than ordinary players.
(C) It is more compact than other players.
(D) It is more shock-resistant than ordinary players.

7 Who most likely is Susan Robinson?

(A) A customer
(B) A musician
(C) An employee of Whimmy Electronics
(D) The president of Whimmy Electronics

PART 7

Questions 1-3 refer to the following article.

Rodeo Times

Tuesday, November 24

We are pleased to announce the construction of a new renewable energy manufacturing facility in Emeryvill. The city council just approved the construction of the new 3-billion-dollar state-of-the-art plant. The city actively persuaded INSU Energy to locate their facilities in Emeryville. This was done without the use of any incentives or tax credits. In other words, it did not cost taxpayers any money to entice the company to come to Emeryville. Other cities have spent millions of dollars in incentives trying to attract businesses to their cities, but we do not believe in that. We promoted the city by highlighting our skilled workforce and high quality of living. This combined with our enthusiastic spirit attracted INSU Energy to our city.

1. What is the purpose of this article?
   (A) To explain the benefits of solar energy
   (B) To announce the construction of a new plant
   (C) To explain renewable energy
   (D) To explain tax incentives to businesses

2. How much money did Emeryvill spend to attract INSU Energy?
   (A) $ 4 million
   (B) $ 5 million
   (C) $ 6 million
   (D) No tax money

3. What was one of the most attractive elements to entice the business to Emeryvill?
   (A) Low crime rate
   (B) Low tax rate
   (C) Favorable climate
   (D) A highly trained work force

Questions 4-7 refer to the following e-mail.

From: Tony Stark
To: All Staff
Date: Wed 13 January
Subject: Congratulations on a job well done!

Dear Team,

I am happy to start the New Year with great news. Charger Industries, one of the companies we have been targeting, has agreed to tie up with us. This is our second new client contract in January.

Charger is noteworthy because they have a fairly sizable account with us and they have made a large down payment. Whenever we acquire clients like this who respect our consulting services, it says a lot about our reputation. Let's make it our goal to get five more clients by next quarter.

I am incredibly fortunate to have such an excellent and ambitious team. To show my gratitude, I would like to invite you all to lunch next Thursday. Thanks again for all your hard work!

Tony Stark
Highbrow Software
Founder and Chief Executive Officer

---

4 Why is Mr. Stark happy?

(A) An important contract has been signed.
(B) A quarterly goal has been surpassed.
(C) A project has been finished before the deadline.
(D) An employment policy has been put into effect.

5 The word 'fairly' in paragraph 2, line 1, is closest in meaning to

(A) equally
(B) kindly
(C) quite
(D) hard

6 According to the e-mail, what does Mr. Stark want his company to do in the future?

(A) Expand its offices
(B) Offer new services
(C) Attract more customers
(D) Hire five employees

7 What will e-mail recipients be invited to do?

(A) Participate in a professional seminar
(B) Attend a celebratory activity
(C) Join a talent contest
(D) Vote for teammates for an award

DAY 12 독해 집중 연습

PART 7

Questions 1-2 refer to the following schedule.

Alternative Energy Conference

May 5, 9:00 A.M. to 5 P.M.
Expo Center / San Francisco, CA

Schedule		Attendance Policy
9:00 A.M. – 9:30 A.M.	Breakfast and greetings	optional
9:30 A.M. – 10:00 A.M.	This year's agenda	required
10:00 A.M. – 11:00 A.M.	Address by Professor John Chambers of Stanford University	By invitation only
11:00-A.M. – 12:00 P.M.	Address by United Nations Ambassador on climate change	required
12:00 P.M. – 1:00 P.M.	Lunch	optional
1:00 P.M. – 2:00 P.M.	Demonstration of new technologies	required
2:00 P.M. – 3:00 P.M.	Address and demonstration by Solar-Tech Inc.	required
3:00 P.M. – 4:00 P.M.	Demonstration of tidal wave generation from Hydro Industries of Denmark	optional
4:00 P.M. – 5:00 P.M.	Questions and answers session of all officers and industry representatives	optional

1 What type of demonstration will Hydro Industries of Denmark give?

(A) The latest solar advances
(B) Climate change
(C) Ultra capacitors
(D) Tidal wave generation

2 What is scheduled for 11:00 A.M.?

(A) Address by the CEO
(B) Lunch break
(C) Demonstration by Solar Tech
(D) Speech by United Nations Ambassador

Questions 3-5 refer to the following instructions.

Battery Maintenance

Congratulations on the purchase of your new electric car. One of the most important things is proper maintenance of the batteries. You can extend the lifespan of your batteries up to 10 years by maintaining them properly. The batteries have a ten-year warranty, but only if the owner maintains them according to these instructions.

Recharge your batteries after each use. The car is provided with a smart charger, which will prevent the batteries from being overcharged. The smart charger will detect the voltage levels in the batteries and taper the amperage down to the appropriate levels. The smart charger also provides what is known as a 'trickle charge', which will maintain batteries at their peak charging capacities when not in use. We recommend the use of a 220-volt system for the charging, although a 110-volt system can be used. However, the 220 volt is faster and more efficient.

3. What are the instructions for?

(A) How to drive a car
(B) Charging electric batteries
(C) How to care for car engines
(D) How warrantees are determined

4. What should users always do?

(A) Put water in the batteries
(B) Add acid to the batteries
(C) Recharge batteries after every use
(D) Test the batteries every day

5. According to the instructions, what is the recommended voltage for charging?

(A) 110 volts
(B) 220 volts
(C) 12 volts
(D) It is not specified.

DAY 13 독해 집중 연습

PART 7

Questions 1-3 refer to the following letter.

Dear Mr. Watson,

I am writing to you in reference to problems we are experiencing with your company in foam rubber deliveries to our furniture plants around the United States. As you know, we have five different furniture manufacturing plants around the United States, and your foam rubber is required for 75% of our furniture products. However, in the last thirty days, delays of your foam rubber shipments have forced our plants to cease production. This is unacceptable and we need to have your assurance that this practice will cease at once. Otherwise, we will be forced to cancel our supply agreement with Acme Foam Rubber and switch to another company. Thank you for your understanding in this matter.

Tom Brokaw
Director of Logistics
Savannah Furniture Inc.

1. What is the purpose of this letter?
   (A) To increase sales of furniture
   (B) To increase sales of foam rubber
   (C) To complain about deliveries of foam rubber
   (D) To report about the shipping problem.

2. What is the result of the delayed shipment?
   (A) It causes production to be stopped.
   (B) It causes increases in prices.
   (C) It is inconvenient for all.
   (D) It causes relocation of the plant.

3. What will Mr. Brokaw do if the problems are not resolved?
   (A) He will offer more time.
   (B) He will negotiate the prices.
   (C) He will find another manufacturer.
   (D) He will develop another product.

Questions 4-6 refer to the following article.

Tips and tricks to maximize your productivity in the workplace

Even after a full night of sleep, it is common to feel tired or stressed when spending all day behind a desk. Fortunately, there are several things you can do to maintain your energy level and keep yourself stress-free during the day. Best of all, some of these "tricks" are absolutely free.

Remain active
A lack of physical activity can often lead to drowsiness or tired muscles. According to a research by Winnie Manson, M.D, people who remain physically active during the day feel more clearheaded and process information much faster. So, go outdoors and take a five-minute walk every few hours. If that is not possible because of weather or location, then take it indoors. Climbing stairs can be especially invigorating.

Drink lots of water
Dehydration can be a common cause of daily tiredness. In a recent study at Michigan University, researchers found that drinking at least eight glasses of water a day helped students maintain greater mental clarity and focus for the whole day. Keep a bottle or container of water near you for easy access, and drink before you even feel the need to.

Connect with nature
Keep a potted plant in your workspace. Research has concluded that people who keep fresh flowers or green plants in their office receive a number of benefits. They create more original and innovative ideas, experience a greater sense of positivity, and breathe cleaner air. Palms, ivy or ferns are easy-to-care for plants.

4. What advice is given to readers?

   (A) Develop a hobby
   (B) Plant a vegetable in the garden
   (C) Take short walks during the day
   (D) Eat a healthy snack in the afternoon

5. What can be inferred about drinking water?

   (A) It can prevent tiredness.
   (B) Cold water is better than warm water.
   (C) It doesn't help you focus.
   (D) You should drink water when you feel thirsty.

6. According to the article, what can increase creativity?

   (A) Drinking more water
   (B) Having plants nearby
   (C) Exercising regularly
   (D) Getting more sleep

DAY 14 독해 집중 연습

PART 7

Questions 1-3 refer to the following announcement.

We are pleased to announce the grand opening of Empire Bank in the financial district of New York City. Empire Bank is the result of a merger between Bank of the West and Great Western Bank. Empire Bank's assets exceed one hundred billion dollars. The merger of Bank of the West and Great Western Bank provides nationwide service for our customers. We now have bank branches in all fifty states of the United States. The opening of Empire Bank Branch in New York City symbolizes a landmark for our company. Empire Bank also has a strong securities trading division. Eagle Securities will provide a full range of trading options and stock trading for our banking customers. As a gesture of appreciation to our new customers, we are offering free checking accounts to our customers for life. The public is invited to the grand opening on Friday, July 5 at 9 A.M.

1. What division of Empire Bank provides stock trading?
   (A) America Securities
   (B) Bank of the West
   (C) Empire Bank
   (D) Eagle Securities

2. In how many states does Empire Bank have branches?
   (A) 35 states
   (B) 45 states
   (C) 49 states
   (D) 50 states

3. What does Empire Bank offer new customers?
   (A) A fifty dollar US Savings Bond
   (B) Coffee and cake
   (C) Free stock trading account
   (D) Free checking accounts

Questions 4-6 refer to the following schedule.

Appointment Calendar of John H. Hastings, CEO of Consolidated Financial Services, Inc.

Monday June 21	8:00 A.M. to 11:00 A.M. 1:00 P.M. to 5:00 P.M.	Meeting with stockholders Conference with Chamber of Commerce
Tuesday June 22	8:00 A.M. to 10:00 A.M. 2:00 P.M. to 4:00 P.M.	Meeting with vice presidents Meeting with director of Labor Relations regarding union contract
Wednesday June 23	8:00 A.M. to 11:30 A.M. 1:00 P.M. to 5:00 P.M.	Meeting with freight forwarder Meeting with Beneto Steel CEO on supply contract
Thursday June 24	8:00 A.M. to 10:00 A.M. 2:00 P.M. to 4:00 P.M.	Meeting with Heather Jones, Mayor of San Felipe Presentation to the Order of Masons
Friday June 25	8:00 A.M. to 10:00 A.M. 2:00 P.M. to 3:00 P.M.	Breakfast with shareholders Keynote Address to graduation class of Pacific University

4   What is this schedule for?

(A) The sales representative of Consolidated Financial Services
(B) The personal assistant of the CEO
(C) The manager of sales of Consolidated Financial Services, Inc.
(D) The CEO of Consolidated Financial Services

5   When will there be a meeting with the Mayor of San Filipe?

(A) On Monday
(B) On Tuesday
(C) On Thursday
(D) On Friday

6   What is scheduled for Friday at 8:00 A.M.?

(A) Breakfast with shareholders
(B) Breakfast with the board of directors
(C) Breakfast with the vice presidents
(D) Breakfast with the Chamber of Commerce

DAY 15 독해 집중 연습

PART 7

Questions 1-4 refer to the following article.

Upcoming Road Renovation on Casanville Bridge

2 July — The much-anticipated road reconstruction on Casanville Bridge will be underway next month. This renovation will widen the roads by adding one additional lane both ways, allowing the vehicles to travel at a faster pace. Until the construction work is over, heavier traffic congestion is to be expected. Last Saturday, The Saint Juste Transportation Agency (SJTA) reported that they will undertake road construction on Casanville Bridge on Monday, August 3. – [1] –.

To avoid the rush hours, roadwork will be performed in three shifts. (Weekdays: 11 A.M. to 5 P.M. and 10 P.M. to 5 A.M. Weekends: 10 A.M. to 4 P.M. and 9 P.M. to 7 A.M.) – [2] –.

– [3] –. Bridge renovation will be completed in three weeks. In accordance with the situation, SJTA advises motorists not to get on the Casanville Bridge, but instead take Forest Avenue or Ponoma Street, both of which will lead to Van Waals Bridge, thus allowing you to reach the other side of the river. – [4] –.

---

1 For whom is the article primarily intended?

(A) Travel agents
(B) International tourists
(C) Construction workers
(D) Local Drivers

2 In which of the positions marked [1], [2], [3] and [4] does the following sentence best belong?

"As stated above, both lanes on the bridge will experience slow-moving traffic, and consequently, drivers will have to face temporary discomfort due to traffic delays."

(A) [1]
(B) [2]
(C) [3]
(D) [4]

3 What is indicated about the roadwork?

(A) It will cause traffic to be slower than it used to be.
(B) It will result in the closure of Casanville Bridge.
(C) It will take over several months to be completed.
(D) It will include repair work.

4 What action does the SJTA recommend?

(A) Making a detour
(B) Avoiding rush hours
(C) Driving at a lower speed
(D) Not using Casanville Bridge

Questions 5-8 refer to the following online chat.

Operator [2:30 P.M.] Good afternoon. Customer service agent; How can I help you?

Ross Dickerson [2:31 P.M.] Recently, I bought a mobile phone, Milky Way M3, but I have had trouble with some touchscreen issues. The touchscreen is not working as expected.

Operator [2:32 P.M.] Sir, please tell me about the issue in detail. What exactly makes you feel uncomfortable?

Ross Dickerson [2:34 P.M.] It didn't accept anything when I typed. And I received a phone call but I couldn't answer it as the swipe didn't work at all.

Operator [2:35 P.M.] It appears that the touchscreen becomes unresponsive. Please follow these steps. First, connect your device to your computer. Second, restore your mobile phone back to factory settings.

Ross Dickerson [2:40 P.M.] Yes. I've already done that. Sadly, nothing has been changed in that process.

Operator [2:42 P.M.] If that is the case, there is one option. Your device is still under warranty. You could exchange your mobile phone for a refurbished one.

Ross Dickerson [2:43 P.M.] Please tell me what to do.

Operator [2:45 P.M.] Please ship your product to our center. And we can send you a postage-paid box right away, or you can drop off your mobile phone at our nearby authorized service provider.

5. Why did Mr. Dickerson contact Customer Service?

   (A) To place an order
   (B) To return an item
   (C) To have technical assistance
   (D) To report delivery delays

6. According to the chat, what is suggested about Dickerson's mobile phone?

   (A) It can be fixed immediately.
   (B) Its warranty has been already expired.
   (C) It is delivered to the wrong address.
   (D) Its touchscreen is damaged.

7. What is the solution the operator recommends about the device?

   (A) Fix it at a nearby service center
   (B) Send in for replacement
   (C) Get a full refund
   (D) Replace a touchscreen

8. At 2:42 P.M., what does the operator mean when she writes, "If that is the case"?

   (A) She tries to suggest an alternative.
   (B) She apologizes for the inconvenience.
   (C) She wants to encourage him to extend the warranty.
   (D) She makes up for the problem by giving a discount coupon.

PART 7

Questions 1-5 refer to the following flyer and e-mail.

The 6th Semi-Annual Gerry Garcia Arts Festival
10-12 August

The Gerry Garcia Arts Festival (GGAF), sponsored by the Psychedelic Arts Guild, has a surprise for everyone. The events, encompassing over three days, will showcase artworks by celebrated artists and mini concerts by local musicians and actors. Food and crafts will be for sale as well as activities for children.

Below is an incomplete list of activities and events:

▶ Friday, 10 August, 1:00 P.M., West wing Art Gallery
   Initial showing of Johann Strauss' "Faces around Me." Display runs through 15 September.

▶ Saturday & Sunday, 11 and 12 August, 10:00 A.M.-6:00 P.M., Fire station picnic area. Young kids arts and crafts.

▶ Saturday, 11 August, 6:00 P.M., Balboa Outdoor Theatre (In the event of rain: Cortez Auditorium) Concert by the Irish Orphan Choir (back by popular demand).
   Tickets required.

▶ Saturday & Sunday, 11 and 12 August, 1:00 P.M.-8:00 P.M. Fallen Heroes Memorial Park. Food and Crafts Market.

▶ Sunday, 12 August, 2:00 P.M. and 8:00 P.M., Savoy Theatre
   The Mata Hari Theatre Ensemble presents "karmic justice" by the renowned writer, John Lloyd. Tickets required.

Tickets go on sale on 1 August. For more details regarding tickets and a full list of events and activities, visit www.ggaf.org.phx.

To: Leah Sharpe <leahsharpe224@ggaf.org.phx>
From: Jasmine McIntyre <jmcintyre@swt.org.za>
Subject: Information
Date: 15 August

Dear Ms. Sharpe:

My gratitude for your giving us the chance to entertain you with music of our orphanage at the Gerry Garcia Arts Festival. It was unfortunate that the weather did not allow us to perform outdoors and fewer people watched our performance. However, many who attended bought copies of our albums or wanted to know if our music was downloadable on popular music Web sites. We really appreciated the positive response we received from the audience.

We hope we can perform again in this festival in the future.

Sincerely,

Jasmine McIntyre
Managing Director
Irish Orphan Choir

---

1 What is NOT an event that will take place during the Arts Festival?

(A) A ballet performance
(B) An arts and crafts display
(C) An art exhibit
(D) A food market

2 When can a play be watched?

(A) On August 1
(B) On August 10
(C) On August 11
(D) On August 12

3 What is said about the festival?

(A) It lasts one week.
(B) It is held twice a year.
(C) It starts at 10:00 A.M. each day.
(D) Tickets can only be purchased online.

4 Why did Ms. McIntyre send Ms. Sharpe an e-mail?

(A) To purchase tickets for an event
(B) To reschedule a performance
(C) To express her gratitude
(D) To decline an invitation

5 What is suggested about the Irish Orphan Choir?

(A) It was its first time to participate.
(B) It performed in the Cortez Auditorium.
(C) It is currently on tour in Ireland.
(D) It gets many visitors to its Web site.

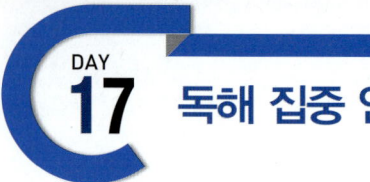

PART 7

Questions 1-5 refer to the following letter and receipt.

Milne Office Supplies

August 10

Williams, Redman
4001 Fifth Ave, Suite 305 Toronto, Ontario M4W 1A7

Account Number: XXXX-3001 / Customer ID: WRA4001305

Dear Mr. Williams,

To express our gratitude for your patronage for the past five years, we have upgraded your Milne Office Supplies (MOS) credit card to the Golden Rewards privilege plan to take effect immediately. This plan features numerous benefits, including an increased credit line of $3,000, cost-free shipment of online purchases over $150, and complimentary passes to special events. Plus, Golden Rewards customers receive a 20 percent discount on a selected category of items monthly by using their MOS credit card. This month, all electronic items are discounted for Golden Rewards customers only. Discounts will be applied at the time of sale and reflected as "SR points" on the receipt.

More details about your upgraded status can be found in the brochure attached. If you have any questions regarding your account, please call toll-free MOS customer services at 709-565-7710, from 10:00 A.M. to 5:00 P.M. Monday to Saturday.

Sincerely,

Oscar Wilde
Director, Card-member Services

Milne Office Supplies
178 E Maple Street, Toronto, Ontario M4W 1A7
Receipt

Printed: July 17. 9:03 A.M. / Customer ID: WRA4001305

Code	Item		Price
CLD974	Orocan high back chair (black)		$129.00
SNW235	Florentine laptop computer (model: 2433CH)		$170.00
KVN291	Grappa computer display cabinet		$430.00
SMR886	Sedgewick standard stapler	12 at $9.00 each	$108.00
SMR810	Canon laser printer		$310.00

Subtotal	$1,147.00
Sales Tax	$113.40
Total paid by credit card XXXX-278	$1,260.40

SR points applied to item numbers SNW235 and SMR810

**No refunds or exchanges will be made on discounted products.
Returns can be made within 30 days of purchase.**

1   What is the purpose of the letter?
    (A) To order a laptop computer and office supplies
    (B) To inform Mr. Williams of changing his credit card
    (C) To advertise a storewide sale of Milne Office Supplies
    (D) To accept Mr. Williams' proposal

2   According to the letter, what is implied about Mr. Williams?
    (A) He attended an auction held by MOS.
    (B) He made an online purchase at MOS.
    (C) He has been a long time customer.
    (D) He spent a total of $3,000 on his previous order.

3   For what product did Golden Rewards customers receive a 20% discount in July?
    (A) Computers and peripherals
    (B) Writing tools
    (C) Office furniture
    (D) Office supplies

4   In the letter, the word "applied" in paragraph 1, line 8, is closest in meaning to
    (A) put into effect
    (B) made an appeal
    (C) placed into contact
    (D) worked hard

5   According to the receipt, what true about the purchase?
    (A) The customer received a 10% discount on each item.
    (B) Only exchanges can be made after 30 days from the purchase date.
    (C) Returns can be made without the receipts.
    (D) Refunds are offered for only some of the purchases.

DAY 18 독해 집중 연습

PART 7

Questions 1-5 refer to the following article and letter.

Hampshire Gets dressed

October 30 – It has been difficult not to see the flurry of activities at 34 Macedon Avenue, where national retailer Harold's Haberdashery inaugurated its newest store on October 10 to a large and wonderful crowd. Local shoppers have been excited for the popular clothing that Harold's sells for up to fifty percent off other retailers' prices. The outlet, known for its amazing Sunday sales, took over the former Rochester financial complex and refurbished it to accommodate one of its largest shops so far.

Sigmund Taber, Chairman of the Hampshire Chamber of Commerce, says, "Harold's haberdashery is great for Hampshire. The town will greatly benefit from income tax revenues, and about 30 new jobs have been created." He also says, "Townsfolk are finding it very convenient to have such a great shop in town. We don't really have to travel far to get to the mall in Helmsford to find fine clothing."

Business hours of this store are from 8:00 A.M. to 10:00 P.M. Its south entrance is on Macedon Avenue, and its west entrance is on Duke Street, just off Chestnut Parkway. There is sufficient parking space. However, during the rush hours of this region, it will be very hard to access and leave the parking areas.

Dear Editor,

I read your column on October 30 pertaining to the establishment of Harold's Haberdashery in Hampshire. While the store has greatly been a convenience for the town, it has also become an inconvenience for a number of our longtime residents. Several of us who live on Duke Street are hindered by the heavy traffic in front of our homes. During shop hours there is usually a long line of cars and trucks on Duke Street. Vehicles stop in front of our driveways, making it hard for us to access or leave our own residences. Delivery trucks don't usually use the Macedon Avenue entrance, since Duke Street entrance is nearest to the loading bays.

I realize that there is nothing that Harold's Haberdashery can do about Duke Street entrance. So some residents and I have asked the Hampshire Town Council to put a traffic light at Duke Street and Macedon Avenue intersection. This would make traffic flow more efficiently and offer us some relief. We implore fellow Hampshire residents to help us make our case by participating in the next council meeting on November 30 when this matter will be discussed.

Sincerely,

Leonard Nesmith
Concerned Resident

1 According to the article, why is Harold's Haberdashery popular with shoppers?

(A) Because of its low prices
(B) Because of its customer service
(C) Because of its wide variety of merchandise
(D) Because of its excellent return policy

2 What does Mr. Taber say about Harold's Haberdashery?

(A) It does not have adequate parking spaces.
(B) It benefits Hampshire financially.
(C) It will be opening a branch in Helmsford.
(D) It creates competition with other Hampshire shops.

3 What is suggested about delivery trucks?

(A) Road accidents have increased because of them.
(B) Many of them use Macedon Avenue.
(C) They usually use west entrance of Harold's.
(D) The streets are not crowded with them in the morning.

4 What is Mr. Nesmith's suggestion about the delivery trucks?

(A) They do not use the loading bays.
(B) They should be prohibited from using Duke Street.
(C) They should reduce their business hours.
(D) They often block residents' driveways.

5 What does Mr. Nesmith ask residents to do?

(A) Stop patronizing Harold's Haberdashery
(B) Use public transportation to Harold's Haberdashery
(C) Support a cause to ease traffic congestion
(D) Write a letter to the town councilors

DAY 19 독해 집중 연습

PART 7

Questions 1-5 refer to the following pamphlet, schedule and e-mail.

Asia-Pacific Business Investment Workshop
Hong Kong Municipal Auditorium
Tuesday, November 11

This is a specialized workshop to discuss the latest trend of business investment in Asia-Pacific region. The Asia-Pacific region is one of the fastest growing markets in the world. Renowned presenters will share their insights on various issues. Participants are required to have their names registered to attend the workshop. Those interested to attend have to confirm their participation by emailing to registration@asiapacificworkshop.com on or before October 11. There will be no admission fee for participants.

To avoid any disruption during the event, please arrive at least 30 minutes in advance. The participants will receive press kits and materials available at the registration desk. Please note that due to the limited number of seats for each workshop, the selection of participants will be entirely based on a first come, first served basis.

Time	Presenter	Workshop Title
9:30 A.M.	Martial Graham	Market Outlooks and Economic Perspectives
11:00 A.M.	Coman Lee	Strategic Investment
12:00 P.M.	Lunch Break	
1:00 P.M.	Tachibana Sato	Plan Today for Your Tomorrow
2:30 P.M.	Antonio Griezman	Build a Strong Investing Foundation
4:00 P.M.	Xiu Ying Wang	Risk Management in Investment Decision Making

```
                                    e-mail

From: w.xiuying@wanginvestment.com
To: rashford@asiapacificworkshop.com
Subject: November Workshop
Date: October 3

Dear Mr. Rashford,

I would like to express my sincere gratitude to be a part of this marvelous workshop. My understanding is that a great number of attendees are willing to participate in the November event. I am pretty sure that this event will have a magnificent influence on people and businesses in the region.

I am writing to ask you about the possibility of rescheduling next month's speech. The schedule I received said that I am the last presenter. Unfortunately, I have an important commitment after the lunch break in Hong Kong. So, I have to leave the auditorium no later than 11:30. I have already reported this issue to the organizer, David Solanke. However, perhaps I have not expressed myself very well. So, if possible, please change the schedule and distribute the revised version to all at your earliest convenience.

Sincerely,
Xiu Ying Wang
```

1 What are participants advised to do?

(A) Get to the event early
(B) Pay the registration fee online
(C) Arrange private travel insurance
(D) Turn their mobile off during the workshop

2 Who will deliver a speech about the economic forecast?

(A) Martial Graham
(B) Coman Lee
(C) Tachibana Sato
(D) Antonio Griezman

3 When would Mr. Wang like to speak at the workshop?

(A) 9:30 A.M.
(B) 11:00 A.M.
(C) 1:00 P.M.
(D) 2:30 P.M.

4 What is indicated about Mr. Wang?

(A) He lives in Hong Kong.
(B) He is the organizer of the workshop.
(C) He has an appointment during the workshop.
(D) He recently changed his speech topic.

5 What does Mr. Wang request that Ms. Rashford to do?

(A) Check on the admission fees
(B) Get approval from the hotel
(C) Update an event document
(D) Change workshop location

DAY 20 독해 집중 연습

PART 7

Questions 1-5 refer to the following notice, list and e-mail.

Jason Madison University Communication Center

Are you having problems with communication? How good are we really at communication? Human relationships can be wonderful and sometimes tricky. Discover creative ways of understanding and improving your interaction with others.

A two-day interactive program will focus on improving your communication skills and optimizing your personal and working relationship. Classes will be held in our recently-renovated research lab at the Jason Madison University Communication Center on Thursday and Friday from 5 P.M. to 7 P.M. Those interested in this program may register for one or both sessions. Each session is subject to change due to the number of participants. Payment can be made at the Jason Madison University Communication Center office or through our own Web site: www.jmu.edu/communicationcenter/programs/payment. If you have any questions regarding the program, please contact the instructor Russel Wilson (r.wilson@jmu.edu).

Communication Program List

The highly-intensive two-day program is scheduled as follows.

Session 1 - April 30
Bridging the interpersonal gap & Active listening skills

Session 2 - May 1
Reading body language & Improving management skills

Schedule	Session 1	Session 2	Both Sessions
Jason Madison University Students	$20	$35	$40
Students from other colleges and non-students	$30	$45	$50
Registration after April 5	$40	$55	$70

The program consists of a group discussion and an evaluation section led by experienced psychotherapists. A certificate of attendance will be provided.

e-mail

From: Adrian Monro <amonro1212@ucla.edu>
To: Russel Wilson <r.wilson@jmu.edu>
Subject: Communication program inquiry
Date: April 10

Dear Mr. Wilson,

I am writing to ask you about the program held on April 30. I hope it is not too late to sign up. I just heard about the program from one of my friends who is the student of Jason Madison University. I am interested in learning how to improve my communication skills. Please check and see if there is any room in Session 1. I am also interested in Session 2, but I'm afraid I can't take the program because of my graduation exam.
I would appreciate you letting me know of next program schedule.

Thank you,

Adrian Monro

1. What is the purpose of the notice?
   (A) To confirm program schedule
   (B) To welcome new students
   (C) To promote some classes
   (D) To provide solutions to the problems

2. What is indicated about the Jason Madison University Communication Center?
   (A) It opens every day except for Mondays.
   (B) It is located outside university.
   (C) It was recently remodeled.
   (D) It can be used for the university students only.

3. How much will Mr. Monro probably pay for the program?
   (A) $20
   (B) $35
   (C) $40
   (D) $70

4. How did Mr. Monro learn about the course?
   (A) From an advertisement
   (B) From a friend
   (C) From a bulletin board
   (D) From a psychotherapist

5. What does Mr. Monro ask about?
   (A) Enrollment fee
   (B) Program time schedule
   (C) Availability for admission
   (D) Program change

SECTION 3
Actual Test

READING TEST

In the Reading test, you will read a variety of texts and answer several different types of reading comprehension questions. The entire Reading test will last 75 minutes. There are three parts, and directions are given for each part. You are encouraged to answer as many questions as possible within the time allowed.

You must mark your answers on the separate answer sheet. Do not write your answers in your test book.

PART 5

Directions: A word or phrase is missing in each of the sentences below. Four answer choices are given below each sentence. Select the best answer to complete the sentence. Then mark the letter (A), (B), (C), or (D) on your answer sheet.

101. Please inform ------- right away when Carl from Kirkwood Manufacturing calls.
 (A) me
 (B) my
 (C) mine
 (D) I

102. Although Mr. Park had a(n) ------- schedule, he still found time to supervise and train the new employees.
 (A) false
 (B) sure
 (C) early
 (D) tight

103. Flight 788 to New York took off a couple of hours ------- than expected due to the unexpected mechanical problems in Los Angeles.
 (A) late
 (B) later
 (C) lately
 (D) latest

104. Both West Munster Street ------- Saint Jose Avenue will be closed for the regular safety inspection by the local government next Wednesday.
 (A) and
 (B) or
 (C) so
 (D) like

105. Beeler Office Supplies will be offering ------- on different items for the next 2 months to make room for new products.
 (A) discounts
 (B) discount
 (C) discountable
 (D) discounted

106. Those ------- are interested in participating in the local food fair and symposium should register by April 5.
 (A) when
 (B) from
 (C) who
 (D) since

107. Mr. Steve Otis was ------- to regional manager of the Chicago branch in just 2 years.
 (A) tried
 (B) applied
 (C) promoted
 (D) agreed

108. In compliance with the safety standards in the U.S., UBS Engineering should ------- check the fluid levels of the machinery.
 (A) regular
 (B) regularly
 (C) regularize
 (D) regulars

109 Attached is the document explaining the recently ------- equipment insurance policy for your reference.
(A) driven
(B) issued
(C) influenced
(D) expressed

110 ------- a cafeteria serving casual meals for employees, there are some snack stands on the ground floor.
(A) Just as
(B) In addition to
(C) Otherwise
(D) Because

111 To apply for the position of senior financial consultant, applicants should submit at least two letters of ------- to the personnel department.
(A) recommending
(B) recommend
(C) recommended
(D) recommendation

112 ------- who wants to attend the technical writing seminar must register no later than January 3.
(A) Them
(B) My
(C) Anyone
(D) Whomever

113 ------- the holiday work schedule has already been posted on the company's intranet, paper copies will not be distributed.
(A) Regardless of
(B) Since
(C) In case of
(D) Besides

114 The company's commitment to increasing the productivity of its workforce is expected to have a ------- effect on performance.
(A) benefit
(B) benefits
(C) beneficially
(D) beneficial

115 The items ordered today will be delivered to the address shown on the order form ------- 3 business days.
(A) toward
(B) instead of
(C) within
(D) apart from

116 The exact delivery date of your order ------- on the shipping method you select on the Web site.
(A) have depended
(B) will depend
(C) depending
(D) are depended

117 At the annual stock holders' meeting, Mr. Rio, CEO of the Mellone Corporation, plans on ------- the company's expansion into the European market.
(A) outline
(B) outlined
(C) outlining
(D) outlines

118 There will be some changes to the flight schedules as Phil Airlines and Air Beijing are gradually integrated ------- a single airline company.
(A) of
(B) until
(C) on
(D) into

119 Since the software developers mostly work independently, weekly staff meetings are the only way for them to collaborate with -------.
(A) the same
(B) this
(C) each other
(D) much

120 On July 5, British Broadcasting will start a new program ------- to showcasing amateur performing artists from all over the world.
(A) prepared
(B) dedicated
(C) allowed
(D) compared

121. All employees are asked to ------- with the firm's new policy on internal classified information.
    (A) comply
    (B) fulfill
    (C) perform
    (D) observe

122. The Italian restaurant called Amici, which is not far ------- the business district, is a great place to take clients for dinner.
    (A) on
    (B) with
    (C) about
    (D) from

123. It is advisable for supervisors to inspect thoroughly the materials that have arrived at the construction ------- before signing an invoice.
    (A) engineer
    (B) site
    (C) plan
    (D) industry

124. Articles written by industry analysts ------- inclusion in the summer issue of *Style and Trends* must be submitted before the deadline.
    (A) during
    (B) over
    (C) on
    (D) for

125. The Manchester branch of Simon Sea Food hired six servers ------- in preparing for the busy summer season.
    (A) assisted
    (B) assists
    (C) to assist
    (D) have assisted

126. All the passengers using TRI Airlines are ------- to use battery rechargers while waiting for their flights.
    (A) customary
    (B) welcome
    (C) pending
    (D) expectant

127. No changes to the establishment will be made this time ------- there have been no problems with the evacuation plan during the annual inspection.
    (A) so that
    (B) as soon as
    (C) since
    (D) only

128. Each show at the Incheon International Children's Festival is limited to 120 seats and is filled on a first-come, first-served -------.
    (A) focus
    (B) custom
    (C) quality
    (D) basis

129. Mr. Evans, administrative assistant of the marketing department, is responsible for ------- employees of any changes to meeting schedules.
    (A) recommending
    (B) advising
    (C) offering
    (D) reviewing

130. Ms. Harada's background was so ------- that she was chosen for the managerial position at the Fukui plant.
    (A) qualified
    (B) knowledgeable
    (C) pleased
    (D) impressive

PART 6

Directions: Read the texts that follow. A word, phrase, or sentence is missing in parts of each text. Four answer choices for each question are given below the text. Select the best answer to complete the text. Then mark the letter (A), (B), (C), or (D) on your answer sheet.

Questions 131-134 refer to the following letter.

Vana Novak, Supply Manager
Realto Auto Store
515 S. Chamboard

Dear Ms. Novak,

I am writing to introduce you to a remarkable new tire model from the innovative people at Western Wheel & Tire. I'd like to explain why, ------- of the brand you are now using, you will want to give the new SX 250 tire a try.
131.

First of all, we at Western Wheel & Tire know the SX 250 is the most ------- model on the market because we have already received a large amount of positive customer feedback. -------, the
132.   **133.**
SX250 is currently the best-selling tire in the country, even though it was introduced only a few months ago.

-------. Please see the enclosed pamphlet for more information.
134.

Sincerely,

Devin Di Promo
Marketing Agent

131 (A) regarding
    (B) regardless
    (C) with regards
    (D) possibility

132 (A) promise
    (B) promised
    (C) promising
    (D) promises

133 (A) However
    (B) In addition
    (C) Even though
    (D) Although

134 (A) SX250 is unable to be purchased online at this moment.
    (B) You may donate $300 for the Western Wheel & Tire.
    (C) You are probably very curious about these enthusiastic reviews.
    (D) Customer Service Center opens Monday through Saturday.

Questions 135-138 refer to the following e-mail.

From: Barry Scott <b.scott@huntington.com>
To: Huntington Employee List
Date: October 15
Subject: City Elections

With elections getting closer, we urge all of our employees -------. By voting, you express your voice, especially during citywide and state elections. I understand ------- many of you have children and are unable to find time to vote. As a way to encourage a higher voter ------- and give you all extra time, I would like to offer everyone a half-day off next Friday, October 26. Please vote for your candidate in the morning and be at work before 1 P.M. -------.

135.   136.   137.   138.

I hope you all take advantage of this time to vote. For those who have already voted, enjoy the morning off.

Best regards,

Barry Scott
Chief of Personnel
Hunington International

135 (A) to vote
    (B) voting
    (C) votes
    (D) voted

136 (A) what
    (B) because
    (C) then
    (D) that

137 (A) company
    (B) turnout
    (C) agency
    (D) production

138 (A) Exit poll shows that this election will be a close race.
    (B) For those unable to cast their votes, please report to your supervisors.
    (C) This should be enough time for you all to vote and have lunch.
    (D) Employees are stuck with severe traffic congestion.

Questions 139-142 refer to the following article.

The new construction of the Orange County Airport has been completed despite vehement objections from nearby ------- areas. The new airport is expected to open despite the pertinacious objections of the Newport Beach Homeowners Association. Once the flights begin, opposition from the residents is predicted to become more -------.

The county has stood resolute in the completion of the Orange County Airport (SNA), as it provides a wonderful alternative to Orange County residents that wish to avoid the inconvenience of flying out of Los Angeles International Airport (LAX). The Orange County Board of Commissioners stated the increase in noise levels would be ------- minor, as the airlines will be using the newest jets with quieter engines and noise cancelation technology. The Commissioners are asking the public to be open-minded in the opening of the new one hundred million dollar facility. -------.

139. (A) habitual
 (B) financial
 (C) recreational
 (D) residential

140. (A) additional
 (B) expanded
 (C) eager
 (D) fierce

141. (A) frequently
 (B) relatively
 (C) greatly
 (D) usually

142. (A) The facility was severely damaged by natural disasters.
 (B) It will bring jobs, commerce and tourism to Orange County, thus benefiting everyone.
 (C) The accommodation capacity will increase by 5 percent compared to last month.
 (D) The airlines will go on strike because of the construction.

Questions 143-146 refer to the following memorandum.

To: Human Resources Division
From: Patrick Robinson, VP Personnel
Subject: Recruitment of foreigners for high need positions

As you know, our company has been experiencing problems recruiting qualified engineers and scientists in the various locations for our company. While we are able to hire many of our candidates domestically, we are unable to fill highly specialized positions in engineering and science. Even though we have ------- programs, the shortage is severe. We are asking
143.
employees for any ------- they may have to resolve the situation. They may submit their ideas via
144.
e-mail to my personal e-mail address.

-------. Recent Visa regulations are allowing more American companies to sponsor and hire
145.
foreign workers ------- high levels of expertise.
146.

143 (A) interview
(B) recruiting
(C) training
(D) application

144 (A) suggestions
(B) suggesting
(C) to suggest
(D) suggested

145 (A) One option the company is considering is overseas recruitment of engineers and scientists.
(B) The company is scheduled to relocate its headquarters next month.
(C) The department of human resources is planning to hire more staff.
(D) Our company is struggling to gain a competitive advantage over rival companies.

146 (A) from
(B) with
(C) at
(D) on

PART 7

Directions: In this part you will read a selection of texts, such as magazine and newspaper articles, e-mails, and instant messages. Each text or set of texts is followed by several questions. Select the best answer for each question and mark the letter (A), (B), (C), or (D) on your answer sheet.

Questions 147-148 refer to the following coupon.

Oriental Express Chinese Diner

Dinner specials

$5.59 + tax (reg. price $6.75)

Your options

COUPON	COUPON	COUPON
#1 Beef with Broccoli Served with corn, garlic rice and lemon or apple pie	#2 Spring Wraps Served with blanched string beans, fried rice and lemon or apple pie	#3 Szechuan Chicken Served with lettuce, rice and lemon or apple pie

Valid from 5 P.M. to 9 P.M. weekdays
Only original coupons accepted
Limit one per customer
Good only for options stated in this coupon

---

147 What is indicated about the coupon?

(A) It can be used for any item in the full menu.
(B) It can be used only one time.
(C) It is good for only 30 days.
(D) It is exclusively for couples.

148 What is NOT included in the price of the specials?

(A) Rice
(B) Dessert
(C) Drinks
(D) Vegetables

Questions 149-151 refer to the following article.

PERTH (2 February) – Perth's Ocean Breeze Hotel will once again open its doors under new owners, after being closed for about 3 months. The popularity of the once-famous hotel had diminished, and it was uncertain if the hotel can get back up on its feet again. Past owners who had run the hotel had decided to increase room rates and removed some services and amenities, such as its free breakfast and parking. Accommodation rates went up 20 percent and at the same time, reduced its staff. That made an increasing number of customers disappointed about not having the same level of service that made Ocean Breeze famous for vacationers in the first place. After taking over the hotel six months ago, the new owners contracted Randolph Morehouse to put the hotel back on the map. "The previous owners' decision to make more money by sacrificing its quality has been a terrible mistake on their part" Morehouse was quoted in a recent interview, "starting now, customers will be given excellent coffee and tea service plus free full continental breakfast. And more importantly, we will be offering valet parking at a very reasonable cost and, of course, free Internet service in every room." He also stated a number of the older rooms on the west side had undergone major refurbishing and the lobby has had a complete facelift to make it more warm and inviting. Morehouse is very confident that Ocean Breeze Hotel will once again be the place to go for vacationers and businessmen alike.

149 What is the article's general idea?

(A) A business' major improvement
(B) Plans for a future building renovation
(C) An inauguration of a new hotel
(D) The decline of tourists in Perth

150 Who most likely is Mr. Morehouse?

(A) A restaurateur
(B) A professional traveler
(C) An interior designer
(D) A hotel manager

151 What is NOT stated as a recently added service of the Ocean Breeze Hotel?

(A) Hot beverages
(B) Valet parking
(C) Discounted room rates
(D) A comfortable lobby

Questions 152-153 refer to the following text message chain.

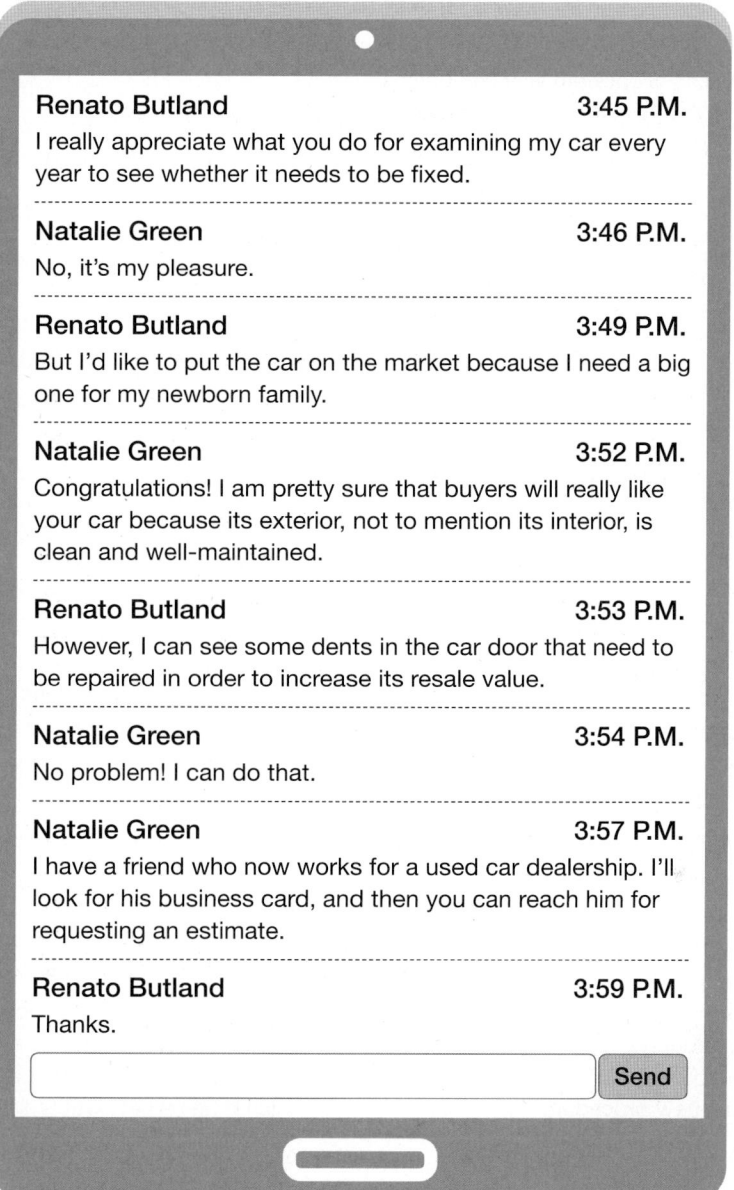

152. What is suggested about Mr. Butland?

(A) He works at a car dealership.
(B) He is an engineer.
(C) He knows someone who could fix car dent issues.
(D) He expects a new arrival in the family.

153. At 3:54, what does Ms. Green mean when he writes, "No problem!"?

(A) She can make dents of the car disappeared.
(B) She can let Mr. Butland know about the car's resale value.
(C) She can put the car on the market for Mr. Butland.
(D) She agrees to sell the car given its conditions.

Questions 154-155 refer to the following e-mail.

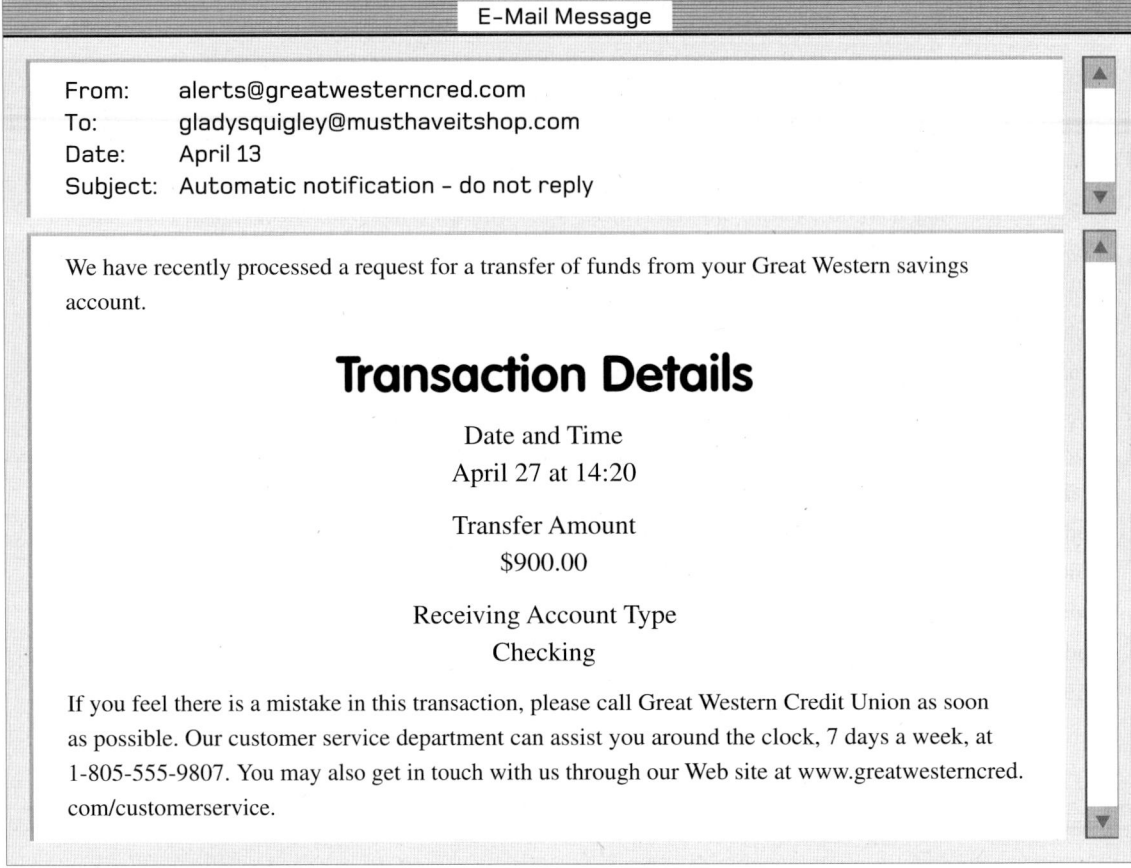

E-Mail Message

From: alerts@greatwesterncred.com
To: gladysquigley@musthaveitshop.com
Date: April 13
Subject: Automatic notification – do not reply

We have recently processed a request for a transfer of funds from your Great Western savings account.

Transaction Details

Date and Time
April 27 at 14:20

Transfer Amount
$900.00

Receiving Account Type
Checking

If you feel there is a mistake in this transaction, please call Great Western Credit Union as soon as possible. Our customer service department can assist you around the clock, 7 days a week, at 1-805-555-9807. You may also get in touch with us through our Web site at www.greatwesterncred.com/customerservice.

154 What is the purpose of this e-mail?

(A) To give her information about a financial transaction
(B) To inquire about her checking account
(C) To demand payment of a bank fee
(D) To explain a new procedure

155 What is stated about Great Western Credit Union's customer service department?

(A) It has changed its hours of operation.
(B) It can be contacted by e-mail.
(C) It is available anytime.
(D) It has a new web address.

Questions 156-157 refer to the following memo.

Hello Everyone,

All employees will be required to attend the service training for our new product line focusing on green technology. The training will be at the Stratford Hotel on Saturday, June 25. Rooms, parking, meals and compensation will be fully provided to all employees.

Please read the following schedule carefully, as you are expected to be at the venue on time. Please do not enter the events late, as this negatively impacts the presentation.

Schedule: 8:00 A.M. - Meet at Red Conference Room downstairs for coffee
8:15 A.M. - Meet the conference speakers
9:00 A.M. - Meet at the Green Room for the company presentation
12:00 A.M. - Break for lunch, serviced in the Oasis Restaurant
14:00 P.M. - Continue with the company presentation
17:00 P.M. - Dismissal

156 What is the main purpose of the conference?
(A) To introduce a new business partner
(B) To appreciate employees' successful outcome
(C) To introduce a new technology
(D) To host a dinner party for employees

157 What is true about the conference?
(A) Those who want to participate in this event should pay for the meal.
(B) Participants should use public transportation since there is no parking space.
(C) The conference will take about 9 hours.
(D) Those who will be late for the conference should notify management beforehand.

GO ON TO THE NEXT PAGE

Questions 158-160 refer to the following advertisement.

NAM

The Native American Museum
122 Onondaga St, Biloxi, Mississippi 90876

We are inviting you to participate in our yearly festival and ceramic sale scheduled Saturday, March 7. Choose from a wide selection of pottery donated by local tribes. All profits go towards the benefit of the museum's upkeep.

The Native American Museum was founded two decades ago in the historic home of nineteenth century tribal chief Wes Studi. The facility showcases an amazing collection of ancient totem poles and Native American artifacts. Walking paths and a stone garden are included in this spectacularly landscaped facility.

A 10 percent discount will be given by the museum's curio shop on the day of the ceramic sale. Operating hours are 10:00 A.M. to 7:00 P.M. Tuesday to Friday, 11:00 A.M. to 4:00 P.M. on weekends. Illustrations by Anna Crow are currently on exhibition and they are open to the general public during regular museum hours through April 6. For further details, visit www.nativeamericanmuseum.org.

158 What is being advertised?
 (A) An inauguration of a facility
 (B) A fund-raising event
 (C) A lecture by Wes Studi
 (D) A sale of Native American artifacts

159 What is stated about The Native American Museum?
 (A) It is remodeling its main gallery.
 (B) It teaches sculpture classes.
 (C) It was recently landscaped.
 (D) It used to be a private residence.

160 What will NOT happen at The Native American Museum on March 7?
 (A) Donations by local tribes will be made.
 (B) A discount will be offered.
 (C) The museum will remain open until 4:00 P.M.
 (D) Illustrations will be showcased.

Questions 161-163 refer to the following e-mail.

TO	Sarah Smith<sarahsmith@aol.net>
FROM	customerservice@azureshoppe.co.au
DATE	21 Feb, 07:03 A.M.
SUBJECT	Purchase number 110958

Dear Ms. Smith,

Listed are the details of your order from Azure RTW Shoppe, Sydney's premier boutique

Purchase order 110958

Description
Item: tube top   Size: 2   Colour: maroon
Quantity: 1   Unit price: $42 Total: $42

Status
In Stock, ready to ship

Subtotal including tax: $42.00
Shipping charge: $3.00
Promotions applied: 20% loyalty discount
Paid by credit card ********6793: $21.90

The items you bought will be shipped within three to five days. A tracking and shipping number will be e-mailed to you when the item leaves our warehouse. If there is a need for some changes regarding this order, please visit www.azureshoppe.co.au, type in your password for your account, and make your changes no later than 4:00 P.M. today.

Thank you for shopping with Azure Shoppe, and we are happy to serve you.

Sincerely yours,

Azure Shoppe, Customer service team

---

161 What is the reason of this e-mail?
  (A) To allow a merchandise to be returned
  (B) To showcase men's clothes
  (C) To confirm a recently bought product
  (D) To announce the opening of a new branch

162 What will Ms. Smith receive from Azure Shoppe within five days?
  (A) An e-mail
  (B) A gift certificate
  (C) A refund
  (D) A receipt

163 What is suggested about Ms. Smith?
  (A) She is entitled to free delivery.
  (B) She changed her order.
  (C) She has an account with Azure Boutique.
  (D) She is a new customer at Azure Boutique.

Questions 164-167 refer to the following e-mail.

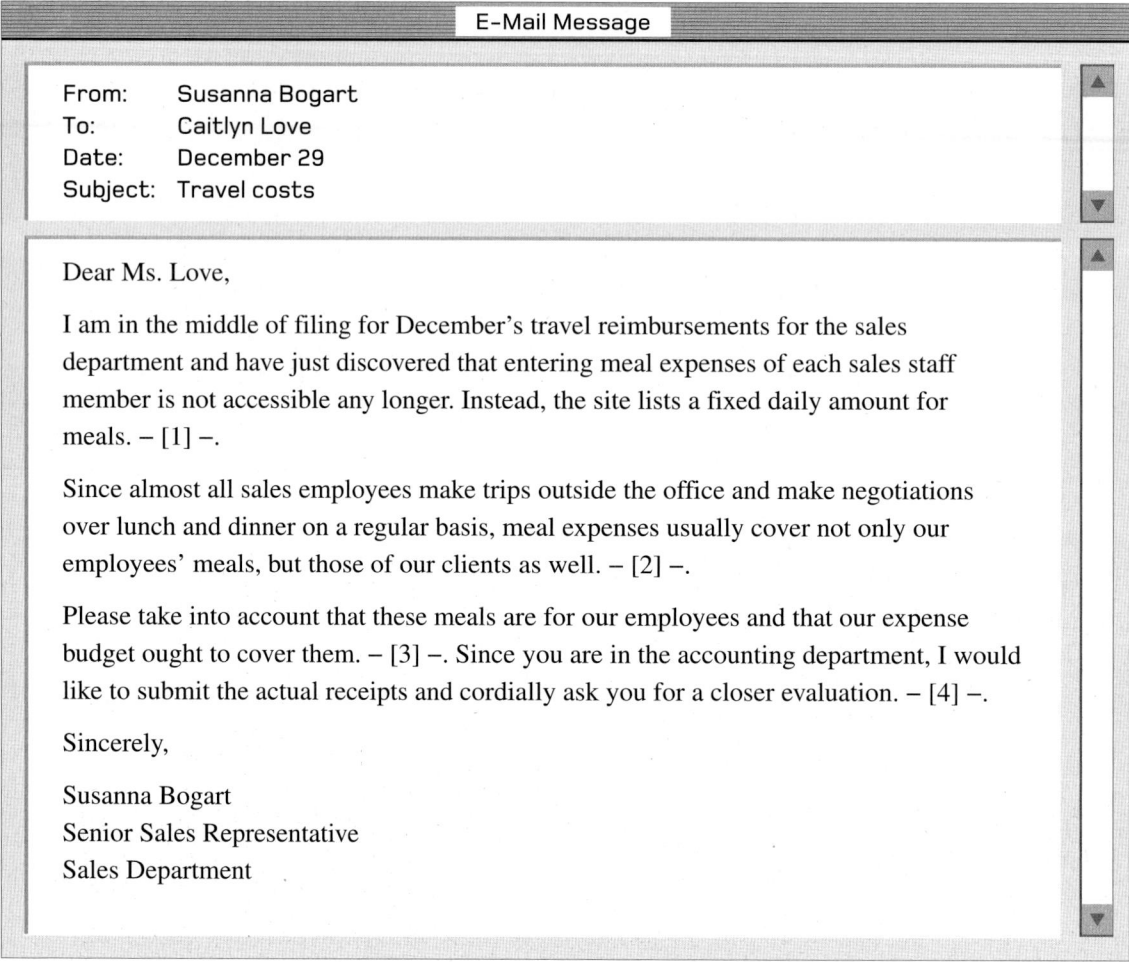

E-Mail Message

From: Susanna Bogart
To: Caitlyn Love
Date: December 29
Subject: Travel costs

Dear Ms. Love,

I am in the middle of filing for December's travel reimbursements for the sales department and have just discovered that entering meal expenses of each sales staff member is not accessible any longer. Instead, the site lists a fixed daily amount for meals. – [1] –.

Since almost all sales employees make trips outside the office and make negotiations over lunch and dinner on a regular basis, meal expenses usually cover not only our employees' meals, but those of our clients as well. – [2] –.

Please take into account that these meals are for our employees and that our expense budget ought to cover them. – [3] –. Since you are in the accounting department, I would like to submit the actual receipts and cordially ask you for a closer evaluation. – [4] –.

Sincerely,

Susanna Bogart
Senior Sales Representative
Sales Department

164 What problem has Ms. Bogart encountered?
(A) She cannot enter certain data through a Web site.
(B) There will be no reimbursement for meal expenses.
(C) She failed to meet a deadline to negotiate a deal with a client.
(D) She is still waiting for employees to submit receipts.

165 According to the e-mail, what does Ms. Bogart want to do?
(A) Arrange for dinner with a client
(B) Be paid back for meal expenses with clients
(C) Propose a new leave policy
(D) Reschedule a sales meeting

166 Who most likely is Ms. Love?
(A) A computer technician
(B) An accountant
(C) A sales director
(D) An event coordinator

167 In which of the positions marked [1], [2], [3] and [4] does the following sentence best belong?

"Due to this circumstance, our sales employees may, or rather must spend notably more than the fixed amount shown on the site."

(A) [1]
(B) [2]
(C) [3]
(D) [4]

Questions 168-171 refer to the following online chat.

Joshua Jamison	[3:30 P.M.]	Hi, I'm Joshua Jamison from the department of human resource. I need a help.
Gabriel Sanches	[3:31 P.M.]	Hi. Sure. What can I do for you?
Joshua Jamison	[3:32 P.M.]	I accessed the intranet system Friday afternoon with no problem. But I was unable to get access to my online account in the morning.
Gabriel Sanches	[3:34 P.M.]	Sorry for the inconvenience caused to you. It might be our recent update over the weekend. We have completed the work at 5 A.M.
Joshua Jamison	[3:35 P.M.]	But whenever I type my password correctly several times, it is always saying the incorrect password. Why has this been happening? I am wondering whether this is just a problem with my own computer or a company-wide problem.
Gabriel Sanches	[3:38 P.M.]	Several employees reported that they had received "access denied" messages. And I am working on that. We have already examined the issue and I must say this system glitch will be resolved by the end of the day.
Joshua Jamison	[3:40 P.M.]	Okay, I understand. I, however, have to download some documents from the intranet in preparation for important presentation before 5 P.M.
Gabriel Sanches	[3:42 P.M.]	Chances are 50/50. Some of the employees said resetting the password would help access the account. If you can't, please call Jason Lee who will help you download files one hour before your presentation.

168 Who most likely is Mr. Sanches?
(A) A bank clerk
(B) A designer
(C) A computer technician
(D) A presenter

169 According to Mr. Sanches, when could Mr. Jamison be able to access his account again?
(A) Friday
(B) 4 P.M.
(C) 5 P.M.
(D) Tomorrow morning

170 Why does Mr. Sanches mention Jason Lee?
(A) He can give a hand to Mr. Jamison.
(B) He is in charge of the IT department.
(C) He is now out for a presentation.
(D) He is responsible for the issue of the intranet connection.

171 At 3:38 P.M., what does Mr. Sanches mean when he writes, "I am working on that"?
(A) He sets up a computer for a presentation.
(B) He learns how to change his password.
(C) He works on web-browsing and homepage-building.
(D) He finds ways to log on to the intranet.

Questions 172-175 refer to the following article.

Major Road Reconstruction in Smithtown

June 25, Smithtown – Starting tomorrow, major roads in Smithtown will go under construction and there will be scheduled lane closures and new traffic control plans for four months until the road work is complete.

The entire project is planned to be executed in three phases. In the first phase, three kilometers of Grimes Boulevard between Sixth Avenue and Seventh Avenue will be repaved. –[1]–. Until the first phase is over, only one lane of the boulevard will be operational Monday to Friday, 9 A.M. to 5 P.M., so the Department of Transportation insists motorists take Victor Boulevard, which meets Grimes Boulevard past Ninth Avenue.

The second phase will begin at the end of July. During the second phase, the expansion of Exit 5A on Dickenson Highway will be underway. This is to take in more traffic as the newly built Vintage Five Outlet has attracted numerous shoppers since January. To alleviate traffic congestion towards the exit, two more lanes will be added on the ramp at Exit 5A. Additionally, the length of the ramps will be extended and straightened so that motorists can enjoy safer driving. –[2]–.

Leonard Cooper, 45, is a resident living on Pasadena Road, which is within a 500-meter radius of Exit 5A. Mr. Cooper has been following the initiative and finds the road reform to be a wise move. –[3]–. He said, "This change should have been made months ago. Now that the ramp will be extended, drivers will have an easier time getting off the highway than before, when the ramp wasn't long enough to allow for slowing down or merging in." He then added, "I hear that this expansion will take up to two months, but I believe it is definitely worth the wait."

The last phase includes additional road maintenance tasks, such as installing luminous road signs for night drivers and restoring damaged guard rails and pavements. Depending on the weather condition, the Department of Transportation estimates that the entire construction process will be completed by October 26 at the earliest. –[4]–.

Fred Peters

172 What is NOT an intended outcome of the initiative?

(A) To alleviate traffic congestion near a shopping center
(B) To secure better visibility of signs at night
(C) To reduce toll costs in Smithtown
(D) To resolve safety concerns in a community

173 Where will crews begin repaving?

(A) On Grimes Boulevard
(B) On Victor Boulevard
(C) On Dickenson Highway
(D) On Pasadena Road

174 How long is the second phase expected to last?

(A) Two weeks
(B) Two months
(C) Five months
(D) One year

175 In which of the positions marked [1], [2], [3] and [4] does the following sentence best belong?

"This pavement work is scheduled to be completed in about two weeks."

(A) [1]
(B) [2]
(C) [3]
(D) [4]

Questions 176-180 refer to the following letter and monthly statement.

Windy City Electric Company

1123 E Branchville St., Chicago, IL 60605

November 6
Ronald Chin
237 Faraday Ave. Apt 6
Chicago, IL 60601
Account Number 56-665-A4

Dear Mr. Chin

Did you know Windy City Electric Company now has a mobile bill-payment system? Since this service started on June 1, hundreds of our valued customers using this service have been very satisfied with the automatic deduction system to manage their bills. By allowing your bank to deduct the amount of your monthly bill from your bank account, you can be sure you will never be late in paying your bills every month without any extra effort from your side.

It's so easy to sign up. Simply, fill out a form, which you can find on our Web site http://www.windycityelectric.com/adform, fill out the form and click "submit" or contact our customer service hotline at 708-555-2234 for help. Once registration is completed, you will be able to pay and examine your bill. We hope this opportunity will be used by you.

Sincerely,

Sandra Smith
Sandra Smith
Customer Service Manager

Windy City Electric Company

Monthly Statement
June

Ronald Chin
237 Faraday Ave. apt 6
Chicago, IL 60601
Account Number 56-665-A4

Last payment made
May 15 - $73.00

Current Charge (Due on June 15)
$79:00

Next Meter Reading Date
July 1

Meter reading should be done on a designated date or your charges will be estimated based on your previous usage.

176 Why was the letter sent to Mr. Chin?
 (A) To inform him of his updated account number
 (B) To advertise a bank
 (C) To explain changes in his recent bills
 (D) To encourage him to sign up for a plan

177 In the letter, what is stated about Windy City Electric Company?
 (A) It is creating a new advertising plan.
 (B) It has improved its customer service department.
 (C) It offers customers another method to pay their bills.
 (D) It has recently changed its Web site address.

178 What should Mr. Chin do if he decides to avail of Ms. Smith's options?
 (A) Make an appointment with her
 (B) Pay a small processing fee
 (C) Send a copy of his most recent bill
 (D) Give a completed form

179 What does Mr. Chin's monthly statement say about him?
 (A) His account existed before automatic bill payment was available.
 (B) He had to adjust a previous meter-reading date.
 (C) He was late in paying one of his bills.
 (D) He should pay additional installation fees.

180 According to the monthly statement, when is Mr. Chin's next payment due?
 (A) June 15
 (B) July 15
 (C) August 22
 (D) September 1

GO ON TO THE NEXT PAGE

Questions 181-185 refer to the following e-mails.

E-Mail Message

From: pcornwallis@dunkirkassoc.com
To: jdreyfus999@giuk.com
Subject: Interview
Date: 12 October
Attachment: Employee manual

Dear. Ms. Dreyfus,

Thank you for visiting our booth at the Liverpool job fair last week. I was glad to have met you and I was very impressed with your experience at Grosvenor International. I am happy for the application you have given me for the position we spoke about.

Human Resources has looked into your application and we would like you to have an interview at our office next week. Below are our available interview dates and feel free to choose the most convenient time for you.

Wednesday, 21 October	Thursday, 22 October	Friday, 23 October
09:00 A.M. or 03:00 P.M.	10:00 A.M. or 01:00 P.M.	09:30 A.M. or 01:00 P.M.

Please go through the employee handbook and prepare any questions regarding our policies. After the interview, our hiring committee will discuss and inform you of our decision on or before Monday, 27 October. If there is something you would like to ask, please let me know.

Regards,

Paris Cornwallis

To: pcornwallis@dunkirkassoc.com
From: jdreyfus999@giuk.com
Subject: Re: Interview
Date: 13 October

Dear Ms. Cornwallis,

Thank you for this opportunity for an interview at Dunkirk and associates. After a number of years as a consultant on several projects, I am anticipating a job managing a team. About the interview schedule, I prefer the afternoon interview so I would like to reserve the 3:00 P.M. slot. One question though, as mentioned last week, for the interview, I may need to bring a list of references complete with contact information of those able to vouch for my ability. That will be no problem at all but I need to know how many I need.

Thank you for giving me the chance to maybe be a part of your company in the future and I am looking forward to seeing you next week.

Sincerely,

Julia Dreyfus

181 How did Ms. Dreyfus find the job opening at Dunkirk and Associates?

(A) From a colleague
(B) From the company's Web site
(C) From a newspaper ad
(D) From a career expo

182 What is Ms. Dreyfus asked to do before her interview?

(A) Prepare a sample of her work
(B) Update her résumé
(C) Read a publication
(D) Pass a background check

183 When will Ms. Deyfus' interview probably be?

(A) On Tuesday
(B) On Wednesday
(C) On Thursday
(D) On Friday

184 Why is Ms. Dreyfus searching for a new career?

(A) Because she is interested in a managerial position
(B) Because she relocated
(C) Because she wants a change of scenery
(D) Because she needs a more suitable schedule

185 What information did Ms. Dreyfus ask for?

(A) Her interviewer's name
(B) The number of references required
(C) The tasks involved in the new job
(D) The interview location

Questions 186-190 refer to the following information sheet and e-mails.

BOSTON HEMISPHERE GOLF CLUB
NEW RESIDENT AND NON-RESIDENT APPLICATION

410 Boston Post Rd #34, Sudbury, MA017776
www.bostonhemispheregolfclub.com, www.bhgolfclub.com

Application process for new resident and non-resident members

1. Residency is defined as having your primary residence solely within the physical boundaries of the Boston Hemisphere.
2. Required documents: a current utility bill or driver's license only. Documents must show applicant's name and current address.
3. New members will not have access to the club facilities until members obtain their membership cards.
4. Once payment is processed, there will be no refunds and a confirmation e-mail will be sent to your e-mail address.

Monthly Membership Dues	New Members [by April 2]	New Members [after April 2]	
Golf Club	$600	$650	A non-resident surcharge of $75 is assessed on all nonresident accounts.
Family Pool	$100	$125	
Fitness Center	$75	$100	

E-Mail Message

From: Eric Dier <e.dier@abase.com>
To: Christian Neves <c.neves@bhgolfclub.com>
Date: April 25
Subject: Membership

Dear Mr. Neves,

I recently examined the membership application form on the Boston Hemisphere Golf Club Web site. What I understand is that the monthly dues are $650 for Boston Hemisphere residents and non-residents have to pay an additional $75. I am not sure, however, which side I should belong to. I am a photographer. I live in Boston Hemisphere from September through January. I spend the rest of the year in Canada. As I live in two different places, I am now holding off my membership application for residents. Would you please check the fact for me whether I qualify for the resident membership? I am already counting down to the big day!

Thank you.

Eric Dier

From	Christian Neves <c.neves@bhgolfclub.com>
To	Eric Dier <e.dier@abase.com>
Date	April 26
Subject	Re: Membership

Dear Mr. Dier,

Thank you for your inquiry. According to our policy, those living in the Boston Hemisphere for at least six months per year are entitled to be a resident member. So, unfortunately, you are not qualified for the rate of resident.

However, you can get several benefits as a member of our golf club. As a member, you have the first opportunity to reserve the desired time to play. You may enjoy our amenities at a 25 percent off of the original price, including swimming pool, tennis court, weight room and etc. Furthermore, golf lessons, club repair, dining and refreshments are offered at a discounted rate to our members.

I ask you to fill out your application form as quickly as possible since our membership is limited to 150. The membership usually fills in April. If you need more information with regard to the membership, please feel free to contact me.

Best regards,

Christian Neves

---

186 What is indicated about the Boston Hemisphere Golf Club?

(A) It has three types of members.
(B) It does not require any information.
(C) Its members have full access to its facilities after becoming a member.
(D) It has no refund policy.

187 Why did Mr. Dier write the first e-mail?

(A) To correct his address
(B) To book a golf lesson
(C) To renew his membership
(D) To request additional information

188 What is NOT mentioned as a benefit of being a member?

(A) Priority scheduling
(B) Equipment repairs
(C) Discounted lessons
(D) Social events

189 How much will Mr. Dier pay for the membership?

(A) $600
(B) $650
(C) $675
(D) $725

190 According to the second e-mail, what does Mr. Neves suggest Mr. Dier to do?

(A) Conduct a survey
(B) Submit an application form online
(C) Join the membership immediately
(D) Go on tours of facilities

Questions 191-195 refer to the following table of contents, online review and e-mail.

Tech Life Magazine
January, Issue 125

Table of Contents

▶ **Page 50**
Cover Story for DES [Digital Electronics Show]
Columnist Franklin Oliver shows us the best 75 apps for everything you could want to do on your mobile phone, from playing games to filing reports.

▶ **Page 73**
Online Business
Specialists and panelists share their insights on the pros and cons of tablet PCs.

▶ **Page 88**
Best Products of DES 2017
Columnist Henderson Lee reports that more than 3,000 companies showcased their products at the Digital Electronics Show. Here are our picks for the best products at the show.

▶ **Page 103**
Clean up Your Passwords
If you haven't changed your most important passwords in a long time, now's the time. Here are the best ways to choose the right passwords.

▶ **Page 118**
Behind the Scenes
Columnist David Jeffrey will take a look at the next year's most anticipated Bluetooth keyboards.

▶ **Page 121**
Recycling Your Old Tech
Columnist Damian Miller explains e-waste is on the rise but you can help combat it by using old PCs and electronics in new ways, or donating them to places that do the right thing.

[Irish291], 3 days ago

When I mention about *Tech Life Magazine*, the first thing is that it is only available in a digital format. This magazine covers a great wide variety of topics, not to mention PCs. It is very informative and entertaining. Given the fact that *Tech Life Magazine* is only 150 pages long, nearly all of this are dedicated to information about technology. The best article that I am satisfied with is the one that is related to the environmental issues. Unfortunately, the magazine is well organized but does not take advantage of the linking options so that you cannot easily navigate through the various related articles with just a click of your mouse.

E-Mail Message

FROM: Subscription department <customerservice@techlive.com>
TO: Jane Sinclair <j.sinclair@spx.com>
DATE: May 2
RE: Subscription issues

Dear Jane Sinclair,

Thank you for your recent subscription from *Tech Life Magazine*. We are sorry you have experienced a problem with your billing or payment. Bills are sent monthly. If you receive two consecutive bills after sending your payment, please write us and include a copy of your billing statement receipt with your letter.

If you should encounter a problem with your subscription, please do not hesitate to contact us. We want you to enjoy your subscription to our *Tech Life Magazine*. Thank you.

Best regards,

Alison Brie
The manager of Subscription Department

---

191 What section of the magazine contains points of view from various experts?
(A) Cover Story for DES
(B) Online Business
(C) Best Products of DES 2017
(D) Behind the Scenes

192 Who says about the products that are not yet released?
(A) Franklin Oliver
(B) Henderson Lee
(C) David Jeffrey
(D) Damian Miller

193 According to the review, on what page of the magazine does the reviewer like the most?
(A) Page 50
(B) Page 88
(C) Page 118
(D) Page 121

194 In the review, what is the magazine's weak point?
(A) Its price is a bit expensive.
(B) Its layout is not suitable for online editions.
(C) Its release date is too late.
(D) It does not cover various topics.

195 According to the e-mail, what does Ms. Sinclair inquire about?
(A) Double payment on subscription
(B) Delays in shipment
(C) Damaged products
(D) Subscription extension

Questions 196-200 refer to the following notice and e-mails.

The Fairview County Newspaper is one of the largest monthly newspapers in the City of Oklahoma. The newspaper has a monthly circulation of approximately 12,000. The Fairview County Newspaper is printed in black and white. Seasonal factors would also be considered when setting a price. Advertising rates could change frequently.

If you decide to put an ad in our newspaper, we ask that images be sent to us carefully as any changes after submission are not allowed. Please contact the newspaper's advertising manager Susan Schmidt (s.schmidt@fairviewnewspaper.com) for an exact quote.

Advertising Rate for *the Fairview County Newspaper* [February]			
SIZE	ONE ISSUE	SIX ISSUES	TWELVE ISSUES
Quarter page	$300	$1,500	$2,800
Half page	$500	$2,500	$4,500
Full page	$1,100	$5,000	$9,900

E-Mail Message

FROM: Heidi S. Kim <H.S.Kim@ideabox.com>
TO: Susan Schmidt <s.schmidt@fairviewnewspaper.com>
DATE: February 25
SUBJECT: Advertising in the Fairview County Newspaper
ATTACHMENT: Fairview_County_Newspaper_layout

Dear Ms. Schmidt,

Please check the attached file about my advertisement. I am planning to place an advertisement in your newspaper. However, I have little confidence that it does really work. I have to use caution as we are on a limited budget. I decide to start out with a half page for six issues. As far as I know, half page for six issues is currently priced at $2,500. It seems that the project about advertisements in the local newspaper for small businesses is subsidized by the government. Is there any way to receive a discount? If there is, please let me know.

Thank you.

Heidi S. Kim

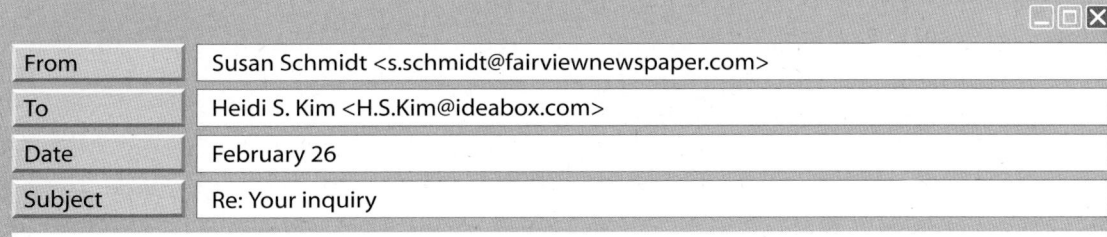

From	Susan Schmidt <s.schmidt@fairviewnewspaper.com>
To	Heidi S. Kim <H.S.Kim@ideabox.com>
Date	February 26
Subject	Re: Your inquiry

Dear Ms. Kim,

You might be wondering if putting an advertisement in the local newspaper is worthwhile. Also, you might be curious about your ad actually reaching your customers. Advertising in the Fairview County Newspaper is the most effective way of reaching hundreds of thousands of households in Fairview County and neighboring communities once a month.

Sadly, the government does not grant support to our newspaper. Good news is, as you are our new customer, we could provide a 20 percent discount on our standard advertisement fees.

We look forward to doing business with you.

Sincerely,

Susan Schmidt
Advertising Manager

196 What is the purpose of the notice?
(A) To encourage subscription
(B) To provide a potential client with some information
(C) To explain the monthly charge for a newspaper
(D) To cancel an advertisement

197 What is indicated about advertising in *the Fairview County Newspaper*?
(A) It uses various types of colors.
(B) Its images can be revised.
(C) It has seasonal rates.
(D) It has been distributed across the nation.

198 What does Ms. Kim ask for in the first e-mail?
(A) Reduced advertisement fees
(B) Cancellation of subscription
(C) Change in advertisement layout
(D) Monthly circulation

199 How much will Ms. Kim likely be charged?
(A) $500
(B) $1,500
(C) $2,000
(D) $2,500

200 In the second e-mail, the word "grant" in paragraph 2, line 1 is closest in meaning to
(A) give
(B) acknowledge
(C) receive
(D) know

스피킹시험도 트렌드를 따라가야 한다!
라이브인강은 단연, 플랜티라이브!

플랜티라이브는 언제 촬영한지도 모르는 온라인 강의를 제공하지 않습니다.

▶ **인터넷 강의! 왜 촬영 일자를 따져야 하나요?**
토익 스피킹 시험은 한 달에 4~8회, 하루 1~5회의 시험이 진행됩니다. 시험 출제 경향은 약 2개월마다 바뀌고 있어서, 개인 학습자가 혼자서 파악하기는 어렵습니다. 아무리 유명 강사의 인터넷 강의라고 해도 촬영 일자가 오래된 경우에는 최신 경향을 반영할 수 없습니다. 인터넷 강의! 반드시 촬영 일자를 확인하세요.

▶ **매일 촬영, 매일 업로드**
현장 강의를 매일 촬영하여 당일 업로드

▶ **스타강사의 현장강의를 인강으로**
토스, 오픽 유명 강사의 현장 감동을 그대로 전달

www.plantlive.co.kr

新토익을 대비하는 가장 현명한 선택!

• 나혼자 끝내는 新토익 실전서 •

신토익 LC+RC 5회분 + 해설집

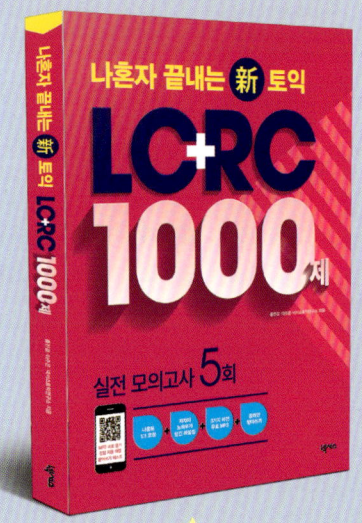

신토익 LC+RC 3회분 + 해설집

실제 시험지가 봉투 안에 쏙~

나혼자 끝내는 新토익 LC+RC 1000제

- ✓ 한 권으로 끝내는 신토익 실전 모의고사 5회분 수록
- ✓ 해설집을 따로 구매할 필요가 없는 LC+RC 합본 실전서
- ✓ 저자의 노하우를 담아 문제의 키워드를 단숨에 파악하는 알짜 해설 수록
- ✓ 실전용·복습용·고사장 버전의 3종 MP3 무료 다운로드(www.nexusbook.com)

나혼자 끝내는 新토익 실전 모의고사 3회분(봉투형)

- ✓ 실제 시험지 형태 그대로, 신토익 실전 모의고사 3회분 수록
- ✓ 문제의 키워드를 단숨에 파악하는 알짜 해석·해설 무료 다운로드(www.nexusbook.com)
- ✓ 실전용·복습용·고사장 버전의 3종 MP3 무료 다운로드(www.nexusbook.com)

나혼자 끝내는 신토익 LC+RC 1000제 | 홍진걸·이주은 지음 | 2017년 6월 출간 | 364페이지
나혼자 끝내는 신토익 실전 모의고사 3회분 | 김랑·박자은·임철, 넥서스토익연구소 지음 | 2017년 7월 출간 | 144페이지

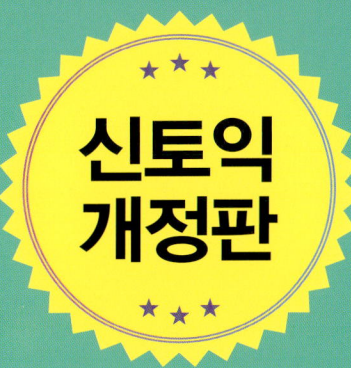

신토익 개정판

20일 만에
끝내는
가장 빠른
토익 솔루션

플랜티 어학연구소 지음

정답 및 해설

토익 한번에 끝내기 RC

• 깔끔한 문제 풀이 전략 & 풍부한 실제 문제 수록
• 정확하게 핵심만 콕콕 짚어 주는 문제 해설 포인트
• 매일매일 섹션별·단계별 학습으로 문법, 독해, 어휘 완성

넥서스

TOEIC 신유형 개정판

20일 만에 끝내는
가장 빠른 토익 솔루션

플랜티 어학연구소 지음

정답 및 해설

토익 한 번에 끝내기 RC

넥서스

Section 1

Grammar

DAY 01 주어와 동사

○ 비법 적용 연습   본문 p.19

PART 5	1 (B)	2 (D)	3 (A)	4 (C)	5 (A)
	6 (B)	7 (D)	8 (B)	9 (A)	10 (A)

1
해석 올해 리더십 과정에 참석하기 위해서 인사과에 참석 여부를 다음 주 월요일 전에 알려 주세요.

해설 please부터가 주절이 된다. 주어와 동사가 있어야 하는데 명령문에서 주어는 생략될 수 있다. 명령문의 생략된 주어는 you인데 2인칭 주어에는 동사에 -s를 붙이지 않으므로 명령문의 시제는 항상 현재가 된다. 따라서 정답은 (B)이다.

어휘 attend 참석하다 human resources department 인사부 participation 참가

2
해석 수요일 아침에 HD Vision의 대표 이사는 유럽 시장에서의 확대 계획을 발표했다.

해설 빈칸 앞에 주어가 있고 뒤에는 목적어가 있으므로 동사 자리이다. 동사 형태 (A), (D) 중에서 주어가 3인칭 단수이므로 (A)는 수 일치에서 오답이다. 따라서 정답은 (D)이다.

어휘 expansion 확장, 확대

3
해석 참가자들은 떠나기 전에 피부 관리의 새로운 제품에 대한 설문지를 제출해야 한다.

해설 주어 자리가 빈칸이므로 동사인 (C)는 제외한다. submit의 주체는 사람이 되어야 하므로 (A), (B) 중에서 의미상 정답이 (A)임을 알 수 있다.

어휘 submit 제출하다 survey form 설문지

4
해석 저조한 판매 성과에도 불구하고, 이사는 다음 해에 대해서 여전히 낙관적이다.

해설 관사(the) 뒤는 명사 자리이다. 따라서 (C)가 정답이다. (A)도 형용사 외에 명사로 쓸 수 있지만 의미상(지령, 지시, 명령) 맞지 않다.

어휘 despite ~에도 불구하고 sales performance 판매 실적 optimistic 낙천적인, 긍정적인

5
해석 연간 운영비용을 줄이는 것은 매니저의 중요한 일들 중 하나이다.

해설 빈칸을 뒤의 명사(costs)를 수식하는 형용사 자리로 보고 분사 형태인 (D)를 정답으로 생각할 수도 있지만 그렇게 되면 문장의 주어는 costs가 되고 단수 동사(is)와 수 일치가 어긋나게 된다. 따라서 동명사 (A) Reducing이 costs를 목적어로 취하면서 주어가 되는 문장이 자연스럽다.

어휘 annual 매년의, 연간의 operating costs 운영비 priority 우선사항, 우선, 우선권

6
해석 우리가 전체 비용을 받을 때까지 당신의 등록은 처리되지 않을 것입니다.

해설 빈칸은 주어 자리이며 앞에 소유격(your)이 있으므로 명사를 찾아야 한다. 선택지 중에 (B)만이 명사이다.

어휘 receive 받다 full payment 완납, 완불 process 처리하다

7
해석 출발 시간의 연기는 대부분 좋지 않은 기상 상황이나 예상치 못한 기계적인 문제들 때문이다.

해설 빈칸은 문장의 주어 자리이므로 명사를 찾아야 한다. delay는 동사 또는 명사로 쓰이는데, 명사로 쓰일 때는 가산 명사, 불가산 명사 모두 쓰일 수 있다. 동사가 are(복수 동사)이기 때문에 복수 형태의 주어 (D) Delays가 정답이다.

어휘 departure time 출발 시간 due to ~에 때문에 unexpected 예상 밖의, 예상치 못한

8
해석 HAAY Shipping Company는 당신이 요청한 서비스들을 배송하기 위해서 당신의 개인정보를 수집하고 사용한다.

해설 빈칸은 주어(HAAY Shipping Company) 뒤의 동사 자리이다. 등위접속사 and를 기준으로 앞, 뒤의 품사가 같아야 한다. and 뒤에 uses라는 동사가 있으므로 빈칸도 현재 시제가 와야 한다. 따라서 (B)가 정답이다.

어휘 shipping 운송, 배송 personal information 개인정보, 신상정보 deliver 배달하다 request 요청하다

9
해석 우리 회사의 대부분의 신입 사원들은 1년간의 수습 기간을 완료해야 한다.

해설 조동사(must) 뒤에는 동사원형이 와야 한다. 따라서 정답은 (A)이다.

어휘 new hire 신입 사원 probation 수습 (기간)

10
해석 도시의 외곽으로 본점을 이전하는 것은 필요한 공간을 얻기 위해서 상당히 추천할 만하다.

해설 빈칸 뒤에 관사를 포함한 명사가 오기 때문에 빈칸은 the central office를 목적어로 취하면서 주어가 될 수 있는 동명사 (A)가 정답이다.

어휘 central office 본사 outskirt 변두리, 교외 recommend 추천하다, 권고하다 obtain 얻다, 획득하다

DAY 02 목적어 · 보어 · 수식어

비법 적용 연습
본문 p.23

PART 5	1 (C)	2 (A)	3 (D)	4 (B)	5 (D)
	6 (B)	7 (D)	8 (D)	9 (C)	10 (D)

1
해석 국제 공항에서 새롭게 소개된 교통 시스템은 상당히 인상적이다.

해설 be동사 is 뒤의 보어 자리이다. 보어 자리에는 명사 또는 형용사가 오는데 빈칸 앞에 부사 quite가 있으므로 빈칸에는 부사의 수식을 받는 형용사가 와야 한다. 선택지의 형용사 (B), (C) 중에서 주격 보어 자리이므로 주어와의 관계가 능동인지 수동인지 확인해야 한다. 능동의 관계이므로 정답은 (C) impressive이다.

어휘 transportation 수송, 운송 impress 깊은 인상을 주다

2
해석 훈련생이 필요할 때 언제든지 감독관에게서 조언을 구하는 것은 바람직하다.

해설 seek이 타동사이므로 빈칸은 목적어 자리이다. 목적어 자리에 올 수 있는 명사 (A), (B) 중에 (B)는 단수 가산 명사로서 정답이 되려면 빈칸 앞에 한정사가 있어야 한다. 따라서 정답은 (A)이다.

어휘 desirable 바람직한 trainee 교육을 받는 사람, 수습 seek 찾다, 구하다 supervisor 감독관

3
해석 Goodman 씨에 의해서 조직된 새로운 광고 캠페인은 매우 성공적이었다.

해설 be동사인 was 뒤의 보어 자리이다. 빈칸 앞에 very(부사)가 있으므로 부사의 수식을 받는 형용사가 정답이다. 선택지에서 (D)만이 형용사이다.

어휘 campaign 캠페인, (사회, 정치적 목적을 위한 조직적인) 운동, 활동 organize 준비하다, 정리하다

4
해석 우리가 당신의 서면 확인서를 받을 때까지는 당신이 사용할 회의실은 배정되지 않을 것이다.

해설 빈칸 앞에 [소유격(your)+분사(written)]가 왔으므로 빈칸은 명사 자리이다. 선택지에서 (B)만이 명사이다.

어휘 receive 받다 conference room 회의실 assign (일, 책임 등을) 맡기다, 배정하다

5
해석 문 옆에 기재된 지시사항들은 비상 대피에 대한 절차를 설명하고 있다.

해설 관사(the) 뒤의 명사 자리이다. 선택지에서 (B), (D)가 명사인데 의미상 '절차'를 뜻하는 (D)가 정답이다.

어휘 instruction 설명, 지시, 지시사항 post 게시하다, 공고하다 outline 개요를 설명하다 emergency 비상 evacuation 피난, 대피 proceeds (거래, 투자에 의한) 수입, 이익, 순익 procedure 진행, 절차, 순서

6
해석 더 나은 배급과 낮은 인터넷 비용이 사업들을 더욱 이익이 나게 만들었다.

해설 동사 made는 5형식이 가능한 동사이다. 따라서 빈칸은 목적격 보어 자리가 된다. 보어 자리에 들어갈 수 있는 명사와 형용사 중에서 목적어와의 관계를 보면 businesses(사업)와 profit(이윤)은 동격이 될 수 없으므로 형용사 (B) profitable이 정답이다.

어휘 distribution 분배, 배부

7
해석 새로운 근무 시간은 가게들이 11시 혹은 자정까지 문을 열게 해 줄 것이다.

해설 keep은 5형식이 가능한 동사이다. 빈칸은 목적격 보어 자리이고, open은 동사 외에도 형용사(열려 있는)로 사용할 수 있으므로 (D)가 정답이다.

어휘 working hours 근무 시간

8
해석 생산 시설의 관리자들은 작업 과정이 생산적일 수 있도록 계속 유지해야만 한다.

해설 to부정사의 동사는 동사의 성질을 그대로 가지고 있으므로 keep은 5형식 문장의 성질을 가지고 있다. 따라서 빈칸은 목적격 보어 자리가 되고 work procedures와의 관계를 통해 보어 자리에 형용사 (D) productive가 정답임을 알 수 있다.

어휘 manufacturing 제조업 facility 시설 work procedure 작업 절차

9
해석 필요한 시간과 노력을 줄이는 측면에서 합동 조사팀이 더욱 효율적으로 여겨진다.

해설 5형식의 수동태 문장이다. consider는 목적어 뒤에 목적격 보어가 올 수 있는 5형식 문장인데 5형식 문장이 수동태가 될 경우, 목적격 보어 자리에 있던 명사 혹은 형용사가 수동태형 동사 뒤에 남게 된다. 여기서도 are considered 뒤의 빈칸은 목적격 보어 자리이다. Joint research teams와 관계가 동격이 아니므로 형용사 (C)가 정답이다.

어휘 joint 합동의 consider 고려하다, (~을 ~로) 여기다 reduce 줄이다, 감소시키다

10
해석 미국에서 가장 큰 패스트푸드 브랜드인 King Brothers는 확장의 일환으로 GBS 사의 인수를 계획하고 있다.

해설 동사(plans) 뒤는 목적어 자리이다. 동사인 (A)를 제외하고 명사인 (B)는 빈칸 뒤에 명사가 또 있기 때문에 제외한다. plan은 목적어 자리에 to부정사를 목적어로 취하는 동사이므로 (D)가 정답이다.

어휘 expansion 확장, 확대 acquire 인수하다

DAY 03 명사

○ 비법 적용 연습 본문 p.28

PART 5	1 (B)	2 (D)	3 (D)	4 (B)	5 (B)
	6 (B)	7 (D)	8 (C)	9 (D)	10 (C)

1
해석 모든 방문객들은 시설에 입장하기 전에 적어도 한 가지의 신분증을 제시할 것이 요구됩니다.
해설 전치사(of) 뒤는 명사 자리이다. 선택지에서 (B)만이 명사이다.
어휘 require 요구하다 present 제시하다 facility 시설 identification 신분증

2
해석 품질 관리 직책에 대한 모든 지원자들은 2주 이내에 이메일을 통해서 회신을 받을 것입니다.
해설 every(형용사) 뒤에는 단수 가산 명사가 와야 한다. (C), (D)가 모두 단수가산 명사인데 의미상 (D)가 정답임을 알 수 있다.
어휘 quality control 품질 관리 managerial position 관리직

3
해석 직원들은 업무 시간이 이달 나머지 기간 동안 효력을 미칠 거리는 통지를 받았다.
해설 전치사(for)와 관사(the) 뒤의 명사 자리이다. 선택지에서 (D)만이 명사이다.
어휘 inform 통지하다, 알리다 business hour 업무 시간 be in effect 시행되다

4
해석 각각의 프로그램이 끝나고 나면 과정 평가가 완료되어야 하고, 평가를 위해 강사들에게 제출되어야 한다.
해설 주어 자리이므로 빈칸 앞의 course와 더불어 복합명사를 이루는 (B) evaluation이 정답이다. (C)는 단수 가산 명사이므로 앞에 관사나 소유격이 필요하다.
어휘 complete 완성하다, 끝마치다 submit 제출하다 instructor 강사

5
해석 새로운 장치가 설치된 이래로 생산이 크게 증가되었다.
해설 has been 동사 앞의 주어 자리이다. 따라서 명사 (B)가 정답이다. (A)는 의미도 어색하고 가산 명사이므로 단독으로 쓸 수 없다.
어휘 equipment 장비, 장치 install 설치하다 increase 증가시키다, 증가하다

6
해석 Koon 박사의 결과는 다른 연구원들의 실험 결과에 대한 해석과 달랐다.
해설 명사의 소유격은 명사에 ['s]를 붙이는데 s로 끝나는 명사는 [']만을 붙인다. 소유격 뒤에 명사를 써야 하므로 (B), (C) 중에서 의미가 적절한 (B)가 정답이다.
어휘 finding 결론 different from ~와 다른

7
해석 좋은 본보기가 되는 출석 기록을 유지하는 사람들은 올해 보너스를 받을 자격을 가지게 된다.
해설 동사(maintain) 뒤에 형용사(exemplary)의 수식을 받는 복합명사 attendance records(출석 기록)가 적절하다.
어휘 maintain 유지하다 record 기록 eligible for (자격, 연령 등의 조건이 맞아서) ~을 가질 수 있는

8
해석 다가오는 홍보 행사들은 현재 개발 중인 제품들에만 초점을 맞출 것이다.
해설 전치사(under) 뒤는 명사 자리이다. (D)도 명사이지만 가산 명사인데 관사가 없으므로 오답이다. (B)는 동명사이지만 타동사가 동명사가 되는 경우 동사의 성질을 가지고 있어서 동명사 뒤에 목적어가 필요하다. 따라서 정답은 (C)이다.
어휘 upcoming 다가오는, 곧 있을 promotional 홍보의, 판촉의

9
해석 Smart Life는 새로운 착용하기 적합한 장치들을 위해 효과적인 광고 전략을 만들었다.
해설 빈칸은 명사 자리로서 앞의 advertising과 더불어 복합명사가 되는 advertising strategy(광고 전략)가 적절하다.
어휘 effective 효과적인 wearable 착용하기 적합한

10
해석 다른 대안이 없었기 때문에 우리는 새로운 복사기에 추가적인 2,300달러를 소비했다.
해설 there is/are ~는 '~이 있다'라는 표현으로 뒤에는 명사가 와야 한다. 또한 빈칸 앞에 형용사 no가 있으므로 '대안'이라는 뜻의 alternative가 정답이다.
어휘 spend (시간, 돈을) 소비하다 since ~때문에

DAY 04 대명사

○ 비법 적용 연습 본문 p.33

PART 5	1 (D)	2 (D)	3 (B)	4 (A)	5 (A)
	6 (D)	7 (B)	8 (B)	9 (B)	10 (A)

1
해석 Rhodora의 승진 후에, 그녀는 모든 지역 지점들의 운영을 책임지게 될 것이다.
해설 선택지가 모두 she에서 나온 대명사들이고 격이 다르므로 주어 자리에 들어갈 수 있는 주격(she)과 소유대명사(hers)가 정답이 될 수 있다. 의미상 그녀의 것(hers)은 부적절하므로 정답은 (D) she이다.
어휘 promotion 승진 responsible for ~에 책임이 있는 operation 운영 regional 지역의 branch 지사, 분점

2
- 해석 모든 시간제 근로자들은 그들의 직속상관에게 그들이 일한 시간을 알려야 한다.
- 해설 빈칸 앞에는 관계대명사(형용사절 접속사) 목적격 that 또는 which가 생략되어 있다. 따라서 빈칸 뒤에 동사(worked)가 있으므로 빈칸은 주어 자리이다. 따라서 정답은 (D)이다. 여기서 they는 all the part-time employees를 받는다.
- 어휘 part-time employee 시간제 근무자 inform 통지하다, 알리다 immediate supervisor 직속상관

3
- 해석 그의 첫 번째 영화의 성공에 영감을 받아, Shin 씨는 즉시 속편을 계획하기 시작했다.
- 해설 전치사(of) 뒤에는 대명사의 목적격을 써야 하지만 여기서는 빈칸 뒤에 명사(movie)가 있으므로 명사를 수식하는 소유격 (B) his가 정답이다.
- 어휘 inspire 영감을 주다, 격려하다 sequel 속편

4
- 해석 Beck 박사가 연구 논문을 완성하자마자, 그것은 사본을 만들기 위해서 그의 조수 연구자에게 전해질 것이다.
- 해설 빈칸은 주어 자리이다. 따라서 주격은 (A) it이 정답이다. 재귀대명사 (B)는 주어 자리에 혼자 들어갈 수 없으며, (C) other는 형용사이므로 오답이다. (D) them은 목적격이다.
- 어휘 as soon as ~하자마자 research paper 연구 논문 forward 보내다 assistant 조수

5
- 해석 각 부서의 이사들은 누가 세미나에서 발표를 할지를 그들 스스로 결정할 것이다.
- 해설 재귀대명사 -self는 주어와 목적어가 같을 때 목적어 자리에 쓸 수 있다. 문제에서는 주어가 Directors이므로 목적어 자리에 재귀대명사 themselves가 정답이다.
- 어휘 director 이사, 감독 department 부서 make a presentation 발표하다

6
- 해석 장비를 조사할 때 장비에 부착되어 있는 체크리스트에 어떤 기술적인 결함이라도 기재해 주십시오.
- 해설 빈칸은 명사(failures)를 수식하는 형용사 자리이다. (B) where은 의문사 혹은 접속사로 쓰이므로 오답이고, (C) every는 형용사로는 쓰이나 대부분 뒤에 단수 명사가 온다. some과 any의 경우 some은 긍정문에서 any는 부정문, 의문문, 조건문에서 '약간의', '몇몇의'라는 뜻으로 쓰이나 any가 긍정문에 쓰이는 경우에는 뜻이 '어떤 ~라도'이며 some과 같이 확실한 존재를 의미하기보다는 불확실한 존재를 의미할 때 쓰인다. 문제에서 기술적인 문제가 꼭 있다기보다는 문제가 있을 수도 없을 수도 있는 상황이므로 (D) any가 정답이다.
- 어휘 inspect 점검하다, 검사하다 equipment 장비 record 기록하다 attach 첨부하다, 붙이다

7
- 해석 이 사업 모델은 혜택과 위험을 둘 다 포함하고 있으므로, 이 사업에 관심이 있는 사람들은 각 요소를 나머지 다른 요소와 주의 깊게 비교해야 한다.
- 해설 혜택과 위험을 비교해야 한다는 의미이므로 두 가지 것 중에서 하나를 대명사 one으로 받으면 나머지 하나는 the other로 받아야 한다. 따라서 정답은 (B)이다. (A) other는 형용사로 쓰며, (D) the one은 '바로 그 한 가지 것'이란 뜻으로 의미상 부적절하다.
- 어휘 benefit 이득, 혜택 risk 위험 involve 포함하다 weigh (결정을 내리기 전에) 따져보다, 저울질하다

8
- 해석 Gloria는 회사에서 그녀의 32년간의 근무에 대해서 은퇴 만찬에서 공로상을 받을 것이다.
- 해설 빈칸 뒤에 명사를 수식하는 소유격이 와야 한다. 따라서 정답은 (B)이다.
- 어휘 receive 받다 lifetime achievement award 공로상 retirement 은퇴 banquet 연회, 만찬

9
- 해석 당신이 언제 도착하는지를 저에게 알려 주셔서 제가 당신을 데리러 갈 사람을 준비할 수 있게 해 주세요.
- 해설 동사(let) 뒤에 목적어 자리이므로 목적격 (B) me가 정답이다. 사역동사 let 다음의 목적격 보어 자리에는 to를 생략하고 원형부정사를 쓴다. 소유대명사 mine(나의 것)도 목적어 자리에 들어갈 수 있지만 의미상 어색하다.
- 어휘 arrange 정리하다, 준비하다

10
- 해석 Gonzales 씨는 모레 회의로부터 돌아올 것이지만, 인사부 이사인 Delgado 씨는 다음 주까지는 그와 만나지 않을 것이다.
- 해설 전치사 뒤의 목적어 자리이므로 목적격을 쓴다. 따라서 목적격인 (A) him이 정답이다. 전치사 뒤에 목적격 자리에 재귀대명사(-self)도 쓸 수 있지만 재귀대명사는 주어와 동격이 되는 경우에 쓸 수 있다.
- 어휘 human resources department 인사부

DAY 05 형용사

○ 비법 적용 연습 본문 p.39

PART 5	1 (C)	2 (B)	3 (D)	4 (A)	5 (B)
	6 (C)	7 (D)	8 (C)	9 (B)	10 (B)

1
- 해석 우리 팀은 동아시아 시장으로의 성공적인 확장 덕분에 이번 분기 예상 이윤에 대해서 낙관적이다.
- 해설 선택지가 모두 형용사이고 빈칸은 보어 자리이므로 의미상 '낙관적인'이라는 뜻의 (C)가 정답이다. (A) 공상적인, 관념적인 (B) 기꺼이 하는 (D) 단정적인, 고집하는
- 어휘 project 계획하다, 예상하다 revenue 수입, 수익 quarter 분기 expansion 확장, 확대

2
- 해석: 다음 주부터 모든 직원들은 사내에서는 신분증을 반드시 착용해야 한다.
- 해설: 선택지가 수량 형용사들로 구성되어 있으면 빈칸 뒤 명사에 주의한다. staff members는 복수 명사인데 every, each, either는 형용사로 쓰여 뒤에 명사가 올 때 단수 명사가 온다. 뒤에 복수 명사가 오는 (B) all이 정답이다.
- 어휘: premises 부지, 구내

3
- 해석: Burke 씨는 국제 녹색 에너지 회의에서 기조연설을 했고, 나는 연설이 매우 유익하다는 것을 알게 되었다.
- 해설: find는 5형식 문장이 가능한 동사이므로 빈칸은 목적격 보어 자리이다. 보어 자리에 들어갈 수 있는 명사와 형용사 중에서 빈칸 앞에 very(부사)를 보고 부사의 수식을 받는 형용사 (D)가 정답임을 알 수 있다.
- 어휘: keynote speech 기조연설 green energy 그린 에너지, 친환경 에너지

4
- 해석: 웹 사이트에 모아진 모든 개인 정보들은 기밀로 유지되어야 한다.
- 해설: remain은 2형식 동사이므로 빈칸은 보어 자리이다. 따라서 명사와 형용사 중에서 (C)는 명사로 주어와 동격이 되지 못하므로 빈칸은 형용사 보어가 와야 한다. 의미상 '기밀의'라는 뜻의 (A)가 정답이다.
- 어휘: gather 모으다 remain 유지하다

5
- 해석: 거의 20년 전에 세워진 KMP 항공사는 특히 사업차 출장을 가는 사람들을 위해서 다양한 서비스들을 제공한다.
- 해설: '다양한'이란 뜻의 a wide range of는 형용사로 쓰이며 여기서 range는 array, variety, selection으로 바꿔 쓸 수 있다. 뒤에는 대부분 복수 명사가 온다.
- 어휘: establish 설립하다 a range of 다양한

6
- 해석: Jump High의 부사장은 몇몇 지점들이 여름 시즌 동안에 연례 검사를 위해 일시적으로 문을 닫을 것임을 알렸다.
- 해설: close는 형용사로 쓰일 경우 '(시간적, 공간적으로) ~과 가까운', '밀집한', '친밀한' 등의 뜻이지만 이 문장에서는 의미상 부적절하다. 동사로 쓰일 경우 '(가게를) 닫다', '(영업을) 폐쇄하다'의 뜻이므로 수동형인 closed가 적절하다.
- 어휘: vice president 부사장 branch 지사, 분점 annual inspection 연례 검사, 연례 조사

7
- 해석: 모든 컴퓨터 부품들과 다른 관련 사무용품들은 각 사무실에 지정된 사물함에 보관되어야 한다.
- 해설: 빈칸은 명사 앞 형용사 자리이므로 의미상 '관련된'이라는 뜻의 (D)가 정답이다. alike는 형용사로 '비슷한, 동등한'이라는 뜻이 있지만 명사 앞에서 수식하는 것이 아니라 서술적 용법으로만 사용된다.
- 어휘: component 요소, 부품 office supplies 사무용 소모품 store 저장하다, 보관하다 designate 지정하다

8
- 해석: 런던에서 가장 많이 방문되는 관광명소에 관한 모든 정보는 〈London Life〉의 최신호에서 알 수 있다.
- 해설: 선택지가 모두 형용사이므로 해석을 통해서 풀어야 한다. 주격 보어 자리이므로 주어(information)와의 관계를 통해 '정보를 이용할 수 있다'가 적절하다. 따라서 정답은 (C) available이다.
- 어휘: regarding ~에 관하여 attraction 명소, 관광명소 issue (잡지, 신문 같은 정기 간행물의) 호

9
- 해석: 지점 관리자들은 매일 업무를 위해 필요한 용품들을 구매할 책임이 있다.
- 해설: be동사 뒤에 보어 자리이므로 형용사가 와야 한다. 의미상 '~에 대해 책임을 지다'라는 뜻의 be responsible for가 적절하다.
- 어휘: purchase 구매하다 daily task 매일의 업무

10
- 해석: Smith 씨가 오후 3시 30분에 일본에서 온 고객과 급한 미팅이 있기 때문에 3시 15분 미팅을 좀 더 늦은 시간으로 재조정해 주세요.
- 해설: 빈칸은 time(명사)를 수식하는 형용사 자리이다. 선택지 모두 형용사이므로 해석을 통해 정답을 골라야 한다. 의미상 (B)가 정답이다. (A) 최근의 (B) 보다 늦은, 후에 (C) (보통 거리나 깊이에 대해) 더 멀리 (D) (명사를 수식하는 한정적 용법으로 the와 함께 쓰며) 다음의, 다음에 오는
- 어휘: reschedule 일정을 변경하다 urgent 긴급한, 시급한

DAY 06 부사

○ 비법 적용 연습 본문 p.44

PART 5	1 (C)	2 (A)	3 (B)	4 (A)	5 (D)
	6 (C)	7 (C)	8 (C)	9 (A)	10 (A)

1
- 해석: Jefferson 씨는 GRN 제품들의 정시 배송을 주로 책임진다.
- 해설: 선택지가 모두 부사이므로 해석을 통해서 정답을 골라야 한다. '주로 책임진다'라는 뜻이 자연스러우므로 정답은 (C)이다. (A) 느리게 (B) 거의 (C) 주로 (D) 다양하게
- 어휘: responsible for ~에 책임이 있는 on time 정시에 delivery 배달

2
- 해석: Lukas 씨는 내일이 마감일이기 때문에 연간 판매 보고서를 빨리 완성하라고 요청받았다.
- 해설: Mr. Lukas부터 sales report까지 이미 완전한 문장이므로 뒤에 나올 수 있는 품사는 대부분 수식어이다. since부터 tomorrow까지도 부사절이므로 수식어절이 된다. 따라서 동사 complete를 수식하는 부사 quickly가 정답이다.
- 어휘: complete 완료하다, 끝마치다 annual 매년의, 연간의 sales report 판매 보고서 due 만기가 된

3

해석 새로운 연구에 따르면 파트 타임으로 일하는 사람의 수가 지난 5년 동안 급격하게 증가했다고 한다.

해설 선택지가 모두 부사이므로 부사 어휘 문제이다. 여기서 부사는 has risen(~이 증가하다)을 수식하므로 의미상 dramatically(급격하게)가 정답이다. (A) 효율적으로 (C) 공개적으로 (D) 급하게

어휘 suggest 제안하다, 제시하다 rise 증가하다

4

해석 작년 세미나 동안에 제안된 세계 은행의 직원 복지 정책들이 이미 시행되고 있다.

해설 빈칸은 have와 p.p. 사이의 부사 자리이다. 의미상 '이미'를 뜻하는 (A)가 정답이다. (C) 곧 (D) 훨씬, 단연코.

어휘 employee 고용인 benefit (회사에서 급여 외에 받는) 특전, 수당 propose 제안하다 implement 시행하다

5

해석 어제 기자회견에서 Chang 씨는 그녀가 창업한 회사가 Jin Education에 의해 인수되었다는 것을 공식적으로 발표했다.

해설 선택지가 모두 부사이므로 동사(announced)를 수식하는 적절한 의미의 부사를 써야 한다. (A) 습관적으로 (B) 외부적으로 (C) 주의 깊게 (D) 공식적으로

어휘 press conference 기자회견 announce 공표하다, 알리다 found 설립하다 acquire 얻다, 취득하다, 매입하다

6

해석 회사의 대표 이사인 David Lindarton 씨는 이번 분기의 형편없는 판매량이 회사의 주식 가격에 부정적인 영향을 미치지 않을 거라고 확신했다.

해설 조동사(will)과 동사(affect) 사이의 부사 자리이다. 따라서 정답은 (C)이다. (A) 상대방, 적수 (B) 부정적인 (D) 변경

어휘 confident 자신감 있는, 확신하는 affect 영향을 미치다 stock 주식

7

해석 모든 기계가 수리된 후에 Crimpson 생산 시설은 곧 다시 문을 열 것이 예상된다.

해설 동사 reopen을 수식하는 부사 자리이다. 의미상 '곧 다시 문을 열 것이다'가 적절하므로 (C)가 정답이다. (A) 초기에 (B) 동등하게 (C) 곧 (D) 거의

어휘 machinery 기계, 기계류 repair 수리하다 facility 시설 expect 예상하다, 기대하다

8

해석 Grand 호텔의 지점들은 모두 중심가에 위치해 있어서 손님들이 주요 관광명소에 쉽게 갈 수 있게 해 준다.

해설 be동사와 p.p.(즉, 수동태) 사이가 빈칸이라면 빈칸은 부사 자리이다. 따라서 정답은 (C)이다.

어휘 branch 지사, 분점 locate 위치시키다 provide A with B A에게 B를 제공하다 access 접근 tourist attraction 관광명소

9

해석 시상식이나 회사 만찬과 같은 행사를 전문적으로 준비하는 그 회사는 특히 큰 행사들을 위해서 임시 직원들을 종종 고용한다.

해설 specializing ~ banquet은 수식어이므로 The company(주어)와 arranges(동사) 사이는 부사가 와야 한다. 따라서 정답은 (A)이다.

어휘 specialize 전공하다, 전문적으로 다루다 organize 준비하다, 조직하다 award ceremony 시상식 banquet 성찬, 연회 arrange (일을) 처리하다, 마련하다 temporary staff 임시 직원

10

해석 성공한 영화감독인 Charles Pearson의 팬들이 그의 이전 영화의 속편을 열렬히 기다리고 있다.

해설 주어(Fans)와 동사(await) 사이는 부사 자리이다. 따라서 정답은 (A)이다.

어휘 await 기다리다 sequel 속편 previous 이전의

DAY 07 전치사

○ 비법 적용 연습 본문 p.49

PART 5	1 (C)	2 (D)	3 (C)	4 (A)	5 (C)
	6 (B)	7 (B)	8 (D)	9 (D)	10 (A)

1

해석 Wyoming Communications의 모든 직원들은 스트레스 관리에 관한 3월 7일 세미나에 참여하라고 초대받았다.

해설 on/about/as to/as for/regarding/concerning/in regard to/with respect to는 모두 '~에 대해서, 관해서'라는 뜻의 전치사이다. 따라서 정답은 (C)이다.

어휘 employee 고용인 attend 참석하다 management 관리

2

해석 Betty는 해외여행의 지출 보고서를 제외한 모든 지출 보고서들을 승인할 책임이 있다.

해설 those는 대명사로서 앞의 명사(expense reports)를 받는다. 따라서 대명사를 앞 문장과 연결시키기 위해 전치사가 필요하므로 정답은 (D) except이다. (A) aside(부사)는 from과 같이 써서 전치사로 '~을 제외하고'라는 뜻이다.

어휘 responsible for ~에 책임이 있는 approve 승인하다, 인가하다 expense report 지출 보고서

3

해석 Hale 씨가 그녀의 프로젝트를 위해 쓴 추가 시간에도 불구하고, 그녀는 마감일까지 그녀의 서류를 끝낼 수 없었다.

해설 선택지가 전치사와 접속사로 구성된 경우 빈칸 뒤에 [주어+동사]가 있는지를 확인해야 한다. hours와 Ms. Hale 사이에 형용사절 접속사(관계대명사)의 목적격 which 또는 that이 생략되어 있으므로 빈칸 뒤에는 명사(hours)만 있는 것이다. 따라서 빈칸은 전치사가 와야 한다. (A)와 (C) 중에서 의미상 '~에도 불구하고'가 적절하므로 (C)가 정답이다.

어휘 be unable to ~할 수 없는 deadline 마감일

4
- 해석 일련의 회의들의 안건이 첫 번째 회의 전에 모두에게 나누어졌다.
- 해설 명사(the first meeting) 앞의 전치사 자리이다. 의미상 '~ 전에'라는 뜻이 적절하므로 (A)가 정답이다. (C)는 owing to 형태가 되면 '~ 때문에'라는 뜻이다. (B) ~에 호의적으로 (D) ~의 경우에 대비해서
- 어휘 agenda 의제, 안건 a series of 일련의 distribute 분배하다, 나누어 주다

5
- 해석 T&T Advertising에서의 임금 인상은 연례 직원 평가에 기초한다.
- 해설 지정된 장소나 비교적 작은 장소에 쓸 수 있는 전치사는 at이 적절하다.
- 어휘 wage 임금 increase 인상 based on ~에 기초하는, 기반하는 annual employee evaluation 연례 직원 평가

6
- 해석 경영 자문위원들이 런던으로부터 도착할 때 그들은 재무 자료와 같은 기밀문서들에 접근할 수 있을 것이다.
- 해설 의미상 arrive라는 동사와 함께 쓰이는 방향 전치사 (B) from(~로부터)이 정답이다.
- 어휘 consultant 상담가, 자문위원 confidential 비밀의, 기밀

7
- 해석 수일간의 협상 후에 Rousch Drinks와 H&H Chemicals는 새로운 연구 계획들에 대한 합의에 이르렀다.
- 해설 시간의 명사(days of negotiations)와 적절하게 쓰일 명사는 After(~후에)이다.
- 어휘 negotiation 협상 reach 도달하다 agreement 합의 regarding ~에 관하여 initiative 계획

8
- 해석 Cerabo Electronics의 착용 가능한 장비의 판매가 지난 5년간 2배가 되었다.
- 해설 현재완료(have doubled)와 함께 쓰이는 표현을 묻는 문제이다. in/for/over the past/last는 '지난 ~ 동안에'라는 뜻이다. 따라서 정답은 (D)이다.
- 어휘 wearable 착용 가능한 double 2배가 되다

9
- 해석 당신이 첫 번째 임무를 완수하자마자 추가적인 지시사항을 위해서 Cager 씨에게 연락 하십시오.
- 해설 for further instructions는 '추가 지시사항을 위해서'라는 뜻이다. 따라서 정답은 (D)이다.
- 어휘 as soon as ~하자마자 complete 완성하다 assignment 과제, 임무 instructions 지시사항

10
- 해석 Lindstein 씨는 4번의 경력 개발 회의 중 하나에 모든 직원이 등록하기를 요청하는 공지 사항을 게시판에 올렸다.
- 해설 resister for(= sign up for)는 '~에 등록하다'라는 뜻이다. 따라서 정답은 (A)이다.
- 어휘 post 게시하다, 공고하다 notice 공고문 register 등록하다

DAY 08 동사의 종류와 형태

○ 비법 적용 연습   본문 p.54

PART 5	1 (D)	2 (B)	3 (C)	4 (D)	5 (B)
	6 (D)	7 (B)	8 (A)	9 (D)	10 (A)

1
- 해석 브루스가 좋은 관리자이기는 하지만 할 줄 아는 외국어가 없다는 것이 그의 승진을 막고 있다.
- 해설 어휘 문제로 'A가 B하는 것을 막다'라는 뜻의 prevent A from B가 적절하다. (A) ~을 위협하다(threatens A with B: A를 B를 가지고 협박하다) (B) ~을 훔치다(steal A from B: A에게서 B를 훔치다) (C) 분배하다
- 어휘 although ~에도 불구하고 inability 무능, 불능 move up 승진하다, 출세하다

2
- 해석 Cogin's Business Consulting 사는 작은 사업체들을 위해 맞춤화된 인력 관리 방법을 제공하는 것에 특화되어 있다.
- 해설 빈칸은 동사 자리인데 목적어 대신 전치사(in)가 있으므로 in과 함께 쓸 수 있는 자동사로 specialize in(~에 특화되다)이 있다. 따라서 정답은 (B)이다. (C) facilitate 가능하게 하다 (D) utilize 활용하다
- 어휘 customize 주문 제작하다 staff 직원을 제공하다

3
- 해석 관리자들은 모든 건설 인부들이 현장에서 새로운 안전 규정을 따라야 한다는 것을 확실히 해야 한다.
- 해설 빈칸은 동사 자리인데 동사 뒤에 목적어가 아닌 전치사 with가 있기에 with와 어울리는 자동사 (C) comply(~을 따르다, ~에 순응하다)가 정답이다.
- 어휘 make sure ~을 확실히 하다 construction 건설, 공사 safety regulation 안정 규정 on site 현장의, 현지의

4
- 해석 정규 근무 시간이 건물의 보수공사가 완료되자마자 재개될 것입니다.
- 해설 resume은 자동사와 타동사로 모두 쓰일 수 있다. 여기서는 자동사로 '~이 다시 시작되다'라는 뜻이다.
- 어휘 business hours 영업 시간 complete 완료하다

5
- 해석 Torrex 사의 대리인이 Pam 씨에게 유망한 새 땅이 매물로 나왔다는 것을 알렸다.
- 해설 (A), (C), (D)와는 달리 (B) inform은 명사절 that을 바로 목적어로 취하기보다는 '~에게'라는 간접 목적어를 쓰고 나서 that절을 직접 목적어로 받는다. 이런 동사로는 inform, notify, convince, assure, tell, remind, advise 등이 있다.
- 어휘 agent 대리인 promising 유망한 lot 지역 for sale 판매 중인

6
- 해석 모든 계약서는 지역 법과 규제를 회사가 준수한다는 것을 확실히 하기 위해 법무부서에 의해 검토되어야 한다.
- 해설 '반드시 ~하게 하다'라는 뜻의 ensure는 that(명사절)을 목적어로 취하는 3형식 동사로 쓰일 수 있다.
- 어휘 contract 계약 review 재검토하다 in compliance with ~에 따라, ~에 응하여

7
- 해석 상업은행의 역할은 주로 일반인들로부터 예금을 받아서 그중 일부를 투자하는 것으로 구성된다.
- 해설 빈칸 뒤의 부사(primarily)는 수식어이므로 배제하고, 그 뒤의 of를 보고 동사 뒤에 목적어가 아닌 전치사가 오는 자동사를 선택해야 한다. consist는 전치사 of와 함께 쓰이므로 정답은 (B)이다. (D)도 자동사이지만 cooperate with의 형태로 사용된다. (A) spread 펼치다 (D) cooperate 협력하다
- 어휘 primarily 주로 accept 받아들이다 deposit 예금 the general public 일반대중 invest 투자하다

8
- 해석 기술팀 이사인 Kelvin은 10월 2일에 새로운 화상 회의 시스템에 대한 다음 연수를 예정했다.
- 해설 schedule은 타동사로 '~을 예정하다, ~을 스케줄에 넣다'라는 뜻이므로 정답은 (A)이다. (D) present 수여하다
- 어휘 teleconference (원격) 화상 회의

9
- 해석 고객들은 지난 2월의 서비스 장애 후에 SA Telecom이 취한 방법들에 대해서 우려를 표시했다.
- 해설 빈칸 뒤에 목적어 concern이 오기 때문에 타동사 자리이다. (A) focus는 타동사로 쓰일 때 '(빛 등을) 초점에 모으다'라는 뜻이고, (B) appear는 자동사, (C) apply는 타동사로 쓰일 때 '~을 ~에 적용하다, 응용하다'의 뜻이므로 오답이다. 타동사 express는 concern과 함께 '걱정을 표현하다'란 뜻이므로 (D)가 정답이다.
- 어휘 concern 걱정, 우려 take measures 대책을 강구하다, 조치를 취하다

10
- 해석 Cook 씨가 급한 미팅이 있어서 우리는 그를 대신해 Victoria를 추천한다.
- 해설 빈칸은 동사 자리로 동사 어휘 문제이다. (A)는 타동사로 '~을 추천하다, 권하다', (B)는 '~을 강요하다', (C)는 '~을 상기하다, 기억하다' (D)는 '~을 발명하다'라는 뜻이다.
- 어휘 urgent 긴급한 fill in for 대신하다

DAY 09 수 일치

비법 적용 연습 본문 p.59

PART 5
1 (B)	2 (C)	3 (A)	4 (A)	5 (A)
6 (C)	7 (D)	8 (C)	9 (A)	10 (D)

1
- 해석 선명한 영사기는 명확하게 표시되는 음영을 가진 사진을 만들어낸다.
- 해설 projector(주어)가 단수이므로 동사도 단수 동사가 되어야 한다. 3인칭 단수 주어에는 동사에 -s를 붙인다. 따라서 정답은 (B)이다.
- 어휘 high-contrast 선명한, 고대비의 defined 모양을 분명히 나타내는

2
- 해석 새로운 온라인 회계 솔루션은 Duway 사의 재정 보고서들의 오류의 수를 상당히 감소시켰다.
- 해설 동사 자리이므로 (B), (C) 중에서 (B)는 주어(3인칭 단수)와 수 일치가 맞지 않으므로 오답이다.
- 어휘 accounting 회계 significantly 상당히 corporation 기업

3
- 해석 공사 현장의 오직 절반의 근로자들만이 버스를 타고 출퇴근을 한다.
- 해설 half는 of 뒤에 오는 명사에 따라서 수 일치를 한다. 뒤에 복수 명사 the workers가 있으므로 복수 동사 (A)가 정답이다.
- 어휘 construction site 공사 현장 commute 통근하다

4
- 해석 데이터 분석 회의에 참석하는 데 관심이 있는 사람은 누구든지 이번 달말 전에 Glenn에게 연락을 해야 한다.
- 해설 who부터 forum까지가 형용사절로 빈칸(주어 자리)을 수식하고 있다. 형용사절의 동사(is interested)가 단수이므로 정답은 (A)이다. 재귀대명사 (B), (C)는 주어 자리에 쓸 수 없으며 (D) Those는 뒤에서 수식하는 구나 절이 있으면 '~하는 사람들'이라는 뜻인데 수 일치에서 어긋나므로 오답이다.
- 어휘 be interested in ~에 관심이 있는 join 합류하다

5
- 해석 우리의 새로운 기술은 인도의 숙련된 기술자들의 외부 도움을 받아서 캐나다에서 개발되었다.
- 해설 빈칸은 주어 자리이다. 단수 동사(was)를 보고 단수 명사인 (A)가 정답임을 알 수 있다.
- 어휘 off-site 떨어진, 부지 밖의

6
- 해석 Hopkins 의료센터에 있는 연구원들은 전자기기들을 사용하는 것이 인간의 뇌에 미치는 영향을 연구해 왔다.
- 해설 이 문장의 주어는 Researchers(복수 주어)가 되며 빈칸 뒤에 목적어(the effect)가 있으므로 능동태가 되어야 한다. 따라서 현재완료인 (C)가 정답이다. (A)는 수 일치에서 어긋나고, (B)는 동사가 아니며 (D)는 수동태라서 오답이다.
- 어휘 effect 영향

7
해석 기술 지원팀의 이사인 Andrew Sato 씨는 사무기계의 적절한 사용에 대한 모든 교육 세미나에 대해 책임을 질 것이다.
해설 쉼표 사이에 있는 Director of Technical Support는 앞에 나온 Mr. Andrew Sato와 동격을 나타낸다. 따라서 빈칸은 동사 자리이며 주어가 단수이므로 (D)가 정답이다.
어휘 responsibility 책임 proper 적절한 assume 맡다

8
해석 기술의 최근 발전으로 인해 지역 지점들은 서로 더 쉽고 빠르게 의사소통할 수 있게 되었다.
해설 recent(형용사)가 수식하는 명사(주어) 자리이다. (A), (C), (D)가 주어 자리에 들어갈 수 있지만 복수 동사(have)를 보고 복수 주어 (C)를 선택해야 한다.
어휘 regional 지역의 branch 지사, 분점 communicate 의사소통하다

9
해석 많은 Bowden Energy의 직원들이 전기를 아끼고 건강 유지를 위한 노력으로 승강기 대신 계단을 이용한다.
해설 A number of 뒤에는 복수 명사가 오고 이 복수 명사가 주어가 되므로 빈칸은 복수 동사가 와야 한다. 따라서 정답은 (A)이다.
어휘 a number of 많은 in an effort to ~하기 위한 노력으로

10
해석 12월 23일에 예정된 연례 회사 연회를 위한 초대장이 모든 직원들에게 보내졌다.
해설 주어 자리가 빈칸이고 동사는 복수 동사(have been sent)이므로 복수 주어가 와야 한다. 따라서 정답은 (D)이다. scheduled는 여기서 동사의 역할이 아닌 형용사(분사)의 역할을 하므로 주어와의 수 일치와 관계가 없다.
어휘 annual 연간의, 매년의 banquet 연회, 성찬

DAY 10 태

○ 비법 적용 연습   본문 p.64

PART 5	1 (A)	2 (D)	3 (C)	4 (D)	5 (C)
	6 (C)	7 (B)	8 (B)	9 (B)	10 (D)

1
해석 P&G Chemical Lab의 방문자들은 항상 우리의 홍보 직원과 동행해야 한다.
해설 조동사(must) 뒤 동사원형 자리인데 타동사 accompany 뒤에 목적어가 없고 대신 by가 있으므로 수동태 문장이 되어야 한다. 따라서 정답은 (A)이다.
어휘 public relation 홍보 representative 대표 at all times 항상 accompany 동행하다

2
해석 Deutsche Motor Imports의 직원 안내서는 업무 관련 회사의 전화번호들을 포함하고 있다.
해설 동사 자리이며 주어가 단수이기에 (A)는 수 일치에서 오답이다. (C), (D) 중에서 타동사(contain) 뒤에 목적어(a list)가 있으므로 능동의 동사 (D)가 정답이다.
어휘 handbook 안내서 work-related 일과 관련된 contain 들어 있다

3
해석 Pierson 지하철역이 5월 말까지 수리로 인해 문을 닫습니다.
해설 여기서 close는 '~을 닫다(영업을 하지 않다)'라는 뜻의 동사로 쓰여야 하고, 능동적으로 무엇을 닫는 주체가 아닌 닫히는 것이므로 수동태 (C)가 정답이다.
어휘 repair 수리

4
해석 제조업체는 카메라 렌즈에 대한 보증 기간을 6개월까지 연장했다.
해설 동사 자리이고 주어가 단수이므로 수 일치에서 (A)는 오답이다. 빈칸 뒤에 목적어(the warranty period)가 있으므로 수동태 (B)도 오답이다. 따라서 정답은 현재완료 시제의 (D)이다.
어휘 manufacturer 제조자, 생산 업체 warranty period 보증 기간

5
해석 다른 지점으로 이동하고자 하는 신청자들은 이번 주 말까지 서류를 제출해야 한다.
해설 조동사(must) 뒤의 동사원형 자리이다. 빈칸 뒤에 목적어가 있으므로 능동의 (C)가 정답이다.
어휘 applicant 지원자 transfer 옮기다, 이동하다 branch 지사

6
해석 Lutz Mobile의 대변인이 회사의 모든 스마트폰은 만약 기계적인 문제가 있다면 적절하게 수리될 것이라고 보장했다.
해설 부사(properly)를 빼고 앞에 be동사가 오고 타동사(repair) 뒤에 목적어가 없으므로 수동태 (C)가 정답이다.
어휘 spokesperson 대변인 guarantee 보장하다, 보증하다

7
해석 이 모임의 목적은 8월 15일에 열리는 무역 박람회를 위해 Copenhagen으로 가는 당신 팀의 여행의 세부 사항과 예산을 확인하기 위해서입니다.
해설 빈칸 앞의 to는 to부정사(형용사적 용법)의 to이므로 빈칸은 동사원형이 먼저 와야 한다. hold(타동사) 뒤에 목적어가 없으므로 정답은 수동태 (B)이다.
어휘 confirm 확정하다, 확실히 하다 trade fair 무역 박람회

8
해석 고객 관리와 판매 분야에서 이전 경험이 있는 사람들에게 공석에 고용될 수 있는 더 좋은 기회가 주어질 것이다.
해설 빈칸 뒤에 목적어(the better chance)가 있어서 능동태 같지만 give는 4형식이 가능한 동사로서, 간접 목적어와 직접 목적어 2개의 목적어를 가질 수 있다. 따라서 수동태가 되어도 직접 목적어가 남을

수 있으므로 정답은 (B)이다.

어휘 previous 이전의 vacant 비어 있는

9

해석 Dunham Titan 2000 XG는 신뢰가 가는 트럭이지만, 몇몇 전문가들은 트럭의 의자들이 엉망으로 디자인되었다고 주장한다.

해설 poorly(부사를 제외하고 빈칸 앞에 be동사 are가 있고 뒤에 목적어가 없으므로 타동사 design은 수동태 형태가 되어야 한다. 따라서 정답은 (B)이다.

어휘 reliable 믿을 수 있는, 신뢰할 수 있는 expert 전문가

10

해석 회사의 자선 행사에 기여하고 싶은 직원들은 Gregory Moreland 사무실 앞에 붙은 자원봉사 명단에 등록할 것을 제안합니다.

해설 invite는 목적격 보어 자리에 to부정사를 취할 수 있으며, 이 경우 [주어+invite+목적어+to부정사]가 수동태가 되면 [목적어+be invited to부정사] 형태가 된다. 따라서 정답은 (D)이다.

어휘 contribute 기부하다, 기여하다 charity 자선 sign up 등록하다

DAY 11 시제

비법 적용 연습

본문 p.68

PART 5	1 (D)	2 (A)	3 (B)	4 (B)	5 (B)
	6 (A)	7 (C)	8 (A)	9 (B)	10 (C)

1

해석 스쿨버스는 교문 앞에서 30분마다 출발한다.

해설 동사 자리이므로 수 일치–능동태/수동태–시제의 순으로 확인한다. (A)는 주어가 단수인데 복수 동사가 왔으므로 수 일치가 맞지 않고, (B)는 depart가 자동사이므로 수동태로 쓸 수 없다. (C), (D)는 시제의 차이인데 every 30 minutes처럼 반복적으로 일어나는 행위는 현재 시제를 쓰므로 (D)가 정답이다.

2

해석 기타 연주자 Carlos Santana는 지난 일요일에 Los Angeles 자선 콘서트에서 젊은 음악가들과 함께 그의 대표곡들을 연주했다.

해설 동사 자리이므로 동사가 아닌 (C)를 제외하고, last Sunday에서 과거 시제임을 알 수 있다. 따라서 정답은 (A)이다.

어휘 charity 자선

3

해석 Cassel 박사가 Zurich 물리 연구소의 수석 연구원으로서 은퇴할 때가 되면 그는 연구실의 명성을 상당히 증가시킬 것이다.

해설 By the time은 시제 문제의 힌트로서 [by the time+현재 시제, 미래완료 시제]가 된다. 또한 [by the time+과거 시제, 과거완료 시제]도 기억하자.

어휘 retire 은퇴하다 laboratory 연구소 reputation 명성

4

해석 제품개발팀은 경쟁업체의 신제품이 그들의 작업 원형을 쓸모없게 만든 후에야 앞 다투어 혁신적인 아이디어를 찾기 시작했다.

해설 주절이 과거(began)이므로 after 이하의 절도 과거 시제가 와야 한다. 따라서 정답은 (B)이다.

어휘 scramble for 앞 다투어 ~하다 prototype 원형 obsolete 쓸모가 없는 render (어떤 상태가 되게) 하다

5

해석 기한까지 대여한 책을 반납하지 않은 도서관 이용자들은 연체료를 부과 받을 것이다.

해설 동사 자리이므로 수 일치–능동태/수동태–시제 순으로 정답을 찾아야 한다. charge는 charge A B(A에게 B를 부과하다)라는 4형식 동사로 쓰일 수 있으므로 late fees(직접 목적어)가 있어도 수동태가 될 수 있다. 주어(library members)가 연체료를 부과하는 주체가 아니라 받는 객체이므로 수동태가 정답이다.

어휘 due date 만기일 late fee 연체료

6

해석 Winex Japan의 Demon's Lair가 롤플레이 게임으로 온라인에 진출할 때쯤 되면 기술자들이 베타 테스트에서 보고된 모든 오류들을 고쳤을 것이다.

해설 빈칸은 동사 자리이다. (A), (B), (C)는 모두 능동태이므로 시제의 차이임을 알 수 있다. [By the time+현재 시제, 미래완료 시제] 구문이므로 정답은 (A) will have corrected이다.

어휘 official 공식적인

7

해석 Trey Jones는 Columbia 대학에 34년 전에 들어갔는데, 이것이 그를 Burrows School 응용과학대에서 가장 오래된 교수진 구성원으로 만들었다.

해설 빈칸은 동사 자리이다. ago를 통해서 과거 시제 문장임을 알 수 있다. 따라서 정답은 (C)이다.

어휘 faculty 교수단, 교수들 applied science 응용과학

8

해석 회사가 노동조합 구성원들에게 주말에 시간 외 근무를 하라고 요청한다면 회사는 반드시 근무자들에게 음식과 음료를 제공해야 한다.

해설 시간, 조건의 부사절에서는 미래 시제 대신에 현재 시제를 써야 한다. if(접속사)가 이끄는 조건에 대한 부사절이므로 현재 시제인 (A) asks가 정답이다.

어휘 union 조합, 연합 beverage 음료

9

해석 지난 주말에 TV에 광고가 나간 이래로 우리는 무수한 질문들을 받아 왔다.

해설 [Since+과거 시제]가 왔으므로 현재완료 시제임을 알 수 있다. 따라서 정답은 (B)이다.

어휘 countless 셀 수 없이 많은, 무수한 inquiry 질문 advertisement 광고 air 방송되다

10

해석 Malcom Merchant Marine이 차량 수송 부서를 구조 조정했을 때 상당한 수의 직원들이 회사에서 다른 부서로 배정을 받았다.

해설 빈칸은 동사 자리이다. (A)는 뒤에 목적어가 있는데 수동태라서 오답이고, (B)는 주절의 동사가 과거(were)인데 현재 시제를 썼으므로 이 문장의 시제로 적절하지 않다. 따라서 정답은 (C)이다.

어휘 considerable 상당한 assign 배정하다 restructure 구조조정하다

DAY 12 부정사

○ 비법 적용 연습 본문 p.73

PART 5	1 (C)	2 (B)	3 (D)	4 (C)	5 (D)
	6 (A)	7 (A)	8 (C)	9 (D)	10 (D)

1

해석 Boston 관광 사무소는 도시의 역사적인 장소에 위치해 있는 호텔들과 식당들을 방문객들이 애용할 수 있게 유도한다.

해설 invite(동사)는 목적어 뒤에 목적격 보어를 취할 수 있는 5형식 동사이다. 이 경우 목적격 보어로 to부정사가 나올 수 있다. [invite+목적어+to부정사: 목적어가 to부정사 하게 요청하다]

어휘 historic 역사적인 patronize 애용하다

2

해석 이 지역에 다양한 새로운 식당들로 인해 경쟁이 심화되고 있지만, Romano's Bistro는 여전히 사업차 방문한 많은 고객들을 모으고 있다.

해설 to부정사는 동사가 형용사의 역할을 할 수 있게 해 준다. 여기서 customers to stay in business(사업차 방문한 고객들)처럼 to stay가 customers를 수식하는 형용사의 역할을 한다.

어휘 various 다양한 attract 끌어 모으다

3

해석 Miller 씨는 다음 달에 열릴 연간 기술 세미나를 위해 회사의 강당을 사용할 수 있는 허가를 요청했다.

해설 빈칸 앞의 명사(permission)를 수식하는 형용사적 용법으로 사용할 수 있는 to부정사가 정답이다. 따라서 정답은 (D)이다.

어휘 request 요청하다 permission 허락 auditorium 강당 hold 개최하다

4

해석 직원의 사기를 향상시킬 노력으로 이사회는 새로운 보상 프로그램의 시행을 계획하고 있다.

해설 effort(명사)는 뒤에서 to부정사가 형용사적 용법으로 쓰여 effort를 꾸미는 형식으로 많이 쓰인다. [in an effort+to부정사]는 '~하기 위한 노력으로'라는 뜻이다.

어휘 morale 사기, 의욕 implement 시행하다

5

해석 이동 통신 업체들은 새로운 고객을 모으기 위해서 할인과 다양한 혜택에 종종 의존한다.

해설 '~하기 위해서'라는 뜻의 to부정사가 적절하다. 따라서 정답은 (D)이다.

어휘 depend on ~에 의존하다 various 다양한

6

해석 우리 제품 개발팀은 공식적인 제품 출시 기자 회견을 위해 마감일을 맞추려고 그들이 할 수 있는 모든 것을 다 하고 있다.

해설 빈칸 앞에 있는 조동사 can만 보고 동사원형이 정답이라고 생각할 수 있지만 빈칸 앞의 they can은 이 문장에서 everything을 수식하는 형용사절이다. 따라서 빈칸 앞까지 문장의 의미가 완벽하므로 빈칸부터는 수식어가 되어야 한다. '~하기 위해서'라는 뜻의 to부정사 (A)가 정답이다.

어휘 deadline 마감기한 launch 시작하다, 출시하다 press conference 기자 회견

7

해석 시장에 나와 있는 모든 제품들의 디자인, 특징, 가격을 비교하기 위해서 우리 웹 사이트에 방문해 주세요.

해설 Please ~ Web site까지 문장의 의미가 완벽하다. 따라서 빈칸 뒤부터는 수식어이다. to부정사의 부사적 용법(~하기 위해서)이 적절하다.

어휘 appliance (가정용) 기기

8

해석 조합의 중역들은 새로운 직원들을 환영하기 위해서 6월 1일에 일찍 오라는 요청을 받았다.

해설 request는 목적격 보어 자리에 동명사가 아닌 to부정사를 취한다. 따라서 [request+목적어+to부정사]가 수동태가 되면 [be requested+to부정사] 형태를 취하게 된다.

어휘 union 조합, 연합 executive 간부, 이사 request 요청하다

9

해석 과정을 신속하게 처리하기 위해 모든 서류에 제품 이름과 일련번호를 적어 주세요.

해설 please부터가 주절이 되므로 쉼표 앞의 문장은 부사가 되어야 한다. 따라서 빈칸은 부사적 용법의 to부정사(~하기 위해서)가 적절하다.

어휘 include 포함하다 expedite 신속히 처리하다 serial number 일련 번호

10

해석 계절적 수요의 증가에 대처하기 위해서 인사과는 몇 명의 새로운 직원들을 고용할 생각이다.

해설 intend(동사)는 목적어 자리에 to부정사와 동명사 중에 to부정사만을 취한다. (B)는 빈칸 뒤에 명사(employees)와 충돌하므로 정답일 수 없다. 따라서 정답은 (D)이다.

어휘 cope with ~에 대처하다 personnel 인사과, 인원, 직원들

DAY 13 동명사

○ 비법 적용 연습   본문 p.78

PART 5
1 (B)　2 (D)　3 (C)　4 (A)　5 (C)
6 (A)　7 (B)　8 (B)　9 (C)　10 (A)

1
해석 Gleason 씨는 7월 사업 회의에서 잠재적 대체 투자 옵션들을 둘러보기를 기대하고 있다.
해설 look forward to의 to는 전치사의 to이다. 따라서 to 뒤에는 명사 상당어구가 나와야 하는데 빈칸 뒤에 명사(options)가 있으므로 이 명사를 목적어로 가지는 동명사 (B)가 정답이다.
어휘 look forward to ~을 기대하다, 고대하다 potential 가능성이 있는, 잠재적인 alternative 대안

2
해석 사업 발표 동안에 잠재 고객들을 불편하게 만드는 것을 피하기 위해서 복잡한 배치를 사용하는 것을 자제해 주세요.
해설 avoid(동사) 뒤에 목적어 자리이지만 뒤에 명사(clients)가 있으므로 빈칸은 동명사 자리이다. 따라서 정답은 (D)이다.
어휘 avoid 피하다 prospective 장래의 retrain from ~을 자제하다, 삼가다 complicated 복잡한 layout 배치

3
해석 우리의 선임 상담가인 Anthony Dinozo는 작은 규모의 사업 고객들에게 맞춰진 광고 전략들을 제공하는 것을 총괄한다.
해설 전치사(for)와 명사(strategies) 사이에 동사와 명사의 성질을 모두 가지는 동명사 (C)가 정답이다.
어휘 responsible for ~에 책임이 있는 customized 개인의 요구에 맞춘 advertising 광고 strategy 전략

4
해석 대학교 외부에서 열리는 모든 행사들은 사전 공지 없이 취소될 수 있음을 알아 두십시오.
해설 be subject to의 to는 전치사의 to이다. 따라서 빈칸은 명사 자리이다. 빈칸 뒤에 목적어가 없으므로 동명사 (B)는 오답이다.
어휘 aware 알고 있는 premises (한 사업체가 소유, 사용하는 건물이 딸린) 부지 be subject to ~될 수 있는

5
해석 새로 도입된 생산 라인에서의 불량률 증가에 대해 우리에게 경고한 것이 우리가 공장의 모든 기계를 검사하는 것을 가능하게 했다.
해설 빈칸은 문장에서 주어 자리이다. 그리고 빈칸 뒤 us(목적격)가 있으므로 동명사 (C)가 정답이다.
어휘 defect rate 불량률 assembly line 생산 라인

6
해석 도쿄 지점은 기존 직원들과 새로운 직원들을 교육시키는 데 많은 시간을 쓴다.
해설 [spend+시간/돈+동명사]는 '~하는 데 시간/돈을 쓰다'라는 뜻이다.
어휘 plenty of 많은 recruit 신입사원

7
해석 정부 관광 사무소들이 국제 관광객들을 유치하기 위해 끊임없이 새로운 방법을 찾는 것은 필수적이다.
해설 전치사(of)와 명사(tourists) 사이의 명사 자리이다. 물론 형용사 (D)도 문법상 맞기는, '매력적인 국제 관광객들의 새로운 방법'은 의미상 어색하다.
어휘 crucial 중대한, 결정적인 consistently 지속적으로

8
해석 십만 명 이상이 참가한 국제 록 페스티벌을 준비한 것이 올해 가장 어려운 프로젝트였다.
해설 빈칸은 동사(was)의 주어 자리이다. 따라서 명사 상당어구가 들어가야 하지만 빈칸 뒤에 명사(festival)가 있으므로 동명사 (B)가 정답이다.
어휘 challenging 도전적인, 도전 의식을 북돋우는

9
해석 잡지 회사의 유통 부서는 빠르고 훌륭한 서비스를 제공하는 데 헌신한다.
해설 [be dedicated(= devoted) to: ~에 헌신하다]에서 to는 전치사의 to이다. 따라서 빈칸은 명사 상당어구가 와야 한다. (A) 명사는 뒤의 명사(service)와 충돌하므로 오답이다.
어휘 circulation 유통 division (조직의) 분과, -부 dedicated 헌신적인, 전념하는 responsive 즉각 대응하는

10
해석 Francis Taylor는 그의 팔레트 칼과 붓 위에 페인트의 양을 다양하게 함으로써 자신의 작업에서 흥미로운 패턴과 질감을 만들었다.
해설 전치사(by)와 명사(the amount) 사이의 동명사 자리이다. 형용사로 뒤에 명사(amount)를 수식하는 방법은 뒤의 관사(the) 때문에 할 수 없다. [관사+형용사+명사]
어휘 texture 질감

DAY 14 분사

○ 비법 적용 연습   본문 p.82

PART 5
1 (C)　2 (A)　3 (B)　4 (A)　5 (D)
6 (D)　7 (C)　8 (B)　9 (B)　10 (C)

1
해석 Mitsukoshi 백화점의 정책은 고객들이 구매 제품에 대해서 만족하지 못한다면, 2주일 이내에 어떤 상품이든지 반품하거나 환불을 받을 수 있다는 것이다.
해설 be동사(are) 뒤에 p.p. 형태를 취하는 수동태 be satisfied with (~에 만족하다) 표현을 알면 쉽게 풀 수 있다.
어휘 patron 고객 satisfactory 만족스러운

SECTION 1_Grammar ≫ 013

2

해석 지난 토요일에 새 제품 개시 기념 발표에 감명을 받아서, Forrester Investment 은행은 Packard Company의 G-1 Tablet PC를 500개 주문하기로 결정했다.

해설 분사구문이다. 분사구문에서 능동의 분사와 수동의 분사를 구별하는 방법은 다른 절의 주어를 가지고 와서 분사와의 관계를 보는 것이다. Forrester Investment Bank와 impress(인상을 주다)의 관계가 다른 누군가에게 인상을 주는 것이 아니라 은행이 인상을 받은 것이므로 수동의 분사 p.p.가 정답이다.

어휘 launch 시작하다, 출시

3

해석 나쁜 날씨가 지난밤의 정전을 유발했고, 몇몇 주민들이 전기 없이 방치되었다.

해설 반대 절의 주어(Inclement weather)와 분사(leave)의 관계를 보면 나쁜 날씨가 주민들을(목적어) 능동적으로 남겨 둔 것이고, 또 분사는 동사의 성질을 가지고 있기 때문에 빈칸 뒤에 목적어(residents)를 보고 능동의 분사(-ing)를 선택할 수 있다.

어휘 inclement 날씨가 좋지 못한 blackout 정전 resident 거주자 electricity 전기

4

해석 재무 분석에 대해 석사 학위를 획득한 후에 Brown 씨는 고위 분석 직책에 가장 유망한 후보들 중 하나로 여겨진다.

해설 분사구문. 주절의 주어(Mr. Brown)와의 관계를 보고, 또 빈칸 뒤에 목적어(degree)를 보면 능동의 분사가 들어가야 하는 것을 알 수 있다. (C), (D)는 수동의 분사 형태이므로 오답이다.

어휘 master's degree 석사 promising 유망한 candidate 후보자 analyst 분석가

5

해석 모든 Frontier Telecom 고객들은 각각의 가족 구성원들의 매달 요금을 보여 주는 새로운 통합 월별 고지서를 검토하는 것이 좋습니다.

해설 new(형용사)와 statement(명사) 사이에 들어갈 수 있는 품사는 형용사이다. 분사는 동사가 형용사가 된 것이므로 정답은 (D)이다.

어휘 encourage 격려하다 respectively 각각, 각자

6

해석 그의 서류는 그곳에 빨리 도착해야 하기 때문에 Tom은 오토바이 배달 서비스를 요청했다.

해설 concern(~를 걱정스럽게 만들다)과 Tom(주절의 주어)의 관계를 봤을 때, Tom이 누군가를 걱정하게 만드는 것이 아니라 걱정이 되어지는 것(=걱정하는 것)이므로 수동의 분사(p.p.)가 정답이다. (ex) I am concerned about you. (나는 당신을 걱정한다.)

어휘 forward 주다, 수여하다 request 요청하다

7

해석 Ford의 Kansas City 공장의 평균 생산 시간이 제3세대 자동 조립 시스템의 도입 이래로 거의 절반이 되었다.

해설 단어와 단어 사이가 '-'로 연결된 많은 경우 두 단어를 형용사 취급한다. 또 빈칸은 형용사가 되어야 명사(assembly system)를 수식할 수 있다. 따라서 분사 (C)가 정답이다.

어휘 halve 반으로 줄이다, 이등분하다 assembly 조립

8

해석 MOTA 중공업은 제안된 원자력 공장을 위한 잠재적 부지들의 위치를 찾기 위한 지역 부동산 업체와 함께 일하고 있다.

해설 관사(the)와 명사(nuclear power plant) 사이의 형용사(분사) 자리이다.

어휘 real estate 부동산 potential 가능성이 있는 nuclear power plant 원자력 발전소

9

해석 Hopkins 병원의 정책은 환자의 정보는 관련된 환자들의 서면화된 동의 없이는 공개되지 않는다는 것을 확실하게 명시하고 있다.

해설 전치사(without)와 명사(consent) 사이는 1. 동명사(writing) 자리일 수도 있지만 2. 분사(written)로 명사(consent)를 수식할 수도 있다. 따라서 둘 중에서 해석을 통해 문제를 풀어야 한다.

어휘 indicate 나타내다, 명시하다 disclose (특히 비밀이던 것을) 밝히다, 폭로하다 consent 동의

10

해석 한국에서 국제결혼과 대한 대중의 시선들이 변화하고 있는 것이 고무적인 징후이다.

해설 빈칸은 형용사 자리로 명사(signs)를 수식한다. '격려되는'이라는 뜻의 (B)와 '고무적인'이라는 뜻의 (C) 중에서 해석을 통해서 (C)가 정답임을 알 수 있다.

어휘 sign 징후, 조짐

DAY 15 접속사

비법 적용 연습   본문 p.86

PART 5	1 (A)	2 (D)	3 (A)	4 (D)	5 (B)
	6 (A)	7 (D)	8 (D)	9 (C)	10 (A)

1

해석 사무실 자동화 교육 과정들이 Colors United 사의 정직원과 파트타임 직원 모두에게 열려 있다.

해설 빈칸 앞에 both가 왔으므로 상관접속사(both A and B) 문제이다. 따라서 정답은 (A)이다.

어휘 automation 자동화

2

해석 MOMA 미술역사 수업의 참석자들은 재료와 용품들의 비용을 지불하기 위해서 첫 번째 수업 전에 소액의 비용을 지불해야 한다.

해설 등위접속사(and)는 접속사를 기준으로 앞뒤에 같은 형태가 와야 한다. 앞에 명사(materials)가 왔으므로 (D)가 정답이다. (C)도 명사지만 가산 명사이므로 관사 a와 함께 와야 한다.

어휘 participant 참석자, 참가자 nominal 아주 얼마 안 되는 defray (비용, 경비 등)을 부담하다, 지불하다 expense 비용

3

해석 우리는 Jones & Brown 쇼핑몰이 7월 1일부터 가격은 낮추고 멤버십 할인율은 높일 것을 알려 드리게 되어 기쁩니다.

014

해설 빈칸 앞의 [동사+목적어(lower prices)]와 빈칸 뒤의 [동사+목적어(raise membership discount rates)]를 연결하는 등위접속사 (A) and가 정답이다.

어휘 raise 높이다, 인상하다 effective 효과적인, 실질적인 as of ~부터

4

해설 Nishimoto 씨는 Wiseman 씨나 Yoon 씨 중 한 명이 다음 주 무역 박람회에 참석해야 한다고 추천했다.

해설 상관접속사 문제이다. 빈칸 뒤의 or와 어울리는 것은 (D)이다.

어휘 recommend 추천하다, 권고하다 attend 참석하다, 참가하다

5

해설 지역 판매 매니저로 승진하기 위해서 직원들은 더 많은 책임을 맡으려는 의지와 지난 수년 동안 판매 실적이 뛰어나야 한다.

해설 빈칸 앞뒤로 명사(sales record, a willingness)가 왔으므로 상관접속사가 적절하다. '~에 더하여'라는 뜻의 상관접속사 as well as는 앞뒤로 같은 품사가 와야 한다.

어휘 promote 승진시키다 regional 지역의 possess 소유하다 outstanding 뛰어난, 걸출한 willingness 기꺼이 하는 마음 take responsibility 책임을 지다, 책임을 맡다

6

해설 우리의 온라인 책자는 종합적입니다만 특정한 품목들은 모든 가게에서 취급하지 않을 수도 있습니다.

해설 문장과 문장을 연결할 수 있는 접속사가 필요하다. 빈칸 앞뒤 문장이 서로 대조를 이루고 있으므로 정답은 (A) but이다.

어휘 comprehensive 포괄적인, 종합적인 available 이용 가능한

7

해설 우리 인테리어 전문가들은 방을 꾸밀 때 영사기를 사용할지, 큰 화면의 TV를 사용할지를 결정하는 것을 도와준다.

해설 빈칸 앞에 whether가 왔으므로 정답은 (D) or이다. whether A or B는 'A인지 B인지'라는 뜻이다.

어휘 decorate 꾸미다

8

해설 중앙 재해 안전 대책 위원회는 10개의 민간 기업들과 12곳의 기관 출신의 이사들로 구성되었다.

해설 빈칸 앞의 명사(firms)와 뒤의 명사(agencies)를 연결할 접속사 자리이다. 따라서 정답은 (D)이다.

어휘 private firm 사기업 government agency 정부 기관, 정부 관계 기관

9

해설 회사의 갱신된 작업장 증진 제안서는 인금 인상과 확장된 직원 복지 시설들을 포함하지 않았다.

해설 neither와 함께 쓰이는 상관접속사 (C) nor가 정답이다.

어휘 renewed 재개된, 갱신된 include 포함하다 expand 확장하다 welfare 복지 facility 시설

10

해설 Autobahn 렌터카는 재미를 위해서든 사업을 위해서든 상관없이 자동차 대여를 적절한 가격에 쉽게 할 수 있게 하는 다양한 가격 정책을 제공한다.

해설 빈칸 앞에 whether가 왔으므로 정답은 (A) or이다. whether A or B는 'A든지 B든지'라는 뜻이다.

어휘 a range of 다양한 rate 요금 affordable (가격이) 알맞은

DAY 16 관계사

○ 비법 적용 연습   본문 p.91

PART 5	1 (D)	2 (D)	3 (B)	4 (C)	5 (C)
	6 (D)	7 (A)	8 (D)	9 (C)	10 (A)

1

해설 사실 확인 과정은 보고되고 있는 정정 신청서의 증가하는 수 때문에 개정될 것이다.

해설 being을 분사로 보고 applications(명사)를 수식할 수도 있고, 빈칸 앞에 which are(관계대명사+be동사)가 생략되었다고 볼 수도 있다.

어휘 revise 수정하다 due to ~ 때문에 correction 수정 application 신청서

2

해설 황사 인식에 관한 지난주 회의에서 말했던 날씨 전문가는 올해의 아시아 환경 저널리즘상 후보에 올랐다.

해설 빈칸부터 awareness까지 형용사절. 선행사(specialist)를 보고 사람을 판단하고 빈칸 뒤의 형용사절 안에서 주어가 없으므로 주격 관계대명사를 고른다.

어휘 awareness 의식, 인식 nominate (후보자로) 지명하다, 추천하다

3

해설 이력서와 자기소개서에 5월 11일이나 그 이후의 소인이 찍힌 지원자들은 채용 과정에서 고려되지 않는 것을 알아 두십시오.

해설 선행사(applicants)를 보고 사람을 판단하고 빈칸 뒤의 문장에서 소유격이 빠진 것을 보고 whose를 선택한다. 소유격이 빠진 것을 알 수 있는 다른 방법은 명사 앞에 관사가 없는 것을 보면 된다.

어휘 applicant 지원자 résumé 이력서 cover letter 자기소개서 postmark (우편물의) 소인

4

해설 고객들은 그들이 원본 영수증만 가지고 있다면 만족스럽지 않은 물건에 대해서 전액 환불을 받을 수 있다.

해설 형용사절 접속사(관계대명사)는 전치사와 함께 형용사절을 이끌 수 있는데 따라서 선행사(merchandise)를 보고 사물임을 알고, 그리고 전치사(with) 뒤는 목적어 자리이므로 목적격 관계대명사 which가 정답이다.

어휘 receive 받다 full refund 전액 환불 merchandise 물품, 상품 satisfied 만족스러운 receipt 영수증

5
- 해석 우리 실험실들에서 일하는 직원들은 항상 보호 의복을 입는 것이 요구된다.
- 해설 분사(working)로 명사(employees)를 수식한다고 보거나 employees 뒤에 who are(주격 관계대명사+be동사)가 생략되었다고 볼 수도 있다.
- 어휘 laboratory 실험실 protective clothing 방호복 at all times 항상

6
- 해석 9월 이래로 운행 중인 새로운 지하철 라인이 도시의 22개의 정류장을 맡고 있다.
- 해설 선행사(line)와 빈칸 뒤 형용사절에서 주어가 없는 것을 보고 which가 정답임을 알 수 있다.
- 어휘 operate 작동되다, 가동하다

7
- 해석 총무부는 모든 직원들에게 5월 3일부터 적용될 개정된 보상금 정책을 발표했다.
- 해설 선행사(policy)를 보고 사물임을 알고, 그리고 빈칸 뒤에 주어가 없으므로 선행사가 사람이든 사물이든 가리지 않는 that이 정답이다.
- 어휘 general affairs department 총무부 announce 공표하다, 알리다 revised 수정된 take into effect 시행되다

8
- 해석 조사 동안에 인터뷰했던 대부분의 사람들이 추가적인 차가 필요하지 않다고 말했다.
- 해설 선행사(people)와 빈칸 뒤에 주어가 없으므로 주격 관계대명사가 정답이다.
- 어휘 additional 추가적인, 추가의

9
- 해석 우리의 New Jersey 지점으로 전근 가는 데 동의한 품질 관리부 부장들은 회사의 비용으로 전체적인 이사에 관한 도움을 받을 것이다.
- 해설 동사 자리처럼 보이지만 will receive(동사)가 있으므로 빈칸은 Managers(명사)를 수식하는 형용사(분사) 자리이다. 혹은 빈칸 앞에 who are(주격 관계대명사 + be동사)가 생략되었다.
- 어휘 transfer 옮기다, 이동하다 relocation 재배치, 이전

10
- 해석 Agostino Audios는 대량생산 제품들뿐만 아니라 수제 시스템을 파는 천재 오디오 개발업자인 Daniel Agostino가 소유하고 있다.
- 해설 선행사(developer)와 빈칸 뒤 형용사절에 주어가 없는 것에서 who가 정답임을 알 수 있다.
- 어휘 own 소유하다 genius 천재 developer 개발자, 개발업자 mass-produced 대량 생산의

DAY
17 명사절 접속사

○ 비법 적용 연습   본문 p.96

PART 5	1 (A)	2 (C)	3 (C)	4 (C)	5 (A)
	6 (A)	7 (A)	8 (A)	9 (D)	10 (C)

1
- 해석 버려지는 종이를 줄이기 위해서 선생님들은 꼭 필요한 것만 프린트하도록 다시 알려 드립니다.
- 해설 print(동사) 뒤의 목적어 자리이다. 빈칸 뒤에 동사(is)가 있으므로 빈칸부터 명사절로 묶어야 한다. 선택지에서 what만이 명사절 접속사이므로 정답은 (A)이다.
- 어휘 remind 상기시키다, 일깨우다 reduce 줄이다

2
- 해석 12월 둘째 주 말까지 가장 많은 판매 수치를 달성하는 사람 누구든지 간에 10,000달러의 현금과 함께 올해의 공로상을 받게 될 것이다.
- 해설 빈칸부터 December까지가 동사(will receive)의 주어가 되는데 achieves라는 동사가 있으므로 빈칸에 명사절 접속사가 필요하다. (A), (C)가 명사절 접속사이고 whose는 '누구의 것', whoever는 '누구든지 간에'라는 뜻이므로 의미상 (C)가 정답이다. 또 명사절 접속사 whose가 '누구의 것'이라는 뜻을 가질 경우 나머지 명사절은 완벽한 문장이 나와야 하므로 whose는 문법적으로도 오답이다.
- 어휘 achieve 달성하다, 성취하다 sales figure 판매 수치, 판매액

3
- 해석 고객들을 가장 기쁘게 하는 것은 식당 종업원들의 즉각적인 서비스들이었다.
- 해설 빈칸부터 most까지가 주어 자리이고 주어 안에 pleased(동사)가 있으므로 명사절로 묶어야 한다. 명사절 접속사 that은 나머지 명사절의 문장이 완벽해야 하는데 빈칸 뒤 문장은 주어가 없는 불완전한 문장이므로 (C)가 정답임을 알 수 있다.
- 어휘 please 기쁘게 하다 responsiveness 민감, 반응성

4
- 해석 관련된 대다수 거주자들이 재개발에 동의할지 아닐지는 중요한 문제이다.
- 해설 빈칸부터 development까지가 주어 자리이므로 명사절로 묶어야 한다. (A), (C)만 명사절 접속사인데 의미상 '~인지 아닌지'라는 뜻인 (C)가 정답이다.
- 어휘 majority 대다수 resident 거주자 critical 중요한

5
- 해석 국제 체육인 협회의 보조를 받은 최근 한 연구에 따르면 왼손잡이 선수들이 대부분의 스포츠 행사에서 더 좋은 성과를 얻는다고 한다.
- 해설 동사(suggests) 뒤의 목적어 자리이다. 목적어 자리에 동사(are)가 있으므로 빈칸은 명사절 접속사 자리이다. 빈칸 뒤 명사절이 완벽한 문장이므로 (B) which를 제외하고 의미상 (A)가 정답임을 알 수 있다.
- 어휘 recent 최근의 sponsor 후원하다 left-handed 왼손잡이의 achieve 달성하다, 성취하다 performance 실적, 성과

1

해석 이번 분기의 판매가 예상만큼 높을 거라는 경우에만, Hoshiro Designs는 일본에서 선두 그래픽 디자인 회사들 중 하나로서 부상하는 것을 예상한다.

해설 동사가 2개(are, anticipates)가 있으므로 접속사가 필요하고 빈칸부터 projected까지를 부사절로 묶어야 한다. (A), (D)는 전치사 (B)는 부사이고 (C)는 '~라는 경우에만'이라는 접속사이므로 정답은 (C)이다. (D) 다음에

어휘 quarter 4분의 1, 사분기 project 예상하다 anticipate 예상하다 leading 선두의

2

해석 방문객들은 실험실에 들어갈 때 전자장치들의 전원을 끄는 것이 요청된다.

해설 분사구문이다. when(접속사) 뒤에는 visitors are(주어와 be동사)가 생략되어 있다.

어휘 turn off (전기, 가스, 수도 등을) 끄다 laboratory 실험실

3

해석 그 밴드가 마침내 공연이 가능하다는 것을 확인해 주었기 때문에, 야외 콘서트가 6월 11일 일요일에 예정되었다.

해설 부사절 접속사 자리이다. (B), (C) 중에서 해석을 통해서도 구할 수 있고 so that은 부사절 접속사이지만 문두에는 잘 나오지 않는다. 따라서 '~때문에'라는 뜻의 (B)가 정답이다.

어휘 confirm 확실하게 하다 availability 가능성

4

해석 Kendal 사가 단지 9개월 동안 사업을 해 왔지만 매우 빠르게 수익을 내게 되었다.

해설 부사절 접속사 자리이므로 전치사 (D)를 제외하고, 의미상 '~에도 불구하고'라는 뜻의 (A) although가 정답이다.

어휘 in business 사업을 하는 profitable 수익성이 있는

5

해석 Danawala 씨가 그 직책을 받아들이는가에 상관없이, 우리는 적어도 두 명 이상의 의사들을 채용해야 한다.

해설 부사절 접속사 whether는 뒤에 or not과 함께 쓰일 수 있고, '~이든지 아니든지 상관없이'라는 뜻이다. 따라서 정답은 (A)이다.

어휘 accept 받아들이다 hire 고용하다 physician 의사; 내과 의사

6

해석 그녀가 거기에 반드시 있어야 하는 것은 아니지만 Hagger 씨는 지역 세미나에 참석할 계획이다.

해설 문장 처음부터 seminar까지 문장이 끝났으므로 빈칸부터는 수식어. 빈칸 뒤에도 문장이 있으므로 접속사 자리인데 전치사인 (C)를 제외하고 (A), (B), (D)에서 해석을 통해서 정답을 결정한다.

어휘 attend 참석하다, 참가하다 regional 지역의

6

해석 도움이 필요한 사람 누구든지 어떤 문제를 가지고 있든지 간에 청소년 상담 센터에 오시는 것을 환영합니다.

해설 동사(is) 앞의 주어 자리이다. 그 안에 동사(needs)가 있으므로 빈칸은 명사절 접속사가 와야 한다. If는 명사절 접속사이지만 주어 자리에 명사절 접속사로 쓰일 수 없으므로 오답이고 (A), (B)는 모두 불완전한 문장을 묶어 명사절로 만들 수 있는데 의미상 '도움이 필요한 사람 누구든지'이므로 (A) Whoever(누구든지 간에)가 정답이다.

어휘 adolescent 청소년

7

해석 어떤 마케팅 전략이 당신의 회사에 가장 적합한지를 선택하는 것은 다양한 조사가 필요하다.

해설 동명사(choosing)의 목적어 자리에 명사절(빈칸부터 company까지)이 있는데 which(어떤), what(무슨), whose(누구의)와 같은 명사절 접속사는 접속사 바로 뒤의 명사(marketing strategies)를 수식하면서 동시에 명사절로 묶을 수 있으므로 정답은 (A)이다.

어휘 strategy 전략 suit ~에 어울리다, 적합하다 a range of 다양한

8

해석 Vasquez 씨가 새로운 계획을 이끌기에 최선의 후보자인지는 결정하기 쉽지 않다.

해설 동사(determine) 뒤의 명사절 자리이다. (A), (B) 중에서 빈칸 뒤의 문장이 완전하므로 (A)가 정답이다.

어휘 determine 결정하다 candidate 후보자 initiative 계획

9

해석 그의 자리에서 물러날 것인지 아닌지를 질문 받았을 때, Engle 씨는 할 수 있는 한 그의 일을 오래하고 싶다고 말했다.

해설 동사(asked) 뒤의 목적어 자리이다. '~인지 아닌지'라는 뜻으로 명사절로 묶을 수 있는 접속사는 (D)이다.

어휘 resign 사직하다, 물러나다 intend to ~할 의도이다, 생각이다

10

해석 연구비를 받는 사람이 누구든지 간에 즉시 필요한 일을 시작할 수 있을 것이다.

해설 빈칸부터 fund까지가 주어 자리이다. 명사절로 묶을 수 있는 whatever, whichever, whoever 중에서 연구비를 받는 것은 사람이므로 (C) Whoever가 정답이다.

어휘 research fund 연구비

DAY 18 부사절 접속사

○ 비법 적용 연습 본문 p.100

| PART 5 | 1 (C) | 2 (B) | 3 (B) | 4 (A) | 5 (A) |
| | 6 (D) | 7 (A) | 8 (B) | 9 (A) | 10 (C) |

7

해석 건설이 완료되자마자, Ridge Manufacturing의 지점 사무실에서 일하고 있는 직원들은 새로운 본사로 이사할 것이다.

해설 접속사 자리이므로 부사 (B), (C), (D)는 오답이다. 또 아직 건설이 완성된 건 아니지만 is finished라고 현재 시제를 쓴 이유가 시간에 대한 부사절이기 때문이므로 시간에 대한 접속사 (A)가 정답이다.

어휘 move into ~로 이동하다 headquarters 본사

8

해석 최초 신청서가 사무실에 오자마자 당신은 어떤 추가적인 서류도 제공하길 요구받지 않을 것이다.

해설 빈칸부터 office까지 부사절이 되어야 하며, 등위접속사 (D)를 제외한 나머지 중에서 (A)는 부사절로 쓰일 경우 반드시 whether A or B 구문이나, whether or not 구문으로 써야 하므로 문법적으로 오답이다. (C) As if는 '마치 ~인 것처럼'이라는 뜻이므로 의미상 어색하다. 따라서 정답은 (B)이다.

어휘 initial 처음의, 최초의 application 지원서 documentation 서류

9

해석 Business Notes의 보고에 따르면 합병 발표 후에 ViStar의 주식 가격이 폭락했다.

해설 빈칸 뒤에 명사가 있으므로 전치사 자리이다. 부사인 (B)와 접속사인 (D)를 제외하고 '~ 후에'라는 뜻의 (A)가 적절하다.

어휘 plummet 곤두박질치다, 급락하다 merger 합병

10

해석 비용을 우편으로 보낼 때, 송장의 위 부분을 포함해 주십시오.

해설 분사구문이다. 빈칸 앞에는 you are (일반적인 주어 + be동사)가 생략되었다고 볼 수 있다. payment를 보내는 능동적인 분사가 들어가야 하므로 (C)가 정답이다.

어휘 include 포함하다 invoice 송장

DAY 19 비교급과 최상급

● 비법 적용 연습   본문 p.104

PART 5	1 (C)	2 (A)	3 (B)	4 (A)	5 (D)
	6 (C)	7 (C)	8 (D)	9 (C)	10 (B)

1

해석 조사 결과물에서 설문 조사에 참여한 사람들이 예상보다 새로운 Nautilus 1000 Diamond Speakers의 디자인에 훨씬 더 호의적으로 반응했다는 것이 나타났다.

해설 원급/비교급/최상급을 말하기에 앞서 우선 품사는 앞에 자동사 (responded)가 있으므로 부사가 되어야 한다. (A), (C) 중에서 앞에 비교급을 수식하는 부사 even과 뒤에 than을 보고 비교급을 정답으로 고른다.

어휘 participant 참가자 respond 반응하다 expect 예상하다, 기대하다

2

해석 자동차 판매가 6월에 5.8% 떨어졌는데, 이것은 예상보다 더 낮은 수요를 보여 준다.

해설 명사(demand)를 수식하는 형용사 자리이며 뒤에 than이 있으므로 비교급을 골라야 한다. 따라서 (A)가 정답이다.

어휘 drop 떨어지다 anticipate 예상하다

3

해석 Mahin Motors의 새롭게 개시된 자동차들은 경쟁자들의 그것들보다 훨씬 인상적으로 여겨진다.

해설 consider(5형식 동사)의 수동태 문장이다. 5형식 목적격 보어 자리에 있던 형용사가 수동태가 되면 be p.p. 뒤에 남을 수 있다. 선택지에서 형용사 (B)가 정답이다.

어휘 launch 시작하다, 출시 consider (~을 ~로) 여기다, 간주하다

4

해석 새로운 LZ3 스마트폰은 현재 시장에 나와 있는 많은 다른 모델들과 같은 카메라 기능들을 가지고 있다.

해설 [the same ~ as] 표현이다. as 뒤에는 동일한 대상이 나온다.

어휘 feature 특징 current 현재의

5

해석 와인 코르크 마개를 병에서 따면 가능한 한 빨리 와인을 마셔야 한다.

해설 as ~ as 원급 비교인데 as 사이에는 형용사 또는 부사가 온다. 앞 문장을 보고 빠진 품사를 쓰면 된다. 이 문제에서는 we ~ it까지 문장이 끝났으므로 빈칸은 부사 (D)가 와야 한다. 원급 비교에 -er, -est 등 비교급과 최상급 표현을 쓸 수 없다.

어휘 remove 제거하다

6

해석 이용 가능한 모든 배달 선택 사항 중에서, Langston Bike Messenger Service가 도시 안의 누군가에게 물건을 보내는 가장 빠른 방법이다.

해설 빈칸 앞에 the가 있는 것 이외에도 Among all the ~ available에서 3개 이상의 방법들 중에서 나오는 부분이 최상급의 힌트가 된다. 따라서 정답은 (C)이다.

어휘 available 이용 가능한 designated 지정된

7

해석 증가하는 연료 비용 때문에 우리 회사가 그 어떤 때보다 이윤을 내기가 어렵게 만들고 있다.

해설 빈칸은 make(5형식 동사)의 목적격 보어 자리이다. 따라서 형용사가 가능하고, 빈칸 뒤에 비교급의 힌트인 than이 있으므로 (C)가 정답이다.

어휘 fuel 연료 profitable 수익성이 있는

8

해석 Eurolink Telecom의 이사회는 도입하여 운영하기 쉽다는 것을 인정하며 Sopa의 제안서가 아닌 Aming의 제안서를 어제 채택했다.

해설 be동사 뒤의 보어 자리이다. 따라서 형용사가 와야 하므로 easy(형용사)의 비교급은 easier이다. (A) 쉬움, 덜어 주다

어휘 proposal 제안, 제안서 admit 인정하다

9
- 해석 점점 더 많은 회사들과 공공기관들이 새것보다 훨씬 덜 비싸기 때문에 재활용 토너 카트리지로 교체하고 있다.
- 해설 be동사(is) 뒤에 보어 자리이다. 앞에 less가 왔으므로 형용사가 들어가야 한다. 따라서 정답은 (C)이다.
- 어휘 public institution 공공 기관

10
- 해석 우리의 마케팅 부서 이사는 단골 고객층을 만드는 것이 새로운 고객층을 만드는 것보다 훨씬 중요하다고 항상 강조한다.
- 해설 비교급의 than이 있으므로 비교급을 만들기 위한 more이 정답이다.
- 어휘 executive 이사, 간부 stress 강조하다 essential 필수적인

DAY 20 가정법과 도치

비법 적용 연습   본문 p.108

PART 5	1 (B)	2 (A)	3 (C)	4 (B)	5 (A)
	6 (A)	7 (A)	8 (C)	9 (B)	10 (A)

1
- 해석 Vasquez 씨가 그의 의사를 이사회 구성원들에게 분명하게 전달했더라면 그렇게 심한 반대에 직면하지는 않았을 것이다.
- 해설 가정법 과거완료는 [주어+would+have p.p., if+주어+had p.p.]이다. 빈칸 뒤에 목적어가 없으므로 수동의 (B)가 정답이다.
- 어휘 bitter 격렬한 intention 의도 confront 직면하다

2
- 해석 당신이 새로운 스마트폰을 샀더라면 당신은 지금쯤 그것을 즐기고 있을 것이다.
- 해설 가정법 과거완료와 가정법 과거가 섞여 있는 혼합가정법으로 [If+주어+had p.p., 주어+would+동사원형]의 형태를 가지며 과거의 일이 현재까지 영향을 미치는 경우이다.

3
- 해석 만약 당신이 모든 법률 서류들을 포함한 꾸러미를 받는다면 그 서류가 당신에게 전달된 것을 우리에게 알려 주세요.
- 해설 가정법이 아니라 조건문이다. 조건문에서 중요한 문법은 조건에 대한 부사절에서는 미래 시제를 말하더라도 현재 시제로 써야 한다는 것이다. 따라서 정답은 (C)이다.
- 어휘 legal 법적인, 법률의 forward 보내다

4
- 해석 세미나 동안에 문제가 있는 어떤 직원이라도 로비에 있는 업무 지원 센터에 와 주세요.
- 해설 가정법 미래 [If+주어+should+동사원형, 주어+will(can, may, should)+동사원형] 형태에서 if가 생략된 문장으로 if가 생략되면 주어와 동사의 도치가 일어난다. participant가 주어, have가 동사인 것이 힌트가 된다.
- 어휘 participant 참가자

5
- 해석 그의 헌신이 없었더라면 그들은 Parthenon 계획에서 추가적인 자금 지원을 얻지 못했을 것이다.
- 해설 첫 번째 문장이 가정법 과거완료에서 if가 생략된 구문이므로 빈칸은 [would, should, could, might+have p.p.] 형태가 와야 한다. 앞의 had it not been for (=If it had not been for)는 "~이 없었더라면"의 뜻을 가지는 가정법 표현이다.
- 어휘 devotion 헌신 award 수여하다 additional 추가적인 funding 자금, 재정적 지원

6
- 해석 모든 이사회 구성원들이 만장일치 결정에 도달한 후에야 그 기업은 위스키 생산부서의 구조조정을 시작했다.
- 해설 [only+부사(구, 절)]는 강조를 위해서 문장 앞으로 나올 수 있고 이럴 경우, 주어와 동사의 도치가 일어난다. 이 문장의 원래 주어는 the firm이고 빈칸은 동사 자리이지만 앞에 did(대동사)가 나간 것을 볼 때 과거 동사가 있었다. 하지만 이미 did가 시제를 표시했으므로 빈칸은 다시 동사원형이 와야 한다.
- 어휘 reach 도달하다 unanimous 만장일치의 division (조직의) 분과, -부, -국

7
- 해석 만약 그 고객이 그 도시의 주요 백화점들의 카드 할인 정책에 대해서 알았더라면 그는 더 빨리 멤버십에 등록할 결정을 했을 것이다.
- 해설 가정법 과거완료 문장이다. 따라서 주절에 would have p.p.가 있으므로 if절에는 had p.p.가 와야 한다.
- 어휘 sign up for ~을 신청하다, 등록하다

8
- 해석 만약 기차 사고가 그렇게 빨리 보고되지 않았더라면 모든 승객들은 시기적절한 의료 치료를 받을 수 없었을 것이다.
- 해설 가정법 과거완료 문장이다. if절에 had p.p.가 있으므로 주절은 would have p.p.가 와야 한다. 따라서 (C)가 정답이다.
- 어휘 timely 시기적절한

9
- 해석 만약 회사의 제안서가 조금만 더 자세했더라면, Kawasaki 철강 회사는 지금쯤 철강 분야에서 우리의 단독 공급업체가 되었을 것이다.
- 해설 혼합가정법 문장이다. 앞에는 가정법 과거완료가 나오고, 주절은 가정법 과거가 나오는 문형이다. 따라서 정답은 (B)이다.
- 어휘 detail 상세히 열거하다 sole 유일한, 단독의

10
- 해석 시장 분위기가 주식 시장에서 당신의 돈을 투자하는 데 더 나빴던 적은 거의 없다.
- 해설 주어와 동사의 도치가 생기는 경우 중에 부정어가 강조를 위해서 문장의 문두로 나오는 경우가 있다. 여기서도 have(동사)가 the market atmosphere(주어)보다 먼저 나와 있는 것을 보고 도치임을 알 수 있다. 부정어가 나오는 경우에 이 형태가 가능하므로 선택지에서 부정어가 Seldom(거의~않다)이 정답이다.
- 어휘 atmosphere 분위기 stock 주식

DAY 01 주제 · 목적 문제

○ 비법 적용 연습 본문 p.111

| 1 (D) | 2 (A) | 3 (A) | 4 (C) | 5 (C) |
| 6 (B) | | | | |

1-3

정전

10월 20일 화요일 10시부터 일련의 정전이 Broadway 지역에서 Marina Bay 지역까지 발생할 것입니다. 이 정전은 1시간 정도 지속되겠지만, 몇몇 경우에는 좀 더 오래 지속될 수 있습니다. 이 정전은 주말을 제외하고 영업일을 기준으로 대략적으로 5일 동안 지속될 것입니다.

이 정전의 원인은 30년 이상 된 것으로 추정되는 기존 송전선을 업그레이드하기 위해서입니다. 업그레이드의 목적은 시민들의 안전 외에도 노후화된 송전선에 의해서 야기될 수 있는 다른 추가적인 문제를 피하기 위해서입니다. 공사 중에 조금만 불편을 감수해 주시면 이 보수 작업이 끝났을 때 안정되고 끊김 없는 전력 공급을 약속드리겠습니다.

시민 여러분께 전력과 관련된 업무를 정전 전에 완료하시거나, 전력이 복구될 때까지 기다려 주시기를 권고드립니다. 불편을 드리게 되어 사과 말씀드리며, 양해와 이해를 부탁드립니다.

어휘 electric power interruption 정전 a series of 일련의 expect 예상하다, 기대하다 last 계속되다, 지속되다 approximately 대략, 약 working day 근무일 power line 송전선 estimate ~라고 여기다, 평가하다 cause ~을 일으키다 avoid 피하다 age 노후하다 bear with ~을 참을성 있게 대해 주다, ~가 말하는 것을 끝기 있게 듣다 in progress 진행 중인 steady 꾸준한 uninterrupted 중단되지 않은 maintenance 유지, 보수 the public 일반 대중 restore 복구하다, 회복하다 apologize for ~에 대해 사과하다 inconvenience 불편 consideration 사려, 숙고, 배려 electronic gadget 전자 제품 affect ~에 영향을 미치다

1
해석 기사의 목적은 무엇인가?
(A) 유지 보수 일정을 잡기 위해
(B) 현재의 문제를 설명하기 위해
(C) 불편함에 대해 사과하기 위해
(D) 프로젝트를 대중에게 알리기 위해

해설 주제 문제이다. 영어의 문장은 대부분이 두괄식이므로 주제는 대부분 첫 번째 문장, 혹은 두 번째 문단의 첫 번째 문장에서 언급되는 경우가 많다. 하지만 첫 문단을 보고 정답을 확실하게 고를 수 없다면 다른 문제를 모두 푼 후 마지막에 푸는 것이 확실한 주제를 알 수 있는 방법이 된다. 이 문제는 첫 문장에서 앞으로 정전이 있을 것임을 말하고 있고, 마지막 문단에서 "The public: 시민"에게 권고하는 내용이 나오므로 정답은 불편에 대해 사과를 하기 위한 글이라기보다는 시민에게 정전 계획에 대해 알리는 것이 목적인 글이라고 볼 수 있다.

2
해석 프로젝트가 언제 완료되는가?
(A) 월요일
(B) 화요일
(C) 금요일
(D) 토요일

해설 세부 사항 문제. 화요일에 시작해서 5일 동안 진행된다고 했지만, 주말을 제외한 working days(영업일)에만 진행된다고 하였으므로 그 다음 월요일에 공사가 완료되게 된다.

3
해석 이 기사에 암시되지 않은 것은 무엇인가?
(A) 시민들은 현재 정전을 겪고 있다.
(B) 일부 지역은 정전이 한 시간 이상 계속될 수 있다.
(C) 근로자들은 공사 중에 전자 기계 장치를 꺼야 한다.
(D) 전력 차단은 토요일과 일요일에는 영향을 주지 않는다.

해설 추론 문제이다. 추론 문제는 지문에 나와 있는 내용을 이용해서 지문에 나와 있지 않은 선택지의 내용을 고르는 것이지만, 대부분은 지문의 내용을 패러프레이징한 수준에서 크게 벗어나지는 않는다. (B)번은 in some cases may stretch longer(몇몇 경우에는 한 시간 이상 진행될 수 있다)부분을, (C)번은 The public is encouraged to complete their electricity-related duties before the interruption(정전 전에 전기와 관련된 작업을 마쳐 주기를 권고한다) 부분을, (D)번은 with no interruptions on weekends(주말에는 정전이 없다) 부분을 패러프레이징했다고 볼 수 있다.

4-6

수신: Oscar Wilde Literary Guild
〈oscarwildliteraryguild@wea.com〉
발신: James Takahashi 〈jtakash@smail.com〉
제목: 75회 Oscar Wilde 기념 행사
날짜: 7월 17일

Oscar Wilde의 수집가 여러분과 팬 여러분께,

Oscar Wilde 협회는 Oscar Wilde의 수집가 여러분과 팬 여러분에게 문을 열었고, Oscar Wilde의 기념품에 대한 경매를 발표했습니다. 경매는 수요일 오전 10시에서 오후 2시, 목요일 오전 10시에서 오후 12시에 열릴 것입니다. 매우 제한적인 수의 물건이 경매에 나올 것이며, 판매하는 개인 물건의 최소 가격은 Oscar Wilde의 생존해 계신 친족들에 의해 결정될 것입니다. 제품에 대한 사전 선별이 있을 것이며, 개인적인 기념품도 입찰에 나올 수 있지만 손으로 직접 기록한 원고는 대중이 입찰할 수 없습니다.

이 독점적인 행사에는 단지 몇 분의 참석자만이 참여가 가능하므로, 이 경매 좌석을 얻으시려면 이 이메일에 회신해 주십시오.

어휘 commemorative 기념의 foundation 재단, 협회 announce 발표하다, 알리다 a series of 일련의 auction 경매, 경매로 팔다 memorabilia 수집품 hold 개최하다 relative 친척 pre-screening 사전 검열 bidding (경매의) 가격 제시, 입찰, 호가 manuscript 원고 off limits 사용이 금지된 attendee 참석자 exclusive 독점적인, 배타적인 admiration 존경, 찬양 soroptimist 국제 여성 기업인 buff 전문가 auctioneer 경매인

4

해석 이메일을 보낸 이유는?
(A) Oscar Wilde에게 존경을 표하기 위해
(B) 문학 클럽 회의 일정을 잡기 위해
(C) 판매 품목에 대한 정보를 제공하기 위해
(D) 특별 휴일을 알리기 위해

해설 "The Oscar Wilde foundation has opened its doors to collectors and fans of Oscar Wilde and has announced a series of auctions of Oscar Wilde memorabilia.: Oscar Wilde 협회는 Oscar Wilde의 수집가 여러분과 팬 여러분에게 문을 열었고, Oscar Wilde의 기념품에 대한 경매를 발표했습니다."에서 앞으로 있을 경매에 대해 이야기할 것임을 알 수 있고, 글 전반적으로 경매에 대한 자세한 정보를 제공하고 있다.

5

해석 회원들은 누구일 것 같은가?
(A) 프리랜서 예술가들
(B) 갤러리 주인들
(C) 문학 애호가들
(D) 경매인들

해설 추론 문제이다. 작가의 물건을 파는 기념 행사를 가지는 것을 홍보하고 있으므로 문학에 관심이 많은 애호가들(Literature buffs)이 멤버일 가능성이 높다.

6

해석 판매하는 품목이 아닌 것은?
(A) 옷
(B) 원고
(C) 생활용품
(D) 타이핑한 노트

해설 세부 사항 문제이다. 키워드는 not for sale이다. handwritten manuscripts are off limits라는 문장에서 off limits가 '배제된다'라는 뜻이므로 manuscripts는 판매하지 않는다는 것을 알 수 있다.

DAY 02 육하원칙 문제

○ 비법 적용 연습   본문 p.114

| 1 (D) | 2 (A) | 3 (A) | 4 (D) | 5 (A) |

1-3

소형화 토론회
2014년 3월 5일

소형화를 효율적으로 하는 방법은 무엇이며, 또 어디에서부터 시작해야 할까요? 주택 판매에 대한 준비를 언제, 어떻게 해야 할까요? 퇴직 후 내 삶의 방식은 어떻게 될까요?

부동산 중개업자들의 재정적 지원을 받은 소형화 토론회는 현재의 지역 부동산 경향과 효과적인 주택 판매 전략, 퇴직 후의 이상적인 생활을 위한 행동 계획을 세우는 법을 주제로 진행될 것입니다.

장소: Constitution Hill
주소: 1 Centenary Avenue, Northmead NSW 2152
날짜: 2014년 3월 5일 수요일
시간: 오전 11시-오후 1시
등록 마감 시간: 2014년 3월 4일 화요일

어휘 downsize 줄이다, 축소하다 efficiently 효율적으로 retirement 은퇴 financially 재정적으로 property 재산 feature 주제로 하다, 특징으로 삼다, 특별히 포함하다 real estate 부동산 effective 효과적인 strategy 전략 action plan 상세한 사업 계획 venue 장소, 발생 장소 cut-off 마감, 중단

1

해석 행사에서 다루지는 주제가 아닌 것은?
(A) 부동산 경향
(B) 주택 판매 기법
(C) 노후 생활을 위한 계획
(D) 리모델링 아이디어

해설 세부 사항 문제이다. 특징들이 모여 있는 문단을 고른 후 하나씩 오답을 소거해 나간다. current local area real estate trends에서 (A)를, effective home selling strategies에서 (B)를, how to create an action plan for living your ideal retirement lifestyle에서 (C)를 찾을 수 있다.

2

해석 잠재 고객들은 언제까지 등록해야 하는가?
(A) 행사 하루 전날
(B) 행사 며칠 전
(C) 행사 당일
(D) 등록 마감 날짜가 없다.

해설 세부 사항 문제로 키워드는 "When, register"이다. "Registration cut-off: Tuesday 4th of March 2014"과 "Date: Wednesday 5th of March 2014"를 보고 행사 하루 전날까지 등록할 수 있다는 것을 알 수 있다.

3

해석 정보에 따르면, 누가 행사를 후원하는가?
(A) 부동산 중개인
(B) 생활 방식 전문가
(C) 퇴직자
(D) 주택 구입자

해설 "The Downsizing Workshop financially supported by property sales professionals"에서 property sales professionals는 Real estate agents로 패러프레이징될 수 있다.

4-5

든든한 은퇴 후 삶
Pittwater Palms의 상점들과 편의 시설로부터
걸어갈 수 있는 곳에서 사는 삶을 상상해 보세요.

현혹되지 마세요. 은퇴 후의 삶은 세상으로부터 여러분을 단절시키는 것을 의미하는 것이 아닙니다. 사실, Pittwater Palms에서 여러분은 이전 삶에서보다 더 든든해질 것입니다. Avalon의 바로 중심부에서

자립과 친교의 삶을 즐기세요. 생활 속에서 이용 가능한 여러 가지 선택 사항과 제공되는 다양한 사회적, 오락적 활동을 통해, 오늘은 내일을 위해 계획을 시작해야 할 시간입니다.

시설을 둘러보기 위해 방문하시려면 우리에게 전화 주시고, 어떻게 Pittwater Palms가 여러분의 은퇴 후 삶을 풍성하게 할 수 있는지를 알아보세요.

Pittwater Palms
82 Avalon Parade, Avalon, NSW 2107
13 AVEO (13 28 36) www.avewo.com.au

어휘 amenity 생활 편의 시설 mislead 호도하다, 오도하다 cut somebody/something off (from somebody/something) ~을 (~에서) 단절시키다 independence 독립, 자립 heart 중심; 심장 a selection of 다양한 available 이용 가능한 a range of 다양한 arrange 마련하다, 준비하다, (일을) 처리하다 inspection 점검 enrich 풍부하게 하다, 부유하게 만들다

4
해석 이 광고는 누구를 대상으로 하는가?
(A) 다른 사람들로부터 독립을 갈망하는 사람들
(B) Avalon을 떠나고 싶어 하는 사람들
(C) 여가 활동을 좋아하는 사람들
(D) 현지 회사에서 일하는 사람들

해설 추론 문제이다. For whom으로 시작되는 문제는 이 글의 예상되는 독자를 묻는 것이다. 제목이 "A Retirement That Is Well Connected"로 든든한 은퇴 후 삶에 대한 글이므로 읽는 사람은 언젠가는 일을 그만두고 은퇴할 가능성이 있는 (D) 그 지역의 회사에서 일을 하는 사람들이 적절하다.

5
해석 잠재 고객이 시설 방문 일정을 잡을 수 있는 방법은 무엇인가?
(A) 전화를 걸어서
(B) 웹 사이트를 방문해서
(C) 직원에게 개인적으로 문의해서
(D) 그들 스스로를 부유하게 만들어서

해설 세부 사항 문제이다. 잠재적인 고객이 방문 예약을 할 수 있는 방법은 글의 초반보다 후반에 많이 언급되는 내용이다. "Call us to arrange an inspection"에서 inspection=visit로 패러프레이징되어 있다.

DAY 03 일치 · 불일치 문제

비법 적용 연습   본문 p.117

| 1 (C) | 2 (D) | 3 (A) | 4 (A) | 5 (B) |

1-2

발신: Anytime&Anywhere Service Team
⟨service@anywhereanytime.co.de⟩
수신: Kenneth Schneider⟨schneider79@smile.co.de⟩
날짜: 10 August
제목: 새로운 서비스 프로그램

Schneider 씨,

저희 Anytime&Anywhere 사는 고객의 요구를 더 잘 반영하기 위한 새로운 서비스 제도를 도입할 것입니다. 저희는 메일을 통한 무제한 DVD 서비스와 무제한 스트리밍 서비스를 두 개의 개별적인 제도로 나눌 것입니다.

이제부터 우리의 고객은 선택권을 가지게 됩니다.

1안: 월 6.99달러에 무제한 스트리밍 서비스(DVD 서비스 제한)
2안: 월 6.99달러에 한 번에 2개 대여가 가능한 무제한 DVD 서비스(스트리밍 서비스 제한)

이 두 서비스를 다 누릴 수 있는 가격은 한 달에 13.98달러입니다(6.99달러+6.99달러). 만약 당신이 현재 사용 중인 서비스 제도(무제한 DVD와 스트리밍)를 계속 유지하고 싶으시다면, 위에 언급된 새로운 요금으로 계속 이어지질 것이기 때문에 아무것도 하실 필요가 없습니다. 이 요금은 2014년 9월 1일 이후에 부과될 것입니다.

하지만, 당신은 Your Account의 Plan Change를 방문함으로써 쉽게 무제한 스트리밍 서비스나 무제한 DVD 서비스, 혹은 둘 다를 변경하거나 취소할 수 있습니다.

우리는 당신이 가족 오락에 있어서 선택권이 많이 있다는 것을 알고 있으며, 저희 서비스를 이용해 주신 데 대해 감사드립니다. 지금까지와 마찬가지로, 질문이 있으시면 주저 없이 1-888-436-5453번으로 저희에게 전화 주세요.

The Anytime & Anywhere Team

어휘 reflect 반영하다, 반사하다 separate 나누다 unlimited 무제한의, 무한정의 streaming 스트리밍(인터넷으로 음성이나 영상을 실시간으로 재생하는 것) at-a-time 한 번에 charge (상품, 서비스에 대한) 요금 home entertainment 가정용 오락 feel free to do 거리낌 없이 ~ 하다 promote 홍보하다 subscription 구독 currently 현재, 지금 extra charge 추가 비용

1
해석 이 이메일의 목적은 무엇인가?
(A) 새로운 스트리밍 서비스를 홍보하기 위해
(B) 과다 청구에 대해 사과하기 위해
(C) 고객들에게 가격 변동을 알리기 위해
(D) 멤버들이 그들의 구독 기간을 갱신하도록 권장하기 위해

해설 목적 문제. 글의 목적은 대부분 글의 초반에 언급된다. 이미 서비스를 사용하고 있는 기존 사용자에게 요금 제도 변화에 대해서 공지하고 있는 글이므로 (C)가 정답이다.

2
해석 Schneider 씨에 관해 암시하고 있는 것은 무엇인가?
(A) 그는 현재 한 달에 13.98달러를 지불하고 있다.
(B) 그는 새로운 고객이다.
(C) 그는 추가 요금 없이 현재 서비스를 유지할 수 있다.
(D) 그는 웹 사이트에서 자신의 서비스를 바꿀 수 있다.

해설 you can easily change or cancel ~ by going to the Plan Change page in Your Account.에서 "당신은 Your Account의 Plan Change를 방문해서 쉽게 ~ 변경하거나 취소할 수 있다"고 했으므로 온라인상에서 스스로 현재 정책을 바꿀 수 있다는 것을 추론할 수 있다. (A) 변경된 후의 가격은 13.89달러이지만 현재 가격은 알 수 없다. (B) Schneider씨는 새로운 고객이 아니라 기존 고객이다. (C) 변경된 가격으로 계속 연장을 할 수 있다고 했으나 추가 요금이 없는지는 알 수 없다.

3-5

World of Hobbits

World of Hobbits는 Hubert Abernathy의 작품이고, 그는 많은 작품을 만든 온라인 게임 개발자로서 겨우 일 년 전에 Blizzard gaming platform에서 이 게임을 시작했는데 현재까지 전 세계로부터 56,000명의 게이머를 모았다. 대부분이 JRR Tolkien이 쓴 "반지원정대"의 팬인 10대가 이 성공의 중심에 있다.

게임의 이야기는 대략적으로 반지 원정대 시리즈의 네 번째 책에서 따왔다. 이 온라인 게임은 일반적으로 평균적인 청소년보다 지적인 수준이 높은 젊은이에게 매우 인기가 있다.

엄청난 규모의 이 게임이 진행되는 웹 사이트는 더 큰 목표 시장에 자신들의 10대 겨냥 제품을 광고하기 원하는 기업들에게 있어서 굉장히 중요하다.

지금까지, 자신들의 제품을 광고하는 기업들은 이 게임이 쌓아 온 제품의 노출에 굉장히 만족하고 있다. 그리고, 이 게임이 광고 분야에서 매우 성공적이라는 사실이 증명되었기 때문에, Abernathy 씨는 10대와 특히 이 연령대를 목표로 하는 광고업자들을 위해 더 성공적이고 인기가 있을 것이라고 약속하는 새로운 온라인 게임을 만들 것이다.

어휘 prolific 화가, 작가 등이 다작하는 launch 시작하다, 출시하다 platform (사용 기반이 되는 컴퓨터 시스템, 소프트웨어) 플랫폼 barely 겨우, 거의 garner (정보, 지지 등을) 얻다 mainstay (of sth) (무엇의 존재, 성공을 가능하게 하는) 중심 loosely 대충, 막연하게 adapt 적응하다, 개작하다, 각색하다 fellowship 유대감 appealing 매력적인, 흥미로운 intellectual ability 지적 능력 adolescent 청소년 massive 대량의, scale 규모 teen-oriented 10대를 겨냥한 target market 표적 시장 satisfied with ~에 만족한 exposure 노출, 폭로, 알려짐 age bracket 연령층 release 발매하다, 발표하다, 개봉하다

3

해석 기사의 주제는 무엇인가?
(A) 광고주들이 만족하고 있다.
(B) 그 책 시리즈는 많은 팬이 있다.
(C) 이 게임을 즐기는 십 대가 제품을 더 많이 구매한다.
(D) Tolkien은 새 소설을 출간할 것이다.

해설 주제 문제. 전반적인 내용은 Hobbits 게임이 청소년들에게 크게 인기를 끌어서 Hobbits 게임에 제품을 광고하는 광고주들이 매우 만족하고 있다는 내용이다. 특히, "So far, companies advertising their products have been very satisfied with the exposure this game has garnered."에서 주제를 확인할 수 있다. 이 글은 책에 대해 이야기하려는 것이 아니므로 (B)와 (D)는 오답이고, 이 게임을 하는 10대가 물건을 더 많이 샀다는 언급은 없으므로 (C)도 오답이다.

4

해석 첫 번째 단락 네 번째 줄에 나온 단어 "mainstay"와 의미가 가장 가까운 것은?
(A) 기초
(B) 청중
(C) 반박하는 사람들
(D) 성인

해설 동의어 찾기. 문장에서 mainstay는 '(~의 존재나 성공을 가능하게 한) 중심'이라는 뜻이다. 따라서 '기초, 기본, 근간'이라는 뜻의 base가 정답이다.

5

해석 이 게임에 대해 언급되지 않은 것은?
(A) 청소년들은 이 게임을 사랑한다.
(B) 성인들은 종종 이 게임을 한다.
(C) 그 게임은 세계 각 국에서 성공적이었다.
(D) Abernathy 씨는 새로운 게임을 만들 것이다.

해설 (B) 성인에 대해서는 지문에서 언급된 것이 없다. (A) "Teens who mostly are fans of the Lord of the Rings series of books written by JRR Tolkien are generally its mainstay."에서 청소년들이 이 게임을 매우 좋아한다는 것을 알 수 있다. (C) "has so far garnered 56,000 gamers worldwide"에서 전 세계적으로 성공했음을 알 수 있다. (D) "Mr. Abernathy will be creating a new online game"에서 Abernathy 씨가 새로운 게임을 개발할 거라는 사실을 알 수 있다.

DAY 04 추론 문제

비법 적용 연습 본문 p.120

| 1 (D) | 2 (B) | 3 (A) | 4 (B) | 5 (C) |

1-3

요즘 우울한가요?

- 우리의 공인된 심리학자들이 자상하고 협조적인 분위기에서 매우 전문적이고 개별적인 서비스를 제공할 것입니다.
- 삶의 변화에 적응하는 것, 걱정, 우울, 스트레스, 사람 사이의 관계 문제, 약물 남용, 정신적 충격과 같은 문제에 대해 도움을 드립니다.
- 심각한 상황에 처해 있으시다면 즉각적인 도움이 제공됩니다.
- 고통을 줄이고, 당신의 대처 능력을 증진시키며, 효과적인 해결책을 향해서 나아가고, 궁극적으로 삶의 안정을 되찾기 위해서 함께 노력합니다.

주 정부에서 운영하는 건강 보험 상환이 가능합니다.

Balanced Psychological Services
전화: 9877-4998 혹은 0416-884-0394
www.balancedps.com

어휘 feel down 우울해 하다 registered (공식) 등록된, 등록한 psychologist 심리학자 provide 공급하다 individualized 개인적으로 compassionate 동정적인 supportive 지지하는 assistance 도움, 원조 concern 걱정, 근심 adjustment 적응 anxiety 걱정 depression 우울 substance abuse 약물 남용 trauma 정신적 충격 immediate 즉각적인 alleviate 경감하다 distress 고통 coping skills 대처 기술 resolution 해결책 regain 되찾다 stability 안정 medicare 의료 보험 제도(미국의 노인의료보험제도로 65세 이상의 노인과 장애인에게 의료비의 50%를 지원하는 제도) reimbursement 상환 mentally handicapped 지적 장애가 있는 efficient 효율적인 one-on-one 일대일의 consultation 상담 care about ~을 염려하다 facility 시설 be entitled to ~할 자격이 부여되다

1

해석 이 공고문은 누구를 대상으로 하는가?
(A) 심리학자

(B) 지적 장애인
(C) 의학 전문가
(D) 감정적으로 문제를 겪고 있는 사람들

해설 For whom으로 시작하는 질문은 대부분 이 글을 읽는 독자에 대해서 묻는 것이다. 제목에서부터 감정적으로 문제를 겪고 있는 사람들을 위한 글임을 알 수 있다. mentally handicapped people은 심리적으로 문제가 있는 것이 아니라 뇌에 문제가 있는 지적 장애를 말하므로 오답이다.

2

해설 심리학자에 관해 암시하지 않은 것은 무엇인가?
(A) 그들은 매우 효율적이고 빨리 일을 한다.
(B) 그들은 일대일 상담을 제공한다.
(C) 그들은 환자들의 행복에 관심을 갖는다.
(D) 그들은 환자들의 생활 방식을 지지해 줄 수 있다.

해설 Not 문제는 선택지의 키워드를 하나씩 지문에 있는지 확인해야 한다. (B)는 일대일 상담을 해 준다는 것인데 이는 지문에 나오지 않는다.

3

해설 이 기사에서 지불 방법에 대해 언급된 것은?
(A) 정부는 치료비를 지불할 수 있다.
(B) 환자는 나중에 지불할 수 있다.
(C) 시설은 저렴한 비용으로 제공될 수 있다.
(D) 몇몇 환자들은 무료로 치료 받을 수 있다.

해설 범위를 "payment methods"로 정해 주었으므로 지문의 "State-run health insurance reimbursements available" 부분을 선택지와 맞추어 간다. 주 정부에서 운영한다고 하므로 나라가 치료비를 지불해 주는 것을 알 수 있다.

4-5

카펫을 사실 분들 주목하세요!

호주의 일류 카펫 생산 업체인 Carpet Right는 또 다른 최고 품질의 카펫 50,000제곱미터를 급하게 처분하기로 했습니다. 100% 뉴질랜드 울로 꼬아 만든 털과 특별한 질감이 나도록 만들어진 고리 모양으로 만든 털, 사이잘 섬유와 플러시 천으로 만든 털, 선염(실을 염색한) 나일론 등이 포함되어 있습니다. 모두 엄청나게 단단하고, 최고의 품질 등급을 받았습니다.

이전에는 본 적이 없는 가격!
*40%까지 절약할 수 있습니다!

모든 카펫은 지금 재고가 있고, 당신의 편의에 따라 보관해 드릴 수 있습니다. 서두르세요! 재고가 있는 동안에 모든 가게에서 이 가격으로 구매 가능합니다.

* 오직 선별된 제품 라인만 가능

BELROSE
Warehouse
56 Clide St. Niangala Cl(Homemakers Supa Centre 옆)

어휘 leading 일류의 manufacturer 제조자, 생산 업체 pile (카펫의) 표면, 털 textured 특별한 질감이 나도록 만들어진 loop (실이나 끈 등의) 고리, 털로 만들어진 고리 sisal 사이잘삼(용설란 과의 풀로 밧줄을 만드는 재료로 쓰임) plush 플러시 천(벨벳과 비슷하며, 길고 부드러운 보풀이 있는 비단) solution dyed nylon 선염 나일론(원료 상태에서 염색을 한 나일론) heavy duty 튼튼한 in stock 비축되어, 재고 at one's convenience ~가 편리한 때에

4

해설 이 글은 어디서 볼 수 있겠는가?
(A) 카펫 카탈로그
(B) 신문
(C) 경영학 교재
(D) 카펫 사용 설명서

해설 추론 문제이다. 좋은 카펫을 싼 가격에 구매할 수 있다는 광고이므로 신문 광고에서 볼 수 있을 것이다. 카펫 카탈로그나 카펫 사용 설명서에 할인 광고를 싣지는 않으므로 함정에 빠지지 않도록 유의한다.

5

해설 광고에 대해 암시되는 것은?
(A) 부가가치세가 포함되어 있다.
(B) 모든 품목을 40% 할인한다.
(C) Carpet Right는 카펫의 재고를 처분하고 싶어 한다.
(D) 이 세일은 오직 한 장소에서만 한다.

해설 암시 문제도 대부분 선택지의 키워드를 패러프레이징만 잘하면 쉽게 맞출 수 있다. "Carpet Right, has chosen to urgently clear another 50,000m² of top quality carpets."에서 clear(처리하다)를 dispose of(처리하다, 처분하다)로 패러프레이징한 것이므로 (C)가 정답이다. tax에 대한 언급은 없고, 모든 제품을 40% 할인하는 것이 아니라, 선별된 제품만 40%까지 할인을 받을 수 있는 것이다. 모든 점포에서 이 할인 행사를 진행하고 있다.

DAY 05 동의어 문제

비법 적용 연습   본문 p.123

| 1 (B) | 2 (B) | 3 (D) | 4 (D) | 5 (A) |
| 6 (B) | 7 (C) |

1-4

Office Solutions
편리하고 편안한 사무실이 꼭 비싸야 하는 것은 아닙니다

대부분의 기업은 사업에서 나중에는 못 쓰게 될 사무 가구와 사무 용품에 예산의 많은 부분을 사용합니다. 그들의 사무실을 꾸미는 데 불필요하게 지출된 많은 돈이 있다는 것을 알기 때문에, Office Solutions의 사주들은 사업장을 꾸미는 효율적인 방법을 소개하고자 회사를 만들었습니다. 지난 20년간 영업을 하면서, Office Solution은 나라 전역에 18개의 지점을 내었고, Los Angeles에 2개의 새로운 지점을 열 계획을 가지고 있습니다.

Office Solutions는 중고 가구와 장비를 사서 수리하고, 그것을 고객에게 임대해 드립니다. Office Solutions는 합리적인 가격으로 제공하는 것 외에도 고객의 매일의 필요에 적합한 장비와 가구를 추천함으로써 돈을 절약할 수 있게 도와 드립니다. Office Solutions는 책상과 파일 캐비닛뿐만 아니라 컴퓨터와 프린트, 복사기, 팩스도 임대합니다. 회사는 또한 모든 임대 전자 제품이 좋은 상태를 유지하게 하기 위해서 숙련되고 기술이 뛰어난 기술자들을 보유하고 있습니다.

그래서 만약 새로운 사업을 시작하시거나, 단순히 추가로 장비가 필요하시다면, 예산의 많은 부분을 사무용품이나 가구에 쓰는 것을 피하실 수 있습니다. 지금 (619) 285-2923으로 전화하세요.

어휘 come at ~에 이르다 equipment 장비 obsolete 더 이상 쓸모가 없는, 구식의 furnish (가구를) 비치하다, 제공하다 cost-efficient 비용 효율적인 lease 임대하다 affordable (가격이) 알맞은 assist 돕다, 도움이 되다 ensure 보장하다

1
해석 광고에서 새로운 사업주들에 관해 말하는 것은 무엇인가?
(A) 그들은 실내 장식을 하는 데 문제가 있다.
(B) 그들은 비용의 대부분을 사무기기에 소비한다.
(C) 그들은 다른 사무실의 중고 기기를 구입한다.
(D) 그들은 직원들을 현명하게 관리하는 방법을 모른다.

해설 say 혹은 mention 문제는 지문에 나온 내용을 그대로 패러프레이징한 선택지를 찾는 문제이다. "Most businesses spend a large part of their budget on office furniture and equipment"를 (B)번의 "사무용품에 그들의 지출의 대부분을 쓴다"로 패러프레이징했다.

2
해석 첫 번째 단락 두 번째 줄에 나온 단어 "obsolete"와 의미가 가장 가까운 것은?
(A) 오래된
(B) 사용 불가능한
(C) 관측된
(D) 비싼

해설 동의어 문제는 꼭 그 단어가 들어가 있는 문장을 해석한 후, 문장 안에서 단어의 뜻을 확인해야 한다. "will later become obsolete in their businesses"에서 obsolete는 후에 "사용할 수 없어 쓸모가 없어진다"는 뜻이므로 정답은 (B)이다.

3
해석 Office Solutions는 회사의 비용 절약에 어떻게 도움을 주는가?
(A) 사무실의 가구를 판매함으로써
(B) 직접 공급 업체를 소개함으로써
(C) 대량 구매에 할인 혜택을 제공함으로써
(D) 적절한 장비에 대해 조언을 해줌으로써

해설 세부 사항 문제로 키워드인 "How, save money"를 기억하고 지문에서 찾는다. "saving money by recommending the most suitable equipment and furniture for their day-to-day needs"에서 가장 적절한 장비를 추천해 준다고 했으므로 (D)가 정답이다.

4
해석 Office Solutions에 대해 언급되지 않은 것은?
(A) 20년 동안 운영되어 왔다.
(B) 장비를 관리할 기술자를 보유하고 있다.
(C) 중고 장비를 구매한다.
(D) 무료 배송 서비스를 제공한다.

해설 NOT 문제이지만 about 뒤에 범위가 지문 전체이므로 선택지의 키워드를 보고 지문에서 나올 때마다 바로 정답/오답을 선택하고 넘어가야 한다. (A)는 "Open for the past 20 years"에서, (B)는 "It also maintains a team of experienced and skilled technicians who ensure that all leased electronic equipment is in good working condition"에서, 그리고 (C)는 "Office Solutions buys and repairs used furniture and equipment"에서 언급되었으므로 오답임을 알 수 있다.

5-7

이 지역 전설의 사업가 은퇴

Frank Plimpton은 매우 희귀한 사업가이다. 그는 많은 고객의 이름을 알고, 직원들에게 높은 봉급과 스톡옵션을 제공하며, 다섯 개나 되는 Mary's 슈퍼마켓의 모든 직원에게 유급 휴가를 제공한다. 그는 이 지역에서 전설이다. 그의 성공은 당연하고, 존경받을 만하다. 어제는 그가 일을 하는 마지막 날이었다. 5개의 체인과 40년이 넘어서야 마침내 그는 휴가를 가질 것이다.

Plimpton은 어머니의 이름을 딴, 자신만의 식료품점인 Mary's를 열겠다는 비전 하나를 가지고 Yorktown에 왔다. 그의 모친은 그가 여전히 소중하게 여기는 친절과 너그러움을 가르쳐 준 분이다. 그의 상냥함과 성실함은 사업이 크는 데 큰 도움이 되었고, 그는 1960년에 옆 동네인 Springfield에 가게를 열었다.

그는 이 모든 성공에도 불구하고 여전히 작고, 고객이 환영받는 분위기를 가진 상점의 중요성을 강조했다. 그 후 그는 그 지역에 4개의 상점을 더 열었다. 그리고 그곳은 광고를 하지 않는 전국에서 유일한 상점이 되었다. Plimpton은 차라리 직원들에게 그 돈을 사용하겠다고 말한다. 그리고 그는 그의 고객들은 이미 자신의 가게를 친구들에게 소문을 내 줄 만큼 좋게 여기고 있기 때문에 그에게 있어서는 입소문이 가장 효과적이라고 말한다.

어휘 legend 전설 retire 은퇴하다 rare 드문 stock option 스톡옵션 deserve ~할 만하다, ~할 자격이 된다 satellite store 분점 kindness 친절 generosity 너그러움 cherish 소중히 여기다 demeanor 태도, 행위 flourish 번영하다 neighboring 이웃의 stress 강조하다 importance 중요성 word-of-mouth 입소문 effective 효과적인 value ~을 소중히 여기다 fame 명성 prominent 주목을 끄는, 두드러진

5
해석 Plimpton 씨에 대해 암시된 것은 무엇인가?
(A) 자신의 상점이 작고 친숙한 분위기이기를 원했다.
(B) 어머님께 돈을 드리기 위해서 돈을 벌기를 원했다.
(C) 지역에서 가장 인기가 좋은 상점을 갖고 싶어 했다.
(D) 사업가로서의 명성을 얻고 싶어 했다.

해설 세부 내용 문제이다. 글의 후반부의 "Even with all that success, he still stressed the importance of small, welcoming stores."에서 작고, 고객이 환영받는 느낌이 들도록 하는 것을 중요하게 생각한다는 것을 알 수 있다. 따라서 정답은 (A)이다.

6
해석 두 번째 단락 세 번째 줄에 있는 단어 "demeanor"와 가장 의미가 가까운 것은?
(A) 추론 능력
(B) 태도
(C) 너그러움
(D) 의도

해설 동의어 찾기 문제이다. Part 7의 어휘 문제는 문맥상 이해하는 것이 중요하다. 위 지문에서 demeanor 앞에 "his friendly"라는 표현을 볼 수 있으므로 이와 가장 잘 어울리는 (B)가 정답이 된다.

7

해석 대부분의 사람들은 Mary's 슈퍼마켓을 어떻게 찾게 되는가?
(A) TV 광고를 통해서
(B) 주목을 끄는 위치 덕분에
(C) 다른 고객의 추천으로
(D) Plimpton 씨와 관련된 신문 기사를 통해서

해설 지문 후반부의 "word-of-mouth is most effective for him, since his customers value his business enough to tell their friends to go there"에서 사람들이 자신의 친구들에게 Mary's에 가보라고 추천하기 때문에 입소문이 가장 효과적이라는 내용을 찾을 수 있으므로 다른 고객의 소개, 추천으로 슈퍼마켓을 찾게 된다는 의미인 (C)가 정답이 된다. 광고를 하지 않는다고 지문에 등장하므로 TV 광고는 오답이 된다.

DAY 06 편지 / 이메일

○ 비법 적용 연습   본문 p.126

| 1 (D) | 2 (A) | 3 (A) | 4 (C) | 5 (B) |

1-3

발신: Caren Doles〈carend@hatmail.com〉
수신: Doy Chanders〈doychanders@superfurniture.com〉
날짜: 1월 1일, 수요일, 오후 2시 24분
제목: 주문 번호 255671

Chanders 씨께,

저는 최근에 DIY 침대 한 개와 의자 두 개, 컴퓨터 책상 두 개를 구매했습니다. 하지만 제가 주문하지 않은 식탁이 침대와 의자들과 함께 배송되었습니다. 그래서 수령하자마자, 저는 당신의 고객 서비스 직원 중 한 명에게 전화를 했고, 그는 저에게 배달된 제품들은 주문서에 적혀 있는 것에 따라 정확히 배달되었다고 알려 주었습니다.

제가 이 식탁을 시내에 있는 당신의 지점 중 하나에 가져다 놓겠습니다. 당신이 이 문제를 해결해 주고, 저에게 제가 주문한 책상을 보내 주신다면 정말 감사하겠습니다. 만일의 경우에 대비해서, 구매 주문서의 사본을 첨부합니다.

협조에 감사드립니다.

Caren Doles

어휘 DIY (Do-It-Yourself) 가정용품의 제작, 수리, 장식을 직접 하는 것 on receipt 받는 즉시 customer service representative 고객 서비스 상담원 inform 알려주다 corresponding to ~에 상응하는, 일치하는 itemize 항목별로 적다, 명세서를 작성하다 delivery order 화물 인도 지시서 appreciate 고마워하다 settle up 결말짓다, 처리하다 in case ~의 경우에 대비해서 attach 첨부하다 purchase order 구매 주문서 cooperation 협조

1

해석 이 이메일의 목적은?
(A) 사무용 가구를 주문하기 위해
(B) 전액 환불을 요청하기 위해
(C) 제품에 대해 문의하기 위해
(D) 문제를 해결하기 위해

해설 문제점 찾기 문제이다. 대부분 문제점은 글의 후반보다 초반에 제시되고 후반에는 그 문제의 해결책에 대한 내용이 주로 나온다. 이 글에서 문제점은 주문한 제품과 다른 제품이 배달된 것이므로 (D) "문제를 해결하기 위해서"가 정답이 된다.

2

해석 이메일에 첨부된 것은?
(A) 주문서
(B) 영수증
(C) 송장
(D) 안내 책자

해설 세부 사항 문제이다. e-mail에 첨부된 자료를 물어보는 빈번히 출제되는 문제 유형이다. include라는 단어가 지문에서는 attach, accompany, send with, enclose와 같은 단어로 패러프레이징 될 수 있다.

3

해석 Doles 씨가 다음에 할 일은 무엇인가?
(A) 상품을 반품한다.
(B) 고객센터에 전화를 한다.
(C) 새 가구를 주문한다.
(D) 웹 사이트에 방문한다.

해설 세부 사항 문제이다. 문제에서 키워드를 찾고 그 단어를 역으로 지문에서 찾아서 풀 수 있다. 이 문제에서의 키워드는 do next이므로 "미래의 행동"이 언급된 "I will drop the kitchen table(주방 테이블을 반납하겠다)"을 패러프레이징한 (A)가 정답이다.

4-5

8월 10일
Chris Allen
6325 Brownsville Avenue
Pittsburgh, PA 14739

Allen 씨께,

당신이 시설에 대해서 질문한 7월 23일자 이메일을 받았습니다. 저는 약 20년 전에 이 사업을 시작했고, 저희 호텔 손님들로부터 최상의 평가를 받아 왔습니다. 저와 저희 직원들은 저희 서비스와 시설에 대해 큰 자부심을 느낍니다. 저는 당신이 원하는 모든 것이 공급되는 여기에서 즐거운 시간을 보내게 될 것을 확신합니다.

요청하신 것처럼, 가격 책자를 첨부합니다. 9월 15일부터 11월 14일 사이에, 저희는 주중 숙박에 대해서 30%의 할인을 제공합니다. 방을 예약하시려면 335-3293번으로 저희 지배인인 Andy Smith 씨에게 연락하시거나 그저 클릭 몇 번으로 예약할 수 있는 저희 웹 사이트(www.thebestinn.com)를 방문해 주세요. 최소한 숙박 2주 전에는 예약하시길 바랍니다.

질문이 있으시면 주저 말고 연락 주십시오.

감사합니다.
Robin Hober

어휘 be in receipt of ~을 받다 inquire about ~에 대해 묻다, 알아보다 take pride in ~에 자부심을 느끼다 confident 자신감 있는, 확신하는 request 요청하다 attach 첨부하다 brochure 책자 accommodation 숙박 시설 reserve ~을 예약하다 book 예약하다, 예매하다 suggest 제안하다 in advance 미리

4

해석 Hober 씨는 누구인가?
(A) 호텔 종업원
(B) 관리자
(C) 호텔 주인
(D) 호텔 투숙객

해설 세부 사항 문제이다. Hober 씨가 키워드이다. 지문에서 Hober 씨가 이 편지를 쓴 사람임을 확인 후, I(나)로 시작하는 부분에서 정답이 나올 것을 예측할 수 있다. "I started this business almost two decades ago: 나는 약 20년 전에 이 사업을 시작했다"와 "My staff members and I take great pride in ~: 나와 내 직원들은 ~에 자부심이 있다" 부분에서 호텔 소유주임을 알 수 있다. 또한 호텔의 소유주이므로 employee(직원)는 아니고, supervisor는 Andy Smith이다.

5

해석 특별 할인은 얼마 동안이나 제공되나?
(A) 3개월
(B) 2개월
(C) 30일
(D) 2주

해설 세부 사항 문제이다. 키워드는 How long과 special offer이다. "Between September 15 and November 14: 9월 15일에서 11월 14일 사이"라고 했으므로 패러프레이징하면 2개월이 된다.

DAY 07 제품 광고

○ 비법 적용 연습   본문 p.129

| 1 (C) | 2 (C) | 3 (B) | 4 (D) | 5 (B) |

1-3

이것 중 어떤 것도 포기하지 마세요: 넓은 공간과 스타일

정가: 150달러
할인가: 100달러, 무료 배송
크기: 17인치
색상: 검정, 갈색, 회색
*세 가지 색상 모두 재고 있음

이 품목은 포장이 된 상태로 배송되며, 선물용 포장은 되지 않습니다.
- 100% 폴리에스테르
- 18인치 높이
- 12인치 넓이
- 딱 맞게 조정이 가능한 시스템은 13인치에서 15.6인치의 휴대용 컴퓨터에 맞춰 크기 조절이 가능
- 모든 업무적 요구를 맞출 수 있는 태블릿 주머니를 포함한 앞주머니 구성
- 뒷면에 깔린 냉각 충전재는 안정감과 열 조절 기능 제공
- 스마트 끈은 이동의 용이성을 위해 위한 수직 손잡이 위로 내려감
- 안전한 지퍼 형식의 숨겨진 주머니 두 개

특별한 가격과 제품 행사
- 신용 카드로 제품을 구입하시면, 20달러 할인을 받게 될 것입니다.
- 8월 10일에서 23일까지 구매하시는 모든 분께 세 자리 숫자 자물쇠가 무료로 제공됩니다.

어휘 spacious 넓은 free shipping 무료 배송 in stock 재고가 있는 note 주목하다, (중요하거나 흥미로운 것을) 언급하다 ship (배나 다른 운송 수단으로) 실어 나르다, 수송하다 packaging 포장 gift-wrap 선물용으로 포장하다 adjustable 조정[조절] 가능한 custom fit 고객 맞춤형의 padding 충전재 comfort 편안, 안락 heat regulation 열 제어 upright 똑바른, 수직의 slide over ~으로 미끄러져 내려가다 mobility 이동성 stash 숨겨 두는 장소; 숨겨 두다 promotion 홍보 accommodate 수용하다, ~에 적합하게 하다

1

해석 무엇을 광고하고 있는가?
(A) 노트북
(B) 세 자리 숫자 자물쇠
(C) 배낭
(D) 여행가방

해설 세부 사항 문제. "Perfect fit adjustable system provides custom fit for 13-15.6" laptops: 딱 맞게 조정이 가능한 시스템은 13인치에서 15.6인치의 휴대용 컴퓨터에 맞춰 크기 조절이 가능"하다는 점에서 휴대용 컴퓨터용 가방을 광고하고 있음을 알 수 있다. 서류 가방(suitcase)은 heating regulation과 같은 기능이 필요 없으므로 정답이라고 보기 어렵다.

2

해석 신용 카드로 지불할 때 한 개당 얼마를 지불해야 하는가?
(A) 150달러
(B) 100달러
(C) 80달러
(D) 20달러

해설 신용 카드로 결제하면 20달러를 할인 받는다고 했고, 행사 가격이 100달러이므로 80달러를 내야 한다.

3

해석 광고에서 언급되지 않은 것은 무엇인가?
(A) 상품은 세 가지 색상이 있다.
(B) 어떤 크기의 휴대용 컴퓨터라도 크기에 맞게 조절할 수 있다.
(C) 일정 기간 동안 선물이 제공된다.
(D) 주머니가 여러 개 있다.

해설 모든 크기가 아니라 "13인치에서 15.6인치까지의 휴대용 컴퓨터"에 맞는 가방이라고 했으므로 (B)가 정답이다.

4-5

매매

단층집(현 거주자 있음)
위치: 2378 Clairemont Avenue
San Diego, California
평수: 1,050 제곱피트
가격: 13만 달러(협상 가능)

이전에 주인이 있었고, 전 소유주가 극진히 아꼈던 이 집에는 침실 2개와 화장실 한 개, 넓은 일광욕실이 있습니다. 이 집에는 또한 주말 바비큐 파티를 하기에 더할 나위 없이 알맞은 뒷마당과 작은 차 두 대를 주차할 수 있는 주차장이 있습니다. 새로운 생활을 막 시작한 작은 가족에게 완벽한 장소입니다.

추가적인 정보를 얻고 싶으시면 주저하지 마시고 (619) 286-9934번으로 Ericka Matthews(중개업자)에게 전화 주세요.

정말 구매하실 의향이 있는 분과 직접 구매하실 분만 연락 바랍니다. 부동산 중개업자는 연락하지 말아 주세요.

> **어휘** occupy (공간, 지역, 시간을) 차지하다 square feet 평방피트 negotiable 협상 가능한 pre-owned 중고의, 다른 사람이 소유하고 있던 spacious 널찍한 sunroom 일광욕실 parking area 주차장 hesitate to ~ 하기를 주저하다 real estate agent 부동산 중개업자 priority 우선권 reside 거주하다

4

해석 이 건물의 특징이 아닌 것은?
(A) 일광욕실
(B) 주차장
(C) 뒷마당
(D) 발코니

해설 Not/True 문제 중 간단히 풀 수 있는 문제. 선택지의 명사를 먼저 보고 지문에서 하나씩 소거해 나간다. (A)는 a spacious sunroom에서, (B)는 a parking area good for 2 small cars에서, (C)는 a comfortable backyard ideal for weekend barbecues에서 찾을 수 있다.

5

해석 광고에 언급된 것은?
(A) 부동산 업자들은 우선권을 받을 것이다.
(B) 할인이 있을 것이다.
(C) Matthews 씨가 그곳에 산다.
(D) 이 집은 임대가 가능하다.

해설 Price: $130,000 (negotiable)에서 negotiable(협상 가능)을 (B)번에서 discount로 패러프레이징한 것이다.

DAY 08 구인 공고

비법 적용 연습   본문 p.132

| 1 (D) | 2 (B) | 3 (A) | 4 (A) | 5 (D) |

1-2

MS 출판사 직원 채용

편집자 (SYDNEY 지사)
* 대학 졸업생, 저널리즘이나 기타 관련된 과목 전공자
* 뉴스 방송 업계에서 2년 이상의 편집 경험
* 평균 이상의 영어 집필 능력
* 레이아웃이나 페이지 디자인에 관한 지식을 가진 분 우대
* 저녁이나 주말에도 기꺼이 일할 수 있고, 매일의 마감 압박에 견딜 수 있는 사람

회계 보조(CANBERRA 지사)
* 회계 감사나 일반 회계에 최소 3년 이상의 경력을 가진 회계학이나 회계 직무 졸업생
* 정리를 잘하고, 성숙하며, 책임감이 강한 사람
* 최소한의 감독으로도 일할 수 있고, 성실하며, 성과 지향적인 사람
* 필요한 경우 추가 근무를 할 수 있는 사람

관심 있는 지원자들은 자신의 이력서를 아래의 이메일 주소로 보내거나

wagnerronaldo@mspublications.com

이력서와 성적 증명서, 유효한 신분증을 직접 아래의 주소로 가져오세요.

THE 2ND FLOOR, LOUIE R. PRIETO PRESS BUILDING, 9 Pirie St. Fyshwick ACT 2609

> **어휘** publication 출판 copy editor 편집자 major in ~을 전공하다 preferably 되도록이면, 선호하는 layout 레이아웃, 지면 배정 willing to 기꺼이 ~하는 thrive 번창하다 deadline 기한, 마감기한 accounting 회계(업무) accountancy 회계직, 회계업무 audit 회계 감사 well-organized 정리가 잘 된 mature 성숙한 supervision 감독 hardworking 근면한, 부지런히 일하는 work overtime 초과 근무를 하다, 시간 외로 일하다 require 필요로 하다, 요구하다 applicant 지원자 requirement 요구 조건 previous 이전의 related field 관련 분야 bachelor's degree 학사 학위 proficiency 기량, 능숙

1

해석 편집자 자리를 위한 자격 요건으로 언급되지 않은 것은?
(A) 관련 분야에서의 경력
(B) 학사 학위
(C) 글쓰기 실력
(D) 레이아웃 및 페이지 디자인에 관련된 지식

해설 requirement(요구 조건)와 preference(선호 사항)를 구분하는 문제. (D)번은 선호되는 조건이지 꼭 있어야 하는 요구 조건은 아니다.

2

해석 관심 있는 사람들은 어떻게 회계 보조 자리에 지원할 수 있는가?
(A) 이력서를 팩스로 보낸다.
(B) 필요 서류를 이메일로 보낸다.
(C) 회사의 웹 사이트에 방문한다.
(D) 캔버라 사무실에 전화한다.

해설 "send their resumes to wagnerronaldo@mspublications.com: wagnerronaldo@mspublications.com으로 이력서를 보내세요"라고 했으므로 이메일로 서류를 보내라고 한 (B)와 같은 내용이다.

3-5

J&P Design
James and Pett Design Company

우리는 우리의 독특하고 표현이 풍부한 디자인에 대한 증가하는 수요를 맞추기 위해서 최근에 New York 지점을 개점하였습니다. 그래서 우리는 내부 부서 간의 서신과 외부와의 서신을 처리하고, 다양한 종류의 서류, 메일을 다루고, 관리자와 이야기하기를 원하는 전화를 처리할 수 있으며, 컴퓨터와 소프트웨어의 정기적인 유지 보수 역시 책임질 관리직 보조가 필요합니다. 사무용품을 구매하고, 감독관과 다른 관리자들의 여행 일정을 잡는 것도 포함됩니다. 관심이 있는 지원자들은 적어도 3년의 관리직 경력이 있어야 하고, 컴퓨터와 다른 사무 장비를 매우 잘 다뤄야 합니다. 뛰어난 구술 및 작문 실력도 요구됩니다. 2년제 대학 학위는 필수 조건입니다. 하지만, 4년제 대학 학사 학위를 우대합니다. 이 도전적인 직책은 무엇이든 할 수 있다는

자세와 꼼꼼함을 겸비한 후보자들에게 적합합니다. 회사가 보너스와 높은 수준의 기본급을 제공합니다.

이 직책에 관심이 있으시면, www.jpdesign.com을 방문하셔서, 온라인 신청서를 작성하시고, 이력서와 추천서 한 부를 첨부하여 제출해 주세요.

어휘 branch 지사, 지점 meet demand 요구를 충족시키다, 수요를 충족시키다 expressive 표현력이 풍부한, 표현하는 expertise 전문 기술, 지식 in need of ~을 필요로 하고 administrative 관리상의, 행정상의 aide 보좌관 interdepartmental 부처 간의 external 외부의, 밖의 correspondence 서신 deal with 다루다, 처리하다 a range of 다양한 responsible for ~에 책임지고 있는, 책임이 있는 routine 정례적인, 일상의 maintenance 유지, 보수 office supplies 사무용품 travel arrangement 여행 준비 applicant 지원자 familiar with ~에 친숙한, 익숙한 verbal 말의 associate's degree 2년제 학사 학위 prerequisite (무엇이 있기 위해서는 꼭 필요한) 전제 조건 bachelor's degree 학사 학위 prefer 선호하다 challenging 도전적인, 모험적인 suit 어울리다 candidate 후보자 can-do attitude 의욕적인 태도 base salary 기본급 fill out application 신청서를 작성하다 recommendation letter 추천서

3

해석 어떤 직종이 광고되고 있는가?
(A) 사무 보조
(B) 웹디자이너
(C) 부서 관리자
(D) 관리자의 비서

해설 광고하는 대상이나 제품은 글의 초반에 나온다. "So we are in need of an Administrative Aide"에서 Administrative Aide가 Office assistant로 paraphrasing 되었는데, office assistant(사무 보조원)라는 것은 바로 뒤에 나오는 "who is able to process interdepartmental and external correspondence, ~ of computers and software. Ordering office supplies ~." 등의 내용을 통해 알 수 있다.

4

해석 광고에서 언급되지 않은 것은?
(A) 예상 급여 범위
(B) 회사의 위치
(C) 자리 지원 방법
(D) 자리의 특정 직함

해설 선택지의 키워드를 기억하면 바로 정답과 관련된 지문 부분을 찾을 수 있다. (B)는 "We have recently opened a New York branch"에서, (C)는 "please visit www.jpdesign.com, fill out an online application and click "submit" with your résumé and one recommendation letter attached" 부분에서, (D)는 "we are in need of an Administrative Aide"를 보고 (A)가 정답임을 알 수 있다.

5

해석 자리의 책무로 언급된 것은?
(A) 회의 일정 관리
(B) 고객과의 만남
(C) 견학 안내
(D) 사무용품 구매

해설 직원을 채용하는 글에서 빈번하게 나오는 문제가 responsibility(업무)와 requirement(자격 요건)에 관한 것이다. "Ordering office supplies"를 보고 (D)를 정답으로 고를 수 있다.

DAY 09 공지, 안내, 정보

○ 비법 적용 연습   본문 p.135

| 1 (C) | 2 (C) | 3 (D) | 4 (C) | 5 (B) |

1-3

아시다시피, 최근에 저희는 시설을 확장했습니다. 수영장을 추가로 짓고, 헬스클럽을 확장했으며, 무료 돌봄이 서비스를 제공합니다. 건설 비용을 충당하려면, 2월 1일부터 가족 회원 회비를 25달러 인상해야 합니다. 이제 Slim Gym은 수영과 웨이트 리프팅, 아이스 스케이팅, 에어로빅을 가족 회원 모두에게 제공합니다. 심지어 인상된 가격도 주에서 제공하는 가격 중 가장 낮은 가격에 속합니다. 이미 회원 갱신을 하신 분들은 다음 갱신 날짜까지 인상된 25달러가 적용되지 않을 것입니다. 현재의 멤버십 비용으로 시설을 이용하고 싶으시다면, 이번 달 말 전에 귀하의 멤버십을 갱신하시기 바랍니다. 귀하의 지원에 감사드리며, 가족의 건강을 위한 장소로써 Slim Gym을 선택해 주시길 희망합니다.

어휘 expand 확장하다 add 더하다, 첨가하다 pool 수영장 offset 상쇄, 상쇄하다 effective 효력이 있는 renew 갱신하다 assess (가치, 양)을 평가하다 additional 추가의 appreciate 감사하다 patron 단골손님 register for ~을 등록하다 instructor 강사

1

해석 공지를 작성한 이유는?
(A) 피트니스 센터의 재개장을 알리기 위해
(B) 부가 서비스를 광고하기 위해
(C) 회원들에게 회비 인상을 알리기 위해
(D) 고객들의 지속적인 지원에 감사하기 위해

해설 글의 주제를 묻는 문제이다. 초반에 "we must increase our family membership fees by $25, effective February 1"를 통해서 회비 인상이 주제인 것을 알 수 있다.

2

해석 이 공지는 누구를 대상으로 하는가?
(A) 새로운 회원들
(B) 에어로빅 강사들
(C) 기존 체육관 이용자들
(D) 무료 회원들

해설 For whom으로 시작되는 문제이므로 이 글의 대상을 묻고 있다. 갱신(renew)을 해야 하는 대상이 이 글의 주요 독자일 것이므로 (C) 기존 체육관 이용자들이 정답이다.

3

해석 인상된 회비를 지불하지 않고 시설을 이용하려면 고객들은 무엇을 해야 하는가?

(A) 2월 1일에 회원 자격 갱신
(B) 에어로빅 수업 등록
(C) 강사에게 문의
(D) 이번 달에 갱신

해설 세부 사항 문제로 질문은 인상된 비용 없이 이용할 수 있는 방법을 묻고 있는데, "If you want to use the facility at the current membership fee, please renew your membership before the end of this month."에서 이번 달 말까지 갱신하면 되는 것을 알 수 있다. 새로운 가격이 적용되는 것이 "effective February 1"이므로 그 전달은 1월이 된다.

4-5

발신: Jimmy Clint 관리부
수신: 전 직원
제목: 결근 정책 및 절차

겨울이 다가옴에 따라 저희는 혹독한 날씨로 인한 결근과 관련된 우리의 정책을 상기시켜 드리려 합니다. 겨울철 추운 날씨에 안전한 운전을 위해서 당신의 차량을 점검하기에는 지금이 적기입니다. 저희는 직원의 안전이 가장 큰 관심사입니다. 우리는 사무실을 완전히 폐쇄해야 했던 적이 거의 없었습니다만, 도로 상태가 운전하기에 너무 위험했을 때는 그렇게 해 왔습니다.

출근을 해야 하는지 아닌지 확실하지 않다면, 직원 상담 직통 전화인 555-5555로 전화 주세요. 혹독한 날씨나 다른 비상사태의 경우에 회사 운영 시간에 대한 정보를 제공합니다. 직원들은 회사가 공식적으로 운영이 될 때는 출근해야 합니다. 만약 출근을 할 수 없다면, 상관에게 개인 휴가를 쓰겠다는 것을 알려야만 합니다.

어휘 absence 결근, 결석 approach 다가가다, 다가오다 remind A of B A에게 B를 일깨우다, 상기시키다 regarding ~에 관해서 due to ~때문에 severe 심각한 rarely 거의 ~하지 않다 hazardous 위험한 report to 출근하다 hotline 긴급 직통 전화 concerning ~에 관하여 notify 통지하다 알리다 take a day off 휴가를 내다

4
해설 공지는 주로 무엇에 관한 것인가?
(A) 안전한 출근을 위한 자동차 준비
(B) 심각한 기상 조건
(C) 결근 관련 정책
(D) 직원 안전

해설 글의 주제를 묻는 문제이다. 초반에 "we want to remind you of our policy regarding absence due to severe weather conditions"를 보고 결근에 대한 회사 정책을 내용으로 글이 전개될 것을 알 수 있다.

5
해설 만약 직원들이 출근할 수 없을 경우 그들은 어떻게 해야 하는가?
(A) 직원 상담 전화로 연락한다.
(B) 그들의 관리자에게 연락한다.
(C) 안전한 출근을 위해 그들의 차를 준비한다.
(D) 도로 상황에 관한 정보를 수집한다.

해설 세부 사항 문제이다. 키워드는 "unable to come to work" 부분임을 기억하고 지문에서 비슷한 내용이 나오면 그 부분을 정독한다. "if you are unable to be at work, you must notify your supervisor that you are taking a personal day off"를 보고 (B)를 정답으로 고른다.

DAY 10 기사

○ 비법 적용 연습   본문 p.138

1 (B)   2 (C)   3 (C)   4 (C)   5 (D)
6 (D)

1-3

Mona Vale 사업 박람회

Mona Vale 시 의회는 사람들이 살며, 일하며, 즐기며, 쇼핑하고 싶은 장소를 만드는 것에 전념해 왔습니다. 성장하는 지역 경제는 생기 있는 지역 사회를 만드는 데 필수적인 요소입니다. Mona Vale 사업 박람회가 사업가들과 시민들에게 이 목표를 이루기 위해 함께 일할 수 있는 멋진 기회를 제공할 것입니다.

날짜: 9월 19일 금요일
장소: Bay View 골프 클럽
시간: 오전 8시 30분부터 오후 5시까지

이 하루 동안의 사업 박람회는 Mona Vale을 지역적으로 홍보할 것이고, 지역 사업자들에게 업무상 관계를 구축하고, 자신들의 제품과 서비스를 홍보할 좋은 기회를 제공할 뿐만 아니라, 전문 연설가로부터 지역을 더 매력적으로 만드는 방법과 관광 산업, 산업 기술에 대한 일련의 패널 대담을 들을 것입니다. 패널 연설자들의 약력이 소개되어 있는 이 흥미로운 팸플릿을 한 번 살펴보세요.
박람회에 대해 더 많은 정보를 원하시면, 아래의 웹 사이트를 방문해 주세요. www.pittwater.nsw.gov.au

어휘 fair 박람회, 설명회 City Council 시 의회 committed to ~에 전념하는 critical 대단히 중요한 vibrant 활기찬 accomplish 성취하다 showcase 소개하다, 전시하다 regionally 지역적으로 place making 건물이나 지역을 더 매력적으로 만듦 craft 기술, 솜씨, (수)공예 network 업무상의 관계를 구축하다 take a look at ~을 한 번 보다 booklet 팸플릿 biography 약력, 전기 inaugurate ~을 개시하다 hold 개최하다 councilor 의원 have a speech 연설하다 detailed 자세한 post 게시하다

1
해설 이 기사는 무엇을 시사하는가?
(A) 새로운 커뮤니티가 개설될 것이다.
(B) 지방 정부가 공식 행사를 개최할 것이다.
(C) 다수의 의원들이 연설을 할 것이다.
(D) 자세한 일정이 게시될 것이다.

해설 "City Council of Mona Vale is committed to creating a city where people want to live, work, play and shop."에서 시 의회가 지역을 더 좋게 만들기 위해서 노력하고 있다고 언급했고, 이 부분의 City Council이 (B)의 local government로 패러프레이징되었다. 또 "Mona Vale Business Fair는 official event로 패러프레이징되었다.

2
해설 이 행사에 참여하지 않는 사람은 누구인가?
(A) 전문 발표자들
(B) 기업인들
(C) 골프 선수들

(D) 패널들

해설 세부 사항 문제로 키워드는 의문사 Who와 attend, event이다. "Mona Vale Business Fair is an exciting opportunity for businesses and citizens to work together to accomplish the goal."부분에서 (B) Businessmen이 참석할 것임을 알 수 있고, "Mona Vale locally ~ include a series of panel talks ~ craft industries from expert presenters"에서 (A) Expert presenters, (C) Panel members가 참석할 것임을 알 수 있다. 골프 클럽에서 사업 박람회가 열리지만, 골퍼들을 위한 행사는 아니므로 (C)가 정답이다.

3

해설 세 번째 단락 첫 번째 줄에 나온 단어 "showcase"와 의미가 가장 가까운 것은?
(A) 열다
(B) 모방하다
(C) 보여 주다
(D) 디자인하다

해설 동의어 문제이다. 여기서 showcase는 '보여 주다, 전시하다' 등의 의미이므로 (C)가 정답이다.

4-6

Everglades 양서류 보호 구역

Everglades 양서류 보호 구역이 어제 양서류 애호가들에게 새로운 명소를 개장을 했습니다. 세계 각지에서 온 30개 이상의 양서류 전시와 더불어, 방문자들에게 어떻게 악어가 살고, 번식하며 생존하는지를 교육해 주는 악어 농장이 보호 구역의 최신 시설입니다. 전에는 동물원의 소형 인공 호수였던 이곳에 위치한 농장에는 50마리 이상의 민물 악어들이 서식하고 있습니다.

더욱이, 방문객은 수중 관측 구역에서 유리를 통해 동물들을 가까이에서 볼 기회를 가질 수 있습니다. 새로운 지역에는 포획된 양서류 번식을 위해서 사용되는 연구 시설도 있습니다. 이것은 보호 구역 관리소와 Durban 생물학 연구소 교수들과 협력을 통해서 가능해졌습니다. 이 농장은 멸종 위기에 처한 야생 동물 보존의 중요성을 강조하기로 계획되었는데, 요즘은 많은 사람들이 이 점을 간과하고 있습니다. 동물들은 어떻게 보이든, 혹은 영화에서 어떻게 묘사되든지 간에, 우리 환경을 위해서 필요하기 때문에 어른들과 아이들이 야생 동물을 돌보는 것의 중요성을 알아야 합니다.

방문객에게 야생 동물의 진가를 더 잘 알게 하기 위해 보호 구역에서는 손님들이 직접 새끼 악어를 돌볼 수 있는 인큐베이터 구역을 개장했습니다. 보호 구역에서는 이번 주말에 악어와 멸종 위기에 처한 다른 파충류를 다룬 다큐멘터리 영화를 상영할 것입니다. 야생 동물 보호나, 보호 구역의 개장 시간, 비용에 대해 관심이 있는 분은 www.evergladesmarine.org를 방문해 주세요.

어휘 amphibian 양서류 preserve 보호하다; 보호지역 launch 시작하다, 출시하다 attraction 명소 breed 새끼를 낳다, 번식하다 stand on ~에 위치하다 man-made 인공의 house 수용하다, 보관하다 freshwater 담수, 민물 observatory 관측소 captive 사로잡힌, 억류된 envision 상상하다, 마음속에 그리다 highlight 강조하다 wildlife 야생 동물 extinction 멸종 overlook 간과하다 essential 필수적인 portray 그리다, 묘사하다 appreciation 감상 incubation 부화, 배양 feature 특별히 포함하다, 특징으로 삼다 breed 사육하다 commercial 상업적인 conserve 보호하다, 보존하다 endangered species 멸종 위기의 종

4

해설 이 기사는 신문의 어느 부분에서 찾을 수 있는가?
(A) 스포츠
(B) 의견란
(C) 지역 소식
(D) 과학 및 기술

해설 질문은 '신문의 어떤 면에 이 기사가 실릴 수 있을까'라는 것이다. "Everglades Amphibian Preserve"라는 기관 이름에서 Everglades라는 지역을 말하고 있으므로 정답은 (C)이다. 운동, 과학 및 기술, 의견은 모두 해당 사항 없으므로 오답이다.

5

해설 누가 이 보호 구역이 새 시설을 구축하는 데 도움을 줬는가?
(A) 기자들
(B) 정부
(C) 농부들
(D) 과학자들

해설 세부 사항 문제로 의문사 who외에도 help build가 키워드이다. "through a partnership between the preserve management and professors from the Durban Biological Institute" 부분에서 교수들이 관리자들과 파트너를 이루어서 이 프로젝트를 가능하게 만들었으므로 (D) 과학자들이 정답이다.

6

해설 악어 농장에 대해 언급된 것은 무엇인가?
(A) 상업적인 판매를 위해 동물을 사육할 것이다.
(B) 다큐멘터리 영화를 위해 동물을 제공할 것이다.
(C) 과학자들에 의해서만 이용될 것이다. **(D) 멸종 위기에 처한 종을 보존하는 데 도움이 될 것이다.**

해설 "The farm is envisioned to highlight the importance of protecting wildlife in danger of extinction,"을 통해 이 악어 농장이 멸종 위기에 처한 동물의 보존을 도와줄 것임을 알 수 있다. 동물을 상업적으로 판매하는 것이 아니므로 (A)는 오답, 다큐멘터리를 찍기 위해 동물들을 공급해 주는 것이 아니므로 (B)는 오답, 과학자들만 이용하는 것이 아니므로 (C)는 오답이다.

DAY 11 양식 및 기타 지문

○ 비법 적용 연습   본문 p.141

| 1 (B) | 2 (C) | 3 (B) | 4 (D) |

1-2

승객			
Patty Hearst			
항공사 – Worldspan Airlines		2014년 5월 19일 월요일	
항공기 번호	2227	확인 번호	YIE88G
좌석 등급	Economy		
출발	Gatwick 공항 London, 영국 터미널 N	오후 12시 5월 19일 월요일	
도착	Atlanta Hartsfield-Jackson 공항 국제공항 Atlanta, GA 미국	오전 2시 15분 5월 20일 화요일	
좌석	배정되지 않음	경유:	0
식사	식사 제공	거리:	4213
항공기	MD10	비행 시간:	09:15

* 쉽게 깨지거나 손상되는 물건, 현금, 귀중품, 사업 서류들, 개인적인 약품, 휴대용 컴퓨터, 카메라, 휴대 전화 등은 짐에 넣어 부치실 수 없으며, 비행기에 가지고 타셔야 합니다. Worldspan 항공사는 이 규정을 어김으로써 발생하는 분실이나 파손에 대해 어떤 법적 책임도 지지 않습니다.

| 비행 상태 | 지도 / 운행 방향 | 달력에 추가 | 온라인 수속 |

어휘 flight 항공편, 비행 assign 지정하다 stopover 경유 meal 식사 aircraft 항공기 fragile 부서지기 쉬운 perishable 잘 썩는 valuables 귀중품 liable 법적 책임이 있는 violation 위반

1
해설 이 일정에서 언급되지 않은 것은?
(A) 여행 거리
(B) 좌석 번호
(C) 터미널
(D) 항공기 종류

해설 표와 같은 구성으로 되어 있는 글은 선택지를 보고 지문에서 하나씩 오답을 소거해 나가면 된다. (A)는 "Mileage: 4213"에, (C)는 "Terminal N"에, (D)는 "Aircraft: MD10"에 명시되어 있지만, (B)는 "Not Assigned"로 아직 배정되지 않았다.

2
해설 부치는 수화물에 대해 알 수 있는 것은?
(A) 깨지기 쉬운 물품은 반드시 포장해야 한다.
(B) 개인 약품은 부치는 짐에 넣을 수 있다.
(C) 전자 제품은 부치는 짐에 넣을 수 없다.
(D) 1인당 20킬로그램이 허용된다.

해설 checked luggage라는 키워드를 지문에서 찾으면 "Fragile or perishable items, ~ laptop, camera, mobile phone and etc. cannot be transported as checked baggage and should be carried with you on the plane"에서 laptop, camera, mobile phone 등은 승객이 가지고 타야 한다고 했으므로 (C)가 정답이다.

3-4

Runner's world Magazine	구독 취소를 신청하신 것에 대해 유감스럽게 생각합니다. 정식으로 구독 취소를 하시려면, 이 카드를 기입하셔서 이메일로 저희에게 보내 주세요. 감사합니다.
	이름: Fred Durst
	주소: 478 Elm St. Oakland, CA
	이메일: fredurst@aol.com
	전화: (692) 647-3377
Irvin Blvd. Mission Viejo California www.runnersworld.com	취소 사유 □ 가격 ■ 내용 □ 서비스 의견: 저는 이 구독을 무료로 받았었는데, 제 취미가 아니어서 취소하고 싶어요.

어휘 regret 유감스럽게 생각하다 subscription 구독 fill out 기입하다 formally 공식적으로 fill out ~을 기입하다 cancellation 취소 content 내용 for free 무료로

3
해설 Durst 씨는 왜 구독을 취소하길 원하는가?
(A) 그는 잡지가 너무 비쌀 것이라는 것을 알았다.
(B) 그는 달리는 것을 좋아하지 않는다.
(C) 그는 다른 도시로 이사를 한다.
(D) 그는 다른 구독을 하고 있다.

해설 취소하는 구체적인 이유를 묻는 문제이다. "I received this subscription for free and I wish to cancel it because this is not my hobby."에서 이유를 찾을 수 있는데, 잡지의 제목이 "Runner's world Magazine"이라고 했고, 이것이 내 취미가 아니라고 했으므로 달리는 것을 즐기지 않는다는 것을 알 수 있다.

4
해설 Durst 씨는 자신의 구독을 취소하기 위해 무엇을 해야만 하는가?
(A) 잡지사 사무실에 전화한다.
(B) 전화 조사에 답변한다.
(C) 일반 우편을 통해 정보를 보낸다.
(D) 양식을 완성하고 〈Runner's World〉로 보낸다.

해설 세부 사항 문제이다. 키워드는 What to cancel이다. "To formally cancel your subscription, please fill out this card and e-mail it back to us.: 공식적인 취소를 위해서, 이 카드를 기입해서 저희에게 다시 이메일을 보내 주세요."에서 정답을 찾을 수 있다.

DAY 12 연계 문제

○ 비법 적용 연습   본문 p.144

1 (B)	2 (A)	3 (C)	4 (C)	5 (B)
6 (B)	7 (C)	8 (C)	9 (D)	10 (B)

어휘 honored 명예로운, 유명한 partake 참가하다; 먹다 prairie 대초원 restoration 복원, 복구 achieve 달성하다, 성공하다 collaboration 공동 작업, 협력 display 전시 treat 대접, 접대, 음식 thereafter 그 후에 wilderness 황야, 황무지 refreshment 휴양, 상쾌함; 다과 terrain 지형, 지역 binoculars 쌍안경 participate in ~에 참여하다, 참가하다 confirm 확실히 하다, 확정하다 availability 가능성 no later than 늦어도 ~까지는 prohibit 금지하다 regularly 규칙적으로 register for ~을 등록하다 arrange for ~을 계획하다, 준비하다 venue 발생 장소 propose 제안하다

1-5

지역 사회 행사

9월 9일
기념식 - 오전 10시
가이드와 함께하는 하이킹 - 오전 11시 30분
293th St. Just west of La Union Rd.

*대초원 복원의 지휘권이 군으로부터 RSCP로 넘어감에 따라 정부 기관과 지역 사회 자원봉사자의 협력으로 이루어낸 초원 복원을 축하하기 위해 유명한 초청 연사와 시 공무원이 모일 것입니다.

* 우천 시: 예정된 기념식, 전시품, 음식은 Bronton 공립 도서관 옮겨질 것입니다.

* 가이드가 인솔하는 무료 하이킹: 유명한 Hubo Gatton의 통솔로 진행되는 첫 번째 하이킹이 11시 30분에 있고, 나머지 하이킹은 Dui, Pinn과 Alkan에 의해서 통솔될 것입니다. 마지막 하이킹은 오후 1시 30분에 출발합니다.

* 대초원의 황무지를 경험해 보고 싶은 가족, 학생, 모든 사람에게 좋습니다.

* 하이킹 외의 즐길 거리: 전시물을 볼 수도 있고, 유용한 지도와 문헌들을 얻을 수 있으며, 맛있는 음식을 먹을 수 있습니다.

* 하이킹을 성공적으로 마치기 위한 복장: 자연 지형에서 하이킹을 할 수 있는 옷을 입고 당신의 경험을 즐기세요. 샌들이나 반바지, 민소매 티셔츠는 추천하지 않습니다.

발신: Tylor Watson <tylorwatson889@unimail.com>
수신: Daniel Graham <danielgraham@brontontown.org>
날짜: 9월 13일
제목: 다가오는 행사

Graham 씨께,

최근에 저와 가족들은 Bronton 지역 사회 센터에서 진행했던 대초원 하이킹 행사에 참여했습니다. 저는 하이킹을 하는 동안 매우 즐거운 시간을 보냈으며, 잊을 수가 없는 경험을 했습니다. 그래서, 저희 회사 대표님께 제가 그곳의 가이드인 Hubo Gatton 씨와 함께 했던 엄청난 경험을 다시 하기 위해 직원들을 데리고 하이킹을 가야 한다고 제안했고, 대표님은 제 제안을 받아들였습니다. 그래서 저는 Gatton 씨가 저와 제 가족을 위해 해 줬던 것처럼 우리를 안내해 줄 수 있는지 묻기 위해 Gatton 씨의 전화번호나 이메일 주소를 알고 싶습니다. 회사 하이킹은 10월 2일에 같은 장소에서 개최될 것입니다. 여행과 호텔 비용은 회사가 지불할 것이고, 그가 참여한다면 수당도 지불할 것입니다.

그의 연락처를 이메일로 보내 주시거나, 늦어도 9월 19일까지 그가 이 일을 할 수 있는지 확인해 주십시오.

Tylor Watson

1

해석 안내문에 따르면, 이 정보는 누구를 대상으로 하는가?
(A) 시 공무원
(B) 지역 주민
(C) 외국인 학생
(D) 관광 가이드

해설 안내문의 대상을 물었으므로 첫 번째 지문을 읽고 풀어야 한다. For whom으로 시작되는 문제는 글의 독자를 추론하는 문제이다. 제목이 Community Event이므로 지역 사회 행사이고, "Good for families, students and all those who want to experience prairie wilderness"에서 학생, 가족들에게 적합하다고 했으므로 (B) 지역 주민들을 대상으로 하고 있음을 알 수 있다.

2

해석 안내문에 근거해 볼 때, 다음 중 어느 것이 사실인가?
(A) 두 그룹 이상의 등산객이 있을 것이다.
(B) 슬리퍼와 민소매 티셔츠는 금지된다.
(C) 하이킹은 Bronton 공립 도서관에서 출발할 것이다.
(D) 행사가 정기적으로 개최될 것이다.

해설 True 문제로 전체 지문이 범위가 되는 시간이 많이 걸리는 문제이다. (A)가 "First hike at 11:30 led by the honored guest, Hubo Gatton; others thereafter by Dui, Pinn, and Alkan. Last hike leaves at 1:30 P.M."을 읽고, 안내하는 사람이 4명이므로 하이킹하는 사람들이 두 그룹 이상 있다는 것을 판단할 수 있다. (B)는 "Flip flops, shorts and tank tops not recommended."에서 추천되지 않는다고 했지 prohibit(금지된다)이라고 하지는 않았으므로 옳은 내용이 아니다.

3

해석 Watson 씨는 몇 시에 하이킹을 하였는가?
(A) 오전 10시
(B) 오전 11시
(C) 오전 11시 30분
(D) 오후 1시 30분

해설 Mr. Tylor가 나오는 글은 두 번째 글이므로 이제 두 번째 글을 읽기 시작한다. 힌트는 "repeat the great experience I had with your guide Mr. Hubo Gatton"이라고 했으므로 첫 번째 글에서 Hubo Gatton이 이끌었던 하이킹을 찾으면 된다. "First hike at 11:30 led by the honored guest, Hubo Gatton"을 보면 오전 11시 30분인 것을 알 수 있다.

4

해석 Tylor Watson 씨가 이메일을 쓴 목적은 무엇인가?
(A) 하이킹 프로그램에 등록하기 위해
(B) 공동체 행사를 준비하기 위해
(C) 몇 가지 정보를 요청하기 위해
(D) 전에 있었던 행사에 대해 자신의 대표 이사에게 알리기 위해

해설 연계 문제 이후의 문제들은 두 번째 글에 답이 나올 확률이 높다. "So I would like to ask for Mr. Gatton's contact number or an e-mail address to see"를 보고 연락처를 알기를 원한다는 것을 알 수 있다.

5
해설 이메일에서 추론할 수 있는 것은?
(A) Tylor Watson 씨는 전에 Hubo Gatton 씨에게 이메일을 보낸 적이 있다.
(B) Tylor Watson 씨는 제안한 하이킹 장소를 이미 방문했었다.
(C) 회사는 야유회를 다녀왔다.
(D) 직원과 그 가족은 행사에 참가할 수 있다.

해설 "I suggested to my company CEO that we go hiking with our employees to repeat the great experience I had with your guide Mr. Hubo Gatton"에서 Mr. Tylor는 이미 이 하이킹을 해 보았고 좋아서 다른 사람에게 추천한 것이므로 (B)가 정답이다.

6-10

품질 보증

NTGX 노트북 컴퓨터 품질 보증은 모든 모델에 적용됩니다. (New Tech의 어떤 지점에서든 숙련된 기술자에 의해 제공되는 100% 관리 프로그램)

기본 관리 프로그램: 구매 후, 일 년 이내에 컴퓨터나 부속 제품이 파손되거나 제품을 잃어버리신 경우, 제품을 수리하거나 교환받을 자격을 가지게 됩니다. 위에 언급한 문제가 발생할 때마다, 우리의 어떤 지점이든 관계없이 New Tech 서비스 센터를 방문하셔서, 간단한 서류를 작성하시어 제품에 대해 보상을 요구하시면 됩니다. 정책에 따라서, 수리나 교환은 영업일 기준 2일 이내에 완료될 것이고, 집으로 제품이 무료 배송될 것입니다.

우수 관리 프로그램: 추가적으로 40달러만 더 내시면, New Tech의 우수 관리 프로그램을 구매하실 수 있고, 이것은 보상 기간을 추가적으로 12개월 연장해 드립니다. 기본 관리 서비스 기간인 첫 6개월 이내에 언제든지 우수 관리 프로그램을 구매하실 수 있습니다. 더 많은 정보를 원하시면, www.newtech.com/warranty/premiumcare에 방문하시거나 229-4854-0039로 전화 주세요.

발신: Kuger Smith〈ks1122@eskbroadcasting.com〉
수신: servicedepartment@newtech.com
날짜: 12월 12일
제목: 접수 번호 (223GE1224)

관계자분께,

몇 주 전에, 제 컴퓨터의 인터넷 접속에 문제가 생겨서 12월 2일에 제 사무실 근처의 New Tech 서비스 센터에 수리를 요구했습니다. 다음 날, 귀사의 어떤 서비스 직원에게 전화를 받았는데, 그는 저에게 컴퓨터는 곧 수리될 것이고, 저의 우수 관리 프로그램에 의해서 보장될 것이라고 했습니다. 하지만, 저의 요구에 대한 어떤 다른 소식도 듣지 못하고 있습니다. 가능한 한 빨리 메일에 답신을 주시면 감사하겠고, 제 노트북 컴퓨터를 언제 돌려받을 수 있는지 알려 주십시오.
감사합니다.

Kuger Smith

어휘 warranty 보증 applicable 적용되는 eligible for ~에 자격이 있는 operate 작동하다 seasoned 노련한 eligible for ~할 자격이 있는 replacement 교체, 대체, 교체물 file a claim 요구하다 file out 기입하다 in compliance with ~에 따라, ~에 응하여 be completed 마무리되다 extend 확장하다 coverage 보상 범위 the following day 다음 날 service representative 서비스 직원 damaged 손상된 estimate 견적 describe ~을 설명하다 faulty 결함이 있는 inquire ~을 묻다, 알아보다 employee 고용인 original 원래의

6
해설 이 보증서는 누구를 대상으로 하는가?
(A) New Tech 서비스 센터의 기술자
(B) 최근에 컴퓨터를 구매한 소비자
(C) 영업 직원
(D) 컴퓨터 업그레이드를 원하는 사람

해설 첫 번째 글의 의도된 독자가 누구인지를 묻고 있다. New Tech 사에서 구입한 새 컴퓨터에 대한 보장 프로그램 안내로 보장 프로그램의 종류와 보상받을 수 있는 방법에 대해 설명하는 내용이다. 따라서 New Tech 사에서 (B) 최근에 컴퓨터를 구매한 사람들이 이 글의 주요 독자가 될 것이다.

7
해설 서비스 센터에서 불가능한 서비스는 무엇인가?
(A) 프리미엄 관리 계획 구매
(B) 무료 배송 서비스
(C) 손상 제품 당일 수리
(D) 제품 교체

해설 (C)에서 수리를 해 주는 것은 맞지만, "a repair or replacement will be completed within two working days"라고 했으므로 당일 수리가 아니라 2일 이내에 수리라고 해야 맞다.

8
해설 고객은 문제가 생기면 무엇을 해야 하는가?
(A) 웹 사이트를 방문한다.
(B) 서비스 센터에 전화한다.
(C) 컴퓨터를 서비스 센터로 가져간다.
(D) 온라인 양식을 작성한다.

해설 세부 사항 문제이다. 문제가 생기면 고객이 어떻게 해야 되는지를 묻는 문제이고 "Whenever you have problems mentioned above, you can visit any of our New Tech service center and file a claim by filling out a simple form."에서 알 수 있듯이 우선 New Tech service center로 컴퓨터를 가지고 와야 한다.

9
해설 Smith 씨가 이메일을 보낸 이유는 무엇인가?
(A) 환불을 요청하기 위해
(B) 제품 몇 개의 견적을 요청하기 위해
(C) 결함 제품을 설명하기 위해
(D) 그의 요청에 대한 처리 상황을 문의하기 위해

해설 두 번째 글의 주제 문제이다. 글의 뒷부분 "However, I haven't received any other news regarding my claim. It will be very much appreciated if you reply to this e-mail"에서 곧 수리가 될 것이라고 말을 들었지만 연락이 없어서 어떻게 진행되고 있는지를 알고 싶어 한다는 것을 알 수 있으므로 (D)가 정답이다.

10

해석 Smith 씨에 대해 가장 사실인 것은?
(A) New Tech의 직원이었다.
(B) 컴퓨터의 첫 보증서는 만료되었다.
(C) 그녀의 컴퓨터를 전에 고친 적이 있다.
(D) 컴퓨터를 사용한 지 6개월이 되지 않았다.

해설 연계 문제이다. 우선 문제에서 Smith 씨가 나오고 있는데 이 사람은 두 번째 글에서만 언급되고 있다. 두 번째 글의 "will be covered by my Premium Care Plan"을 보고 이 사람이 Premium Care Plan을 등록했다는 것을 알 수 있고, 첫 번째 글에서 "this plan extends your coverage for an additional 12 months."라고 했으므로 Basic Care Plan이 끝나고 Premium Care Plan의 보장을 받고 있다는 것을 알 수 있다.

DAY 13 문장 삽입

비법 적용 연습   본문 p.149

| 1 (B) | 2 (D) | 3 (A) | 4 (A) |

1-4

Noa Engineering & Construction

10월 22일
Monolith 건설
39-43 Sands Street, Kennedy Town,
Hong Kong

Theodor Yi 씨에게,

지난 5년간 Noa Engineering & Construction에서 저의 관리 하에 있었던 전 직원인 James Chun을 추천하기 위해서 이 편지를 씁니다. 잠재력 있는 졸업 예정자로서 Chun 씨는 인턴으로 저희 회사와 처음 함께 했습니다. 그의 잠재력을 안 우리는 그가 Linden 대학교를 졸업하자마자 싱가포르에 있는 저희 본사에 정규직으로 재빨리 채용했습니다. 그 이후로 단 5년 만에 그는 프로젝트 매니저로 승진하였고, 현재 두각을 나타내고 있습니다.

투철한 책임감을 가지고, Chun 씨는 스스로를 지략 있는 직원으로 증명해 왔으며, 많은 주요 고객을 저희 회사로 끌어 왔습니다. 이것은 그의 노력이 저희 회사를 이전보다 더욱 인정받게 만드는 데 기여했기 때문에 높이 평가하는 점입니다. 그는 나라 안팎의 작업을 지휘했는데, 주로 동남아시아의 관광 지역에서 활동했습니다. 그뿐 아니라, 그의 꼼꼼함 덕분에 Chun 씨는 지난여름에 중요한 건설 프로젝트의 예산과 일정을 계획하고 조직할 때 가장 인상적인 모습을 보여 줬습니다.

Chun 씨가 저희 회사를 떠난다는 것은 저에게 정말 아픔이지만, 저희는 그가 홍콩에서 새로운 시작을 하는 것을 응원합니다. Noa에서 그의 직무 수행은 뛰어났으며, 우리는 그를 그리워할 것입니다. 그가 어디에서 일하든지 훌륭한 자산이 될 것이라는 데에는 의심의 여지가 없습니다. 그의 직업의식은 견줄 것이 없으며, 따라서 당신의 직원 중 하나로 그를 고용하는 것은 현명한 선택입니다. Chun 씨에 대해 더 많은 정보를 원하신다면, 성실한 답변을 드리겠습니다.

Anes Kim
경영 이사

어휘 prospective 장래의, 유망한 superb 최고의, 최상의 noteworthy 주목할 만한, 괄목할 만한 oversee 감독하다 primarily 주로 meticulousness 꼼꼼함 root for ~을 지지하다 doubt 의심, 의혹 ethic 윤리 sincerest 가장 진심 어린, 진실된 specialize in ~을 전문으로 하다 headquarters 본사 permanent 영구적인 opportunity 기회

1

해석 왜 Kim 씨가 Yi 씨에게 연락하는가?
(A) 추천서를 요청하려고
(B) 전 직장 동료에 대해 이야기하려고
(C) 공석에 대해 알려 주려고
(D) 인턴 프로그램의 결과를 논의하려고

해설 편지 글 초반에 James Chun이라는 인물의 채용을 추천한다는 내용이 있고, 전반적인 내용을 봤을 때 Chun이 회사를 그만 두고 이직을 계획 중인 것으로 보아 정답은 (B)이다.

2

해석 Chun 씨에 대해서 암시된 것은 무엇인가?
(A) Hong Kong에서 일을 시작했다.
(B) 회사에 능력 있는 직원들을 데려오는 데 일조했다.
(C) 10년 동안 프로젝트 매니저로 일했다.
(D) 졸업 전에 일을 시작했다.

해설 졸업 예정자로 인턴으로서 처음 일을 시작했다고 했으므로 (D)가 정답이다.

3

해석 Noa Engineering & Construction에 대해서 추론할 수 없는 것은?
(A) 도로 건설 전문 기업이다.
(B) 이전보다 지금 더 사업 분야에서 알려졌다.
(C) 본사는 싱가포르에 있다.
(D) 때때로 인턴에게 정규직 자리를 제공한다.

해설 (B)는 his efforts contributed to making our company more recognized than ever before 부분에서, (C)는 we were quick to offer him a full-time position at our head office in Singapore, (D)는 right after Mr. Chun graduated from Linden University라고 명시된 부분을 통해 추론할 수 있으나, (A)에 대한 내용은 편지에서 찾을 수 없다.

4

해석 [1], [2], [3], [4]로 표시된 부분 중에서 다음 문장이 들어가기에 가장 알맞은 곳은?

"그 이후로 단 5년 만에 그는 프로젝트 매니저로 승진하였고, 현재 두각을 나타내고 있습니다."

(A) [1]
(B) [2]
(C) [3]
(D) [4]

해설 주어진 문장은 입사 후 커리어에 대해서 설명하는 부분에 들어갈 수 있는 문장이다. in just five years라는 '기간'이 나오므로 입사 이후의 내용에 해당한다. 이에 관련된 내용은 첫 번째 문단 마지막이 가장 적절하다. 따라서 (A)가 정답이다.

DAY 14 의도 파악

○ 비법 적용 연습 본문 p.152

1 (D) 2 (A)

1-2

Jillian Coles [11:19]
다음 주에 동료를 위해 은퇴 기념 파티를 열어주려고 해.

Brian McGrady [11:22]
그럼, 행사를 하기 전에 초대장을 주문해야겠네.

Jillian Coles [11:23]
네가 좋은 인쇄 회사를 추천해 줄 수 있다고 들었어.

Brian McGrady [11:28]
응. 동료 중 한 명이 최근에 사표를 제출했거든. 그래서 같은 일을 해 본 적이 있어.

Brian McGrady [11:29]
내가 초대장을 주문한 회사는 다양한 초대장 종류를 제공하고 있어. 네가 할 일은 단지 선택 페이지에서 버튼을 클릭하는 것이야.

Jillian Coles [11:30]
난 카드에 그의 사진을 붙이는 것처럼 기억에 남는 무언가를 하고 싶어.

Brian McGrady [11:31]
안타깝게도 그렇게는 못 할 거야. 그 회사는 웹 사이트에 있는 디자인만 출력할 수 있어.

어휘 host a party 파티를 주최하다 turn in 제출하다 resignation 사직, 사직서 a variety of 다양한 memorable 기억에 남을 만한

1

해석 Coles 씨에 대해 알 수 있는 것은 무엇인가?
(A) 동료를 위해 파티를 열었다.
(B) 퇴직을 할 것이다.
(C) 현재 인쇄 회사에서 일하고 있다.
(D) 초대장에 사진을 넣고 싶어 한다.

해설 11시 30분 내용에서 사진을 넣고 싶어 한다는 것을 알 수 있다. 따라서 정답은 (D)이다. 파티를 아직 열지 않았으므로 (A)는 오답이다.

2

해석 11시 31분에 McGrady 씨가 "안타깝게도 그렇게는 못 할 거야"라고 쓸 때 그 의도는 무엇인가?
(A) 이 인쇄 회사에서 주문 제작 카드를 만들 수 없다.
(B) 은퇴 기념 행사가 다른 일정으로 인해 열리지 않을 것이다.
(C) 웹 사이트가 점검 중이다.
(D) 인쇄 회사가 폐업했기 때문에 주문을 할 수 없다.

해설 가장 마지막에 웹 사이트에서 제공하는 것만 출력할 수 있기 때문에 사진을 넣거나 하는 식의 주문 제작 카드는 만들 수 없다는 것을 의미한다. 따라서 (A)가 정답이다.

DAY 15 삼중 지문

○ 비법 적용 연습 본문 p.154

| 1 (B) | 2 (B) | 3 (C) | 4 (C) | 5 (A) |
| 6 (C) | 7 (B) | 8 (C) | 9 (A) | 10 (C) |

1-5

Jessica's Catering Service

Jessica's Catering Service는 샌프란시스코 롬바드, 잭슨빌, 디비사데로에서 최고의 케이터링 서비스를 제공합니다. 비즈니스 모임, 개인, 기업 행사, 생일, 결혼, 기념 행사와 같은 다양한 이벤트를 완벽하게 준비할 수 있도록 도와 드립니다. 만약에 귀하께서 이런 행사를 개최하신다면 진정으로 기억에 남고 특별한 행사가 될 수 있도록 4개의 공간이 준비되어 있습니다. 저희의 최고 이벤트 코디네이터가 여러분의 니즈에 딱 맞는 독특한 식사 경험을 하실 수 있도록 도와 드릴 것입니다. 더 많은 정보를 원하시거나 질문이 있으시면 언제든지 724-266-8001 또는 이메일 events@jessicas_cateringservice.com으로 연락 주시기 바랍니다. 최소 2주 전에 미리 예약을 하시기를 권합니다.

Jessica's Catering Service에 오신 것을 환영합니다.

샌프란시스코 Jessica's Special Room을 선택해 주셔서 감사합니다. Jessica's는 다양한 행사 요구를 만족시키고 있습니다. 또한 저희는 완벽한 고객 맞춤형 케이터링 메뉴를 제공하고 있습니다. 4개의 방 종류를 선택하실 수 있습니다: Rockhopper Suite, Gentoo Hall, Emperor Hall, Royal Garden

방	특징	수용 인원
Rockhopper Suite	강당 스타일 평면 스크린 TV 2대, LED 프로젝터 시설 완비	15명
Gentoo Hall	연회장 스타일 바 설치, 스페셜 리넨 제공	40명
Emperor Hall	최신 시청각 시스템 및 조절식 조명	100명
Royal Garden	옥외 파티오에서 이국적인 식사 경험	150명

발신자: shinohara@yakuruwringle.com
수신자: events@jessicas_cateringservice.com
일자: 11월 15일
제목: 정년 퇴임식

Jessica's Catering Service 직원분들께,

제 동료 중 한 분의 정년 퇴임식을 열 계획인데 Jessica's Catering Service를 이용하려고 생각하고 있습니다. 제 동료인 Johansson 씨가 작년 9월에 비즈니스 행사를 개최하기 위해서 귀사의 서비스를 이용했었습니다. Johansson 씨가 직원분들의 서비스에 너무 만족했습니다. 그래서 저에게 강력하게 귀사를 추천해 줬습니다.

행사는 12월 12일에 예정되어 있고 오후 7시에 시작해야 합니다. 대략 80명에서 100명의 사람들이 참석할 것으로 생각하고 있습니다. 기억에 남을 만한 연설을 보여줄 수 있는 대형 모니터와 사운드 시스템이 필요합니다.

만약에 Johansson 씨의 추천으로 할인을 받을 수 있는지 곧바로 알려주시기 바랍니다. 어떻게 진행할지 결정하는 데 도움이 될 것입니다.

Takeuchi Shinohara
크리에이티브 디렉터, Yakuru Wringle

어휘 specialize in ~을 전문으로 하다 premier 최고의 business gathering 비즈니스 모임 corporate 기업의 host 주최하다, 개최하다 sincerely 진정으로, 진심으로 dining 식사 be tailored to ~에 맞춰진 cater for ~의 요구를 만족시키다 function 행사, 기능 fully-customized 완벽한 맞춤형의 be equipped with ~로 갖춰지다 state-of-the-art 최신의 integrated 통합된 audiovisual 시청각의 adjustable 조절할 수 있는 exotic 이국적인, 독특한 open-air 옥외 retirement ceremony 정년 퇴임식 proceed 진행하다

1
해석 광고의 목적은 무엇인가?
(A) 서비스 비용 할인을 알리기 위해
(B) 서비스를 홍보하기 위해
(C) 새로운 종류의 케이터링 서비스를 소개하기 위해
(D) 두 회사의 합병을 알리기 위해

해설 케이터링 업체가 서비스를 홍보하는 글이다. 따라서 정답은 (B)이다.

2
해석 모든 다이닝 룸에 대해 언급된 것은 무엇인가?
(A) 오디오 시스템이 있다.
(B) 다양한 행사를 위해 설계되었다.
(C) 실내에 있다.
(D) 무료 주차 서비스를 제공한다.

해설 방이 총 4개가 나오는데 공통적인 내용이어야 한다. (A), (C)처럼 모든 방을 설명할 수 없는 것은 답이 될 수 없다. 모두 다양한 행사를 할 수 있으므로 정답은 (B)이다.

3
해석 Shinohara 씨의 요구를 가장 충족시키는 방은 무엇인가?
(A) Rockhopper Suite
(B) Gentoo Hall
(C) Emperor Hall
(D) Royal Garden

해설 연계 지문 문제이다. 대략 80명에서 100명의 인원이 참석할 것이고 대형 모니터와 사운드 시스템이 필요하다고 했다. 따라서 수용 인원이 100명이며 audiovisual system이 있는 (C)가 가장 적합하다.

4
해석 Johansson 씨에 대해 언급된 것은 무엇인가?
(A) 매달 행사를 개최한다.
(B) Jessica's Catering Service에서 일한다.
(C) 케이터링 서비스를 이용했다.
(D) 직장 동료가 작년에 은퇴했다.

해설 Johansson 씨가 케이터링 업체를 이용하고 너무 만족스러워서 소개를 해 준 내용이 나온다. 이를 통해 서비스를 이용했다는 (C)가 정답임을 알 수 있다.

5
해석 Shinohara 씨가 요청한 것은 무엇인가?
(A) 방 요금 협상
(B) 텔레비전 추가
(C) 시간 연장
(D) 특별 메뉴

해설 이메일 마지막 부분에서 소개를 통해 '할인'을 받을 수 있는지 알려 달라고 했다. 따라서 정답은 (A)이다.

6-10

http://www.microearbuds.com

MICRO EARBUDS 시리즈 출시!

無케이블. 無와이어. 無방해.

더 나은 사운드는 이제 시작일 뿐입니다. 우리의 목표는 새로운 프리미엄 이어폰, 헤드폰, 스피커 제품군을 만들어서 고객들이 불편함 없이 더 긴 시간 동안 음악을 즐길 수 있도록 도와 드리는 것입니다. 10년 이상의 연구를 통해 놀라울 정도로 정교하고 훌륭한 사운드를 얻게 되었습니다.

오늘 주문하시면 무료 배송 혜택을 드립니다!

MICRO EARBUDS 무선 헤드폰 재고 있음 279.95달러 배송 가능: 영업일 1~3일	MICRO EARBUDS 무선 이어폰 재고 있음 147.95달러 배송 가능: 영업일 5~7일
MICRO EARBUDS 무선 스피커 재고 없음 200.00달러 배송 불가	MICRO EARBUDS 노이즈 캔슬링 헤드폰 재고 있음 300.00달러 배송 가능: 영업일 1~3일

http://www.microearbuds.com

| 홈 | 특징 | 제품 | FAQs | 리뷰 |

모든 무선 헤드폰에서 최고의 제품입니다.
수개월 동안 무선 헤드폰 여러 제품을 찾아봤습니다. 완벽한 무선을 위한 끝도 없는 검색을 한 후 Micro Earbuds 무선 헤드폰이 제가 바로 찾던 그 제품이었습니다. 이 제품은 아무런 주변 소음의 방해 없이 음악을 듣기 원하는 사람들에게 추천합니다. 음질은 놀라울 정도로 훌륭했고 웹 사이트에 기술되었던 것과 정확하게 일치합니다. 사실 시장에 출시된 다른 동일 제품군과 비교했을 때는 가격이 다소 비쌉니다. 하지만 이 무선 헤드폰은 가격을 지불할 만한 가치가 있습니다. 광고된 대로 배터리는 10시간 이상 지속됐습니다. 헤드폰이 정말로 녹음되었던 소리 그대로 전달해 줍니다.

발신자: Jenny Brown <jennybrown@smail.com>
수신자: 고객 서비스 <customerservice@microearbuds.com>
제목: 지점 위치 문의
일자: 9월 15일 화요일

최근에 제 딸 생일 선물로 MICRO EARBUDS 무선 헤드폰을 구매했습니다. 딸이 참 좋아했어요. 이 헤드폰으로 음악을 듣고 나서 제 딸이 다른 종류의 제품 구입에 관심을 가지게 되었어요. MICRO EARBUDS에서 출시한 노이즈 캔슬링 헤드폰을 고려하고 있어요. 하지만 MICRO EARBUDS 제품은 저희들이 직접 체험해 볼 수 있는 상점을 찾기가 매우 어려워요. 홈페이지에서 제가 있는 위치에서 가장 가까운 지점을 찾으려고 해도 어떠한 정보도 얻을 수 없었어요. 어디에서 찾을 수 있는지 알려 주세요.

Jenny

어휘 release 발매하다 distraction 방해 segment 단편, 조각, 부분 extended 확장된 discomfort 불편함 in stock 재고 있음 out of stock 재고 없음 remarkably 놀라울 정도로 firsthand 직접

6
해설 웹 사이트에서 구매할 수 없는 제품은 무엇인가?
(A) MICRO EARBUDS 무선 헤드폰
(B) MICRO EARBUDS 무선 이어폰
(C) MICRO EARBUDS 무선 스피커
(D) MICRO EARBUDS 노이즈 캔슬링 헤드폰

해설 무선 스피커를 제외하고는 모두 In stock이라고 명시되어 있다. 따라서 Out of stock이라고 명시된 (C)가 정답이다.

7
해설 온라인 리뷰에서 리뷰어가 제품을 추천하는 이유는 무엇인가?
(A) 적절한 가격 때문에
(B) 성능 때문에
(C) 배송 정책 때문에
(D) 디자인 때문에

해설 리뷰에서 제품에 대해 가장 강조한 것은 음질이었다. 따라서 정답은 (B)이다. 가격은 다소 비싸다고 했으므로 (A)는 오답이다.

8
해설 이메일에 따르면 생일 선물은 얼마인가?
(A) 147.95달러
(B) 200.00달러
(C) 279.95달러
(D) 300.00달러

해설 연계 지문 문제이다. 딸의 생일 선물로 무선 헤드폰을 샀기 때문에 정답은 (C)이다.

9
해설 Brown 씨가 고객 서비스 센터에 요청한 것은 무엇인가?
(A) 위치 확인
(B) 배송 방법 변경
(C) 웹 사이트 제품 업데이트
(D) 제품 반송

해설 이메일 제일 마지막 줄에서 정답을 찾을 수 있다. 직접 체험해 보고 구입하고 싶은데 상점 위치를 찾을 수 없다는 내용과 위치를 알려 달라고 하는 내용이 나온다. 따라서 정답은 (A)이다.

10
해설 이메일 두 번째 문단 두 번째 줄 "직접"이라는 뜻과 가장 유사한 단어는?
(A) 합리적으로
(B) 부응해서
(C) 직접
(D) 거의

해설 firsthand는 directly와 동일한 표현이다. '직접'이라는 뜻으로, 이 뜻을 모른다고 해도 글에서 experience라는 표현을 사용해서 상점에 가서 경험해 보겠다는 힌트가 있으므로 의미를 알 수 있다. 따라서 정답은 (C)이다.

DAY 16 독해 유형 연습 1

비법 적용 연습 본문 p.158

| 1 (D) | 2 (A) | 3 (B) | 4 (D) | 5 (D) |
| 6 (D) | 7 (C) | 8 (A) | | |

1-3

West Coast Home Opportunities 신용 조합

저희는 집을 구입하는 것뿐만 아니라 사람들이 자신의 집에서 거주할 수 있도록 돕는 일을 합니다.

저희는 대출 산업과 대출자 사이의 대출 방식의 변화를 선도해 왔습니다. 어려움에 처한 고객들을 위해 저희는 63만 명의 대출자들이 자신의 집을 지킬 수 있도록 1,000억 달러 이상을 담보 대출로 변경하여 제공하고 있습니다.

집을 구매하실 준비가 되신 고객을 위해서 저희는 그분들이 성공적인 주택 보유자가 될 수 있도록 확실히 대출을 받을 수 있게 조치를 취하고 있습니다. 또 우리는 채무자의 책임감으로 대출을 해 줄 것입니다. 즉, 숨겨진 비용이나, 당황스러운 상황이 없고, 모든 대출자가 대출금을 갚을 능력이 있다는 것을 완전하게 확신합니다.

보시다시피, 우리는 고객에게 집을 구매하도록 하는 것만큼 많이 고객이 집을 계속 보유할 수 있도록 신경을 씁니다. 고객들이 원하는 것을 얻지 못한다면, 저희도 실패하는 것입니다.

저희는 항상 사람들이 자기에게 맞는 방식으로 집을 구매할 수 있도록 재정적으로 사람들을 도왔던 것처럼 오늘도 준비가 되어 있습니다. 준비가 되셨다면, 1-888-995-6745번으로 전화하세요.

어휘 take the lead 선두에 서다, 솔선수범하다 lending 대출, 대여 in need 어려움에 처한, 궁핍한 modify 변경하다, 수정하다 mortgage 담보 대출, 주택 담보 대출 keep up 계속 유지하다 take steps 조치를 취하다 enable ~을 할 수 있게 하다 confidence 자신(감), 확신 finance 대출하다, ~에 자금을 공급하다 subsidizer 보조금 지급자 foreclosure 압류, 담보권 행사

1
해석 이 회사의 종류는 무엇인가?
(A) 부동산 회사
(B) 정부가 후원하는 주택 보조금 지급자
(C) 담보 대출 압류 회사
(D) 은행

해설 회사의 종류를 묻는 문제로 이 글은 일종의 광고라고 할 수 있다. "we're offering to modify over 100 billion dollars in mortgages to help keep up to 630,000 borrowers in their homes", "to make sure people are getting loans that enable them to be successful homeowners", "to help people finance their homes in ways that are right for them" 등을 통해 집 구매 후에도 대출자가 자신의 능력으로 대출금을 계속 지불할 수 있도록 적절한 대출을 해 주는 곳임을 알 수 있다. 주택 담보 대출을 해 주는 곳은 은행이다. 보조금을 지급해 준다는 내용은 없다.

2
해석 이 회사에 대해 언급된 것은 무엇인가?
(A) 사람들이 집을 소유하기를 원한다.
(B) 작은 매장 주인들에게 인기가 있다.
(C) 대출을 갚을 수 있는 사람들을 선호한다.
(D) 천억 달러를 잠재적인 주택 구매자들에게 대출한다.

해설 글 전체에서 회사가 고객이 집을 구매하고 보유할 수 있게 도와주는 역할을 한다고 말하고 있으므로 (A) "회사는 사람들이 집을 소유하기를 원한다"가 정답이다. 주택 담보는 집을 살 것 같은 사람이 아니라 집을 사는 사람들에게 대출을 해 주는 제도이다.

3
해석 정보에 따르면, 왜 West Coast Opportunities는 대출 산업이 바뀌길 원하는가?
(A) 좀 더 많은 돈을 사람들에게 빌려 주고 싶어서
(B) 사람들이 성공적 주택 보유자가 되는 것을 원해서
(C) 가장 큰 대출 회사가 될 원해서
(D) 어떤 놀랄 만한 일이 생기는 것을 원하지 않아서

해설 세부 사항 문제이다. 문제의 "want to change the lending industry" 부분은 지문의 "lead to change how the lending industry works"에서 찾을 수 있고, 문제는 변화를 이끌어 가는 이유를 묻고 있다. 지문 중간 부분의 "people are getting loans that enable them to be successful homeowners"에서 집을 구매하고자 하는 사람들이 성공적인 주택 보유자가 될 수 있도록 적절한 대출을 받게 해 주고 싶어서가 그 이유임을 알 수 있다.

4-8

행사 세부 사항
힐링의 여정에 있는 여성들을 지원하는 지역의 음악가들

뮤즈 축제가 무엇인가요? 뮤즈 축제는 지역의 재능있는 여성 음악가를 축하하는 신 나는 밤입니다. 작년 여성 센터의 프로그램을 지원하기 위해서 저희는 만 달러 이상을 모금했습니다.

여성 센터는 지원 단체나 상담 서비스 동료를 위한 서비스 및 취업을 하거나 취업 상태를 유지를 위한 도움을 제공합니다. 작년 한 해 307명의 여성이 저희 문을 두드렸고 3,273건의 지역 여성의 정보나 지원 또는 소개 요청 전화를 받았습니다. 저희 서비스의 긍정적인 영향은 고객들로부터의 반응에서 보입니다.
"여성 센터는 저의 안식처입니다. 당신은 두 팔 벌려 제 모습 있는 그대로를 받아주셨습니다. 제가 제 스스로를 믿지 못할 때, 절 믿어주셨습니다. 하시는 일 지속적으로 부탁드리고요, 절대 멈추지 말아 주세요."

200명 이상이 작년에 저희 뮤즈 페스트에 참여해 주셨고, 우리 공동체의 멋진 재능에 놀랐습니다. DJ Donna Lovejoy, Marra Koren, Lori Yates & Buckshot Bebee, Melissa Marchese (Weekend Riot Club) 그리고 Gillian Nicola가 올해 참여하는 음악가들입니다. 그리고 이들은 공연하게 되어 매우 들뜬 상태입니다. 이 행사는 11월 7일 금요일 East King Street 95번가에 위치해 있는 Braddocks Arts Theatre에서 열릴 것입니다.

질문이나 문의 사항이 있으시면, develop@intervalhousehamilton.org로 Annie Horton에게 연락 주시기 바랍니다.
뮤즈 축제에 대한 질문이 있으신가요? Hamilton 여성 센터로 연락 주시기 바랍니다.

어휘 journey 여정 celebrate 축하하는 talented 재능이 있는 raise 모금하다 peer 동료 assistance 도움, 원조 maintain 유지하다 employment 고용 referral 위탁 invariably 변함없이 reflect 반영하다 haven 안식처 inaugural 첫 wow 열광시키다 perform 공연하다 venue 행사 장소

4
해석 행사에 대해 주로 언급된 것은 무엇인가?
(A) 학대 속에서 살아남은 사람들이 여는 콘서트이다.
(B) 자선의 목적으로 하는 것이다.
(C) 시민의 안전을 홍보한다.
(D) 청중들을 치료하는 힘이 있다.

해설 Local artisans and musicians supporting women in their healing journey 부분에서 여성의 힐링을 위한 행사라는 것을 알 수 있다. 공연자로 참여하는 사람들의 목적을 나타내는 부분으로서 이 행사의 내용을 설명해 주고 있다. (A) 학대 받는 사람들이 공연하는 것이 아니며, 재능 있는 여성 음악가를 지원하는 데 목적이 있으므로 (B)도 오답이고, (C)는 언급된 내용이 아니다.

5
해석 누가 이 행사에서 공연할 예정인가?
(A) 전국 각지에서 온 예술가와 음악가
(B) 록밴드
(C) 국제적으로 유명한 여성 가수
(D) 그 지역 출신의 탤런트

해설 글의 초반에 공연자로 참여하는 사람들 앞에 local이라는 수식어가 붙은 내용을 바탕으로 그 지역의 사람들이라는 것을 알 수 있다. 따라서 정답은 (D)가 된다.

6

해석 여성 센터가 하지 않는 일은 무엇인가?
(A) 상담 서비스 제공한다.
(B) 지원 단체를 후원한다.
(C) 여성 고용 확보에 도움을 준다.
(D) 여성에게 쉼터를 제공한다.

해설 지문의 중반에서 여성 단체에서 하는 일을 나열해 놓았다. 하지만 (D)의 경우 이용자들의 피드백이 나온 부분에서 haven(안식처)이라고 이야기한 부분을 이용한 오답 선택지가 된다. 따라서 정답은 (D)가 된다.

7

해석 이 페스티벌은 전에 몇 번이나 개최됐는가?
(A) 매년
(B) 두 번
(C) 한 번
(D) 없음

해설 글의 후반부에서 Over 200 hundred people attended our inaugural Muse Fest last year라고 이야기하고 있다. 작년에 첫 회가 열렸다는 것을 알 수 있으므로 정답은 (C)이다.

8

해석 추가적인 정보를 위해 누구에게 연락해야 하는가?
(A) Horton 씨
(B) Koren 씨
(C) Yates 씨
(D) Nicola 씨

해설 글의 후반부 For any questions or inquiries please contact Annie Horton에서 정답의 힌트를 찾을 수 있다. 따라서 정답은 (A)이다.

DAY 17 독해 유형 연습 2

○ 비법 적용 연습 본문 p.161

| 1 (D) | 2 (B) | 3 (C) | 4 (B) | 5 (D) |

1-3

Choy's Chinese Chow

바쁜 스케줄 속에서 사시나요? 식사를 준비할 시간이 없으신가요? 요리하는 것이나 겨우 한 끼를 해결하기 위해 슈퍼마켓의 긴 줄에 서서 기다리는 것에 지치셨나요?

San Francisco에서 가장 큰 동양 요리 음식점인 Choy's Chinese Chow는 당신의 사무실이나 학교, 기숙사, 가정집도 가리지 않고 바로 문 앞까지 무료로 배달하고 있습니다.

Bay 지역에서 40년 이상 운영 중인 저희 식당은 일주일 내내 밤과 낮을 가리지 않고 배달을 해 드립니다.

당신의 주문 양과 사시는 지역에 따라 배달 소요 시간은 다를 수 있다는 것을 알아 두십시오. 배달 서비스를 이용하기 위해서는 최소 3가지 이상의 음식을 주문하셔야 합니다.

메뉴에 대한 더 자세한 특별한 요청 사항이 있으시면, 무료 전화인 1-800-976-CHOW로 연락 주세요.

어휘 oriental 동양의 free delivery 무료 배달 doorstep 현관 dormitory 기숙사 deliver 배달하다 note ~에 주목하다, 주의하다 depend on ~에 달려 있다 avail of ~을 이용하다 reside 살다 preparation 준비 distance 거리 accommodate 수용하다

1

해석 이 광고는 누구를 대상으로 하는가?
(A) 파티를 계획 중인 고객들
(B) 먼 거리에 거주하는 사람들
(C) 직장인들
(D) 바쁜 사람들

해설 세부 사항 문제이다. For whom으로 시작되는 문제는 이 글의 독자를 묻는 문제가 많다. 여기서도 초반에 "Having a tight schedule? No time to prepare your meals?"를 보고 정답을 추론할 수 있다. 식사를 직접 해서 먹기에 부담이 되는 (D) 바쁜 사람들이 정답이다.

2

해석 Choy's의 특징이 아닌 것은?
(A) 24시간 배달
(B) 온라인 주문
(C) 식사 준비
(D) 전화 주문

해설 간단한 NOT 문제이다. (A)는 "we can deliver day or night"을 읽고 알 수 있는 내용이고, (C)는 식사를 직접 만들어 먹기 귀찮은 사람들에게 식사를 제공해 주는 것이므로 오답이며 (D)는 "For more information about our menu and special requests, call toll free 1-800-976-CHOW"를 읽고 오답인 것을 알 수 있다.

3
해석 Choy's Chinese Chow에 대해 말하고 있는 것은?
(A) San Francisco에 새 지점을 열었다.
(B) 음식을 30분 이내로 배달한다.
(C) 배달 시간은 거리와 양에 달려 있다.
(D) 특별 요구 사항은 받지 않는다.

해설 문제에 say 혹은 mention이 등장하면 언급된 세부 사항을 묻는 문제이다. 지문에 잘 패러프레이징되어 있는 선택지를 찾아야 한다. (C) "배달 시간은 주문의 거리와 양에 달려 있다."가 지문의 "actual delivery time may vary depending on the size of your order or the location of your address" 부분과 같은 의미이다.

5
해석 Gasik 씨에 대해 나타나 있는 것은 무엇인가?
(A) 7월 12일에 물건을 받았다.
(B) Big Green World의 단골 고객이다.
(C) 물건의 반품을 원한다.
(D) 빠른 배송을 받기 위해 돈을 결제했다.

해설 영수증의 후반쯤 "express shipping(overnight delivery)"라는 문구를 볼 수 있다. 또한 지불 상태를 나타내는 부분에서 이미 결제가 이루어졌다는 것을 알려 주고 있으므로 정답은 (D)가 되며 단골 인지는 알 수 없고, 가장 매력적인 오답인 (A)의 경우 배송을 한 날짜이지 도착한 날짜가 아니다. overnight delivery가 되었으므로 물건을 받은 날짜는 배송한 다음 날인 7월 13일이 된다.

4-7

Big Green World
158 Huánuco St
Uluru NSW 5445
문학 및 교육 자료 온라인 판매점

고객: Hannah Gasik
배송지 주소: 53 Stingray Street, Cucamonga CA 5609
주문 번호: 11245 (7월 9일 오전 9시 43분에 주문)

수량	품목	가격
1	〈Dog Days: Angel Lassick의 단편 컬렉션〉	22달러
1	〈피아노 기초: Glenda Owynne-Johnson〉	31달러
1	〈야구의 기술과 훈련: 미국 야구 코치 협회〉	20달러
	중간 합계 금액	53달러
	세금	5.3달러
	특급 우편 (익일 배송)	7달러
	주문 총액	85.30달러
	지불 상태	(결제 완료)

배송 일자: 7월 12일 오후 3시 45분

저희 회사를 이용해 주셔서 감사합니다. 귀하는 사용하지 않은 물건을 30일 이내에 반품이 가능하며, 반품 시 영수증 원본이나 구매 증명을 포함시켜 주시기 바랍니다. 반품 규정에 대한 자세한 정보는 저희 웹 사이트 www.biggrennworld.com.au/returns를 참고해 주시기 바랍니다.

어휘 literary 문학의 educational 교육적인 shipping 배송 quantity 수량 subtotal 중간 합계 express shipping 빠른 배송 payment 지불 original receipt 원본 영수증 proof 증명 policy 정책 musical instrument 악기 regular customer 단골 고객

4
해석 Big Green World는 어떤 종류의 물건을 판매하는가?
(A) 애완동물 용품
(B) 경영 관련 교재
(C) 악기
(D) 운동 용품

해설 무엇을 판매하는 회사인지 묻고 있다. 영수증의 초반을 보면 "Online dealer of literary or educational materials"라고 어떤 회사인지를 밝히고 있으며, 이후 구매 항목은 모두 책 제목이다. Big Green World는 책을 파는 서점이므로 경영 관련 교재를 팔 것임을 알 수 있다.

DAY 18 독해 유형 연습 3

○ 비법 적용 연습 본문 p.163

1 (B)	2 (A)	3 (B)	4 (A)	5 (D)
6 (D)	7 (B)			

1-3

Chula Vista 신용 협동조합
Quick n' Eazy 자동차 대출

Chula Vista 신용 협동조합의 'Quick n' Eazy' 자동차 대출과 함께 하시면 당신의 생애 첫 자동차 소유가 쉬워집니다. 이번 겨울, 버스를 기다리면서 왜 추위에 떨어야 하나요? 바로 이것이 우리가 첫 구매자 프로그램을 통해 당신에게 꿈의 자동차를 소유할 수 있는 기회를 드리는 이유입니다.

저희는 새 차 구매를 위해 세워 놓은 당신의 예산에 맞출 수 있는, 일 년에 이자를 최하 3.95%까지 내려 드릴 수 있는 대출 상품이 있습니다. 계약금은 필요하지 않습니다. 이 상품은 7년 미만의 중고차를 위한 대출로도 이용 가능합니다.

차를 소유하기 위해서, 당신이 해야 할 것은 딱 세 가지 쉬운 단계를 거치는 것입니다. 첫 번째, 저희의 웹 사이트를 방문하시어, 대출 아이콘을 누르시고, 대출 신청 서류를 내려 받으세요. 이 서류를 작성해서 제출하세요. 다음, 대출 승인과 신용 조사 결과를 위해 3일을 기다려 주세요. 그리고 마지막으로 저희의 신용 조사관들에 의해 당신의 대출이 승인되면, 대리점에 가서서 당신 취향의 자동차를 요구하시면 됩니다.

또한 도시 곳곳에 있는 저희 지점 어디라도 개인적으로 방문하실 수 있고, 당신을 도울 수 있는 저희 직원과 함께 서류를 작성하실 수 있습니다.

*이 행사는 12월 20일까지만 유효합니다.
*이율은 당신의 현재 신용 등급에 따라 달라질 수 있습니다.

어휘 down payment 착수금, 계약금 avail 도움이 되다 used car 중고차 application 지원서 application form 지원서 fill out 기입하다 approval 승인 credit 신용 investigation 조사 dealership 대리점 claim 주장하다 suit 어울리다, 적합하다 citywide 전 도시의 interest rate 이율 vary 다양하다 based on ~에 근거하여 standing 지위, 평판, 순위표 borrower 대출자 open an account 계좌를 개설하다 credit assessment 신용 평가

1

해석 이자율에 대한 사실은 무엇인가?
(A) 3% 미만으로 떨어질 수 있다.
(B) 대출의 신용 기록에 따라 결정된다.
(C) 국가 경제에 따라 증가할 수 있다.
(D) 다른 은행들보다 높다.

해설 우선 지문에서 키워드인 "interest rates"를 찾아야 한다. "Interest rates may vary based on your current credit standings."에서 이율이 고객의 현재 신용 등급에 따라서 달라질 수 있다고 했으므로 (B)가 정답이다.

2

해설 광고에 따르면, 대출자로부터 요구되지 않는 것은 무엇인가?
(A) 그들의 지점 중 한 곳에서 계좌 개설하기
(B) 양식 완성하기
(C) 웹 사이트 방문하기
(D) 신용 평가 대기하기

해설 문제에서 세 가지 단계를 말하고 있는 부분을 찾으면 된다. (C) Visiting a Web site는 "First, visit our Web site"에, (B) Completing a form은 "Fill this out and submit it"에, (D) Waiting for a credit assessment는 "wait three days for the loan approval and credit investigation results"에 나타나 있으므로 요구되지 않은 것은 (A)이다.

3

해석 프로모션에 대해 얘기하고 있는 것은?
(A) 계약금이 필요하다.
(B) 시간 제한이 있다.
(C) 모든 지점에서 가능한 것이 아니다.
(D) 자동차 대리점에서 신청할 수 있다.

해설 세부 사항 문제이다. 키워드는 promotion이다. "This promotion is good until December 20 only"라고 하면서 시간적 제한이 있음을 말하고 있다. "No down payment is required."에서 (A)가 오답임을, "at any of our branches citywide"에서 (C)가 오답임을 확인할 수 있다. dealership에서는 자동차를 구매하는 것이지 자동차 대출을 해 주는 것은 아니므로 (D)도 오답이다.

4-7

Double Wishbone 출판사
125 Bath Road, Trafalgar, London N1 ORW

Olga Kuzminski
453 Merrion Square, Dublin, Ireland

Kuzminski 씨께

지난주에 저희와 상의하기 위해 시간을 내어 London에 와 주신 것에 대해 정말 감사드립니다. 당신에게 칼럼 편집자 자리를 제안할 수 있어서 기쁩니다. 당신의 경력과 지식이 우리에게 큰 자산이 될 것이라 확신합니다. 당신의 추천서도 매우 인상적이었습니다. 인사 담당자와 회의 끝에, 우리는 당신에게 아래의 고용 관련 혜택을 제공하기로 결정했습니다.

봉급: 연봉 4만 2천 파운드
혜택: 이주 지원 비용 6천 파운드, 2주간 유급 휴가, 퇴직금
보너스: 1천 파운드부터 5천 파운드까지 성과에 따른 연 2회의 보너스

당신이 필요한 실질적인 정보와 세부 사항을 포함한 계약서가 이 편지에 포함되어 있습니다. 추가적인 정보가 필요하시면, annhath@doublewishpub.co.uk로 이메일을 보내 주세요.

첨부된 계약서를 읽으시고 동의하시면, 표시된 모든 곳에 서명하시고 저에게 메일로 보내 주세요. 나중에 참고하실 수 있도록 본인 보관용 사본을 만들어 두세요. 우리는 계약서를 받은 후, 당신의 일주일 교육 일정을 잡을 것입니다.

정말 감사하고, 장차 당신과 함께 일하게 되기를 기대합니다.

Ann Hathaway
편집장, Double Wishbone 출판사

어휘 gratitude 감사 take the time 시간을 내다 confer with ~와 상의하다 certain 확실한 impressed 감명 받은, 인상 깊게 생각하는 reference 추천서 Human Resources Chief 인사 관리 부장 relocation 이주, 이전 allowance 비용 paid holiday 유급 휴가 retirement 은퇴 annual 일 년의 contract 계약, 계약서 indicated 표시된 impressed with ~에 감명 받은 fill a position 자리를 채우다 expense 비용 paid vacation 유급 휴가 yearly 연간의 supplemental 추가의 allowance 허가; 비용, 수당

4

해석 Hathaway 씨는 Kuzminski 씨에게 왜 편지를 썼는가?
(A) 그녀에게 고용 조건을 알려 주기 위해
(B) 그녀에게 자신이 그녀의 추천서에 깊은 인상을 받았다는 것을 말하기 위해
(C) 자리를 채우기 위해
(D) 추가 정보를 요청하기 위해

해설 주제 문제이다. "Why ~ write" 역시 편지의 목적을 묻는 문제로 초반의 "We are very glad to offer you the position of column editor"에서 같이 일하자는 제안을 하고 있고 "we have decided to offer you the following employment package"에서 제공되는 채용 혜택을 알려 주고 있으므로 (A)가 정답이다.

5

해석 계약서 내용에 포함되지 않은 것은?
(A) 이사 비용
(B) 반 달 유급 휴가
(C) 연간 두 번의 보너스
(D) 보충 교육

해설 간단한 NOT 문제이다. "to offer you the following employment package:" 아래에 제공하는 계약 관련 내용이 나온다. (A)는 "relocation allowance of £6,000에서, (B)는 "Two weeks paid holiday"에서, (C)는 "Two annual bonuses"에서 찾을 수 있다.

6

해석 Kuzminski 씨가 편지를 읽은 후에 할 행동은 무엇인가?
(A) 즉시 비행기를 타고 아일랜드에 간다.
(B) 추가 정보를 제공하기 위해 런던으로 간다.
(C) 그녀의 허가를 기다린다.
(D) 서류를 몇 개 보낸다.

해설 글을 읽고 난 후에는 편지를 쓴 사람이 요청한 대로 하게 되는 것이 대부분이므로 편지에서 요청한 사항(ask, request, demand, recommend)을 그대로 답으로 고른다. "Once you have read and agreed to the attached contract, please sign it on all the indicated areas and mail it to me."에서 정답을 찾을 수 있다. 필요한 서류를 보내라고 했으므로 (D)가 정답이다.

7
해석 Hathaway 씨는 누구이겠는가?
(A) 런던의 직업소개소 직원
(B) 회사의 부서 책임자
(C) 출판사의 소유주
(D) 인사 담당자

해설 세부 사항 문제로 키워드는 "Ms. Hathaway"이다. 이 사람의 이름이 편지 맨 아래에 언급되어 있으므로 Ms. Hathaway는 편지를 쓴 사람이고, 그 아래에 있는 것이 이 사람의 직책이다. "Chief Copy editor"라고 되어 있으므로 chief를 보고 head로 패러프레이징한 것을 고른다.

DAY 19 독해 유형 연습 4

○ 비법 적용 연습   본문 p.167

| 1 (D) | 2 (C) | 3 (C) | 4 (A) |

1-2

2014년 4월 29일

Siva 씨께,

환영합니다! Woculus에 보내 주신 당신의 지원서가 합격하였습니다. 우리는 우리의 편집자의 한 명으로 당신을 고용하게 되어 기쁩니다.

제가 지난번에 말씀드린 것처럼, Woculus의 비전은 사업가와 마케터, 영업 사원들이 자신들의 사업을 위해서 첨단 기술을 유용하게 사용할 수 있는 방법을 한 곳에서 다 배울 수 있는 통합 사이트가 되는 것입니다.

우리 웹 사이트의 게시물들은 조사가 잘 되어 있고, 실용적이며, 양도 많습니다. 인터넷 상에서 전도유망한 블로그로서 우리는 우리의 독자들에게 최고 수준의 게시물을 제공하고자 꾸준히 노력할 것입니다. 만약 인터넷 상에 우리가 관심을 가지고 있는 어떤 분야라도 더 좋은 자료가 있다면, 우리는 우리의 일을 잘 못하고 있는 것입니다.

아래에 당신의 로그인 정보들이 있습니다.:
아이디: Don Siva
비밀번호: siVA2013

전 Woculus 팀은 당신과 매우 전문적인 업무 관계를 기대하고 있습니다. 그리고 우리의 독자들에게 더 나은 서비스를 제공할 수 있도록 가능한 한 모든 방식으로 당신을 도울 준비가 되어 있습니다.

Donald Warchowsky
편집장

어휘 application 지원서 approve 인가하다, 승인하다 proud 자랑스러워하는 one-stop 한 군데에서 모든 것을 처리하는 profitably 이익이 되게 practical 현실적인, 실용적인 up and coming 유망한, 진취적인, 활동적인 constantly 변함없이 strive 노력하다, 애쓰다 audience 청중, 관중, 시청자 recruit 모집하다 accept 받아들이다 claim 요구하다 useful 유용한

1
해석 이 편지의 목적은 무엇인가?
(A) 사업을 홍보하기 위해
(B) 편집자를 모집하기 위해
(C) 새로운 사업을 환영하기 위해
(D) 신입 사원을 받아들이기 위해

해설 전형적인 주제 문제는 정답이 초반에 바로 언급된다. "Welcome! Your application to Woculus has been approved. We are proud to have you as one of our editors."라는 부분에서 편집자로서 고용되었다는 사실을 전하고 있으므로 (D)가 정답이다.

2
해석 회사에 대해 언급되지 않은 것은 무엇인가?
(A) 게시물은 잘 조사되어 있다.
(B) 그 분야에서 최고라고 주장한다.
(C) 일을 잘하고 있지 않다.
(D) 블로그는 실용적이고 내용이 풍부하다.

해설 전체 지문 NOT 문제이므로 지문이 길면 선택지를 먼저 훑고 들어가면 편하게 풀 수 있다. (A), (D)는 "Our posts are well-researched, practical and rich."에서 동시에 언급되고 있고, (B)는 "If there is a better post about any of our areas of interest on the Internet, we are not doing our job well"에서 당사보다 더 좋은 웹 사이트가 있다는 것은 일을 제대로 하지 못하고 있다는 뜻이라고 말하고 있으므로 최고의 회사가 되고 싶다고 해석할 수 있다.

3-4

수신: 고객 서비스 부서
Sears 가전제품
Duluth, Michigan

2주 전에 저는 귀사의 봄 카탈로그를 보고 주문했던 동봉된 가지치기용 가위를 받았습니다. 제 친구 중 한 명이 저에게 귀사의 제품이 다른 회사의 제품보다 훨씬 좋고 내구성도 강하다고 말했습니다. 하지만, 제 경우에는 그렇지가 않았습니다. 가지치기용 가위로 하는 일로써는 상대적으로 쉬운 일인 라일락 덤불을 손질하고 있는데 가위의 손잡이가 두 동강이 나버렸습니다. 보증서에는 만족하지 못할 경우, 전액 환불을 받을 수 있다고 적혀 있습니다. 그래서 하자가 있는 가위를 다시 돌려보냅니다. 그리고 운송료를 포함한 제 돈을 환불받기를 원합니다. 가위 영수증과 배송비 영수증을 동봉합니다. 수표와 이 편지에 적힌 제 주소로 수표를 보내 주세요.

Mary White

어휘 receive 받아들이다 enclosed 동봉된 pruning shears 가지치기하는 가위, 전지 가위 durable 내구성이 강한 turn out: ~인 것으로 드러나다, 판명되다 trim 다듬다, 손질하다 relatively 상대적으로 warranty 보증서 indicate 나타내다 entitled to ~할 권리가 있는 full refund 전액 환불 shipping cost 배송비 receipt 영수증 faulty 결함이 있는 request 요청하다 estimate 견적

3
해석 이 편지는 왜 쓰여졌는가?
(A) 제품의 결함을 알리기 위해
(B) 주문을 취소하기 위해
(C) 전액 환불을 받기 위해
(D) 견적을 요청하기 위해

해설 전형적인 불만을 표시하는 글로 글의 목적(대부분 환불이나 교환)은 주로 마지막에 나온다. 여기서도 "I want my money refunded, including my shipping costs"라고 하면서 글의 후반에서 전액 환불을 요청하고 있다.

4

해석 Sears는 편지를 받은 후 무엇을 할 것인가?
(A) 그녀의 돈을 보낸다.
(B) 영수증을 요청한다.
(C) 회사를 방문한다.
(D) 보증서를 취소한다.

해설 "The terms of the warranty indicate that if I am not satisfied, I am entitled to receive a full refund." 부분에서 보증서에 전액 환불을 보장한다고 쓰여 있고, "Please send the check to my home address"에서 고객이 전액 환불을 요청하고 있으므로 회사가 할 일은 환불을 해 주는 일이다.

DAY 20 독해 유형 연습 5

○ 비법 적용 연습   본문 p.169

| 1 (B) | 2 (C) | 3 (D) | 4 (C) | 5 (B) |
| 6 (B) |

1-3

수신: 부서와 구매 담당자
발신: Kent Feldstein
날짜: 1월 7일
제목: 재생지와 관련된 요청
참조: 이 메모를 읽은 후에 다른 사람에게도 전달해 주세요.

저는 우리 부서가 염소가 없는 재생지의 사용을 회사의 규정으로서 채택해야 한다고 요청하기 위해 이 메모를 씁니다. 재생지를 사는 것은 우리 회사가 환경을 보호하고, 친환경적인 물품 조달 방식을 채택하고 있는 많은 세계적인 대기업의 행보에 참여할 수 있는 간단하고 편리한 방법입니다.

우리나라에서는 프린트용이나 필기용으로 만들어지는 종이의 90% 이상이 여전히 새로운 나무로 만들어지고 있습니다. 비 재생지를 재생지로 대체하면 1톤에 17그루의 나무를 살리고, 화학 재료나 천연 자원을 덜 사용하며, 공기와 물의 오염을 줄여줍니다. 품질이 좋은 재생지는 다용도로 사용이 가능합니다. 사실, 재생지는 세계에서 가장 좋은 제지 공장에서 만들어집니다. 재생지는 인쇄기와 복사기, 레이저 프린터, 컴퓨터, 삽입기, 그 외의 다른 사무 장비에 사용하는 데 있어서 비 재생지만큼 경쟁력이 있습니다. 재생지는 비 재생지보다 가격이 훨씬 더 합리적입니다.

어휘 request 요청, 요구 사항 recycled paper 재생지 adopt 채택하다 chlorine-free 염소가 없는 standard 기준 convenient 편리한 procurement 조달, 입수 practice 실행; 행하다, 실천하다 substitute 대신하다, 대체하다 chemical 화학 물질 natural resource 천연 자원 pollution 오염 widely 광범위하게 available 이용 가능한 paper mill 제지 공장 perform 실행하다 competitively 경쟁적으로 printing presses 인쇄기, copier 복사기 equipment 도구, 장비 reasonably 합리적으로 content 내용물 encourage 권고하다 state 말하다, 밝히다 pros and cons 장점과 단점 ecologically 생태학적으로

1

해석 이 편지는 왜 쓰여졌는가?
(A) 직원들에게 재생지를 사용하도록 권장하기 위해
(B) 부서에서 재생지를 사용할 것을 요청하기 위해
(C) 재생지의 장단점을 말하기 위해
(D) 재생지와 비 재생지를 비교하기 위해

해설 주제가 초반에 언급되는 전형적인 주제 문제이다. 초반에 "I am writing to request that our department adopt the use of recycled chlorine-free paper as the standard for our company."를 통해 부서에서 재생지의 사용을 요청하고 글의 후반부에는 재생지의 좋은 점을 나열하여 그 이유를 설명하고 있다.

044

2
해석 메모에 따르면, 비 재생지에 비해 재생지의 이점은 무엇인가?
(A) 더 간단하고 편리하다.
(B) 주요 기업들이 재생지 사용을 선호한다.
(C) 많은 천연자원을 아낀다.
(D) 비 재생지보다 성능이 좋다.

해설 세부 사항 문제로 키워드는 benefit이다. "Every ton of recycled paper substituted for non-recycled paper saves 17 trees, uses fewer chemicals and natural resources, and reduces air and water pollution."에서 재생지가 natural resources를 절약한다는 것을 알 수 있다.

3
해석 글쓴이가 재생용지의 사용에 대해 언급하지 않은 것은 무엇인가?
(A) 회사의 돈을 절약할 수 있게 해 준다.
(B) 환경 친화적이다.
(C) 광범위하게 이용된다.
(D) 더 편리하다.

해설 NOT 문제는 True 문제에 비해 훨씬 간단히 그리고 정확히 풀 수 있다. 왜냐하면 선택지 중 3개는 올바른 내용을 전달하기 때문이다. 따라서 선택지를 먼저 읽고 지문을 보면 바로 지문과 일치하는 선택지를 오답으로 지울 수 있다. (A)는 "Recycled paper is much more reasonably priced than paper without recycled content"에서 (B)는 "Every ton of recycled paper substituted for non-recycled paper saves 17 new trees"에서 (C)는 "Recycled paper performs as competitively as non-recycled sheets in printing presses, copiers, laser printers, computers, inserters, and other office equipment."에서 찾을 수 있으므로 정답은 (D)이다.

4
해석 이 광고의 주 목적은 무엇인가?
(A) 광고 책자에 완제품을 보여주기 위해
(B) 잠재 고객에게 큰 할인을 제공하기 위해
(C) 광고에 출연할 집을 찾기 위해
(D) 고객들에게 무이자 융자에 대해 알리기 위해

해설 "We need clients with homes in your area to "show them off."에서 이 글의 주제인 집을 가지고 있는 고객들을 찾아서 고객의 주방을 새롭게 설치한 후에 그것을 홍보 수단으로 사용하고 한다는 것을 알 수 있다. (C)가 "광고에서 특집으로 다루어질 집을 찾기 위해서"란 뜻으로 주제와 일치한다.

5
해석 마지막 문장에서, 두 번째 문단 세 번째 줄의 단어 '견적서'와 의미가 가장 가까운 것은?
(A) 발언권
(B) 견적
(C) 반복
(D) 언급

해설 "free design and quote" 무료 디자인과 견적서를 얘기하고 있으므로 견적서의 또 다른 단어인 estimate가 정답이다.

6
해석 광고로부터 추론할 수 있는 것은?
(A) 무료 배달이 가능하다.
(B) 고객은 반드시 제품 후기를 제공해야 한다.
(C) 고객의 주방은 TV 광고에 나타날 것이다.
(D) 지불은 크리스마스 전에 이루어져야 한다.

해설 추론(infer) 문제이다. 지문과 선택지를 읽고 가장 적절한 것을 추론해서 풀어야 하지만 대부분 지문과 같은 내용을 패러프레이징한 것이 정답이다. "We may also need your testimonial when completed."에서 새로운 부엌을 설치한 후에 고객 상품평이 필요하다는 것을 알 수 있으므로 (B)가 정답이다.

4-6

모두가 원하는 주방을 전시합니다!
정상가의 70%

Kitchener's Kitchen에는,

다양하고 인상적인 최신식 주방 마감재와 디자인이 있습니다. 저희는 이러한 것들을 귀하의 지역에 자랑할 집을 소유한 고객이 필요합니다. 우리는 주방을 새로 설치하고 제품 책자에 실을 사진을 찍어야 합니다. (이것은 세트를 짓는 것보다 싸고, 실제 집에 있는 주방이 더 보기 좋기 때문입니다.) 우리는 또한 모든 것이 완성되었을 때, 당신의 상품평이 필요합니다.

더불어 무이자 융자가 가능합니다.

서두르십시오. 크리스마스 전에 배달을 받으시려면 지금 주문하세요. 무료 디자인과 견적서를 받아 보시려면 1-800-826-1446(24시간)으로 지금 전화하시거나 www.kitcheners.com을 방문하세요.

어휘 impressive 인상적인 range of 다양한, ~의 범위 client 고객 show off 과시하다 brochure 소책자 install 설치하다 testimonial 추천서, 추천의 글 interest 이자 financing 융자, 대출 delivery 배달 quote 견적서 potential 잠재적인 feature 특징으로 하다, ~을 특집으로 하다 appear on ~에 나타나다 payment 지불

Section 2

1. Part 5·6 유형 연습

DAY 01

본문 p.176

1 (C)	2 (D)	3 (A)	4 (C)	5 (D)
6 (D)	7 (B)	8 (B)	9 (D)	10 (D)
11 (D)	12 (B)	13 (C)	14 (A)	

1
- 해석: 직원들의 근무 시간을 상당히 줄여 줄 수 있는 새로운 소프트웨어가 개발 중이다.
- 해설: 빈칸은 동사 자리이다. that부터 time까지는 형용사절이고 주어(New software)에 맞는 동사가 필요하다. 선택지에서 (C)만이 동사이다.
- 어휘: considerably 상당히

2
- 해석: 지난 주말 Las Vegas의 채용 박람회에 수천 명의 기술 전문가들이 왔었다.
- 해설: '~이 있다(과거 시제는 ~이 있었다)'라는 의미의 표현은 There is/are이고, 뒤에 명사가 나오며 동사의 수 일치는 뒤에 나오는 명사에 맞춘다. 시제는 과거이고 빈칸 뒤에 복수 명사(thousands of technical experts)가 왔으므로 (D)가 정답이다.

3
- 해석: 이 새로운 스마트폰 어플리케이션의 주요 기능은 모든 서류의 양식을 열고 프린트할 수 있는 것이다.
- 해설: 빈칸은 명사 자리이다. 동사가 is이므로 단수 명사인 (A)가 정답이다.
- 어휘: function 기능, 기능하다(작용하다)

4
- 해석: 당신이 구매한 음식의 정확하고 빠른 배달을 위해서, 제공되는 꼬리표에 당신의 주소를 적으세요.
- 해설: To부터 foods까지는 부사구이므로 무시하고, 빈칸부터가 주절이 되는데 동사가 없으므로 빈칸은 동사 자리이다. 문장 앞에 동사가 들어가는 명령문이므로 동사원형인 (C)가 정답이다.
- 어휘: ensure 보장하다 purchase 구매하다

5
- 해석: 일반적인 시청자들의 경향에 대해 집중한 Kacey 씨의 연구와 달리, 나의 연구는 Massachusetts 주 지역의 15세에서 19세 사이의 시청자들의 TV 채널 선택 경향을 더 특별히 다루고 있다.
- 해설: 빈칸은 주어 자리이다. 해석상 주격(I)보다 소유대명사(mine)가 적절하다. 여기서 mine은 my study 대신 쓰였다.
- 어휘: concentrate on 집중하다 tendency 경향, 동향

6
- 해석: 요즘 약간의 운동조차 몸무게를 조절하는 데 도움이 되는 것으로 알려져 있다.
- 해설: 가주어(it)와 진주어(that이 이끄는 명사절) 구문이다. 주어가 너무 긴 경우 가주어 it을 문장 앞에 쓰고 진주어를 문장 끝으로 보낸다.
- 어휘: beneficial 유익한, 이로운

7
- 해석: 첨부된 설문지를 완성해서 가능한 한 빨리 우리 직원에게 제출해 주세요.
- 해설: and(등위접속사) 앞의 문장에 동사가 없으므로 빈칸은 동사 자리이고 주어가 없는 명령문이므로 동사원형을 써야 한다.
- 어휘: questionnaire 설문지

8
- 해석: 표가 매진이 되면, 박스 오피스 정책은 대기자 명단을 만들기를 시작하고 취소가 발생한 경우, 고객들에게 전화하는 것이다.
- 해설: there is/are (~이 있다) 뒤에는 명사가 와야 한다. 선택지에서 (B)만이 명사이다.
- 어휘: patron (특정 상점 등의) 고객, 후원자

9
- 해석: 미지급 금액은 즉시 지불되어야 하며, 그렇지 않으면 우리는 당신의 계좌를 닫고 이용하고 있는 서비스를 중단시켜야 합니다.
- 해설: 조동사(must) 뒤는 동사원형이 온다. 빈칸 뒤에 목적어가 없으므로 수동태 형태가 와야 한다. 따라서 정답은 (D)이다.
- 어휘: outstanding amount 미지급 금액 discontinue 중단하다

10
- 해석: 위원회의 새로운 의장은 아직 정해지지 않았지만, 임명 위원회는 후보자를 세 명으로 줄였다.
- 해설: be동사(been) 뒤에 올 수 있는 동사 형태는 현재분사형(-ing) 아니면 과거분사형(p.p.)이다. 여기서는 타동사(choose)를 써야 하는데 목적어가 없으므로 수동의 be p.p. 형태가 와야 한다.
- 어휘: nomination 지명, 임명 narrow down 좁히다, 줄이다 candidate 후보자

11-14

발신: donotreply@wmusic.com
수신: paulcarter@exmail.com
제목: 확인서, Wire Music
날짜: 9월 10일

친애하는 Carter 씨,

최고의 음악 스트리밍 서비스인 Wire Music을 이용해 주셔서 감사합니다. 이 이메일은 Wire Music에 관한 귀하의 구독에 관한 확인 이메일입니다. 귀하께서는 프리미엄 패키지를 선택하셨습니다. 귀하의 거래는 완료되었고, 지금부터 귀하께서는 매달 무제한 음악 다운로드를 즐기실 수 있습니다. 그리고 또한 뮤직 비디오와 인터뷰도 모든 멤버들에게만 독점적으로 제공합니다. 이 모든 서비스들이 매달 단지 5.99달러입니다. 저희는 매월 5일에 이 금액을 신용 카드에 청구할 것입니다. 만약 귀하께서 서비스를 끝내고 싶으시다면, customersupport@wmusic.com으로 이메일을 통해 구독 종료 요청을 보내 주세요.

Wire Music

어휘 confirmation 확인 transaction 거래 unlimited 무제한의 via ~을 매개로, ~에 의해

11
해설 어휘 문제이다. (A) 지원, (B) 복잡, (C) 취소, (D) 가입, 구독 중에서 앞에서 Wire Music을 이용해 주셔서 감사하다는 내용과 뒤에서 프리미엄 패키지를 선택했다는 내용을 통해 (서비스, 잡지 등의) 가입, 구독을 뜻하는 (D)가 정답임을 알 수 있다.

12
해설 be동사 are 뒤에 보어로 형용사 available이 왔으므로 빈칸은 이 형용사를 수식할 수 있는 부사 자리이다. 따라서 부사 (B)가 정답이다.

13
해설 (A) 이 패키지는 또한 저희의 주간 소식지 구독을 포함합니다.
(B) 불행히도, 이번에는 귀하의 납입금을 처리할 수 없습니다.
(C) 저희는 매월 5일에 이 금액을 신용 카드에 청구할 것입니다.
(D) 귀하께서는 판매 전문가에게 메일을 보냄으로써 저희의 스트리밍 서비스에 등록할 수 있습니다.
해설 바로 앞에서 서비스의 금액에 대해서 언급하고 있으므로 이와 관련된 내용이 빈칸에 적절하다. 따라서 (C)가 정답이다.

14
해설 (A) 중단하다, 파기하다, (B) 자금을 보충하다, (C) 향상시키다, (D) 설치하다 중에서 빈칸 뒤에 나오는 un-subscription(구독 종료)를 통해 정답이 (A)임을 알 수 있다.

DAY 02 본문 p.178

1 (B)	2 (C)	3 (A)	4 (A)	5 (D)
6 (C)	7 (A)	8 (B)	9 (D)	10 (A)
11 (B)	12 (D)	13 (D)	14 (A)	

1
해석 Elliot 씨는 8월에 그녀의 현 직책에서 물러나겠다는 계획을 언급했지만, 후임자는 아직까지 찾지 못했다.
해설 빈칸 앞에 동사(has mentioned)가 왔으므로 목적어 자리이다. 명사인 (B), (C) 중에서 해석상 (B)가 정답이다.
어휘 mention 언급하다 retire 퇴직하다 successor 후임자

2
해석 Arthur D. Stowa Consulting의 Koh 씨는 우리의 새로운 내부 전산망 시스템을 어떻게 사용하는지를 모든 사람들에게 이해시키는 면에서 도움이 되었다.
해설 be동사(was) 뒤의 보어 자리이며 보어 자리에는 명사 또는 형용사가 들어 간다. 명사(help)가 보어가 되려면 주어(Mr. Koh)와 동격이 되어야 하는데 그렇지 않으므로 형용사인 (C)가 정답이다. (B)는 가산 명사인데 관사가 없어서 오답이다.

3
해석 인체 구조에 대한 역사 박물관의 10번째 전시회가 다음 달부터 대중에게 공개될 것이다.
해설 open은 형용사로 '개방되어 있는', '누구나 참여할 수 있는'이라는 뜻이다. 특히 'open to the public'의 표현으로 많이 쓰인다.
어휘 human anatomy 인체 구조

4
해석 새로운 뮤지컬 <황혼 후 새벽까지>의 제작자들은 쇼에 대한 엄청난 수요 때문에 한 달간 더 공연하기로 결정했다.
해설 빈칸은 뒤에 명사가 있으므로 전치사 자리이다. 의미상 '~ 때문에'가 적절하므로 (A)가 정답이다. (B)는 접속사, (C)는 부사, (D) 접속사로 오답이다.
어휘 overwhelming 압도적인, 강력한

5
해석 대다수의 Cook County의 주민들은 유서 깊은 Shackenberg Mansion 바로 옆에 새로운 스포츠 복합 단지의 건설에 대해 반대 의사를 표현했다.
해설 동사(have expressed) 뒤의 목적어 자리이므로 '반대'라는 뜻의 명사 (D) opposition이 정답이다. (B)는 동명사로 타동사의 성질을 가지고 있으므로 뒤에 목적어가 필요하다.
어휘 historic 역사적으로 중요한 oppose 반대하다

6
해석 국도 유지 관리부는 운전자들에게 젖은 도로에서 조심하라고 권고한다.
해설 be동사 뒤의 보어 자리이다. 명사 혹은 형용사가 오면 되지만 motorists와의 caution의 관계가 동격이 되지 않으므로 형용사인 (C)가 정답이다.

7
해석 우리 회사는 유능한 직원들을 유지하는 수단으로 뛰어난 혜택들을 제공합니다.

해설 동사 offers의 목적어이자 형용사 outstanding의 수식을 받는 명사가 필요하므로 (A)가 정답이다.

어휘 outstanding 뛰어난, 두드러진

8
해석 지난 반년 동안 이윤의 감소를 경험했음에도 불구하고, Lockhart & Gardner 사는 내년에 새로운 세 명의 변호사를 고용할 생각이다.

해설 관사 the 뒤의 품사를 묻는 문제이다. 관사 뒤는 명사 자리이므로 (B)가 정답이다.

어휘 attorney 변호사 intend 의도하다, 생각하다

9
해석 긴자에 있는 Tony Borelli의 본점은 이 지역으로 옮겨온 다른 가게들과의 늘어나는 경쟁에도 불구하고 고객들로부터 인기를 유지하고 있다.

해설 빈칸 뒤에 동사는 없고 명사만 있으므로 전치사 자리이다. 접속사인 (B), (C)를 제외하고 전치사 중에서 의미상 '~에도 불구하고'가 적절하다. 따라서 정답은 (D)이다.

어휘 flagship store (체인점의) 본점, 주력 상점

10
해석 고객과 좀 더 좋은 관계를 만들기 위해서, 우리는 판매 직원들이 매우 세부적으로 제품 개발에 대해서 알게 할 필요가 있다.

해설 keep은 5형식 문장이 가능한 동사로 목적어(our sales representatives) 뒤에 목적격 보어(명사, 형용사)가 올 수 있다. 명사(information)는 목적어와의 관계가 동격이 아니므로 오답이다. 따라서 '숙지한', '능통한'이라는 뜻의 형용사 (A) informed가 정답이다.

어휘 sales representative 판매 직원 informant 정보원, 정보 제공자

11-14

Cameron 태국 레스토랑

Cameron 씨가 North Sydney 대학을 졸업할 때까지 그의 교수는 그를 Pam Plaza에 있는 Sri Thai Kitchen의 총매니저로 추천해 왔었다. Sri Thai Kitchen은 다양한 태국 음식을 제공하는데, 예를 들면 Tom Yum Goong(매콤한 새우 수프), Som Tum(매운 그린 파파야 샐러드), Tom Kha Kai(코코넛 수프에 닭 요리), 그리고 다른 전통 요리들이 있다. 이 지역의 많은 태국 음식점의 주인들은 그들의 판매를 늘리는 방법과 영어와 태국어를 할 줄 아는 능력 있는 매니저를 구하는 방법을 고민해 왔다. 그들은 지역 신문에 2개 국어에 능통한 매니저를 찾는 광고를 게재했다. Cameron 씨가 총 매니저로 고용되자마자, 그는 현재의 근무 환경을 보다 서양식으로 바꿀 것이고, 해외 손님뿐만 아니라 지역 손님들을 끌기 위해서 노력할 것이다.

어휘 complete 완성하다, 끝마치다 recommend 추천하다, 권고하다 general manager 총지배인 carry (가게에서 품목을) 취급하다 concerned with ~에 관심이 있다 boost 북돋우다, 신장시키다 qualified 자격이 있는 as soon as ~하자마자, ~하자 곧 working environment 근무 환경

11
해설 접속사 문제이다. [By the time + 과거 동사, 과거완료 동사]를 알아야 한다. 따라서 정답은 (B)이다.

12
해설 복수 동사(have)이므로 주어도 복수가 되어야 하는데 문맥상 빈칸 앞의 Many Thai restaurant와 이어질 수 있는 명사가 필요하다. 따라서 복수 명사 (D) owners가 정답이다.

13
해설 (A) 그들은 주말에 레스토랑을 닫기로 결정했다.
(B) 메뉴 가격이 10퍼센트 인상될 것이다.
(C) 고객은 3일 전에 미리 예약을 해야 한다.
(D) 그들은 지역 신문에 2개 국어에 능통한 매니저를 찾는 광고를 게재했다.

해설 빈칸 앞에서 태국 음식점 주인들이 판매를 늘리는 방법과 2개 국어를 할 수 있는 매니저를 구할 방법을 모색하고 있다고 했으므로 빈칸에는 '방법'에 대한 내용이 나와야 한다. 따라서 지역 신문에 광고를 냈다고 하는 (D)가 정답이다.

14
해설 change A to(into) B는 'A를 B로 바꾸다, 변경하다'라는 뜻이다.

DAY 03
본문 p.180

1 (C)	2 (D)	3 (D)	4 (B)	5 (B)
6 (C)	7 (A)	8 (D)	9 (B)	10 (B)
11 (B)	12 (D)	13 (C)	14 (A)	

1
해석 발주 후에 당신의 구매 내역을 보관하기 위해서 주문 확인서를 출력하세요.

해설 목적어 자리에 order(주문)와 함께 쓸 수 있는 복합명사 order confirmation(주문 확인서)이 적절하다. 따라서 정답은 (C)이다.

어휘 order placement 발주

2
해석 6월 6일 이후에 받은 주문들에는 소액의 처리 비용이 추가될 것이다.

해설 to 뒤에 빈칸이 있으면 전치사의 to와 to부정사의 to를 구분하는 문제이다. to부정사라면 빈칸 뒤에 목적어가 와야 하는데 그렇지 않으므로 전치사 to임을 알 수 있다. 빈칸에는 명사 자리인데 (A)도 명사이지만 가산 명사이므로 관사와 함께 와야 한다. 따라서 복수형인 (D)가 정답이다.

어휘 nominal fee 아주 적은 수수료

3
해석 효율적인 제품을 찾는 고객들에 대한 인식 운동으로 BBDO Media는 합리적인 대안을 제공한다.

해설 빈칸 앞에 관사(a)와 형용사(reasonable)가 왔으므로 명사 자리이다. 선택지 중에 명사인 alternative(대안)는 가산 명사이다.

어휘 reasonable 합리적인 alternate 번갈아 나오다

4

해석 Sawamura 씨의 지역 매니저 자리로의 승진이 오늘 팀 미팅에서 발표되었다.

해설 전치사(of) 다음에 형용사(regional)가 왔으므로 빈칸은 명사 자리이다. 선택지에서 (B)만이 명사이다.

5

해석 Phariva 보험사에 현재 공석들이 회사 자체의 웹 사이트와 몇몇 인터넷 구직 사이트에서 발표되었다.

해설 빈칸은 주어 자리이므로 앞의 명사(job)와 함께 복합명사를 이루는 job openings(공석들)이 적절하다.

6

해석 Shuster 씨는 최근 전시 기간 동안에 참여자들의 근면과 헌신에 대해서 그녀의 감사를 표했다.

해설 동사(expressed)의 목적어이자 소유격(her) 다음에 오는 명사가 와야 한다. 선택지에서 (C)만이 명사이다.

어휘 dedication 헌신 appreciate 고마워하다

7

해석 모든 고급 회계 과목들의 수강료는 한 명당 250달러이다.

해설 뒤의 명사(fee)와 함께 복합명사를 이루는 enrollment fee(등록비, 수강료)가 적절하다.

어휘 advanced 고급의, 상급의 enroll 등록하다

8

해석 서명된 합의서는 언급된 모든 약관에 대한 계약자들의 동의를 나타낸다.

해설 소유격(contractor's) 뒤는 명사 자리이다. 선택지에서 (D)만이 명사이다.

어휘 indicate 나타내다 terms and conditions 조건, 약관, 조항

9

해석 당신이 한 예약에 대한 어떤 변경 사항이든 적어도 리조트에 도착하기 2일 전에 완료되어야 한다는 것을 명심하세요.

해설 소유격(your) 뒤는 명사 자리이다. 선택지에서 (B)만이 명사이다.

어휘 keep in mind 명심하다, 마음에 새기다 at least 적어도

10

해석 Shoppico의 웹 사이트는 고객들에게 현재 시장에 나와 있는 오디오 제품들의 후기와 가격 비교를 제공한다.

해설 빈칸은 명사 자리인데 선택지 중에서 (B)만이 명사이다. comparison은 price와 함께 쓰이면 '가격 비교'라는 뜻의 복합명사가 된다.

어휘 compare 비교하다

11-14

수신: 전 직원
발신: Dennis Baird
제목: 새로운 전화 시스템 교육
날짜: 11월 21일

회사는 인터넷을 기반으로 한 새로운 전화 해결법을 다음 달부터 도용하기로 결정했습니다. 기술팀 직원들이 필요한 장비들을 모든 회의실을 시작으로 설치하기 시작할 것이고, 이번 달 말까지는 모든 다른 사무실들에도 설치 완료될 것입니다. 새로운 시스템으로의 전환이 원활하기 위해서, 기술팀이 진행할 직원 교육 과정이 월요일 오후 2시와 수요일 오전 11시에 예정되어 있습니다. 두 과정 모두 301호실에서 진행됩니다. 이 한 시간 과정 동안 새로운 장비에 대한 시연이 있을 것입니다. 그러므로 모든 직원들이 이 과정들 중 하나에 참석하는 것은 필수입니다. 참가는 연례 실적 평가에 고려 대상이 될 것입니다. 만약 고객들과의 중요한 약속이 있으시다면, 상사들 중 한 명에게 이번 주 말까지 알려 주세요. 이 과정들에 대한 세부적인 정보는 회사 게시판에 공지될 것입니다.

어휘 employ 고용하다, 이용하다 ensure 보장하다 transition 이동, 변화, 전환 take place 발생하다 demonstration (작동 과정이나 사용법에 대한 시범) 설명, 시연 mandatory 의무적인, 법에 정해진 attend 참석하다

11

해설 어휘 문제이다. (A) hold on (대기하다), (B) 설치하다, (C) 회신하다, (D) ~을 구하다(찾다) 중에서 '직원들이 필요한 장비들을 설치하기 시작할 것이고'가 적절하므로 정답은 (B)이다.

12

해설 대명사가 주어 자리에 들어가야 하는데 대명사는 명사를 대신하기 위해 쓰여지므로 앞의 내용을 참고하여 월요일과 수요일에 교육이 2번 있으므로 (D) Both로 받아야 한다.

13

해설 선택지는 모두 (접속)부사들인데 접속부사는 접속사처럼 두 문장을 연결할 수는 없지만 끊어진 두 문장의 [의미]를 연결할 수는 있다. 따라서 접속부사가 들어갈 자리라면 앞뒤 문장을 모두 해석하고 두 문장의 관계에 맞는 접속부사를 써야 한다. 문제에서는 "장비가 주어질 것이다"라는 원인과 "모든 직원들이 참석해야 한다"라는 결과를 말하고 있으므로 thus(그래서, 그러므로)가 적절하다.

14

해설 (A) 참가는 연례 실적 평가에 고려 대상이 될 것입니다.
(B) 회사가 세션과 관련된 더 많은 직원을 고용할 것입니다.
(C) 일정은 사전 통보 없이 변경될 수 있습니다.
(D) 기술 부서장이 새로운 부사장으로 임명될 것입니다.

해설 빈칸 바로 앞에서는 참가하는 것이 의무라고 했고, 뒤에서는 만약에 다른 일로 인해 참가하기 어렵다면 상사에게 알리라는 내용이 이어진다. 따라서 빈칸에는 '참가'와 관련된 내용이 와야 하므로 (A)가 정답이다.

DAY 04

본문 p.182

1 (D)	2 (A)	3 (B)	4 (C)	5 (D)
6 (C)	7 (D)	8 (A)	9 (D)	10 (B)
11 (D)	12 (B)	13 (A)	14 (C)	

1
- 해석 Johansson 씨는 뉴스 방송 분야에서 뛰어난 경력을 가지고 있으므로, 그녀는 이 직책에 매우 적합하다.
- 해설 선택지의 대명사들이 모두 인칭이 다르므로 앞의 어떤 명사를 받는지를 알아야 한다. Ms. Johansson을 받는 것이므로 (D)가 정답이다.
- 어휘 outstanding 뛰어난

2
- 해석 사무실을 떠나기 전에 Patel 씨를 위한 사업 보고서를 출력해서 그녀에게 전송해 주세요.
- 해설 전치사(to) 뒤의 빈칸은 목적어 자리이다. 재귀대명사 (B)는 주어와 목적어가 같을 때 쓸 수 있으므로 오답이고, (D) 소유대명사(그녀의 것)는 의미상 어색하다. 따라서 정답은 (A)이다.

3
- 해석 회사의 새로운 대표 이사는 그녀의 혁신적인 전략 계획 수립 때문에 국제적으로 칭송을 얻고 있다.
- 해설 전치사 뒤의 빈칸은 목적어 자리인데 빈칸 뒤에 명사 목적어(strategy planning)가 있으므로 소유격이 오는 것이 적절하다. 따라서 정답은 (B)이다.
- 어휘 praise 칭송, 찬사

4
- 해석 당신이 새로운 배터리를 구입할 때, 새로운 배터리에 대한 추가적인 20%의 할인을 위해서 출납원에게 이 상품권을 보여 주세요.
- 해설 앞의 명사를 받을 때 단수는 대명사 one으로 복수는 ones로 받을 수 있다. 여기서는 batteries를 받으므로 복수의 ones가 적절하다.
- 어휘 voucher 상품권, 쿠폰

5
- 해석 만약 당신의 픽업 트럭이 내일까지 준비되지 않는다면, 새 아파트로 이사할 때 우리 트럭을 이용하세요.
- 해설 빈칸은 동사(use)의 목적어 자리이며 [소유격 + 명사 = 소유대명사]이므로 our pickup truck을 ours로 받을 수 있다.

6
- 해석 Cahill 씨는 제출 마감일을 맞추기 위해서 스스로 사업 보고서를 편집했다.
- 해설 by oneself는 on one's own과 같은 의미로 '스스로, 혼자의 힘으로, 혼자서'라는 뜻이다.
- 어휘 compile 엮다, 편집하다 submission 제출

7
- 해석 새로 뽑힌 직원들 모두는 대표 이사가 주최하는 환영 파티에 초대받았다.
- 해설 주어 자리에 들어가는 대명사여야 하므로 형용사(every)는 제외하고 most와 all은 뒤의 명사 employees와 함께 복수 주어가 되므로 동사(was)와의 수 일치에서 어긋난다. 하지만 each는 각각이라는 단수 대명사가 되므로 정답은 (D)이다.
- 어휘 show up 나타나다

8
- 해석 아파트 복합 단지의 거주자들은 스스로 자신들의 재활용 정책을 홍보하기 위해서 전단지를 만들기로 결정했다.
- 해설 재귀대명사의 용법 중에서 강조의 용법은 강조하는 단어(residents) 바로 뒤나 문장 맨 뒤에 쓸 수 있다.
- 어휘 flyer 전단지

9
- 해석 건설 재료들을 구매하기 위한 올해의 수치들이 지난 3년간의 수치들과 꽤 유사하다.
- 해설 that과 those는 뒤에서 수식하는 구나 절이 있다면 앞의 명사를 받을 수 있다. that은 단수 명사, those는 복수 명사를 받는다. 여기서는 figures를 받는 것이기에 (D)가 정답이다.
- 어휘 figure 수치 preceding 이전의

10
- 해석 월정액 지하철 표가 출퇴근하는 사람들에게 가장 경제적인 방법이지만, 다른 것들도 가능하다.
- 해설 빈칸은 주어 자리이다. 한 가지 방법을 제시하고 다른 방법들(other options=others)도 있다는 의미이므로 (B)가 정답이다. ones는 앞에 받을 수 있는 복수 명사가 없으며, '몇몇의, 약간의'라는 뜻의 some과 any도 오답이다.

11-14

날짜: 1월 11일
수신: Eugene Landy
발신: Cam Dunkan
제목: 숙박

Landy 씨에게,

저는 1월 7일에 당신이 Minetta Inn에 숙박해 주신 것에 대해 감사드립니다. 우리는 당신이 숙박 기간을 즐겁게 보냈기를 희망합니다. 우리가 고객 만족에 가치를 두고 있기 때문에, 우리가 당신의 요구 사항을 얼마나 만족시켰는지를 알기 위해 첨부된 설문조사를 조금만 시간을 내서 채워주신다면 정말로 감사하겠습니다. 그러면 저희가 기존 가격에서 최대 10퍼센트 할인되는 할인 쿠폰을 드리도록 하겠습니다.
질문이 있으시면 바로 연락 주십시오. 다음에 또 이 지역에 방문할 계획이시라면 다시 뵙기를 희망합니다.

Cam Dunkan, 총지배인
Minetta Inn
1-223-342-0101

- 어휘 value 소중하게 생각하다 satisfaction 만족 fill out 기입하다 survey (설문)조사 attach 첨부하다 hesitate 망설이다

11
해설 편지를 쓴 날짜가 1월 11일인데 Mr. Landy가 이곳을 방문한 날짜는 지문에서 1월 7일이라고 했으므로 과거 동사 (D)가 정답이다.

12
해설 빈칸은 know의 목적어 자리이다. 빈칸 뒤에 동사(met)가 있으므로 명사절 종속접속사가 필요하다. (B), (C) 중에서 빈칸 뒤에 well이라는 부사가 접속사 바로 뒤로 나와 있는데 이렇게 문장을 절로 묶어주는 종속접속사들 중에서 접속사 뒤로 형용사나 부사를 끌어올 수 있는 접속사는 how 관련 접속사들이다. 따라서 정답은 (B)이다.

13
해설 (A) 그러면 저희가 기존 가격에서 최대 10퍼센트 할인되는 할인 쿠폰을 드리도록 하겠습니다.
(B) 고객 설문조사를 실시할 예정입니다.
(C) 그 후에 프런트 데스크에서 최신 프로모션에 등록하실 수 있습니다.
(D) 그러면 1년 동안 구독하실 수 있는 쿠폰을 받으실 수 있습니다.

해설 빈칸 앞에 설문조사를 작성해 달라고 요청하고 있으므로 이를 작성하면 그에 따른 '혜택'에 대한 내용이 나오는 것이 적절하다. 따라서 (A)가 정답이다. 구독에 대해서는 언급되어 있지 않기 때문에 (D)는 오답이다.

14
해설 앞의 동사 contact를 수식하는 부사 자리이다. 의미상 (C)가 정답이다. (A) 균등하게 (B) 강력하게 (C) 직접 (D) 이전에

DAY 05
본문 p.184

1 (B)	2 (A)	3 (D)	4 (C)	5 (D)
6 (B)	7 (B)	8 (B)	9 (C)	10 (D)
11 (B)	12 (A)	13 (D)	14 (B)	

1
해설 정치 칼럼니스트인 Folly Byun은 야당에 대한 논쟁거리가 될 새로운 책을 출간했다.

해설 형용사(new) 앞의 부사 자리처럼 보이지만 book을 수식하는 형용사가 들어갈 수도 있다. 형용사 controversial이 의미적으로 수식하는 것은 new가 아니라 명사(book)이므로 (B)가 정답이다.

어휘 controversy 논란

2
해설 컴퓨터화된 회계 교육 과정에 등록한 사람이 거의 없었기 때문에, 과정은 다음 달로 연기되었다.

해설 명사(people)를 수식하는 형용사 자리이므로 부사인 (B), (D)는 먼저 제외한다. (C)는 불가산 명사를 수식하므로 오답이다. 따라서 정답은 (A)이다.

어휘 sign up for ~을 신청하다 computerize 컴퓨터화하다, 컴퓨터에 저장하다 postpone 연기하다 barely 간신히, 가까스로

3
해설 대중들이 공청회에서 제시된 각각의 문제들에 대해서 토론할 시간이 있을 것이다.

해설 issue(문제)가 가산 명사이므로 all이 오면 복수 형태(issues)가 와야 한다. most of 역시 뒤에 복수 명사가 와야 하므로 오답이다. 또한 most of는 뒤에 명사를 쓰려면 the가 같이 와야 한다. each 뒤에는 단수 명사가 오므로 정답은 (D)이다.

어휘 public hearing 공청회

4
해설 전 회장 Patel 씨의 새롭게 출판된 자서전이 많은 논란의 대상이 되고 있다.

해설 빈칸 뒤의 명사(debate)를 수식하는 형용사 자리이다. 부사인 (A), (B)를 제외하고 복수 명사와 함께 쓰는 (D)도 오답이다. 따라서 정답은 (C)이다.

어휘 autobiography 자서전

5
해설 Iomantu 섬에 최근에 개장한 Peninsula 리조트는 아이를 가진 가족들에게 매력적인 다양한 활동들이 특징이다.

해설 be동사 뒤의 보어 자리(명사, 형용사)이다. activities와 attraction이 동격이 아니므로 형용사 (D)가 정답이다.

어휘 feature 특징으로 삼다

6
해설 Grayson Global은 다양한 고객층에 우리의 제품을 소개할 활동적인 판매 직원을 고용하기를 원한다.

해설 명사(sales representative)를 수식하는 형용사 자리이다. 선택지에서 (B)만이 형용사이다.

어휘 sales representative 판매 직원

7
해설 Bethiad Apparel은 적절한 가격에 높은 품질의 아동복을 제공하는 가족이 운영하는 기업이다.

해설 명사(prices)를 수식하는 형용사 자리이다. (B), (D) 중에서 의미상 '가격이 적절한'이라는 뜻의 (B)가 정답이다.

어휘 afford 여유가 되다

8
해설 국제 광산업에 관한 며칠간의 토론 끝에, TS 홀딩스의 이사진들은 시장에 상당한 양의 금액을 투자하기로 결정했다.

해설 명사(sum)를 수식하는 형용사 자리이다. (B), (C) 중에서 (B)는 '양, 정도가 상당한', (C)는 '사려 깊은'이라는 뜻이므로 의미상 정답은 (B)이다.

어휘 mining industry 광산업

9
해설 Smithson 국제 장학금 신청서는 선발 위원회에 적시에 제출되어야 한다.

해설 timely는 -ly로 끝나지만 형용사이다. 숙어로 in a timely manner(=fashion)는 '시기적절한 때'라는 뜻이다.

어휘 application 신청서

10

해석 Kaneko 수입 회사는 Tokyo와 Osaka의 광역 지역으로 Gallo 선글라스를 유통시킨다.

해설 빈칸은 명사(area)를 수식하는 형용사 자리이다. 선택지에서 (D)만이 명사이다.

어휘 distribute 분배하다, 유통시키다

11-14

새롭게 단장한 멜버른 도서관이 12월 23일 오전 7시에 공식적으로 대중들에게 다시 문을 엽니다. 새로운 탄생을 기념하는 리본 절단식이 중요 <u>고위</u> 인사들과 함께 열립니다.
사서 총괄인 Menitez Brown은 새로운 대중매체 분야가 이 계획의 주요 목적이었고, 도서관 이용자가 사용할 수 있도록 수천 가지의 시청각 자료들을 <u>수용</u>할 것이라고 말했습니다.
도서관 이용자들에게 새롭게 추가된 시설을 효과적으로 이용하는 법을 알려 주기 위해서 일련의 강습회가 예정되어 있고, 그중에 먼저 이 이용객들이 학술 연구의 목적으로 새로운 시설을 사용하는 법에 대해 <u>특별히 다루게 될 것입니다. 나머지 강습은 디지털 자료 접근을 위한 새로운 기기들을 활용하는 방법에 초점을 둘 것입니다.</u>

어휘 celebrate 축하하다, 기념하다 dignitary 고위 관리 parton 고객 utilize 이용하다, 활용하다

11

해설 빈칸은 명사(dignitaries)를 수식하는 형용사 자리이다. 의미상 '중요한 고위 관리'라는 뜻이 적절하므로 정답은 (B)이다. (A) 근면한 (B) 중요한 (C) 전문가 (D) 형식적인

12

해설 동사 자리 어휘 문제이다. '~을 수용하다'라는 뜻의 (A)가 정답이다. (D)는 '~을 구성하다'라는 의미의 자동사로 [consist of+명사]의 형태로 써야 한다. (B) ~을 분배하다 (C) (상자나 용기에) ~을 넣다

13

해설 빈칸 앞의 which는 형용사절로 앞의 명사 workshops를 받아 주며, 아직 workshops가 열리지 않은 것이므로 미래 시제의 (D)가 정답이다.

14

해설 (A) 도서관 보수 공사 동향에 대해서 배우게 될 것입니다.
(B) 나머지 강습은 디지털 자료 접근을 위한 새로운 기기들을 활용하는 방법에 초점을 둘 것입니다.
(C) 도서관 규정 준수에 관한 주제가 논의될 것입니다.
(D) 참가자들은 목소리를 낮추는 것의 중요성에 대해 알아야 합니다.

해설 빈칸 앞에 일련의 강습회가 있을 것이라고 했고 먼저 학술 연구의 목적으로 새로운 시설을 사용하는 법에 대한 강습회가 있을 것이라고 했다. 따라서 이어서는 나머지 강습에 대한 내용이 와야 적절하므로 (B)가 정답이다.

DAY 06
본문 p.186

1 (C)	2 (C)	3 (B)	4 (C)	5 (B)
6 (A)	7 (B)	8 (C)	9 (B)	10 (B)
11 (A)	12 (C)	13 (D)	14 (A)	

1

해석 아파트의 다른 세입자들을 방해하지 않기 위해서 볼륨을 조금만 줄여 주세요.

해설 동사 + 목적어(put the volume down)까지 문장의 의미가 완벽하고 빈칸이 put down(동사)을 수식하는 것이 적절하므로 부사 자리이다.

어휘 so as to ~하기 위해서 tenant 세입자 slightly 약간, 조금

2

해석 우리 도시가 겪고 있는 재정적인 위기는 새롭게 선출된 시장과 그의 직원들에 의해서 신속하게 해결되어야 한다.

해설 빈칸 앞에 수동태(be addressed)가 있고 뒤에 전치사가 있으므로 부사인 (C)가 정답이다.

어휘 urgent 긴급한, 시급한

3

해석 우리 모임에 새로운 일원이 되기 위해서, 그저 웹 사이트의 신청서를 작성해 주시기만 하면 됩니다.

해설 빈칸 뒤에 동사가 있지만 빈칸은 주어 자리가 아니라 부사 자리이다. 주어가 없는 명령문으로, simply가 동사(complete)를 수식하는 구조이다.

어휘 simplicity 간단함, 평이함

4

해석 시 위원회 구성원들 사이에 프로젝트 작업이 공평하게 분배되었다.

해설 빈칸 앞이 수동태로 완벽한 문장 형식은 갖췄으므로 빈칸은 부사 자리이다. even은 형용사로 '공평한'이란 뜻이다.

어휘 evenness 반반함, 평등, 균등

5

해석 Stafford 시 계획 위원회는 공연이 시작되기 전에 Wilshire 공원의 모든 문들에 재활용 쓰레기통을 전략적으로 배치할 것이다.

해설 조동사와 동사원형 사이에는 부사가 온다. 따라서 정답은 (B)이다.

6

해석 Stanford Consulting Group은 가장 중요한 잠재 고객들에게 당신의 제품을 창의적으로 홍보하는 전략을 당신에게 제시할 것이다.

해설 빈칸은 뒤의 동명사(promoting)를 수식한다. 동명사는 동사의 성질이 남아 있으므로 부사가 수식한다.

어휘 desirable 바람직한, 호감 가는

7

해석 우리의 수석 인사과 이사인 Jason Park은 헌신적인 직원을 고용하는 것과 그들을 붙잡고 있는 것이 회사의 미래를 위해서 똑같이 필수적이라는 것을 알고 있다.

해설 be동사(are) 뒤에 형용사 보어(critical)가 있으므로 이 형용사를 수식하는 부사가 적절하다.

어휘 dedicated 전념하는, 헌신하는   retain 유지하다, 보유하다

8

해석 온도가 거의 2주 동안 높게 유지된 후에 오늘 결국 약간 떨어졌다.

해설 자동사(drop)를 수식하는 부사 자리이다. 따라서 정답은 (C)이다.

9

해석 출장 중인 분들로부터 영수증이 전달되면, 신속하게 처리하여 지출 기록을 정확하게 해야 한다.

해설 수동태 다음에 빈칸이 있으므로 동사를 수식하는 부사 자리이다. 따라서 정답은 (B)이다.

어휘 precisely 정확하게

10

해석 이사회는 새로운 회사의 제품 라인을 위해 어떤 상표를 사용할지를 아직 결정하지 못했다.

해설 already는 긍정문에 쓰이기에 오답이며, soon은 해석상 어색하다. still과 yet은 둘 다 부정문에서 '아직'이라는 뜻을 가지지만 still은 부정어 앞에 오고, yet은 부정어 뒤에 온다. 따라서 정답은 (B)이다.

11-14

Lopez 씨에게,

우리는 귀하께서 반송하신 우비를 받았습니다. 물건과 함께 원래 영수증을 동봉하지 않으셔서, 저희는 이 우비가 우리의 가게들 중에서 구매되었는지를 확인할 수가 없습니다.

최대한 빨리 1-800-982-1096로 전화하셔서 고객 관리 직원 중 한 명에게 연락 주세요. 반품을 처리하기 위해서 귀하에게 몇 가지 질문을 드릴 것입니다. 추가적으로 저희의 반송에 관한 정책은 전액 환불을 위해서 영수증이 필요하다는 것에 유의해 주세요. 구매하셨다는 증거 없이는, 반송하신 제품의 교환으로 매장에서 사용하실 수 있는 포인트만 제공될 수 있습니다. 이 포인트는 온라인이나 매장에서 물건의 가장 최근 판매 가격으로 발급됩니다.

응답을 해 주시기 바랍니다. 반품이 원활하게 처리될 수 있도록 도울 수 있기를 바랍니다. 전화 주세요.

E&C 고객 서비스팀

어휘 merchandise 상품   receipt 영수증   purchase 구매하다   process 처리하다   proof 증거   in exchange for 교환으로, ~대신에

11

해설 어휘 문제이다. '결정하다, 확인하다'라는 뜻의 (A)가 정답이다. (B) 조직화하다, 조정하다, 꾸미다 (C) 배열하다, 준비하다 (D) 정착하다, 놓다, 결정하다

12

해설 전치사 어휘 문제이다. (A) ~ 위에, ~을 넘어서 (B) ~에 대항해서, ~에 기대서 (C) ~ 없이 (D) ~에도 불구하고

13

해설 동사 자리 문제이다. 수 일치에서 (C)를 제외하고 (A), (B), (D)가 모두 수동태이므로 시제를 고려하면 [이 포인트는 온라인이나 매장에서 물건의 가장 최근 판매 가격으로 발급됩니다]는 내용은 일반적인 사실을 말하므로 현재 시제가 정답이다.

14

해석 (A) 반품이 원활하게 처리될 수 있도록 도울 수 있기를 바랍니다.
(B) 무료 배송의 혜택을 받으실 자격이 있습니다.
(C) 올 8월에 만료되는 보증 기간을 연장해 드리겠습니다.
(D) 프로모션 행사로 상품권을 받으실 것입니다.

해설 물건을 반품했지만 영수증이 동봉되지 않아서 반품이 진행되고 있지 않은 상황이다. 따라서 '반품'이 원활하게 처리될 수 있도록 도와 드리겠다는 (A)가 정답이다.

DAY 07
본문 p.188

1 (D)	2 (C)	3 (B)	4 (B)	5 (A)
6 (A)	7 (C)	8 (C)	9 (A)	10 (D)
11 (C)	12 (B)	13 (A)	14 (B)	

1

해석 Willard 대학 극장은 최신식 음향과 조명 장비를 설치하는 비용 때문에 내년에 표 가격을 올릴 것이다.

해설 전치사와 접속사를 구분하는 문제이다. 빈칸 뒤에는 동사는 없고 명사만 있으므로 전치사 자리임을 알 수 있다. 의미상 '~ 때문에'라는 뜻의 (D) due to가 정답이다.

어휘 state-of-the-art 최신의, 최첨단의

2

해석 모든 Howrett-Packard 직원들은 목요일 오후 5시까지 직원 만족도 설문지를 완성해야 한다.

해설 모두 전치사이므로 뒤의 명사와의 관계를 본다. 의미상 '목요일 오후 5시까지 완성해야 하는 것'이므로 정답은 (C)이다.

어휘 fill out 기입하다

3

해석 매표소는 공연 시작 20분 전에 표 판매를 중지한다.

해설 twenty minutes before the start of the show(공연 시작 20분 전)라는 표현을 알아 두자. 여기서 before를 prior to로 바꿀 수 있고, 만약 after로 바꾸면 공연 후 20분이 된다.

4

해석 Freedom Trail 위원회는 일요일과 월요일을 제외하고 매일 Boston 지역의 역사적인 장소들의 투어를 인도한다.

해설 전치사 자리로 의미상 '~을 제외하고'라는 뜻의 except가 적절하다.

5
해석 Inter-Continental Hotel Taipei에 예약을 확인하기 위해서 24시간 이내에 이 이메일에 회신해 주세요.

해설 since는 의미상 어색할 뿐만 아니라 그 뒤의 시간 표현은 시점이 나와야 하는 반면에 within은 24 hours처럼 기간이 나와야 한다는 것을 알아야 한다.

어휘 guarantee 보장하다, 확실하게 하다

6
해석 사무용품들은 우편 보관소 옆의 저장 수납실에 저장된다.

해설 명사 앞 전치사 자리이므로 down을 제외하고 의미상 '~의 옆에'라는 뜻의 (A)가 적절하다.

7
해석 목록에 없는 판매 제품의 할인된 가격들은 판매 운영 부서로부터 얻을 수 있다.

해설 전치사 어휘 문제이다. (A) ~ 쪽으로 (B) ~를 제외하고 (C) ~로부터 (D) ~아래에서

어휘 obtain 얻다

8
해석 광고 캠페인의 세부적인 정보는 보조 상무이사에 의해서 제공될 것이다.

해설 수동태 다음에 빈칸이므로 '~에 의해서'라는 의미의 (C) by가 적절하다.

9
해석 Deshields 씨는 경영진들이 그녀의 국제 마케팅 분야에서 광범위한 경력으로부터 혜택을 얻을 수 있다는 것을 그들이 알 수 있도록 노력했다.

해설 benefit은 전치사 from과 어울린다. '~으로부터 혜택을 얻다'라는 뜻이다. 따라서 정답은 (A)이다.

어휘 extensive 아주 넓은

10
해석 장소나 시간의 변화에 대한 공지 사항들은 컨벤션 센터의 로비에 설치된 게시판에 게시될 것이다.

해설 '~에 관해서'라는 뜻의 전치사 'concerning'이 적절하다.
(concerning = regarding = as to = as for = about = on)

어휘 bulletin board 게시판 set up 설치하다

11-14

Ashley Winston
630 W. 5th Street.
Los Angeles, CA 90071

Winston 씨에게,

Jillian Mitchell이 7월 1일부로 Los Angeles 지점에 합류하게 된 것을 알리게 되어 기쁩니다.
그녀는 지난 5년간 기업 관련 변호사 아래에서 일했던 Henderson & Carney로부터 우리 회사로 왔습니다. Mitchell 씨는 국내 혹은 국외 저작권법에 매우 정통하며, 우리가 그녀를 고용하게 된 것이 정말 다행이라고 생각합니다. 그녀와의 미팅을 희망하시면, 962-235-2580로 연락하시면 됩니다.
그녀는 매우 헌신적이고 재능 있는 변호사입니다. 그녀의 이전 고용주인 Carney 씨는 그녀를 놓치게 된 것이 너무 아쉽다고 했습니다. 그녀는 앞으로 귀하의 가장 훌륭한 자산이 될 것입니다. 그녀는 중국 휴대폰 회사와 관련된 소송에서 큰 도움이 될 것입니다. 귀하께서도 그녀를 좋아했으면 좋겠네요.

William Simmons
Sonberg & Simmons

어휘 inform 통지하다, 알리다 attorney 변호사 knowledgeable 아는 것이 많은, 많이 아는 domestic 국내의, 가정의 copyright 저작권, 판권 dedicated 전념하는, 헌신적인 talented 재능 있는 litigation 소송

11
해석 해석과 함께 (B), (D)는 자동사로 쓰이므로 바로 목적어가 오기보다는 전치사 뒤에 목적어가 오게 된다. (A) '지명하다'는 의미상 오답이다. (A) 지정하다 (C) 합류하다

12
해석 knowledgeable(박식한)을 수식하는 부사 자리이다. (A) 모호하게 (B) 매우 (C) 희망차게 (D) 조심스럽게

13
해석 wish는 목적어 자리에 동명사가 아닌 to부정사를 목적어로 취한다.

14
해석 (A) 그녀는 인수 합병 계약에 대해서 경험이 거의 없습니다.
(B) 그녀는 앞으로 귀하의 가장 훌륭한 자산이 될 것입니다.
(C) 변호사로 일을 시작하면서 저작권 부서로 발령받을 것입니다.
(D) 최근에 그녀는 다른 지역으로 이사했습니다.

해설 빈칸 앞에서는 이전 직장 상사가 Mitchell 씨를 긍정적으로 평가했고 빈칸 뒤에서는 그녀가 큰 도움이 될 것이라고 했다. 따라서 그녀가 훌륭한 자산이 될 거라는 (B)가 적절하다.

DAY 08

본문 p.190

1 (B)	2 (A)	3 (D)	4 (D)	5 (C)
6 (D)	7 (C)	8 (B)	9 (A)	10 (A)
11 (D)	12 (C)	13 (A)	14 (C)	

1
해석 지난 10년 동안 SSC 자동차는 북미의 3대 슈퍼카 생산업체 중 하나로서 꾸준히 지위를 차지하였다.

해설 has와 함께 쓰일 수 있는 동사 형태는 과거분사(p.p.) 형태뿐이다.

2
해석 모든 직원들은 생산 과정이 기계 오작동에 의해서 방해를 받고 있다면 현장 감독관에게 알려야 한다.

해설 speak와 respond는 자동사로 목적어를 취하기 위해서 전치사(to)가 필요하다. inquire 역시 대부분 about과 함께 자동사로 쓰인다.

어휘 interrupt 방해하다, 가로막다 malfunction (기계 등) 오작동, 고장

3
해석 정부가 후원하는 국제 마라톤 이벤트가 9월 20일에 열릴 것이고, 모든 시민들은 참여하는 것이 요청된다.

해설 invite는 목적어 뒤에 to부정사를 취할 수 있으며 수동태가 되면 be invited to부정사(~하는 것이 요청된다)의 형태로 쓰일 수 있다. 따라서 정답은 (D)이다.

4
해석 호텔 밖으로 나가실 때, 안내 데스크에 방 카드 키를 맡겨 주세요.

해설 빈칸은 주어가 없는 명령문의 동사 자리이다. 명령문의 동사는 동사원형을 쓰므로 정답은 (D)이다.

5
해석 우리의 웹 사이트를 사용하는 데 어려움을 겪는 손님들은 무료 전화번호로 고객 지원 직원들과 통화하는 것을 권합니다.

해설 동사 자리인데 빈칸 뒤에 목적어가 아닌 전치사(with)가 있으므로 자동사를 써야 한다. 선택지에서 (C)번이 자동사이다.

어휘 toll-free number 수신자 부담 전화(toll-free 무료의)

6
해석 많은 회사들과 법률 회사들이 정부의 최신 세금 개정안 중에서 3가지 조항들에 대해 강하게 비판했다.

해설 have와 함께 쓸 수 있는 동사 형태는 과거분사이다. 형용사(critical)로 뒤의 목적어를 수식할 수 없는 이유는 중간에 관사(the)가 있기 때문이다.

어휘 provision 공급, 제공/조항 criticize 비판하다, 비평하다

7
해석 Cote 제약 회장은 최근의 국제 판매 문제들이 기업의 장기 국제 확장 계획들에 영향을 미치지 않게 했다.

해설 사역동사(let, have, make)는 목적어 뒤 목적격 보어 자리에 원형부정사를 쓴다.

8
해석 우리의 계약자들에 의해 제공된 대부분의 테스트 엔진 부품들이 현재 적용되는 품질 기준을 맞추는 데 실패했다.

해설 자동사 comply with 문제이다. adhere도 자동사이지만 adhere to(~을 준수하다)의 형태로 쓰인다. belong도 대부분 to와 함께 '~에 속한다'의 의미를 가진다.

어휘 belong to ~에 속하다 approach 다가가다, 접근하다

9
해석 대표 이사는 매년 열리는 전문성 개발과 훈련 세미나들이 모든 직원을 많은 분야에서 지식과 전문 기술을 넓힐 수 있게 도와준다는 것에 자신이 있었다.

해설 that절(명사절)의 동사는 help이다. 준사역동사인 help는 목적격 보어 자리에 to부정사나 원형부정사가 올 수 있다.

어휘 expertise 전문 지식(기술)

10
해석 수석 재정이사와 총무부 이사는 내년 예산 인상에 대한 제안에 대해서 꽤 다르게 반응했다.

해설 react는 자동사로 '~에 반응하다'라는 의미를 가지며 전치사구(to+명사)가 뒤따른다. 자동사는 수동태로 쓰일 수 없고 (D) reacts는 수가 일치하지 않으므로 정답은 (A)이다.

어휘 react 반응하다

11-14

발신: Benjamin Willis
수신: Yoon-sung Kim
보낸 시간: 2월 28일 오후 2시 45분
제목: 고객님의 문의 사항

Kim 씨에게,

Evermates Agency에서 상담가들이 제공하는 중매 서비스에 대해서 문의해 주셔서 감사합니다. 우리는 여성분들과 남성분들 모두가 만족할 수 있는 중매 이벤트를 만드는 데 특화되어 있습니다. 저희는 수많은 경력이 있고, 저희 전문가들은 좋은 외모와 재정적인 안정을 가진 남녀에 대한 방대한 자료를 가지고 있습니다. 간단히 말해, Evermates는 당신이 원하는 이성을 만나는 데 가장 적합니다.

저희는 당신을 만나 개인적 취향을 알고 나서, 첫 번째 만남을 주선하겠습니다. 저희의 노하우와 전문성은 개인적인 정보를 다루고 모든 만남들에 대해서 기밀을 유지하는 것에 의해 증명됩니다. 고객들은 또한 저희 기관의 중매 전문가와 상담한 1주일 이내에 첫 번째 만남을 가지는 것을 보장받습니다.

저희 전문가들은 당신이 만족할 수 있는 관계를 발전시킬 수 있도록 도울 것입니다. 추가적인 도움이 필요하시면 저희에게 알려 주십시오.

Benjamin Willis
수석 중매 상담사

어휘 inquire 질문하다, 묻다 matchmaking 결혼 중매 specialize in ~을 전문으로 하다 plenty of 많은 vast 방대한, 막대한 financial stability 금융 안전성 suited 어울리는 confidentiality 비밀

11
해설 접속부사 자리는 앞 문장과 뒤 문장의 해석을 통해서 문제를 푼다. 앞 문장들의 내용을 빈칸 뒤의 문장이 정리하고 있으므로 (D) In short(간략히 말해서)가 정답이다. (A) 그렇지 않으면 (B) 예를 들어 (C) 그럴더라도

12
해설 and 앞에 명사(know-how)가 있으므로 빈칸에도 명사가 와야 한다. (A) 직업, (B) 전문가, (C) 전문성이 모두 명사인데 문맥상 (C)가 정답이다.

13
해설 전치사 어휘 문제이다. within은 시간의 전치사로 쓰일 때 기간의 명사(one week)를 취하며 시점의 명사는 취하지 않는다. (B) ~ 가운데

14
해석 (A) Evermates Agency는 업계 선두 주자입니다.
(B) 30분도 걸리지 않을 것입니다.
(C) 저희 전문가들은 당신이 만족할 수 있는 관계를 발전시킬 수 있도록 도울 것입니다.
(D) 다음 신청서를 작성해 주셔야 합니다.
해설 빈칸 뒤에 추가적으로 도움이 필요하면 알려 달라고 했으므로 빈칸에는 어떤 도움이 되는지에 대한 내용이 와야 한다. 따라서 (C)가 정답이다. (A)는 글 초반에 나올 수 있는 내용이므로 오답이다.

DAY 09
본문 p.192

1 (C)	2 (A)	3 (A)	4 (A)	5 (D)
6 (D)	7 (C)	8 (B)	9 (B)	10 (B)
11 (B)	12 (B)	13 (A)	14 (B)	

1
해석 우리의 충전식 배터리에 대한 최근 조사에서 새로운 주력 스마트폰에 들어가는 새롭게 발명된 배터리가 동종의 배터리들보다 훨씬 좋은 성능을 발휘하는 것이 밝혀졌다.
해설 빈칸은 명사절 that안의 동사 자리이다. 주어가 단수 명사(battery)이므로 동사도 -s를 붙인 단수 동사가 와야 한다.
어휘 rechargeable 재충전되는 flagship 주력 상품

2
해석 지난주 금요일에 뉴욕시 통근자들은 42번 도로에서 전복된 트럭 때문에 어쩔 수 없이 우회로를 이용해야만 했다.
해설 동사(were)가 복수 동사이므로 주어도 복수가 되어야 한다. 따라서 복수 명사 (A) commuters가 정답이다.
어휘 alternate route 대체 도로, 우회로 flip 뒤집다

3
해석 우기와 예상치 못한 법적인 문제들이 두 번째 Illinois 주 과학 센터의 건설의 가장 큰 장애물로 놓여 있다.
해설 동사 자리이므로 수 일치-능동/수동태-시제의 순서로 선택지를 확인하면 복수 주어이므로 (B), (C)는 오답이고 빈칸 뒤에 목적어가 있으므로 수동태인 (D)도 오답이다.
어휘 pose 제기하다

4
해석 Paris로 가는 고속 기차들은 주중에는 D 승강장에서 오전 10시에만 출발합니다.
해설 주어가 복수 명사(trains)이므로 동사도 복수 동사여야 한다.
어휘 depart 출발하다

5
해석 Thorpe Industrial Design 사는 개별적 고객의 요구에 맞춘 모든 종류의 디자인 서비스를 제공한다.
해설 design 뒤에 명사(services)를 또 쓸 수 있는 것은 복합명사이다. 빈칸 뒤의 that 절은 형용사절로 빈칸에 들어갈 명사를 수식하고 형용사절의 동사(match)가 복수 동사이므로 빈칸의 명사도 복수 명사가 되어야 한다.

6
해석 이 사업 제안서의 세부 사항들은 지난 목요일 모임에서의 전략 토론의 결과물이다.
해설 주어가 details(복수 명사)이므로 동사도 복수 동사이다.

7
해석 생산 전문가에 의해서 제공된 제안들이 전체 생산율을 증가시킬 것이라 예상된다.
해설 이 문장의 동사는 복수(are)이므로 주어도 복수 명사(suggestions)가 되어야 한다.
어휘 overall 전체의

8
해석 지난 3년 동안에 환불을 요구하는 고객의 수가 엄격하게 품질 기준을 맞춘 우리의 계속적인 노력 때문에 지속적으로 감소했다.
해설 빈칸은 동사 자리이고 주어는 복수 명사(refunds)가 아닌 the number(~의 수)가 되므로 단수 동사를 써야 한다. 〈The number of 복수 명사 + 단수 동사〉이므로 복수 동사인 (C), (D)는 오답이다. (A), (B)는 시제가 다른데 for the past/last ~는 현재완료 시제와 함께 쓰이므로 정답은 (B)이다.
어휘 steadily 꾸준히 strict 엄격한

9
해석 Packard-Dewitt의 거의 절반의 직원들이 전철로 직장에 통근한다.
해설 적절한 동사 형태를 고르는 문제인데, 수 일치를 해야 할 명사는 half가 아니라 the employees이다. 전체 중 일부분을 나타내는 표현에서는 예를 들어 일부분을 나타내는 some, any, 99%, 1%, 2/3, the rest, all이 중요한 것이 아니라 그 뒤에 나오는 명사에 의해서 수 일치가 정해진다. employees가 복수 명사이므로 빈칸도 복수 동사가 들어가야 한다.
어휘 commute 통근하다

10
해석 푸드코트에서 제공되는 채소들의 신선도는 공급업체에 따라서 매우 많이 다르다.
해설 〈전치사+명사〉는 수식어이므로 이 문장의 주어는 freshness(불가산 명사)이다. 따라서 동사도 단수 동사가 와야 한다.
어휘 vary 다양하다

11-14

발신: Paul Mitchell
수신: Delilah Simpson
날짜: 10월 15일 목요일
제목: 귀하의 문의 사항

Simpson 씨에게,

귀하의 회사를 위해서 새로운 웹 사이트를 만드는 것에 대해서 이메일로 질문을 주셔서 감사합니다. 우리는 다양한 요구 사항을 가지고 있는 고객들을 위한 맞춤 제작된 웹 사이트를 제공하는 것에 특화된 웹 디자인 회사입니다.

우리는 각각의 사이트의 독특한 콘셉트에 특별히 주목해 만들어진 웹 사이트를 제공합니다. 더불어, 모든 고객의 요구에 맞는 내용들에 신중하게 집중합니다. CCD에서 저희는 잘 만들어진 웹 사이트가 고객들을 매료시킬 수 있다고 확실히 믿습니다. 귀하께서 목적을 달성하는 것을 돕기 위해서 저희의 매우 숙련된 전문가들이 창조적인 그래픽과 맞춤 생산된 프로그램을 가지고 아름답고 효율적인 디자인을 제공합니다.

몇몇 샘플과 귀하께서 요청하신 최초 무료 견적서를 첨부합니다. 귀하께서 웹 사이트를 만드는 데 저희 회사를 고려해 주셔서 감사합니다. 곧 귀하와 사업을 할 수 있기를 희망합니다.

Paul Mitchell
수석 광고 PD
Chicago Commercial Design Ltd.

어휘 inquiry 질문 specialize in ~을 전문으로 하다 customize 주문 제작된 various 다양한 offer 제공하다 pay attention 주목하다, 관심을 갖다 contents 내용물 contribute 기여하다 functional 실용적인

11
해설 전치사(in)와 명사(Web sites) 사이의 동명사 자리이다. '웹 사이트를 고객들에게 제공하는 것'으로 해석이 된다.

12
해설 타동사(believe) 뒤에 목적어 자리에 명사절이다. what과 that 중에서 빈칸 뒤의 명사절이 완벽한 문장이므로 that이 정답이다.

13
해설 명사(specialists)를 수식하는 형용사 자리이다. '매우 자격을 갖춘'이라는 뜻의 highly qualified가 가장 적절하다.

14
해설 (A) 저희 서비스에 만족하지 못하셨었다면 환불해 드리겠습니다.
(B) 몇몇 샘플과 요청하신 최초 무료 견적서를 첨부합니다.
(C) 지원 마감일은 11월 15일입니다.
(D) 저희 웹 사이트에 프리젠테이션 파일을 업로드해 주시기 바랍니다.

해설 이 글은 웹 디자인 회사가 웹 사이트 제작에 대해 문의한 것에 대한 답장을 보내는 것이다. 따라서 샘플과 함께 견적서를 보내 주겠다는 (B)가 가장 적절하다.

DAY 10   본문 p.194

1 (D)	2 (B)	3 (B)	4 (D)	5 (B)
6 (A)	7 (D)	8 (B)	9 (A)	10 (C)
11 (D)	12 (D)	13 (A)	14 (B)	

1
해석 〈Healthcare Today〉 잡지의 최신 설문 조사에 따르면 우리 회사는 이 나라에서 일할 만한 10대 고용주들 중 하나로 알려져 있다.
해설 능동/수동태 문제이다. 빈칸은 동사 자리이고, 빈칸 뒤에 목적어 역할을 할 수 있는 명사가 없기 때문에 수동태를 써야 한다. 따라서 정답은 (D)이다.
어휘 according to ~에 따르면

2
해석 이번 주의 우리 백열전구 배송이 폭풍과 동해안의 기후로 난항을 겪고 있으며 동해안은 현재 허리케인이 한창 진행 중이다.
해설 능동/수동태 문제이다. 빈칸에는 동사 interrupt에 대한 목적어 역할을 하는 명사가 없기 때문에 수동태로 써야 한다. 따라서 정답은 (B)이다.
어휘 currently 현재 in the middle of ~도중에, 중간에 interrupt 방해하다, 가로막다

3
해석 우리의 새로운 회사 매거진은 매달 초에 발행되고 해외를 포함한 모든 회사 지점에 배포될 것이다.
해설 능동/수동태 문제이다. 주어진 빈칸에는 조동사 will 다음에 동사원형을 써야 하고 동사 자리 뒤에 목적어가 없기 때문에 수동태를 써야 한다. 따라서 정답은 (B)이다.
어휘 publish 출판하다, 발행하다 distribute 분배하다

4
해석 직원 비용에 대한 금액 상환은 인사부에서 제공 가능한 적절한 서류를 제출한 후에 이루어질 것이다.
해설 수동태 문제이다. 조동사 will 다음에 동사원형을 써야 하며 빈칸 뒤에 목적어가 없기 때문에 수동태를 써야 한다. 따라서 정답은 (D)이다.
어휘 reimbursement 변제, 상환 submission 제출 appropriate 적절한

5
해석 승무원에 의한 안전 시범은 캡틴의 발표와 함께 진행될 것입니다.
해설 동사 문제이다. 주어진 빈칸은 동사를 써야 하며 의미적으로 미래의 의미가 적합하므로 will be preceded를 쓴다. be는 조동사 없이 원형이 쓰일 수 없으므로 (A)는 오답이다.
어휘 safety demonstration 안전 시범 precede ~에 앞서다

6

해석 FTA의 통과로 미국의 농업 무역은 첫 번째 해에는 100%, 두 번째 해에는 200%가 상승할 것으로 예상된다.

해설 〈expect+목적어+목적보어[to부정사]〉는 〈be expected+to부정사〉로 바꿀 수 있고 의미는 '~할 것으로 예상된다'이다.

어휘 passage (법안의) 통과 agricultural 농업의

7

해석 어떤 직원도 보안 직원에게 자신의 ID 카드를 보여 주지 않고, 주요 오피스 빌딩에 들어갈 수 없습니다.

해설 수동태 문제이다. 빈칸은 be동사 뒤의 분사가 나오는 자리인데, 빈칸 뒤에 목적어가 없기 때문에 수동태로 써야 한다. 따라서 정답은 (D)이다.

어휘 permit 허가하다, 허가

8

해석 인사 부서는 많은 수의 지원자들로 인해 다음 달 말에서야 인터뷰를 받게 될 모든 지원자들에게 알리게 될 것이다.

해설 능동태 문제이다. 주어진 빈칸은 be동사 뒤에 오는 분사 자리이며 목적어인 all candidates가 있기 때문에 능동형인 notifying이 와야 한다.

어휘 candidate 후보자 notify 알리다, 통보하다

9

해석 Texas의 Austin에 있는 우리의 연구 개발 실험실은 새로운 울트라 축전기를 개발해 왔고 이는 배터리들을 대체하고 백만 번 넘게 다시 충전될 수 있다.

해설 능동태 문제이다. 주어진 빈칸에는 앞에는 be동사가 있고, 뒤에는 목적어 new ultra capacitors가 있기 때문에 능동 형태의 분사 developing을 쓴다.

어휘 capacitor 축전기 replace 교체하다, 대체하다 recharge 재충전하다

10

해석 우린 태양광과 기계적으로 동력을 얻는, 두 가지 형태의 전원을 가지고 있는 가장 새로운 손전등을 홍보할 것이다.

해설 능동태 문제이다. 주어진 빈칸은 동사를 써야 하는 자리이며 목적어인 flashlights가 있기 때문에 능동의 형태인 will be promoting을 쓴다. (A), (B)는 be동사 뒤에 나올 수 있는 동사 형태가 아니다.

어휘 mechanically 기계로, 기계적으로 flashlight 손전등 form 종류, 유형, 방식

11-14

세계적인 선두 화학 회사들 중의 하나인 NOS Chemicals가 변화를 만들 준비가 되어 있는 야망 있고, 갓 졸업한 대학 졸업생들을 위한 몇몇 공석들을 중국에 가지고 있습니다. 이전 경력은 전혀 필요 없습니다.

모든 필요한 훈련은 회사에 의해서 제공될 것입니다. 성공적인 후보자들은 뛰어난 의사소통 기술과 문제 해결 능력을 가지고 있어야 합니다. 경제학이나 마케팅에 관한 교과 과정이 필요하지는 않지만, 혜택을 받을 수는 있습니다.

많은 열정이 있는 분들이 이 기회를 이용하실 거라 예상합니다. 이런 직책에 지원을 하시려면, 당신의 이력서를 www.noschemicals.com을 통해 인사과에 보내 주세요. 그러면, 채워서 회신하셔야 하는 지원서를 받으실 겁니다.

더 많은 세부 사항을 위해서, 저희의 웹 사이트에 방문해 주세요.

어휘 leading 선두의 vacancy 결원, 공석 ambitious 야심 있는 make a difference (~에) 영향이 있다 candidate 후보자 possess 소유하다 advantageous 이로운, 유리한 apply for ~에 지원하다 human resources department 인사부 application 지원서

11

해설 어휘 문제이다. 바로 뒤 문장에서 모든 필요한 훈련(training)을 제공한다고 했으므로 이전 경력(experience)이 필요 없는 것이 적절하다. (A) 연장 (B) 지원 (C) 시도

12

해설 우선 접속사 자리이므로 전치사 (A)를 제외하고 의미상 '~에도 불구하고'가 적절하므로 (D)가 정답이다.

13

해설 (A) 많은 열정이 있는 분들이 이 기회를 이용하실 거라 예상합니다.
(B) 지원자들은 최소 5년 이상 전문 경험이 있어야 합니다.
(C) 지원서는 저희 데이터베이스에 1년간 유지될 것입니다.
(D) 인턴은 인터뷰를 위한 마감 시간에 맞춰야 합니다.

해설 빈칸 앞에서는 주로 지원 자격에 대해 나와 있고 뒤에는 지원하는 방법에 대해 나오고 있다. 따라서 빈칸에는 지원을 장려하는 내용이 올 수 있는데 많은 열정이 있는 분들이 지원할 거라고 예상한다는 (A)가 정답이다.

14

해설 뒤에 목적어(an application)이 있어서 능동태가 필요한 것처럼 보이지만 send는 4형식 동사라서 목적어가 2개 올 수 있다(간접목적어, 직접목적어). 해석상 신청서를 채워서 다시 보내려면(to complete and return) 우선 신청서를 받아야 하므로 수동태(be sent)가 나와야 한다. 수동태 (B), (C), (D) 중에서 선택하는 시제 문제가 되며 아직 발생하지 않은 사건이므로 미래 시제를 써야 한다.

DAY 11

본문 p.196

1 (C)	2 (C)	3 (C)	4 (D)	5 (C)
6 (A)	7 (D)	8 (A)	9 (B)	10 (D)
11 (C)	12 (B)	13 (A)	14 (B)	

1
해석 판매 부서는 우리의 마케팅과 판매 사원들을 교육시키기 위한 새로운 교육 지침을 썼다.

해설 동사 시제 문제이다. 주어진 빈칸은 동사를 써야 하는 자리이며 주어가 단수이기 때문에 (A)는 오답이며, (C) wrote를 쓸 수 있다.

2
해석 기획위원회는 빌딩의 인증의 승인에 대해 투표하기 위해 화요일 밤 7시에 모일 것이다.

해설 동사 시제 문제이다. 주어진 빈칸은 동사를 써야 하며 미래를 나타내는 will convene이 정답이다. (D) have convened는 현재완료 시제인데 특정 시간을 나타내는 표현인 on Tuesday night at 7 P.M.과 함께 쓰일 수 없다.

어휘 convene 소집하다

3
해석 회담이 시작되면, 연설자는 회사 전체의 새로운 방향에 대해 이야기할 것이다.

해설 동사 시제 문제이다. 주어진 빈칸은 동사를 써야 하며 접속사 once 다음에는 현재형이 미래 시제를 대신하기 때문에 starts를 쓴다.

어휘 direction 방향

4
해석 20년 전에 회사가 설립된 이래로, 창조적인 마케팅 전략들에 의해서 원동력을 얻는 계속적인 성장을 해 왔다.

해설 Since 뒤에 과거 시제(20 years ago)가 나오면 주절에서 현재완료 시제가 온다.

어휘 found 설립하다, 세우다 fuel 연료를 공급하다, 부채질하다

5
해석 새로운 대표 이사가 회사에 합류한 후에, 그는 획기적인 상품들의 연구 개발의 중요성을 알리기 시작했다.

해설 동사 시제 문제이다. 주어진 빈칸은 주어 the new CEO 다음에 쓸 수 있는 동사가 필요한 자리이고 주절의 동사가 과거형(began)이므로 종속절도 과거형 동사여야 한다.

어휘 join 가입하다, 합류하다 innovative 획기적인

6
해석 이사회는 지난밤에 만나 광고에 추가로 80만 달러를 지출하기로 했다.

해설 동사 시제 문제이다. 빈칸은 동사를 써야 하는 자리이며 과거를 나타내는 부사인 last night이 있기 때문에 met를 쓴다.

어휘 elect ~하기로 결정하다; 선출하다

7
해석 우리가 관리자로부터 건물 계약서를 받았을 때, 중요한 서류가 사라졌다.

해설 동사의 시제 문제이다. 주어진 빈칸은 동사를 써야 하는 자리이며 접속사 by가 이끄는 절이 과거형 received이며 주절의 내용은 더 이전에 일어난 사실이므로 과거 완료형을 쓴다.

어휘 disappear 사라지다

8
해석 회사의 이사회는 워싱턴주 Seattle에 새로운 생산 시설을 건설하는 것의 가능성에 대해 토의하기 위해 금요일에 모였다.

해설 동사의 시제 문제이다. 주어진 문장의 빈칸은 동사를 써야 하며 의미적으로 단순현재는 의미상 어색하며 과거형이 와야 한다.

어휘 assemble 소집하다

9
해석 회사는 충전식 스마트폰의 반도체의 조달을 위한 새로운 협력체를 선정했으며 스마트폰은 좀 더 효율적인 서비스를 제공하게 될 것이다.

해설 동사 문제이다. 빈칸은 문장의 동사가 필요한 자리이며 주어가 the company로 단수이기 때문에 select는 답이 될 수 없다. 과거형인 selected가 적합하다.

어휘 vender 판매 회사 procurement 조달, 입수

10
해석 Jones 씨는 다른 회사의 직책을 맡으면서 영업 부사장직에서 물러날 것이다.

해설 동사 문제이다. 주어진 빈칸은 동사를 써야 하는 자리이며 의미적으로 미래형 동사를 써야 하므로 will resign을 쓴다.

어휘 resign (직책에서) 물러나다

11-14

Com&Com Furniture
5 Lowanna Place Hornsby
New South Wales 2077 Australia
1월 12일

고객님께

저는 여러분의 사무실을 위한 현대식 가구의 새 제품군을 소개하고자 합니다. Com&Com Furniture는 업무자가 편하게 일하는 동시에 효율적으로 일할 수 있도록 <u>고안된</u> 몇 개의 새 책상 의자 세트를 개발하였습니다.
저희는 고객님들의 건강을 소중히 여기고 신경 쓰기 때문에, 우리의 신체에 꼭 맞는 완벽한 디자인을 위해서 의학 전문가 몇 명을 고용했습니다. <u>게다가,</u> 저희 새 책상 세트는 어떤 기밀문서든 보관할 수 있는 작은 금고를 갖추고 있어서 여러분이 지문으로 이 금고를 이용할 수 있는 유일한 사람입니다. 여러분이 그것들이 어떻게 생겼는지 궁금하시면 저희 웹 사이트에 방문하셔서 제품을 클릭하셔서 제품 페이지에 방문해 주세요. <u>저희는 현재 모든 저희의 제품을 할인해서 판매하고 있습니다.</u> 더 자세한 정보를 알고 싶다면 망설이지 마시고 1-330-499-5583번으로 전화 주시기 바랍니다.

Matthew Gleason
마케팅 이사

어휘 line 제품군 comfortably 편하게 efficiently 효율적으로 value 소중하게 여기다 expert 전문가 be equipped with ~를 갖추고 있다 safe 금고 confidential 비밀의, 기밀의 finger print 지문

11
해설 동사의 태를 고르는 문제이다. 〈design+목적어+목적보어(to부정사)〉는 '~를 ~하도록 고안하다'라는 뜻이다. 관계대명사 that 앞의 new desks sets and chairs는 고안되는 대상이므로 동사 design과 의미적으로 수동 관계에 있다. 따라서 (C) are designed가 정답이다. (B)는 조동사 없이 be동사가 원형으로 쓰였으므로 정답이 될 수 없다.

12
해설 빈칸 앞뒤는 내용상 의학 전문가를 고용해서 인체 공학적인 디자인을 갖췄다는 내용과 기밀문서를 저장할 수 있는 금고를 갖췄다는 두 개의 제품 특징이 나열되고 있다. 따라서 개별적인 사실을 나열할 때 쓰이는 접속부사인 (B) Additionally가 정답이다. (C)의 In addition to는 전치사이기 때문에 뒤에 명사가 나와야 하는데, 바로 주어(our new desk sets)가 나오므로 빈칸에 들어갈 수 없다.

13
해설 문맥에 알맞은 동사를 고르는 문제이다. 문맥상 기밀문서를 보관하는 금고에 지문을 통해서만 접근할 수 있다는 뜻이므로 (A) access가 정답이다.

14
해설 (A) 이메일에 동봉된 양식에 기입해 주세요.
(B) 저희는 현재 모든 저희의 제품을 할인해서 판매하고 있습니다.
(C) 최대 동시 접속자 수로 인해 웹 사이트 이용이 일시적으로 제한되고 있습니다.
(D) 이 신청서와 함께 첨부된 편지를 읽어 주세요.
해설 빈칸 앞에서 웹 사이트를 방문해 보라는 내용이 나오므로 이 웹사이트에서 할 수 있는 일이 나오는 것이 적절하다. 제품을 할인해서 판매하고 있다는 (B)가 정답이다.

DAY 12
본문 p.198

1 (A)	2 (C)	3 (A)	4 (A)	5 (A)
6 (C)	7 (A)	8 (B)	9 (A)	10 (B)
11 (C)	12 (C)	13 (A)	14 (C)	

1
해석 티켓 판매 개선을 위한 노력의 일환으로, 항공사는 승객이 미리 티켓을 구매할 시, 50%를 절약할 수 있는 저렴한 요금 프로그램을 발표했다.
해설 부정사 문제이다. 명사인 effort를 수식해 줄 수 있는 to부정사를 써야 하는 자리이다.

2
해석 우리는 전체 유틸리티 비용 중 적어도 25%까지는 절감하기 위하여 에너지 관리 회사를 고용했다.
해설 부정사 문제이다. 에너지 관리 회사를 고용한 것은 비용을 줄이기 위한 것이므로 목적을 나타내는 부사적 용법의 to부정사가 필요하다.
어휘 overall 종합적인, 전체의

3
해석 이달의 사원으로 지명된 각각의 회사원들은 매년 있는 12월 31일 파티에서 영광이 돌려질 것입니다.
해설 빈칸 앞에 is가 있고 빈칸은 주어(Each employee)에 대한 보어여야 한다. 예정을 나타내는 to부정사인 (A) to be가 정답이다.
어휘 name 명명하다, 지명하다

4
해석 우리 회사의 제일의 목표는 고객 서비스이므로, 관리자들은 소비자들의 불만을 대할 때 마땅한 모든 조치를 취하도록 권고한다.
해설 부정사 문제이다. 동사 advise 다음에는 부정사를 써야 하므로 to 다음에 동사원형인 exercise를 써야 한다.
어휘 due diligence 적절한(마땅한) 조치

5
해석 미국의 2대 자동차 회사는 최근 새로운 하이브리드 자동차를 개발하기 위해 함께 협력하자는 내용의 동의서에 서명했다.
해설 빈칸 앞까지 완전한 문장 구조를 갖추고 있다. 빈칸은 앞의 agreement를 수식해 줄 수 있는 to부정사의 형용사적 용법이 들어갈 수 있다. 따라서 정답은 (A)이다.
어휘 automaker 자동차 회사

6
해설 항공사는 New York과 Seattle 사이의 운항의 실행 가능성에 대한 조사를 실시할 것이다. 그 결과는 5월 1일에 발표될 것이다.
해설 빈칸은 동사 need 다음에 쓰일 수 있는 부정사를 써야 한다. need는 '~할 필요가 있다'라는 의미로 뒤에 to부정사를 목적어로 취한다.
어휘 viability 실행 가능성

7
해설 우리 회사는 우리의 포장재에 대한 설계 및 판매를 위해 Consolidated Container와 다음 달부터 협력하기로 결정했다.
해설 동사 decide 다음에는 목적어로 to부정사를 써야 하기 때문에 to partner를 쓴다.

8
해설 항공사는 12월 1일, Orange County와 Lake Tahoe 사이에 서비스를 복원하기를 원한다.
해설 want 다음에는 목적어로 to부정사를 취하기 때문에 to restore를 쓴다.
어휘 restore 회복시키다

9
해설 이 트레이닝 과정의 목적은 이 요구가 많은 업종에서 직원들이 고객들을 좀 더 잘 모시는 것이 가능하도록 하는 것이다.
해설 be동사 뒤에 보어 자리에 to부정사(명사적 용법)가 들어간 형태이다. 보어 자리는 명사, 형용사 또는 to부정사나 동명사 같은 명사 상당어구

어휘 demanding 요구가 많은

10
해석 다른 주로의 이동에 대한 회사 방침에 질문을 가지고 있는 사원들은 인사부서와 연락하고 Karen White와 이야기해 볼 것을 요청한다.
해설 동사 ask는 to부정사를 목적어로 취하기 때문에 to speak를 쓴다.
어휘 interstate 주와 주 사이, 주간의

11-14
Your Diners의 대표 이사인 Raymond 씨는 첫 번째 분점으로 자리를 잡은 그의 20년 된 체인점 식당이 3달 후에 시카고에서 다시 문을 열 것이라고 발표했다. 그 내부 수리 프로젝트는 식당과 주차 공간을 포함한다.

Raymond 씨는 그 식당의 문을 다시 여는 것을 기념하기 위해서 요리 경연 대회를 개최할 것을 계획 중인데, 이 대회에서 우승자는 그의 요리를 새 메뉴에 올릴 수 있는 기회를 갖게 될 것이다. 우승자는 Raymond 씨가 3일간에 걸쳐 지도하는 요리 수업도 받게 될 것이다. Raymond 씨는 조언을 요청받자, 대회 참가자가 기억해야 할 가장 중요한 요소는 그의 식당이 영양 요소를 매우 중요하게 여긴다는 점이라고 말했다. 1등 우승자는 5,000달러뿐만 아니라 Your Diners의 주방장이 될 수 있는 기회를 가질 것이다.

어휘 diner (소규모의) 식당 establish 설립하다 satellite 분점의 renovation 내부 수리 consist of ~으로 구성되다 complete 끝마치다 cuisine 요리 factor 요인 contestant (대회의) 참가자 cherish 소중히 여기다 nutritional 영양분의

11
해설 빈칸 앞에 소유격(its)이 있고, 그 뒤에 명사(project)가 있다. 따라서 빈칸에는 형용사나 합성어를 만들 수 있는 명사가 들어갈 수 있는데, (C) renovation은 project와 결합해서 '보수 공사 프로젝트'라는 의미의 합성어를 만들 수 있다.

12
해설 hold는 '행사나 대회를 개최하다'라는 의미가 있으므로 뒤의 a cooking contest와 결합할 수 있다. 따라서 정답은 (C)이다.

13
해설 (A) 우승자는 Raymond 씨가 3일간에 걸쳐 지도하는 요리 수업도 받게 될 것이다.
(B) 많은 식당에서 메뉴를 업데이트 하기를 원한다.
(C) Raymond 씨는 지역 특산 요리를 메뉴에 추가할 것이다.
(D) 식당은 인기 메뉴는 유지하면서 독특한 메뉴를 선보일 것이다.
해설 빈칸 바로 앞에서 우승자에게 주어지는 혜택을 언급하고 있다. 따라서 also가 나오며 우승자에게 주어지는 또다른 혜택을 언급하는 (A)가 가장 적절하다.

14
해설 이 문장의 동사(said)는 뒤의 that절(목적어)과 이어지며, 빈칸부터 advice까지는 하나의 부사절 역할을 한다. 의미상 시간 부사절이 생략된 분사구문의 형태가 자연스럽다. 따라서 정답은 (C)이다.

DAY 13
본문 p.200

1 (C)	2 (C)	3 (D)	4 (B)	5 (D)
6 (C)	7 (B)	8 (B)	9 (C)	10 (A)
11 (D)	12 (C)	13 (B)	14 (C)	

1
해석 우리 회사는 프로그램 작동이 가능한 온도 장치를 사용함으로써 빌딩 온도를 조절하여 빌딩의 유지비용을 줄여 왔다.
해설 동명사 문제이다. 전치사 by 다음에는 명사와 동명사를 모두 쓸 수 있지만 빈칸 뒤에 명사 temperatures가 있기 때문에 동명사를 써야 한다. 따라서 정답은 (C)이다.
어휘 regulate 규제하다, 조절하다 thermostat 자동 온도 조절 장치

2
해석 이 회사는 6월 1일부터 150명의 새로운 승무원 채용에 대한 지원서 수락을 시작할 것입니다.
해설 동사 begin은 to부정사와 동명사를 목적어로 취하기 때문에 (C) accepting이 정답이다.
어휘 application 지원서 flight attendant 승무원

3
해석 LED 상품의 엄청나게 많은 주문을 받자마자 우리는 전체 생산량을 늘리기 위해 두 번째와 세 번째 근무조를 고용하기로 결정하였다.
해설 동명사 문제이다. 전치사 upon 다음에 명사나 동명사 형태가 와야 하므로 (D) receiving이 정답이다.
어휘 massive 거대한, 엄청나게 큰 shift 근무조 overall 전체의

4
해석 회사는 도심 지역에 가맹점들 중 몇몇을 개조하는 것을 고려 중이다.
해설 동사(is considering) 뒤의 목적어 자리이다. 동사 consider는 목적어 자리에 동명사를 취하므로 정답은 (B)이다.
어휘 remodel 개조하다 franchise store 가맹점

5
해석 우리는 당신이 여행을 위해 Best Value Guided Tours를 선택해 준 것에 감사를 표하고자 합니다.
해설 전치사(for) 다음에는 명사 또는 동명사가 온다. 빈칸 다음에 명사(Best Value Guided Tours)가 왔으므로 빈칸은 동명사 자리이다. 따라서 정답은 (D)이다.

6
해석 우리는 당신의 새로운 제품에 정말 관심이 있고, 그것에 대해서 더 많이 알게 되기를 고대하고 있습니다.
해설 look forward to에서 to는 전치사로 뒤에 명사나 동명사가 와야 한다. 따라서 정답은 (C)이다.
어휘 be interested in ~에 관심이 있다 look forward to ~를 바라다, 기대하다

SECTION 2_Part 5·6 유형 연습 » 061

7

해석 새로운 회사 로고를 개발함으로써, MAC 전자는 회사와 제품들에 대한 대중들의 인지도를 높일 수 있을 것이다.

해설 전치사(By)와 명사(logo) 사이의 동명사 자리이다. developing이 형용사로 logo를 수식할 수 없는 이유는 빈칸 뒤에 관사(a)가 있기 때문이다. 따라서 정답은 (B)이다.

어휘 public awareness 대중의 인지도

8

해석 관리 과정에서 지시 사항을 제공하는 것과 더불어 개정된 훈련 모듈은 새로운 직원들을 격려해야 한다.

해설 전치사(in addition to)와 명사(instruction) 사이의 동명사 자리이다. 따라서 정답은 (B)이다.

어휘 instruction 설명, 지시 managerial 경영의, 관리의 encouragement 격려

9

해석 홍보과 이사는 진행 중인 홍보를 통해 회사의 이미지를 증진시킬 책임이 있다.

해설 전치사(for)와 명사(image) 사이의 동명사 자리이다. 따라서 정답은 (C)이다.

어휘 ongoing 계속 진행 중인 publicity 홍보

10

해석 Sherwood는 사전에 고객들에게 통지 없이 무료 사은품을 바꿀 권한을 가지고 있다.

해설 전치사(without)와 명사(customers) 사이의 동명사 자리이다. 물론 형용사(notified)로 명사(customers)를 수식할 수도 있지만 해석상 어색하다. 따라서 정답은 (A)이다.

어휘 reserve 가지다 in advance 미리 notify 알리다

11-14

보내는 이: Revera Computer ⟨sales@reveracomputer.com⟩
받는 이: 모든 단골 고객
보낸 날짜: 11월 12일
제목: 여러분의 돈을 주머니에 보관하세요.

저희의 물품 목록이 더 다양해졌습니다! Revera Computer는 이제 저희 소중한 고객님들께 모든 종류의 브랜드 제품을 제공하게 되었습니다. 저희는 RCR 카드를 소지하고 계신 저희 단골 고객들께 훨씬 더 많은 혜택을 드림으로써 이번 변화를 축하하고자 합니다. 카드를 소지한 분들께는 모든 주문에 대한 무료 배송뿐만 아니라, 11월 30일까지 저희 매장에서 모든 컴퓨터 제품을 300달러 이상 구매하신 경우 10%의 할인을 제공해 드립니다. 저희 웹 사이트 www.reveracom.com을 방문하셔서 '회원'을 클릭하셔서 멤버십 카드를 신청하세요.

이 이메일은 고객님으로부터 요청이 없었으므로 자동적으로 생성됩니다. 이메일 뉴스 레터 구독을 취소하고 싶으시다면 이곳을 클릭하세요.

Revera Computer

어휘 loyal 충성스러운 expand 확장하다 shipping 배송 bearer (카드, 여권 등의) 소지자 generate 생성하다 automatically 자동적으로

11

해설 문맥에 맞는 적절한 명사 어휘를 고르는 문제이다. 두 번째 문장에서 고객에게 더 다양한 브랜드의 컴퓨터 제품을 제공하게 되었다는 내용으로부터 첫 번째 문장은 물품 목록(inventory)이 확장되었다는 의미가 되어야 한다. 따라서 정답은 (D)이다.

12

해설 빈칸 바로 앞 문장에서 단골 고객에게 더 많은 혜택을 제공한다는 내용이 언급되었다. 따라서 무료 배송 이외에도(in addition to) 10%의 할인이 제공된다는 내용이 자연스러우므로 정답은 (C)이다.

13

해설 고객들에게 발송되는 이메일이므로 여기서 이메일을 받는 상대방인 고객은 you로 지칭될 수 있다. 따라서 정답은 (B)이다.

14

해석 (A) 귀하께 보내는 첫 번째 이메일입니다.
(B) 정보 요청의 이용 가능성을 확인하기 위함입니다.
(C) 이메일 뉴스 레터 구독을 취소하고 싶으시다면 이곳을 클릭하세요.
(D) 무료로 저희 월간 뉴스 레터를 구독하실 수 있습니다.

해설 바로 앞에서 고객의 승인 없이 자동적으로 보내지는 이메일이라는 내용이 나온다. 이 뒤에는 우선적으로 보내고 혹시라도 구독하기 싫으면 취소해도 된다는 말이 올 수 있다. 따라서 (C)가 정답이다.

DAY 14

본문 p.202

1 (C)	2 (C)	3 (B)	4 (B)	5 (C)
6 (B)	7 (C)	8 (A)	9 (B)	10 (C)
11 (D)	12 (C)	13 (B)	14 (B)	

1

해석 직원들이 최신 전화번호와 주소를 업데이트 해 놓는 것은 중요하다.

해설 과거분사 문제이다. keep은 목적어 뒤에 목적보어를 취하는데 형용사, 분사가 올 수 있다. 전화번호와 주소는 업데이트되는 대상이므로 과거분사인 (C)가 정답이다.

어휘 current 현재의

2

해석 우리 컴퓨터는 기술자들이 메모리를 업데이트하기 전까지 새롭게 개발된 회사 소프트웨어를 실행할 수 없다.

해설 분사 문제이다. 명사 corporate software를 수식하는 분사가 와야 하는 자리이며 '새롭게 개발된 회사 소프트웨어'라는 뜻이므로 수식을 받는 명사와 분사의 의미 관계가 수동인 과거분사를 써야 한다. 따라서 정답은 (C)이다.

어휘 be unable to ~할 수 없다 run 운영하다, 실행하다

3
해석 우리 회사는 최고의 에너지 보존 장치를 가지고 있고 세계적으로 인정 받는 회사인 Energy Star 재단과 계약을 체결하였다.

해설 분사 문제이다. 명사인 firm을 수식하는 자리에는 분사를 써야 하는데 현재분사인 recognizing은 의미적으로 능동이기 때문에 적합하지 않다. 따라서 수동의 의미인 '인정을 받다'라는 뜻의 과거분사 형태인 recognized가 정답이다.

어휘 foundation 재단 recognize 알아보다, 인정하다 conservation 보호, 보존, 관리

4
해석 첨부된 메모는 그 의미가 약간 애매모호하니 목표가 더 뚜렷하게 나타나게 다시 제출해 주세요.

해설 과거분사 문제이다. 빈칸 다음에 있는 memo를 수식해 줄 수 있는 분사가 와야 하는 자리이며 의미적으로 수동의 의미인 '첨부된'이 적절하므로 attached가 정답이다.

어휘 ambiguous 모호한 resubmit 다시 제출하다 objective 목적, 목표

5
해석 우리는 우리 회사의 사원들이 이번 해 100만 달러 이상을 자선 업체에 기부한 것을 발표하게 되어 자랑스럽다.

해설 동사 문제이다. have 다음에 과거분사형인 contributed를 써서 현재완료 문장이 된다. 따라서 정답은 (C)이다.

6
해석 Allen 씨는 기존의 프린터를 새로운 것으로 교체하는 것이 비용 효율적이라는 것을 알았다.

해설 빈칸은 뒤의 명사(printers)를 수식하는 분사 자리이다. exist는 자동사이므로 existed는 어색하다. 현재분사 형태인 existing은 '기존의'라는 뜻이다. 따라서 정답은 (B)이다.

어휘 cost-effective 비용 효율이 높은 replace 대신하다, 대체하다

7
해석 David Shaffer이 최고의 고객 서비스 덕에 이달의 직원상을 받게 되었다는 것을 발표하게 되어 기쁩니다.

해설 형용사 문제이다. be동사 뒤에는 형용사가 와야 하고 주어가 사람이기 때문에 과거분사 형태인 pleased를 쓴다.

어휘 outstanding 뛰어난, 두드러진

8
해석 다음 주부터 상점에서 판매될 저희 회사의 새로운 태양 에너지 제품인 Old Time Lantern에 대한 소개서가 동봉되어 있으니 읽어 보시기 바랍니다.

해설 과거분사 문제이다. 명사인 letter를 수식할 수 있는 형용사를 써야 하며 의미적으로 '동봉된'이라는 수동의 의미가 되어야 하기 때문에 정답은 (A) enclosed이다.

어휘 opposite 반대의 absent 결석한 innocent 무죄의

9
해석 경영진은 시의회에 의해 그들의 제안이 거부되었다는 소식을 듣고 아주 실망했다.

해설 주어 the management는 '경영진'이라는 뜻이므로 사람 명사를 주어로 사용하는 분사 (B) disappointed가 정답이다.

어휘 management 경영진 proposal 제안 reject 거부하다

10
해석 거의 모든 영화 평론가들이 시사회에서 그 새 스릴러 영화가 재미있다는 것을 알았다.

해설 동사 find는 [find+목적어+목적격 보어]의 구문으로 사용되기 때문에 빈칸은 동사 find의 목적격 보어 역할을 하는 형용사나 분사를 써야 한다. 감정 표현 분사인 interesting은 주어가 사물일 때 또는 재미있는 사람을 나타낼 때 사용한다. 따라서 정답은 (C)이다.

어휘 critic 비평가, 평론가 preview 시사회

11-14

Mathew Smith
1519 Walnut Ave
Antioch, CA 94883

Joanna Evens
Personnel Director
Oasis Health Club
Las Vegas, NV 89154

Evens에게,

저는 Oasis 헬스클럽의 개인 트레이너 자리에 지원하기 위해 이력서를 보냅니다. 저는 Manhattan의 Tropics 헬스클럽에서 개인 트레이너로서 5년 동안 일을 했습니다. 저는 그곳에 있는 동안 두 권의 운동에 관한 책을 냈는데, 두 권 다 독자들로부터 좋은 반응을 얻었습니다. 저는 또한 몇 번 건강 채널의 TV 쇼에 출연하여 많은 연예인들에게 그들의 요구 사항에 맞게, 집에서도 하기 쉬운 운동을 추천했습니다. 몇 달 후, 그들은 모두 저에게 메일을 통해서 그들이 꿈꿔 왔던 몸을 가지게 되었다고 말하면서 저에게 감사를 표시했습니다. 저는 저의 전문 지식이 귀하의 헬스클럽에 큰 도움이 될 것이라고 믿고 있습니다. 그 직책을 위한 인터뷰가 언제인지 알려 주시기 바랍니다. 저는 귀하의 헬스클럽에 많은 새 고객들을 모을 수 있는 많은 아이디어가 있습니다. 가능한 한 빨리 귀하와 이런 아이디어에 대해서 공유하고 싶습니다. 귀하로부터 소식을 들을 수 있기를 바랍니다.

Mathew Smith

어휘 submit 제출하다 position 자리, 직위 response 반응 routine 정해진 틀 celebrity 유명 인사 of help 도움이 되는(= helpful)

11
해설 문맥에 맞는 명사 어휘를 고르는 문제이다. 이 글의 목적은 Oasis 헬스클럽에 입사 지원을 위해 쓴 편지이므로 (D) employment가 적절하다.

12
해설 received는 타동사이므로 뒤에 목적어, 즉 명사가 와야 한다. 빈칸이 명사인 responses 앞에 놓였으므로 responses를 꾸며주는 형용사가 와야 한다. 따라서 (A)나 (C)가 들어가야 하는데, (A)는 '가장 좋아하는'의 의미로 문맥상 의미가 어색하다. 정답은 '호의적인'이라는 의미의 (C) favorable이다.

13

해설 빈칸은 문맥상 인터뷰가 예정된 날짜를 묻는 내용인데, 〈will+be+-ing〉는 미래에 예정된 일을 나타낼 때 사용될 수 있다. 따라서 정답은 (B)이다.

14

해설 (A) 제 프리젠테이션을 준비하는 데 많은 시간을 할애했습니다.
(B) 가능한 한 빨리 귀하와 이런 아이디어에 대해서 공유하고 싶습니다.
(C) 저는 라스베이거스 대회에 참가했습니다.
(D) 저는 운동 프로그램을 진행한 경험이 있습니다.

해설 바로 앞문장이 핵심 힌트다. 많은 아이디어가 있다고 했으므로 이와 관련된 내용이 다음에 나와야 한다. 이런 아이디어에 대해 공유하고 싶다는 (B)가 정답이다.

DAY 15

본문 p.204

1 (C)	2 (A)	3 (D)	4 (B)	5 (D)
6 (D)	7 (C)	8 (B)	9 (A)	10 (A)
11 (C)	12 (A)	13 (A)	14 (B)	

1

해설 모든 영업 사원들은 회사가 후원하는 연금 또는 직원의 지분 프로그램에 가입할 수 있다.

해설 등위접속사 문제이다. 빈칸에는 두 개의 명사인 the company sponsored annuity와 the employee shareholding programs 두 개 중에서 선택을 할 수 있는 등위접속사를 써야 하며 의미상 (C) or이 적절하다.

어휘 annuity 연금 shareholding 주식 보유량

2

해설 대표 이사는 그의 회사를 매각하고 새 사업을 시작하는 것을 진지하게 고려 중이다.

해설 빈칸은 consider의 목적어가 되는 동명사 selling off와 and를 통해 연결되어 있다. 등위접속사와 연결되는 것은 같은 형식이어야 한다. 즉, 형용사는 형용사끼리, 부사는 부사끼리, 동명사는 동명사끼리, to부정사는 to부정사끼리 연결되어야 한다. 따라서 starting이 정답이다.

어휘 sell off (싼 가격에) 매각해 버리다

3

해설 UPC 배송은 효율적인 일정 관리와 배분 시스템을 이용해서 배송 지연을 최소화했다.

해설 명사 문제이다. 등위접속사 and를 기준으로 앞에 명사가 왔으므로 뒤에도 명사가 와야 한다. 의미상 '배포'를 의미하는 distribution이 정답이다.

어휘 minimize 최소화하다

4

해설 100명이 넘는 사원들이 LA 지사로 전근을 요구하였지만 그곳에는 오직 10명의 자리만 있다.

해설 등위접속사 문제이다. 두 개의 문장을 연결하는 접속사가 필요한 자리이며 의미적으로 빈칸 앞의 문장과 뒤의 문장이 서로 대조를 이루고 있으므로 (B) but이 정답이다.

어휘 transfer 전근 opening 빈자리, 공석

5

해설 직원들은 Gold Star 의료 보험이나 Silver Star 의료 보험에 등록할 수 있지만 고용주 개인 분담금 한도가 한 달에 887달러라는 것을 명심해야 한다.

해설 등위접속사의 의미 선택 문제이다. 빈칸 앞뒤로 2가지 서로 다른 의료 보험이 나오므로 의미상 선택을 나타내는 등위접속사 (D) or이 정답이다.

어휘 sign up for ~를 신청하다 keep in mind ~를 명심하다 contribution 개인 분담금 cap (액수의) 한도

6

해설 마케팅 부서와 판매 부서 모두 'Old Time Lantern'의 새로운 광고 프로그램에 착수할 것이다.

해설 상관접속사 문제이다. 빈칸 뒤에 and로 짝을 이룬 명사가 나오므로 '둘 다'를 의미하는 (D) both가 정답이다.

7

해설 Sear 전자 직원들은 국경일 바로 전이나 후에 휴일을 가짐으로써 더 긴 휴가를 떠날 수 있다.

해설 상관접속사 문제이다. 주어진 빈칸에는 or와 쌍을 이룰 수 있는 either를 써야 한다.

어휘 national holiday 국경일

8

해설 디트로이트 공장이나 보스톤 공장 둘 다 추가적인 직원이 필요하지 않지만 LA 공장은 20명의 노동자를 고용할 계획이다.

해설 상관접속사 문제이다. 빈칸 앞부분에 Neither가 있으므로 이와 짝을 이루는 (B) nor가 정답이다.

9

해설 파일럿 지원자는 자격증뿐만 아니라, 항공 산업에서의 넓은 경험이 있어야 한다.

해설 상관접속사 문제이다. 빈칸 뒤의 but also와 짝을 이룰 수 있는 상관접속사는 'A뿐만 아니라 B 또한'을 의미하는 not only ~ but also 이다. 따라서 정답은 (A)이다.

어휘 extensive 아주 넓은, 대규모의 certificate 자격증 aviation 항공

10

해설 조합의 직위에 고용된 엔지니어들은 고용인 조합에 가입하거나 고용된 날짜로부터 30일 이내에 멤버십을 거절해야 한다.

해설 상관접속사 문제이다. 빈칸 앞부분에 나오는 상관접속사 either와 짝을 이루는 (A) or가 정답이다.

어휘 union 조합 decline 거절하다

11-14

받는 이: 모든 직원들
보내는 이: John C Charter, VP Personnel
보낸 날짜: 9월 21일
주제: 직원 항공 혜택

첨부된 직원 항공 혜택 개정안인 SOP Personnel Policy 21-340을 주목하여 주십시오. 회사는 직원 항공 혜택 프로그램의 제약을 풀어 확대 가족까지 포함하도록 하였습니다. 즉시 효력이 있으며, 모든 직속 가족들과 확대 가족들은 항공권을 받을 자격이 있습니다. 이 혜택들은 회사원이 정직원 채용으로 계약을 한 기간에만 효력이 있다는 것에 유의하십시오.
이 티켓들은 직원이 회사에서 퇴직하는 순간 즉시 만료될 것입니다. 친척들이 여행하기 적어도 2주 전에 직원들은 HR-21-340을 제출하도록 요구됩니다. 이 서류는 부서의 부서장에게 서명을 받아야 합니다. 그것은 최종 승인을 위해 인사부서에 제출되어야 합니다. 이 서류가 승인이 되면, 직원들은 공항에서 유효한 여권과 함께 제시되어야 하는 탑승권을 받을 것입니다. 질문이 있으시면 내선 번호 8766번으로 전화 주세요.

어휘 attach 첨부하다 revision (법, 규칙의) 개정 policy 정책 liberalize (규제를) 풀다 extended family 확대 가족 effective 효력을 발휘하는 immediately 즉시 immediate 직계 혈통의 eligible 자격을 갖춘 tenure 재직 기간 full time employment 상근직 고용 terminate 끝내다, 종료하다 prior to ~에 앞서서 pass 탑승권, 입장권 extension 내선 번호

11
해설 혜택 기간이 적용되는 것은 고용 기간 동안이어야 한다는 것이 자연스러우므로 (C) during이 적절하다.

12
해설 직원이 회사를 그만 두는 순간 혜택이 만료되는 것이므로 적절한 부사는 '즉시'라는 의미의 (A) immediately이다.

13
해설 (A) 그것은 최종 승인을 위해 인사부서에 제출되어야 합니다.
(B) 그것은 새로운 직책에 대한 자격을 입증합니다.
(C) 여행 경비를 반영하는 수정 사항에 대한 어떠한 요청이라도 알려주셔야 합니다.
(D) 여행 혜택 프로그램을 향상시킬 수 있는 방안이 보고되어야 합니다.
해설 빈칸 앞에는 서명을 받아야 한다는 내용이 나오고 뒤에는 승인 후 절차에 대해 나오고 있다. 따라서 빈칸에는 서명을 받은 후의 절차에 대한 설명이 나와야 하므로 (A)가 정답이다.

14
해설 비행기에 탑승할 때 여권과 함께 탑승권이 제시되어야(presented) 하므로 정답은 (B)이다.

DAY 16

본문 p.206

1 (A)	2 (D)	3 (C)	4 (B)	5 (D)
6 (B)	7 (A)	8 (D)	9 (D)	10 (B)
11 (C)	12 (C)	13 (A)	14 (D)	

1
해석 다가오는 새해 파티에 참가하고 싶은 직원은 확실한 예약을 위해 적어도 12월 15일까지 최대한 빨리 답장을 해야 한다.
해설 관계대명사 문제이다. 앞의 선행사 all employees(사람)를 받는 주격 관계대명사 (A) who가 정답이다.
어휘 participate in ~에 참가하다 upcoming 다가오는 RSVP (프랑스어 Répondez s'il vous plaît를 줄인 것) 회답 주시기 바랍니다(please reply)

2
해석 직원들이 인사부에서 로비에 붙인 메모에 대해 질문하고 있다.
해설 관계대명사 문제이다. 빈칸 앞의 선행사 a memo를 부가 설명해 주는 관계대명사 (D) that이 정답이다.
어휘 human resources department 인사부

3
해석 Vector Design의 많은 직원들은 비행기 표와 호텔 요금이 높은 휴가철 성수기에는 휴가를 떠나는 것을 피한다.
해설 빈칸에 관계사가 들어가는 경우, 관계사절이 이끄는 절에서 주어나 목적어 같은 성분이 빠져 있으면 관계대명사가, 모든 성분이 갖춰져 있으면 관계부사가 들어간다. 빈칸 뒤의 절은 〈주어, 동사, 보어〉가 완벽하게 갖춰진 절이므로 빈칸에는 관계부사가 들어가는데, 선행사(the peak of the holiday season)가 시간을 나타내므로 when이 적절하다.
어휘 peak 정점, 최고조

4
해석 지난달 업데이트된 이 회사의 새로운 웹 사이트는 고객이 자신만의 제품을 디자인하고 그것들을 온라인에 올릴 수 있도록 해 줄 것이다.
해설 관계대명사 문제이다. 선행사인 the company's new Web site를 받을 수 있는 관계대명사가 필요하다. 빈칸 앞에 쉼표가 있으므로 (B) which가 정답이다.

5
해석 BTS IT Solutions는 최근 어떤 삭제 파일이라도 완벽하게 복원시킬 수 있는 새로운 소프트웨어를 개발했다.
해설 빈칸 뒤의 절은 빠진 성분 없이 완벽하므로 주격 관계대명사나 목적격 관계대명사는 올 수 없다. 선행사인 new software는 삭제된 파일을 복구시킬 수 있는 도구이므로 도구를 나타내는 전치사와 함께 쓰인 with which가 적절하다.
어휘 restore 복구하다 perfectly 완벽하게

6

해석 부서의 매니저들과 감독관들의 이번 분기 미팅은 Hilton에서 열릴 것이고 그곳에서 우린 직원들의 의욕을 개선시킬 방안에 대해 토의할 것이다.

해설 빈칸 뒤의 문장은 빠진 것 없이 완벽하며 빈칸 앞에 장소가 왔으므로 장소를 나타내는 관계부사 (B) where가 정답이다.

어휘 quarterly 분기별 morale 사기, 의욕

7

해석 시장 분석을 담당하는 Jenna Harrison은 조사 팀과 임무의 할당을 토론하기 위해서 만나기를 바라고 있다.

해설 빈칸부터 analysis까지가 관계대명사절(계속적 용법) Jenna Harrison을 부연 설명한다. Jenna Harrison(선행사)이 사람이고 나머지 형용사절에서 주어가 없으므로 주격 관계대명사 (A) who가 정답이다.

어휘 be in charge of ~를 맡다, 담당하다 allocation 할당, 할당량

8

해석 PIC Communications 사는 5명의 그래픽 아티스트를 최근에 고용했는데, 그들 모두가 여성이다.

해설 쉼표를 기준으로 2개의 문장이 있으므로 빈칸은 접속사 자리이고 앞의 선행사(artists)를 받는 형용사절 접속사 자리이다. 선행사는 사람, 전치사 뒤에 빈칸이 있으므로 목적격 관계대명사인 whom을 써야 한다.

9

해석 NY Fine Art Center에서 현재 그림들이 전시되고 있는 Michael Stevens는 가장 영향력 있는 미술가들 중에 한 명으로 여겨진다.

해설 빈칸부터 Center까지가 형용사절이다. 선행사(Michael Stevens)가 사람이고 나머지 형용사절에서 빠진 것이 없으므로 소유격이 정답이 될 수 있다.

10

해석 10일 이내에 서명이 되지 않은 어떤 계약서라도 자동으로 폐기되며, 다시 협상되어야 한다.

해설 빈칸부터 days까지가 형용사절이다. 선행사(agreement)가 사물이고 나머지 형용사절에서 주어가 없으므로 주격 관계대명사 which가 정답이다.

어휘 discard 버리다, 폐기하다

11-14

최근 풍력 사용의 세계적인 증가로 인해 캘리포니아 주 퍼먼트에 있는 Apex 풍력 시스템은 노스다코다 주 샬롯에 있는 Beta 대체 에너지사와 합병을 하기로 결정했다. 합병은 Apex 사가 캐나다를 포함한 전체 북아메리카 대륙에게 서비스를 제공할 수 있도록 해 주기 때문에 Apex에게 더 유리해질 것이다. Beta 대체 에너지사는 캐나다에서 풍차 시스템 운영을 허가 받았고 캐나다 에너지국과의 조달 계약을 실행하고 있다. Apex는 미에너지국에서 공인된 공급자이다. 두 회사의 합병이 끝난 후, 두 회사는 활동의 중복을 없애고, 시스템의 운영을 간소화할 것이다. 이번 합병은 풍력 발전 기술을 새로운 단계로 끌어올릴 것으로 기대되고 있다.

어휘 wind power 풍력 merge with ~와 합병하다 advantageous 이익이 되는 license ~을 허가하다 windmill 풍차 fulfill (의무를) 이행하다 procurement (물품의) 조달, 공급 vender 공급업체 duplication 중복 streamline 간소화하다 operation 운영

11

해설 빈칸은 주어(Apex Wind Energy Systems of Fremont, California)에 대한 동사 자리이다. 따라서 수가 일치하지 않는 (A)는 수 일치에서 오답이며 동사 형태가 아닌 (B)도 오답이다. 수와 태, 시제 면에서 (C)가 적절하다.

12

해설 빈칸 앞에 전체 북아메리카 대륙(entire North American continent)이 언급되므로 뒤에는 '캐나다까지 포함되는'이라는 의미가 되도록 including이 들어가야 한다. including은 '~를 포함하여'라는 의미의 전치사이다.

13

해설 문맥상 적절한 동사를 고르는 문제로, 뒤에 and와 연결되는 동사인 streamline이 있는데, 이는 '간소화하다'라는 동사이다. 따라서 문맥상 '중복을 없애다'라는 의미가 될 수 있는 (A) eliminate가 정답이다.

14

해석 (A) 경쟁력을 약화시킬 것이다.
(B) 그들의 사업이 자연에 악영향을 미칠 것이다.
(C) Apex는 많은 업무량으로 인해 고통받을 것이다.
(D) 이번 합병은 풍력 발전 기술을 새로운 단계로 끌어올릴 것으로 기대되고 있다.

해설 빈칸 앞에서는 합병으로 인한 장점에 대해서 언급하고 있다. 따라서 풍력 발전 기술을 새로운 단계로 끌어올릴 것이라는 (D)가 정답이다. (D)를 제외하고는 모두 부정적인 영향에 대한 내용이다.

DAY 17 본문 p.208

1 (C)	2 (A)	3 (A)	4 (A)	5 (C)
6 (A)	7 (C)	8 (B)	9 (C)	10 (C)
11 (C)	12 (A)	13 (D)	14 (B)	

1

해석 비즈니스 서류 작성 세미나에 참석을 희망하는 사람은 누구든지 이번 달 말까지 등록을 해야 한다.

해설 빈칸은 wishes에 대한 주어인데 뒤에 또 동사(must register)가 나오므로 빈칸이 이끄는 절은 명사절을 이끄는 말이 들어가야 한다. (A), (B)를 정답에서 제외하고, 주어 자리이므로 Whoever(누구든지 간에)가 정답이다.

어휘 register 등록하다

2

해석 최근에 발표된 연구에 의하면 대부분의 피부 관리 제품들이 피부를 지킨다는 면에서 거의 같은 품질을 가지고 있다고 한다.

해설 동사가 2개 있으므로 빈칸은 접속사 자리이며 indicate(동사) 뒤의 목적어 자리이다. 따라서 명사절이 되어야 하고, (A)와 (C)가 명사절 접속사인데 빈칸 뒤에 명사절 문장이 완벽한 문장이므로 what(불완전한 문장을 명사절로 묶는 접속사)은 올 수 없다. 따라서 정답은 (A)이다.

어휘 indicate 나타내다, 보여주다

3

해석 조사에 참가한 사람들은 아무리 작은 것이라도 그들의 마음에 떠오르는 무엇이든지 간에 말하라고 요청 받았다.

해설 say의 목적어가 필요한데 빈칸 뒤에 문장이 있으므로 명사절로 묶어야 한다. 따라서 정답은 (A)이다. whenever도 접속사이긴 하지만 부사절 접속사로 오답이다.

어휘 come to one's mind 생각이 나다, 떠오르다 regardless of ~에 상관없이

4

해석 Redmond Foundation 검토 위원회는 어떤 교육 기관에 자금 지원을 할지 결정하기 위해서 화요일에 만날 것이다.

해설 의미상 '어떤 교육 기관에 자금 지원을 할지'라는 뜻이므로 (A) which가 정답이다. which가 뒤의 명사(educational organization)를 수식하면서 to부정사와 함께 명사 상당어구로 쓰이고 있다. [의문사+to부정사]는 명사 역할을 함을 알아 두자.

5

해석 최근 경기 침체 때문에 대표 이사는 생산 공장이 새로운 비용 절감 계획을 시행해야 한다고 발표했다.

해설 동사(announced) 뒤의 목적어 자리에 완벽한 문장이 오므로 불완전한 문장을 묶어서 명사절로 만드는 (B)는 오답이다. (C)와 (D) 중에서 의미상 (C)가 정답임을 알 수 있다.

어휘 downturn 감소, 하락 implement 시행하다 cost-cutting 비용 절감

6

해석 GSEM 에너지는 이사진 회의 동안에 Osaka에 새로운 사무실을 열지 말지에 대해 결정해야 한다.

해설 [의문사 + to부정사]는 명사의 역할을 할 수 있다. 이와 마찬가지로 [whether + to부정사]는 '~할지 말지'라는 의미의 명사 상당어구로 쓰일 수 있다. 하지만 if는 뜻은 같지만 to부정사와 함께 명사로 쓰일 수 없다. 따라서 정답은 (A)이다.

어휘 the board of directors 이사회

7

해석 우리는 경영진이 지방 정부와 이 문제를 여전히 토론하고 있기 때문에 우리의 3번째 지점이 어디에 위치될 것인지 아직 확신할 수 없다.

해설 be sure 뒤의 명사절을 묻는 문제이다. 빈칸 뒤의 명사절은 완벽한 문장이므로 (B)는 정답이 될 수 없다. 의미상 '어디에 위치될 것인지'라는 뜻이므로 정답은 (C)이다.

8

해석 충분한 좌석을 확보하기 위해서 우리는 누가 공항에서 무료 셔틀 서비스를 이용할지를 확인해야 한다.

해설 determine 뒤는 목적어 자리이다. 명사절로 묶어야 하는데 (A), (B), (C) 중에서 의미상 '누가 이용할지를'이 적절하므로 정답은 (B)이다. that은 완벽한 문장을 묶어야 하므로 주어가 없는 문장을 묶을 수 없다.

어휘 determine 알아내다, 밝히다

9

해석 고객들을 가장 기쁘게 하는 것은 식당으로부터 제공되는 품질 좋은 음식과 서비스들이다.

해설 동사(was) 앞은 주어이므로 명사절로 묶어야 하며 (A), (C) 중에서 의미상 '~하는 것'이 적절하고 빈칸 뒤가 완벽한 문장이 아니므로 (C) What이 정답이다.

10

해석 직원 설명서는 새로운 직원들이 회사의 규정에 대해서 알아야 하는 것을 설명한다.

해설 동사(explains) 뒤는 목적어 자리인데 빈칸 뒤의 문장에서 know의 목적어가 빠져 있으므로 불완전한 명사절을 묶는 (C), (D) 중에서 의미상 '알아야 하는 것'이 적절하다. 따라서 정답은 what이다.

어휘 handbook 편람, 안내서 regarding ~에 대하여

11-14

Amtrak의 미국 관광 여행권

저희는 여행객들이 90일 이상 Amtrak을 이용해서 북아메리카의 어느 곳이든 여행할 수 있는 〈The See American Pass〉라고 불리는 새 여행 프로그램을 소개하게 되어서 매우 기쁘게 생각합니다. 〈The See American Pass〉를 이용함에 있어서 아무런 제약이 없으며 유일하게 제약 받는 것이 있다면 그저 여행자의 상상력뿐입니다. 이 새 프로모션은 미국 역사상 전례 없는 일입니다. 또한 우리는 군인, 학생, 노인에게 여행권의 20%를 할인해 줍니다. 90일 간의 〈The See American Pass〉는 단 150달러입니다! 이 값은 오늘날 여행 산업에서 들어보지 못했던 것입니다. 이것은 돈을 아낄 수 있는 투자입니다! 한 가지 주의할 사항이 있다면 시간입니다. 저희는 이 여행권을 5월 1일부터 시작해서 단 1주일 동안만 제공할 것입니다. 그 이후에는 판매가 되지 않을 것입니다. 〈The See American Pass〉는 다른 할인이나 판촉 상품과 결합해서 사용할 수 없음을 알려 드립니다.

어휘 limit 제한 senior citizen 노인 investment 투자 caveat 통고, 경고

11

해설 동사의 알맞은 시제를 고르는 문제이다. 관광객들이 여행을 할 수 있는 상

품을 홍보하는 글로 문맥상 미래 시제가 되어야 하므로 정답은 (C)이다.

12
해설 이 새로운 프로모션은 미국 역사상 전례가 없었다고(unprecedented) 해야 의미가 자연스러우므로 정답은 (A)이다.

13
해석 (A) 여행 패키지 프로그램에 투자할 수 있습니다.
(B) 가족이나 친구에게 이것을 소개해 줄 수 있습니다.
(C) 이 프로그램은 정부 보조금으로 만들어졌습니다.
(D) 이 값은 오늘날 여행 산업에서 들어보지 못했던 것입니다.
해설 빈칸 앞의 only $150와 뒤의 a money saving investment를 통해 가격이 저렴하다는 것을 알 수 있다. 따라서 가격의 저렴함을 강조하는 (D)가 정답이다.

14
해설 5월 1일부터 시작해서 일주일 동안 여행권이 판매되는 것이므로 (B) beginning이 정답이다.

DAY 18
본문 p.210

1 (B)	2 (D)	3 (D)	4 (A)	5 (C)
6 (A)	7 (B)	8 (D)	9 (B)	10 (C)
11 (B)	12 (A)	13 (D)	14 (C)	

1
해석 컴퓨터 기술자는 다른 사용자가 컴퓨터 시스템을 사용하는 동안에도, 새로운 소프트웨어를 설치할 수 있다.
해설 접속사 문제이다. 2개의 문장을 연결하는 접속사 자리이기 때문에 부사절 접속사 (B) while이 정답이다.
어휘 install 설치하다

2
해석 비록 축구 결승전이 폭우 때문에 잠시 중단되었지만 대부분의 관중들은 경기가 끝날 때까지 경기장을 떠나지 않았다.
해설 빈칸 뒤에는 두 개의 절이 연속적으로 나오므로, 빈칸에는 두 개의 절을 이어줄 수 있는 접속사가 필요하다. 두 개의 절은 내용상 서로 대조 관계를 이루므로 양보의 부사절 접속사 Though가 가장 적절하다.
어휘 be interrupted 잠시 중단되다 audience 관중

3
해석 일단 Consolidated Container의 인수에 대한 승인을 받고 나면, 우리는 작업을 보다 효율적으로 하기 위해 두 회사의 시설을 결합할 것입니다.
해설 접속사 문제이다. 두 개의 문장을 연결할 수 있는 접속사를 써야 하며 의미상 부사절 접속사인 '일단 ~한다면'이라는 once가 적절하다.
어휘 approval 승인 acquisition 인수

4
해석 우리가 확인서를 받자마자 주문들은 그 주소로 바로 보내질 것이다.
해설 부사절 접속사 자리이다. 접속부사인 (C)를 제외하고 (A), (B), (D)에서 해석을 통해서 문제를 푼다. 의미상 '~하자마자'가 적절하므로 정답은 (A)이다.
어휘 confirmation 확인서 right away 즉시

5
해석 우리 상품들이 처음에는 비쌀 수 있지만, 이들은 에너지를 아낌으로써 시간에 따라 비용을 아껴 나간다.
해설 접속사 문제이다. 두 개의 문장을 연결하는 접속사 자리이며 의미상 양보의 절을 이끄는 부사절 접속사인 Even though가 정답이다.
어휘 initially 처음에

6
해석 Karen 씨가 계획대로 그녀의 출장에서 사무실로 돌아온다면 회의 일정에는 변화가 없을 것이다.
해설 접속사 자리이다. 접속부사인 (C)를 제외하고 (A), (B), (D) 중에서 해석을 통해 문제를 푼다. 의미상 조건을 나타내는 (A)가 정답이다.

7
해석 모든 직원들은 사용하지 않을 때는 회의실의 불을 끄는 것이 요청됩니다.
해설 빈칸부터 in use까지를 부사절로 묶는 것이 해석상, 문법상 더 적절하다. (A), (B) 중에서 해석을 통해서 정답을 도출한다. (A)는 '~가 아니라면'의 의미로 문맥상 맞지 않고 (B)가 정답이다.

8
해석 모든 사원들이 새로운 London 사무실로 이적하였으므로, 우리는 이제 교육과 절차들을 개선시키는 데 집중할 수 있다.
해설 두 개의 절이 연결되어 있기 때문에 부사절 접속사인 (D)가 정답이다.

9
해석 회사가 작년에 상당한 돈을 절약했기 때문에 우리는 모든 직원들에게 일괄적으로 10%의 임금 인상을 할 수 있다.
해설 동사 saved가 있는 절 앞에는 접속사가 필요하고 문장의 구성에 영향을 주지 않는 부사절 접속사가 필요하다. 빈칸에는 의미적으로 '~이기 때문에'가 되어야 하므로 Since가 정답이다. So는 부사절 접속사이지만 문장의 처음에 쓰이면서 문장을 이끄는 역할은 할 수 없다.
어휘 considerable 상당한 across the board 전반에 걸쳐

10
해석 저희 상점의 정책은 제품이 하자가 없는 경우 어떤 교환이나 환불도 해 드리지 않는다는 것입니다.
해설 빈칸 뒤의 절은 앞절과 자연스럽게 연결되려면 'if the product is not defective (제품이 하자가 없는 경우)'의 의미가 되어야 한다. if ~ not은 unless로 바꿔 쓸 수 있으므로 정답은 (C)이다.
어휘 policy 정책 defective (제품이) 결함이 있는

11-14

연례 직원 피크닉이 New Jersey의 Newark에 있는 Riverside 공원에서 있을 예정입니다. 이 연례 피크닉은 작년에 우리 직원들의 놀라운 헌신에 바칠 것입니다. 여러분 모두가 알다시피, 작년은 우리 회사가 가장 이익이 발생했던 해였습니다. 게다가, 질 좋은 제품을 만들고 뛰어난 고객 서비스를 제공한 것은 모두 우리 종업원들의 헌신과 노력 때문이었습니다. 이것이 우리 회사에 최고의 사람들을 찾기 위하여 직원 모집, 급여와 이익에 많은 양의 투자를 하는 이유입니다. 이 직원 피크닉을 후원하게 되어 기쁩니다. 우리 회사는 모든 음식과 음료 그리고 여흥을 제공할 것입니다.

어휘 profitable 수익성 있는 dedication 전념, 헌신 sponsor 후원하다, 지원하다

11
해설 주어진 빈칸은 동사를 써야 하며 미래의 의미를 가지고 있기 때문에 미래 시제를 써야 한다. 의미상 능동태가 아니라 수동태가 되어야 하므로 정답은 (B)이다.

12
해설 dedicate A to B(A를 B에게 바치다)는 A is dedicated to B와 같이 수동태로 만들 수 있다.

13
해설 주어진 문장의 빈칸에는 '~하기 위하여'라는 부사적 용법의 to부정사를 써야 하기 때문에 정답은 (D)이다.

14
해설 (A) 대신, 연수 과정은 토요일까지 미뤄질 것입니다.
(B) 회사 이익이 지난 5년간 증가하였습니다.
(C) 우리 회사는 모든 음식과 음료 그리고 여흥을 제공할 것입니다.
(D) 면접은 성공적인 모집 절차의 핵심입니다.
해설 전체적으로 직원 피크닉에 대한 내용이고 빈칸 바로 앞에는 피크닉을 후원하게 되어 기쁘다는 내용이 나온다. 따라서 마지막으로 음식, 음료 등 회사에서 할 수 있는 일을 언급한 (C)가 정답이다.

DAY 19

본문 p.212

1 (C)	2 (C)	3 (A)	4 (C)	5 (C)
6 (C)	7 (C)	8 (D)	9 (B)	10 (A)
11 (B)	12 (C)	13 (B)	14 (C)	

1
해석 승무원이 되는 것은 지원자들이 예상했던 것보다 더 어렵고 혹독한 일이다.
해설 형용사 비교급 문제이다. 주어진 빈칸은 be동사 다음에 보어로 형용사를 쓸 수 있으며 '~보다'라는 의미의 than이 뒤에 쓰이고 있기 때문에 비교급을 쓴다.
어휘 rigorous 철저한, 엄격한 recruit 지원자 anticipate 예상하다, 예측하다

2
해석 Texas 주 공장 Austin을 시작하기 전에, 우리는 높은 펌프를 이용하는 것보다 일반적인 에어컨으로 온도를 낮추는 것이 더 저렴한지 결정해야 한다.
해설 형용사의 비교급 문제이다. 빈칸 앞에 나온 비교급 표현인 cheaper와 짝을 이루는 비교급 표현인 '~보다'라는 의미를 가지고 있는 than이 정답이다.
어휘 conventional 통상적인, 일반적인

3
해석 새롭게 설계된 Sadler LED 캠핑용 랜턴은 예전보다 내구성이 좋고 방수가 된다는 측면에서 더 탄탄한 구조를 가진다.
해설 형용사 비교급 문제이다. 뒤쪽에 than이 오므로 형용사의 비교급을 써야 하는 자리이다. 따라서 정답은 (A)이다.
어휘 durable 내구성이 좋은 waterproof 방수의

4
해석 최근의 한 연구는 시골보다 대도시에서 더 많은 범죄가 발생한다는 사실을 보여 준다.
해설 more와 함께 비교급을 나타내는 than을 써야 한다.
어휘 commit 저지르다, 범하다 rural 시골의

5
해석 Sydney 오페라 하우스는 여태껏 내가 본 것 중에서 가장 인상적인 건물이다.
해설 최상급 문제이다. '여태껏 ~한 것 중 가장 ~한'은 〈최상급~I've ever+과거분사〉를 쓴다. 따라서 정답은 (C)이다.
어휘 impressive 인상적인, 감명 깊은

6
해석 우리 회사는 전체 항공 산업에서 가장 높은 고객 서비스를 제공하고 있으며 제시간에 도착하는 것에서도 최고이기 위해 노력한다.
해설 형용사 최상급 문제이다. 빈칸은 명사 level 앞에 쓸 수 있는 형용사를 써야 하는 자리이며 정관사 the 뒤에 쓰기 때문에 형용사의 최상급을 쓴다.
어휘 be committed to ~에 전념하다

7
해석 우리의 새 광고 간판은 시내의 모든 간판들 중에 가장 밝은데 이것은 지난주 뉴스팀의 헬리콥터 비행에서 밝혀졌다.
해설 형용사 최상급 문제이다. 정관사 the는 최상급과 함께 사용된다.

8
해석 이 새 선반은 가격은 훨씬 저렴하지만 이전 것만큼이나 튼튼하다.
해설 비교급 cheaper 앞에서 비교급을 강조하는 부사 자리이므로 much가 정답이다.
어휘 durable 내구성 있는, 오래가는

9
해석 둘 중에서 위원회는 실현시키기가 더 쉽다고 언급하면서 Raven 씨의

계획을 선택했다.

해설 〈the+비교급+of the two〉는 '둘 중에서 더 ~한'이라는 뜻의 표현이다.

어휘 alternative (2개의 것 중) 한쪽

10
해설 직원들에게는 SOP로 알려진 회사의 표준 행동 절차 매뉴얼에 보다 익숙해지는 것이 장려되었다.

해설 형용사 문제이다. 빈칸 앞에 more이 왔으므로 형용사인 familiar가 정답이다.

11-14

Moody's Business.com에 대하여
Moody's Business.com은 경제, 재정, 지역 그리고 산업 연구의 주도적 독립적인 제공자입니다. 비즈니스, 정부와 전문가들의 다양한 계획과 정보의 필요를 위해 설계되었습니다.
저희 서비스는 금융, 산업, 현지 시장 분석을 포함합니다. 무디 비즈니스 닷컴의 정보와 서비스는 전략적 계획, 위기 관리, 투자 조사와 같은 다양한 방면에서 활용됩니다. 우리는 은행과 많은 회사들을 포함하여 전 세계에 3,000명 이상의 고객들이 있습니다.
본사는 호주의 수도 캔버라에 있습니다. 저희는 또한 런던, 뉴욕 그리고 홍콩에 지사를 유지하고 있습니다. 더 많은 정보를 위하여 저희 웹사이트인 www.moodysbiz.com으로 방문해 주십시오.

어휘 independent 독립적인 diverse 다양한

11
해설 주어진 문장의 빈칸에는 주어인 Moody's Business.com을 뒤에서 수식하는 분사가 필요한 자리이다. 의미적으로 이 자리에는 과거분사형인 designed가 와야 한다. 따라서 정답은 (B)이다.

12
해설 주어진 빈칸은 전치사가 들어가야 하는 자리로 의미적으로 '~을 넘는'이라는 의미가 와야 적합하므로 정답은 (C)이다.

13
해설 (A) 이 기업은 데이터 관리 플랫폼을 찾는 데 도움을 주기 위해 만들어졌습니다.
(B) 본사는 호주의 수도 캔버라에 있습니다.
(C) 이 회사는 신규 사업가들에게 유익한 자원입니다.
(D) 저희는 고객에게 마케팅 솔루션을 제공합니다.

해설 바로 뒤에 나오는 also가 힌트가 된다. 런던, 뉴욕, 홍콩에도 지사가 있다는 얘기는 다른 곳에도 사무실이 있다는 뜻이며 다른 지사를 말하기 전에 먼저 본사를 언급하는 것이 적절하다. 따라서 정답은 (B)이다.

14
해설 주어진 문장에 들어갈 수 있는 적합한 어휘는 '~을 유지하다'라는 의미의 maintain이다. 따라서 정답은 (C)이다. (A) 주장하다, (B) 연장하다, (D) 편집하다

DAY 20
본문 p.214

1 (D)	2 (C)	3 (B)	4 (C)	5 (C)
6 (D)	7 (B)	8 (C)	9 (C)	10 (D)
11 (D)	12 (B)	13 (A)	14 (C)	

1
해석 첨부된 것은 당신이 다음 사업 회의 전까지 검토하고 승인해야 하는 예산 보고서다.

해설 문장의 의미가 '예산 보고서가 첨부되다'이므로 강조를 위해 문장 첫머리로 이동한 과거분사 attached를 써야 한다. 주어 역할의 명사 자리로 혼동하지 않도록 주의해야 한다. 명사 attachment가 주어로 빈칸에 오면 명사 the budget report가 보어가 되어서 '첨부(attachment) = 보고서(report)'의 의미가 되기 때문에 문장이 틀리게 된다. 명사 보어는 반드시 주어와 의미가 동격이 될 때만 사용할 수 있다.

2
해석 당신의 발표가 좀 더 구체적이었더라면, 당신이 우리 회사와의 계약을 따냈을 것이다.

해설 주절 동사의 형태로 문장이 가정법 과거완료 구문인 것을 알 수 있다. 접속사 if가 생략된 도치 구조이므로 Had를 써야 한다. (A) If를 쓰면 과거분사 been이 동사 역할을 하게 되어서 틀리고, (D) If had는 접속사가 생략되지 않은 상태에서는 도치가 발생할 수 없기 때문에 오답이다.

어휘 specific 구체적인, 명확한

3
해석 생산팀이 일을 예정대로 마칠 수 있으면 배송 마감일을 맞출 수 있을 텐데.

해설 주절의 동사가 could meet이기 때문에 가정법 과거 구문인 것을 알 수 있다. 가정법 과거 구문에서 be동사는 were로 써야 한다. (C) is가 오면 일반 조건문(~이라면)이 되기 때문에 주절의 동사는 미래나 현재 시제가 와야 한다.

4
해석 우리가 교육에 더 많이 투자했더라면, 학교에서 발생하는 많은 청소년 범죄들을 예방할 수 있었을 것이다.

해설 주절 동사의 형태가 would have prevented이므로 가정법 과거완료 구문이다. 가정법 과거완료의 if절의 동사는 [had + p.p.] 형태로 써야 한다. (A) spent는 가정법 과거 구문으로 주절이 〈would/could+동사원형〉 형태로 와야 한다. (B) spend는 조건문에 사용되어야 하고 주절에 현재 시제나 미래 시제가 온다.

어휘 juvenile 청소년의 take place 발생하다, 일어나다

5
해석 그가 변호사 시험을 합격했더라면, 그는 가난한 사람들을 돕는 변호사가 되었을 것이다.

해설 if절이 가정법 과거완료이므로 (C)가 정답이다. (A) will은 일반 조건문인 경우에 쓸 수 있다.

어휘 bar exam 사법고시, 변호사 시험

6

해석 만약 새로운 제품이 더 일찍 소개된다면, 지금쯤에는 고객들에게 더 호의적으로 받아들여질 텐데.

해설 문장의 내용은 제품이 더 이전에 받아들여졌다면(과거 사실의 반대를 가정), 지금쯤에는 고객들이 이 상품에 호의적인 반응을 보낼 것이라는 (현재 사실의 반대) 내용으로 혼합 가정법을 사용해야 한다. 따라서 if 절의 동사가 〈had+p.p.〉 형태라도 주절의 동사는 〈would/might/could+동사원형〉형태가 되어야 한다.

어휘 favorably 호의적으로

7

해석 당신의 표에 대해서 추가적인 정보가 필요하시면, 항공사 카운터에 판매 대리인에게 상담하세요.

해설 가정법 미래의 공식은 〈If+주어+should+동사원형, 주어+will/can/may/should]+동사원형〉인데 여기서 If가 생략되면 주어와 동사의 자리가 바뀌는 도치가 일어난다.

8

해석 회사가 올해의 판매 목표를 초과했을 뿐만 아니라, 새로운 수익 기록을 만들었다.

해설 Not only와 같은 부정어가 강조를 위해서 문장 맨 앞으로 나오면 주어와 동사가 도치된다. 뒤에 but을 보고도 not only ~ but (also) 구문인 것을 알 수 있다.

어휘 exceed 넘다, 초과하다 revenue 수익

9

해석 당신이 요청한 지난 전략 계획 회의의 회의록 사본이 동봉되어 있습니다.

해설 보어의 도치 문제이다. 보어의 강조를 위해서 보어를 문장 맨 앞으로 보내고 주어와 동사를 도치시킨 구문이다.

어휘 enclose 동봉하다, 에워싸다 minutes 회의록

10

해석 개정된 세법에 대해 궁금한 점이나 관심이 있다면, 편안하실 때 회계부서로 부담 갖지 말고 연락해 주세요.

해설 가정법 미래에서 if가 생략되고 should가 주어와 자리를 바꾼 형태이다.

어휘 revise 변경하다, 수정하다

11-14

회사는 새로운 판매 장려 프로그램의 창설을 알려 드리게 되어 기쁩니다. 5월 1일부터 영업부에 잠재 고객 명단을 제출하는 모든 사원들은 100달러를 받을 것입니다. 이 명단은 상업 거래 계정의 실질적인 개설로 이어져야 할 것입니다. 게다가, 회계 연도 마지막까지 가장 많은 고객 명단을 확보한 사원에게는 경비 전액이 지원되는 2주간의 하와이 여행이 상으로 수여됩니다. 이 프로그램은 승진에 중요한 역할을 할 것입니다.
저희는 직원들의 근무에 매우 만족하고 있으며, 이것이 우리 회사의 지속적인 성장의 열쇠라는 것을 굳게 믿고 있습니다.

어휘 creation 창조, 창작, 창설 sales lead 잠재적으로 고객이 될 만한 회사들의 명단 stipend 봉급, 급료 sustainable 지속 가능한

11

해설 주어진 빈칸은 형용사가 와야 하며 주어가 사람이기 때문에 과거분사형인 pleased를 써야 한다. 따라서 정답은 (D)이다.

12

해설 주어진 빈칸에는 앞에 the가 있으므로 형용사의 최상급을 써야 한다. 따라서 정답은 (B)이다.

13

해설 (A) 이 프로그램은 승진에 중요한 역할을 할 것입니다.
(B) 연례 업무 수행평가가 실시될 것입니다.
(C) 회사에서 본사 이전을 발표할 것입니다.
(D) 직원들은 현황에 대한 지식과 이해의 수준을 유지할 것입니다.

해설 빈칸 바로 앞에서 가장 성과가 좋은 직원에게 하와이 여행을 보내준다고 했으므로 빈칸에는 '상'과 관련된 내용이 나오는 것이 적절하다. 따라서 '승진'이 언급된 (A)가 적절하다.

14

해설 주어진 빈칸에는 형용사가 와야 한다. 직원들의 근무로 만족감을 느끼게 되었으므로 과거분사형인 satisfied를 써야 한다. 따라서 정답은 (C)이다.

2. 실전 랜덤 연습

DAY 01 본문 p.218

1 (B)	2 (C)	3 (A)	4 (C)	5 (D)
6 (C)	7 (A)	8 (B)	9 (D)	10 (B)
11 (D)	12 (C)	13 (A)	14 (A)	15 (D)
16 (A)	17 (C)	18 (C)	19 (C)	20 (B)

1
- 해석 Andy Garcia는 랩 음악을 새로운 차원으로 끌어올리려고 노력함으로써 다른 음악가들과 그 자신을 차별화했다고 말했다.
- 해설 주어와 목적어가 같은 대상일 경우 목적어 자리에 재귀대명사를 쓴다.
- 어휘 state 진술하다 elevate 올리다 heights 수준

2
- 해석 당신의 뛰어난 노력과 지식이 없었다면 Texco 계좌를 얻을 수 없었을 것이다.
- 해설 명사 effort and expertise를 수식하는 형용사 자리이다. 의미상 '뛰어난, 특출한'이라는 뜻의 (C)가 정답이다. (A) 전체의 (B) 많은 (D) 경비가 포함된
- 어휘 succeed 성공하다 expertise 지식

3
- 해석 우리는 당신이 새로운 비디오가 추가되었는지를 알기 위해서 주기적으로 확인할 것을 추천합니다.
- 해설 check를 수식하는 부사 어휘 문제이다. 의미상 '주기적으로'라는 뜻의 (A)가 정답이다. (B) 부수적으로 (C) 무기한으로 (D) 상당하게
- 어휘 recommend 추천하다

4
- 해석 CNA 프로젝트에 참여한 사람 누구든지 이번 달 말까지 그들의 계획의 개요를 제출하는 것이 요구된다.
- 해설 동사가 2개(is, requested)이므로 빈칸은 접속사 자리이다. 따라서 정답은 (C)이다.
- 어휘 involve 참여하다 request 요청하다 submit 제출하다 outline 개요

5
- 해석 기름 가격의 예상치 못한 상승으로 인해 대다수의 지역 회사들은 예산 부족에 직면하고 있다.
- 해설 동사 자리는 수 일치-능동/수동-시제 순서로 확인한다. 주어가 복수이므로 (B)는 수 일치에서 맞지 않고 뒤에 목적어가 있으므로 수동태 (A), (C)는 오답이다.
- 어휘 rise 상승 budget 예산

6
- 해석 신문 배송 부서는 최고의 서비스를 제공하는 것에 전념한다.
- 해설 be committed to 명사/동명사: ~에 전념하다
- 어휘 circulation 배송, 순환 department 부서 provide 제공하다

7
- 해석 다가오는 대중매체 캠페인은 현재 개발 중인 제품에 초점을 맞출 것이다.
- 해설 전치사(under) 뒤의 명사 자리이다.
- 어휘 upcoming 다가오는 currently 현재

8
- 해석 우리가 교체 부품들이 즉시 보내져야 한다고 요청했지만, 이번 주말 전까지는 도착하지 않는다는 통보를 받았다.
- 해설 빈칸은 접속사 자리이므로 (C) 접속부사는 오답이다. (D)는 접속사 중에서 등위접속사이므로 역시 오답이다. 의미상 '~에도 불구하고'라는 뜻의 (B)가 정답이다.
- 어휘 replacement 대체 inform 알리다

9
- 해석 비교적 적은 양의 자금을 가지고 몇 년 전에 시작한 많은 소프트웨어 기업들은 요즘 매우 성공을 거두고 있다.
- 해설 be동사(are) 뒤의 보어 자리이다. 앞에 부사(extremely)가 있으므로 부사의 수식을 받는 형용사 (D)가 정답이다.
- 어휘 firm 회사 relatively 상대적으로 capital 자금

10
- 해석 제품 정보를 포함한 홍보 책자는 포장 안에 포함되어 있다.
- 해설 제품 정보(product information)라는 복합명사를 알면 쉽게 풀 수 있다.
- 어휘 pamphlet 홍보책자 include 포함하다

11
- 해석 우리가 이 결정을 내리기 위해 더 오래 기다리면 기다릴수록 대중에게 그것을 발표기는 더 어려울 것이다.
- 해설 '~하면 할수록 ~하다'라는 뜻의 [the+비교급, the+비교급] 구문이다.
- 어휘 decision 결정 announce 발표하다

12
- 해석 그녀의 남편이 Tokyo로 전근을 가게 되었기 때문에 그녀 역시 전근을 신청했다.
- 해설 접속사 자리이다. 빈칸부터 Tokyo까지가 부사절이므로 부사절 접속사 (A), (C) 중에서 '~ 때문에'라는 뜻의 (C)가 정답임을 알 수 있다.
- 어휘 transfer 옮기다

13
- 해석 이 기계를 수리하시고자 한다면, 기본 안전 예방책을 반드시 따라 주시기 바랍니다.
- 해설 복합명사 문제다. 복합명사는 기본적으로 두 단어의 관계가 용도, 목적이라면 사용할 수 있다. 첫 번째 단어인 safety '안전'과 가장 잘 어울리는 명사는 (A)이다.
- 어휘 attempt 시도하다 safety precaution 안전 예방책

14
- 해석: Yamamoto 씨는 내가 그를 복도에서 만났을 때 막 나를 부르려고 했다고 말했다.
- 해설: be about to부정사: 막 ~ 하려고 하다
- 어휘: hallway 복도

15
- 해석: 원래 오후 2시에 시작하기로 예정되었던 워크숍이 스케줄이 중첩되어서 취소되었다.
- 해설: 빈칸 뒤의 분사를 수식하는 부사 자리이다. 따라서 정답은 (D)이다.
- 어휘: workshop 워크숍 call off 취소하다 conflict 중첩

16
- 해석: 도심가의 증가하는 임대 비용 때문에 우리 회사는 외곽으로 이전하기로 결정했다.
- 해설: rents(임대 비용)를 수식하는 형용사 자리이다. '증가하는'이라는 뜻의 분사 (A)가 정답이다. (C)도 분사 형태지만 arise는 자동사로 p.p. 형태의 분사는 쓸 수 없다.
- 어휘: due to ~로 인해서 downtown 도심가 suburb 교외

17
- 해석: 그는 제안된 마감일 전에 수정된 프로젝트 설명서를 마무리하는 것을 실질적으로 예상할 수 없다.
- 해설: 관사(the)와 명사(deadline) 사이의 형용사 자리이다. (B), (C)가 분사의 형태인데 deadline과 propose의 관계가 수동의 관계이므로 과거분사가 정답이다.
- 어휘: realistically 실질적으로 revise 개정하다 specification 상세 설명서 deadline 마감 기한

18
- 해석: 프로젝트에 엄청난 양의 돈이 투자되었다는 사실에도 불구하고, 그것은 실패하였다.
- 해설: the fact that ~의 that은 동격의 that이다. the fact와 that절은 동격이다. 명사절이 왔으므로 빈칸은 전치사가 와야 한다. 의미상 '~에도 불구하고'라는 뜻의 (C) Despite가 정답이다.
- 어휘: a great deal of 많은 양의 invest 투자하다 failure 실패하다

19
- 해석: 주말에 예정된 야외 음악 축제가 다음 주 수요일까지 연기되었다.
- 해설: 어휘 문제이다. '축제가 연기되었다'라는 의미이므로 (C)가 정답이다. (A) 축약하다 (B) 파기하다, 제거하다 (D) 예정하다
- 어휘: outdoor 야외 festival 축제

20
- 해석: 고객들의 불만 때문에, Hong Kong Airlines는 정책을 변경하고 이제 승객 당 두 개의 서류 가방을 허용합니다.
- 해설: change의 목적으로 적절한 목적어(명사) 어휘 문제이다. '정책을 변경하다'라는 뜻의 (B)가 정답이다. (A) 수용, 숙소 (C) 처리 (D) 정책, 척도, 단위
- 어휘: complaint 불만, 항의 allow 허가하다 passenger 승객

DAY 02
본문 p.220

1 (C)	2 (A)	3 (B)	4 (A)	5 (A)
6 (C)	7 (C)	8 (A)	9 (D)	10 (B)
11 (D)	12 (C)	13 (D)	14 (B)	15 (D)
16 (D)	17 (A)	18 (C)	19 (A)	20 (C)

1
- 해석: 비행기에서 내리기 전에 개인적인 소유물이나 소지품을 위해서 머리 위 사물함을 확인해 주세요.
- 해설: 시간, 조건의 부사절에서는 미래 시제를 대신해 현재 시제를 쓴다.
- 어휘: aircraft 비행기 overhead 머리 위에 compartment 사물함 effect 소지품 belonging 소유물

2
- 해석: AHJ Comtech는 지역 경제지로부터 3년 연속으로 상을 받았다.
- 해설: third consecutive year(= three consecutive years)는 '3년 연속으로'라는 뜻이다.
- 어휘: win ~(상 등)을 타다 award 상

3
- 해석: 당신이 머무르시는 동안에 비서 서비스가 필요하시다면 호텔 접수담당자에게 연락을 주세요.
- 해설: during(전치사) 다음에 명사 자리인데 뒤에 명사 stay가 있으므로 빈칸은 명사 앞의 소유격 자리이다. 따라서 정답은 (B)이다.
- 어휘: secretarial 비서직의 contact 연락하다 receptionist 접수담당자

4
- 해석: 고객들은 불만 사항의 종류를 고객 서비스부서에 최대한 자세하게 묘사할 것이 요구된다.
- 해설: 비교급 as ~ as 사이에는 부사 혹은 형용사가 들어갈 수 있다. 여기서 빈칸은 동사 describe를 수식하므로 부사 (A)가 정답이다.
- 어휘: encourage 권장하다 describe 묘사하다 complaint 불만사항 Customer Service Department 고객 서비스부서

5
- 해석: 회사는 훈련 과정을 개선시키기 위해서가 아니라 최신 기술을 채택하고 적용하기 위해서 돈을 투자했다.
- 해설: [not A but B]는 'A가 아니고 B'라는 뜻이므로 (A)가 정답이다.
- 어휘: adopt 적용하다 install 설치하다 latest 최신의 improve 향상시키다 procedure 과정

6
- 해석: 지난달 동안의 광범위한 내부 수리의 결과로서 우리는 현재 우리의 고객들에게 훨씬 더 좋은 서비스를 제공할 수 있다.
- 해설: 해석과 함께 offer가 간접 목적어와 직접 목적어를 모두 취하는 4형식 동사라는 것이 단서가 된다.
- 어휘: result 결과 extensive 광범위한 renovation 개조

7
해석 현재 임대가 가능한 2개의 침실을 가진 아파트가 없다.
해설 '~을 위한, ~을 위해서'라는 뜻의 전치사 (C) for가 정답이다.
어휘 available 가능한 lease 임대

8
해석 Autoland Company는 마루를 자동으로 쓸고 닦으며 노동력을 줄여 주는 기계를 최근에 출시했다.
해설 floor와 관련 있는 동사를 찾아야 한다. 앞에 sweep이 왔기 때문에 의미상 '닦다'라는 뜻의 (A)가 정답이다. (B) 붓다 (C) 흐르다 (D) 누르다
어휘 recently 최근 introduce (제품을) 출시하다 labor-saving 노동 절감 sweep 쓸다

9
해석 Southern Hill 백화점의 최고의 품질을 위한 오래된 헌신이 회사에게 남다른 명성을 안겨 주었다.
해설 소유격(store's)와 형용사(longstanding) 의 수식을 받는 명사 자리이다.
어휘 longstanding 오래 지속되는 earn 얻다 distinguished 남다른, 구별된 reputation 평판

10
해석 다음번에는 대가가 큰 오해를 피하기 위해서 보고서를 좀 더 명확하게 써 주세요.
해설 report까지 문장은 완벽한 구조를 갖추므로 빈칸은 write(동사)를 수식하는 부사 자리이다. more 뒤에는 원급 형태인 (B)가 올 수 있다.
어휘 avoid 피하다 costly 소개가 큰 misunderstanding 오해

11
해석 Lee 박사를 기념하는 공식적인 저녁 식사를 위해서 초대장이 메일로 보내질 것이다.
해설 주어 자리가 빈칸이므로 명사가 정답이고 (C)는 단수 명사인데 관사가 없으므로 오답이 된다.
어휘 formal 공식적인 honor 기념하다

12
해석 구성원은 미결제된 금액이 없으면 회원 자격을 갱신할 수 있는데, 미결제 금액이 있는 경우 갱신이 거절될 것이다.
해설 접속사 자리이다. (A) 전치사, (B) 접속부사를 제외하고 (C), (D)에서 해석을 통해서 정답을 찾는다.
어휘 renew 갱신하다 outstanding 미지불된 payment 지불금 deny 거부하다

13
해석 추천되는 운동의 종류는 개인의 나이와 건강 상태에 따라서 굉장히 다양하다.
해설 빈칸은 vary(다양하다) 를 수식하는 부사 자리이다. (A) 기꺼이 (B) 기분 좋게 (C) 다정하게 (D) 상당히
어휘 vary 다양하다 depending on ~에 따라서 condition 상태, 조건 individual 개인

14
해석 마케팅 매니저는 그가 제안한 변경 사항에 대한 확실한 대답을 받기 전까지 일을 계속할 수 없었다.
해설 빈칸 앞에는 형용사절 접속사(관계대명사)의 목적격이 생략되어 있다. 따라서 빈칸은 새로운 문장의 시작인 주어 자리이다.
어휘 receive 받다 definite 확실한 propose 제안하다

15
해석 판매 이사는 그의 팀 구성원들에게 상담가가 해 준 추천 사항들 중 어떤 것도 무시당하는 일이 없도록 당부했다.
해설 동사 자리 어휘 문제이다. (A) 행동하다 (B) 참석하다 (C) 작동하다 (D) 무시하다
어휘 make sure 확실히 하다 none of 아무것도 ~하지 않다 consultant 상담가

16
해석 우리의 최신 발명품을 위한 안전 시스템이 마지막 단계에 도달했다 .
해설 마지막(final)의 수식을 받는 명사자리 문제. (A) 길 (B) 현장 (C) 초안 (D) 단계
어휘 security 보안 invention 발명 reach 도달하다

17
해석 고객들의 다양한 요구에 맞추기 위해서, Twin's Market은 다양한 제품을 제공한다.
해설 meet the needs: 요구사항에 맞추다
어휘 In order to ~하기 위해 diverse 다양한 offer 제공하다 variety of 다양한

18
해석 우리 가게에 있는 모든 가구들이 엄청난 주의를 기울인 수제품들이기 때문에, 우리는 당신이 무엇을 선택하든 간에 최고의 만족을 줄 것을 보증한다.
해설 that 절의 주어는 명사절이다. 빈칸부터 choose까지가 명사절인데 (A), (B), (D)는 부사절 접속사이다.
어휘 since ~이기 때문에 furniture 가구 handcrafted 손으로 만들어진 guarantee 보장하다 utmost 최고의 satisfaction 만족

19
해석 선구적인 조사 프로젝트는 첫 해에 20,000달러어치의 가치가 있는 상을 받았다.
해설 worth가 돈의 액수 앞에 쓰이면 '(~ 정도 돈의) 가치가 있는'이라는 뜻이 된다.
어휘 research 조사

20
해석 지역 통신 회사는 3달간 지불 기한이 지난 어떤 계좌라도 취소할 것이다.
해설 계좌를 취소할 것이라는 내용과 three months 뒤에 쓸 수 있는 형용사 어휘 문제로 (C)가 가장 적절하다. (A) 비싼 (B) 영구적인 (C) 지급 기한이 지난 (D) 중요하지 않은
어휘 local 지역의 cancel 취소하다 account 계좌

DAY 03

본문 p.222

1 (B)	2 (B)	3 (A)	4 (D)	5 (A)
6 (B)	7 (C)	8 (A)	9 (D)	10 (C)
11 (A)	12 (B)	13 (D)	14 (A)	15 (B)
16 (A)	17 (D)	18 (D)	19 (A)	20 (B)

1
- 해석 이사는 조사 제안서들이 이번 달 말까지 제출될 것을 예상했다.
- 해설 by the end of는 '~의 말까지'라는 뜻이므로 정답은 (B)이다.
- 어휘 expect 기대하다 proposal 제안서 turn in 제출하다

2
- 해석 Janet의 가게는 그녀 자신만의 브랜드가 베일을 벗을 1월 28일에 공식적으로 문을 열 것이다.
- 해설 〈소유격+own+명사〉는 '자신만의 …'를 의미한다.
- 어휘 officially 공식적으로 unveil 베일을 벗다 brand 브랜드

3
- 해석 오늘 밤 Carter Center에서 젊은 피아니스트의 공연은 지난밤의 실수를 만회할 수 있는 재능을 보여 주었다.
- 해설 뛰어난 재능이 실수를 만회할 수 있게 해 준 것이므로 (A)가 정답이다. (B) 집중 (C) 서술, 묘사 (D) 정보
- 어휘 performance 공연 demonstrate 보여주다 talent 재능 make up for 만회하다

4
- 해석 두 개의 유명한 생산업체들이 더 큰 하나의 업체로 합병하는 것은 날카로운 비판을 받을 것으로 예상된다.
- 해설 〈It(가주어) that 절(진짜 주어)〉 문장 형태이다. 따라서 빈칸 뒤에는 목적어가 없는 것이므로 수동태 형태의 동사가 필요하다.
- 어휘 merger 합병 renowned 유명한 manufacturer 생산업체 draw 끌어내다 sharp 날카로운 criticism 비평

5
- 해석 해외 여행자들은 제한 구역에서 카메라의 사용에 대한 다양한 정부의 규제에 대해서 알아야 한다.
- 해설 government regulations(명사)를 수식할 형용사 자리이다.
- 어휘 overseas 해외의 traveler 여행가 be aware of ~을 알다 regulation 규제 restricted 제한된

6
- 해석 다음 주 월요일부터 National Health Association은 Richmond Clinic에 소속된 건강 전문가들에 의해서 수행되는 조사들의 결과를 공개할 것이다.
- 해설 healthcare는 형용사로 '건강 관리의, 의료의'라는 뜻이 있다. 따라서 빈칸은 명사 자리가 되어야 한다. (C)는 '직업'이라는 뜻으로 의미상 어색하다. (D)는 가산 명사인데 관사가 없어서 오답이다.
- 어휘 survey 설문조사 conduct 시행하다

7
- 해석 우리 사무실이 최근에 이전을 해서 위에 출력된 우리의 새로운 메일 주소로 연락해 주세요.
- 해설 recently는 '최근에'라는 의미가 있으며, 과거 시제, 현재완료 시제와 함께 쓰일 수 있다.
- 어휘 address 주소 above ~위에

8
- 해석 익명의 기부가 아이들을 위해서 없어서는 안 될 많은 것들을 지역 고아원이 살 수 있게 해 주었다.
- 해설 a great number of: 많은
- 어휘 anonymous 익명의 donation 기부 enable 가능하게하다 orphanage 고아원 indispensable 없어서는 안 되는

9
- 해석 현지 농부들이 충분한 옥수수와 밀을 제공할 수 없었기 때문에, 북부 텍사스 지역의 제과점들이 다른 출처를 통해서 재료를 사야 했다.
- 해설 접속사 자리이다. (C)는 등위접속사이므로 오답이고, (B), (D) 중에서 해석을 통해서 정답을 구한다.
- 어휘 farmer 농부 supply 제공하다 wheat 밀 ingredient 재료

10
- 해석 사건에 대해서 더 이상 말하는 것을 거부하면서 회장은 기자 회견장을 떠났다.
- 해설 분사구문 문제이다. 접속사는 생략 되었고 주절의 주어(the president)와 종속절의 주어가 같으면, 종속절의 주어를 생략할 수 있다. 빈칸 뒤에 to부정사라는 목적어가 있으므로 능동의 분사(C)가 정답이다.
- 어휘 comment 언급하다 further 더 이상 president 회장 press conference 기자 회견

11
- 해석 우리 회사는 제품 품질을 높이기 위해서 한 달 이상을 보냈고, 다행히도, 계약자들은 이제 만족한다.
- 해설 and(접속사) 뒤에 문장이 완벽하므로 빈칸은 부사 자리이다.
- 어휘 spend 사용하다 enhance 높이다[향상시키다] contractor 계약자

12
- 해석 Harper Pharmaceutical은 모든 직원들이 근처의 헬스클럽에 회원증을 가질 자격이 있음을 알리게 되어 기쁩니다.
- 해설 tell은 that절을 직접 목적어로 바로 받기보다는 간접 목적어(~에게)를 쓴 후에 that절을 직접 목적어로 받는다. 반면 announce는 뒤에 바로 that절이 올 수 있다.
- 어휘 be pleased 기쁘다 eligible 자격이 있는 nearby 근처의

13
- 해석 우리의 자선 행사는 높은 참석률을 가졌기 때문에, 우리는 기부금 목표에 도달했다.
- 해설 donation과 함께 복합명사로 쓸 명사 어휘 문제. (A) 목적지 (B) 의견 (C) 기관 (D) 목표
- 어휘 charity 자선 attendance 참석자 수

14

해석 일본의 연간 무역 흑자가 20억 달러를 초과했고, 내년에는 더 커질 것이 예상된다.

해설 in excess of ~을 초과한

어휘 annual 연간 trade 무역 surplus 흑자 excess 초과

15

해석 도로 건설 프로젝트를 위한 제안서를 검토한 후에, 회장은 Kim 박사의 제안서를 가장 적절한 선택으로 결정했다.

해설 choice(명사)를 수식할 형용사 자리이다.

어휘 review 검토하다 choice 선택

16

해석 이번 달에만 Heavenly 체육관은 새로운 이용자들에게 한 달에 30달러만큼 저렴한 금액으로 수영장을 포함한 모든 시설의 사용을 제공하고 있다.

해설 $30(금액)를 수식할 수 있는 형용사 자리. much는 의미적으로 금액이 높다는 의미이므로 오답이고 less는 비교급으로 as ~ as (원급비교) 사이에 들어갈 수 없다.

어휘 facility 시설

17

해석 서울에서 열리는 국제 교육 회의에 참석을 희망하는 사람들은 이번 달에 등록을 해야 한다.

해설 빈칸부터 Seoul까지가 형용사절이다. [Those who ~]는 '~하는 사람들'이란 뜻을 가진 표현이므로 익혀 두도록 한다.

어휘 attend 참석하다 conference 회의, 대회 register 등록하다, 신청하다

18

해석 Baker 씨가 서비스에 대해서 실망했기 때문에, 현장 감독은 지난 며칠 동안 직원들의 행동을 계속 주시해 왔다.

해설 (A)~(D)는 수 일치와 능동/수동태가 다 맞기 때문에 최종적으로 시제를 확인해야 한다. 주절의 시제가 현재완료 진행형이고 의미상 빈칸에는 과거의 의미가 적절한 자리이므로 과거 동사를 쓴다.

어휘 disappointment 실망 behavior 행동

19

해석 만약 당신이 직업을 빨리 잡기를 원하신다면 당신이 즉시 모든 직업 인터뷰를 보는 것이 중요하다.

해설 여기서 빈칸은 보어 자리가 아니라 보어는 전치사(in)+명사 (interviews)가 보어의 역할을 한 것이다. 따라서 빈칸은 부사 자리이다.

어휘 critical 중요한 interview 면접

20

해석 실망스럽게도 Saito 씨는 그녀의 아이디어가 나쁘지 않았음에도 불구하고 형편없는 발표를 했다.

해설 to my dismay: 실망스럽게도

어휘 dismal 서투른, 형편없는 presentation 발표

DAY 04

본문 p.224

1 (B)	2 (C)	3 (D)	4 (A)	5 (B)
6 (B)	7 (B)	8 (A)	9 (D)	10 (D)
11 (D)	12 (B)	13 (B)	14 (A)	15 (D)
16 (A)	17 (B)	18 (C)	19 (B)	20 (C)

1

해석 새로운 차는 훌륭한 핸들링과 거의 모든 지형에 대처할 수 있는 굉장한 힘을 가졌다.

해설 both 뒤에 빈칸 하나를 사이에 두고 두 개의 명사구가 연결되어 있다. 따라서 상관접속사 both A and B가 가장 적절하다. 따라서 정답은 (B)이다.

어휘 cope with 대처하다 terrain 지형

2

해석 당신의 차를 회사 건물에 주차하길 원하신다면 앞 유리에 주차 허가증을 붙여놓아야 합니다.

해설 목적어(a parking permit)와 함께 쓰는 동사 자리이다. 의미상 '주차 허가증을 붙이다'가 적절하므로 (C)가 정답이다. (A) 동봉하다 (B) 밀다 (D) 주다

어휘 park 주차하다 property 소유(영토, 건물) permit 허가증 windshield 앞 유리

3

해석 가능한 파손을 막기 위해서 당신은 매우 믿을 만한 기계를 구매해야 한다.

해설 are(be동사) 뒤에 보어 자리이다. 앞에 highly(부사)가 있으므로 부사의 수식을 받는 형용사 (D)가 정답이다.

어휘 possible 가능한 breakdown 파손 purchase 구매하다

4

해석 내일 아침 일찍 노동부 장관은 그의 혁신적인 일자리 창출 계획의 시작을 발표하기 위해서 기자 회견을 열 것이다.

해설 hold a press conference: 기자 회견을 열다

어휘 Labor Minister 노동부 장관 press conference 기자 회견 publicize 알리다 launch 시작, 개시 innovative 혁신적인 creation 창조

5

해석 철저한 의료 검사 후에 의사는 폐암 진단을 내렸다.

해설 관사(a) 뒤의 명사 자리이다.

어휘 thorough 철저한 medical 의학적인 patient 환자 lung cancer 폐암 diagnose 진단하다

6

해석 우리의 경제 상황을 고려했을 때, 우리는 회사를 닫는 것 이외에 다른 선택의 여지가 없다.

076

해설 other는 형용사로 뒤에 1. 복수 명사, 2. 불가산 명사가 온다. (A)는 단수 가산명사가 오고, (C)는 any 뒤에 관사(the)가 어색하며 (D)는 대명사이므로 오답이다.

어휘 considering ~를 고려할 때 financial 경제적인 situation 상황

7

해석 건강 전문가들은 고객들을 보호하기 위해서 패스트푸드 사업을 면밀하게 통제하고 있다.

해설 주어와 동사 사이에 부사 자리이다. 따라서 정답은 (B)이다.

어휘 control 통제하다 industry 산업 protect 보호하다

8

해석 연설을 준비하기 위해서 단지 20분만 주어졌기 때문에, Peter는 실수를 상당히 많이 했다.

해설 분사구문 문제이다. 접속사는 생략되었고 주절의 주어(Peter)와 같은 종속절의 주어도 생략되었다. 내용상 종속절의 시제가 주절의 시제보다 앞서므로 완료 분사구문이 들어가야 한다.

어휘 prepare 준비하다 speech 연설 considerable 상당한

9

해석 어떤 서류든지 위조하려는 시도는 단기간에 고소로 이어질 수 있다.

해설 전치사(in) 뒤의 명사 자리이다. (B)도 명사이지만 의미상 어색할 뿐 아니라 관사가 없으므로 오답이다.

어휘 attempt 시도 falsify 위조하다 document 문서 period 기간

10

해석 Brown 씨는 고객과의 급한 미팅 때문에 직원 회의에 결석했다.

해설 absent from ~에 결석하다, 빠지다

어휘 be absent 결석하다 urgent 급한 client 고객

11

해석 보고서의 결론은 정부가 소비를 격려하기 위해서 세금을 낮춰야 한다는 것이다.

해설 was(be동사) 뒤에 보어 자리에 명사절이 들어간 구문이다. 명사절의 선택은 나머지 명사절이 완전한지 여부에 따라 달라진다. (A), (B), (C)는 뒤에 불완전한 문장이 나오고, (D)는 뒤에 완전한 문장을 명사절로 묶어 준다. 빈칸 뒤의 명사절은 완전하다.

어휘 conclusion 결론 report 보고서 lower 낮추다 tax 세금 stimulate 자극시키다 consumption 소비

12

해석 추가 근무를 하는 직원들은 사무실을 떠날 때, 모든 컴퓨터를 꺼야 한다.

해설 빈칸은 동사 자리가 아니라 staff를 수식하는 분사 자리이다. 동사는 are requested이다.

어휘 overtime 초과 근무 turn off 끄다 leave 떠나다

13

해석 시간적 제약 때문에 위원회 구성원들은 생산적인 결론에 이르지 못했다.

해설 '시간적인 제약'을 뜻하는 time constraints가 적절하다. 따라서 정답은 (B)이다.

어휘 committee 위원회 fruitful 생산적인

14

해석 많은 직원들은 그들이 수행할 일들을 다양화함으로써 그들의 일의 단조로움을 깨려고 노력한다.

해설 [전치사(by)+빈칸+명사(the tasks)]의 빈칸에는 동사와 명사의 성질을 모두 가진 동명사가 정답이다.

어휘 monotony 단조로움 task 업무 undertake 수행하다

15

해석 경제 상황에 대한 우울한 예상에도 불구하고, 한국 거래소의 거래 규모는 어제보다 약간 높았다.

해설 higher를 수식하는 부사 어휘 문제이다. (A) 각각, 존경하는 (B) 최근에 (C) 이전에 (D) 약간

어휘 in spite of ~에도 불구하고 dismal 우울한 economic 경제적인

16

해석 제품에 대한 어떠한 질문이든 고객 서비스 부서에 연락하세요.

해설 가정법 미래 [If+주어+should+동사원형, 명령문] 구문을 알아두자. 명령문이 가정법 미래의 힌트가 될 수 있다. 또 가정법에서 if가 생략되면 주어와 동사의 도치가 일어난다.

어휘 concerning ~에 대한

17

해석 불법 어획을 막기 위해서, 정부는 다가오는 어획철에 추가적인 해안 경비원을 고용하기로 결정했다.

해설 fishing season을 수식하는 형용사 어휘 문제이다. (A) 일으키는, 발생시키는 (B) 다가오는 (C) 결과로 초래된 (D) 발전하는

어휘 prevent 예방하다 illegal 불법의 hire 고용하다 coast guard 해안 경비원

18

해석 Washington 씨는 회의에 참석할 수 없을 것이고, Monroe 씨도 참석 못할 것이다.

해설 긍정문에 동조하는 표현은 so를 쓰지만, 부정문에 동조하는 표현에서는 neither를 쓴다. 예를 들어 I don't like a cat.은 Neither do I.로 받아야 한다.

어휘 be able to ~이 가능하다 attent 참석하다

19

해석 작년에 취임한 이래로 정부는 대중을 걱정시키는 고용 정책에 대한 몇 몇의 변경 사항을 만들었다.

해설 선택지가 수량형용사들로 구성되어 있다. a lot of가 뒤에 복수 명사가 올 수 있고, (C), (D)는 불가산 명사가 와야 한다.

어휘 take office 취임하다 employment 고용 policy 정책 concern 걱정시키다

20

해석 Office Box가 현재 공사 중이기 때문에, 길 아래에 있는 약국을 이용하세요.

해설 is(현재 시제)와 under construction이 힌트가 된다. (A) 쉽게 (B) 분명히 (C) 현재 (D) 극도로

어휘 construction 공사 alternative 대안

SECTION 2_실전 랜덤 연습 » 077

DAY 05

본문 p.226

1 (D)	2 (C)	3 (B)	4 (C)	5 (A)
6 (C)	7 (B)	8 (A)	9 (D)	10 (C)
11 (B)	12 (B)	13 (A)	14 (A)	15 (C)
16 (A)	17 (C)	18 (D)	19 (C)	20 (D)

1
- 해석 인터뷰했던 대부분의 학생들이 학기 중의 방학이 너무 짧았다고 말했다.
- 해설 빈칸부터 interviewed까지는 형용사절이다. 선행사(students)가 사람이고 빈칸 뒤에 동사가 있으므로 주격의 who가 정답이다.
- 어휘 a majority of 대다수의 term 학기

2
- 해석 추운 날씨와 최근에 내린 눈 때문에 스키 시즌이 3월 말까지 지속될 것이다.
- 해설 동사 어휘 문제이다. '지속될 것이다'라는 뜻이므로 (C) last가 정답이다. (A) 만기되다 (B) 끝내다 (D) 참다
- 어휘 season 시즌 until ~까지

3
- 해석 뉴욕에서는 당신이 서양 또는 동양 음식을 원하든지에 상관없이 선택은 다양하다.
- 해설 be동사 뒤에 보어 자리이다. '다양한'이라는 뜻의 형용사 (B) varied가 정답이다.
- 어휘 western 서양의 eastern 동양의

4
- 해석 다른 근무자들과 비교하여 직원들을 평가하는 것은 개인적인 형편을 기반으로 해야 한다.
- 해설 전치사(in) 뒤의 명사 자리이다. in comparison with는 '~와 비교하다'라는 뜻이다.
- 어휘 evaluate 평가하다 be based on ~에 기반하다 circumstance 상황

5
- 해석 고객들은 10,000달러를 초과한 금액을 해외로 보낼 때 은행 지점장으로부터 특별한 승인을 받아야 한다.
- 해설 부사절을 분사구문으로 만들 때에는 부사절의 주어가 주절의 주어와 같은 경우 주어를 생략하고 동사를 -ing형으로 만든다. 접속사는 의미를 명확히 하기 위해 남겨놓기도 한다.
- 어휘 specific 특정한 approval 승인 abroad 해외

6
- 해석 우리 공장에서 관리자들은 직원들이 정시에 오고, 조립 라인이 순조롭게 돌아가도록 하는 것에 상당한 시간을 쓴다.
- 해설 [spend+시간+-ing] 구문 안에서 명사 time을 수식하는 형용사 자리이다. '상당한'이라는 뜻의 (C) considerable이 정답이다. (B)도 형용사인데 '사려 깊은'이라는 뜻이므로 어색하다.
- 어휘 supervisor 관리자 on time 정시에 assembly line 생산 라인 smoothly 순조롭게

7
- 해석 좋은 책을 읽는 것은 마치 신체에 조화를 가져오는 영양적으로 균형 잡힌 식사를 하는 것과 같다.
- 해설 balanced(형용사) 앞의 부사 자리이다. 부사가 바로 뒤 형용사를 수식한다.
- 어휘 balanced 균형이 잡힌 meal 식사 harmony 조화

8
- 해석 영양실조가 만연한 몇몇 나라에서 Peace Corps는 사람들의 결핍된 식사를 보충하기 위해서 비타민을 자주 배포한다.
- 해설 어휘 문제이다. '결핍된 식사를 보충하다'라는 뜻이므로 정답은 (A)이다. (B) 부과하다 (C) 추구하다 (D) 더하다
- 어휘 malnutrition 영양실조 prevalent 만연하다 frequently 자주 distribute 배포하다 meager 결핍된 diet 식단, 식사

9
- 해석 의료원은 그녀가 환자의 고통에 무관심한 것을 보고 그녀를 간호사로서 고용하지 않기로 결정했다.
- 해설 명사 어휘 문제이다. '환자의 고통에 무관심한 것'이라는 뜻이므로 (D)가 정답이다. (A) 망설임 (B) 낙심 (C) 본의 아님
- 어휘 clinic 의료원 discover 발견하다 suffer 고통

10
- 해석 뉴질랜드의 시민권 소유자들이 시간 내에 등록하지 않는다면, 그들은 투표할 자격이 없을 것이다.
- 해설 [be eligible to부정사] / [be eligible for 명사] ~할 자격이 있다
- 어휘 holder 소유자 citizenship 시민권 register 등록하다 vote 투표하다

11
- 해석 가게에서 화난 고객들을 다룰 때 판매원은 급한 문제가 해결되자마자 그들을 돕겠다고 정중하게 안심시켜야 한다.
- 해설 reassure을 수식하는 부사 어휘 문제로 '정중하게 안심시키다'가 적절하므로 정답은 (B)이다. (A) 잠재적으로 (C) 가능하게 (D) 진보적으로
- 어휘 deal with 다루다 anxious 흥분한, 화난 salespeople 판매원 reassure 안심시키다 matters 문제 address 다루다

12
- 해석 올해 정부가 사람들의 금연을 위해 펼친 캠페인은 성공적이었음이 증명되었다.
- 해설 be동사 뒤의 형용사 어휘 문제이다. '캠페인이 성공적이었다'라는 뜻이므로 (B)가 정답이다. (A) 계승하는 (C) 호화로운 (D) 순종적인
- 어휘 prevent A from B A를 B로부터 막다, 보호하다 prove 증명하다

13
- 해석 많은 금융 우려에도 불구하고 많은 사람들은 그 회사가 국내 시장보다 해외 시장에 많은 중점을 둘 것으로 예상한다.
- 해설 동사 자리이다. many가 대명사로 쓰였으므로 복수 동사가 와야 한다. (A), (C) 중에서 빈칸 뒤에 목적어(명사절 that)가 있으므로 능동태가 되어야 한다. 따라서 정답은 (A)이다.
- 어휘 despite ~에도 불구하고 emphasis 강조 foreign 외국의 domestic 국내의

14
- 해석 이번 주말까지 Jackson 씨에게 올해 연간 판매 보고서의 사본을 제출해 주세요.
- 해설 명사 어휘 문제이다. '사본을 제출하다'가 적절하므로 (A)가 정답이다. (B) (잡지 등의) 호 (C) (책 형태의) 판 (D) 표시
- 어휘 submit 제출하다 annual 연간 by ~까지

15
- 해석 기술 전문가들은 소프트웨어의 진보가 가까운 미래에 계속될 것이라고 예측했다.
- 해설 in the foreseeable future: 예측 가능한 미래, 가까운 미래
- 어휘 predict 예측하다 enhancement 발전 continue 계속되다

16
- 해석 회사 직원들이 계속해서 임금 인상을 요구했지만 3년이 넘도록 승인되지 않았다.
- 해설 동사 request(요청하다)를 수식하는 부사 자리이다. '계속해서 요구하다'라는 뜻이므로 정답은 (A)이다. (B) 정확하게 (C) 엄청나게 (D) 짧게, 잠깐
- 어휘 raise 인상 grant 승인하다

17
- 해석 경찰은 불가사의하게 실종된 배의 선원들로 추정되는 3구의 시신을 발견했다.
- 해설 빈칸은 뒤의 형용사(missing)를 수식하는 부사 자리이다. 따라서 정답은 (C)이다.
- 어휘 body 시체 crew 선원 missing 실종된

18
- 해석 Twilight Charity는 가난한 지역의 아이들을 교육시키고 지원하기 위한 목표를 가진 기관이다.
- 해설 형용사절 접속사 자리이다. 앞의 선행사(organization)가 사물이고 뒤의 명사(mission) 앞에 관사가 없으므로 소유격 (D)가 정답이다.
- 어휘 organization 기관 educate 교육하다 support 보조하다 poverty 가난

19
- 해석 회장은 직원들에게 직장에 있는 모든 컴퓨터는 오로지 사무용으로만 사용되어야 한다는 것을 상기시켰다.
- 해설 for official use: 공식적인 용도
- 어휘 remind 상기시키다 official 공식적인

20
- 해석 모든 질문들은 면접관이 방을 떠나기 전까지 차례로 대답되었다.
- 해설 one after another: 잇따라서, 차례로
- 어휘 interviewer 면접관 answer 대답하다

DAY 06
본문 p.228

1 (C)	2 (B)	3 (D)	4 (D)	5 (B)
6 (C)	7 (D)	8 (B)	9 (C)	10 (A)
11 (A)	12 (C)	13 (A)	14 (A)	15 (D)
16 (A)	17 (A)	18 (D)	19 (D)	20 (C)

1
- 해석 회장은 선출된 이래로 매년 대중교통 시스템의 재건을 추천하고 있다.
- 해설 동사 자리이다. 뒤에 목적어가 없으므로 수동태의 (C)가 정답이다.
- 어휘 recommend 추천하다, 권고하다 rebuild 다시 세우다, 재건하다 transportation 수송, 운송

2
- 해석 Robert 박사의 치료사로서 이전 경력이 자원봉사 현장에서 그녀에게 큰 도움이 될 것이다.
- 해설 동사 help 뒤에 목적어 자리이다. 따라서 정답은 (B)이다. 재귀대명사는 주어와 목적어가 같아야 목적어 자리에 쓸 수 있는데 이 문장의 주어는 experiences이므로 오답이다.
- 어휘 previous 이전의 therapist 치료 전문가 greatly 대단히 volunteer 자원봉사자

3
- 해석 지난겨울에 온 기록적인 양의 비 때문에 올해 물이 부족할 가능성은 낮다.
- 해설 관사(a)와 형용사(low) 뒤의 명사 자리이다. 따라서 정답은 (D)이다. (B)는 '유사성, 닮음'이라는 뜻으로 의미적으로 오답이다.
- 어휘 amount 총액, 양 shortage 부족 likelihood 가능성

4
- 해석 Jeff는 우리가 작은 광고 회사와 함께 일해야 한다고 생각하는 반면에, Jessica는 큰 회사가 더 좋을 거라고 생각한다.
- 해설 접속사 자리이다. 등위접속사 and를 제외하고 의미상 '~하는 반면에'라는 뜻의 (D)가 정답이다.
- 어휘 advertising 광고

5
- 해석 오토바이를 타기 전에 당신의 헬멧이 확실히 조여졌는지를 확인하세요.
- 해설 〈be+p.p.〉 사이의 빈칸은 동사를 수식하는 부사 자리이다. 따라서 정답은 (B)이다.
- 어휘 helmet 헬멧 fasten 매다, 채우다 completely 완전히, 전적으로

SECTION 2_실전 랜덤 연습 » 079

6

해석 만약 Brown 씨가 선출된다면 이 프로젝트는 철저한 검토를 겪게 될 것이다.

해설 가정법 미래는 〈If+주어+should+동사원형, 주어+will+동사원형〉 구문인데 가정법에서 If가 생략되면 주어 동사의 자리가 바뀌는 도치가 일어난다. 따라서 정답은 (C)이다.

어휘 elected 선출된 undergo 겪다, 받다 thorough 철저한 review 검토

7

해석 당신의 이력서에 쓰인 어떠한 잘못된 정보도 자동 불합격으로 이어질 수 있다.

해설 빈칸 뒤에 이미 동사가 있으므로 빈칸은 동사가 아닌 information을 수식하는 분사 자리이다. 따라서 정답은 (D)이다.

어휘 misleading 오해의 소지가 있는 result in ~(한 결과)를 낳다 disqualification 자격박탈, 불합격

8

해석 David Collins는 단지 6개월 전에 우리 회사에 입사했지만 그는 이미 최고의 판매원이 되었다.

해설 부사 어휘 문제이다. already는 대부분 긍정문에 쓰는 반면 yet은 have yet to(아직~않다) 구문을 제외하면 대부분 의문문이나 부정문에 쓰인다.

어휘 salesperson 판매원

9

해석 그의 이전 성공 때문에 이사는 그가 일을 잘할 수 있을까 하는 어떤 의심할 이유도 없었다.

해설 빈칸은 reason(명사)을 수식하는 형용사 자리이다. 앞에 부정어(not)가 있기 때문에 (C)가 정답이다. few는 형용사일 때 뒤에 복수 명사가 와야 한다.

어휘 previous 이전의 doubt 의심, 의혹

10

해석 회사를 위해 열심히 일한 Michael White는 올해의 사원으로 뽑혔다.

해설 worked(자동사) 뒤의 부사 자리이다. hard와 hardly는 둘 다 부사지만 의미상 (A) hard(열심히)가 정답이다.

어휘 be selected as ~로 선발(선택)되다 employee 사원

11

해석 이 직책의 모든 지원자들은 늦어도 금요일 7시까지 들어와야 한다.

해설 at the latest: 늦어도

어휘 applications 지원(신청)자

12

해석 입국 신고서를 가지고 있지 않은 어떤 승객이라도 승무원으로부터 하나를 얻을 수 있다.

해설 obtain(동사) 뒤 목적어 자리이다. 앞서 나온 a landing card(단수)를 받는 (C) one이 정답이다.

어휘 landing card 입국 신고서 flight attendant 승무원

13

해석 2층에 있는 모든 컴퓨터실은 추후 공지가 있을 때까지 수리를 위해서 사용이 중지될 것이다.

해설 until further notice: 추후 공지 때까지

어휘 be closed for ~을 위해 닫다 renovations 수리, 혁신 further 추가의 notice 공지

14

해석 구조대원들은 난파선의 생존자들을 위한 광범위한 탐색을 할 것이지만 생존자가 없을까 우려되었다.

해설 관사(an)와 search(명사) 사이의 형용사 자리 어휘 문제이다. '광범위한 탐색'이라는 뜻이므로 (A)가 정답이다. (B) 경비가 포함된 (C) 배타적인 (D) 걱정되는, 불안한

어휘 rescue 구조, 구출 conduct 행동하다 shipwreck 난파, 조난 사고 fear 두려워하다

15

해석 작년에도 또 다시 수많은 관광객들이 Yellowstone 국립공원의 숨 막히는 장관에 매료되었다.

해설 수동태 어휘 문제이다. '관광객이 매료되었다'는 뜻이기 때문에 (D)가 정답이다. (A) 할당된 (B) 발표된 (C) 짜증난

어휘 tourist 관광객 breathtaking (놀라워서) 숨이 멎는 듯한 view 경관

16

해석 당신이 어떤 식으로 그것을 보든지 간에 어린 나이에 올림픽 동메달을 딴 것은 놀랄만한 업적이다.

해설 부사절을 이끄는 접속사를 고르는 문제이다. (B) However의 경우 부사절로 사용할 경우 이후에 형용사나 부사가 같이 나와야 하며, (C)의 경우 '~할 때마다' 또는 '~할 때는 언제든지'의 의미로 이후 주절의 내용과 어울리지 않는다. (D)의 경우 불완전한 문장과 함께 사용되어야 하기 때문에 위 문장에서는 오답이다. 따라서 정답은 '어떤 식으로 그것을 보든지 간에'라는 의미를 완성하는 (A)가 정답이다.

어휘 bronze 청동 remarkable 놀라운 achievement 업적, 성취 however 그러나

17

해석 회사가 Parker 씨의 국제 무역 경험으로부터 혜택을 얻을 수 있는 것에는 의심의 여지가 없다.

해설 benefit from: ~로부터 혜택을 얻다

어휘 doubt 의심, 의혹 benefit 유익하다 international 국제적인 trade 거래, 무역

18

해석 병사들은 그들이 상황에 대처하는 매우 효과적인 방법으로 인해 칭찬을 받았다.

해설 very(부사)의 수식을 받는 형용사 자리로 (C), (D) 중에서 way와의 관계가 능동이므로 (D) impressive가 정답이다.

어휘 soldiers 군인, 병사 commend 칭찬하다 deal with 다루다

19

해석 만약 당신의 정규 근무 시간 동안 사고가 발생했다면 장애 보험에 의해 보상될 것이다.

해설 관사(the) 뒤의 명사 자리이다. (A)도 명사지만 의미상 어색하다.

어휘 occur 일어나다, 발생하다 regular 규칙적인, 정기적인 duties 직무, 직책 cover 보상하다 disability 장애 insurance 보험

20

해석 Honeycutt는 마침내 뉴욕에서 가장 가치 있는 지역으로 본사를 옮길 자금상의 여유가 생겼다.

해설 piece of land를 수식하는 형용사 어휘 문제이다. '가장 바람직한 지역'이라는 뜻이므로 정답은 (C)이다. (A) 끌 수 있는 (B) 상당한 (D) 세울 수 있는

어휘 afford ~할 여유가 되다 headquarters 본사 desirable 바람직한

DAY 07

본문 p.230

1 (C)	2 (D)	3 (D)	4 (A)	5 (D)
6 (D)	7 (A)	8 (B)	9 (A)	10 (C)
11 (B)	12 (C)	13 (C)	14 (B)	15 (D)
16 (A)	17 (C)	18 (C)	19 (D)	20 (B)

1

해석 회사 정책은 직원들이 그들이 원할 때마다 직원 휴게실을 사용하는 것을 가능하게 만들었다.

해설 진목적어(to부정사) 앞의 의미상의 주어 자리이다. 의미상의 주어는 [for+명사(대명사)]이므로 정답은 (C)이다.

어휘 policy 정책 possible 가능한 staff lounge 직원 휴게실

2

해석 Jackson 교수는 새로운 보존 계획이 이 지역의 야생 동물의 수를 두 배로 늘릴 거라고 예상한다.

해설 동사 자리이다. (C)는 수동태이므로 that절(명사절)이 뒤에 목적어로 올 수 없다. 따라서 능동의 (D)가 정답이다.

어휘 preservation 보존 wild 야생의 region 지역, 지방 anticipate 예상하다

3

해석 술집에서 술을 마시기로 한 사람은 누구든지 최소한 18살이어야 한다.

해설 관사(a) 뒤의 명사 자리이다.

어휘 consume 소모하다, 마시다 minimize 최소화하다

4

해석 매 근무를 시작하기 전에 서명을 하세요. 그렇지 않으면 일한 시간이 당신의 봉급에 정확하게 반영되지 않을 수 있습니다.

해설 세미콜론(;)은 마침표에 가깝기 때문에 빈칸은 접속사가 아닌 접속부사가 와야 한다. 의미상 '그렇지 않으면'이라는 뜻의 (A) otherwise가 정답이다.

어휘 sign 서명하다 shift 교대 근무 accurately 정확히 reflect 반영하다 nevertheless 그렇기는 하지만 whereas ~한 반면에

5

해석 유감스럽지만 경영진은 방안에 남겨두고 가신 소지품에 대해서는 책임을 질 수 없다.

해설 빈칸 뒤에 쉼표(,)가 있고 빈칸 뒤는 완벽한 문장 구조를 갖추고 있으므로 빈칸은 부사 자리가 되어야 한다. 따라서 정답은 (D)이다.

어휘 management 경영진 accept 받아들이다 responsibility 책임 belongings 소유물

6

해석 우리는 경제가 내년에 훨씬 성장할 것이라 예상된다고 해도 새로운 직원을 지금은 채용할 생각이 없다.

해설 빈칸 뒤에 절이 오기 때문에 문장을 연결하는 접속사 자리임을 알 수 있다. (C), (D) 중에서 의미상 '~한다고 해도'라는 뜻의 (D)가 정답이다.

어휘 intend to ~할 작정이다 forecast 예측하다 significantly 상당히 regardless of ~에 상관없이

7

해석 많은 경제학자들은 소비재의 가격이 증가하는 것에 대해 증가하는 세금을 탓했다.

해설 blame A for B: A를 B에 대해서 탓하다

어휘 economist 경제학자 consumer goods 소비재

8

해석 인사과 부장은 그의 퇴직일이 다가옴에 따라 복잡한 감정을 경험했다.

해설 관사(a)와 명사(array) 사이의 형용사 자리이다. '어쩔 줄 모르는'이라는 뜻의 bewildering이 정답이다.

어휘 retirement 은퇴 an array of 다수의

9

해석 친환경적인 태양 에너지의 잠재적인 매력을 규명하기 위한 노력으로서 우리는 전국적인 조사를 시행하고 있다.

해설 관사(the) 형용사(potential) 뒤의 명사 자리이다. 따라서 정답은 (A)이다.

어휘 establish 설립하다 potential 잠재적인 environmentally friendly 친환경적인 nationwide 전국적인 appeal 매력

10

해석 Stephen Covey에 의해서 디자인 된 몇몇 제품들은 내수보다 해외에서 더 인기가 있다.

해설 부사 overseas와 반대되는 의미인 (C) locally가 정답이다. 그리고 빈칸 앞의 are 뒤에는 popular가 생략되었다고 볼 수 있다.

어휘 overseas 해외에 locally 현지에서

11

해석 Local Plan은 2007년과 2008년 사이에 추가적인 2,000개의 새

로운 주택들을 감안한 것이다.

해설 〈make allowance for+명사〉는 '~를 감안(참작)하다'라는 뜻이다.

어휘 allowance 감안, 허용량 dwelling 주택 omission 생략, 누락 impression 인상 elimination 제거, 배제

12

해설 노조 구성원들은 처음에는 새로운 노동 계약서에 대해서 동의했으나 마지막에는 거부했다.

해설 in the end와 반대되는 의미로 '초기에, 처음에'라는 뜻의 initially가 정답이다.

어휘 union 조합 agree to ~에 대해 합의하다 labor 노동 reject 거부하다 initially 처음에 strictly 엄격히

13

해설 우리는 그렇게 어려운 협상 동안 매우 협조적이었던 당신에게 감사합니다.

해설 being은 be동사가 동명사가 된 것이지만 여전히 be동사의 성질을 가지고 있다. 따라서 빈칸은 보어 자리이다. so의 수식을 받는 형용사 (C)가 정답이다.

어휘 negotiation 협상 cooperative 협력하는

14

해설 당신이 이 나라에 처음 온 이래로 10년이 지났다는 것이 놀랍다.

해설 빈칸부터 country까지 명사절이다. (A), (B), (D)가 명사절 종속접속사인데 (A), (D)는 불완전한 문장을 묶어서 명사절로 만들기 때문에 오답이다. 따라서 정답은 (B)이다.

어휘 unbelievable 믿기 어려울 정도인

15

해설 방 예약 단가는 정기적으로 바뀌기 때문에 더 자세한 정보는 호텔 측에 직접 상의해 주세요.

해설 on a regular basis(= regularly)는 '정기적으로'라는 뜻이다.

어휘 consult 상담하다 directly 곧장 detailed 상세한 vary 다르다, 달라지다

16

해설 앞으로의 게임쇼 참가자들은 부착된 설문지를 채워주세요.

해설 〈ask+목적어+to부정사〉는 수동태로 고치면 〈be asked to부정사〉 형태가 된다.

어휘 prospective 장래의, 유망한 contestant 참가자 attached 첨부된 questionnaire 설문지

17

해설 긴 휴가에서 돌아온 후에 나는 동료들 중 한 명이 사임한 것을 알게 되었다.

해설 resign은 자동사이므로 수동태 (A), (B)는 오답이다. 알게 된 시점 (realized: 과거동사)보다 사임한 것이 더 과거에 일어난 일이므로 대과거가 와야 한다. 따라서 과거완료의 (C)가 정답이다.

어휘 colleague 동료 resign 사직하다

18

해설 부분적인 납입금이 이번 달 말까지 보내져야 한다. 그렇지 않으면 추후 조치가 취해 질 것이다.

해설 명사(payment) 앞의 형용사 자리이다. 따라서 정답은 (C)이다.

어휘 further 추가의 partial 부분적인

19

해설 계약이 만료되기 10일 전에 세입자들은 임대를 갱신할 것인지 아닌지를 서면으로 통보해야 한다.

해설 명사 자리 어휘 문제이다. '서면 통보'라는 뜻이므로 (D)가 정답이다. (A) 축약 (B) 휴가, 허가 (C) 선언

어휘 expires 만료되다 tenant 세입자 submit 제출하다 renewal 갱신

20

해설 관리팀은 인터뷰가 회의실에서 진행될 것이라고 발표했다.

해설 conduct an interview: 인터뷰를 진행하다

어휘 board room 회의실 alert 알리다 engage 사로잡다 protect 보호하다

DAY 08

본문 p.232

1 (A)	2 (A)	3 (B)	4 (C)	5 (B)
6 (B)	7 (B)	8 (B)	9 (B)	10 (B)
11 (B)	12 (C)	13 (A)	14 (B)	15 (A)
16 (D)	17 (A)	18 (D)	19 (B)	20 (D)

1

해석 많은 고객들이 다양한 제품을 제공하는 이 웹 사이트를 통해서 가구를 구매한다.

해설 동사 자리이다. 빈칸 뒤에 목적어가 있으므로 수동태 (C)는 오답이다. 따라서 정답은 (A)이다.

어휘 a wide range of 광범위한, 다양한

2

해석 좀 더 철저한 검사를 한 후 우리는 처음에는 찾지 못했던 계약서의 많은 오류들을 발견했다.

해설 명사(examination)을 수식하는 형용사 자리이다. 따라서 정답은 (A)이다.

어휘 examination 조사, 검사 flaw 결함 detect 발견하다

3

해석 비행기는 다음 달 초부터 뉴욕과 샌프란시스코 사이의 매일 운항을 재개할 것이다.

해설 daily service를 목적어로 받기에 의미상 적절한 어휘는 (B) resume(재개하다)이다.

어휘 depart 떠나다, 출발하다

082

4

해석 양측이 며칠 전에 진행되었던 독립적 중재의 결과를 기다리고 있다.

해설 형용사(independent) 뒤의 명사 자리이다. 따라서 (C)가 정답이다. (D) 중재자도 명사지만 which was conducted(얼마 전에 시행된)와 어울리지 않는다.

어휘 independent 독립적인 arbitration 중재

5

해석 집의 난방을 위해서 많이 기름에 의존하는 Northeast 지역의 가정 난방비가 작년 동안에 두 배가 되었다.

해설 over the past year은 현재완료 시제의 힌트가 되고 또 double은 자동사로 쓸 수 있으므로 능동의 (B)가 정답이다.

어휘 region 지역 rely on ~에 의존하다 heavily 심하게, 아주 많이

6

해석 2명의 대표 이사가 회사의 합병을 매듭짓기 위해 공식적인 계약서에 서명하려고 만났다.

해설 관사(a) 뒤에 가산명사로 쓸 수 있는 명사는 (B)뿐이다. 의미상으로도 '합병'이 가장 자연스럽다. (A) 법인 설립 (C) 융합 (D) (영토의) 합병

어휘 formal 공식적인

7

해석 우리의 이익을 극대화하기 위해서 우리는 잠재 고객들에게 더욱 적극적으로 따라 붙을 필요가 있다.

해설 clients까지 이미 완벽한 문장이므로 뒤로는 수식어이다. more는 여기서는 부사로 썼으므로 빈칸도 부사 (B)가 정답이다.

어휘 maximize 극대화하다 profit 이익 pursue 추구하다, 뒤쫓다 aggressively 적극적으로

8

해석 이 아파트 건물의 세입자들 모두가 이 지역에서 가장 큰 부동산 업체인 Brenda Housing에 의해서 독점적으로 고지서를 받는다.

해설 (A)는 최상급 표현으로 '가장 ~한'이라는 뜻이므로 오답이고, (C), (D)는 대명사로 주어 자리에 나올 때 단수 취급해야 하므로 동사 are와 수 일치가 맞지 않아 오답이다. 따라서 정답은 (B)이다.

어휘 bill 청구서를 보내다 exclusively 독점적으로 developer 개발업자

9

해석 4월 미팅의 회의록이 미팅의 주제의 관점에서 봤을 때 이치에 맞지 않는 것 같다.

해설 make sense: 이치에 맞다

어휘 minutes 회의록 in light of ~에 비추어 agenda 안건, 주제

10

해석 3분기의 초기 보고서들은 우리 상점들의 판매가 작년 이래로 20퍼센트 증가해 온 것을 보여준다.

해설 year를 수식하는 형용사 자리인데 since가 '~이래로'라는 뜻이므로 과거의 시점과 비교를 해야 한다. 과거의 형용사인 (B) previous가 정답이다.

어휘 initial 처음의 previous 이전의

11

해석 여행 일정표에 따르면 관광객들은 Pimentel 섬으로 가는 보트 여행을 즐기게 될 Coosa 만으로 향해 떠나는 것이 예정되어 있다.

해설 leave for는 '~를 향해 떠나다'라는 의미가 있다. towards는 '~을 향해서'라는 뜻이 있는데 이 경우 Coosa Bay가 목적지가 아니라 '그 쪽을 향해서'라는 뜻이므로 정답은 (B) for이다.

어휘 itinerary 일정 leave for ~로 떠나다

12

해석 만약 새로운 마케팅 전략이 그렇게 성공적이지 않았다면 그들은 은행으로부터 그렇게 많은 금융 지원을 받을 수 없었을 것이다.

해설 가정법 과거 완료 구문 [If+had+p.p., 주어+would have p.p.]가 사용되었으므로 정답은 (C)이다.

어휘 strategy 전략 financial 금융의, 재정의

13

해석 많은 가게 주인들은 공휴일을 준수하기 위해서 내일 가게를 닫을 것이다.

해설 전치사 뒤의 명사 자리이다. (A), (D) 중에서 '준수'라는 뜻의 (A)가 정답이다. (D)는 '관찰'이라는 뜻이라서 어색하다.

어휘 local shop 지역 상가 in observance of ~를 준수하여

14

해석 Purustan의 그림인 Olympia는 최근에 가장 인상적인 그림 중에 하나로 칭송받는다.

해설 pieces를 수식하는 형용사 자리이다. 선택지에서 (B)만이 형용사이다.

어휘 admired 존경받는

15

해석 30년이 넘는 기간 동안 First National 은행은 고객들에게 투자금을 관리하기 위해 필요한 전문 지식과 조언을 제공해 왔다.

해설 은행이 고객들에게 줄 수 있는 것은 '전문 지식'이므로 정답은 (A)이다.

어휘 investment 투자 reimbursement 환급 conversion 전환, 개조

16

해석 우리의 호텔은 매일 전체적인 방 청소를 하고 이틀에 한 번 당신의 냉장고를 보충한다.

해설 '이틀에 한 번'이라는 뜻의 every other day가 적절하므로 정답은 (D)이다.

어휘 housekeeping service 집안 청소 서비스 replenish 다시 채우다, 보충하다

17

해석 우체국은 국경일을 제외하고 매일 아침 8시에서 저녁 6시까지 문을 연다.

해설 전치사 어휘 문제이다. 접속사 (D)를 제외하고 의미상 '~을 제외하고'라는 뜻의 (A) except가 정답이다. (B) ~를 위해서 (C) ~하는 동안

어휘 except ~를 제외하고는

18
해석 후보자들 중 아직 아무도 선택되지 않았지만 경제를 전공한 사람들이 뽑힐 기회가 가장 높다.
해설 be동사 뒤의 동사 형태 중에서 목적어가 없으므로 수동태의 구조가 적절하다. 따라서 정답은 (D)이다.
어휘 none 아무도 (아니다) candidate 후보자 major in ~을 전공하다

19
해석 전자 통신을 사용하는 가장 매력적인 장점 중의 하나는 집에서 편안하게 일할 수 있다는 것이다.
해설 명사 어휘 문제이다. 집에서 일하는 것은 가장 큰 '장점' 중의 하나이므로 정답은 (B)이다.
어휘 attractive 매력적인 advantage 이점 comfort 안락, 편안

20
해석 공석에 빨리 지원하는 것은 그 어떤 것도 보장해 줄 수는 없지만 좋은 인상을 줄 수는 있다.
해설 주어 자리이다. 동사가 단수이며 to부정사의 명사적 용법으로 '공석에 지원하는 것'이라는 뜻의 (D)가 정답이다. to부정사는 단수 취급한다.
어휘 guarantee 보장하다, 약속하다 impression 인상, 느낌

DAY 09

본문 p.234

1 (A)	2 (C)	3 (B)	4 (C)	5 (C)
6 (B)	7 (A)	8 (D)	9 (A)	10 (B)
11 (A)	12 (D)	13 (B)	14 (C)	15 (B)
16 (A)	17 (C)	18 (C)	19 (C)	20 (A)

1
해석 이 일을 처리하기 위해 회계 부서와 마케팅 부서 둘 다 함께 협력해야 한다.
해설 상관접속사 both A and B를 묻는 문제이다.
어휘 accounting department 회계부서 cooperate 협력하다 handle 다루다

2
해석 Scott Bond는 30년 전에 A&C 사에 입사했고 이것이 그를 이 회사에서 가장 오래 일한 직원으로 만들었다.
해설 동사 자리이다. 주어가 단수이므로 (A)는 수 일치에서 오답이다. 뒤에 목적어가 있으므로 수동태 (D)는 오답이다. ago라는 과거 시제의 힌트가 나오므로 (B)가 정답이다.
어휘 long-serving 장기 근무한

3
해석 경영진은 근무 시간을 줄이자는 노조의 제안에 만장일치로 동의할 것이 예상된다.
해설 agree(자동사)와 on(전치사) 사이이므로 동사를 수식하는 부사 자리이다. (B), (D) 중에서 '만장일치로'라는 뜻의 (B)가 정답이다. (D)는 '때 이른, 시기상조의'라는 뜻이다.
어휘 suggestion 제안 decrease 줄다, 줄이다 unanimously 만장일치로

4
해석 우리 가게들 중 한 곳에서 200 달러 이상을 소비한 고객에게 카메라를 무료로 제공할 것이다.
해설 동사 자리 어휘 문제이다. '카메라를 무료로 준다'라는 뜻이므로 (C)가 정답이다. (A) 만들다 (B) 통제하다 (D) 복구하다

5
해석 이 시장의 선두 기업으로서 우리는 당신이 우리의 서비스에 만족할 것이라고 확신한다.
해설 be content with: ~에 만족하다
어휘 confident 자신감 있는 potential 잠재적인 potent 강한 content 만족하는 constant 지속적인

6
해석 로마에 있는 폐허들 중에서 가장 잘 보존되어 있고, 가장 인상적인 건축물은 콜로세움이다.
해설 형용사(impressive)가 수식하는 명사 자리이다. 선택지에서 (B)만이 명사이다.
어휘 ruin 폐허 well-preserved 잘 보존된

7
해석 우리는 모든 방들이 우리 고객들을 위해서 가능하면 최대한 깨끗하게 유지될 수 있게 한다.
해설 원급 비교 as와 as 사이에는 형용사나 부사가 오는데 앞에 오는 동사를 보고 형용사/부사를 구분한다. stay는 2형식 동사로 뒤에 보어가 오기 때문에 형용사 (A)가 정답이다.
어휘 stay 유지하다

8
해석 새로운 고용 정책이 실제적으로 실업률을 줄일지는 두고 볼 일이다.
해설 [It remains to be seen whether ~]은 '~은 두고 볼 일이다'라는 뜻이다.
어휘 remain 계속 ~이다, 남다 rate of unemployment 실업률

9
해석 허리케인에 의해서 야기된 피해의 정도를 조사하기 위해서 긴급 모임이 열린다.
해설 관사(the) 뒤의 명사 자리이다. 선택지에서 (A)만이 명사이다.
어휘 extent 정도, 규모 damage 피해

10
해석 공장 노동자들은 지난주에 발휘된 새로운 규정을 따르는 것에 익숙해지고 있다.
해설 [be(get) used to: ~에 익숙해지다]에서 to는 전치사이다. 따라서

빈칸은 명사 혹은 동명사가 나와야 한다. 따라서 정답은 (B)이다. (D)도 동명사이지만 수동의 형태이므로 오답이다.

어휘 regulation 규칙, 규정

11
해석 국회위원들은 농업 보조금에 관한 제안된 정책에 만장일치로 반대했다.

해설 동사 자리 문제이다. 빈칸 뒤에 목적어가 있으므로 능동의 (A)가 정답이다.

어휘 legislator 입법자, 국회의원 unanimously 만장일치로 reject 반대하다 agricultural 농업의 subsidy 보조금

12
해석 노동조합 회비는 산업 분야에 따라서 다양하다는 것을 알아 두세요.

해설 note(동사) 뒤의 목적어 자리이다. 빈칸에 접속사가 들어가서 뒤 문장을 명사절로 묶어야 한다. 전치사 (A), (B)를 제외하고 (C)는 명사절로 묶을 수는 있지만 불완전한 문장을 묶기 때문에 오답이다. 따라서 정답은 (D)이다.

어휘 vary 서로 각기 다르다 concerning ~에 관한

13
해석 기술 분야의 진보들은 예상보다 많은 수익을 기업인들에게 가지고 왔다.

해설 전치사 어휘 문제로 분야를 나타내는 전치사는 (B) in이다.

어휘 advance 진보 entrepreneur 기업가

14
해석 이 시스템은 유지보수에 대한 점검이 규칙적으로만 수행되면 사용자에게 품질 좋은 서비스를 제공할 것이다.

해설 부사절 접속사 자리이다. 선택지가 모두 부사절 접속사인데 의미상 '~하는 한'이라는 뜻의 (C)가 정답이다.

어휘 quality 고급의, 양질의 maintenance 유지보수

15
해석 우리 회사는 앞으로 몇 년 후에 새로운 경영 기술들을 채택할 필요가 있다.

해설 need to에서 to는 to부정사이다. 따라서 빈칸에는 동사원형이 들어가야 한다. (A) 등록하다 (D) 교체하다

16
해석 이 사원의 동양의 미는 세계 각지의 많은 관광객을 끌어들인다.

해설 동사 어휘 문제이다. '많은 관광객을 끌어들이다'는 뜻이므로 (A)가 정답이다. (B) 계약하다 (C) 철회하다 (D) 연장하다

어휘 oriental 동양의 temple 사원

17
해석 Telicka 씨가 서류를 검토한 후에만 승인이 이뤄질 것이다.

해설 [only+부사]가 앞으로 나와서 도치된 문장이다. '~을 검토하다'라는 뜻의 look into가 정답이다. (A) look out(조심하다) (B) look after(~을 돌보다) (D) look back(뒤돌아보다)

어휘 approval 승인

18
해석 검사들은 부패와 관련이 있다고 밝혀진 어떤 정부 관리에 대항해서도 단호하게 대처할 것이다.

해설 act가 '행동을 취하다'라는 자동사이므로 뒤에는 이를 수식하는 부사가 나온다. 따라서 정답은 (C)이다.

어휘 prosecutor 검사, 검찰관 against ~에 반대하여 corruption 부패

19
해석 양측은 계약서의 조건에 동의하기 위한 공통된 기반을 마침내 찾았다.

해설 common ground까지 문장이 완벽하므로 이후로는 수식어 자리이다. 의미상 to부정사의 부사적 용법 '~하기 위해서'가 적절하다.

어휘 common ground 공통점, 공통 기반 terms of ~의 조건

20
해석 판매 부장은 오후 이사회 미팅에서 판매를 증가시키기 위한 장기간의 전략의 개요를 설명할 것이다.

해설 long-term(형용사)의 수식을 받는 명사 자리이므로 (A)가 정답이다. (C)도 명사지만 의미상 어색하다.

어휘 outline 개요를 서술하다 long-term 장기적인 increase 증가시키다

DAY 10
본문 p.236

1 (D)	2 (A)	3 (C)	4 (B)	5 (D)
6 (A)	7 (A)	8 (D)	9 (D)	10 (D)
11 (B)	12 (B)	13 (C)	14 (B)	15 (C)
16 (D)	17 (A)	18 (B)	19 (A)	20 (C)

1
해석 마케팅 부서의 주요 목표는 고객들이 회사에 대해서 알게 하는 것이다.

해설 keep은 5형식 동사이므로 빈칸은 목적격 보어 자리이다. 명사와 형용사 중에서 (B) information은 customers와 동격이 아니므로 형용사가 들어가야 한다. customers와 inform의 관계가 수동이므로 과거분사 (D)가 정답이다.

어휘 primary 주된, 주요한 objective 목표, 목적

2
해석 허가 없이 고기를 잡는 어부들은 상업적인 이익을 위해서 그것을 팔수도 없고, 위안 삼아 그것을 소비할 수도 없다.

해설 상관접속사 neither A nor B가 쓰인 문장이다.

어휘 fisherman 어부 permit 허용하다 neither 어느 것도 아니다 commercial 상업의 gain 이익

3
해석 새로 임명된 매니저는 모든 정책 변경 사항을 그의 상관에게 직접 보고하도록 지시받았다.

해설 changes까지 완벽한 문장 구조이므로 빈칸부터는 수식어이다. report(동사)를 수식하는 부사 (C)가 정답이다.
어휘 newly 최근에 appoint 임명하다 instruct 교육하다 supervisor 관리자

4
해석 많은 양의 전문 지식 없이 고객이 원하는 것을 완전히 만족시키는 것은 불가능하다.
해설 〈it(가주어)+to부정사(진주어)〉 구문이다. to 뒤에는 동사원형이 나와야 하기에 정답은 (B)이다.
어휘 fully 완전히 satisfy 만족시키다

5
해석 Norton Motors에 의해서 생산되고 배급되는 최신 자동차는 매우 훌륭하게 디자인 되었다.
해설 빈칸과 distributed가 앞의 명사 vehicle을 수식하는 분사이다. 따라서 과거분사형의 (D)가 정답이다.
어휘 distribute 나누어주다, 분배하다 manufacture 제조(생산)하다

6
해석 제품의 품질이 불만족스러운 고객들은 즉시 매니저에게 말해야 한다.
해설 뒤에 목적어가 오므로 타동사를 골라야 한다. '말하다'의 뜻인 (A)가 정답이다. (B)는 자동사이므로 뒤에 바로 목적어가 올 수 없고 전치사가 필요하다.
어휘 unsatisfied 불만족스러운 at once 즉시, 당장

7
해석 Lewis 씨의 사임이 받아들여지자, 인사과 부장은 새로운 광고 이사를 찾기 시작했다.
해설 빈칸 앞에 소유격이 왔으므로 빈칸은 명사 자리이다. 선택지에서 (A)만이 명사이다.
어휘 executive 이사, 경영간부 resignation 사임, 사직

8
해석 그녀는 그가 두 달 전에 그녀에게서 빌린 책을 돌려줘야 한다고 요구했다.
해설 제안, 요청, 충고, 명령의 뜻을 가진 동사 뒤에 나오는 that절의 동사는 앞에 should가 생략된 형태로 주어에 상관없이 동사원형이 와야 한다. 따라서 정답은 (D)이다. 주어진 문장은 요청을 나타내는 동사 request 대신 make a request의 형태로 쓰였다.
어휘 request 요구하다, 요청하다

9
해석 이 제품의 전국적 배급은 주로 얼마나 배송망이 좋은지에 달려 있다.
해설 nationwide의 수식을 받는 명사 자리 어휘 문제이다. '전국적인 배급'이라는 뜻이므로 (D)가 정답이다. (A) 기여 (B) 귀속 (C) 찬사
어휘 nationwide 전국적인 largely 크게, 대체로 depend on ~에 달려 있다 distribution 분배, 분포

10
해석 휴일에 우리가 방문했던 장소들 중에서 나이아가라 폭포가 가장 인상적이었다.
해설 빈칸 앞에 the가 있고 뒤에 형용사가 나오는 것으로 보아, 최상급임을 알 수 있다. 따라서 정답은 (D)이다. of the places처럼 범위를 주는 표현도 최상급의 힌트가 될 수 있다.

11
해석 최신 의학 연구에 따르면 암으로 죽는 사람의 수가 지난 10년 동안 급격하게 늘었다.
해설 문장의 주어는 the number of people 즉, 사람들의 '수'가 되므로 단수 동사 중에서 골라야 한다. (A)와 (D)는 오답이며, 끝에 for the past ten years를 근거로 완료 시제의 (B)가 정답이다.
어휘 medical 의학의, 의료의 research 연구, 조사

12
해석 경찰은 범죄 현장에서 하나의 단서도 찾지 못했다.
해설 clue를 목적어로 받는 동사 자리 어휘 문제이다. '단서를 찾다'라는 뜻이므로 (B)가 정답이다. (A) 망명하다 (C) 상호작용하다 (D) 연락하다
어휘 clue 단서, 실마리 crime scene 범죄 현장

13
해석 우리는 Lennox 씨가 다음 주부터 회계 부서를 담당할 것을 발표하게 되어 매우 기쁩니다.
해설 '~하게 되어 기쁘다'란 뜻의 [be pleased to부정사] 구문이다. 따라서 정답은 (C)이다.
어휘 in charge of ~를 담당하는 accounting department 회계부

14
해석 치어리더들은 열정을 가지고 운동선수들을 응원하여 운동선수들이 시합에서 더 잘하고 마침내 게임에서 승리했다.
해설 전치사(with) + such(형용사) + 명사 자리. (A)는 단수가산 명사인데 관사가 없으므로 오답이다.
어휘 enthusiasm 열광, 열정 eventually 결국

15
해석 나의 주된 걱정거리는 우리가 어떻게 이 비싼 프로젝트의 자금을 마련할 수 있을까 하는 것이다.
해설 concern(걱정, 염려)을 수식하는 형용사 자리이다. '나의 주된 걱정거리'라는 뜻이므로 (C)가 정답이다. (A) 명망 있는 (B) 중요한, 유명한 (D) 예비의
어휘 finance 자금을 대다 costly 많은 돈이 드는 concern 우려, 걱정

16
해석 아이들이 잠들기 전에 보기 위해서 Cohen 씨는 모든 저녁 약속을 취소했다.
해설 의미상 '잠들기 전에 보기 위해서'가 적절하므로 정답은 (D)이다. (A)는 의미가 어색하고 뒤에 목적어가 있기 때문에 수동형인 (B), (C)는 오답이다.
어휘 in order to ~하기 위하여 cancel 취소하다

17
- 해석 모든 공항 보안 요원들은 테러리스트의 공격에 어떻게 대처해야 하는지에 대한 특별 훈련을 받는다.
- 해설 전치사(in) 뒤에 명사가 와야 하므로 명사의 역할을 하는 〈의문사+to부정사〉가 정답이다.
- 어휘 security staff 보안 요원 deal with ~을 다루다 calmly 고요히, 침착하게

18
- 해석 당신의 도움이 없었더라면 이것을 정시에 끝낼 수 없었을 것이다. 그래서 당신은 많은 칭찬을 받을 자격이 있다.
- 해설 명사 어휘 문제이다. '칭찬을 받을 자격이 있다'라는 뜻이므로 (B)가 정답이다. (A) 보완하다 (C) 시행하다 (D) 실행
- 어휘 deserve ~을 받을 만하다 compliment 칭찬

19
- 해석 당신은 봉투의 우측 상단 구석에 이 우표를 붙여야 한다.
- 해설 this stamp를 목적어로 가지는 동사 자리이다. '우표를 붙이다'라는 뜻이므로 (A)가 정답이다 (B) 괴롭히다 (C) 갈등 (D) 반영하다
- 어휘 stamp 우표 upper 위쪽의 affix 부착하다

20
- 해석 이것이 제품 안전에 관심이 있는 고객들이 자주 물어보는 질문의 목록이다.
- 해설 빈칸은 뒤의 asked(분사)를 수식하므로 부사 자리이다. 따라서 (C)가 정답이다.
- 어휘 client 고객 frequently 자주, 흔히

DAY 11 본문 p.238

1 (C)	2 (C)	3 (D)	4 (B)	5 (A)
6 (C)	7 (D)	8 (A)	9 (A)	10 (D)
11 (C)	12 (B)	13 (B)	14 (D)	15 (C)
16 (A)	17 (D)	18 (C)	19 (B)	20 (A)

1
- 해석 Two Hearts Bakery의 특별 할인 판매는 다음 토요일에 시작될 것이다.
- 해설 next Saturday에서 미래 시제 (C)가 정답임을 알 수 있다.
- 어휘 sale 할인 판매

2
- 해석 Great Golf Courses 잡지의 편집자는 가장 좋아하는 골프 코스에 대해 글을 쓰기 위해서 유명한 골프 선수를 초대했다.
- 해설 courses(명사) 앞의 소유격 자리이다. 따라서 정답은 (C)이다.
- 어휘 editor 편집자

3
- 해석 워싱턴 지점에서 온 다음의 메시지를 Smith 씨의 사무실로 전송해 주세요.
- 해설 의미상 메시지의 출처를 나타내는 전치사가 와야 하므로 정답은 (D)이다.
- 어휘 forward 전달하다

4
- 해석 매니저는 직원들에게 그들이 아무리 바쁘더라도 일하는 동안에 최소한 두 시간에 한 번씩은 쉬라고 요청한다.
- 해설 "아무리 ~하더라도"라는 뜻의 부사절 접속사 no matter how(= however)가 적절하다. 따라서 정답은 (B)이다.
- 어휘 crew 승무원, 직원 at least 최소한

5
- 해석 호텔에서 나가시기 전에 고객 만족도 서류를 작성해 주세요.
- 해설 동사 자리이다. 명령문이므로 동사원형 (A)가 정답이다.
- 어휘 check out 나가다, 체크아웃하다 complete 완성하다

6
- 해석 새롭게 단장한 저희 컨벤션 센터는 미팅이나, 회의, 그리고 연회와 같은 여러분의 다음 번 행사에 완벽히 안성맞춤입니다.
- 해설 suit(적합하다)를 수식하는 부사 자리이다. 의미상 '완벽히 잘 들어맞는다'라는 뜻이 적절하므로 (C)가 정답이다. (A) 느리게 (B) 점진적으로 (D) 심하게
- 어휘 renovate 개조하다, 수리하다 suit 적합하다 conference 회의(학회) banquet 연회, 만찬

7
- 해석 Smith 씨는 제한된 여행 예산과 효율성 때문에 개인 승용차 대신에 대중교통을 이용하고 싶어 한다.
- 해설 would like to는 '~하고 싶다'라는 표현으로 뒤에 동사원형을 쓴다. 따라서 정답은 (D)이다.
- 어휘 public transportation 대중교통 private vehicle 개인 승용차 limited 한정된, 제한된 travel budget 여행 예산 efficiency 효율성

8
- 해석 우리는 당신이 주간 직원 회의에서 다음 시즌 제품들에 대해 시연해 주기를 원한다.
- 해설 의미상 '~의'이라는 뜻의 전치사 (A) of가 적절하다.
- 어휘 give a demonstration 시연하다 weekly staff meeting 주간 직원 회의

9
- 해석 Johnson 씨는 컴퓨터 기술자와 상담 후에 새롭게 설치된 하드웨어가 가진 문제를 쉽게 해결했다.
- 해설 unit까지 의미가 완벽하고 빈칸이 앞의 동사 solved를 수식하므로 부사 자리이다. 따라서 정답은 (A)이다.
- 어휘 newly 최근에, 새로

10
- 해석 Kayan Chemicals는 지난주에 Geneva 사와 3백만 달러의 계약서에 서명했다.
- 해설 빈칸 앞에 형용사가 있으므로 명사가 들어가야 한다. (C)는 복수 명사이므로 앞의 부정관사(a)와 맞지 않다. 따라서 정답은 (D)이다.
- 어휘 million 100만

11
- 해석 우리는 지난 화요일에 데스크톱 컴퓨터를 주문했지만 그것은 다음 주 금요일까지 발송되지 않았다.
- 해설 Friday를 수식할 수 있는 형용사로 의미상 '다음 금요일'이 적절하므로 following(=next)이 정답이다.
- 어휘 ship 발송하다

12
- 해석 Krause 씨가 좋은 평가를 받았기 때문에 그녀는 총괄 매니저로 승진할 기회가 있다.
- 해설 접속사 자리이므로 전치사 (C), (D)는 정답에서 제외한다. (A)는 접속사이지만 문장 맨 앞에는 잘 쓰이지 않는다. '~ 때문에'라는 의미인 (B)가 정답이다.
- 어휘 evaluation 평가 promote 승진시키다

13
- 해석 16세 이하의 아이들은 Benson 미술관을 방문할 때 부모 또는 보호자와 동행해야 한다.
- 해설 상관접속사 either A or B가 쓰인 문장이다.
- 어휘 accompany 동반하다, 동행하다 guardian 보호자

14
- 해석 Oliver Sports Injury Clinic은 지난 10년 동안 뛰어난 기술적, 전문적 성과들에 대해 상을 받았다.
- 해설 동사 자리이다. 주어가 단수이며 뒤에 목적어가 오므로 선택지 모두 수일치와 능동/수동태는 맞다. over the past ten years에서 현재완료 시제임을 알 수 있으므로 정답은 (D)이다.
- 어휘 award 상 outstanding 뛰어난, 두드러진 achievement 업적, 달성, 성취한 것

15
- 해석 Hess 사의 3분기 순이익은 2012년에 오천만 달러까지 급격히 증가했다.
- 해설 주어(net income)와 동사(increased) 사이에서 동사를 수식하는 부사 자리이다. 선택지에서 (C)만이 부사이다.
- 어휘 net income 순이익

16
- 해석 판매 목표를 달성하기 위해서 직원들은 스스로 효율적으로 일을 해야 한다.
- 해설 '혼자의 힘으로, 스스로'라는 뜻의 on one's own(=by ~ self)가 적절하다.
- 어휘 achieve 달성하다 effectively 효과적으로 on one's own 스스로

17
- 해석 회사는 올해의 최우선 사항으로 Community Health Projects에 자금 조달하는 것을 꼽았다.
- 해설 명사 어휘 문제이다. '최우선 사항'이라는 뜻이므로 (D)가 정답이다. (A) 변화 (B) 적응 (C) 조항, 준비
- 어휘 fundraising 기금 모금, 자금 조달

18
- 해석 기존 시설의 확장으로 인해 우리는 더 많은 제품을 만들 수 있었다.
- 해설 관사(the) 뒤에 명사 자리이다. 선택지에서 (C)만이 명사이다.
- 어휘 owing to ~ 때문에 existing 기존의, 현재 사용되는 facility 시설(기관) produce 생산하다

19
- 해석 안전상의 이유로 공장 직원들은 발가락 부분이 철로 만들어진 신발과 헬멧을 항상 착용해야 한다.
- 해설 '항상'이라는 뜻의 at all times(=all the time) 표현이 적절하므로 정답은 (B)이다.
- 어휘 steel-toed (발가락을 보호하기 위해) 철로 만들어진

20
- 해석 라스베이거스와 같이 급격히 성장한 도시에서 지난 5년간 사무실 공간을 경제적으로 사용하는 것이 증가해 왔다.
- 해설 use(명사)를 수식하는 형용사 자리이다. 선택지에서 (A)만이 형용사이다.
- 어휘 rapidly 빨리, 급속히, 신속하게, 순간적에 economical 경제적인

DAY 12
본문 p.240

1 (B)	2 (C)	3 (A)	4 (D)	5 (B)
6 (A)	7 (A)	8 (D)	9 (A)	10 (C)
11 (B)	12 (A)	13 (A)	14 (A)	15 (B)
16 (C)	17 (D)	18 (D)	19 (A)	20 (C)

1
- 해석 현지 공장은 모든 직원들을 위해 안전 규정을 최근에 발표했다.
- 해설 '안정 규정'이라는 뜻의 복합명사 safety regulations가 적절하다.
- 어휘 local 현지의 issue 발표하다/공표하다 regulation 규정

2
- 해석 환불 절차를 밟기 위해서 모든 정보와 영수증을 제출해야 한다.
- 해설 refund까지가 부사 역할을 해야 하는데 process가 동사로 쓰였으므로 to부정사의 부사적 용법으로 만들면 된다.
- 어휘 process 진행시키다 submit 제출하다 even as ~하는 바로 그 순간에

3
해석 Benson 사에서 우리는 직원들 사이의 건강과 행복을 증진시킬 책임이 있다고 믿는다.
해설 관사(a) 뒤의 명사 자리이다. (D)는 복수 명사이므로 부정관사(a) 뒤에 올 수 없다. 따라서 정답은 (A)이다.
어휘 promote 증진시키다

4
해석 Green Technology는 차세대 기술로의 성공적인 전환을 이루었다.
해설 명사 어휘 문제이다. 빈칸 뒤에 '차세대 기술'이 나오므로 '전환'이라는 뜻이 적절하다. 따라서 정답은 (D)이다. (A) 연기, 보류 (B) 협력 (C) 위치
어휘 process 공정

5
해석 부지배인은 직원 모임에서 개정된 종이 재활용 정책을 설명할 것이다.
해설 뒤의 명사(policy)를 수식하는 형용사 자리이다. policy와 revise의 관계는 수동이므로 과거분사 형태인 (B)가 정답이다.
어휘 assistant manager 대리, 부팀장, 부지배인 policy 정책

6
해석 대학교 모금 행사에 PedEx 사의 David Johnson 씨가 가장 후한 기부를 하였다.
해설 형용사(generous) 뒤의 명사 자리이다. (C)는 의미상 뒤에 나오는 was made와 어울릴 수 없으므로 (A)가 정답이다.
어휘 generous 후한, 너그러운 fundraising 모금, 자금 조달

7
해석 Wilson 씨는 그녀의 팀 구성원들에게 수요일 오후까지 업데이트 된 리포트를 읽을 것을 상기시켰다.
해설 전치사 어휘 문제이다. 리포트를 읽는 것은 특정 기한까지 완료되어야 하는 것이므로 '~까지'라는 뜻의 전치사 (A) by가 정답이다.
어휘 remind 상기시키다

8
해석 Larry Miller Automobiles는 판매를 증진시키기 위해서 강력한 광고 캠페인을 시작할 것이다.
해설 동사 자리 어휘 문제이다. 목적어로 campaign을 받을 수 있는 동사는 '시작하다'는 뜻의 (D) launch이다.
어휘 intense 극심한, 강렬한

9
해석 사업 분석가들이 최고 수준의 협상에 관한 최근의 뉴스들에 근거해서 Grand Tech와 Albertson Works 사의 합병을 조심스럽게 예상하고 있다.
해설 부사 자리 어휘 문제이다. predict(예상하다)를 수식하는 부사로 '조심스럽게 전망했다'는 뜻이 되어야 하므로 (A)가 정답이다. (B) 실수로 (C) 동등하게 (D) 단단히
어휘 predict 예측하다 merger 합병 negotiation 협상

10
해석 공사 현장의 진행 중인 문제로 인해 지역 회사는 새로운 안전 대책들을 도입했다.
해설 명사(problems)를 수식하는 형용사 자리 어휘 문제이다. '진행 중인 문제'라는 뜻이므로 (C)가 정답이다. (A) 통제된 (B) 용해된 (D) 배려심 있는
어휘 site 현장, 부지 measures 방안, 방법, 조치 ongoing 진행 중인

11
해석 지난주에 배달 된 상품은 카탈로그에 나온 제품의 색깔과 일치하지 않았다.
해설 ones는 앞의 명사(merchandise)를 받고 이 명사를 수식하는 분사 어휘 문제이다. 뒤에 in the catalog가 있으므로 pictured(사진이 실린)가 정답이다.
어휘 merchandise 상품 match 부합하다, 일치하다 exposed 노출된

12
해석 우리는 직원들 사이의 협력을 강화할 방법을 논의할 것이다.
해설 enhance가 타동사이므로 뒤에 목적어가 와야 한다. 선택지에서 목적어로 올 수 있는 것은 명사 (A)이다.
어휘 enhance 높이다, 향상시키다 cooperation 협력, 합동, 협동 cooperative 협력하는, 협동하는 cooperate 협력(합동)하다

13
해석 예산 리포트 제출 마감일이 빠르게 다가오고 있기 때문에 우리는 정시에 끝내기 위해 추가 시간을 일해야 한다.
해설 동사 어휘 문제이다. deadline(마감일)과 rapidly(빠르게)를 통해 '다가오다'라는 뜻의 (A)가 정답임을 알 수 있다.
어휘 now that ~이기 때문에 submit 제출하다 on time 시간대로

14
해석 회사 규정에 따르면 공장 안에서는 안전 고글과 헬멧을 항상 착용해야 한다.
해설 부사 어휘 문제이다. '항상 착용해야 한다'라는 뜻이므로 (A)가 정답이다. (B) 거의 (C) 면밀하게 (D) 강력하게
어휘 state 명시하다 factory floor 공장의 작업장

15
해석 이전 버전과 비교했을 때 새로운 소프트웨어는 속도와 품질을 더욱 강조했다.
해설 빈칸은 emphasis(명사)를 수식하는 형용사 자리이다. 형용사 (B), (D) 중에서 앞에 compared to가 나오므로 비교급 (B)가 의미상 자연스럽다.
어휘 previous 앞의, 이전의 place (중요성, 가치 등을) 두다 emphasis 강조, 역점, 주안점

16
해석 합의서가 유효하기 위해서 다음 정보는 완성되어야 한다.
해설 be동사 뒤의 보어 자리이다. 의미상 주어가 agreement이므로 보

어 자리에는 형용사가 오는 것이 적절하다. 따라서 정답은 (C)이다.
어휘 complete 완료하다, 마무리하다 validate 유효하게 하다 validity 유효함 valid 유효한

17
해석 고객 충성도를 높이기 위해 우리는 고객들의 증가하는 기대치를 충족시키거나 능가해야 한다.
해설 고객 충성도(customer loyalty)라는 복합명사가 적절하다.
어휘 meet 충족시키다, 부응하다 exceed 초과하다, 초월하다 expectation 예상, 기대

18
해석 회사는 초기 비용이 높기는 했지만 시작부터 많은 이윤을 낼 수 있었다.
해설 접속사 자리이다. (A)는 전치사, (B), (C)는 부사이므로 정답은 '~일지라도'라는 뜻의 (D)가 정답이다.
어휘 at the very beginning 애당초에, 처음에 start-up costs 초기 비용

19
해석 새로운 컴퓨터 장비는 이번 달 말에 설치될 예정이다.
해설 '장비는 설치될 예정이다'라는 뜻이므로 '설치하다'라는 뜻의 (A) set up이 적절하다. (B) 습관이 붙다 (C) 항복하다 (D) 내려놓다
어휘 equipment 장비, 용품 be supposed to ~하기로 되어 있다

20
해석 의료 장비는 다른 첨단 장비와는 달리 주의해서 다뤄야 한다.
해설 전치사 어휘 문제이다. '~와는 달리'라는 뜻의 (C)가 정답이다.
어휘 handle 다루다, 처리하다 high-tech equipment 첨단 장비

DAY 13 본문 p.242

1 (A)	2 (B)	3 (A)	4 (C)	5 (A)
6 (B)	7 (B)	8 (C)	9 (A)	10 (B)
11 (A)	12 (B)	13 (C)	14 (D)	15 (C)
16 (C)	17 (C)	18 (D)	19 (A)	20 (A)

1
해석 부동산 회사는 땅의 견적을 내기 위해서 다음 달에 올 것이다.
해설 [be ~ing]의 동사 형태는 진행형과 함께 가까운 미래 시제를 나타내기도 한다. 따라서 정답은 (A)이다.
어휘 real estate company 부동산 회사 estimate 판단, 평가 property 재산, 소유물

2
해석 최근에 고용된 요리사는 그의 혁신적인 요리법 때문에 많은 긍정적인 피드백을 받았다.

해설 명사(recipe) 앞의 소유격 자리이다. 따라서 정답은 (B)이다.
어휘 recently 최근에 innovative 혁신적인

3
해석 회사는 월요일 오후 3시에 모든 근무조들을 위해서 안전 절차와 장비 사용에 관한 필수 세미나들을 시행할 것이다.
해설 morning, afternoon, night 등의 앞에 요일이 오면 전치사는 on을 쓴다.
어휘 conduct 실시하다 mandatory 의무적인, 필수의, 필수적인 procedure 절차 shift 근무조

4
해석 2개의 스마트폰 모델이 다른 선택 사항들을 특징으로 하지만, 보기에는 거의 동일하다.
해설 identical을 수식하는 부사 자리이다. near도 부사로 '가까이에'라는 뜻이 있지만 의미상 어색하다. 따라서 '거의'라는 뜻의 nearly가 정답이다.
어휘 feature 특징으로 삼다, 특징을 이루다

5
해석 재생 가능 에너지에 관한 David 박사의 제안서에 대한 광범위한 검토를 수행한 후에 예산 위원회는 그의 프로젝트에 전면적인 자금 지원을 결정했다.
해설 명사(review)를 수식하는 형용사 자리이다. 따라서 정답은 (A)이다.
어휘 proposal 제안서 renewable 재생 가능한 funding 자금, 자금 제공(재정 지원) extensive 대대적인, 광범위한

6
해석 우리의 책자 형태의 카탈로그는 컴퓨터 산업에서 고객들이 구입할 수 있는 제품 목록들이 부분적으로만 담겨 있다.
해설 the 다음에 빈칸이 있으므로 명사 자리이다. 관계사절의 are available과 연결될 수 있는 명사는 products이다.
어휘 contain 포함하다 partial 부분적인

7
해석 회사의 매니저들은 마케팅 부서의 사람에 의해서 칭찬을 받았다.
해설 have been praised로 수동태 문장이고 by 뒤의 명사가 능동태 문장의 주어이므로 praise(칭찬하다)할 수 있는 주체는 사람이어야 한다.
어휘 praise 칭찬하다 perform 수행하다, 실시하다 performance 공연, 연주회

8
해석 뮤지컬 공연 동안 어떤 누구도 콘서트 장에 들어가는 것이 허락되지 않는다.
해설 전치사 어휘 문제이다. '뮤지컬 공연 동안에'라는 뜻이 적절하므로 정답은 (C)이다. (A) ~ 사이에 (B) ~에 관해서 (D) ~의 안으로
어휘 allow 허락하다, 용납하다

9
해석 매니저에 따르면 우리는 판매 이윤 건을 다루면서 시작할 것인데, 이윤

이 작년 이래로 20퍼센트 떨어졌다.

해설 빈칸은 형용사절 접속사 자리이다. 앞의 선행사(revenue)가 사물이고 빈칸 뒤에 형용사절에 주어가 없으므로 주격 관계대명사 which가 정답이다.

어휘 address 고심하다, 다루다 revenue 수익

10
해석 회사 규정은 각각의 부서가 스스로의 사무용품을 주문할 책임이 있다고 확실하게 명시한다.

해설 state(명시하다)를 수식하는 부사 어휘 문제이다. (A) 매우 (B) 확실히 (C) 느리게 (D) 다양하게

11
해석 200명 이상의 라디오와 텔레비전 아나운서들이 연간 회의에 참석하기 위해서 Benson 회의 센터에 모였다.

해설 center까지 문장 구조가 완전하므로 빈칸부터는 수식어이다. to부정사는 부사적 용법으로 쓰일 때 '~하기 위해서'라는 뜻이다.

어휘 gather 모이다, 모으다

12
해석 공식적인 연회가 소묘 대회 우승자를 축하하기 위해서 금요일 저녁에 열릴 것이다.

해설 be held(열리다) 할 수 있는 주체는 reception(연회) 뿐이다.

어휘 formal 정식, 공식의 honor 존중하다, 존경하다, 예우하다 drawing 소묘

13
해석 동봉된 책자는 Green Thumb Landscaping Service에 의해서 제공되는 서비스를 자세히 설명한다.

해설 빈칸은 brochure(명사)를 수식하는 형용사 자리이다. enclose와 brochure의 관계가 수동이므로 과거분사가 정답이다.

어휘 enclosure 동봉된 것 enclose 동봉하다 clearly 분명히, 명확하게

14
해석 시장 분석가들은 다가올 해의 스마트 폰의 판매의 증가를 예측했다.

해설 analyst(분석가)가 하는 일은 예측하는(predict) 일이다.

어휘 forthcoming year 다가오는 해 earn 돈을 벌다 inspect 점검하다, 검사하다

15
해석 Hendrickson 씨는 그가 중복되는 스케줄 때문에 회장의 저녁 파티에 초대장을 거절해야 하는 것을 유감스러워했다.

해설 scheduling conflict(일정이 중복되는 경우)라는 복합명사가 적절하다.

어휘 regret 후회하다, 유감스럽게 생각하다 decline 거절하다, 사양하다

16
해석 해외 여행자들은 해외에 나가기 전에 그들의 여권이 유효한지를 확인하도록 권고된다.

해설 advise는 목적격 보어 자리에 to부정사를 취하는 동사로 수동태 형태가 되면 〈be advised to부정사〉 형태를 가진다.

어휘 valid 유효한 abroad 해외로 register 기재하다, 신고하다 praise 칭찬하다

17
해석 Ace Trading 사는 모든 부서에 자금 지원의 공평한 분배를 위해서 재정 상담가인 John Anderson을 고용했다.

해설 관사(a)와 형용사(fair) 뒤의 명사 자리이다.

어휘 ensure ~하게 하다, 보장하다 fair 타당한, 공평한 funding 자금

18
해석 Northwest Air는 라스베이거스를 떠나는 모든 비행기들이 심각한 날씨 상황 때문에 연착될 것을 보고했다.

해설 weather conditions를 수식하는 형용사 자리이다. (A) 평가된 (B) 출발한 (C) 빈번한 (D) 심한, 혹독한

어휘 report 발표하다, 전하다

19
해석 매니저 자리에 지원한 300명의 지원자들 중에서, Graham 씨보다 인상적인 자격을 가진 사람은 거의 없다.

해설 주어 자리에 대명사가 들어가야 하므로 (C)는 오답이고, (B), (D)는 의미상 오답이다.

어휘 applicant 지원자 impressive 인상적인 qualifications 자격 요건

20
해석 U-Hall Transport는 운송 중에 발생할 수 있는 제품의 파손을 막기 위해서 각별한 주의를 기울이며 파손되기 쉬운 물건들을 다룬다.

해설 각별한 주의를 가지고 다루어야 하는 제품들은 fragile(파손되기 쉬운)한 제품들이다.

어휘 handle 다루다, 처리하다 extreme 극도의, 각별한 deliberate 의도적인 cautious 신중한 industrious 근면한, 부지런한

DAY 14

본문 p.244

1 (D)	2 (C)	3 (B)	4 (A)	5 (D)
6 (A)	7 (B)	8 (C)	9 (B)	10 (B)
11 (A)	12 (D)	13 (A)	14 (D)	15 (B)
16 (B)	17 (A)	18 (B)	19 (D)	20 (B)

1
해석 직원들은 그들의 비행기가 공항에 도착하자마자 육상 교통편을 마련하기 위해서 지역 사무실에 전화해야 한다.

해설 (A), (B), (C)는 의미적으로 어색할 뿐 아니라 자동사로 많이 쓰이는 동사들이다. 따라서 바로 목적어(ground transportation)가 나올 수 있는 타동사 (D) arrange가 정답이다.

어휘 local office 지역 사무실, 출장소 ground transportation 육상 교통 proceed 진행하다

2
해석 새로운 생산 시설을 위한 계획을 꼼꼼히 검토한 후에 안전 조사관들은 몇 가지 추천을 해 주었다.
해설 동명사 reviewing 수식할 부사 자리이다. (A) 신념을 가지고 (B) 심각하게 (C) 주의 깊게 (D) 극도로
어휘 manufacturing facility 생산 시설 inspector 조사관, 감독관 recommendation 권고, 추천

3
해석 재정 분석가들은 추가적인 연구가 완료될 때까지, 이용 가능한 자료들이 신중하게 해석되어야 한다고 강조했다.
해설 빈칸 앞 내용은 완벽한 문장 구조를 갖추고 있으므로 빈칸은 부사 자리이다.
어휘 financial analyst 금융 전문가, 분석가 emphasize 강조하다 interpret 해석하다 cautious 조심스러운, 신중한 cautiously 조심스럽게 caution 조심 cautionary 충고성의, 경고성의

4
해석 최근 구직 인터뷰 동안에 면접관들은 후보자들의 기술적인 경력 부족에 놀랐다.
해설 (B)는 few 뒤에 복수 명사가 와야 하므로 정답이 될 수 없다. 나머지 선택지들 중에서 의미적으로 '적절한 기술적 경험의 부족(the lack of experience)'의 의미를 만들 수 있는 (A)가 정답이다.
어휘 interviewer 면접관 candidate 지원자, 응시자 so few 너무 극소수의 hardly any 거의 ~ 없는 least 가장 적은, 최소의

5
해석 영화 〈Harpy's Journey〉가 긍정적인 평가를 받았기 때문에, HJ Studios는 속편을 만들 계획이다.
해설 접속사 자리이므로 (A)를 제외한 나머지 접속사 중에서 의미상 '긍정적인 평가를 받았기 때문에'라는 뜻이므로 (D)가 정답이다.
어휘 sequel 속편 owing to ~ 때문에

6
해석 회사는 수입은 증가했지만, 수익이 고위 관리들의 기대를 충족시키지는 못했다.
해설 meet one's expectations ~의 기대를 충족시키다
어휘 achieve 달성하다, 성취하다 earning 수입

7
해석 World Handy I-6 핸드폰은 그것의 많은 유용한 특징들 때문에 시장에서 가장 경쟁력 있는 모델들 중 하나이다.
해설 models(명사)를 수식하는 형용사 자리이므로 (B)가 정답이다.
어휘 competitor 경쟁자, 경쟁 상대 competitive 경쟁을 하는 competitively 경쟁적으로, 서로 앞다퉈 competition 경쟁

8
해석 퇴임하는 부회장 Peter Smith는 그의 가까운 동료들만을 위해 열린 개인 저녁 식사에서 그의 퇴임을 축하했다.
해설 for his closet colleagues를 수식하는 부사 자리이다. (A) 점진적으로 (B) 거의 (C) 오로지, 배타적으로 (D) 이전의
어휘 outgoing 물러나는, 나가는 celebrate 기념하다, 축하하다 retirement 은퇴, 퇴직 colleague 동료

9
해석 Brown 씨는 그가 새로운 고객들과 점심 모임을 가지는 동안 제안된 프로젝트를 설명했다.
해설 동사 자리이다. 앞에 동사(explained)의 시제가 과거 시제이므로 과거를 나타낸 (B)가 가장 적절하다.
어휘 explain 설명하다, 해명하다

10
해석 지난 10년 동안에, Detroit Motors는 자동차 산업 분야에서 최고의 고객 서비스를 제공하는 것으로 명성을 쌓아 왔다.
해설 관사 뒤 명사 자리이다. 고객에게 최고의 서비스를 제공하여 '명성(reputation)'을 쌓아 온 것이므로 정답은 (B)이다.
어휘 automotive 자동차의 destination 목적지, 도착지 reputation 평판, 명성 renewal 재개, 부활 transfer 이송, 이적

11
해석 운동화를 추천해 줄 수 있는 잘 알려진 운동선수를 고용함으로써, Trend Lead Group은 30%의 판매 성장을 예상하고 있다.
해설 전치사 어휘 문제이다. 의미상 수단을 나타내는 전치사 (A) by가 정답이 된다. (B) ~위로 (C) ~에 대해서 (D) ~로, ~에게
어휘 endorse 지지하다, 홍보하다

12
해석 Smith 씨는 KCU Finance가 그들의 경쟁 업체가 하기 전에 유럽 국가들로 사업을 확장하는 것을 고려하는 것이 유리할 것이라고 믿었다.
해설 be동사 뒤의 보어 자리이다. 앞의 주어 it은 가주어로 뒤의 to부정사가 진짜 주어가 되고 진주어는 명사 보어와 동격이 될 수 없으므로 형용사 (D)가 정답이다.
어휘 consider 고려하다 rival 경쟁자

13
해석 예상치 못한 상황 때문에 Provo Dance 사는 Varsity 극장에서의 오늘 공연을 취소해야만 했다.
해설 unforeseen circumstances는 '예상치 못한 상황'이라는 뜻이다. 따라서 정답은 (A)이다.
어휘 be forced to ~하도록 강요받다, 강요당하다 qualification 자격 classification 분류, 유형, 범주 instance 사례, 경우

14
해석 Manning 씨는 효율적이고 뛰어난 전문성을 가지고 그의 고객의 때늦은 요청들을 해결했다.
해설 빈칸은 전치사 뒤의 명사 자리인데 (A), (B), (D)가 모두 명사이다. (D)

가 '전문성'이라는 의미로 문맥에 가장 잘 어울린다.

15
- 해석 지난달에 승인된 새로운 안전 규정들은 모든 직원들이 건설 현장에서 안전 모자와 안전 장비들을 착용해야 한다고 지시한다.
- 해설 동사 자리 어휘 문제이다. (A) 모으다, 조립하다 (B) 지시하다 (C) 조사하다 (D) 조직하다

16
- 해석 대부분의 인사과 직원들이 4월 회의에 참여할 것이기 때문에 그들은 회사의 야유회가 5월로 연기되는 것을 선호한다.
- 해설 〈prefer that+주어+(should)+동사원형〉 구문이다. should가 생략되므로 빈칸은 동사원형이 나와야 하고 수동태 형태인 (B)가 정답이다.
- 어휘 human resources department 인사부 postpone 연기하다, 미루다

17
- 해석 고객 요청을 더 효율적으로 처리하기 위해 5명의 추가적인 고객 서비스 직원들이 지난달에 고용되었다.
- 해설 be handled(처리되다)를 수식하는 부사 자리이다. (A) 효율적으로 (B) 거의 (C) 대부분 (D) 특히
- 어휘 representative 대리인

18
- 해석 Morgan 사의 조사관들은 내년의 경제 동향을 예측하기 위해서 국제 자료들로부터 포괄적인 정보를 모은다.
- 해설 information을 수식하는 형용사 자리이다. 의미상 '포괄적인 정보'가 적절하므로 정답은 (B)이다. utmost는 '최고의'라는 뜻으로 대부분 앞에 정관사 the가 온다. (C) 최종적인 (D) 근면한
- 어휘 utmost 최고의, 극도의

19
- 해석 다르게 언급되지 않는 이상, 이 웹 사이트에 올려 진 내용들은 Breeden Pharmacy의 독점적인 자산이다.
- 해설 property(자산)을 수식하는 형용사 자리이다. (A) 제한적인 (B) 관찰력 있는, 준수하는 (C) 사려 깊은 (D) 독점적인
- 어휘 unless ~하지 않는 한, ~이 아닌 한

20
- 해석 이 기계는 직원들이 있는 동안 오전 8시부터 오후 5시까지 운영되게 프로그램 되어 있다.
- 해설 접속사 자리이므로 전치사 (A)를 제외하고 (B), (C), (D) 중에서 의미상 (B)가 가장 적절하다.
- 어휘 whereas (두 가지 사실을 비교, 대조할 때 씀) 다른 것들은 though (비록) ~이긴 하지만[인데도/일지라도]

DAY 15
본문 p.246

1 (D)	2 (B)	3 (B)	4 (C)	5 (B)
6 (A)	7 (A)	8 (C)	9 (B)	10 (C)
11 (D)	12 (D)	13 (A)	14 (A)	15 (C)
16 (D)	17 (A)	18 (C)	19 (D)	20 (D)

1
- 해석 John은 승진 후에 인사부를 책임질 것이다.
- 해설 빈칸 뒤에 동사가 있으므로 주어 자리이다. 따라서 주격의 (D) he가 정답이다.
- 어휘 be responsible for ~에 책임이 있는

2
- 해석 은퇴할 예정인 수석 요리사인 Anderson 씨는 음식 조리법에서 효율적이고 창조적인 것으로 명성이 높다.
- 해설 상관접속사 both A and B를 묻는 문제이다.
- 어휘 reputation 명성 recipe 조리법

3
- 해석 Baek Electroic의 최신 TV 모델은 이전의 모델들보다 선명한 영상을 만들어낸다.
- 해설 빈칸 앞에 주어가 있고 뒤에 목적어가 있으므로 빈칸은 동사 자리이다. 주어가 단수이므로 (B)가 정답이다.
- 어휘 latest 최근의, 최신의 display 영상, 디스플레이 previous 이전의

4
- 해석 추가 정보를 위해서 www.bestshopping.com으로 우리의 웹 사이트에 방문할 수 있다.
- 해설 정보를 얻으려는 목적 때문에 웹 사이트에 방문하는 것이므로 목적을 나타내는 전치사 for가 와야 한다.
- 어휘 further 추가의

5
- 해석 K-pop 대회를 위한 참가작들은 10월 20일까지 제출되어야 한다.
- 해설 주어 자리이다. 선택지에서 (B)만이 명사이다. entry는 '참가작'이라는 뜻이다.
- 어휘 competition 경쟁, 대회 submit 제출하다

6
- 해석 Dunning 은행의 고객들은 그들의 직장에서 언제든 계좌 정보에 쉽게 접근할 수 있다.
- 해설 조동사(can)와 동사원형(access) 사이의 부사 자리이다. 따라서 정답은 (A)이다.
- 어휘 workplace 직장 easily 쉽게

SECTION 2_실전 랜덤 연습 » 093

7

해석 Simpson Electronics의 대표 이사는 훌륭히 자신들의 일을 해온 판매 직원들을 축하했다.

해설 work(일, 업무)를 수식하는 형용사 어휘 문제이다. '훌륭한 일을 한 직원들을 칭찬했다'라는 뜻이므로 (A)가 정답이다. (B) 관심을 가진 (C) 감사하는 (D) 완전한

어휘 chief executive officer 대표 이사, 최고경영자 congratulate 축하하다

8

해석 안타깝게도 Han 씨는 무역 회의에 참석할 수 없지만 Johnson 씨가 그 회의에서 회사를 대표할 것이다.

해설 빈칸 앞까지 문장이 완벽하므로 빈칸은 부사 자리이다. 선택지에서 거기에'라는 뜻의 부사 (C)가 정답이다.

어휘 regrettably 안타깝게도 represent 대신(대표)하다

9

해석 Street 미술 전시회는 나쁜 날씨 때문에 연기될 것이다.

해설 빈칸 뒤에 명사가 나오므로 빈칸에는 전치사가 와야 한다. 접속사 (A)를 제외하고 '~ 때문에'라는 뜻의 (B)가 정답이다.

어휘 exhibition 전시회 even though 비록 ~일지라도 besides ~외에, 게다가

10

해석 인적자원부에서 Charlton 씨의 서류 처리가 지연되는 것은 그가 새로운 사업을 시작하는 것을 방해할 수 있다.

해설 prevent A from B: A가 B하는 것을 막다

어휘 deal with ~을 처리하다 prevent 막다 launch 시작하다 enhance 높이다, 향상시키다

11

해석 Joan 씨는 그 분야에서 훌륭한 20년간의 경력을 가진 후에도, 여전히 회계학 학생들을 가르칠 시간을 내고 있다.

해설 20년이 지난 후에도 시간을 내서 학생들을 가르치고 있는 의미에서 still(여전히)이 의미적으로 적절하다. (A)가 부사로 쓰일 때는 '한때'라는 뜻인데 과거 시제와 함께 쓰이고, yet은 부정문, 의문문에서 쓰인다.

어휘 mentor 가르치다, 조언해주다 outstanding 뛰어난, 훌륭한 career 경력 field 분야

12

해석 Choi 씨의 헬스클럽은 Neo Fitness Trend 세미나에 참석하는 모든 직원들에게 여행을 위해서 준비를 하라고 요청했다.

해설 타동사 make 뒤의 목적어(명사) 자리이다. 선택지에서 (D)만이 명사이다.

어휘 request 요청하다 arrangement 준비

13

해석 그 직책의 지원자들은 모두 매우 경험이 많은 사람이었지만 Ruben 씨의 인터뷰가 가장 인상적이었다.

해설 be동사(was) 뒤의 보어 자리이다. 따라서 '인상적인'이라는 뜻의 형용사 (A)가 정답이다.

어휘 applicant 지원자 experienced 경험을 갖춘

14

해석 자격증이나 허가증을 신청하기 전에 우리 웹 사이트를 방문하셔서 우리가 정한 요구 사항을 확인해 주세요.

해설 관사(a) 뒤의 명사 자리이다. 따라서 정답은 (A)이다. (B)도 명사지만 '허가해 주는 사람'이라는 뜻으로 의미상 어색하다.

어휘 prior to ~에 앞서 permit 허용하다 requirement 요구사항

15

해석 Lee 씨는 Blue Peel 상품의 품질 보증 과정을 주로 담당한다.

해설 in charge of를 수식하는 부사 어휘 문제이다. '주로 담당하다'라는 뜻이므로 (C)가 정답이다. (A) 천천히 (B) 거의 (D) 다양하게

어휘 in charge of ~을 맡아서 quality assurance 품질 보증 process 과정

16

해석 DMC 사의 모든 직원들은 그들이 일한 시간을 기록해야 한다.

해설 빈칸 앞에는 형용사절 접속사(관계대명사)의 목적격(which, that)이 생략되어 있다. 따라서 새로운 주어가 필요하므로 (D) they가 정답이다.

어휘 record 기록하다

17

해석 마감일이 임박했기 때문에 Harry 씨는 2분기 판매 리포트를 빨리 수정하라고 요청 받았다.

해설 빈칸 앞까지 문장이 완벽하므로 빈칸에는 수식어가 들어가야 함을 알 수 있다. edit를 수식할 수 있는 부사 (A)가 정답이다.

어휘 around the corner 임박한, 아주 가까운 edit 수정하다 quarter 4분의 1; (1년의) 분기

18

해석 KS Telecommunications의 모든 직원들은 육체적, 정신적 건강 유지에 관한 5월 18일 워크숍에 참석하는 것을 권고 받았다.

해설 뒤에 동명사가 왔으므로 전치사 자리이다. '~에 관해서'라는 뜻의 on(=regarding/concerning/as to/as for/about)이 정답이다.

어휘 maintain 유지하다 physical 육체의 mental 정신의

19

해석 Dong-Pyo Electronics의 마케팅 팀은 처음에는 신제품 홍보에 대해 문제들이 있었지만 지금은 모든 것이 해결 되었다.

해설 처음(initially)과 반대로 '지금은 모두 해결되었다'라는 뜻이다. now에서 현재 시제 또는 현재완료 시제임을 알 수 있고 뒤에 목적어가 없으므로 수동태형의 (D)가 정답이다.

어휘 initially 처음에 correct 바로잡다

20

해석 오늘밤 TIC 밴드의 콘서트에 참석할 계획이라면 좌석이 제한되어 있기 때문에 오늘 표를 구매하는 것이 좋을 것이다.

해설 보어 자리 형용사 어휘 문제이다. 의미상 '좌석이 제한되다'라는 뜻이므로 (D)가 정답이다. (A) 가이드가 안내하는 (B) 시기적절한 (C) 이른 빨리

어휘 seating 좌석

DAY 16

본문 p.248

1 (D)	2 (D)	3 (D)	4 (D)	5 (C)
6 (B)	7 (B)	8 (D)	9 (A)	10 (A)
11 (D)	12 (B)	13 (A)	14 (A)	15 (B)
16 (C)	17 (C)	18 (C)	19 (D)	20 (A)

1
- 해석 새로운 회사 정책은 회계 직원들에게 회사에서 일할지 아니면 집에서 일할지 선택하는 데 있어서 더 많은 선택권을 줄 것이라고 예상된다.
- 해설 whether(종속접속사)은 명사절로 문장을 묶을 수 있고 또 to부정사와 함께 쓰여 명사의 역할도 할 수 있다.
- 어휘 flexibility 융통성 accounting 회계

2
- 해석 당신의 서명은 만약 당신의 차가 고장 났을 때, BSW 자동차 회사 서비스 센터에 전화하는 것에 동의했다는 것을 의미한다.
- 해설 정비 센터에 전화하는 경우는 자동차가 고장 났을 때다. 따라서 '고장 나다'라는 뜻의 (D)가 정답이다.
- 어휘 signature 서명 imply 나타내다 hang up 끊다 turn down 거절하다

3
- 해석 참석한 모든 구성원들은 연구 발표 후 바로 질문할 수 있는 기회를 얻을 것이다.
- 해설 부사 shortly, immediately, right 등은 after 또는 before 앞에 쓰여서 '바로'라는 의미를 갖는다. 따라서 정답은 (D)이다.
- 어휘 immediately 즉시

4
- 해석 Simpson 씨는 뉴욕에 있는 그녀의 인테리어 디자인 작업실에서 고객들에게 새롭고 현대적인 실내 장식 방식에 대해서 조언을 합니다.
- 해설 여기서 at은 '~에서'라는 작은 장소를 뜻하는 전치사이므로 장소 명사인 studio(스튜디오, 작업실)가 정답이다.
- 어휘 modern 현대의 decor (실내) 장식

5
- 해석 지역 위원회는 Dennis Avenue에 예정된 쓰레기 매립지에 대해 걱정하는 모든 지역 주민들을 공청회에 초대할 계획이다.
- 해설 '~을 걱정하다'는 be concerned about을 쓴다. 따라서 정답은 (C)이다.
- 어휘 resident 거주자, 주민 landfill 쓰레기 매립지 public hearing 공청회

6
- 해석 책 곳곳에 있는 많은 그림들이 독자들이 본문을 이해하는 데 도움을 준다.
- 해설 전치사 어휘 문제이다. throughout은 '(시간적) ~동안 내내' '(공간적) ~의 구석구석에, 전역에'라는 뜻이다. 따라서 정답은 (B)이다.
- 어휘 aid 돕다 text 본문

7
- 해석 ABC Supplies의 마케팅 직원 자리를 위한 이상적인 지원자는 창의적이어야 하고 사회성 있는 성격이어야 한다.
- 해설 빈칸 앞에 관사와 함께 형용사(sociable)가 왔으므로 형용사의 수식을 받는 명사 자리이다. 따라서 정답은 (B)이다.
- 어휘 ideal 이상적인 representative 직원, 대리인 sociable 사교적인

8
- 해석 Smart Box 사의 직원들은 스마트폰의 새로운 포장 아이디어를 발전시켰다.
- 해설 어휘 문제이다. packaging idea를 목적어로 하며 '아이디어를 발전시켰다'라는 뜻이므로 (D)가 정답이다.
- 어휘 packaging 포장

9
- 해석 조사팀의 직원들은 BOB Cosmetics의 생산 비용을 줄일 수 있는 몇몇의 매우 효과적인 방법을 제안했다.
- 해설 매우(highly)와 방법(measures) 사이에서 부사의 수식을 받는 형용사 자리이다. 의미상 '매우 효과적인 방법'이 적절하므로 (A)가 정답이다.
- 어휘 suggest 제안하다 highly 매우 measures 방법 production costs 생산 비용

10
- 해석 워싱턴 DC의 지하철 통근자들을 위한 여름 일정표가 6월 13일에 공표될 것이다.
- 해설 동사 자리는 수 일치-능동/수동-시제 순으로 살펴봐야 한다. 주어가 복수(schedules)이므로 (D)는 오답이며 빈칸 뒤에 목적어가 없으므로 능동태 (B), (C)도 오답이다. 따라서 정답은 (A)이다.
- 어휘 commuting 통근

11
- 해석 Anderson 씨는 Max Finance의 성공을 위한 그녀의 한결같이 놀라운 헌신으로 인해 최근 지역 매니저로 승진했다.
- 해설 remarkable을 수식하는 부사 어휘 문제이다. (A) 정확하게 (B) 함께 (C) 거의 ~ 없다 (D) 한결같이
- 어휘 remarkable 놀랄만한 contribution 기여

12
- 해석 새로운 축구 경기장의 디자인이 매력적이기는 하지만 위치는 교외 지역에 사는 사람들에게 접근성이 좋지 않다.
- 해설 be동사 뒤 보어 자리에 형용사. attractive(매력적인)과 attracted(매료되는) 중에서 주어(design)와의 관계를 볼 때 (B) attractive가 적절하다.
- 어휘 accessible 접근 가능한

13
- 해석 Bear Technologies는 모든 생산 기계에서 작업장 안전성을 최고로 높은 수준으로 유지한다.
- 해설 명사 어휘 문제이다. high와 함께 많이 쓰이고 maintain이란 동사와도 많이 쓰이는 standard(기준, 표준, 수준)가 정답이다.
- 어휘 workplace 직장 manufacturing 생산, 제조

14
해석 Perris Inc.는 Zebra Auto가 자회사의 SUV의 매력을 확대하기 위한 급박한 요구에 대해 논의하기 위해 특별 주주 총회를 가질 것이다.
해설 소유격(auto's)과 needs(명사) 사이에는 형용사가 와야 한다.
어휘 discuss ~를 논하다 urgent 긴급한 appeal 매력

15
해석 조사팀 직원들은 판매 부서 동료들로부터 그들의 프레젠테이션이 받은 좋은 반응을 전혀 예상하지 못했다.
해설 진행형에서 be동사와 –ing 사이에 빈칸이 있으면 부사가 정답이다. 따라서 정답은 (B)이다.
어휘 response 반응 division 부서 fully 완전히, 충분히

16
해석 시 도서관이 운영 시간을 연장할 것이기 때문에 시민들은 시설에 출입을 더 많이 할 것이다.
해설 hours(운영 시간)를 extend(연장하다)해야 시민들이 도서관을 더 많이 이용할 수 있다. 따라서 정답은 (C)이다.
어휘 access 입장

17
해석 도시 지도자들은 비록 하수 시설을 설치하는 것의 비용이 상대적으로 비싼 것 같지만, 이 설치가 지역 사회에 도움이 될 것에 동의했다.
해설 even though로 연결된 두 개의 절은 의미적으로 상반된 내용이 나와야 한다. 즉 설치비용이 많더라도 지역 사회에 이익이 된다는 (beneficial) 내용이 나와야 하므로 정답은 (C)이다.
어휘 installation 설치 conclusive 결정적인 drainage 배수 relatively 비교적

18
해석 Hello Food의 커피 용기들은 제품을 신선하게 유지하는 목적만큼 외관을 좋게 만들기 위해서 알루미늄 포장지에 분리되어 포장된다.
해설 'A 하는 것만큼 B 하다'라는 뜻의 [as much A as B] 구문이다.
어휘 separately 따로따로 foil 알루미늄 포장지 appearance 모습, 외관

19
해석 Sun Publication 사는 9월 6일에 현지의 서점들에게 13만권의 책을 배달했는데 이것은 계약서 상의 의무를 두 달 먼저 달성한 것이다.
해설 13만권의 책을 배달하는 것이 계약서상에 나와 있던 의무(계약조건)이었다.
어휘 fulfilling 성취감을 주는 contractual 계약상의 surplus 과잉 indication 말 forecast 예측 obligation 의무

20
해석 Mango Travel은 최고의 비행 편과 숙박 시설을 제공할 뿐만 아니라 사고 없는 여행을 제공하기 위해서 꼼꼼하게 일정들을 계획한다.
해설 plan(계획하다)를 수식하는 부사 자리 어휘 문제이다. 최고의 서비스와 말썽 없는 여행을 위해서는 세심하게(meticulously) 계획을 짜야 하므로 정답은 (A)이다.

어휘 ensure 반드시 ~하게 하다 accommodation 숙박시설 meticulously 꼼꼼하게, 세심한 considerably 많이, 상당히 enormously 엄청나게, 대단히 compatibly 적합하게

DAY 17
본문 p.250

1 (C)	2 (B)	3 (C)	4 (C)	5 (B)
6 (B)	7 (B)	8 (B)	9 (A)	10 (D)
11 (C)	12 (D)	13 (A)	14 (D)	15 (D)
16 (B)	17 (D)	18 (C)	19 (B)	20 (C)

1
해석 새롭게 개발된 자료 시스템은 MEGA 사의 디지털 문서에서의 오류를 상당히 줄였다.
해설 문장에 동사가 없으므로 빈칸은 동사 자리이다. (B), (C) 중에서 (B)는 수 일치에서 맞지 않으므로 정답은 (C)이다.
어휘 developed 개발된 reduce 줄이다, 줄어들다

2
해석 Simpson 씨는 안전 규정이 잘 지켜지고 있는지 점검하기 위해서 디트로이트에 있는 공장을 정기적으로 방문한다.
해설 locate는 타동사로 '~를 위치시키다'라는 의미가 있어서 뒤에 목적어를 가질 수 있다. locate는 목적어를 주어 위치로 이동해서 수동태로 만들 수 있다. 빈칸부터 basis까지 the plan를 수식하는 관계사절인데, 관계사와 be동사가 생략된 분사구 형태로 the plant를 꾸며주고 있다.
어휘 on a regular basis 정기적으로 safety rule 안전 규정 observe 준수하다 locate 위치시키다

3
해석 AZ Supermarket은 Seeley 아파트 복합 단지 근처 건물 안에 4번째로 문을 여는 상점이 될 것이다.
해설 뒤에 장소 명사가 왔으므로 '~ 근처'라는 뜻의 near가 적절하다. between이나 among은 뒤에 복수 명사가 와야 하므로 (A), (B)는 오답이다.
어휘 complex 복합 단지

4
해석 우리는 현재 12시간 근무조로 기꺼이 일할 수 있는 사람을 찾고 있다.
해설 근무조(shift)는 night shift, day shift, weekend shift 등으로 쓰일 수 있다.
어휘 willingly 자진해서 shift 교대 근무

5
해석 Manchester에 본거지를 둔 Bobby's Hamburger는 현지의 음식 제공 업체들과 좋은 관계를 맺어 왔다.
해설 relationship을 목적어로 받기 적절한 동사는 develop이다.
(A) ~을 야기하다 (C) ~을 실행하다 (D) ~을 예약하다.
어휘 relationship 관계 supplier 공급업자

6
해석 몇몇 고객들은 SAC Electronics의 카탈로그 제품 설명에 대한 충분한 세부 사항이 없다고 불평했다.
해설 '제품 설명서'를 뜻하는 복합명사 product descriptions이 적절하다.
어휘 complain 불평하다 description 설명

7
해석 이번 주의 Good Morning Today 신문의 기사 중 하나가 재택 근무하는 직원들의 수가 대략 10년 전 이래로 급속하게 증가하고 있다고 보도했다.
해설 rise, decrease, increase 등과 함께 많이 쓰는 부사로 rapidly, sharply, dramatically 등이 있다. 따라서 정답은 (B)이다.
어휘 efficiently 능률적으로 dramatically 극적으로 openly 터놓고 hastily 급히

8
해석 수리가 필요한 제품 오작동이 있다면 유지보수 팀으로 직접 요청서를 제출해 주세요.
해설 malfunction(오작동)이 있는 제품은 '수리(repairing)'가 필요하다. 따라서 정답은 (B)이다.
어휘 equipment malfunction 기기 오작동

9
해석 고객 서비스 센터에 제안된 대부분의 변화들이 이미 시행되었다.
해설 부사 자리이다. (C)는 '곧'이라는 의미로 시제에서 적절하지 않다. (D) by far는 대부분 최상급을 수식하는 부사로 많이 쓴다. (A) already는 완료시제와 쓰일 수 있는 부사이다.
어휘 implement 시행하다 a great deal 다량으로 by far 훨씬

10
해석 고객들은 서핑보드를 가지고 Family 호텔 앞의 해안을 거닐든지 고급 요트를 타고 안내원과 함께 여행을 즐길 수 있다.
해설 빈칸 뒤의 주어가 앞 문장의 주어와 같아서 생략된 것을 보고 등위접속사 자리임을 알 수 있다. (B), (D) 중에서 의미상 (D)가 정답이다.
어휘 explore 답사(탐험)하다 surfboard 서핑보드 guided tour 안내원이 딸린 관광 yacht 요트

11
해석 최근에 설치된 초고속 열차 시스템 덕분에 먼 도시까지 출장을 쉽게 관리할 수 있다.
해설 be동사(is) 뒤의 보어 자리이다. 앞의 부사 easily의 수식을 받는 형용사 (C)가 정답이다.
어휘 distant 먼 manageable 관리할 수 있는

12
해석 Paul 박사는 너무 많은 의학 직원들이 실험실로 샘플들을 가져와 달라고 요청하기 때문에 항상 자신이 직접 그들과 만날 수는 없다.
해설 전치사 뒤의 목적격 자리이다. 따라서 목적격인 (D)가 정답이다. 여기서 them은 representatives를 받는다. 빈칸 뒤의 himself는 강조의 재귀대명사이다.
어휘 representative 대표(자), 직원 laboratory 실험실

13
해석 GAD 사의 새로운 수력 펌프 시스템은 고객 요구에 맞춰서 임대와 구매가 모두 가능할 것이다.
해설 복합명사 문제이다. '고객의 요구(demand)에 맞춰서'라는 뜻이므로 (A)가 적절하다.
어휘 lease 임대차 계약 payment 지급금 convention 회의

14
해석 판매의 꾸준한 성장세가 소매 판매의 어려운 시즌을 예상했던 산업 분석가들을 놀라게 했다.
해설 형용사 어휘 문제이다. 뒤에 나오는 slow와 대비되는 형용사가 들어가야 사람들을 놀라게 할 수 있다. 따라서 '꾸준한'이라는 뜻의 (D)가 정답이다. (A) 짧은 (B) 형편없는 (C) 사실상의
어휘 astonish 놀라게 하다 retail 소매 virtual 사실상의 steady 꾸준한

15
해석 남성복 가게의 수석 매니저로서 Watson 씨는 모든 할인 판매 행사에 대해 책임을 맡을 것이다.
해설 동사 자리이다. (C), (D) 중에서 주어가 단수이므로 (C)는 수 일치에서 오답이다. 따라서 정답은 (D)이다.
어휘 responsibility 책임 assume 맡다

16
해석 저녁 시간 동안에 더 많은 매출을 창출하기 위해서 VRP 식당은 Swan 백화점 건너편의 Ruby Street로 이전할 것이다.
해설 '건너편'이라는 뜻의 전치사 (B)가 정답이다.
어휘 generate 발생시키다

17
해석 Eastern Zoo를 둘러쌀 울타리가 재활용 재료들을 이용해서 설치될 것이다.
해설 빈칸은 형용사절의 동사 자리인데 아직 fence가 설치되지 않았으므로 앞으로 둘러쌀 것이라는 미래 시제가 되어야 한다. 따라서 정답은 (D)이다.
어휘 fence 울타리 enclose 둘러싸다 recycled 재활용된

18
해석 Town 은행의 고객들은 고객 서비스 부서에 최근에 설치된 새로운 컴퓨터 시스템에 거의 영향을 받지 않았다.
해설 〈be+p.p.(수동태)〉 사이에 빈칸이 있으면 부사가 정답이다. 따라서 정답은 (C)이다.
어휘 unaffected 영향을 받지 않은 largely 주로

19
해석 David Institute 위원회의 구성원들은 추가적인 강의들을 위한 제안된 예산 변경에 대해 한 시간 동안 심사숙고했다.
해설 동사 어휘 문제이다. deliberate는 형용사와 동사가 같은 형태로 형용사로 '심사숙고하는', 동사로는 '심사숙고하다'라는 뜻이다.
어휘 committee 위원회 lecture 강의 mediate 중재하다 regard

~으로 여기다 suppose 생각하다

20

해석 환경 부처는 국가의 이익을 위해서 그린벨트 지역에 제한적인 접근을 허락했다.

해설 빈칸은 동사(allow)와 목적어(access) 사이이므로 목적어인 명사를 수식하는 형용사 자리이다. 따라서 분사 형태의 형용사 (C)가 정답이다.

어휘 access 접근 for the sake of ~을 위해서 restricted 제한된

DAY 18

본문 p.252

1 (B)	2 (D)	3 (A)	4 (B)	5 (C)
6 (B)	7 (C)	8 (B)	9 (C)	10 (D)
11 (C)	12 (A)	13 (A)	14 (B)	15 (C)
16 (A)	17 (B)	18 (D)	19 (D)	20 (B)

1

해석 2개의 주요 안경알 제조회사의 합병으로 국가의 가장 큰 맞춤 안경 생산업체가 탄생될 것이다.

해설 형용사(largest) 뒤에 명사 자리이다. 따라서 정답은 (B)이다. (A), (C)도 명사로 쓸 수 있지만 의미상 어색하다.

어휘 merger 합병 customizable 맞춤형의

2

해석 Dennis 씨는 오늘 오후 기자 회견에서 Son Tech는 그 회사를 인수했다고 공식적으로 발표했다.

해설 news conference(기자 회견)에서 발표한 내용은 공식적(formally)으로 한 것이다.

어휘 customarily 일상적으로 externally 외부적으로 observantly 주의 깊게 formally 공식적으로

3

해석 Nelson 씨는 수년간 잡지 글은 써 왔지만, 잡지 편집자로서는 짧은 시간 동안 일해 왔다.

해설 접속사 자리이므로 전치사 (B)를 제외한다. 빈칸 앞뒤가 서로 반대의 이야기이므로 양보의 접속사 even though(= although, even if, though)가 정답이다.

어휘 essay (짧은) 글 even though 비록 ~일지라도 despite ~에도 불구하고

4

해석 장래의 학생들은 정직원과 파트 타임 직원 프로그램이 둘 다 많은 혜택이 있기 때문에 하나를 다른 하나와 신중하게 비교해야 한다.

해설 2개의 선택 사항 중에서 one(하나)를 제외한 다른 하나는 the other로 쓴다. 따라서 정답은 (B)이다.

어휘 prospective 장래의 weigh 따져보다

5

해석 Allen 씨는 원래 초안보다 상당히 더 경쟁력이 있는 노래의 개정된 형태를 발견하게 되어 기뻤다.

해설 빈칸은 뒤의 형용사 competitive를 수식하므로 부사가 와야 한다. 선택지에서 (C)만이 부사이다.

어휘 revised 수정된 competitive 경쟁력 있는 draft 초안

6

해석 Simon 씨는 기자 회견에서 MIS Company가 정유 공장을 확장하는 계획을 진행할 것이라고 발표했다.

해설 빈칸 앞에 동사 move가 나왔으므로 '앞으로 발전시켜 나아가다'라는 뜻의 move forward가 적절하다. 따라서 정답은 (B)이다.

어휘 enlarge 확대하다 refinery 정유 공장 altogether 완전히, 모두

7

해석 몇몇 Olive Photography 고객들은 새로 나온 Jenssen 카메라가 사용하기 편리하지 않기 때문에 사기를 꺼린다고 말했다.

해설 '~하기를 꺼리다, 주저하다'라는 뜻의 be reluctant to가 적절하다. (A) 의혹을 갖는 (B) 불확실한 (D) 걱정하는

어휘 consider ~라고 여기다 user-friendly 사용하기 편리한

8

해석 한국에 있는 Merci 호텔은 관광 명소와의 근접성 때문에 항상 만원이다.

해설 '~로의 근접성'이라는 뜻의 proximity to가 적절하다. 따라서 정답은 (B)이다.

어휘 owing to ~때문에 attraction 명소 exclusion 제외 proximity 가까움, 근접성

9

해석 연예 기획사 관계자 Long 씨는 그가 대표하는 예술가들을 위한 능숙한 협상으로 유명하다.

해설 명사 어휘 문제이다. 의미상 '능숙한 협상'이라는 뜻이므로 (C)가 정답이다. (A) 협력 (B) 행동 (D) 말

어휘 skillful 숙련된

10

해석 Sera는 해외 여행을 위해 보고서를 제외하고 모든 비용 보고서를 승인하는 것을 책임진다.

해설 전치사 자리이다. (B) 접속사 (C) 부사를 제외하고 의미상 '해외 여행 보고서를 제외하고'가 적절하므로 (D)가 정답이다.

어휘 be responsible for ~에 책임이 있다 approve 찬성하다 additionally 게다가

11

해석 판매 매니저 직책은 장애물 앞에서의 근성과 예상치 못한 직무들이나 어려움을 맡을 수 있는 의지를 요구한다.

해설 명사 어휘 문제이다. 의미상 '장애물 앞에서의 근성'이 적절하므로 (C)가 정답이다. (A) 참석 (B) 풍부 (D) 빈번함

어휘 in the face of ~에 직면하여 obstacle 장애물 willingness (~하려는) 의지

12
- 해석 Tony 금융사는 고객 포트폴리오의 가치를 극대화하기 위해서 변동에 대해 안정적인 장기 투자를 추천한다.
- 해설 빈칸은 be동사 뒤의 보어(형용사, 명사) 자리이다. 주어와 동격이 아니므로 형용사 자리이다. '안정적인'이라는 뜻의 (A) secure가 정답이다.
- 어휘 fluctuation 변동 portfolio 보유 중인 각종 금융 자산 secure 안전한

13
- 해석 조사 결과는 시 위원회가 지역 사업가들이 개정된 토지 이용 규제법에 대해서 가지고 있는 문제들을 적절하게 해결하지 못했다고 전했다.
- 해설 address(해결하다, 시행하다)를 수식하는 부사 자리 어휘 문제이다. (B) 불쾌하게 (C) 대략적으로 (D) 상호적으로
- 어휘 resident 주민 regarding ~에 관하여 zoning law 토지 이용 규제법 adequately 충분히

14
- 해석 런던의 창고를 확장하는 것은 저장 용량의 30 퍼센트의 증가를 가져올 것이다.
- 해설 result in 뒤에 나오는 전치사 목적어이면서 30 percent의 수식을 받는 명사 자리이다. increase는 동사/명사 모두 가능하므로 명사형인 (B)가 정답이다.
- 어휘 expand 확장하다 storehouse 창고 capacity 용량

15
- 해석 Ohio Industries의 회장은 최근 수익의 감소가 회사의 주식 가격에 부정적으로 영향을 미치지 않을 것으로 확신했다.
- 해설 조동사(will)와 동사원형(affect) 사이의 부사 자리이다. 선택지에서 (C)만이 부사이다.
- 어휘 profit 이익, 수익 adversely 반대로, 불리하게

16
- 해석 지난 6년 동안 Harry Wilson 재단은 Bradford에 있는 Dawson 의약 연구 협회에 상당한 기부를 해왔다.
- 해설 donations(기부)를 수식하는 형용사 자리이다. 의미상 '상당한 기부'가 적절하므로 (A)가 정답이다. (B) 만족해하는 (C) 발생시키는 (D) 획득한
- 어휘 donation 기부

17
- 해석 Park 박사가 그의 연구에 바친 추가적인 시간에도 불구하고, 그는 마감일 전에 그의 연구를 끝낼 수 없었다.
- 해설 Dr. Park contributed to his project는 형용사절로 앞의 명사 hours를 수식하고 있다. 따라서 빈칸은 접속사가 아닌 전치사가 들어가야 된다. (A), (B) 중에서 의미상 '~에도 불구하고'라는 뜻의 (B)가 정답이다.
- 어휘 contribute to ~에 기여하다. in spite of ~에도 불구하고 as if 마치 ~인 듯이 even though 비록 ~일지라도

18
- 해석 많은 단골 고객들이 있었기에 Blue Gift Shop은 지금까지 이 지역에서 새로 들어온 가게들의 엄청난 경쟁을 버텨왔다.
- 해설 동사 자리이다. 뒤에 목적어가 있으므로 능동의 (D)가 정답이다.
- 어휘 fierce 험악한, 격렬한 withstand 견뎌내다

19
- 해석 King 박사는 그녀의 발표 동안 어떻게 과학자들과 농부들이 지역 보전 노력의 성공에 필수적일 수 있는지를 설명했다.
- 해설 '성공을 위해 필수적인'이라는 의미가 적절하므로 (D)가 정답이다. (A) 근면한 (B) 준비된 (C) 전시된
- 어휘 diligent 근면한 integral 필수적인

20
- 해석 구성원들이 다가오는 일련의 회의를 준비하는 것을 돕기 위해서 안건은 첫 회의 전에 구성원들 각자에게 분배되었다.
- 해설 전치사 어휘 문제이다. 준비를 하려면 회의 전에 안건이 전달되어야 한다. 따라서 (B) prior to(=before)가 정답이다.
- 어휘 agenda 안건, 주제 distribute 분배하다 in favor of ~에 찬성하여 prior to ~에 앞서 owing to ~때문에 in case of ~의 경우

DAY 19
본문 p.254

1 (D)	2 (D)	3 (C)	4 (A)	5 (C)
6 (D)	7 (A)	8 (B)	9 (B)	10 (A)
11 (B)	12 (B)	13 (C)	14 (A)	15 (B)
16 (C)	17 (C)	18 (C)	19 (B)	20 (C)

1
- 해석 서울 박람회의 가장 유명한 행사는 요리 경연 대회이다.
- 해설 '요리 대회'라는 뜻의 복합명사 cooking competition이 적절하다. 따라서 정답은 (D)이다.
- 어휘 competitive 경쟁력 있는

2
- 해석 이 제품의 구매자들은 포장 안의 내용물을 서늘하고 건조한 곳에 보관해 주세요.
- 해설 advise는 목적격 보어 자리에 to부정사를 취하고, 수동태가 되면 〈be+advised+to부정사〉 형태가 된다. 따라서 정답은 (D)이다.
- 어휘 contents 내용물 store 저장하다

3
- 해석 국방부는 서해에 새로운 군함의 진수를 발표했다.
- 해설 '진수를 발표했다'라는 뜻이므로 (C)가 적절하다. inform도 '알리다'라는 뜻이 있지만 뒤에 [inform A that절]의 형태로 쓰기 때문에 적절하지 않다.
- 어휘 Ministry of Defense 국방부 warship 군함

4
해석 Lee 씨가 보고서를 끝낸 후에 그것은 Newton 씨에게 제출될 것이다.
해설 빈칸은 주어 자리이고 앞의 report를 받아야 하므로 대명사 (A) it이 정답이다.
어휘 submit 제출하다

5
해석 우리의 감독관인 Rogers 씨는 도쿄에 있는 잠재 고객의 사무실을 방문해달라는 요청을 받았다.
해설 invited(요청 받다)를 수식할 부사 자리이다. '최근에 요청을 받았다'는 뜻이므로 (C)가 정답이다. (A) 면밀하게 (B) 완전하게 (D) 매우
어휘 prospective 장래의

6
해석 ACE Shipping 사에서의 임금 인상은 고과 평가를 기준으로 한다.
해설 뒤에 회사명이 나오므로 '~에서'라는 뜻의 전치사 (D) at이 적절하다. (A) ~로서 (B) ~에(방향전치사) (C) ~위에
어휘 based on ~에 기초를 두다, ~에 근거하여

7
해석 정보 기술부는 모든 직원들이 정기적으로 그들의 컴퓨터 정보들을 백업해 놓아야 한다고 권고했다.
해설 basis(명사)를 수식하는 형용사 자리이다. '정기적으로'라는 뜻의 on a regular basis(= regularly) 표현이 적절하다.
어휘 back up (파일을) 백업하다

8
해석 Mason은 최근 패션 동향에 대한 업무로 인해 폭넓게 여행을 했다.
해설 [made(동사)+his(목적어)+travel(목적격 보어)까지 문장의 의미가 끝났고 빈칸은 travel(동사)을 수식하는 부사 자리이다. 따라서 동사를 수식하는 부사 (B)가 정답이다.
어휘 extensively 광범위하게

9
해석 Miller 씨는 연방 수사국에 개인적인 정보를 제출할지 말지를 결정해야 한다.
해설 or not과 함께 명사절을 이끌 수 있는 whether가 적절하다. 따라서 정답은 (B)이다.
어휘 private 사적인 Federal Bureau of Investigation (미국의) 연방 수사국

10
해석 염두에 둘 것은 모든 여행 경비는 Moore 씨나 회계 부서에 있는 그녀의 동료 중 한 명에게 검토를 받아야 한다.
해설 colleagues를 수식하는 소유격 자리이다. 앞의 명사 Ms. Megan을 받는 her가 적절하다. 따라서 정답은 (A)이다.
어휘 reminder 상기시키는 것 colleague 동료

11
해석 Bella's Sweet은 고객들의 요구에 따라 이제 몇몇 맛있는 새로운 사탕 맛들을 제공한다.
해설 in(전치사) 뒤의 명사 자리이다. '~에 응답하여'라는 뜻의 in response to가 정답이다.
어휘 demand 요구, 수요

12
해석 모든 음식 제품들은 유통 승인이 되기 전에 위생 감독관에게 조사를 받아야 한다.
해설 be동사 뒤에 나올 수 있는 동사 형태 중에서 빈칸 뒤에 목적어가 없으므로 수동태의 be p.p.가 정답으로 와야 한다. 따라서 정답은 (B)이다.
어휘 hygienic 위생적인 distribution 분배, 분포 inspect 점검하다

13
해석 Baek 씨가 10년 동안 Nice Insurance에서 있었기 때문에 그는 지금 우리의 가장 숙련된 직원들 중 한 명이다.
해설 10년을 근무했다고 했으므로 '숙련된 직원'이라는 뜻이 적절하다. '숙련된'이라는 뜻의 experienced, informed, skilled, seasoned 등이 적절하다.
어휘 serve 일하다, 봉사하다 previous 이전의 included 포함된

14
해석 Sanders 씨는 만약 컴퓨터 소프트웨어가 정시에 도착한다면 이번 수요일까지 그녀의 일을 성공적으로 끝낼 수 있다.
해설 접속사 자리이다. (D)는 상관접속사인데 문장에 and가 없으므로 제외하고 (A), (B) 중에서 의미상 (A)가 정답임을 알 수 있다.
어휘 successfully 성공적으로 even ~조차, 훨씬

15
해석 예상치 못한 수리 작업 때문에 정전 공지문이 회사 빌딩 전역에 오늘 아침 일찍 부착되었다.
해설 절이 하나(동사가 하나)이므로 접속사 (C), (D)를 제외하고 빈칸 뒤의 명사가 단수 명사(morning)이므로 this가 정답이다.
어휘 electricity 전력 cutoff 차단, 정지 throughout 도처에

16
해석 Ipswich Town으로부터 도착할 때, 공학 기술자들은 실험실 접근이 허락될 것이다.
해설 빈칸 뒤에 지역명이 나왔으므로 어떤 지역으로부터 왔다는 의미로 from을 쓸 수 있다. 따라서 정답은 (C)이다.
어휘 technician 기술자 laboratory 실험실

17
해석 부잔교가 건설 중인 동안에 여행자들은 Lucky Ferry에 탈 때 주의를 기울이는 것이 요구됩니다.
해설 use(타동사) 뒤에 목적어(caution)를 써서 '주의를 기울이다'라는 뜻이 된다. 따라서 정답은 (C)이다.
어휘 landing (상륙용) 부잔교 under construction 공사 중인 caution 경고, 주의

18

해석 근무 시간 기록표를 아직 제출하지 않은 근로자들은 오늘 저녁 7시 30분까지 제출해야 합니다.

해설 부정문에서 '아직'이라는 뜻의 yet이 적절하다. yet은 보통 부정문이나 의문문에 쓰이는 부사로 부정어 뒤에 쓰인다. 반면에 부정어 앞에 빈칸이 있다면 still을 쓴다.

어휘 hand in 제출하다 rather 꽤, 약간, 상당히

19

해석 모든 직원들은 공장에 들어오기 전에 보호 의복과 안경을 착용해야 한다.

해설 전치사 다음의 빈칸이므로 동명사 어휘 문제이다. '공장에 들어오다'라는 뜻이 적절하므로 (B)가 정답이다. step은 자동사이기 때문에 step into 형태로 써야 한다.

어휘 be required to ~하도록 요구되다 protective 보호의

20

해석 Murrell Labs는 파손된 기계들이 이미 모두 수리되었기 때문에 곧 다시 문을 열 것이다.

해설 부사 어휘 문제이다. '문을 곧 다시 열 것이다'라는 뜻이므로 shortly가 적절하다. (A) 처음에 (B) 공평하게 (D) 거의

어휘 be expected to ~할 것으로 예상되다 machinery 기계(류)

DAY 20

본문 p.256

1 (B)	2 (A)	3 (B)	4 (B)	5 (D)
6 (A)	7 (B)	8 (C)	9 (D)	10 (C)
11 (B)	12 (D)	13 (C)	14 (C)	15 (B)
16 (D)	17 (D)	18 (D)	19 (D)	20 (B)

1

해석 Timon Corporation은 생산 라인을 확장하려는 진행 중인 노력의 일환으로 새로운 사업 기회를 찾는 데 관심이 있다.

해설 명사 어휘 문제이다. 빈칸 뒤에 to가 to부정사의 형용사적 용법으로 쓰였고 effort(명사)가 형용사적 용법을 뒤에 많이 취하는 명사이다. (A) 성장 (C) 증가 (D) 강점

어휘 be interested in ~에 관심이 있다 explore 발굴하다 ongoing 계속 진행 중인 enlarge 확대하다, 확대되다

2

해석 Adams 씨는 그녀가 베를린 대학에서 공부하는 동안 2년 전에 그녀의 회사를 시작했다.

해설 동사 자리 문제이다. 목적어가 있으므로 (D)(수동태)는 오답이 되고, ago 때문에 과거 시제를 써야 한다.

어휘 firm 회사 while ~동안

3

해석 연장 협상 후에, Emson 병원의 회장과 Jason Medical Center의 회장은 새로운 의학 치료에 대해서 동의에 이르렀다.

해설 전치사 문제이다. 동의에 이르는 것은 협상 후에 일어날 수 있는 일이다.

어휘 extended 연장된 counterpart 상대, 대응관계 treatment 치료

4

해석 자전거는 직장까지 통근하는 많은 사람들이 선호하는 교통수단이다.

해설 형용사 자리이다. 동사가 형용사가 된 분사 (B), (D) 중에서 means와 prefer의 관계는 수동이므로 과거분사를 쓴다.

어휘 commute 통근하다 workplace 직장 prefer ~을 좋아하다

5

해석 KS Corporation은 현재 건설 중인 사업장에 더욱 편리한 장소에 새로운 생산 공장들을 열 것이다.

해설 전치사(in) 뒤에 명사 자리이다. that절은 형용사절인데 동사(are)를 보고 선행사(빈칸)가 복수 명사가 되어야 한다는 것을 알 수 있다.

어휘 manufacturing plant 제조 공장 operation 기업, 회사, 사업장 currently 현재

6

해석 당신이 정시에 주문한 제품에 대해서 가격을 지불하면, 우리는 예정대로 당신의 소포를 배송해 줄 수 있다.

해설 빈칸은 2개의 절(동사 2개)을 연결하는 접속사 자리이다. 선택지 중에서 (A)만이 접속사이다.

어휘 on time 정각에, 시간을 어기지 않고 as long as ~하는 한 prior to ~에 앞서 despite ~에도 불구하고 in order to ~하기 위하여

7

해석 내년에 유기농 과일에 대한 더 높은 수요를 예상하고 지역 농부들은 20 퍼센트까지 그들의 수확량이 오르기를 원한다.

해설 농산물의 수확량을 높이는 것은 그만큼의 수요(demand)가 있기 때문이다.

어휘 organic 유기농의 yield 산출량, 수확량 efficiency 효율성 influx 밀어닥침, 밀려듦

8

해석 매달 열리는 자선 행사에 초대장이 모든 40명의 위원회 구성원들에게 보내졌지만, 참석할 수 있는 사람은 거의 없다.

해설 주어 자리 대명사 문제. 접속사인 whoever나 so는 오답 취급한다. 대명사 (A), (D) 중에서 앞에 members라는 복수형 가산 명사를 받을 수 있는 것은 few이다.

어휘 charity 자선 whoever 누구든 few 거의 ~하지 않은

9

해석 Main Corporation의 연간 보고서는 중국에 대한 그들의 수출량이 작년과 비교해서 3.5퍼센트까지 올랐다고 보고했다.

해설 작년 preceding year / 내년 following year

어휘 volume 양, 용량 precede ~에 앞서다, 선행하다

10

해석 Ahn 씨는 학생에 대한 모든 교사들의 자세에 주목하기 위해서 NPPL

Education의 Singapore 지점 이사로 승진되었다.

해설 문장 2개를 연결하는 접속사 자리이다. 상관접속사인 (A), 전치사인 (B)를 제외하고 (C), (D) 접속사 중에서 의미적으로 자연스러운 것은 (C)이다.

어휘 be promoted to ~로 승격되다 focus on ~에 초점을 맞추다 attitude 태도, 자세 nor ~도 아니다

11
해설 인천 국제공항을 드나드는 비행기들은 활주로의 혼잡 때문에 자주 지연된다.

해설 전치사(because of) 뒤의 명사 자리이다.

어휘 frequently 자주, 흔히 postpone 연기하다 runway 활주로 congestion 혼잡

12
해설 이전 회사 연회에서 31명의 작업자들이 회사를 위해 30년 동안 일해 온 것에 대해서 특별한 상으로 표창해 주었다.

해설 recognize는 '1. 인정하다 2. 알아보다 외에도 3. (~의 공로를) 표창하다'라는 뜻도 있다.

어휘 banquet 연회 advocate 옹호하다, 지지하다 assume 추정하다 administer 관리하다

13
해설 그의 프랑스 출장 동안에 Dickens 씨는 거기에서 몇몇 섬유 공급업체들을 잠깐 방문했다.

해설 주어(Mr. Dickens)와 동사(visited) 사이에는 부사 자리이다. 선택지에서 (C)만이 부사이다.

어휘 fabric 직물 supplier 공급자 brief 간단한, 짧은 briefly 간단히

14
해설 혹시나 캐비닛을 설치하는 데 추가적인 시간이 필요하다면 DBC Renovation은 원래 견적서 이상을 청구할 것이다.

해설 가정법 미래에서 If가 생략되면 should가 주어와 도치 된다.

어휘 estimate 추산, 견적서 be required to ~하도록 요구되다 in fact 사실은 through ~을 통해

15
해설 새로운 DX 지역 지점에서 오늘 계좌를 연 새로운 고객들은 2달 동안 서비스 요금을 납부하는 것에서 면제된다.

해설 from과 함께 써서 '면제 받는다'는 뜻의 be exempt from이 적절하다. 따라서 정답은 (B)이다.

어휘 account 계좌 charge 요금 complimentary 무료의 exempt 면제되는 privileged 특권을 가진 offer 제공하다

16
해설 Space 안전 과정에 참가자들 각자는 물에 뜨는 부양 장비를 착용할 것이다.

해설 수동태 표현 중에서 by 이외에 다른 전치사와 함께 쓰는 표현들도 있는데 그 중 하나가 be outfitted with (~을 착용하다)이다.

어휘 flotation (물 위에) 뜸 device 장치, 장비 accustomed 익숙한 donate 기증하다 distribute 분배하다

17
해설 Rexter의 DS340 절단 기계는 그 회사의 산업 제품들 전체를 대표한다.

해설 be동사 뒤에 형용사(representative) 뒤에 전치사(of)를 쓴 [be+형용사+전치사] 구문이다.

어휘 industrial 산업의 represent 대표(대신)하다

18
해설 새로운 작업자들은 다음 주 훈련 과정에 참석하기 전에 작업장 안전 지침을 익혀야 한다.

해설 빈칸 뒤에 재귀대명사(themselves)를 쓴 이유는 주어와 목적어가 같아서 이다. 또 (A), (B)는 '새로운 작업자들이 그들 자신과 친숙하다'라는 뜻이 되므로 어색하다. familiarize A with B: A를 B와 익숙하게 만들다.

어휘 guideline 설명 지침

19
해설 이 이 메일은 현재 절차가 낭비가 심한 이유와 제안된 대체 전략이 어떻게 회사 자원을 절약할 수 있을지를 설명하고 있다.

해설 대체 전략들이 필요하다는 것이 현재 과정에 나쁜 점이 있다는 것이다. 따라서 (D) 낭비가 심하다는 단점을 쓰는 것이 적절하다.

어휘 procedures 절차 alternative 대안의 conserve 아끼다, 보호하다 vacant 비어있는 scattered 드문드문 있는, 산발적인 deserted 사람이 없는, 버려진

20
해설 11월 소식지가 출판될 즈음에는 보수 공사 계약서에 서명할지 말지에 관한 마지막 결정이 이루어질 것이다.

해설 두 개의 절이 이어져 있으므로 빈칸은 접속사가 들어가야 한다. (B), (D) 중 '~할 때 즈음'이라는 의미의 (B)가 자연스럽다.

어휘 whether ~인지 아닌지 maintenance 유지 in order for ~ 하기 위해서 by the time ~할 무렵에는

3. 어휘 집중 연습

DAY 01
본문 p.260

1 (B)	2 (A)	3 (D)	4 (D)	5 (C)
6 (B)	7 (B)	8 (C)	9 (D)	10 (A)
11 (D)	12 (A)	13 (C)	14 (B)	15 (A)

1
- 해석 ATP 식료품 가게는 고객을 위한 다양한 제품으로 매우 유명하다.
- 해설 a (wide) variety of는 '다양한'의 의미가 있으며, 여기서 variety는 selection, array, range 등으로 바꿔 쓸 수 있다.
- 어휘 grocery store 식료품 가게 customer 손님, 고객 plenty 풍부한 양, 많음

2
- 해석 다른 사람들을 방해하지 않기 위해서 극장에 있는 동안에는 전화기의 사용을 자제하세요.
- 해설 refrain은 자동사로 목적어를 취하기 위해서 전치사 from을 쓴다.
- 어휘 refrain 삼가다 disturb 방해하다

3
- 해석 영수증을 가지고 오지 않는다면 당신은 환불을 받을 자격이 없습니다.
- 해설 be eligible for 명사 / be eligible to 동사원형: ~할 자격이 있다
- 어휘 refund 환불 receipt 영수증 dependable 믿을 수 있는 entitle (권리)를 주다

4
- 해석 다행히 Jason Manufacturing은 증가하는 수요를 맞추기 위해서 추가적인 직원들을 고용할 것이 예상된다.
- 해설 증가하는 수요에 맞춰 충원이 예상되므로 '다행히'라는 의미의 부사가 적절하다.
- 어휘 hire 고용하다 additional 추가적인 meet 충족시키다 demand 수요

5
- 해석 Los Angeles로의 비행은 항공 교통 관제나 기후 문제가 없는 한 대략 한 시간 걸린다.
- 해설 부사 자리에 적합한 어휘를 찾는 문제이다. approximately(대략)은 수량 형용사를 수식할 수 있다.
- 어휘 flight 비행 unless ~하지 않는 한 air traffic control 항공 교통 관제 neatly 깔끔하게

6
- 해석 몇몇 사업 분석가들은 세계 경제에 미치는 기름 값 증가의 영향에 대해 이야기했다.
- 해설 (A) 수단, 방법 (B) 효과, 영향 (C) 제안 (D) 추천
- 어휘 industry 산업 analyst 분석가 global economy 세계 경제

7
- 해석 큰 기업은 보수적인 방법을 계속 사용해 왔기 때문에 진보적으로 여겨지지 않는다.
- 해설 5형식 동사의 수동태 형태에서 목적격 보어 자리의 어휘 문제이다. conservative와 반대되는 progressive가 정답이다.
- 어휘 corporation 기업, 회사 conservative 보수적인 profound 심오한 proficient 능숙한 prohibitive 금지하는

8
- 해석 농산물의 신선도를 유지하기 위해서, 모든 제품은 즉시 배달되어야 한다.
- 해설 (A) 최근에 (B) 이전에 (C) 즉시 (D) 대략
- 어휘 freshness 신선함, 생생함 produce 생산물, 농작물 deliver 배달하다 previously 이전에 approximately 대충, 대략

9
- 해석 회사 규정에 따르면, 모든 법적 서류를 승인할 권한은 부서장에게만 주어질 것이다.
- 해설 (A) 등록 (B) 입학 (C) 자격증 (D) 권한
- 어휘 policy 정책, 방침 approve 찬성하다, 승인하다 head (단체, 조직의) 책임자 enrollment 등록 certificate 자격증 authority 권위

10
- 해석 3개월간의 보수 공사 기간 후에, TERA Fitness는 고객을 위해 그들의 원래 일정을 재개했다.
- 해설 (A) 재개하다 (B) 회복하다 (C) 응답하다 (D) 답변하다
- 어휘 renovation 보수 공사 resume 재개하다, 다시 시작하다

11
- 해석 우리 가게의 정책은 모든 주문이 영업일 기준 3일 이내에 고객에게 안전하게 배달되는 것이다.
- 해설 시간 전치사 중에서 '~ 이내로'라는 의미의 within이 정답이다.
- 어휘 working day 영업일

12
- 해석 사무 보조 정직원 자리에 응시한 이력서에는 발생한 순서대로 경력이 기록되어 있어야 합니다.
- 해설 (A) 연대순의 (B) 규칙적인 (C) 최근의 (D) 동시의
- 어휘 applicant 지원자, 신청자 résumé 이력서 assistant 조수, 보조원

13
- 해석 주문한 물품이 특별히 크지 않다면, 저희는 하나의 박스에 넣어 배달할 것입니다.
- 해설 (A) 각각 (B) 효과적으로 (C) 특히 (D) 무작위로
- 어휘 unless 만일 ~이 아니라면

14
- 해석 안전 요원을 고용할 때, 인사과는 후보자들에 대한 모든 유효한 정보를

고려할 것이다.

해설 take into consideration: ~을 고려하다

어휘 security personnel 안전 요원 personnel 인사과 valid 유효한, 타당한 perspective 관점, 시각 speculation 추측, 짐작

15

해설 증가하는 대중의 압박이 결국 회장을 강제로 자리에서 사임하게 만들었다.

해설 (A) (우려스러울 정도로) 증가하는 (B) 올라가는 (C) 곧게 하는 (D) 위협하는

어휘 pressure 압박, 압력 eventually 결국, 끝내 resign 사임하다 mount 증가하다, 올라가다 straighten 똑바르게 하다, 바로 하다 intimidate 겁을 주다, 위협하다

DAY 02
본문 p.262

1 (B)	2 (C)	3 (B)	4 (B)	5 (A)
6 (C)	7 (C)	8 (A)	9 (B)	10 (C)
11 (C)	12 (D)	13 (C)	14 (D)	15 (C)

1

해석 백만 달러 이상의 가치가 있는 TV 곧 나라 전역에 방영될 것이다.

해설 worth를 단지 '가치'라는 뜻으로 외우기보다는 a dollar's worth of change '1달러 가치의 잔돈'식의 구문을 암기하자. ten pounds' worth of books: 10파운드어치의 책

어휘 commercial 광고 air 방송하다 expense (어떤 일에 드는) 돈, 비용 estimation 판단, 평가치

2

해석 Texon Play는 몇몇 나라들에서 첫 2일 동안 새로운 게임의 가격을 인하하기로 결정했다.

해설 해석보다 문법을 알아야 풀 수 있는 문제이다. 빈칸 뒤의 명사는 복수 명사인데 much는 불가산 명사가 와야 하므로 오답이다.

어휘 reduce 줄이다 affluent 부유한 affordable 가격이 적당한

3

해석 당신은 보안상의 이유로 이 시스템에 50메가바이트 이상의 파일들을 첨부할 수 없다.

해설 (A) 할당하다 (B) 첨부하다 (C) 교대하다 (D) 허락하다

어휘 security 보안

4

해석 대형 병원 중 하나에서 경력을 쌓고 싶은 의대 졸업생들은 15년 만에 가장 어려운 직업난에 직면했다.

해설 〈look to+동사원형〉은 '~를 기대하다'는 의미가 있다. (C) considering은 뒤에 오는 목적어 자리에 동명사를 취하지 to부정사를 취하지 않는다.

어휘 graduate 대학 졸업자 pursue 추구하다, (일을) 해나가다 face 직면하다 decline 거절하다 access 접근하다

5

해석 제안서에 만들어진 막판의 몇몇 변경들에도 불구하고 Bostic 사의 대표인 John Malcolm은 그것을 수락하기로 결정했다.

해설 막판에 변화를 줄 수 있는 대상은 제안서(proposal)이다.

어휘 despite ~에도 불구하고 last-minute 막판의 accept 받아들이다 intent 의도 expression 표현 recommendation 추천

6

해석 우리의 새로운 제품들은 전국 300개 이상의 가게에서 합리적인 가격에 구매 가능합니다.

해설 (A) 접근이 가능한 (B) 사려 깊은 (C) 이용 가능한 (D) 믿을 만한

어휘 line (상품의) 종류 reasonable 합리적인

7

해석 기획 부서의 이사인 Durek 씨는 목표 중에 몇 개는 회사의 경제 상황을 고려해서 변경되어야 한다고 제안했다.

해설 (A) 원인 (B) 증거 (C) 목표 (D) 대답

어휘 planning department 기획 부서 in light of ~에 비추어, ~를 고려하여

8

해석 정부 요원은 한 달 후에 이 문제가 얼마나 심각해질 수 있는지 충분히 인식하지 못했다.

해설 understand와 함께 쓰일 수 있는 부사를 고르는 문제로 fully understand(충분히 이해하다)로 활용될 수 있다.

어휘 serious 심각한 current 현재의 approximately 대략 frequently 자주, 흔히 annually 매년, 일 년에 한 번

9

해석 불경기에 맞춰 직원들의 수를 줄였기 때문에, 우리는 더 이상 고객들에게 높은 품질의 상담 서비스를 제공할 수 없다.

해설 해석 이외에도 빈칸 뒤에 간접 목적어(clients)와 직접 목적어(service)가 있는 것을 보고 offer(4형식 동사)가 정답이 될 수 있음을 알아야 한다. 비슷한 뜻의 provide는 〈provide A with B〉의 형태를 가진다.

어휘 downsize 줄이다, 축소하다 personnel (조직의) 인원 no longer 더 이상 ~ 아니다 suggest 제안하다 maintain 유지하다

10

해석 Mica는 지난 분기 프로젝트 기간에 그녀가 보여준 엄청난 헌신 때문에 올해의 직원으로 의심의 여지없이 선택될 것이다.

해설 because of 뒤의 내용에서 확실한 이유를 제시했으므로 앞의 내용은 '의심할 여지 없는'이라는 내용이 오는 것이 자연스럽다. 따라서 undoubtedly가 정답이다.

어휘 contribution 헌신, 기여, 공로 demonstrate 입증하다, (행동으로) 보여주다 slightly 약간, 조금 infirmly 약해져서, 의지가 박약하여

11
- 해석: 당신이 직접 모든 매니저들에게 정책 변경에 대한 이 메모의 사본을 보내야 한다.
- 해설: this memo(이 메모)를 받을 수 있는 명사는 copy(사본)이다.
- 어휘: policy 정책 manager 관리자 dot 점 sign 서명

12
- 해석: 연간 기획 회의에서 내년을 위해 경영진이 세운 최종 판매 수치는 과대평가되었다.
- 해설: overestimate는 '능력, 가능성, 수치, 가치 등을 과대평가하다'라는 의미가 있다.
- 어휘: figure 숫자, 수치 annual 매년의, 연간의 overflow 넘치다 exceed 초과하다 overcome 극복하다

13
- 해석: Wallen 씨는 건설 기간 동안 작업장 근로자들의 조회를 책임지게 될 것입니다.
- 해설: on-site workers 사이에 필요한 것은 coordination(조화, 합동)이다.
- 어휘: hold sb responsible for sth ~에게 ~에 대한 책임을 지우다 on-site 현장의 construction 건설, 공사 promotion 홍보, 승진 distribution 분배 activation 작동, 활성화

14
- 해석: 문제에 대해서 불평을 할 때, 오해가 생기지 않도록 최대한 구체적으로 해야 한다.
- 해설: 최대한 구체적으로 해야 오해가 생기지 않는다. 따라서 정답은 specific이다.
- 어휘: complain 불평하다, 항의하다 make sure 확실하게 하다 in order to ~위하여 misunderstanding 오해, 착오 outstanding 뛰어난 specific 구체적인

15
- 해석: Nagle Research가 여론 조사를 실시하였고, 대략 60퍼센트의 응답자가 회장이 물러나기를 원하는 것으로 나타났다.
- 해설: 여론 조사(poll)의 결과를 표현할 수 있는 동사는 indicate(~로 나타나다, 보여주다)이다.
- 어휘: conduct (특정한 활동을) 하다 respondent 응답자 step down 물러나다, 사직하다 predict 예상하다 indicate 나타내다 assume 추정하다

DAY 03
본문 p.264

1 (A)	2 (C)	3 (B)	4 (A)	5 (B)
6 (D)	7 (A)	8 (B)	9 (C)	10 (D)
11 (C)	12 (D)	13 (A)	14 (B)	15 (C)

1
- 해석: 주요 관광 명소 주변의 소규모 지역 사업장들은 성수기 동안에 추가로 임시직 직원들을 쓰려고 한다.
- 해설: 〈intend+to부정사〉는 '~를 하려고 의도하다'라는 뜻을 가진다. suggest는 목적어 자리에 to부정사가 아닌 동명사를 취해야 하므로 오답이다.
- 어휘: tourist attraction 관광 명소 temporary 임시의 peak season 성수기 intend 의도하다, 생각하다 alleviate 완화하다

2
- 해석: 러시아에서 독일로 회사 본사를 이전하자는 제안은 이사진의 최종 허가에 달려 있다.
- 해설: be contingent on ~: ~에 달려 있다
- 어휘: relocation 재배치 headquarters 본사 authorization 허가 board 이사회 ultimate 궁극적인, 최후의 thoughtful 배려심 있는, 생각에 잠긴 voluntary 자발적인

3
- 해석: 재정 계획과 분석에 대한 마지막 훈련 기간 후에, 모든 훈련생은 가벼운 식사에 초대되었다.
- 해설: refreshments는 '다과'라는 뜻 외에도 '가벼운 식사, 음료'라는 뜻도 가지고 있다.
- 어휘: session (특정 활동을 위한) 시간 analysis 분석 admission 가입, 입장, 입학 expansion 확대, 확장

4
- 해석: H&P Computers는 고객이 온라인 가게에서 구매한 컴퓨터와 다른 부대용품을 수령한 후에 고객에게 비용을 청구할 것이다.
- 해설: (A) 비용을 청구하다 (B) 예상하다 (C) 평가하다 (D) ~을 쓰다
- 어휘: accessory 부대용품 purchase 구매하다

5
- 해석: 우리 웹 사이트에서 내려 받은 할인 쿠폰으로 당신은 한 달에 적게는 40달러로 서비스 계획을 갱신할 수 있다.
- 해설: 빈칸 뒤에 $40이라는 돈이 나오므로 돈을 받을 수 있는 수량 형용사는 much 혹은 little이다.
- 어휘: discount 할인 renew 재개하다, 갱신[연장]하다 petty 사소한, 하찮은

6
- 해석: Josh는 판매 예상 보고서를 끝내기 위해서 연간 판매 기록에 대한 접근 권한을 요청했다.
- 해설: approach는 가산 명사로 빈칸 앞에 관사가 없으므로 오답. 보고서를 끝내기 위해서는 자료의 접근 권한(access)을 요구할 것이다.
- 어휘: projection 예상, 추정 enrollment 등록 approach 접근법, 처리 방법

7
- 해석: 회장은 일본으로부터 온 중요한 고객과의 급한 회의 때문에 이후의 일정을 모두 취소해야 했다.

해설 (A) 다음의, 이후의 (B) 지속 가능한 (C) 성공적인 (D) 미루는

어휘 cancel 취소하다 urgent 긴급한, 시급한 client 고객

8
해석 증가하는 수요에 탄력을 받아, 말레이시아의 코코아 사업은 지난 10년 동안에 급속하게 성장했다.

해설 grow, increase, decrease와 많이 쓰는 부사로 rapidly, sharply, tremendously 등이 있다.

어휘 fuel 부채질하다, 연료를 공급하다 relatively 상대적으로 rapidly 급속하게 roughly 대략, 거의

9
해석 그 전문가들은 모든 판매 자료를 종합한 후에 우리에게 최신 음식 시장 동향에 대한 철저한 분석을 제공했다.

해설 전문가(expert)가 데이터를 종합해서 제공할 수 있는 것은 철저한 분석(through analysis)이다.

어휘 the latest 최신의 foundation 토대, 기초 affirmation 확언, 확인 deployment 전개, 배치

10
해석 모든 건설 인부들은 그들에게 적절하게 맞는 안전 장비들을 착용하는 것이 요구된다.

해설 fit은 '(사람에게 옷이나 장비가) 맞다'라는 의미가 있다.

어휘 protective gear 보호 장비 resemble 닮다, 비슷하다 hold 들다, 갖고 있다 place 놓다, 배치하다

11
해석 새롭게 선출된 대통령은 현재의 경제적 문제를 해결하겠다는 그의 흔들리지 않는 약속을 한 번 더 확인했다.

해설 (A) 관련 없는 (B) 무관심한 (C) 변함없는, 확고한 (D) 부적절한

어휘 elect 선출하다 confirm 확인하다 resolve 해결하다

12
해석 당신의 아파트를 비우기 전에 적어도 30일 전에 미리 관리실에 서면으로 통지를 해 주어야 한다.

해설 서면으로(written) 줄 수 있는 것은 통지(notification)이므로 정답은 (D)이다.

어휘 vacate 비우다, 떠나다 in advance 미리 distribution 분배, 분포 addition 추가된 것, 부가물 completion 완료, 완성

13
해석 연간 재정 회의의 주제는 운영 분석과 미팅 참석자들, 세부적인 회의 일정을 포함한다.

해설 (A) 포함하다 (B) 동봉하다 (C) (돈, 노력을) ~에게 바치다 (D) 등록하다

어휘 agenda 의제, 안건 operation 작업, 운용, 사업 attendee 참석자

14
해석 회사는 증가하는 사업장 사고들을 다루기 위해서 안전 통제 회사에 외주를 맡기기로 결정했다.

해설 해석과 더불어 빈칸 뒤에 목적어가 아닌 with가 있으므로 deal with(~을 다루다)가 정답이다.

어휘 outsource 외부에 위탁하다 safety control 안전 제어 workplace 직장, 업무현장 effect (결과를) 가지고 오다 affect ~에 영향을 미치다 support 지원하다

15
해석 호텔 숙박과 임대 자동차는 운영 위원회에 의해서 자금이 충당될 것입니다만, 추가적인 숙박은 참석자들의 책임입니다.

해설 (A) 응답 (B) 협상 (C) 책임 (D) 협동

어휘 accommodation 숙박 cover 다루다, 포함시키다 participant 참가자

DAY 04
본문 p.266

1 (C)	2 (A)	3 (C)	4 (A)	5 (A)
6 (B)	7 (B)	8 (B)	9 (A)	10 (C)
11 (C)	12 (A)	13 (D)	14 (B)	15 (B)

1
해석 요구되지는 않지만, 네트워크 솔루션에 대한 약간의 경험은 유리하게 적용될 수 있다.

해설 요구 사항(requirement)처럼 필수적인 것은 아니지만 가지고 있으면 도움이 되는 것을 advantage(유리한 점, 이점, 장점)라고 한다.

어휘 adoption 채택, 입양 alleviation 경감, 완화 accumulation 축적, 누적

2
해석 음악계의 거장 G의 특별한 콘서트 표가 우리의 온라인 VOD 스트리밍 서비스를 이용하시는 분들에게 제공될 것이고, 당첨자들은 이번 달 말에 무작위로 선정될 것이다.

해설 (A) 무작위로 (B) 모호하게 (C) 불명확하게 (D) 조심성 없이

어휘 streaming service 스트리밍 서비스

3
해석 무역 센터는 현재 공사 중이고, 대략 2달 후에 완성될 것으로 예상된다.

해설 해석 외에도 is(현재 시제)가 나온 것을 통해서 presently(현재에)를 선택할 수 있다.

어휘 under construction 공사 중 deliberately 고의로, 의도적으로 exclusively 배타적으로, 독점적으로 reluctantly 마지못해

4
해석 지원자들은 온라인 신청서에 있는 박스에 표시함으로써 그들의 직업 선호도를 표시할 수 있다.

해설 (A) 표시하다 (B) 개발하다 (C) 발생시키다 (D) 할당하다

어휘 preference 선호, 선호도 application form 지원서

106

5
- 해석 서류들은 가능한 실수들을 피하기 위해서 정부 조사관에 의해서 꼼꼼하게 검토되어야 한다.
- 해설 close(가까운, 가까이에는 형용사와 부사가 다 되는 단어인데 여기에 -ly를 또 붙여 closely가 되면 '면밀하게, 자세하게'의 의미를 갖는다. highly(매우)도 마찬가지로 high(높은, 높게)는 형용사와 부사가 되는 단어이다.
- 어휘 inspector 조사관, 감독관 avoid 피하다 narrowly 가까스로, 간신히 generally 일반적으로

6
- 해석 SHS Electronics는 GM Tech과의 합병 이후에 반도체 산업의 강력한 경쟁자로 부상했다.
- 해설 (A) 붕괴되다 (B) 부상하다 (C) 혁신을 일으키다 (D) 번역하다
- 어휘 competitor 경쟁자 semiconductor 반도체 merger 합병 emerge 나오다, 모습을 드러내다

7
- 해석 당신은 시설에 들어오기 전에 입구에서 주차 허가증을 받아야 한다.
- 해설 permit은 동사와 명사(허가증)가 모두 가능한 단어이다. parking permit: 주차 허가증
- 어휘 facility 시설 warrant 보증 authority 지휘권, 권한 allowance 용돈; 허용량

8
- 해석 3월 1일부터 새로운 휴가 정책이 작년에 발생한 문제들을 해결하기 위해서 시행될 것이다.
- 해설 policy(정책), change(변화), decision(결정) 등과 함께 쓰는 동사로 implement(시행하다)가 있다.
- 어휘 leave 휴가 realize 깨닫다, 알아차리다 solicit 간청하다 design 고안하다; 디자인하다

9
- 해석 승객들에게 2달 동안 주인이 나타나지 않은 수화물은 어떤 것이든 분실물 센터로 보낼 거라고 공지해 준다.
- 해설 (A) 주인이 나타나지 않은 (B) 보완된 (C) 후보에 오른 (D) 발견된
- 어휘 remind 상기시키다

10
- 해석 당신이 전환할 수 있는 새로운 저축 계획에 대한 세부적인 정보를 위해서 우리의 재정 상담가 중 한 명과 이야기할 수 있다.
- 해설 해석과 함께 빈칸 뒤에 목적어가 아닌 with(전치사)가 있는 것을 보고 자동사 speak를 쓸 수 있다.
- 어휘 savings plan 저축 상품 switch to ~로 전환하다 consultant 상담사

11
- 해석 우리의 숙련된 상담가들은 당신이 계좌를 운영하는 것을 도와줄 수 있다.
- 해설 assist A in[with] B : A가 B 하는 것을 돕다
- 어휘 manage 관리하다 account 계좌 lend 빌려주다 explain 설명하다

12
- 해석 기소 중인 정치가가 관련 업계 사람과 밀접하게 관련되었다는 것은 널리 알려져 있다.
- 해설 A be associated with B: A는 B와 관련되어 있다
- 어휘 prosecution 기소 industry insider 업계 관계자

13
- 해석 당신이 등록한 수업이 마감되거나 이용할 수 없는 경우, 당신의 이름이 자동으로 대기 목록에 들어가게 될 것이다.
- 해설 (A) 상당하게 (B) 간헐적으로 (C) 진보적으로 (D) 자동적으로
- 어휘 be placed on ~에 놓이다

14
- 해석 지난 2년 동안 실업률이 장기간의 경제 침체로 인해 상당히 증가했다.
- 해설 rise, increase, decline, decrease 등과 같이 많이 쓰는 부사로 significantly, dramatically, rapidly 등이 있다.
- 어휘 recession 불경기, 불황 significantly 상당히 fundamentally 원래 impartially 치우치지 않고, 편견 없이

15
- 해석 당신의 서비스를 갱신하고자 하시면 온라인으로 비용을 송금하세요.
- 해설 온라인으로 송금할 수 있는 대상이 선택지 중에서 payment(비용) 밖에 없다. pay는 '급료, 보수'를 의미하므로 오답이다.
- 어휘 remit 송금하다 check 수표

DAY 05
본문 p.268

1 (C)	2 (C)	3 (A)	4 (D)	5 (D)
6 (B)	7 (C)	8 (D)	9 (B)	10 (A)
11 (C)	12 (A)	13 (A)	14 (C)	15 (B)

1
- 해석 Kroll Accounting은 Texas에 있는 새로운 지점으로 전근을 자원한 사람들에게 몇 개의 금전적인 우대를 제공할 것이다.
- 해설 offer(제공할 수 있는) 대상은 monetary incentives(금전적인 장려금)이므로 정답은 (C)이다.
- 어휘 accounting 회계 monetary 통화(화폐)의 format 구성 방식 measure 조치

2
- 해석 온라인 쇼핑의 증가하는 수요에 대응하여, 회사는 웹 디자인과 개발 분야를 전문으로 하는 사람들을 찾고 있다.
- 해설 자동사로 in과 함께 쓰이면서 의미상 가장 적절한 것은 specialize (전문으로 하다)이다.
- 어휘 in response to ~에 반응하여 demand 수요 consider 고려하다 measure 측정하다

3
해석   로스앤젤레스에 본사를 둔, Saint Electronics는 세계적으로 12개 국에 사업체를 둔 기술이 뛰어난 기업이다.
해설   (A) 기술이 뛰어난 (B) 고무된 (C) 증가한 (D) 시행된
어휘   headquarter ~에 본부를 두다

4
해석   이 로션의 향기로운 냄새는 국가적으로 많은 젊은 고객들에게 이전에 없었던 인기를 얻었다.
해설   fragrant(향기로운)과 관련되고 로션(lotion)에서 나올 수 있는 것은 scent(냄새)이다.
어휘   unprecedented 전례 없는 customer 손님, 고객 blaze 화재, 불길 stench 악취

5
해석   몇몇 후기는 새롭게 개봉한 영화가 시각 효과에 과하게 의존하고 있다고 지적했다.
해설   영화가 관객을 끌기 위해 사용할 수 있는 것 중 하나로 visual effects(시각 효과)가 있으므로 정답은 (D)이다.
어휘   release 개봉하다, 출시하다 foreseeable 예측할 수 있는 optical 시력의 unforeseen 예측하지 못한, 뜻밖의

6
해석   당신이 우리의 제품의 샘플을 원한다면 새롭게 단장한 웹 사이트에 방문하세요.
해설   (A) 기대 (B) 견본, 샘플 (C) 모양 (D) 틀
어휘   newly 새롭게 updated 최신의

7
해석   기술적인 문제로 도움이 필요한 고객들은 문제를 자세히 설명해야 한다.
해설   (A) 처리하다, 치우다 (B) 비난하다 (C) 설명하다, 묘사하다 (D) 파생되다, 생겨나다
어휘   technical 기술적인 seek 찾다, 구하다

8
해석   모든 배달 직원들은 상할 수 있는 재료를 확실하게 바로 식당으로 운반해 주십시오.
해설   음식 재료를 빨리 식당에 배송해야 하는 이유는 상하기 쉽기(perishable) 때문이므로 정답은 (D)이다.
어휘   ingredient 재료 promptly 지체 없이, 정확히

9
해석   회사가 생산 과정의 관리를 총괄할 공장 매니저 자리에 적합한 후보자 몇 명을 찾고 있다.
해설   생산 과정을 감독하는 사람은 공장 관리자 (plant manager)이므로 정답은 (B)이다.
어휘   suitable 적합한 candidate 후보자 be in charge of ~를 책임지다 supervise 감독하다 arbitrator 중재자

10
해석   당신은 Science and Technology 박물관에서 자동차 생산의 모든 기술적 진보를 볼 수 있을 것이다.
해설   기술(technological)의 꾸밈을 받고 전치사구 in automobile production의 수식을 받을 수 있는 명사는 advances(진보)이다.
어휘   technological 기술의 automobile 자동차의 production 생산 excavation 발굴 limitation 제약, 제한

11
해석   Krieger Informatics가 수행한 조사에서 고객의 선호가 지난 10년 동안 엄청나게 변화했다는 사실이 밝혀졌다.
해설   illustrate는 '(책 등에) 삽화를 쓰다'라는 의미 외에도 '(실례를 들어) 분명히 보여주다(=show)'의 의미도 있다.
어휘   conduct 수행하다 preference 선호 significantly 엄청나게 amplify 증폭시키다 constitute ~이 되는 것으로 여겨지다, 구성하다 jeopardize 위태롭게 하다

12
해석   50달러의 추가 요금으로 당신은 방을 최고급 객실로 업그레이드 할 수 있다.
해설   방을 최고급 방으로 바꾸려면 추가 요금(charge)이 필요하므로 정답은 (A)이다.
어휘   claim 주장하다, 요구하다 premium 상급의, 고급의 suite (호텔의) 특별실

13
해석   구직 신청자들은 늦어도 3월 27일까지 인사과에 다른 필요한 서류들을 제출해야 한다.
해설   목적어가 documents(서류들)이고 뒤따라 나오는 전치사구가 to the personnel office(인사과로)인 것으로 보아서 제출하다(submit)가 적절하다.
어휘   revise 변경하다, 수정하다 collect 수집하다

14
해석   Steve Marl은 Astella 제약회사의 홍보 담당 이사로 승진했다.
해설   promote는 '~을 홍보하다' 외에도 '승진시키다'라는 의미를 가진다.
어휘   director (회사의) 중역, 이사 public relations 홍보 pharmaceuticals 제약회사

15
해석   수많은 고객들에 의해 걸린 소송들 때문에, 사업 분석가들은 MS 푸드의 식당 가맹점들이 문을 닫게 될 것이라고 예상했다.
해설   빈칸 뒤의 that절 뒤에 나오는 것은 미래에 대한 전망이므로 이 내용에 어울리는 동사는 expect(예상하다)이다.
어휘   lawsuit 소송, 고소 go out of business 폐업하다 expand 확장하다 excuse 양해하다

DAY 06

본문 p.270

1 (A)	2 (D)	3 (C)	4 (D)	5 (C)
6 (A)	7 (A)	8 (C)	9 (C)	10 (C)
11 (D)	12 (C)	13 (A)	14 (A)	15 (C)

1
해석 지난 6개월간의 실험은 부주의하게 실행되어서 의미가 없는 것으로 밝혀졌다.
해설 실험이 의미가 없는 이유는 carelessly(부주의하게)했기 때문이므로 정답은 (A)이다.
어휘 turn out 결국 ~임이 밝혀지다 meaningless 무의미한 neutrally 중립적으로 objectively 객관적으로 reluctantly 마지못해서

2
해석 우리는 현재 높은 품질의 건조한 목재를 꾸준히 제공할 수 있는 믿을 만한 공급 업체를 찾고 있다.
해설 높은 품질의 제품을 꾸준히 제공하는 업체는 reliable(=dependable: 믿을 만한) supplier라고 할 수 있다. reliable은 reliant(=dependant: 의존적인)와 구분해야 한다.
어휘 consistently 끊임없이 accessible 접근 가능한 applicable 적용되는 sustainable 지속 가능한

3
해석 응답자의 약 80%가 우리에게 새로운 제품의 품질이 많이 향상되었다고 말해 주었다.
해설 숫자 앞에 자주 쓰이는 부사로는 nearly, approximately, about, over, more than, less than, roughly 등이 있다.
어휘 respondent 응답자 quality 질, 품질 improve 개선되다 absolutely 틀림없이

4
해석 회사의 스트레스 관리 세미나에 참석을 원하는 사람은 이번 금요일 전에 등록을 해야 한다.
해설 세미나에 참석하기 위해서 미리 취해야 하는 조치는 등록(sign up)이므로 정답은 (D)이다. 〈sign up for + 명사〉는 '~에 등록하다'라는 의미로 쓰이며 〈register for + 명사〉와 의미가 같다.
어휘 participate in ~에 참가하다 stress management 스트레스 관리 forward (메일 등을) 전달하다

5
해석 2월 1일부터 Copen 사의 생산 공장은 대략 2달 걸릴 개조를 위해서 문을 닫을 것이다.
해설 공장이 문을 닫는 이유 중 하나는 개조(renovation) 때문이므로 정답은 (C)이다.
어휘 shut down (공장, 가게의) 문을 닫다, (기계가) 멈추다 fabrication 지어낸 이야기, 거짓말 salvation 구원, 구조

6
해석 20년 전에 만든 휴대 전화 디자인의 특허가 이번 12월에 만기된다.
해설 patent(특허)는 특정 기간이 지나면 만기(expire)되므로 정답은 (A)이다.
어휘 establish 설립하다 intimidate 겁을 주다 specialize 특화하다 volunteer 자원하다, 자발적으로 참여하다

7
해석 회사의 새로운 서비스에 관한 사용자들의 후기는 높은 가격에 대한 몇몇 불평들을 제외하고 대부분 호의적이었다.
해설 호의적(favorable)과 반대되는 명사가 들어가야 하므로 불평(complaint)이 정답이다.
어휘 favorable 호의적인 except for ~를 제외하고 praise 칭찬 objection 이의, 반대

8
해석 파손될 수 있는 물건을 포함한 어떤 꾸러미라도 내부의 내용물에 입힐 수 있는 피해를 막기 위해서 조심스러운 취급이 요구된다.
해설 파손을 막기 위해서는 조심해서(careful) 다룰 수밖에 없으므로 (C)가 정답이다.
어휘 parcel 소포 fragile 부서지기 쉬운 grateful 고마워하는

9
해석 회사는 새로운 분야에 사업을 확장하기 위해서 빠르게 성장하는 유통 회사와 전략적인 제휴를 최근에 설립했다.
해설 recently는 과거 시제, 현재완료와 함께 쓰일 수 있는 부사이다.
어휘 strategic 전략적인 fast-growing 빨리 성장하는 continually 계속해서 frequently 빈번하게 urgently 급하게

10
해석 W&T Dental Clinic은 지역 주민들에게 다양한 치아 관리 서비스를 제공한다.
해설 a wide variety [range, selection, array] of = 다양한
어휘 placement 취업(거주지) 알선, 현장 실습; 설치, 배치

11
해석 회사의 대표 이사인 Wastler은 취임식에서 공장 확장 계획을 수행하겠다는 그의 의지를 표현했다.
해설 (A) 편안함 (B) 증가 (C) 중요성 (D) 의지
어휘 express 나타내다, 표하다 push forward 추진해 나가다 inauguration 취임

12
해석 그 회사는 시장에서 혁신적인 주자로서의 새로운 이미지와 일치하는 일련의 광고들을 시작할 것이다.
해설 회사의 새로운 이미지와 일치하는(match) 광고를 낸다고 하는 내용이 자연스럽다. 정답은 (C)이다.
어휘 launch 시작하다, 개시하다 innovative 혁신적인 compete 경쟁하다 complicate 복잡하게 하다 memorize 암기하다

13
- 해석 우리의 제한된 예산 안에서 큰 프로젝트를 끝내는 것은 약간 어려운 일이다.
- 해설 어떤 계획이나 활동에 들어가는 비용으로 미리 할당해 놓은 것을 budget(예산)이라고 한다.
- 어휘 challenging 도전적인 economy 경제 purse 지갑

14
- 해석 Vinobeach Hotel의 손님들은 방안에 있는 금고에 자신들의 소지품을 안전하게 보관하도록 요청받는다.
- 해설 소지품을 금고(safe)에 보관하는 것은 소지품의 안전을 위한 것이므로 securely(안전하게)가 정답이다.
- 어휘 belongings 소지품, 재산 broadly 넓게 vastly 광대하게 severely 심각하게

15
- 해석 Super Com의 컴퓨터의 가격이 부속품 가격의 하락으로 예상보다 낮아질 것이다.
- 해설 〈비교급 + than anticipated[expected]〉는 '예상했던 것보다 더 ~한'이라는 의미가 있다.
- 어휘 material 재료, 부속품 experiment 실험하다 incline ~쪽으로 기울다

DAY 07   본문 p.272

1 (C)	2 (B)	3 (B)	4 (A)	5 (B)
6 (D)	7 (A)	8 (D)	9 (D)	10 (C)
11 (C)	12 (B)	13 (D)	14 (B)	15 (A)

1
- 해석 이직률 감소는 지난달에 열린 연간 회의에서의 가장 중요한 사안들 중 하나였다.
- 해설 (A) 풍부한 (B) 꾸준한 (C) 중요한 (D) 강한
- 어휘 turnover 이직률, 매출액 reduction 감소

2
- 해석 수요일 세미나는 직원들이 사업의 다른 분야를 이해하는 데 도움을 주기 위해 명확하게 기획되었다.
- 해설 빈칸 뒤에 나오는 'to help the staff members understand'는 세미나에 대한 목적이 될 수 있으므로 목적에 맞게 만들어져야 한다(design). 정답은 (B)이다.
- 어휘 aspect 측면 compile 엮다, 편집하다 eliminate 제거하다 hesitate 주저하다

3
- 해석 오사카 공장의 제조 과정을 단순화하는 노력이 우리의 운영 비용을 감소시켜 줄 것이다.
- 해설 낮은 생산 비용이 나오려면 생산 과정이 단순화(simplify)되어야 하므

로 정답은 (B)이다.
- 어휘 manufacturing process 제조 과정 plant 공장 lower 낮추다 operating cost 운영 비용 contact 연락하다 overweigh ~보다 무겁다[중대하다] progress 과정

4
- 해석 Saito Ginjo의 혁신적인 비용 절감 방법이 올해 2분기 수익의 증가를 야기했다.
- 해설 증가된 이윤을 야기할 수 있는 것은 혁신적인(innovative) 방법이 가장 타당하다.
- 어휘 cutting-cost 비용 절감을 하는 measure 방법, 조치 quarter 분기 potential 잠재적인, 가능성 있는 billable 청구할 수 있는

5
- 해석 원재료의 가격은 지난달에 약간 올랐으나 산업 분석가들은 앞으로 다가오는 달에 급격한 감소를 예상하고 있다.
- 해설 동사 rose(오르다)를 수식하기에 적절한 부사를 찾는 문제로 slightly(약간)가 가장 적절하다.
- 어휘 raw materials 원자재 dramatic 급격한 highly (위상이나 평가를 나타낼 때) 매우 rarely 거의 ~않다 previously 이전에

6
- 해석 다음 달부터 우리는 매달 하는 종이 주문을 10개에서 15개 박스로 늘려야 한다.
- 해설 10개에서 15개로 늘리는(increase) 내용이다.
- 어휘 monthly 매달의, 달마다의 combine 결합하다 maintain 유지하다

7
- 해석 Ayaka의 제과점은 50달러 이상의 제품을 구매하는 사람들에게 다양한 선물을 제공합니다.
- 해설 a (wide) selection of : 다양한
- 어휘 purchase 구입하다 worth ~한 값어치의 selection 선택 pleasure 기쁨 compound 화합물 preference 애호, 좋아하기

8
- 해석 최근 조사는 직원들이 개인적인 문제를 논의하는 데 매일 45분까지 소비한다고 밝혔다.
- 해설 (A) ~을 버리다 (B) 잠깐 기다리다 (C) (주식 등을) 매수하다 (D) (시간을) 소비하다
- 어휘 survey 조사, 연구 up to ~까지 personal matters 개인적인 문제

9
- 해석 선적의 반복되는 지체 때문에 일본의 선적 회사와의 계약은 파기되었다.
- 해설 자꾸만 문제를 일으키는 회사와의 계약을 끝낸다(terminate)는 의미가 자연스러우므로(D)가 정답이다.
- 어휘 shipment 배송 shipping company 운송회사 observe ~을 보다, 목격하다 pretend ~인 척하다

10

해석 경제가 침체기에서 회복하고 있기 때문에 많은 기업들은 올해 이윤이 증가할 것으로 예상하고 있다.

해설 경기 침체(recession)가 끝나고 예상할 수 있는 것은 이윤 증가 (increased profits)이므로 정답은 (C)이다.

어휘 economy 경제 recover 회복하다 recession 침체 discount 할인

11

해석 지난 5년 동안에, 현장 근로자들의 안전 수준이 엄청나게 증가되었다.

해설 문장은 시제가 현재 완료 시제이며 안전 수준이 점차 개선되었다는 내용이다. 현재완료는 과거의 한 시점에서 현재까지 이어지는 변화를 나타낼 때 쓸 수 있다. During the past five years는 '지난 5년 동안'을 의미하므로 현재완료 시제와 잘 어울린다.

어휘 on-site 현장의 enhance 향상시키다 advancing 진격하는, 전진하는

12

해석 정부 기관으로부터 추가적인 자금이 공공 도서관의 새 도서 구입을 위해 할당되었다.

해설 (A) 발표하다 (B) 할당하다 (C) 제안하다 (D) 증명하다

어휘 additional 추가적인 government body 정부 기관 public library 공공 도서관

13

해석 오늘의 위원 모임의 모든 발표자들은 발표를 15분으로 제한하는 요청을 받았다.

해설 문장 뒤에 to 15 minutes(15분까지)가 나오는 것으로 보아 발표 (presentation)를 15분까지로 제한(limit)해야 함을 알 수 있다. 정답은 (D)이다.

어휘 committee 위원회 attend 참석하다 vote 투표하다 follow 따르다

14

해석 반도체 공장의 부지는 좋은 접근성 덕분에 선정되었다.

해설 location(위치)을 수식하는 관련 형용사로 accessible은 '접근하기 쉬운, 사람이 다가가기 쉬운' 등의 뜻을 가진다.

어휘 site 장소, 부지 semiconductor 반도체 excessive 지나친, 과도한 accommodating 선뜻 부응하는, 잘 협조하는 accustomed 익숙한

15

해석 우리는 최근에 판매에서 훌륭한 경력을 가진 매우 재능있는 직원을 고용했다.

해설 strong background를 보고 능력이 좋은 사람인 것을 알 수 있다. 이와 관련된 형용사로는 talented가 있다.

어휘 individual 개인 background 배경 protect 보호하다 annoyed 짜증난 majestic 장엄한

DAY 08 본문 p.274

1 (C)	2 (A)	3 (B)	4 (A)	5 (A)
6 (B)	7 (C)	8 (D)	9 (A)	10 (D)
11 (C)	12 (D)	13 (C)	14 (C)	15 (B)

1

해석 운동은 건강을 위해서 필수적이고, 매일 10분 정도만 걸어도 충분할 수 있다.

해설 운동은 건강에 필수적(essential)인 것이므로 정답은 (C)이다.

어휘 regional 지역적인 grateful 감사하는 final 최종적인

2

해석 일반 식기세척용 비누와 다른 세제들은 자동차의 마무리 손질에 해가 되는 강력한 화학 물질을 포함할 수 있다.

해설 빈칸에 들어갈 단어가 문맥상 dish-washing soap과 비슷한 종류여야 하므로 detergent(세제)가 정답이다.

어휘 contain ~이 들어 있다 insight 통찰력 detonator 기폭장치 inspector 조사원

3

해석 Ace Scientific은 Associated Aircraft와 새로운 레이더 유도 시스템의 판매와 설치에 대한 150만 달러의 계약을 발표하게 되어서 기쁩니다.

해설 문맥상 적절한 동사를 선택하는 문제이다. 빈칸에는 '~을 발표하다'라는 의미의 동사를 써야 하기 때문에 announce를 써야 한다. bargain은 〈bargain about + 명사: ~에 대하여 협상하다〉와 같이 직접 목적어를 취하지 않고 전치사가 필요한 자동사이므로 정답이 될 수 없다.

어휘 contract 계약 installation 설치 enclose 에워싸다, 동봉하다 bargain 협상하다, 흥정하다

4

해석 시 위원회는 도시의 보수 계획을 위한 예산을 상당히 증가시키기로 결정했다.

해설 빈칸에 들어갈 알맞은 부사를 고르는 문제이다. 빈칸의 부사는 해석상 increase를 수식하는 것이 적절하고 substantially(상당히)는 increase를 수식할 수 있다.

어휘 city council 시 의회 budget 예산 renovation 보수, 수리 spontaneously 자발적으로, 자연스럽게 unbiasedly 편견 없이

5

해석 시청에서의 행사 중에 주지사는 Frigs Cameron 씨에게 National Park Ranger 상을 수여했다.

해설 during은 '~동안'의 의미를 가진 전치사로 이와 가장 잘 어울리는 명사는 (A) ceremony가 가장 적절하다.

어휘 award 상 present 수여하다 Governor 주(州) 지사 solution 해결 pleasure 기쁨 constant (수학에서의) 정수, 항수

6
해석 우리 연간 직원 수련회가 Yellowstone 국립공원의 Bear Creek Lodge에서 개최될 것입니다.
해설 동사 의미 선택 문제. '연간 직원 수련회가 열리다'를 의미하는 동사 be held를 써야 한다.
어휘 retreat 수련회; 후퇴, 철수 sustain 지탱하다, 유지하다 support 후원하다, 지지하다

7
해석 올해의 주 행사에서는 그래미 수상자 Maria Cypress를 포함한 유명한 밴드와 가수들이 공연을 한다.
해설 문맥상 적절한 동사를 선택하는 문제이다. 빈칸 앞에는 행사가 나오는 반면, 뒤에는 행사 출연진이 나오고 있다. 따라서 '특징을 이루다, 특집으로 하다'라는 의미의 features가 가장 적절하다.
어휘 observe 관찰하다, 준수하다 transmit 전송하다 secure 확보하다

8
해석 저희는 제품에 대해 고객의 잘못된 사용이나 부주의에 의해 야기된 외부적인 손상에 대해서는 어떤 것도 보상해 드릴 수 없습니다.
해설 피해에 대해서 제품을 보장해 준다(guarantee)는 내용의 동사가 적절하다.
어휘 external 외부의 damage 손상 misuse 남용, 오용 negligence 부주의, 태만 afford 여유가 되다

9
해석 직원들은 매년 고객 서비스에 대한 두 번의 회의에 참석해야 하며 연수 참가 신청서는 직원 게시판에 붙일 것이다.
해설 문맥상 적절한 명사를 고르는 문제이다. 빈칸 앞의 동사가 attend(참석하다)가 나오는 것으로 보아 목적어는 conference(회의)가 되어야 한다.
어휘 customer service 고객 서비스 sign-up sheet 신청서 employee 직원, 고용인 bulletin board 게시판 contribution 공헌, 기여 agenda 의제, 안건 prescription 처방전

10
해석 Ohio에 새 공장을 짓는 것은 1억 달러짜리 계획이며, 그것은 짓는데 2년 이상이 걸릴 것이다.
해설 문맥상 적절한 명사를 선택하는 문제이다. 새 공장을 짓는 것은 대규모 사업 계획이므로 이에 어울리는 단어는 project이다.
어휘 construction 건설 approval 승인 method 방법, 교수법 format 판형, 체재

11
해석 관리 직원 중 한 명이 프린터가 제대로 작동하지 않는 이유를 파악하기 위해 판매 부서로 보내졌다.
해설 work는 '(기계가) 작동하다'라는 의미가 있으며 properly와 함께 쓰여 '정상적으로 작동하다'라는 의미로 쓰인다.
어휘 maintenance 유지, 보수 eloquently 웅변으로, 능변으로 finitely 유한하게, 제한적으로 steadily 지속적으로, 꾸준히

12
해석 최근 국제 유가가 하락한 이유는 아마도 수요의 완화와 원유 공급원의 증가 때문일 것이다.
해설 빈칸 앞뒤의 내용은 각각 결과(국제 유가의 하락)와 원인(수요의 완화와 공급원의 증가)를 나타내는데 probably(아마도)는 이 원인이 추측에 의한 것임을 나타내 주는 부사 역할을 한다.
어휘 decline 감소, 하락 ease 완화, 누그러짐 source 원천, 공급원 nearly 거의 usefully 유용하게 safely 안전하게

13
해석 우리는 올해 말에 사업 파트너와 합병할 것이며, 이로써 우리 시장 점유율은 25% 상승할 것이다.
해설 later는 this year와 함께 쓰이면 '올해 늦게'를 의미하므로 문맥상 later가 적절하다.
어휘 merge with 합병하다 past 과거의, 지나간 next 다음의 afterwards 이후에

14
해석 자산 매각으로 얻은 자금은 Georgia의 새 공장 건설에 쓰여질 것이며 그곳에서 우리 제품에 쓰이는 반도체판을 만들 것이다.
해설 적절한 의미의 전치사를 고르는 문제이다. 자금은 새 공장 건설 용도로 쓰인다고 했으므로 목적이나 이유를 나타내는 전치사 for가 가장 적절하다.
어휘 fund 자금 property 자산 semiconductor 반도체

15
해석 우리는 제품을 사용해도 된다고 판단하기 전에 모든 제품의 안전 점검을 해야 한다.
해설 안전 점검 후에 제품이 사용될 준비(ready)가 된 것에 대해 판단을 내리므로 적절한 답은 (B)이다.
어휘 inspection 사찰, 점검 consider ~라고 여기다 actual 실제의, 현실의 absolute 완전한, 절대적인

DAY 09 본문 p.276

1 (A)	2 (B)	3 (B)	4 (C)	5 (B)
6 (A)	7 (C)	8 (A)	9 (B)	10 (C)
11 (B)	12 (B)	13 (A)	14 (C)	15 (B)

1
해석 JJ Capital의 시장 분석가들은 IT회사들이 앞으로 수년간 빠르게 성장할 것 같다고 언급했다.
해설 likely는 〈be likely to부정사〉의 형태로 '~할 가능성이 크다'라는 의미로 쓰인다. 그 반대 표현은 〈be unlikely to부정사〉이다.
어휘 at a rapid rate 빠른 속도로 observant 관찰력 있는, 준수하는 pertinent 적절한

2
해석 우리 회사는 시장 점유율의 75%를 차지하며, 집과 자동차에 쓰이는 LED 전구의 선두 생산자이다.

해설 시장 점유율의 75%를 차지한다는 것으로 보아 producer를 수식하는 형용사 자리에는 leading이 와야 적절하다.

어휘 producer 생산자 LED bulb LED 전구 automobile 자동차 supply 공급하다 originate ~에서 생기다, 일어나다 incident 일어나기 쉬운 anticipated 예상된, 예견된

3
해석 나는 결국 우리 부서장으로부터 인도로의 3주 휴가를 허락 받았으며 그것은 2주가 넘기 때문에 마케팅 부서의 부서장의 허락이 필요했다.

해설 문맥상 적절한 부사를 선택하는 문제이다. finally는 received permission과 결합해서 '마침내 허락을 받았다'라는 의미로 쓰일 수 있다.

어휘 permission 허락 department director 부서장 approve 승인하다 closely 면밀하게

4
해석 구인 광고는 2년 이상의 업무 관련 경력이 있는 사람들만 자격이 있는 것으로 고려될 것이라고 분명히 명시했다.

해설 qualified는 '자격을 갖춘'이란 뜻이며 qualified candidates(자격을 갖춘 지원자들)처럼 쓰일 수 있다.

어휘 job advertisement 구인 광고 state 말하다, 명시하다 work-related experience 업무 관련 경력 delicate 연약한, 어린 emotional 감정적인 strengthened 강화된

5
해석 그 대학교는 입학하는 모든 학생들에게 태블릿 PC를 지급할 것이라고 기대된다.

해설 빈칸은 동사 자리인데 동사 뒤에 〈목적어+목적보어(to부정사)〉가 나오고 있다. allow는 뒤에 목적어와 to부정사 목적보어를 취할 수 있는 동사이다. give는 간접 목적어와 직접 목적어를 취하는 수여동사이다.

어휘 expect 기대하다 be equipped with ~을 갖추다

6
해석 우리는 새로운 Ohio 공장의 고용을 위하여 추가로 100명의 직원을 채용할 것이며 그 공장은 내년 6월에 완공 예정이다.

해설 Ohio 공장의 고용을 위해서는 직원들을 채용해야(recruit) 하므로 정답은 (A)이다.

어휘 additional 추가적인 employment 고용 be scheduled for ~가 예정되어있다 completion 완료 expand 확장하다 revise 개정하다 converse 대화하다, 의견을 나누다

7
해석 우리 회사는 Laos 공장에 올해 내로 최소한 500명의 직원을 확보해야 하며 모든 직원은 현지의 기계 기술자 연합의 회원이어야 한다.

해설 문장은 연말(the end of the year)까지 500명의 직원 확충을 완료해야 한다는 의미이므로 전치사 by(~까지)가 가장 적절하다.

어휘 membership 회원 자격 machinist 기계 기술자

8
해석 컴퓨터 기술자들이 서버에 바이러스가 있음을 진단하였으며, 따라서 새로운 안티바이러스 소프트웨어의 설치와 업데이트가 필요할 것이다.

해설 diagnose는 '(질병을) 진단하다, (문제의 원인을) 찾아내다'의 뜻이 있으므로 (A)가 정답이다.

어휘 technician 기술자 require 요구하다 installation 설치 antivirus software 바이러스 백신 프로그램 shift 바꾸다 collapse 붕괴하다 respond 응답하다

9
해석 회사가 작년에 상당한 돈을 절약했기 때문에 우리는 모든 직원들에게 일괄적으로 10퍼센트의 임금 인상을 해 줄 수 있다.

해설 빈칸 뒤에 두 개의 절이 연속적으로 연결되어있으므로, 빈칸에는 부사절 접속사가 필요하다. 첫 번째 절에서 상당한 돈을 절약했다는 것은 두 번째 절에 나오는 임금 인상에 대한 이유가 될 수 있으므로 Since가 가장 적절하다. So는 부사절 접속사이지만 문장의 처음에 쓰이면서 문장을 이끄는 역할은 할 수 없다.

어휘 considerable 상당한, 많은 across-the-board 전반에 걸쳐

10
해석 모든 직원들은 건물 보안을 위한 안전 장치로 신원 확인 배지를 달아야 하며, 그것은 입장할 때 보안 경비원들이 확인할 것이다.

해설 신원 확인 배지(identification badge)를 다는 것은 건물의 보안을 지키기 위한 것으로 빈칸에 알맞은 형용사는 protective(보호하는)이다.

어휘 security 보안 upon entry 입장하자마자 security guard 경비원 continuous 계속적인 settled 고정된, 정착한 rival 경쟁관계의

11
해석 기술지원팀 사람들은 연결 실패의 원인이 서버 오류에 있음을 알아냈다.

해설 서버 오류(server failure)로 인한 컴퓨터 문제로 생각할 수 있는 것을 선택지에서 고르면 접속(connection)이 안 되는 것이므로 정답은 (B)가 정답이다.

어휘 determine 알아내다, 밝히다 server (컴퓨터) 서버 relevance 관련성 acquaintance 지인 mixture 혼합

12
해석 소프트웨어 설치를 포함한 새로운 컴퓨터 시스템에 대한 직원 교육은 시작부터 종료까지 3주가 소요될 것이다.

해설 from start to finish: 시작부터 끝까지

어휘 including ~를 포함해서

13
해석 다음 주부터 상점에서 판매될 저희 회사의 새로운 전기 'Old Time Lantern'에 대한 소개서가 동봉되어 있으니 읽어 보시기 바랍니다.

해설 (A) 동봉된 (B) 반대의 (C) 결석한 (D) 무죄의

어휘 regarding ~에 관하여

14
해석 마케팅부의 철저한 광고 캠페인 덕분에 우리의 매우 얇은 노트북 컴퓨

터의 판매가 올해 5천만 달러를 넘어설 것이다.

해설 over는 수량형용사 앞에 쓰여 '(수치가) ~가 넘는, ~이상의'를 의미한다. farther(더 멀리)는 거리를 나타내므로 정답이 될 수 없다.

어휘 reach ~에 이르다, 도달하다 rigorous 철저한, 엄격한 aside from ~를 제외하고 in addition to ~일 뿐만 아니라

15

해석 만약 당신이 잡지를 집으로 배달 받기를 원한다면, 이달 25일 전까지 마케팅 부서에 당신의 주소를 보내 주세요.

해설 날짜 앞에 올 수 있는 전치사는 on, before, after 등이 있다. 선택지 중 before를 넣으면 '25일 전까지 마케팅 부서로 주소를 보내 달라'는 의미가 될 수 있다.

어휘 submit 제출하다

DAY 10

본문 p.278

1 (B)	2 (C)	3 (C)	4 (D)	5 (B)
6 (B)	7 (D)	8 (A)	9 (A)	10 (B)
11 (C)	12 (A)	13 (C)	14 (A)	15 (B)

1

해석 우리 회사의 이익 분배금은 내년 초에 거의 10%가 오를 것이다.

해설 almost는 수량 형용사 앞에 쓰여서 '거의 ~'라는 의미를 나타낼 수 있다.

어휘 profit 이익 sharing 나누기, 공유하기 firmly 확고하게 strongly 강하게 completely 완전히

2

해석 지출과 주유 비용을 줄이기 위해, 모든 직원들은 공무 이행으로 회사 차량을 사용하실 경우, 가장 빠른 길로 다니시길 바랍니다.

해설 기름 값 등 비용을 절약하려면 가장 빠른 길(route)을 이용해야 하므로 정답은 (C)이다.

어휘 official business 공무 expense 비용 total 합계

3

해석 우리 회사는 벌써 목표치의 38%에 달하며 올해의 판매 전망을 넘어섰다.

해설 yet과 already는 모두 현재완료 시제와 자주 쓰이는 부사인데, yet은 부정문, 의문문에서 주로 쓰인다. already는 '이미'라는 뜻으로 '이미 판매 전망을 넘어섰다'라는 의미를 나타낼 수 있다.

어휘 exceed 넘다, 초과하다 projection 예상, 전망 straight 똑바로 even ~조차

4

해석 가족의 규모와 그 필요 사항을 명심하고 보험 상품을 선택할 때는 조심해야 한다.

해설 (A) 지시하다 (B) 지지하다 (C) 요구하다 (D) 선택하다

어휘 insurance 보험 keep in mind 명심하다 need 필요 사항, 욕구

5

해석 성공적인 지도자는 모든 사람들이 환영받고 있음을 느낄 수 있는 열린 정책을 취함으로써, 모든 직원들의 생각들을 수용해야 한다.

해설 문장 후반부에 열린 정책을 취해야(having open door policy) 한다는 문맥으로부터 빈칸에 들어갈 알맞은 말이 'receptive(수용하는)'라는 것을 알 수 있다. be receptive to (~를 수용하는)

어휘 open door policy 열린 정책 feel welcome 환대받고 있음을 느끼다 convinced 확신하는 generous 후한, 너그러운 plausible 타당한 것 같은, 이치에 맞는

6

해석 우리의 최종적인 제품 라인업은 국내 및 해외의 다른 경쟁 업체에 비해 상대적으로 약한 편이다.

해설 relatively는 '상대적으로'의 의미를 지니고 형용사 low 앞에 쓰여 '상대적으로 약한'의 의미를 가질 수 있다.

어휘 product lineup 제품 라인업 in comparison to ~와 비교할 때 competitor 경쟁자 audibly 들리도록 plentifully 많이, 풍부하게 anonymously 익명으로

7

해석 직원이 회사의 다른 부서로 이전하기를 원하는 경우, 그는 부서 책임자 및 관리자의 허가를 얻어야 한다.

해설 (A) 가입하다, 합류하다 (B) 배우다 (C) 보호하다 (D) 얻다

어휘 transfer 옮기다 department 부서 permission 허가 supervisor 관리자, 책임자

8

해석 Thompson 씨는 파리 방문 기간 중에 자동차를 렌트하기로 결심했다.

해설 for the duration of: ~하는 동안에

어휘 rent 빌리다 circumstance 환경

9

해석 인사팀에서 한 연구는 매년 봉급의 증가액이 충분하다는 점을 확인해 준다.

해설 직원들에게 봉급의 증액을 설명할 수 있는 단어는 adequate(충분한)밖에 없다.

어휘 numerous 많은 adjacent 인접한, 가까운

10

해석 해외로 배송되는 모든 수송물은 국제 규정을 준수하는 데 필요한 모든 문서와 서류가 있어야 한다.

해설 국제 규정에 필요한 문서가 필요하다고 했으므로 빈칸에는 compliance(준수, 순응)가 적절하다.

어휘 shipment 수송물; 수송 documentation 서류 international 국제적인 regulation 규정, 규칙 diagnosis 진단 settlement 합의, 해결 criticism 비판, 비평

11

해석 건물의 5층으로 가는 에스컬레이터는 안전 검사를 위해 내일 일시적으로 멈출 것입니다.

해설 shut down을 꾸며줄 수 있는 부사를 골라야 하는데, 안전을 위해서

임시적으로(temporarily) 멈춘다는 의미가 자연스러우므로 정답은 (C)이다.

어휘 escalator 에스컬레이터 safety inspections 안전 점검 formerly 이전에, 예전에 cautiously 조심스럽게

12

해석 연휴 동안의 소매 판매의 급증으로 인해, 지난 12월에 판매량이 절정에 달했다.

해설 연휴 기간 동안의 판매가 급증해서 회사 판매량이 절정에 달했다(peaked)는 내용이 와야 한다. 정답은 (A)이다.

어휘 retail (소비자에게 직접 물건을 파는) 소매 surge 급증, 급등 record 기록하다

13

해석 마케팅 부서 이외에도, 직원의 10%를 해고할 것이며, 이는 다음 달 1일부터 적용될 것입니다.

해설 there will be부터 완전한 문장 구조이기 때문에 그 앞에 오는 말은 전치사구 혹은 부사절이어야 하는데 〈apart from + 명사구〉는 '~이외에도, ~뿐만 아니라'라는 의미가 있다. if were not for는 '~없이는, ~이 없었다면'이라는 의미가 있고 가정법 과거나 과거완료 문장에서 쓰이므로 답이 될 수 없다.

어휘 cut 감축 personnel 인원 take effect 발효하다 rather than ~보다는

14

해석 신입 사원들은 매일 9시에서 5시까지 근무하며, 근무 시간 중 급료가 지불되는 점심시간이 포함됩니다.

해설 빈칸은 the work time 앞에 쓸 수 있는 전치사가 와야 하는 자리인데 근무 시간 중에 점심이 제공되므로 '~하는 동안'이라는 의미의 during이 와야 한다.

어휘 aboard 탑승한

15

해석 고객의 불만 사항을 처리할 때 모든 직원은 표준 운영 절차를 준수해야 한다.

해설 빈칸 뒤의 목적어 procedure(절차)와 결합할 수 있는 동사를 찾아야 한다. 빈칸에는 '(규정, 절차를) 따르다'라는 의미의 follow가 적절하다.

어휘 standard 표준적인 operating procedure 운영 절차 deal with 다루다 complaint 불만

DAY 11

본문 p.280

1 (B)	2 (D)	3 (C)	4 (D)	5 (A)
6 (C)	7 (D)	8 (A)	9 (B)	10 (A)
11 (A)	12 (D)	13 (B)	14 (A)	15 (B)

1

해석 우리 회사는 우리의 재생 가능한 에너지 제품을 시연하기 위해 런던 세계 그린 엑스포에 부스를 설치할 것입니다.

해설 엑스포 부스에서 제품을 가지고 하는 것으로 가장 적절한 것은 시연하는 것(demonstrate)이므로 정답은 (B)이다.

어휘 booth 부스 renewable 재생 가능한 achieve 달성하다, 성취하다 encourage 격려하다 distinguish 구별하다

2

해석 실험 프로젝트에 특별히 배당된 직원들을 제외하고는 그 어떤 직원도 연구 시설에 들어갈 수 없습니다.

해설 (A) ~로서 (B) ~하는 중에 (C) 그래서 (D) ~를 제외하고

어휘 research facility 연구 시설 specifically 분명히, 명확하게 assign 맡기다, 배정하다 lab(=laboratory) 실험실

3

해석 새 비행기의 동체는 전체 무게를 감소시켜 주는 탄소 섬유와 티타늄의 혼합물이다.

해설 빈칸 뒤의 carbon fiber(탄소 섬유)와 titanium(티타늄)은 빈칸 앞의 비행기 동체를 이루는 구성 요소가 될 수 있으므로 빈칸에 들어갈 가장 적절한 단어는 blend(혼합)이다.

어휘 fuselage (비행기의) 동체 carbon fiber 탄소 섬유

4

해석 신제품의 연구와 개발에 관한 모든 질문은 홍보 부서에 해야 합니다.

해설 빈칸에는 questions와 the research and development of our new products 사이에 들어갈 수 있는 것을 고르는 것인데, concerning은 전치사로 '~에 관한 질문'이라는 의미를 만들어 줄 수 있으므로 정답은 (D)이다.

어휘 address 연설하다, 말을 걸다 public relations 홍보 versus ~대, ~에 비해

5

해석 본사는 어제 시내 전체에 영향을 미친 정전 사태로 인해 사람들을 대피시켜야 했습니다.

해설 빈칸 뒤의 a power blackout(정전)은 앞에 나온 대피 상황에 대한 원인이 되므로 빈칸에는 because of가 가장 적절하다.

어휘 corporate 기업의 headquarters 본사 evacuate 대피시키다 blackout 정전 prior to ~에 앞서서 pertaining to ~와 관계된

6

해석 활주로에서 비행기가 지나갈 때, 모든 직원은 보호용 귀마개를 해야 합니다.

해설 빈칸은 명사인 earmuffs(귀마개)를 수식해 줄 수 있는 형용사를 써야 하는 자리이며 네 개의 선택지 중에서 protective(보호를 해 주는)가 가장 자연스럽다.

어휘 earmuff 귀마개, 귀 가리개 tarmac 아스팔트 활주로 absolute 절대적인 savory 맛좋은, 향긋한 expired 만료된, 기한이 지난

7

해석 직원이 통보 없이 결석하는 것은 용납될 수 없고 부적절한 것으로 여겨진다.

해설 형용사 의미 선택 문제. 일반동사 consider 다음에는 보어로 형용사를 써서 의미적으로 '부적절하다'라는 단어가 와야 하므로 improper를 쓴다.

어휘 unacceptable 받아들일 수 없는 concise 간결한, 축약된 equivalent 동등한 submissive 순종적인, 고분고분한

8
해설 휴가 가능 기간을 게시판에 공지하였으니 직원들은 그에 따라 자신의 휴가를 계획해 주시기 바랍니다.

해설 직원들이 휴가를 계획할 때 휴가 가능 기간(vacation eligibility)을 보고 그에 따라 계획을 짜야 하므로 빈칸에 적절한 부사는 accordingly(상황에 부응하여, 상황에 맞춰서)이다.

어휘 eligibility 적격 subsequently 그 뒤에, 나중에 conversely 정반대로, 역으로 assuredly 분명히, 틀림없이

9
해설 새로운 직원 보호 장비는 모든 직원이 사용하기에 적합하며, OSHA에 의해 인증된 것이다.

해설 be suitable for: ~에 적절하다

어휘 protective gear 보호 장비 certify 증명하다 consistent 한결같은, 일관된 accurate 정확한, 정밀한

10
해설 우리가 방금 제작진으로부터 받은 이 새로운 브로셔에 대행사의 새로운 Pan-Europe Tour에 대한 요약이 인쇄되어 있습니다.

해설 주어 자리이며 올 수 있는 단어를 선택해야 하는 문제이다. 브로셔에 인쇄될 수 있는 것은 summary(요약)이므로 정답은 (A)이다.

어휘 brochure 브로셔 registration 등록

11
해설 제품 결함에 대한 조사 결과는 회사 정책에 반하는 지속적인 기준 위반이 있었음을 보여 주었다.

해설 violations of standards(기준 위반)는 company policy(회사의 정책)를 어긴 것이므로 빈칸에 어울리는 어구는 contrary to(~에 반하는)이다.

어휘 investigation 조사 defect 결함 violation 위반, 위배 in place of ~를 대신해서

12
해설 유동적인 휴가를 가지고자 하는 직원들은 상사와 HR부서에 최소 30일 이전에 알려 주어야 합니다.

해설 in advance는 앞에 two days, three weeks 등과 함께 쓰여서 '이틀 전에', '3주 전에' 등의 의미를 가질 수 있다.

어휘 floating holiday 대체휴일, 날짜가 고정되지 않은 공휴일(예: 미국의 추수감사절 - 11월 네 번째 목요일) notify 알리다 ahead of ~에 앞서서 initially 처음에

13
해설 전 세계 매립지에 있는 일반적인 배터리와는 대조적으로 우리의 새로운 태양열 배터리는 매우 친환경적입니다.

해설 as opposed to: ~와는 대조적으로

어휘 eco-friendly 친환경적인 landfill 쓰레기 매립지

14
해설 이 회사가 이번 회계 연도 말까지 14억 달러에 Koontz 사를 구입하고자 한다고 오늘 발표되었습니다.

해설 (A) ~를 하고자 하다 (B) 추구하다 (C) 임명하다 (D) 설명하다

어휘 fiscal year 회계 연도

15
해설 우리 품질 관리 부서는 규정 준수를 보장하기 위해 일 년 내내 걸쳐 상품에 품질 체크를 정규적으로 실시하고 있다.

해설 규정 준수를 철저히 하기 위해서는 정기적으로(regularly) 품질을 체크해야 한다는 것이 자연스러우므로 정답은 (B)이다.

어휘 quality control 품질 관리 quality check 품질 점검 insure 보장하다(=ensure) compliance 준수 essentially 기본적으로 primarily 주로 accessibly 접근 가능한

DAY 12
본문 p.282

1 (C)	2 (A)	3 (C)	4 (A)	5 (A)
6 (B)	7 (A)	8 (B)	9 (A)	10 (B)
11 (C)	12 (C)	13 (A)	14 (D)	15 (A)

1
해설 회사 이사회는 제품 라인을 더욱 다양화할 것을 요구하는 새로운 5개년 계획을 개발할 것입니다.

해설 목적어 plan(계획)과 결합할 수 있는 동사를 고르는 문제이다. develop a plan은 '계획을 개발하다'라는 의미로 쓰일 수 있다.

어휘 board of directors 이사회 call for ~를 요구하다 diversification 다양화, 다양성 product lines 제품 라인, 제품군

2
해설 직원들이 사용하고 열람하는 모든 기록은 기밀 사항이며, 절대 외부로 나가서는 안 된다는 것을 직원들에게 공지합니다.

해설 (A) 비밀의, 기밀의 (B) 제한된 (C) 이전의 (D) 의무적인

어휘 remind 상기하다 disclose 밝히다, 드러내다 party 단체

3
해설 모든 직원은 회사가 기여도에 따라 매년 6%까지 인센티브를 주는 직원 저축 계정을 만들어야 합니다.

해설 savings account(저축 계정)과 결합할 수 있는 동사는 offer와 create가 있는데, 직원 입장에서 계정을 제공하는 것이 아니라 만들어야 하는 것이므로 create가 가장 적절하다.

어휘 match up 부합하다, 맞추다

4
해설 매년 그해의 마지막 날 우리 회사는 전년도의 성공을 축하하기 위해 모든 직원과 그 가족을 위한 전사적 파티를 개최합니다.

해설 빈칸은 동사 자리인데 party와 결합할 수 있는 것을 찾아야 한다. hold a party는 '파티를 열다'라는 뜻인데 매년 직원들과 그 가족들

어휘 New Year's Eve 새해 전날, 한 해의 마지막 날 companywide 전 회사적인 규모의 celebrate 축하하다

5
해석 우리 회사의 상품에 대한 보증은 전체 가전 제품 산업 중에 최고로 인식되고 있다.
해설 문맥상 '~ 중에 최고로 인식된다'라는 의미를 전해야 하며 뒤에 entire가 나오므로 전체 범위를 나타내는 throughout(~전체에 걸쳐서)이 가장 적절하다.
어휘 warranty 제품 보증 entire 전반적인, 전체적인 consumer electronics 가전 제품 industry 산업

6
해석 고객 불만사항은 매우 민감한 문제이며, 즉시 조사되고 처리되어야 합니다.
해설 고객 불만은 즉시 조사되고 처리되어야 하므로 빈칸에는 sensitive(민감한)가 가장 적절하다.
어휘 issue 문제, 사안 investigate 조사하다 immediately 즉시 courteous 공손한, 정중한 competitive 경쟁적인

7
해석 우리 회사의 교육 부서는 일 년 내내 매우 체계적인 프로그램으로 이루어져 있는 워크숍을 후원하는데, 그 프로그램은 직원들이 최소한 25시간의 교육을 받도록 구성되어 있습니다.
해설 빈칸은 과거 분사인 structured를 수식해 줄 수 있는 부사를 써야 하는 자리인데, 선택지 중 highly(매우)는 structured와 결합해서 '매우 구조화된'이라는 의미를 전달할 수 있다.
어휘 sponsor 후원하다 throughout the year 1년 내내 structured 구조가 있는, 구조화된 at least 적어도 hopefully 바라건대 rarely 드물게, 좀처럼 ~ 않는

8
해석 회사는 본사의 식당에 사람이 너무 많이 몰리는 것을 완화하기 위해 추가적인 직원 식당을 지을 것입니다.
해설 식당이 붐비는 것을 막기 위해서 식당을 더 짓는 것이므로 빈칸에는 additional(추가적인)이 가장 적절하다.
어휘 relieve 진정시키다 overcrowding 혼잡 occur 일어나다, 발생하다 infrequent 드문 incidental 부수적인

9
해석 우리의 매출은 낮은 수요와 불리한 시장 상황 때문에 14%나 떨어졌습니다.
해설 문장에서 due to(~ 때문에)는 이유를 나타내는 전치사로 반도체의 낮은 매출의 원인을 설명하는 데 사용되고 있다. 따라서 문맥상 '불리한 시장 환경'이라는 의미를 전달할 수 있는 unfavorable이 빈칸에 올 수 있다.
어휘 demand 수요 market condition 시장 상황 unwilling 꺼리는, 싫어하는, 마지못한 reluctant 꺼리는, 마지못한

10
해석 나는 대통령이 연설을 할 때마다 솔직했던 점을 높이 평가합니다. 그는 빙빙 돌려 말하지 않고, 직접적으로 핵심을 짚어 이야기합니다.
해설 문맥상 빈칸에 들어갈 말은 direct와 의미가 비슷하고, beating around the bush와 반대되는 의미를 만들 수 있는 단어이어야 한다. to the point는 '요점에 들어맞히'이라는 의미를 갖고 있는 표현이다.
어휘 appreciate 진가를 알아보다, 고마워하다 candor 허심탄회

11
해석 시설 정비 부서는 종종 직원에게 깨끗하고 맑은 공기를 제공하기 위해 HVAC 시스템을 진공 청소합니다.
해설 깨끗한 공기를 제공하기 위해서 HVAC(난방, 환기, 공기 조절 시스템)를 청소하는 횟수를 나타내는 부사가 나와야 한다. 따라서 빈칸에는 occasionally가 적절하다.
어휘 maintenance 유지 보수 vacuum 진공청소기로 청소하다 HVAC(=heating, ventilating, and air conditioning) 난방, 환기, 공기 조절 prematurely 시기상조로, 이르게 marginally 가까스로 uncommonly 드물게

12
해석 새로운 태양 LED 램프가 참여 중인 소매업체들에게 한정 수량으로, 7월 17일까지 판매 가능합니다.
해설 July 17 앞에 쓸 수 있는 전치사를 써야 하는 자리이며 의미적으로 '~할 때까지'를 의미하는 단어를 써야 하므로 until을 쓴다. by는 동작의 완료를 의미하므로 오답이다.
어휘 available 구입 가능한 quantity 양 retailer 소매업자

13
해석 우리는 곧 스톡홀름 시내에 있는 새 사무실로 이사 갈 것입니다.
해설 문장은 앞으로의 사무실 이전 계획에 대해 이야기하고 있으므로 미래 시제와 어울릴 수 있는 shortly(곧)가 들어갈 수 있다.
어휘 previously 전에 overly 과하게

14
해석 물의 누수로 인해 인사팀 컴퓨터에 손상이 입혔다는 점이 발견되어, 유지보수 팀이 누출에 대한 원인이 무엇인지 확인하기 위해 노력하고 있습니다.
해설 물의 누수로 문제가 발생해서, 무엇 때문에 물의 누수가 발생됐는지 알아보고 있다는 내용으로 be responsible for는 '~에 대한 원인이 되다'라는 의미가 있다.
어휘 leak 누수, 누출 ascertain 알아내다, 확인하다 transparent 투명한 probable 사실일 것 같은, 개연성 있는

15
해석 최근 설문 조사는 회사원들이 회사를 위해 일하는 데 더 많은 혜택을 원한다는 것을 나타낸다.
해설 주어 자리에 survey(설문 조사)가 있고 빈칸 뒤에 survey의 결과 내용이 나오고 있다. 설문 조사의 결과 등을 표현할 때에는 indicate(나타내다)를 쓸 수 있다.
어휘 benefit 혜택 transfer 전송하다 designate 지정하다, 지명하다

DAY 13

본문 p.284

1 (C)	2 (C)	3 (D)	4 (C)	5 (A)
6 (C)	7 (A)	8 (A)	9 (B)	10 (D)
11 (C)	12 (A)	13 (D)	14 (D)	15 (B)

1
해석 모든 고객들에게 30% 할인된 가격에 우리의 재생 가능한 에너지 제품을 구입할 수 있는 쿠폰이 제공됩니다.
해설 고객에게 쿠폰이 제공된다(be provided)는 내용이 자연스러우므로 정답은 (A)이다. provide A with B는 'A에게 B를 제공하다'는 의미가 있다.
어휘 purchase 구입하다 renewable 재생 가능한 discount 할인 equip 장비를 갖추다

2
해석 우리의 모든 제품에 대한 무료 업데이트를 자주 제공함으로써 고객들이 비싼 소프트웨어 업그레이드 비용을 지불하지 않아도 될 것이다.
해설 (A) 유망한, 전망이 좋은 (B) 수많은 (C) 자주 있는, 빈번한 (D) 자꾸 반복되는

3
해석 모든 신입 사원들은 지원부서의 기술자들 중 한 명에게 복사기 사용법을 배울 것이다.
해설 전치사 의미 선택 문제. 주어진 빈칸은 전치사를 써야 하는 자리이며 의미적으로 '~로부터'라는 from을 써야 한다.

4
해석 회사는 근무 조건, 급여 및 혜택을 포함한 모든 노동 조합의 계약 조항을 준수해야 합니다.
해설 빈칸 뒤에는 계약 조항 내용이 나오고 있다. 이 문맥에 어울리는 표현으로 in compliance with(~를 준수하여)가 있다.
어휘 provision 조항, 규정 combination 조합, 결합 competence 능숙함 fulfillment 이행, 수행, 완수

5
해석 출장 시, 직원들은 250달러를 초과하는 지출에 대해서는 해당 부서 관리자의 허가를 받아야 한다.
해설 출장비에 대해서 허가를 받아야 한다는 문맥이 나오는데, 4개의 선택지 중에서 exceed(초과하다)는 '250달러를 초과하는 비용에 대해 허락을 구해야 한다'는 의미를 만들어주므로 정답은 (A)이다.
어휘 permission 허락 expenditure 지출, 비용, 경비 excel 뛰어나다, 탁월하다 interrupt 방해하다, 가로막다

6
해석 가장 싼 요금으로 비행기 표를 구하려면 출국 전 적어도 60일 전에 표를 구입해야 한다.
해설 ⟨before+명사구⟩ 앞에 60 days, 3 months 등의 표현이 오면 '60일 전에', '3개월 전에' 등의 의미로 쓰일 수 있다.

7
해석 우리 회사의 새 대표 이사는 시내에 있는 Civic 센터 강당에서 7월 17일 금요일에 모든 회사원들 앞에서 연설을 할 것이다.
해설 address는 '형식을 갖춘 연설을 하다'의 의미가 있으며, address a meeting[conference](회의에서 연설하다)와 같이 쓰일 수 있다.
어휘 auditorium 강당 inform 알리다, 통지하다

8
해석 회사에서 5년 이상의 경험이 있는 모든 직원들은 회사의 승진에 특혜를 받을 것이다.
해설 (A) 특혜 (B) 대우; 치료 (C) 이전 (D) 양
어휘 experience 경험 promotion 승진

9
해석 우리 회사는 현재 30억 달러 이상의 세계 판매량을 가지고 있으며, 현재는 소비자들을 위한 피부 관리 제품의 선두 주자이다.
해설 빈칸은 부사 자리인데, '현재 선두를 유지하고 있다'는 의미가 자연스러우므로 정답은 (B)이다.
어휘 consumer 소비자 eagerly 열심히, 간절히

10
해석 관리자급이나 더 높은 자리에 지원하는 지원자들은 적어도 학사 학위는 있어야 한다.
해설 빈칸 뒤에는 지원자들이 갖춰야 할 자격이 나오고 있다. 따라서 문맥상 required가 적절하다. ⟨be required + to부정사⟩는 '~하는 것이 요구되다'라는 뜻을 가진 표현이다.
어휘 applicant 지원자 at least 적어도, 최소한 bachelor's degree 학사 학위 submit 제출하다

11
해석 그 회사는 노조 규약에 대한 협상을 직접 담당하도록 John Brenan을 노동 위원회의 새로운 부회장으로 막 임명하였다.
해설 빈칸 앞에는 직책 이름이, 뒤에는 소속 단체가 나온다. 따라서 주어진 빈칸은 소속을 나타내는 전치사 of를 써야 한다.
어휘 appoint 임명하다 vice president 부회장 union contract 노동조합 규약 negotiation 협상

12
해석 우리 회사의 봄 창고 정리 세일은 이달 말까지 35% 할인된 가격으로 진행될 것이다.
해설 전치사 문제. 명사인 the end of this month 앞에 올 수 있는 전치사를 골라야 하는 문제이며 의미적으로 '~까지'를 의미하는 단어인 until을 써야 한다.
어휘 clearance sale 창고 정리 세일 merchandise 상품

13
해석 John Davis는 소송을 당사자의 합의 하에 해결하였다고 공표하였다.
해설 settle(해결하다)은 a lawsuit와 함께 결합해서 '소송을 해결하다'라는 의미를 나타낼 수 있다.
어휘 lawsuit 소송 out of court 당사자끼리 합의하여

14

해석 우리 회사의 제품 라인의 확장은 우리의 친환경 상품의 판매를 250% 만큼 올릴 것이라 예상된다.

해설 판매를 늘리려면 제품 라인을 확장(expansion)해야 하므로 정답은 (D)이다.

15

해석 주립 소비자 불만 신고센터는 우리의 경쟁사의 상품에 있는 배터리가 불을 낼 소지가 있다고 발표하였다.

해설 (A) 다르다 (B) 발표하다 (C) 취소하다 (D) 지탱하다

어휘 competitor 경쟁자 catch on fire 불붙다

DAY 14
본문 p.286

1 (D)	2 (D)	3 (C)	4 (C)	5 (A)
6 (D)	7 (A)	8 (B)	9 (C)	10 (A)
11 (D)	12 (B)	13 (B)	14 (D)	15 (A)

1

해석 우리의 가구를 홍보하는 새로운 마케팅 프로그램이 통하고 있다는 것은 이달에 1,200만개 이상의 상품이 팔림으로 명백해졌다.

해설 (A) 밝은 (B) 바쁜 (C) 적절한 (D) 명백한

어휘 promote 홍보하다 work 효과 있다 adequate 충분한, 적절한

2

해석 우리 고객은 Oasis 호텔의 손님으로서 그가 투숙한 호텔 방과 고객 서비스에 대해 매우 불만스러워 하였다.

해설 고객(client)이 호텔 방 및 서비스에 대해 불만스러워했다(dissatisfied)는 내용이 자연스러우므로 정답은 (D)이다.

어휘 client 고객 customer service 고객 서비스 impulsive 충동적인 overstate 과장하다

3

해석 우리의 동유럽 상점들은 유럽의 경제 위기로 인해 전체적인 판매의 하락을 보고해 왔다.

해설 economic crisis(경제 위기)로 인해서 생겨날 수 있는 것은 판매의 하락(decline)이므로 정답은 (C)이다.

어휘 overall 전반적인 Eurozone 유로화를 사용하는 유럽 연합 국가 economic crisis 경제 위기 rejection 거절, 거부 denial 부인, 거부, 부정 negation 정반대, 부정

4

해석 열대 기후 덕분에 남아메리카는 미국에 있는 우리의 커피 프랜차이즈들에게 가장 큰 커피의 공급자이다.

해설 (A) 능력 (B) 연습 (C) 공급원 (D) 그룹, 무리

어휘 tropical 열대의 climate 기후 franchise 프랜차이즈

5

해석 소비자 사생활 정책은 소비자가 요청할 경우 메일 발송 리스트에서 그들의 이름을 지워야 한다고 명시한다.

해설 소비자의 사생활 보호 정책이라는 문맥상 소비자의 이름이 메일링 리스트에서 삭제되어야(removed) 의미가 자연스러우므로 정답은 (A)이다.

어휘 privacy 사생활 policy 정책 mailing list 메일 발송 리스트 request 요청하다 replace 대체하다

6

해석 직원들은 시스템의 하자를 보고하는 데 필요한 절차들을 가르쳐주는 메모를 읽어야 한다.

해설 (A) 창조하다 (B) 통보하다 (C) 다르다 (D) 가르쳐주다

어휘 discrepancy 차이, 불일치

7

해석 우리 노동 위원회의 새로운 부회장은 노동 교섭자로 일한 25년의 경험으로 노사 관계법에 매우 익숙하다.

해설 familiarity(익숙함)를 수식할 수 있는 형용사를 고르는 문제이다. broad는 '폭 넓은'의 의미를 가진 형용사로 정답은 (A)이다.

8

해석 우리의 손전등을 위급한 상황에서 사용하라고 권하기도 하지만, 우리 제품은 원래는 일상생활에 사용하도록 디자인되었다.

해설 (A) 자주 (B) 원래 (C) 숫자상으로 (D) 독립적으로

어휘 recommend 추천하다 emergency 비상 상황

9

해석 우리 회사는 재생 가능 에너지와 울트라 축전지에 관한 폭넓은 지식을 가진 기계 공학자를 찾고 있다.

해설 (A) 의견 (B) 능력 (C) 지식 (D) 수집가

어휘 comprehensive 포괄적인 capacitor 축전지 collector 수집가

10

해석 우리 회사는 더 이상 사용하지 않는 여분의 장비를 팔기 위해 최저가 없는 경매를 실시할 것이다.

해설 빈칸 뒤의 that is no longer being used가 정답의 단서이다. 더 이상 사용하지 않는다는 것은 과잉되었기(surplus) 때문일 것이므로 정답은 (A)이다.

어휘 reserve (경매에서의) 최저 가격 sell off ~를 싸게 팔아 치우다 lengthy 너무 긴, 장황한 opportune 적절한, 시의 적절한 brief 짧은, 잠시 동안의

11

해석 직원들은 매주 복사기의 롤러와 드럼을 깨끗이 청소해야 하는데 왜냐하면 이것이 기기들의 수명을 연장시킬 것이기 때문이다.

해설 기계 부품을 청소하는 것은 기계의 수명을 연장시켜(prolong) 줄 것이기 때문에 정답은 (D)이다.

어휘 persist 끈질기게 계속하다 endure 견디다, 참다 enlarge 확대하다, 확장하다

12
- 해석: 직원에게 주는 매우 높은 급여와 혜택을 갖춘 우리 회사의 보수는 전체 산업을 통틀어 최고 중 하나이다.
- 해설: (A) 흥미 (B) 혜택 (C) 제어 (D) 힘
- 어휘: compensation 보상

13
- 해석: 우리의 디지털 카메라는 생산 과정에서 많은 기계 부품을 필요로 하지 않는 새로운 최첨단 기술을 이용하여 개발되었다.
- 해설: (A) 반응 (B) 기술 (C) 결합 (D) 목표
- 어휘: state-of-the-art 최첨단의

14
- 해석: 유통 부서의 부장은 텍사스에 있는 우리의 새로운 공장의 공급망 계획을 검토하였고 그것을 승인하였다.
- 해설: 어떤 계획을 승인(approve)하기 전에는 먼저 검토(review)하는 것이 필요하므로 정답은 (D)이다.
- 어휘: vice president 부회장, 부사장 supply chain 공급망

15
- 해석: 판매 부서의 부장은 이미 샌프란시스코로 가는 것을 예약해 놨으므로 항공편 예약이 마감된 것은 문제가 되지 않았다.
- 해설: 비행기 표 예약이 이미 마감된 것이 문제가 되지 않은 것은 이미 (already) 예약을 완료해 놓았기 때문이다. 정답은 (A)이다.
- 어휘: booked solid(=fully booked) 모두 매진된

DAY 15
본문 p.288

1 (B)	2 (B)	3 (A)	4 (B)	5 (B)
6 (A)	7 (B)	8 (B)	9 (A)	10 (A)
11 (D)	12 (C)	13 (D)	14 (B)	15 (B)

1
- 해석: 우리 회사는 북아메리카 시장에서 100만 개의 LED 전구를 팔겠다는 이번 해의 판매 목적을 아직도 달성하지 못했다.
- 해설: 현재완료의 부정문에서 쓰일 수 있는 부사들로 still, yet등이 있는데 둘 다 '아직'이라는 뜻이지만 yet의 경우 문장 뒤나 have[has] not 뒤에 나올 수 있으므로 빈칸에 올 수 있는 말은 still이다.
- 어휘: reach 도달하다 unit (상품의 개수 단위) 한 개

2
- 해석: 직원 라운지에서 금요일 오전 8시에 신입 사원 환영회가 있을 것이다.
- 해설: (A) 소원을 빌다 (B) 환영하다 (C) 주다 (D) 보다
- 어휘: lounge 라운지, 휴게실

3
- 해석: 저희는 모든 직원에게 판매와 관련된 전문성 개발 세미나에 참석하기를 요청합니다. 선 예약이 필요합니다.
- 해설: 세미나에 참석하기 위해서는 먼저 등록(registration)이 필요할 것이므로 정답은 (A)이다.
- 어휘: enroll 등록하다, 명부에 올리다 influence 영향 operation 운영 significance 중요성, 의의

4
- 해석: 마케팅 부서의 부장은 이번 연도의 우리의 가전 제품의 판매에 대해 매우 낙관적이다.
- 해설: (A) 의욕이 있는 (B) 낙관적인 (C) 선견지명이 있는 (D) 자신 있게 행동하는
- 어휘: regarding ~에 관하여 home appliance 가전 제품

5
- 해석: 우리 회사는 20년 넘게 에너지 절약 소비자 상품에 있어서 선두주자가 되어 왔다.
- 해설: 문장의 시제는 현재 완료(계속적 용법)이며 뒤에 기간(over twenty years)이 나오므로 기간을 나타내는 전치사 for가 나와야 한다.
- 어휘: consumer product 소비자 상품

6
- 해석: 우리의 새로운 향수의 무료 샘플을 받은 모든 소비자들은 우리 상품에 대해 간단한 설문을 하도록 요청받는다.
- 해설: survey(설문 조사)에 대해 응답하다(answer)라는 내용이 나와야 자연스러우므로 정답은 (A)이다. respond나 reply는 to가 필요하다.
- 어휘: complimentary 무료의 perfume 향수

7
- 해석: 최고의 고객 서비스를 보증하기 위해, 모든 직원은 이메일을 주기적으로 확인하고 답장해야 한다.
- 해설: 양질의 고객 서비스를 위해서는 주기적으로(regularly) 메일에 응답을 해야 한다는 내용이 자연스러우므로 정답은 (B)이다.
- 어휘: insure 보장하다 officially 공식적으로 evenly 균등하게

8
- 해석: 모든 신입 사원은 우리 회사의 표준 운용 절차에 대한 일주일간의 교육 수업에 참석하도록 요청받는다.
- 해설: 빈칸 뒤의 class와 함께 결합할 수 있는 동사를 찾아야 한다. '참석하다'라는 의미의 attend가 가장 적절하다.
- 어휘: recruit 신입 사원; 신병 standard 표준의 occur 일어나다, 발생하다 contain ~이 들어있다(함유하다)

9
- 해석: 항공사 직원과 승객의 적절한 비율은 대략 200명의 승객당 1명의 직원이다.
- 해설: (A) 대략 (B) 간단히 (C) 빠르게 (D) 예측할 수 없이

10
- 해석: 주요 공항에 항공편에 대한 수요가 증가함에 따라, 시는 추가적인 활주로를 만들기로 결정하였다.
- 해설: 추가적인 활주로를 건설하는 것은 항공편에 대한 수요가 증가

(increased)했기 때문이므로 정답은 (A)이다.
어휘 elect ~하기로 결정하다 additional 추가적인 runway 활주로 involve 포함하다, 관련 있다

11
해석 모든 직원은 매일 판매 영수증을 외상 매출 관리 부서에 제출해야 한다.
해설 submit(제출하다)의 목적어로 네 개의 선택지 중 receipts(영수증)가 가장 자연스러우므로 정답은 (D)이다.
어휘 submit 제출하다 account receivable 외상 판매[매출] (계정), 미수금

12
해석 공항은 새 레스토랑과 터미널, 티켓 카운터, 짐 찾는 곳을 포함하여 상당한 개조 공사를 하였다.
해설 (A) 성숙한 (B) 생산하는 (C) 상당한 (D) 소모품의
어휘 undergo 겪다 renovation 개조 공사 mature 성숙한, 성숙해지다 consumable 소비재의

13
해석 우리는 세미나 참석을 위해 영업부와 함께 Los Angeles로 가고 싶은 관심 있는 직원을 초대합니다.
해설 along with ~와 함께
어휘 commercial sales 영업부, 판매부

14
해석 우리 회사의 본부는 1976년 5월에 처음 설립되었을 때부터 New York에 위치하고 있다.
해설 주절의 시제는 현재 완료(계속적 용법)이고 빈칸 뒤에 회사 본부가 설립된 시기가 나오고 있다. 따라서 '~이래로 계속 ~했다'라는 의미가 되도록 since가 나와야 한다.
어휘 headquarters 본부 initial 처음의 found 설립하다, 세우다

15
해석 우리는 8월 12일에 있을 국제 대체 에너지 컨퍼런스에 참석하기 위해 일본의 Tokyo로 갈 것이다.
해설 go on a trip to: ~로 여행을 가다
어휘 alternative energy 대체 에너지

DAY 16
본문 p.290

1 (D)	2 (C)	3 (B)	4 (A)	5 (C)
6 (B)	7 (D)	8 (C)	9 (C)	10 (C)
11 (C)	12 (A)	13 (B)	14 (D)	15 (A)

1
해석 우리 회사는 외부에서 고용을 하기 전에 회사 내부의 직원들에게 승진 기회를 제공하자는 신념이 있다.

해설 (A) 발생 (B) 특정한 때, 행사 (C) 행동 (D) 기회
어휘 promotional 홍보의, 승진의

2
해석 우리는 유럽 판매 사무실의 이전 요구를 6월 말에 들어줄 것이며 이때 모든 이전 서류들이 검토될 것이다.
해설 request(요구)와 어울리는 동사를 찾아야 하는 문제이다. accept a request는 '요구를 받아들이다'라는 뜻으로 쓰일 수 있으므로 정답은 (C)이다.
어휘 transfer 이전, 이동 review 검토하다 renovate 개조 공사를 하다

3
해석 우리 고객들은 우리의 상품과 고객 서비스에 매우 만족하고 이는 우리의 최근 소비자 설문에 반영되고 있다.
해설 주어진 문장은 수동태인데, 수동태에서 행위자를 나타내는 전치사는 주로 by(~에 의해서)를 사용한다.
어휘 be satisfied with ~에 만족하다 reflect 반사하다, 반영하다

4
해석 에어컨 계약자에게 들은 가장 최근 소식은 Austin 공장의 냉각 시스템 설치가 5월 21일까지 끝날 것이란 내용이다.
해설 news를 수식할 수 있는 형용사를 찾아야 한다. latest news는 '최근 소식'이라는 의미로 쓰일 수 있는 표현이다.
어휘 contractor 계약자 complete 완료하다 immediate 즉각적인 constant 끊임없는

5
해석 장비와 사람의 부족 때문에 Albers로의 화물 배송이 지연되었다.
해설 빈칸 뒤에 나온 장비와 인력의 부족은 설비 지체의 원인이 되며, 전치사가 들어가야 할 자리이므로 문맥상 due to가 정답이 된다.
어휘 delay 지체, 지연 shortage 부족 in that ~이므로, ~라는 점에서 as for ~에 대해 말하자면 even so 그렇기는 하지만

6
해석 운송부는 모든 발송 소포를 다음날 도착하는 특급으로 보냄으로써 발송에 우선순위를 둔다.
해설 place a priority on: ~에 우선순위를 두다
어휘 ship 배송하다 shipment 배송 outbound 떠나는, 나가는 overnight 밤사이에, 매우 빠른 credit 신용

7
해석 우리의 두 개의 새로운 공장들의 건설로, 확실히 미국에서 납품을 하는 데 가장 높은 등급의 신뢰성을 얻을 수 있을 것이다.
해설 rate(등급)과 결합해서 쓰일 수 있는 명사를 골라야 하는데 선택지 중에서 reliability(신뢰성)은 a high rate of reliability(높은 등급의 신뢰성)과 같이 쓸 수 있다.
어휘 obligation 의무 determination 투지, 결정

8

해석 우리 회사는 Seattle에서 녹색에너지 축제를 주최할 것이고 이는 Seahawks Stadium에서 열릴 것이다.

해설 (A) 머물다 (B) 참고하다 (C) 개최하다, 열다 (D) 가다

어휘 refer 조회하다, 맡기다, 언급하다

9

해석 텔레비전에서 하는 새로운 광고와 마케팅 캠페인 덕분에 우리의 태양광을 사용하는 비상 가로등의 판매가 눈에 띄게 증가하였다.

해설 increase(증가하다)를 수식할 수 있는 부사를 찾아야 한다. 선택지 중에서 dramatically(급격한)가 가장 적절하다.

어휘 emergency 비상 accidentally 우연히 expressively 의미심장하게 eagerly 열심히, 간절히

10

해석 이제 의학 공부를 하고자 하는 학생은 지방에서 10년 동안 일하는 것에 동의할 경우 새로운 대출 프로그램을 이용할 수 있다.

해설 공부를 하고 싶은 학생들에게 대출(financial assistance) 프로그램이 제공될 것이므로 정답은 (C)이다.

어휘 financial assistance 대출, 융자 rural 시골 지역의 association 협회 statement 성명, 진술

11

해석 회사는 공항에서 컨벤션 센터까지 이동 수단이 필요한 모든 직원들을 위해 교통편을 준비할 것이다.

해설 arrange for: (편의를 위해서) ~을 마련하다, 준비하다

어휘 ride 타기, 탑승 convention center 컨벤션 센터

12

해석 연방 정부의 규정에 따라 비행기 조종석에는 오직 자격증이 있는 승무원만 들어가게 허락된다.

해설 규정(regulations)에 따라서 자격을 갖춘(certified) 사람만 조종실에 입장이 허용된다(permitted)는 내용이 자연스러우므로 정답은 (A)이다.

어휘 in compliance with ~에 따라 federal 연방의 cockpit 조종석 associate 연상하다, 어울리다

13

해석 유통 부서의 부장은 우리 상품의 배송을 위해 상당히 향상된 유통망을 구축했음을 발표하였다.

해설 network와 결합해서 쓰일 수 있는 명사를 찾아야 한다. distribution network는 '유통망'이라는 의미로 쓰일 수 있는 합성어이다.

어휘 exception 예외 distribution 배급, 분포 repetition 반복

14

해석 우리 회사의 대표 이사는 총 150만 달러가 자선기금으로 보내졌다고 발표하였다.

해설 150만 달러의 돈을 자선 단체에 '줬다(give)'라는 의미인데, that절 이하가 수동태이므로 give의 과거분사형 given이 들어가야 한다.

어휘 charity 자선 단체

15

해석 비자 발급 조건이 까다로워서 대사관은 그들의 나라에서 일하고자 지원한 사람들 중 적어도 30%를 거절하였다.

해설 까다로운 요구 조건 때문에 30%의 지원자를 '거절하다(reject)'라는 의미가 되어야 하므로 정답은 (A)이다.

어휘 tight 단호한, 엄격한 applicant 지원자 escape 달아나다, 탈출하다 object 반대하다

DAY 17

본문 p.292

1 (C)	2 (A)	3 (C)	4 (C)	5 (D)
6 (D)	7 (A)	8 (C)	9 (D)	10 (C)
11 (B)	12 (A)	13 (C)	14 (A)	15 (B)

1

해석 발송과 수취 담당 부서는 각 부품들이 에어캡 포장재로 분리되어 포장된 경우 손해 배상 청구가 더 낮다는 것을 발견했다.

해설 손해 배상 청구가 낮았다는 문맥에 비춰볼 때 에어캡 포장재로 별도로 (separately) 포장했다는 내용이 자연스러우므로 정답은 (C)이다.

어휘 damage claim 손해 배상 청구 component 요소, 부품 wrap 싸다, 포장하다 jointly 공동으로 diversely 다양하게 partially 부분적으로

2

해석 월례회의가 다가오는 공휴일 때문에 일주일 미뤄졌다.

해설 문맥상 회의 일정이 휴일 때문에 연기된(postponed) 것이므로 정답은 (A)이다.

어휘 monthly meeting 월례회의 upcoming 다가오는

3

해석 사원 라운지를 넓히는 일을 맡은 종합 건설업자가 프로젝트를 위해 150만 달러의 견적서를 발급하였다.

해설 프로젝트에 들어가는 예상 비용을 나타낼 수 있는 단어를 찾아야 한다. 문맥상 estimate(견적서)가 가장 적절하다.

어휘 general contractor 종합 건설업자 in charge of ~를 맡은 expand 확장하다 issue 발급하다 expectation 기대, 예상 emphasis 강조 elimination 제거

4

해석 우리 회사는 Oakland 컨벤션 센터에서 모든 직원을 위한 파티를 열어 창립 25주년을 축하하는 자리를 가질 것이다.

해설 전 직원을 위한 파티를 열어서 25주년을 축하하는(celebrate) 자리를 마련한다는 내용이 자연스러우므로 정답은 (C)이다.

어휘 celebration 축하 memorization 암기, 기억

5
해석 우리 상품은 견고하게 제작되며 고강도 플라스틱으로 감싸져 있어서 매우 믿을 만하다.
해설 견고하게 제작되고 충격에 강한 플라스틱으로 만들어져 있으므로 빈칸에는 reliable(믿을 만한)이 가장 적절하다.
어휘 house 보관하다, 수용하다 high impact plastics 고강도 플라스틱 earnest 성실한 tactful 요령 있는

6
해석 많은 저명한 연예인들이 우리의 서비스에 대해 높은 만족도를 표시했다.
해설 빈칸은 명사인 celebrities(유명 인사)를 수식할 수 있는 형용사 자리이며 의미적으로 '저명한'의 의미를 나타내는 notable이 적합하다.
어휘 celebrity 유명 인사, 유명 연예인 definite 분명한 customary 습관적인, 관례적인 elaborate 정교한

7
해석 낮은 경제적 성장에도 불구하고, 이어지는 해에는 연구와 개발에 대한 투자가 계속될 것이다.
해설 빈칸은 명사 year를 수식하는 형용사를 써야 하는 자리이고 의미적으로 '뒤이은'을 의미하는 형용사 subsequent를 써야 한다. 빈칸 앞에 the가 없이 in이 왔으므로 next는 올 수 없고 followed는 following이 되어야 하므로 오답이다.
어휘 economic growth 경제 성장 follow 따르다

8
해석 대표 이사는 유통과 마케팅, 연구 개발 부서들 사이의 원활한 의사소통의 중요성을 인식하고 있다.
해설 여러 팀 사이에서 일어나는 의사소통의 중요성에 대한 내용이므로 셋 이상의 여럿 사이를 나타내는 전치사 among이 가장 적절하다.
어휘 appreciate 인정하다, 인식하다 importance 중요성 communication 의사소통 logistics 유통

9
해석 모든 직원은 회사 건물에 있을 때 사원증을 항상 보이게 착용해야 한다.
해설 '(옷이나 장신구 등 몸에 걸치는 것을) 착용하다'라는 의미의 동사는 wear를 사용한다.
어휘 visibly 눈에 띄게 on company property 회사의 소유지에서

10
해석 우리의 목표는 우리 분야의 세계 시장에서 가장 높은 위치를 확보하는 것이라고 웹 사이트에 나와 있다.
해설 시장에서 높은 지위를 확보한다는 내용이 자연스러우므로 position (위치, 지위)가 가장 자연스럽다.
어휘 secure 지키다, 보호하다 field 분야

11
해석 현재 우리 회사는 멕시코와 카리브 국가들을 포함한 북아메리카에서 블루투스 기술 분야의 선두 주자이다.
해설 주어진 문장의 빈칸은 명사 앞에 쓰이는 전치사의 자리이며 의미적으로 '~을 포함하여'의 의미로 쓰여야 하므로 including을 쓴다.

어휘 presently 현재, 지금 Caribbean States 카리브 국가들 somewhat 어느 정도, 약간 regarding ~에 관해서

12
해석 회사 간부의 보수는 1년에 2,500만 달러의 가치이다. 그러나 투자의 가치가 있다.
해설 '~할 만한 가치가 있다'라는 표현은 worth를 사용한다. worth는 뒤에 목적어를 취할 수 있는 형용사로 worth the investment는 '투자할 만한 가치가 있다'라는 뜻이다.
어휘 executive 이사, 중역 pay package 보수, 급여 deem ~로 여기다 valued 값어치 있는 prize 소중하게 여기다

13
해석 30일 이상 지속적으로 근무한 직원은 새로운 회사 적금에 가입할 수 있는 자격이 생긴다.
해설 (A) (장비를) 제공하다 (B) 공급하다 (C) ~할 자격이 생기다 (D) 배열하다; 마련하다
어휘 continuous 지속적인 savings plan 저축 상품

14
해석 우리 회사 직원들의 건강을 증진시키기 위해, 회사는 모든 직원과 그들의 가족을 위해 무료로 체육관 회원권을 제공한다.
해설 체육관 회원권을 무료로 제공하는 것은 건강(health)을 증진시키기 위한 것이므로 정답은 (A)이다.
어휘 dimension 크기, 규모 substance 물질

15
해석 회사가 직원 저축 제도에 맞는 수당을 지급하였을 때 회사는 각각의 직원들에게 이메일로 알릴 것이다.
해설 직원들에게 이메일을 통해서 알린다(notify)는 의미여야 하므로 정답은 (B)이다.
어휘 via e-mail 메일을 통해서 present 제시하다

DAY 18 본문 p.294

1 (D)	2 (C)	3 (D)	4 (A)	5 (B)
6 (C)	7 (D)	8 (A)	9 (A)	10 (C)
11 (B)	12 (B)	13 (B)	14 (B)	15 (D)

1
해석 회사의 제도는 같은 부서에 친척인 사원들의 고용을 금지한다. 이 제도는 고용인 매뉴얼에 있다.
해설 (A) 성취할 수 있는 (B) 비슷한 (C) 흥미 있는 (D) 친척의
어휘 forbid 금지하다 division 부서 manual 매뉴얼, 지침서

2
해석 우리는 신용 카드 회사에 수수료를 내야 하기 때문에, 신용 카드 대신

현금으로 지불하는 모든 고객에게 다음 구매에 5퍼센트의 할인을 제공하고 있다.

해설 (A) 배달 (B) 제약 (C) 할인 (D) 갱신

어휘 commission 수수료, 중개료

3

해설 모든 직원은 회사가 후원하는 직원 주식 옵션 프로그램에 등록해야 하고, 그것으로 직원은 매년 주식 보너스를 받게 될 것이다.

해설 enroll in ~: ~에 등록하다

어휘 stock 주식 admit 시인하다, 자백하다 subscribe 구독하다

4

해설 화재 경보가 울리면, 모든 직원은 60초 이내에 빌딩에서 나가야 한다.

해설 빈칸은 명사 sixty seconds 앞에 쓸 수 있는 전치사를 묻는 자리이며 의미적으로 '~안에'를 의미하는 within을 써야 한다.

어휘 fire alarm 화재 경보

5

해설 회사는 프랑스에 새로운 소매 할인점을 찾고 있고 우리의 현지 직원이 전략을 세우고 있다.

해설 '새로운 소매 할인점을 찾는다(seek)'라는 의미가 적절하므로 정답은 (B)이다. look은 바로 뒤에 목적어를 취하지 못하고 for와 같은 전치사가 필요한 동사이다.

어휘 strategy 전략 inquire 묻다, 질문하다

6

해설 판매 보고서는 출력되어 현재 프랑스 백화점을 방문하고 있는 판매 부서의 손에 들려져 있다.

해설 출력될 수 있는 것은 보고서(reports)이므로 정답은 (C)이다.

어휘 at this time 현재, 지금 resource 자원

7

해설 홍보팀 부장은 우리 회사에서 우리의 합병 제안서에 관한 질문에 답할 수 있는 권한이 있는 유일한 사람이다.

해설 빈칸 뒤에 나오는 〈to+명사구〉와 결합해서 쓰일 수 있는 동사를 찾아야 한다. '어떤 질문에 대해서도(to any questions) 응답한다(respond)'라는 내용이 되어야 하므로 정답은 (D)이다.

8

해설 모든 매니저들은 자격증을 받기 위해 필요한 발표 시험을 통과할 수 있다고 기대하고 있다.

해설 be required와 명사(certification) 사이에 빈칸이 있으므로 이 자리는 전치사 자리이다. 문맥상 '자격증을 위해서 필요하다'라는 의미가 되어야 하므로 전치사 for가 가장 적절하다.

어휘 manager 관리자, 매니저

9

해설 내부 감사 직위의 지원자들은 자격이 충분하고 이것은 우리 회사에게 매우 큰 이득이다.

해설 빈칸은 주어 자리인데 보어 자리의 형용사가 well qualified(자격이 잘 갖춰진)이므로 빈칸에 가장 적절한 단어는 applicants(지원자)이다.

어휘 auditor 회계감사관

10

해설 인사부 부장은 모든 매니저에게 월요일에 있는 인종 차별 방지 워크숍에 참여하라고 지시하였다.

해설 빈칸은 '지시하다'라는 의미의 단어를 써야 하므로 instructed를 쓴다. demand(요구하다)는 5형식을 취하지 않고 뒤에 to부정사나 that절을 취하므로 정답이 될 수 없다.

어휘 anti-discrimination 인종 차별 반대(의) intend 의도하다

11

해설 모든 직원은 공항에서 탑승구로 갈 때 여권을 소지하고 있어야 한다.

해설 (A) ~이므로, ~이래로 (B) ~할 때 (C) 충분히 (D) 이후에

어휘 boarding gate 탑승구

12

해설 런던 세미나에 참석하는 직원이 많기 때문에 비행기의 일등석을 쉽게 채울 수 있을 것이다.

해설 빈칸은 동사 fill up을 수식해 줄 수 있는 부사를 써야 하는 자리이고 의미적으로 '쉽게'라는 단어를 써야 하므로 easily를 써야 한다.

어휘 fill up 가득 채우다 softly 부드럽게

13

해설 화물 운송 영업 부서의 부장은 화물 운송업의 이점에 대해 발표할 것이다.

해설 give a presentation on: ~에 대해서 발표하다

어휘 cargo 화물 administration 관리, 행정 profession 직업, 종사자들

14

해설 안전 위원회에 연락을 하여서 혈인성 병원균의 정보 차트의 복사본을 추가적으로 받을 수 있다.

해설 빈칸은 명사 copies(복사본)를 수식해 줄 수 있는 형용사를 써야 하는 자리이다. 네 개의 선택지 중 additional(추가적인)이 가장 적절하다.

어휘 bloodborne pathogen 혈인성(혈액으로 감염되는) 병원균 obtain 얻다

15

해설 화물 부서장은 승객 운송 사업만큼 화물 운송 사업을 촉진시키는 것의 여러 장점들을 열거하였다.

해설 (A) 지지하는 (B) 망친 (C) 자발적인 (D) 많은

어휘 cargo 화물 list 열거하다 advantage 이점, 이익 promote 촉진하다

DAY 19

본문 p.296

1 (C)	2 (B)	3 (D)	4 (C)	5 (B)
6 (D)	7 (C)	8 (D)	9 (C)	10 (B)
11 (C)	12 (B)	13 (C)	14 (D)	15 (A)

1
- 해석 모든 직원은 안전하고 신속하게 건물에서 대피할 수 있도록 지침대로 정확히 비상 탈출 계획에 따라야 한다.
- 해설 지침을 정확하게(exactly) 따라야 신속하고 안전한 대피가 가능할 것이므로 정답은 (C)이다.
- 어휘 emergency exit plan 비상 탈출 계획 prompt 신속한 evacuation 피난 doubly 두 배로 nearly 거의

2
- 해석 그 분야에서의 수년간의 경험을 고려했을 때, Chae 씨는 어려운 고객들의 불평을 다루기에 적합한 사람이다.
- 해설 (A) 흩어지다 (B) 다루다 (C) 연장하다 (D) 맞추다
- 어휘 demanding customer 까다로운 고객

3
- 해석 즉시 빌딩에서 나오지 않는 모든 직원은 자신의 부상에 개인적으로 책임을 져야 할 것이다.
- 해설 빈칸은 형용사 responsible을 수식하는 부사가 와야 하며 의미적으로 '개인적으로 책임을 진다'는 의미가 적절하므로 빈칸에는 personally를 써야 한다.
- 어휘 injury 부상 relevantly 관련되어 realistically 현실적으로 prosperously 번영하여

4
- 해석 모든 직원은 혈액으로 옮겨지는 병원균에 대한 교육을 마쳐야 하는데 이것은 혈액으로 인한 감염이 발생할 경우 직원의 안전을 보장해 준다.
- 해설 목적어 training과 함께 쓰일 수 있는 동사를 선택해야 한다. '안전을 위해서 훈련 과정을 마쳐야(complete)한다'는 내용이 적절하므로 정답은 (C)이다.
- 어휘 insure 보증하다, 안전하게 하다 contamination 감염

5
- 해석 혈인성 병원균 교육을 끝낸 후에 모든 직원은 비상 시의 올바른 처리 방법을 담은 참고 자료의 복사본을 받게 될 것이다.
- 해설 (A) 절차 (B) 복사본 (C) 주제 (D) 말, 암시
- 어휘 blood borne pathogen 혈인성 병원균

6
- 해석 직원의 약 60%가 부서 관리자가 만든 새로운 작업 시간표에 불만이 있는 것으로 밝혀졌다.
- 해설 숫자 앞에 나오는 부사들로는 approximately, nearly, roughly, almost, over, more than, less than 등이 있다.
- 어휘 turn out 드러나다, 밝혀지다 be opposed to ~에 반대하다 coincidently 우연히 desperately 절망적으로 genuinely 진정으로

7
- 해석 감독관은 Los Angeles에서 San Francisco까지 이른 항공편을 탔고 곧 도착할 것이다.
- 해설 flight(비행기)와 함께 쓰일 수 있는 동사 중 take는 '~를 타다'는 의미가 있어서 문맥상 적절하다.

8
- 해석 모든 신입 사원들은 오리엔테이션 세션을 위해서 Sierra 룸에 오전 9시까지 정확하게 도착하여야 한다.
- 해설 오리엔테이션에 늦지 않게 정해진 시간에 정확하게 도착해야 한다는 의미이므로 빈칸에는 '(늦지 않게) 정확한 시간에'를 의미하는 promptly를 써야 한다.
- 어휘 session (특정 활동을 위한) 시간 presently 현재, 지금

9
- 해석 항공사는 San Diego와 Tahoe 호수 사이의 경로 지원서가 거절당한 것에 실망하였다.
- 해설 항공사의 경로 지원이 거절당해서 '실망했다(disappointed)'라는 의미가 적절하므로 정답은 (C)이다. happy, sad, disappointed와 같은 감정 형용사 다음에는 이유를 설명하는 that절을 취할 수 있다.
- 어휘 indebted 감사하는, 고마워하는 eliminate 없애다, 제거하다

10
- 해석 매우 존경받는 스트레스 관리 전문가 중 한 명인 Choi 박사는 직장에서의 스트레스를 다룰 수 있는 방법에 대한 일련의 강의를 하기 위해서 우리 회사를 방문할 것이다.
- 해설 (A) 행동 (B) 강의 (C) 운영 (D) 점수; 요점
- 어휘 highly regarded 높은 평가를 받는 expert 전문가

11
- 해석 직원은 항상 자신의 자동차에 유효한 주차 허가증을 보이도록 비치해 놓아야 한다.
- 해설 주차 허가증을 보이도록 전시해 놓아야 한다는 뜻이므로 display가 정답이다.
- 어휘 valid 유효한 vehicle 탈 것

12
- 해석 그 회사는 안전 성적이 항공 산업 분야에서 최고로 높은 기업 중 하나이고 다양한 정부 기관으로부터 안전 표창장을 받았다.
- 해설 문맥상 항공 산업에서 최고의 안전성을 자랑하는 기업 중 하나라는 의미가 되어야 하므로 among이 적절하다.
- 어휘 airline industry 항공 산업 government body 정부 기관

13
- 해석 지방 공무원 중 한 명인 Chae 씨는 올해 우리의 보조금 신청이 시 위원회에 의해서 마침내 승인되었다고 우리에게 알려주었다.

해설 notify + 목적어 + that절: ~에게 ~를 통보하다
어휘 official 공무원, 임원 grant 보조금 assimilate 완전히 이해하다, 소화하다 retaliate 보복하다

14
해설 스포츠 행사에 참가하는 모든 사람들은 주최측이 그 어떤 법적 책임도 없다는 권리 포기 증서에 사인해야 한다.
해설 스포츠 행사에 참여하는 사람(participants)이 권리 포기 각서에 서명을 하는 것이다.
어휘 waiver 권리 포기 증서 absolve 책임 없음을 선언하다 liability 법적 책임 interviewee 인터뷰를 받는 사람

15
해설 이사회는 증가하는 부채의 심각한 문제를 완화하기 위한 계획을 짜기 위해서 이번 토요일에 회의를 할 것이다.
해설 부채 문제를 해결하거나 완화(alleviate)하기 위해서 회의를 소집한다는 내용이 적절하므로 정답은 (A)이다. 고통이나 교통 혹은 문제를 완화시킬 때(줄일 때) 'alleviate'라는 단어를 쓸 수 있다.
어휘 debt 빚, 부채 annihilate 전멸시키다 domesticate 길들이다 refurbish 재단장하다

DAY 20 본문 p.298

1 (B)	2 (D)	3 (D)	4 (A)	5 (B)
6 (B)	7 (B)	8 (A)	9 (A)	10 (B)
11 (C)	12 (A)	13 (C)	14 (C)	15 (C)

1
해설 새로운 제품을 해외 시장에 소개할 때는 문화적 차이를 고려해야 한다.
해설 (A) 폭발하다 (B) 소개하다 (C) 위치시키다 (D) 반복하다

2
해설 채용 후 12개월이 지나면 모든 직원은 연말 보너스를 받을 자격이 생긴다.
해설 be entitled to부정사: ~할 자격을 가지다
어휘 year-end 연말의 engage 사로잡다, 관계를 맺다 ensure 반드시 ~이게 하다

3
해설 Lee 씨는 겨우 몇 달 전에 고용되었는데, 벌써 회사에서 가장 가치 있는 직원 중 한 명이 되었다.
해설 가치 있는 직원을 valuable employee라고 하고 단골 고객을 loyal customer라고 한다.
어휘 abnormal 비정상적인 loyal 충실한, 충직한

4
해설 높은 품질에도 불구하고 Brill의 최신 모델은 고객들에게 가격이 적당하다고 여겨지지 않았다.
해설 affordable은 '구입하기에 가격이 적절한'이라는 의미이다. reasonable도 비슷한 의미이다.
어휘 correctable 정정 가능한 expendable 소모할 수 있는, 보유할 가치가 없는

5
해설 Vohex Energy는 새로운 정유 공장 건설이 완료된 후에 빠른 성장을 예상하고 있다.
해설 complete는 동사와 형용사가 같은 형태이다. 여기서는 보어 자리에 형용사로 완성된(complete)으로 쓰였다.
어휘 experience 겪다, 경험하다 growth 성장 refinery 정제소, 정제 공장 absolute 절대적인 elusive 찾기 힘든 factual 사실에 기반한

6
해설 나빠진 수익률을 상쇄하기 위해서, D&P Electronics는 앞으로 2년간 20%까지 사업 비용을 줄이기로 결정했다.
해설 수익률을 올리려면 이윤을 창출하는 것과 비용(expenses)을 줄이는 방법이 있으므로 정답은 (B)이다.
어휘 offset 상쇄하다 worsen 더 나빠지다 profit margin (총 매출에서 생산 비용을 뺀) 순이익 tax 세금

7
해설 Choi 씨는 회사의 가장 큰 고객과 계약을 끝낸 후에 주목할 만한 진급을 하게 되었다.
해설 promotion의 의미 중에는 '승진'의 뜻이 있는데 이를 수식해 줄 형용사를 찾는 문제이다. significant는 '중요한, 상당한, 엄청난'이라는 뜻으로 빈칸에 적절하다.
어휘 finalize 마무리 짓다 capable 유능한 proficient 능숙한

8
해설 판매 이윤은 SJ Communications가 서비스를 개선한 후로 지난 6개월간 거의 2배가 되었다.
해설 nearly(거의)는 수량 형용사 이외에도 double(2배가 되다), triple(세 배가 되다)과 같은 동사를 수식할 수 있다.
어휘 revenue 수익 revamp 개선하다 invest 투자하다 release 출시하다

9
해설 새 모니터의 생산은 공장 장비의 기계적인 문제 때문에 연기되었다.
해설 기계적인 문제 때문에 생기는 영향 중 하나는 생산이 연기되는 (delayed) 것이다.
어휘 equipment 장비 provide 제공하다

10
해설 필리핀에 있는 회사의 새 생산 공장은 마지막 안전 점검을 통과하고 나면 운영될 것이다.
해설 마지막(final) 검사를 통과해야 운영을 할 수 있으므로 정답은 (B)이다. numerous는 뒤에 복수 명사가 나와야 하므로 정답이 될 수 없다.

어휘 manufacturing plant 제조 공장 operational 운영되는 facility 시설 inspection 검사 confident 자신감 있는, 확신하는 numerous 수많은

11
해석 그 소규모 회사는 직원들이 열심히 일한 덕분에 심각한 경제 침체로부터 회복할 수 있었다.

해설 열심히 일해서 경기 침체에서 회복한다(recover)는 의미가 적절하므로 정답은 (C)이다.

어휘 downturn 감소, 하락 refrain from 자제하다 stem from ~에서 연유하다

12
해석 최근에 개봉한 Fahey 감독의 영화는 한국에서 일어났던 실제 이야기를 근간으로 하고 있다.

해설 be based on: ~을 기반으로 하다.

어휘 release 개봉하다 direct 감독하다 happen 발생하다

13
해석 국민 건강 관리 프로그램에 관한 기사들은 20년 이상 의약 분야에서 일한 전문가들에 의해 작성되었다.

해설 (A) 묘사 (B) 과정 (C) 산업, 분야 (D) 방향

어휘 article 기사 health care 건강 관리 medical 의학의 description 묘사 course 과정 industry 산업 direction 방향

14
해석 Lomax Tech가 몇 년 동안 상대적으로 훌륭한 판매 기록을 가지고 있지만, 여전히 시장 점유율을 늘리기 위해 고전하고 있다.

해설 (A) 거의 ~ 않다 (B) 좀처럼 ~ 않다 (C) 상대적으로 (D) 약간

어휘 struggle 고전하는, 고군분투하는 market share 시장 점유율

15
해석 의약 실험에서 새로운 의약품이 유방암의 위험을 감소시켜 준다는 사실이 증명되었다.

해설 여기서 risk(위험)는 병에 걸릴 확률을 의미한다.

어휘 prove 증명되다 breast cancer 유방암 clinical testing 임상 실험 reaction 반응 residue 잔여물

DAY 01

4. 독해 집중 연습

본문 p.302

1 (B) 2 (C) 3 (C) 4 (A) 5 (A)

1-2

Citrus Uptown 빌라

Citrus Uptown 빌라는 침실 한 개 혹은 두 개짜리 아파트를 임대합니다. 오션 사이드 도심의 중심에 위치한, 이 새로운 20가구의 아파트, 전문가들에 의해서 설계되었습니다. 완벽한 비즈니스 룸과 수영장, 운동시설, 실내 주차장이 이 복합단지 안에 있으며, 이 모든 시설의 이용은 월세에 포함되어 있습니다. 또한 위치도 완벽한데, Pendleton 다리의 아름다운 경치를 볼 수 있고, 걸어서 몇 분 거리에 영화관과 멋진 식당, 아름다운 공원이 있습니다. 우리의 모델 하우스를 직접 와서 보시고, 우리가 당신께 드릴 수 있는 혜택을 알아가세요. 우리의 임대 담당 직원은 매일 당신이 아파트 복합 단지와 견본 주택을 둘러볼 수 있게 해 드릴 준비가 되어 있습니다.

Citrus Uptown 빌라
17 Basilone Way, Oceanside
818-555-1123
www.citrusuptown.com

어휘 situate (건물을) 짓다, 위치시키다 midst 중앙, 한 가운데 residential 거주하기 좋은 diner 작은 식당; 식사하는 손님

1

해석 광고에서 설명하는 것은 무엇인가?
(A) 판매 중인 별장
(B) 아파트 임대
(C) 사무실 이전 서비스
(D) 지역 관광지

해설 광고하는 대상을 묻는 문제는 대부분 지문의 초반에 언급된다. "Citrus Uptown Villas is now renting out one and two-bedroom condominium units"를 보고 아파트를 임대하고 있는 것임을 알 수 있다.

어휘 relocation 이전

2

해석 독자들은 무엇을 하도록 요청 받았는가?
(A) 계약을 체결한다.
(B) 비용을 지불한다.
(C) 장소를 방문한다.
(D) 임대 계약서를 작성한다.

해설 요청 문제(ask, request, demand, recommend)는 대부분 지문의 후반부에 정답을 찾을 수 있으며 "Come and see for yourself our model units"처럼 명령문에서 정답의 힌트가 나온다.

어휘 close a contract 계약을 체결하다 make a payment 비용을 지불하다 lease agreement 임대 계약

3-5

다용도 사무 프린터

다용도 사무 프린터는 소규모 사무실이나 주택 내 작업실에 매우 편리합니다. 프린터들은 소규모 사무실이나 가정용으로 사용하기에 최고의 선택이 될 것입니다. 이것은 프린터가 요구하는 작은 사용 공간 때문입니다. 다용도 프린터는 프린터와 스캐너 복합 기계입니다. 그래서, 선반 공간이 덜 필요하고 이것이 중요한 사무 공간을 다른 용도로 사용할 수 있게 해 줍니다. 저희는 다른 여러 회사의 다용도 프린터를 시험해 보았고, 이 제품들도 매우 성능이 뛰어나고 편리하다는 것을 알게 되었습니다. 하지만 우리는 WGB 프린터가 모든 기능면에서 우월하다는 것도 알게 되었습니다. 선호도에 따른 조사 결과는 아래와 같습니다.

WGB-145 다용도 프린터는 소매가로 149달러이고, 이 제품은 최고의 전국 소매점에서 판매되고 있습니다. 이 스캔 프로세스는 매우 정교한 복사본을 만들어 냈기 때문에 훌륭했습니다. 흑백과 컬러 프린트는 생생하고 이미지가 산뜻했습니다.

NAV 12-1 다용도 프린터는 소매가로 179달러이고, 이 제품은 대부분 온라인에서 팔리고 있습니다. 이 프린터는 전체 기능 면에서는 인상적이지만, 스캐너의 경우 작은 글자가 약간 흐릿하게 보인다는 점에서 실망스러웠습니다.

HTR 12-4 다용도 프린터는 소매가로 99달러이고, 이 제품은 전국 소매점에서 판매됩니다. 대부분의 기능이 만족스럽지만, 잉크 리필 제품의 가격과 프린트 속도가 느린 것은 당황스러웠습니다. 전체 품질에서 3위에 놓겠습니다.

따라서 전체 품질과 평가 면에서 WGB 다용도 프린터를 추천합니다.

어휘 all-in-one 다용도의 footprint (물건이) 차지하는 공간 free up 해방하다, 풀어주다, 해소하다 capable ~할 수 있는, 유능한 overall 전체적인 favorability 선호도 retail for ~ 가격에 팔리다 retailer 소매업자 vivid 생생한 crisp (이미지가) 맑고 산뜻한 blurry 흐릿한, 모호한 take aback 당황하게 하다

3

해석 이 글의 주제는 무엇인가?
(A) 최상의 컴퓨터
(B) 가장 값싼 프린터
(C) 일체형 프린터에 관한 후기
(D) 새로운 컴퓨터 기술

해설 기사의 주제를 묻는 문제로 첫 문단의 맨 마지막 문장에서 "We are listing the test results in order of favorability."라고 말하면서 다용도 복사기의 성능을 비교하고 있다. 따라서 정답은 (C)이다.

4

해석 글쓴이가 추천하는 모델은 무엇인가?
(A) WGB-145
(B) NAV 12-1
(C) HTR 12-4
(D) BTV-126

해설 세부 사항 문제로 질문의 키워드는 "recommended"이다. 해당하는 내용을 지문에서 찾으면 "we did find the WGB Printer superior in overall functions" 부분과 "we suggest the WGB All-in-One Printer for its overall quality and ratings" 부분에서 WGB-145를 추천하고 있음을 알 수 있다.

5

해석 기사에 언급되지 않은 것은 무엇인가?
(A) 한 장당 비용
(B) 인쇄 품질
(C) 스캔 품질
(D) 잉크 리필 비용

해설 간단한 사실 확인 문제로 지문을 모두 읽기보다는 선택지의 키워드를 찾으면서 지문을 읽는 것이 시간을 절약하는 방법이다. (B)는 "The printing of pages in black and white and color were vivid and crisp."에서, (C)는 "The scanning processor was excellent, revealing very detailed copies."에서 (D)는 "we were taken aback by the cost of ink refills"에서 볼 수 있지만, (A)에 관한 내용은 언급된 부분이 없다.

DAY 02

본문 p.304

| 1 (A) | 2 (B) | 3 (D) | 4 (C) | 5 (A) |
| 6 (B) |

1-3

수신: Victoria Beck, 인사 부장
　　　〈victoriabeck@blackandwhite.com〉
발신: Stuart Barney, 대표 이사
　　　〈stuartbarney@blackandwhite.com〉
제목: 구조 조정에 대한 계획

이사회의 협조를 얻어서 저는 전체 회사 구조를 재정립하는 것을 승인합니다. 지난달에, 우리 회사는 뉴욕의 전략적 사업 컨설턴트에 의해서 회계 감사를 받았습니다. 이 감사에서, 컨설턴트들은 회사의 경영 구조를 재조정할 것을 제안했습니다. 그들에 따르면 우리 회사는 상위 경영진이 너무 많은데, 이 계층은 경영과 의사 결정 과정에서 비효율성을 만들어내는 불필요한 관료주의를 만들어낸다는 것입니다. 그래서, 우리는 5명의 부사장 보조 직책을 없애고, 이 직책을 각각의 부서의 부사장 역할로 전환하겠습니다. 이 변화는 6월 15일부터 실시됩니다. 이 변화가 우리 회사를 더욱 간소하게 만들고 이윤을 내도록 만들어 줄 것입니다.

어휘 structural 구조적인 reorganization 재편성, 개편
in collaboration with ~과 협력해서 audit 감사, 세무 조사
upper management 고위 경영진 layer 층, 단계 bureaucracy 관료주의 inefficiency 비효율성 respective 각각의 take place ~이 발생하다 streamlined 간소화된, 능률화된

1

해석 이메일에서 논의되는 사항은 무엇인가?
(A) 회사 구조 조정
(B) 노조와의 협상
(C) 신입 직원 혜택
(D) 직원들의 뉴욕 전근

해설 주제를 묻고 있다. 첫 문장에서 바로 "a plan to reorganize the entire company structure"라고 언급하면서 주제(구조 조정)를 말하고 있다.

어휘 negotiation 협상 labor unions 노동 조합

2

해석 없어질 직책은 무엇인가?
(A) 상담원
(B) 부사장 보조
(C) 사무직
(D) 임원

해설 세부 사항 문제이다. 문제의 키워드는 position, cut이다. "we are cutting five assistant vice president positions"를 찾으면 바로 풀 수 있는 문제이다.

어휘 clerical 사무직의

3

해석 누가 이러한 변화를 건의했는가?
(A) Stuart Barney
(B) 내부 감사원
(C) Victoria Beck
(D) 사업 전략 상담가

해설 세부 사항 문제로 질문의 키워드인 Who와 recommend를 바탕으로 지문에서 내용을 찾으면 "our company underwent an audit by Strategic Business Consultants of New York City."에서 "Strategic Business Consultants"에서 감사를 받은 것을 알 수 있고, 바로 다음 문장 "In the study, the consultants recommended restructuring of the management pyramid of the company."에서 이 컨설턴트들이 이 조언을 한 것을 알 수 있다.

어휘 internal auditor 내부 감사원

4-6

Brother B-112 프린터를 구매해 주셔서 감사합니다. 상자 안에 무료 잉크 카트리지가 들어 있습니다. 이것은 단지 견본 상품이고 정식으로 사용하기 위해 만들어진 것은 아니기 때문에, 빠른 시간 안에 정식 카트리지로 교체하실 것을 권장합니다. www.brotherprinterink.com에서 쉽게 교체용 카트리지를 구매하실 수 있습니다. 귀하가 근무일로 5일 이내에 잉크 카트리지를 못 받으신다면 무상으로 제공할 것을 약속드립니다. 귀하는 특별 고객으로서 잉크의 첫 구매 시 30%의 할인을 받을 자격이 부여됩니다. 간단하게 코드 2213을 주문하실 때 입력해 주세요. 소매점에서 구매하시는 것이 더 편안하시다면, 모든 우수 컴퓨터 기기 판매점에서 구매가 가능합니다. 하지만 대부분의 소매 상점에서는 우리의 회사 할인을 사용하실 수 없다는 것을 알아 두세요.
귀하의 새로운 프린터에 대해서 질문 사항이나 의견이 있으시면, 24시간 언제라도 기술 지원을 받기 위해 799-334-8897로 전화하시거나, 구매나 계좌와 관련해서는 월요일에서 금요일 오전 8시에서 오후 8시까지 799-334-8899로 연락 주세요.

어휘 entitle ~할 자격을 주다 leading 일류의, 선두의 corporate 기업의 technical 기술적인 aid 도움, 원조

4

해석 이 공지 사항은 누구를 위해 작성되었는가?
(A) 기술 보조 부서의 직원들
(B) 컴퓨터 기술자들
(C) 새 프린터 구매자들
(D) 영업부 직원들

해설 For whom으로 시작하는 문제는 이 글을 읽을 독자를 묻는 문제이고 전체 지문 문제이다. 물론 몇몇 경우에는 초반에 바로 정답을 언급하기도 한다. "Thank you for the purchase of a Brother B-112 printer"로 지문을 시작하고 있으므로 프린터기 구매자들을 위한 글임을 알 수 있다.

5
해설 잉크를 주문하는 것에 대해 어떤 약속을 하고 있는가?
(A) 배송 지연 시 상품은 무료이다.
(B) 잉크 카트리지는 1년까지 지속 가능하다.
(C) 영업 판매원은 항시 대기한다.
(D) 기술자들은 즉각 회신을 할 것이다.

해설 "We guarantee that you will have your ink cartridges within 5 working days or you pay nothing." 부분에서 "영업일 기준 5일 이내에 물건을 배달하고 그렇지 않으면 돈을 받지 않겠다."라고 했으므로 정답은 (A)이다.

어휘 last ~이 지속되다 sales representative 판매 직원 all the time 항시 promptly 즉시

6
해설 고객들은 어떻게 할인을 받을 수 있는가?
(A) 전화 한 통으로
(B) 웹 사이트 상 번호를 기입하여
(C) 컴퓨터 용품 매장에서 구매하여
(D) 쿠폰을 제시하여

해설 세부 사항 문제로 discount를 지문에서 찾는다. "you are entitled to a 30 percent discount off" 부분을 먼저 찾고 바로 다음 문장인 "Simply enter the code 2213"을 보고 2213번을 입력하면 되는 것을 알 수 있다.

어휘 present 제시하다

DAY 03
본문 p.306

| 1 (C) | 2 (C) | 3 (A) | 4 (D) | 5 (A) |
| 6 (B) | 7 (A) | | | |

1-3

옛 도시인 St. Pierre에서, 사람들은 정말 까다로운 고객마저도 만족시키는 다양한 행사와 경험들을 찾을 수 있습니다. St. Pierre는 그 지역의 원주민이 된 순례자들이 1725년에 설립했습니다. 1700년대에 설립된 대부분의 예전 건물들은 오늘날에도 구(舊) 시가지 상업 구역에 남아있습니다. 우리는 여행객들에게 먼저 Mill Creek Grainery 방문을 추천합니다. 이 Mill Creek Grainery는 St. Pierre의 설립과 같은 때에 만들어졌습니다. 이 제분소는 곡식을 갈아 밀가루로 만드는 데 수력을 사용합니다. 정말 놀라운 것은 이 제분소가 수백 년 전에 만들어진 같은 체계와 기술에 의해서 오늘날도 여전히 작동하고 있다는 것입니다. 이것은 요즘에 만들어지는 것보다 과거에 만들어진 것들이 훨씬 좋다는 의견을 입증해 줍니다. 그 당시의 도구와 기구들은 오랫동안 쓸 수 있게 만들어 졌는데, 그것은 그 당시 사람들의 삶과 생존이 그 도구에 달려 있었기 때문입니다. Mill Creek Grainery의 모든 방문객들은 어떤 식으로 빵을 만들어도 맛있는 우리의 신선한 통밀가루 무료 견본품을 받을 것입니다. 이 제분소는 신선한 밀로 만들어진 갓 만든 빵 제품을 제공합니다.

어휘 demanding 까다로운, 요구 사항이 많은 pilgrim 순례자 inhabitant 주민, 서식 동물 mill 제분소, 방앗간 found 설립하다 waterpower 수력 grind 갈다, 빻다 flour 밀가루 grain 곡물 notion 개념 implement 도구, 기구 whole wheat flour 통밀가루 recipe 조리법

1
해설 이 글에서 주로 논의되고 있는 것은 무엇인가?
(A) 신기술 소개
(B) 빵을 구매하는 것
(C) St. Pierre에서의 관광
(D) 수력 작동

해설 지문의 주제를 묻는 문제. 역시 초반에 중점을 두고 문장을 읽어야 한다. "In old town St. Pierre, one can find a large variety of activities and experiences that will please even the most demanding consumer."라고 하면서 St. Pierre 지역에서 참여할 수 있는 행사와 경험에 대해서 이야기하고 있다.

어휘 sightseeing 관광 waterpower 수력

2
해설 Mill Creek Grainery에서 가장 유명한 것은 무엇인가?
(A) 빵집
(B) 건물들
(C) 방앗간
(D) 악기들

해설 문제의 의미는 Mill Creek Grainery에서 가장 유명한 것은 무엇인가에 관한 것인데 "It is truly amazing that the mill still operates today, using the same system and technology that was built hundreds of years ago."라고 하면서 제분소 자체가 아직도 수백 년 전과 같은 방식으로 운영되고 있는 것이 놀랍다고 했으므로 가장 유명한 것은 mill이 된다.

어휘 musical instrument 악기

3
해설 Mill Creek Grainery에서 하는 일은 무엇인가?
(A) 관광객들에게 음식을 제공한다.
(B) 제빵 수업을 제공한다.
(C) 전력을 생산한다.
(D) 쿠키와 음료를 판매한다.

해설 지문 마지막 두 문장에서 관광객들에게 밀가루와 빵을 제공함을 알 수 있다.

어휘 generate 생산하다 electric power 전력

4-7

구독자 여러분께
〈Omega Holistic Health Newsletter〉를 구독해 주셔서 감사합니다. 이달에 우리는 건강을 증진시키기 위해서 자연 허브를 사용하는 방법에 대해 다루고자 합니다. 우리 기사에서 첫 번째로 다룰 허브는 에키네시아입니다. 미국의 인디언들이 처음으로 에키네시아의 의학적 특성에 대해서 발견했습니다. 에키네시아는 감기와 감염에 저항력이 있는 것으로 알려져 있습니다. 연구에서 에키네시아가 자연적인 소독제, 항생제 그리고 면역 체계를 만드는 복합체로서의 역할을 할 수 있다는 것이 증명되었습니다. 이 허브는 대부분 '더블 오' 캡슐로 알려진 캡슐 형태로 먹게 됩니다. 혹은 차나 팅크 형태로도 사용될 수 있습니다. 허브 팅크는 알코올이나 식초에 생허브를 담가서 추출할 수 있습니다. 이 과정은 액체 안에서 허브의 의학적인 특징을 추출해 냅니다.

우리가 다룰 두 번째 허브는 오늘날 골든실이라고 불리는 것입니다. 이것 역시 자연적인 항생제나 피를 맑게 해주는 것으로 여겨지는데, 자주 자연 치료사들에 의해서 감기, 독감, 혹은 간염의 경우 처방됩니다. 주로 더블 오 젤라틴 캡슐 형태를 사용한 가루 형태로 섭취할 수 있습니다. 쓴맛 때문에 대체로 차의 형태로는 섭취되지 않습니다.

어휘 herb 허브, 약초 medicinal property 약효 성분 be known for ~으로 알려져 있다 infection 감염 antiseptic 소독제 antibiotic 항생제 immunity 면역력 compounds 화합물 tincture 팅크 (알코올에 첨가하여 약제로 쓰는 물질) derive 끌어내다, 얻다 soak 담그다, 흠뻑 적시다 vinegar 식초 extract 추출하다 liquid 액체 blood purifier 혈액 청정제 prescribe 처방하다 naturopathic 자연 요법의 physician 의사, 의료진 bitterness 쓴맛

4
해석 이 소식지에서 논의되는 바는 무엇인가?
(A) 의사 고르기
(B) 운동이 주는 혜택
(C) 자연 요법사
(D) 허브의 약물 용도
해설 주제 문제이다. 초반을 읽으면서 "we will be discussing the use of natural herbs to promote health"에서 바로 정답이 (D)임을 알 수 있다.
어휘 naturopathic doctor 자연 요법 치료사

5
해석 더블 오 캡슐은 무엇인가?
(A) 허브 섭취를 위한 캡슐
(B) 복합적인 비타민
(C) 허브들의 혼합
(D) 처방 약품
해설 세부 사항 문제로 키워드는 "double O capsules"이다. 지문에서 바로 찾을 수 있는데 "It is typically taken in capsule form in what are known as 'double O' capsules."에서 대명사 It이 herb를 받으므로 허브를 섭취할 수 있는 하나의 방법이다.
어휘 blend 섞다, 혼합하다

6
해석 허브 팅크란 무엇인가?
(A) 물에 허브 잎을 적시는 것
(B) 허브의 추출액 형태
(C) 허브의 가루 형태
(D) 허브의 표준화된 형태
해설 herbal tinctures를 찾는 세부 사항 문제이다. "Herbal tinctures are derived by soaking the raw herb in alcohol or vinegar."에서 tinctures를 알코올이나 식초에 담근 허브에서 추출할 수 있다고 했으므로 정답이 (B)임을 알 수 있다.
어휘 concentrated 농축된 powdered 가루 형태의

7
해석 왜 보통 골든실을 차로는 마시지 않는가?
(A) 매우 쓰다.
(B) 효과적이지 않다.
(C) 효능을 잃게 된다.
(D) 너무 비싸다.
해설 세부 사항 문제로 의미는 "왜 보통 골든실을 차로는 마시지 않는가?"인데 이렇게 세부적인 문제는 단어 몇 개의 패러프레이징으로 간단하게 지문과 대조해서 풀 수 있다. "Due to its bitterness, it is usually not consumed as a tea."를 보고 쓴맛 때문인 것을 알 수 있다.
어휘 potency 힘, 효능

DAY 04   본문 p.308

| 1 (B) | 2 (A) | 3 (D) | 4 (B) | 5 (A) |

1-2

새 Acer 매트리스 세트 구매를 축하합니다. 저희 매트리스는 최상의 재료와 기술만을 사용하여 만들었습니다. 모든 내용물을 포함하여 저희 매트리스는 미국에서 생산됩니다. 저희 매트리스는 재료와 기술에 관계없이 모든 결함에 대해 20년의 100% 보증 기간을 제공합니다. 보상을 받으시려면 고객님께서는 수리나, 교환, 환불이 가능한 우리의 전국 판매 전문 매장 어디에라도 매트리스를 반품하셔야 합니다. 저희 매트리스가 전체 업계 내에서 가장 강력한 보증 제도를 가지고 있습니다. 대부분의 경쟁 업체들은 단지 비례로만 운영되는 3년의 보증 기간만을 가집니다. 다시 말해, 고객이 그것을 소유한 시간의 양에 따라서 매트리스를 교환하거나 수리하는 비용의 일정 부분을 지불해야 합니다. 예를 들어서 만약 매트리스의 보증 기간이 3년이고 고객이 그것을 2년 후에 반납하면, 겨우 33%의 보증 금액을 교환이나 교체를 위해 고객에게 주는 것입니다. 저희는 이것이 불합리하다고 생각하며, 이것이 저희가 모든 매트리스에 대해서 비례제 없는 100% 환불 제도를 가지고 있는 이유입니다.

어휘 workmanship 솜씨, 기술 component 요소, 부품 warranty 보증 기간 prorate 할당하다, 비례하다 portion 부분 credit 신용 거래, 공제액 unacceptable 수용할 수 없는

1
해석 이 정보는 주로 무엇에 관한 내용인가?
(A) 매트리스의 구성 성분
(B) 매트리스 품질 보증서
(C) 제조 과정들
(D) 침실 부품

해설 정보의 주제를 묻는 문제로 간단하게 첫 문장 "Congratulations on the purchase of your new Acer Mattress set."만 읽고도 B를 고를 수 있다.

어휘 section 부분, 구획

2
해석 이 정보에 따르면, Acer는 매트리스에 대해 어떤 종류의 품질 보증을 제공하는가?
(A) 20년간 100% 보증
(B) 10년간 50% 보증
(C) 20년간 비례 배분
(D) 3년간 비례 배분

해설 우선 Acer가 매트리스 회사이고, 다른 회사가 사용한 기간을 적용해서 보증 금액을 적용하는 반면에 Acer는 20년간 100%의 환불을 해주는 것을 알 수 있다.

3-5

중고 책 판매

후원: Liverpool 도서관의 Liverpool 문학 모임 자원봉사자들
7월 8일에서 10일까지 단 3일간!

거의 새것과 같은 수천 권의 책 중에서 선택하세요! 모든 연령대의 독자를 위한 책이 있습니다.

목요일: 사전 판매
오후 7시 – 오후 8시
입장료 10달러

금요일: 일반 판매
오전 7시 – 오후 4시
* 유명한 작가들의 특별한 강연이 있을 것입니다.

토요일: 판매 마지막 날
오전 10시 – 오후 3시
모든 책이 40% 할인됩니다.

모든 수익은 Hartford Lane의 Liverpool 지역 도서관의 수리와 단장을 위해서 쓰여질 것입니다.

위치: Liverpool 레크리에이션 센터, Main Hall, 42 Grendel Street
질문이 있으세요? 564-7778로 Liverpool 문학 모임 자원봉사 협회의 회장인 Seymour Butts에게 연락하세요.
참조: 이번 판매를 위한 책 기증은 더 이상 받지 않습니다.

어휘 secondhand 중고의 sponsor 후원하다 literary guild 문학 동호회, 문학 협회 mint condition 양호한 상태, 새것과 같은 상태 of all ages 모든 연령대의 admission fee 입장료 renowned 유명한 refurbish 새로 꾸미다

3
해석 판매가 어디에서 이루어질 것인가?
(A) Liverpool 도서관
(B) 지역 서점
(C) Butts 씨의 주택
(D) 레크리에이션 센터

해설 세부 사항 문제로 문제의 키워드는 Where와 sale이다. "Location: Liverpool recreation Center"로부터 (D)가 정답임을 알 수 있다.

어휘 residence 거주, 주택

4
해석 목요일 판매에 대하여 명시된 것은 무엇인가?
(A) 오직 도서관 카드 소지자에게만 해당된다.
(B) 입장료가 있을 것이다.
(C) 지불 방식으로 오직 현금만 인정된다.
(D) 오전에 시행될 것이다.

해설 목요일에 이루어지는 판매에 대한 문제이므로 그 부분을 읽고 선택지에서 하나씩 오답을 소거한다. "$10 admission fee"를 보고 정답이 (B)임을 알 수 있다.

어휘 possessor 주인, 소유주

5
해석 판매되고 있는 도서에 대해 언급된 것은 무엇인가?
(A) 어떤 책은 어린이에게 좋다.
(B) 많은 도서가 양호한 상태가 아니다.
(C) 모든 도서는 협회 회원들에 의해 기부되었다.
(D) 토요일에는 일부 책들이 대체로 할인된 가격에 제공된다.

해설 선택지를 먼저 읽고 지문에서 각 지문의 키워드를 찾는다. "There will be books for readers of all ages."를 보고 모든 연령대를 위한 책이 있다고 했으므로 정답은 (A)이다. 토요일에는 모든 책이 할인된 가격에 제공되므로 (D)는 오답이다.

DAY 05
본문 p.310

1 (C)   2 (A)   3 (D)   4 (A)   5 (C)
6 (D)

1-3

San Francisco 대학의 새로운 시설들

San Francisco 대학 졸업생 협회에 의한 2014 기금 모금 행사 후에, San Francisco 대학의 이사진들이 학생 위원회와 합동하여 모든 돈을 어떻게 써야 할지에 대해서 조사하고 결정했다.

낡은 기념 도서관을 대신할 새 도서관을 2015년 여름 동안 지으려고 계획 중이다. 이 새 도서관은 San Francisco 대학 학생들이 이용할 수 있는 책, 저널, 잡지의 수를 증가시킬 것이다. 학생들이 더 많이 공부할 수 있도록 책상도 제공될 것이다. 더불어, 새 도서관은 온라인 장비를 갖춘 넓어진 컴퓨터실을 몇 개 갖추게 될 것이다.

둘째로, 최신식 스포츠 복합 건물이 대강당 옆에 건축될 것이다. 이 새 복합 건물은 실내 트랙과 올림픽 규격의 수영장, 운동 시설, 큰 체육관을 포함할 것이다.

어휘 fundraising drive 모금 행사 alumni 졸업생 in coordination with ~와 합동해서 state-of-the-art 최신식의 complex 복합 건물 auditorium 강당 gymnasium 체육관

1
해석 이 글의 목적은 무엇인가?
(A) 졸업생 협회를 위한 모금 활동을 하기 위해서
(B) 체육관 개조에 관해 논의하기 위해서
(C) 독자들에게 건설 계획을 알리기 위해서
(D) San Francisco 대학 졸업생 협회의 창립을 알리기 위해서

해설 글의 주제를 묻는 문제로 지문의 초반부의 "board of directors ~ have researched and decided upon ways in which to spend the money"에서 모은 기금을 쓸 방법을 논의했다는 내용이 나오고, 그 아랫부분에서 두 개의 건물 건축에 대한 내용이 나오고 있다.

어휘 raise funds 자금을 모으다

2
해석 새 도서관 시설로서 언급되지 않은 것은 무엇인가?
(A) 갱신된 출입증
(B) 컴퓨터실
(C) 더 많은 도서, 신문, 잡지들
(D) 공부 책상

해설 사실 확인 문제로 우선 문제에서 키워드 new library가 주어졌기 때문에 이 단어를 찾으면 두 번째 문단에서 처음 등장하고 그 이후로 관련된 내용이 나올 것임을 짐작할 수 있다. 이 문단에서 선택지를 하나씩 대입해서 오답을 소거하면 된다.

어휘 access card 출입 관리 카드

3
해석 새 시설을 위한 모금은 어디로부터 왔는가?
(A) 주립 정부의 대출금
(B) San Francisco 대학 졸업생 협회의 기부금
(C) 이전 학생 회장
(D) 2014 모금 활동 캠페인

해설 세부 사항 문제로 자금의 출처를 묻고 있다. "Following the 2014 fundraising drive"를 보고 drive를 campaign으로 바꿔 쓴 것만 알면 풀 수 있는 문제이다. 참고로 (B)의 USF Alumni Association은 지문에 언급이 되어 있지만 "organized by the USF Alumni Association"를 보고 기부를 한 주체가 아니라 행사 주체인 것을 알 수 있다.

어휘 former 이전의

4-6

편집장으로부터

〈Northern Culinary〉의 이번 3월호로 이 잡지가 출판된 지 일 년이 되었습니다. 딱 일 년 전에 우리는 우리의 첫 번째 잡지를 판매했고, 그 이후로, 우리는 지역의 요리법과 관련하여 가장 많이 읽혀지는 잡지 중에 하나로 성장했습니다. 우리의 고객은 20,000명이 되었고, 구독자의 수는 계속해서 증가하고 있습니다. 지역의 미식가들은 우리의 기사에 대해 찬사를 보냈고, 1월에 있었던 Northern Food Festival에서 우리는 "최고의 요리 잡지" 상을 받았습니다. 편집장으로서 우리의 성공에 크게 기여한 모든 분들, 우리의 헌신적인 직원들, 정기 기고자들, 광고주들 그리고 특히 우리의 점점 늘어나는 고객들께 진심으로 감사드립니다.

Erik Bourdain

어휘 culinary 요리의 mark 표시하다 publication 잡지, 출판 subscriber 구독자 foodie 미식가 rave 극찬하다 contribute to ~에 기여하다

4
해석 이 쪽지의 목적은 무엇인가?
(A) 감사를 표하기 위해
(B) 제의를 연장하기 위해
(C) 공헌자를 예우하기 위해
(D) 기부를 간청하기 위해

해설 주제 문제이지만 정답은 전체 지문에 걸쳐서 나오고 특히 맨 마지막에 "I am deeply grateful to ~"에서 편집장이 감사를 전하는 것으로부터 정답이 (A)임을 알 수 있다.

어휘 gratitude 감사 honor ~을 기념하다 solicit 간청하다

5
해석 Northern Culinary에 관해 명시된 것은 무엇인가?
(A) 더 많은 작가를 필요로 한다.
(B) 해외판이 나올 것이다.
(C) 인기가 높아지고 있다.
(D) 광고 비율을 높여왔다.

해설 전체 지문을 읽어야 풀 수 있는 문제이다. "Our customer base has reached 20,000, and that number of subscribers continues to increase."에서 고객층이 계속 성장하고 있다는 내용을 (C)와 같이 인기가 증가하고 있다고 바꿔 썼다.

어휘 rate 운임

6
해석 Northern Food Festival에 대해 언급된 것은 무엇인가?
(A) Bourdain 씨가 축제에서 자신의 요리를 소개했다.
(B) Bourdain 씨가 축제에서 올해의 편집자 상을 수상했다.
(C) 잡지가 그 행사에 대한 자금을 댔다.
(D) 그 행사에서 잡지가 상을 받았다.

해설 정답이 나올 범위를 "Northern Food Festival"로 줄여 주었다. 이것을 지문에서 찾으면 "we were awarded "Best Culinary Magazine""이라고 했고 (D)는 이것을 다른 말로 풀어서 쓴 것이다.

어휘 present 소개하다, 발표하다 cuisine 요리법, 요리

DAY 06 본문 p.312

| 1 (C) | 2 (A) | 3 (D) | 4 (A) | 5 (C) |

SECTION 2_독해 집중 연습 » 133

1-3

수신: 정액 임금을 받는 모든 직원 여러분
발신: William Stevens, 인사과 이사
날짜: 4월 17일
제목: 추가 근무 수당

지금까지 정액 임금을 받는 직원들은 추가 근무 수당을 받지 못했습니다. 하지만 이사진들이 봉급을 받으면서 노조에 속하지 않은 직원들에게 추가 근무 보상 제도를 막 승인하였습니다. 일주일에 40시간 이상 근무를 하는 정액 임금제 직원들은 보상 차원의 휴가를 받게 될 것입니다. 다시 말해서, 만약 직원이 한 달을 기준으로 8시간 이상 추가 근무를 하면, 그들은 휴가 기간이나 휴일에 추가로 8시간의 휴가를 더 받게 될 것입니다. 질문이 있는 직원 여러분은 웹 페이지에서 '인사과'라는 제목 아래에 있는 공식 정책 부분을 읽어 주시길 바랍니다.

어휘 overtime compensation 추가 근무 수당 time off 휴식 in other words 다시 말해서 under the heading ~라는 제목으로 personnel 인사과

1

해석 이 메모의 주제는 무엇인가?
(A) 신입 사원 월급
(B) 노조 직원들의 초과 근무
(C) 초과 근무에 대한 휴가 보상
(D) 고객들의 불평

해설 메모의 주제를 묻고 있다. "the board of directors has just approved an overtime compensation plan for salaried, nonunion employees." 부분에서 추가 근무를 하고, 노조에 가입되지 않은 직원들에 대한 보상 정책이 주된 논제이므로 정답은 (C)이다.

어휘 complaint 불평, 불만

2

해석 새로운 초과 근무 정책이 적용되는 사람은 누구인가?
(A) 정액 임금제 직원들
(B) 노조 직원들
(C) 시간제 근무자들
(D) 경영진들

해설 1번 문제와 같은 부분인 "the board of directors has just approved an overtime compensation plan for salaried, nonunion employees."에서 정확하게 Salaried employees 라고 언급되어 있다.

어휘 hourly worker 시간제 근무자

3

해석 새로운 초과 근무 정책이 제공하는 것은 무엇인가?
(A) 초과 근무에 대한 추가 급여
(B) 시간과 기준 급여의 절반
(C) 병가 연장
(D) 초과 근무에 대한 휴가

해설 "they will be given eight hours of time off that can be added to their vacations or holidays" 부분에서 휴가 기간이나 휴일 기간에 추가적으로 휴가 시간을 얻을 수 있다고 나와 있다.

어휘 a half 이분의 일 sick leave 병가

4-5

발신: Dan McCormick, 인사과 이사
수신: Quidel의 관리팀 직원들
제목: Costa Rica로의 휴가
날짜: 12월 20일

올해 1월 10일에서 20일까지 우리는 당신께 Costa Rica 휴가 패키지를 엄청나게 할인된 가격에 구매할 수 있는 좀처럼 볼 수 없는 기회를 드리고자 합니다. 이 상품은 Costa Rica까지의 비행기 요금과 호텔 숙박 요금이 한 명에 410달러, 두 명에 750달러입니다. 할인 가격은 각각 200달러와 400달러입니다. (가족 할인을 알고 싶으시면 여행사에 문의하세요.)

이 휴가 패키지는 고급 El Verga Rainforest 호텔에서 3일간 묵을 수 있습니다. 또한 이 상품을 이용하는 직원들은 멋진 El Hombre 식당에서 식사를 할 수 있는 현금 20달러(Costa Rica 페소로 환전 가능) 상당의 상품권 세 장을 받게 될 것입니다. 구매와 예약을 하시려면 1월 20일이나 이전까지 1층에 있는 여행사 사무실을 방문해 주세요.

어휘 R&R(= rest and recreation) 휴양 휴식 starting ~부터 rare 드문 airfare 항공료 accommodation 숙박 respectively 각각 avail oneself of ~을 이용하다 voucher 상품권 convertible 전환이 가능한 exotic 이국적인

4

해석 이 메모가 작성된 이유는 무엇인가?
(A) 직원들에게 (할인된 가격으로 여행 갈) 기회를 알리기 위해서
(B) 새로운 여행지를 홍보하기 위해서
(C) 호텔의 개업을 발표하기 위해서
(D) 비행 요금의 변동을 보고하기 위해서

해설 목적을 묻는 문제이다. "we are inviting you to this rare opportunity to buy our popular Costa Rica vacation package at deeply discounted rates."를 보고 이 글이 직원들에게 할인된 가격으로 여행을 갈 수 있는 기회를 제공하는 것임을 알 수 있다. (B)도 여행에 대한 글이지만 새로운 여행지 자체를 광고하는 것은 아니다.

어휘 travel destination 여행 도착지

5

해석 Costa Rica 패키지에 관해 언급된 것은 무엇인가?
(A) 인터넷을 통해 가능하다.
(B) 무료 식사를 포함한다.
(C) 명시된 가격은 1월 20일이 지나면 달라질 것이다.
(D) 2인 이하로만 제한한다.

해설 전체 지문을 범위로 맞게 언급한 것을 찾는 문제. 글의 초반에 "Starting this January 10 to the 20th" 부분과 마지막에 "on or before the 20th of January"를 보고 20일까지 이 행사가 진행되므로 이 날짜 이후에는 가격이 바뀔 것이다.

어휘 indicate 나타내다

DAY 07 본문 p.314

| 1 (C) | 2 (A) | 3 (C) | 4 (D) | 5 (A) |

1-2

NORMA JEAN'S
커피 가게

직장인을 위한 특별 가격 4월 1일~14일

에스프레소 라지	2.25달러 (정가 2.75달러)
렌틸콩 수프 한 컵	2.95달러 (정가 3.75달러)
수프와 서브웨이 콤보	6.25달러 (정가 7.00달러)
작은 찬 음료	1.25달러 (정가 1.85달러)

이 할인 가격은 세 개 지점 모두에 해당됩니다.
특가 상품은 제한 없이 구매할 수 있습니다.
다른 쿠폰이나 할인과 중복해서 사용할 수 없습니다.
할인을 받으려면 제품을 구입할 때 회사 신분증을 제시해야 합니다.

현금, 직불 카드, 신용 카드 모두 사용 가능합니다.
아침 6시에서 저녁 10시까지 매일 영업합니다.

어휘 lentil 렌틸콩, 편두 applicable 적용할 수 있는 debit card 직불 카드

3-5

Giuliani 씨께,

저희는 Oregon 주의 Portland 시내에 Pacific Cascade 치과의 개업을 알리게 되어 기쁩니다. 이 최신식 건물은 건설하는 데 2천 5백만 달러가 넘게 들었습니다. 부모들을 위한 탁아 시설을 갖출 것입니다. 새로운 시설들은 최신 치과 시설을 갖출 것입니다. 최신 장비에는 새로운 블루 라이트 제논 레이저 드릴이 포함됩니다. 이 새로운 레이저 드릴을 사용하는 것의 이점은 엄청납니다. 치과 치료 과정이 마취나 약물 없이 진행될 수 있습니다. 레이저 드릴은 고통을 주지 않고, 어떤 소리도 내지 않습니다. 레이저 드릴을 사용하면 회복 속도 역시 전통적인 드릴이나 마취보다 훨씬 빠릅니다. 이전의 치료에서는 환자가 치료 후 회복을 위해서 하루 혹은 이틀을 쉬어야 했습니다. 하지만 레이저 기술이 이 전형적인 틀을 변화시키고 환자가 직장이나 일상생활로 즉시 돌아갈 수 있게 만들었습니다. 새로운 시설에 당신을 곧 모시기를 희망합니다. 5월 19일 금요일 오후 5시에 예정된 병원 공개일에 당신을 초대합니다. 모든 손님들을 위한 무료 견학과 재밋거리, 그리고 피자가 제공될 것입니다.

Bonnie Dickenson 박사, 치의학 박사

어휘 immense 광범위한, 어마어마한 anesthesia 마취 medication 약물 painless 고통이 없는 emit 내다, 내뿜다 paradigm 전형적인 예 look forward to ~을 고대하다 D.D.S.(Doctor of Dental Surgery) 치의학 박사

1
해석 무엇이 광고되고 있는가?
(A) 음료 메뉴의 확장
(B) 직장인을 위해 최근에 생긴 커피숍
(C) 특정 고객을 위한 가격 할인
(D) 새로 바뀐 영업 시간

해설 광고문은 문장 초반에 대부분 광고 대상과 광고 제품을 언급하고 그 이후는 그 제품의 특징을 소개하는 형식으로 지문이 구성된다. 여기서도 광고 대상과 광고 제품을 지문 초반에 알 수 있다. 즉, "Office worker Specials for April 1-14"로부터 office worker가 선택지에는 certain customers로, specials가 lower prices로 바꿔서 제시되고 있다.

어휘 lower ~을 낮추다

2
해석 Norma Jean의 커피숍에 대하여 언급된 것은 무엇인가?
(A) 다양한 지불 방식이 가능하다.
(B) 한 달간 할인된 가격을 제공한다.
(C) 매일 한 가지 종류의 수프만을 제공한다.
(D) 해외에도 지점을 보유하고 있다.

해설 지문에서 언급된 것을 묻는 문제는 선택지 중에서 지문의 내용을 가장 적절하게 바꿔 쓴 것을 찾는 문제이다. 지문의 "We accept cash, debit cards or credit cards."로부터 (A)가 답이라는 것을 알 수 있다.

어휘 variety of payment 다양한 지불 수단

3
해석 이 편지의 주된 주제는 무엇인가?
(A) 새 드릴링 절차를 발표하기 위해서
(B) 레이저의 이점을 설명하기 위해
(C) 새로운 치과의 개업을 발표하기 위해서
(D) 레이저 드릴과 이전 방식을 비교하기 위해서

해설 주제 문제이다. 글의 초반에 "We are pleased to announce the opening of our new Pacific Cascade Dental Clinic"을 통해 새로운 치과가 생기는 것을 언급하고 있으므로 정답은 (C)이다.

4
해석 편지에는 어떤 종류의 사업이 언급되었는가?
(A) 가정 의원
(B) 정형외과 병원
(C) 심장 전문 의원
(D) 치과 의원

해설 질문의 내용은 어떤 사업이 글에서 언급되고 있는지를 묻고 있는데 전체적으로 치과를 암시하는 힌트를 계속해서 언급하고 있다.

어휘 orthopedics 정형외과 cardiology 심장학

5
해석 편지에 따르면, 레이저 드릴을 사용하는 이점들 중 한 가지는 무엇인가?
(A) 회복 기간을 단축시킨다.
(B) 사용하기 저렴하다.
(C) 충치를 제거할 수 있다.
(D) 잇몸병에 사용할 수 있다.

해설 질문의 키워드는 advantages, laser drill이다. 지문에 여러 가지 좋은 점들이 언급되고 있다. 그중 "The recovery time with laser drills are much faster than traditional drilling and anesthesia."로부터 기존의 전통적인 마취를 통한 방법보다 회복 속도가 훨씬 빠르다는 것을 알 수 있다.

어휘 tooth decay 치아가 썩는 것 gum 잇몸

DAY 08
본문 p.316

| 1 (B) | 2 (A) | 3 (C) | 4 (D) | 5 (B) |

1-3

수신: 모든 Air California 직원들
발신: 대표 이사 John Robert
날짜: 7월 14일

직원 여러분

여러분은 미디어를 통해서 Air California가 Horizon Airways와 제안 받은 합병에 대해 협상 중이라고 읽으셨을지도 모르겠습니다. 많은 Air California 직원들이 저에게 연락해서 이 합병 때문에 직업을 잃게 되는 것이 아닌가 하는 깊은 근심을 표시해 왔습니다. 저는 Air California 직원 여러분께 직원을 해고하는 일은 없을 거라고 확실히 말씀 드립니다. 사실, 저희는 직원의 추가적인 고용을 예상하고 있습니다. 이것은 Horizon Airways가 2년 동안 고용 동결로 인해 직원을 전혀 고용하지 않았기 때문입니다. 결과적으로 회사는 심각한 인원 부족 상태에 있습니다. 합병은 비행 노선 구조의 확장으로 인해 Air California의 사업 전반을 확대시킬 것입니다. Horizon Airways는 Air California의 자회사가 될 것이고 Air California로 알려질 것입니다. 우리 회사 역사의 흥미진진한 시대를 기대합니다.

감사합니다.

대표 이사 John Robert
Air California
Newport Beach, CA

어휘 merger 합병 job loss 실직 eliminate 제거하다 anticipate 예상하다 hiring freeze 고용 동결 consequently 결과적으로 personnel shortage 인원 부족

1
해석 메모의 주제는 무엇인가?
(A) 감원 계획
(B) 항공사 합병
(C) 새로운 항공기
(D) 새 대표 이사의 임명

해설 메모의 주제를 묻는 문제로 "Air California is negotiating with Horizon Airways for a proposed merger" 부분을 보고 항공사들의 합병이 이 글의 주제인 것을 알 수 있다.

어휘 layoff 일시 해고 aircraft 항공기 appointment 임명

2
해석 새로운 회사는 무엇이라 불릴 것인가?
(A) Air California
(B) Horizon Airlines

(C) NorCal Airlines
(D) Air America

해설 세부 사항 문제로 키워드인 What, called를 통해서 정답을 구할 수 있다. "Horizon Air will now become part of the Air California family and will be known only as Air California."에서 합병되는 Horizon Air도 Air California로만 알려질 것이라고 했으므로 회사의 이름으로 적절한 것은 (A)이다.

3
해석 왜 많은 직원들이 대표 이사에게 연락하였는가?
(A) 그들은 전근을 원했다.
(B) 그들은 임금 인상을 원했다.
(C) 그들은 해고에 대해 우려했다.
(D) 그들은 승진을 원했다.

해설 세부 사항 문제로 키워드는 contact이다. "Many Air California employees have contacted me expressing their deep concerns about job losses" 부분을 읽고 바로 (C)를 고를 수 있다.

어휘 transfer 옮기다, 이동하다 raise 임금 인상, ~을 올리다 promotion 승진, 판촉 행위

4-5

CENTER PLACE 호텔

성함: Jonathon Smith
주소: 1556 North First Street, Anaheim, California
전화번호: 714-555-1212
숙박 일자: 4월 12일   객실 번호: 567
방문의 주요 목적
☑ 관광 ☐ 사업 ☐ 회의/그룹 모임

객실	훌륭함	좋음	괜찮음	나쁨
청결	☑	☐	☐	☐
디자인	☐	☑	☐	☐
안락함	☐	☑	☐	☐

의견: 옆방의 소음이 들립니다. 방 사이에 충분한 방음 장치가 없는 것 같습니다.

식당	훌륭함	좋음	괜찮음	나쁨
메뉴 선택	☐	☐	☑	☐
음식의 품질	☑	☐	☐	☐
서비스의 품질	☑	☐	☐	☐

의견: 흔히 접하기 힘든 다양한 생선 요리!

다시 들러 주시겠습니까? 예 ☑ 아니요 ☐

다른 의견
당신의 직원으로부터 받은 따뜻한 고객 서비스에 감사드립니다. 제가 만족하지 못한 한 가지는 공항으로부터 택시를 타고 도착했을 때, 체크인 시간이 길었다는 것입니다. 단지 체크인을 하고 방을 얻기까지 35분을 기다려야만 했습니다. 이런 것은 긴 비행을 마치고 도착했을 때 가장 겪기 싫은 일입니다. 안내 데스크에서 일할 직원을 더 고용하십시오.

이 카드를 안내 데스크에 남겨 주십시오. 감사합니다!

어휘 cleanliness 청결함 sound insulation 방음 장치

1
해석 이 설문 조사는 주로 무엇에 대한 내용인가?
(A) 호텔의 서비스
(B) 항공기 서비스
(C) 서비스 센터의 서비스
(D) 스파의 서비스

해설 설문지의 제목 "Global Airways"나 "flight"를 보고 (B)의 airline을 정답으로 고를 수 있다.

2
해석 이 승객은 글로벌 항공의 어떤 점이 가장 마음에 들지 않았는가?
(A) 비행 중 음식
(B) 긴 티켓 대기 줄
(C) 비행의 지연
(D) 비행기의 뻗는 공간

해설 지문의 Additional Comments에서 "I think the legroom is ridiculous on the flights." 부분에 정답이 나와 있다.

3-5

수신: James Peterson 박사님
〈jamespeterson09@straforduniversity.edu.au〉
발신: Beth Anne George 〈generalmanager@hillahotel.com〉
날짜: 4월 20일
제목: 회신

Petterson 박사님께

Hilla 호텔 35층의 프레지덴셜 스위트 펜트하우스를 요청하시는 이메일을 주신 것에 감사드립니다.
죄송하지만, 호텔에서 전자 관련 회의가 있는 관계로 모든 펜트하우스 객실들이 한 주 내내 예약이 되어 있습니다. 하지만 저희는 박사님께 일반 객실 가격으로 34층에 있는 센터 스위트룸을 제공하고 싶습니다. 귀하께서는 센터 스위트룸도 도시의 어떤 다른 호텔과도 비교할 수 없는 우아함을 가지고 있다는 것을 알게 되실 것입니다. 프레지덴셜 스위트룸과 센터 스위트룸의 유일한 차이점은 센터 스위트룸이 전체적인 크기에서 약간 작다는 것입니다. 저희는 센터 스위트룸에 만족하실 것을 확신하고 귀하를 꼭 손님으로 모시고 싶습니다. 이 객실을 예약하고 싶으시다면, 객실의 예약이 빠르게 마감되고 있으므로 가능한 한 빨리 연락 주시길 바랍니다. 박사님의 계속적인 애용에 감사드립니다.

Beth Anne George
총 지배인, Hilla 호텔

어휘 presidential suite (대통령 급의 인물이 숙박하기 적당한) 귀빈실
reserve 예약하다 rate 비용 unparalleled 비교할 수 없는
A.S.A.P.(as soon as possible) 최대한 빨리 patronage 애용

3
해석 이 이메일의 주된 목적은 무엇인가?
(A) 센터 스위트룸을 예약하기 위해서
(B) 객실 요금에 대하여 문의하기 위해서
(C) Hilla 호텔의 객실 상황을 설명하기 위해서
(D) 회의를 예약하기 위해서

4
해석 Center Place 호텔에 관해 언급된 것은 무엇인가?
(A) 주로 관광객이 이용한다.
(B) 방음 시설이 훌륭하다.
(C) 셔틀을 무료로 제공한다.
(D) 손님들에게 해산물을 제공한다.

해설 사실 관계 파악 문제이다. 지문의 comment 부분 "wide selection of fish dishes"로부터 정답은 (D)임을 알 수 있다.

어휘 mostly 대부분 soundproofing 방음 complimentary 무료의 seafood 해산물

5
해석 왜 고객이 만족하지 못했는가?
(A) 호텔 직원이 친절하지 않았다.
(B) 체크인까지 오래 기다려야 했다.
(C) 레스토랑 음식이 형편없었다.
(D) 호텔 방이 깨끗하지 않았다.

해설 세부 사항 문제로 질문의 키워드는 unhappy이다. 이 단어를 다른 말로 쓴 부분인 "One thing I was not happy about was the long check-in time"로부터 정답이 (B)임을 알 수 있다.

DAY 09
본문 p.318

| 1 (B) | 2 (D) | 3 (C) | 4 (D) | 5 (A) |

1-2

글로벌 항공 고객 만족 평가서

질문	예	아니요
비행기가 제 시간에 출발하고 도착했나요?	×	
발권 담당 직원이 친절했나요?	×	
표를 사기 위해서 줄을 서서 오래 기다리셨나요?	×	
기내 서비스가 만족스러우셨나요?		×
기내 음식이 만족스러우셨나요?	×	
착륙 후 15분 이내에 당신의 짐을 받으셨나요?	×	
비행 동안에 다리를 뻗을 수 있는 공간에 만족하셨나요?		×

추가 의견: 저는 비행 중에 다리를 뻗을 수 있는 공간이 터무니없이 좁다고 생각합니다. 제가 6피트 3인치의 신장인데, 공간의 부족으로 다리를 꼬고 앉을 수가 없었습니다. 완전히 쥐가 날 것 같았습니다. 저는 글로벌 항공이 비행기에 더 많은 승객을 태우려고 노력하기보다는 승객에게 더 많은 공간을 주기를 바랍니다.

어휘 courteous 예의 바른 inflight 기내 landing 착륙 legroom 다리를 뻗을 수 있는 공간 ridiculous 웃기는, 말도 안 되는 cross legs 다리를 꼬다 cramp 경련, 쥐

해설 우선 이 메일의 첫 문장 "Thank you for your e-mail yesterday requesting~" 부분을 보고 이전에 요청 메일이 있었다는 것을 알 수 있고, 이런 종류의 메일은 대부분 질문에 답을 주는 내용이 등장한다. 여기서도 객실의 상황을 설명해 주고 있다는 (C)가 정답이다.

어휘 inquire 문의하다 book 예약하다

4

해석 이메일에 명시된 문제점은 무엇인가?
(A) 세너터 스위트룸이 다 찼다.
(B) 동네에 식당이 많지 않다.
(C) 휴가철이다.
(D) 프레지덴셜 스위트룸이 다 찼다.

해설 어떤 문제점이 있는지를 물어보는 질문은 대부분 지문의 초반에 나온다. "all of the penthouse suites have been reserved"에서 reserved를 선택지에서는 sold out으로 바꿔서 제시하고 있다. 따라서 정답은 (D)이다.

어휘 sold out 매진되다

5

해석 George 씨가 제안한 해결책은 무엇인가?
(A) 세너터 스위트룸을 예약하는 것
(B) 다른 호텔에 객실을 알아보는 것
(C) 환불을 제공하는 것
(D) 다른 날짜에 해당 객실을 예약하는 것

해설 문제점을 제시한 후에 그에 대한 해결책을 제시하는 경우가 대부분인데 이 문제도 "we would like to offer you our Senator's Suite"를 보고 조금 작은 크기의 객실을 제안하고 있다는 것을 알 수 있다.

DAY **10**   본문 p.320

| 1 (B) | 2 (A) | 3 (A) | 4 (D) | 5 (C) |
| 6 (A) | 7 (C) |

1-5

Clint의 여행:
El Paso에서의 24시간
저자: Clint Smith, 전속 작가

4월 9일 – 이번 주에 저는 제 이야기에 단골로 등장하는 이국적인 장소나 먼 지역에 대한 이야기는 잠시 제쳐둘 것입니다. 대신에 저는 우리가 사랑하는 El Paso가 줄 수 있는 것에 대해서 글을 쓸 것입니다. 이것은 우리의 고향에서 가장 멋진 하루를 보낼 수 있는 저의 개인적인 생각입니다.

오전 8시 – 하루를 잘 시작하려면 푸짐한 아침이 당신을 기다리고 있는 Big Mike를 방문하셔야 합니다. 이 식당은 El Paso에 새로 생긴 식당이지만, 길게 줄은 선 고객들이 참을성 있게 식당의 문 밖에서 서 있습니다. 이 식당의 단골 고객으로서, 저는 아침 부리토를 추천합니다. 이 음식 하나로도 오래 기다릴 가치가 있습니다.

오전 10시 – 다음 장소로, 저는 오래된 스페인 풍의 공원 주위를 느긋하게 산책하거나, 자전거를 타시는 것을 제안합니다. 오래된 스페인 풍의 집과 열대 나무의 경치와 풍경은 확실히 당신을 매료시킬 것입니다.

오후 12시 – 점심에 배고픔을 느낄 때, Old Opry 식당이 딱 적당한 식당입니다. 가족이 운영하는 이 식당은 맛있는 가정식 요리로 유명합니다. www.oldopry.com에서 메뉴를 볼 수 있습니다. 주말에 이곳에서 식사를 원하신다면, 예약을 하셔야 하며 예약을 하지 않으면 자주 식당이 손님으로 꽉 차기 때문에 오래 기다리실 수 있습니다. 다른 방법은 음식을 포장하신 후, 그것을 Old Opry에서 가까운 오래된 Spanish Park으로 가져가시는 것입니다.

오후 2시 30분 – El Paso 시민 센터(EPCC)에서 열리는 El Paso 작가 협회에 의해 쓰여진 산문과 시를 특징으로 하는 Torquemada 전시회에 잠시 방문하시는 것으로 El Paso에서 당신의 여행을 마무리하세요. 시는 재미있고 익살맞은 것부터 생각을 하게 하고 영감을 주는 작품까지 다양합니다. 4월 19일에 끝나는 전시회에 가지 못해도 걱정하실 필요가 없어요. 왜냐하면 매달 새로운 것을 전시하기 때문입니다.

El Paso에서 24시간을 더 잘 보낼 수 있는 좋은 의견이 있다면, clintsmith@texsun.com으로 제안해 주세요. 제목으로 "El Paso에서의 24시간"을 쓰시고요.

어휘 set aside 한 쪽에 치워놓다 account (상세한) 설명, 이야기 exotic 이국적인 beloved 사랑하는, 인기 많은 queue (무엇을 기다리는) 줄 leisurely 한가롭게 stroll 거닐다, 산책하다 scenery 경치, 풍경 amaze 놀라게 하다 packed 꽉 차있는 prose 산문 provoking 자극하는 inspiring 고무하는, 격려하는

1

해석 Big Mike 식당에 관해 언급된 것은 무엇인가?
(A) El Paso에 있는 이국적인 장소이다.
(B) 최근에 개업한 식당이다.
(C) 그 지역에서 아주 인기가 많지는 않다.
(D) 아침 식사를 제공하지 않는다.

해설 세부 사항 문제로 키워드는 Big Mike's이다. "this diner is one of El Paso's newest"로부터 최근에 문을 연 식당임을 알 수 있다.

2

해석 첫 번째 문단의 첫째 줄에 있는 단어 "account"와 의미가 가장 가까운 것은?
(A) 설명
(B) 자금
(C) 손님
(D) 걱정

해설 account의 여러 가지 의미 중에서 "I am setting aside my usual account of exotic places and far lands" 문장의 내용상 "이야기"라는 의미가 적절하므로 정답은 (A)이다.

3

해석 Smith 씨의 글에 대해 암시된 바는 무엇인가?
(A) 지역 장소들에 집중하고 있다.
(B) 보통 웃긴 일화를 포함한다.
(C) 한 달에 한 번씩 발행된다.
(D) 신문에서 가장 많이 읽히는 부분이다.

138

해설 전체 지문 암시 문제이다. 지문의 키워드를 꼭 기억해야 쉽게 풀 수 있다. "This is my personal idea of making the most of a nice day in our hometown."은 (A)의 local destination의 다른 표현임을 알 수 있다. 이후 글의 내용도 갈만한 장소들을 하나하나 설명하고 있다.

어휘 ordinarily 일반적으로, 보통 때는 anecdote 일화, 개인적인 진술

4
해설 기사에 따르면, Old Opry에 관해 사실인 것은 무엇인가?
(A) 여러 지점을 가지고 있다.
(B) 점심 때만 영업한다.
(C) 한 기업이 소유하고 있다.
(D) 매 토요일과 일요일은 매우 바쁘다.

해설 질문의 키워드인 Old Opry가 나오는 부분을 지문에서 찾은 후 선택지를 그 부분에 하나씩 비교하면서 정답을 찾는다. "If you plan to dine there on the weekend, better make a reservation, or you will be in for a long wait since the place is often packed." 부분에서 주말(weekend)이 선택지에서 Saturdays and Sundays로, 또 packed가 busy로 바꿔서 제시되어 있다. 따라서 정답은 (D)이다.

5
해설 Smith 씨가 제안한 것이 아닌 것은 무엇인가?
(A) 아침 식사로 특정한 요리를 주문하는 것
(B) Spanish Park에서 산책하는 것
(C) 전시회 정보를 위해 El Paso 시민 센터 웹 사이트를 방문하는 것
(D) 다른 재미있는 El Paso 활동을 제안하는 것

해설 사실 관계 파악 문제로 선택지의 키워드를 하나하나 지문에서 찾아서 비교한다. (C)에서 Web site가 키워드인데 지문에서 Web site가 나오는 부분은 식사 메뉴가 나오는 "Their menu can be viewed online at www.oldopry.com."이지 El Paso 시민 센터에 대한 부분이 아니다.

6-7

Whimmy 전자의 새로운 MP3 태양열 플레이어를 소개합니다!

얼마나 많이 당신의 MP3 플레이어를 통해서 좋아하는 노래를 듣고, 얼마나 많이 듣는 중에 배터리가 나가는 경험을 하셨나요? 얼마나 많이 실수로 MP3 플레이어를 켜 놓았고 또 얼마나 많이 배터리가 소진되는 경험을 하셨나요? 사람들 대부분은 이러한 경험이 있을 것이고, 이 기계의 배터리를 교체해야 하는 것이 매우 짜증나는 일임을 알고 계실 것입니다.

저희의 새로운 태양열을 이용한 MP3 플레이어는 배터리가 필요 없습니다! 대신에, 방의 조명이나 태양에 의해서 충전이 됩니다. 다시는 음악이 필요할 때 좋아하는 음악 없이 지내지 마세요. 지금 Whimmy MP3 플레이어를 구매하십시오! 금요일까지 할인 행사를 합니다! 더 많은 정보를 위해서, 우리의 제품 판매 매니저인 Susan Robinson 씨에게 메일(s.robinson@whimmy.com)이나 전화(1-452-3684)로 연락 주십시오.

어휘 accidently 우연히, 뜻하지 않게 run out 전부 소모되다 frustrating 짜증나는

6
해설 지문에 따르면, Whimmy MP3 플레이어에 관해 사실인 것은 무엇인가?
(A) 현재 할인 판매 중이다.
(B) 일반 MP3 플레이어보다 더 비싸다.
(C) 다른 MP3 플레이어보다 소형이다.
(D) 일반 MP3 플레이어보다 더 충격에 강하다.

해설 사실 파악 문제로 지문의 "It's on sale until this Friday!"로부터 현재 할인 행사 중임을 알 수 있으므로 (A)가 정답이다.

어휘 compact 소형의 shock-resistant 충격 방지의

7
해설 Susan Robinson은 누구일까?
(A) 고객
(B) 음악가
(C) Whimmy 전자의 직원
(D) Whimmy 전자의 사장

해설 문제의 키워드는 Who와 이름 Susan Robinson이므로, 이 이름을 지문에서 찾으면 풀 수 있는 간단한 문제이다. 따라서 정답은 (C)이다.

DAY 11
본문 p.322

| 1 (B) | 2 (D) | 3 (D) | 4 (A) | 5 (C) |
| 6 (C) | 7 (B) | | | |

1-3

로데오 일보
11월 24일 화요일

우리는 Emeryvill의 새로운 재생 에너지 생산 시설의 건설을 알리게 되어서 기쁩니다. 시 의회는 새로운 30억 달러의 최첨단 공장의 건설을 막 승인하였습니다. 시는 Emeryvill에 INSU 에너지의 시설을 유치하기 위해서 적극적으로 INSU 에너지를 설득했습니다. 이것은 장려금이나 세금 공제의 사용 없이 이루어졌습니다. 다시 말하면, 기업이 Emeryvill에 오도록 유도하기 위해서 세금을 사용하지 않았다는 뜻입니다. 다른 도시들은 그들의 도시에 사업을 유치하기 위해서 수백만 달러를 장려금으로 사용했지만 우리는 그것이 옳은 방법이라고 생각하지 않습니다. 우리는 숙련된 노동력과 높은 삶의 질을 강조함으로써 도시를 홍보했습니다. 우리의 열정적인 정신력이 이것과 결합하여 우리 도시에 INSU 에너지를 유치할 수 있게 했습니다.

어휘 renewable energy 재생 에너지 locate 특정 위치에 두다 incentive 장려정책, 우대정책 tax credits 세금 혜택 taxpayer 납세자 entice 유도하다 유인하다 highlight 강조하다 enthusiastic 열정적인

1
해설 이 기사의 목적은 무엇인가?
(A) 태양열 에너지의 이점을 설명하기 위해서
(B) 새로운 공장의 건설을 발표하기 위해서
(C) 재생 가능한 에너지를 설명하기 위해서
(D) 기업들에게 감세 조치를 설명하기 위해서

해설 기사의 주제는 "We are pleased to announce the construction of a new renewable energy manufacturing facility in Emeryville."에서 볼 수 있듯이 새로운 공장의 건설에 대한 내용으로 정답은 (B)이다.

2

해설 INSU 에너지를 유치하기 위해 Emeryvill이 쓴 돈은 얼마인가?
(A) 4백만 달러
(B) 5백만 달러
(C) 6백만 달러
(D) 세금을 사용하지 않음

해설 How much와 동사 spend가 질문의 키워드인데 "This was done without the use of any incentives or tax credits. In other words, it did not cost taxpayers any money"에서 어떤 돈도 쓰지 않은 것을 알 수 있다.

3

해설 Emeryvill에 사업을 유치하는 데 가장 매력적인 요소 중 하나는 무엇이었나?
(A) 낮은 범죄율
(B) 낮은 세율
(C) 우호적인 분위기
(D) 잘 훈련된 노동력

해설 장려금이나 세제 혜택 없이도 기업을 유치할 수 있었던 것은 "our skilled workforce and high quality of living"이 있었기 때문이라고 했다. 여기서 본문의 skilled가 선택지에서는 highly trained로 바꿔 쓰였다.

어휘 favorable 호의적인, 좋은 climate 분위기, 풍조; 기후

4-7

발신: Tony Stark
수신: 전 직원
날짜: 1월 13일 수요일
제목: 훌륭하게 마무리 된 일에 대해서 축하합니다!

팀 멤버 여러분,

새해를 좋은 소식과 함께 시작하게 되어서 기쁩니다. 우리가 목표로 정했던 회사들 중 하나인 Charger Industry가 우리와 함께 일하는 것에 동의했습니다. 이 회사가 1월에 우리의 두 번째 새로운 고객입니다.

Charger는 우리와 꽤 규모가 큰 거래를 하게 된 것과, 큰 계약금을 걸었기 때문에 주목할 가치가 있습니다. 우리의 상담 서비스를 존중하는 이와 같은 고객을 얻게 될 때마다 우리의 명성에 대해 많은 것을 말해 주게 됩니다. 다음 분기까지 5명의 고객들을 더 만드는 것을 우리의 목표로 합시다.

이렇게 훌륭하고 열정적인 팀을 가진 것은 너무 행운이라고 생각합니다. 감사를 표하기 위해서, 여러분 모두를 다음 목요일 점심 식사에 초대하고 싶습니다. 열심히 일해 주셔서 감사합니다.

Tony Stark
Highbrow 소프트웨어
창업주, 대표 이사

어휘 target 목표로 삼다 noteworthy 주목할 만한 sizable 크기가 큰 down payment 착수금, 계약금 acquire 얻다, 획득하다 reputation 평판 incredibly 엄청나게 ambitious 야망이 있는

4

해설 Stark 씨는 왜 행복한가?
(A) 주요한 계약이 체결되었다.
(B) 분기별 목표가 초과 달성되었다.
(C) 프로젝트를 기한 전에 마쳤다.
(D) 고용 정책 효력이 발생되었다.

해설 세부 사항 문제로 happy와 동의어를 우선 찾으면 된다. "I am happy"로 시작하는 첫 번째 문장에 정답이 나온다. 중요한 계약을 성사시킨 것이 기쁜 이유이므로 정답은 (A)이다.

어휘 surpass ~을 능가하다 put into effect 실행하다

5

해설 두 번째 문단의 첫 번째 줄의 단어 'fairly'와 의미가 가장 가까운 것은?
(A) 동등하게
(B) 친절하게
(C) 꽤
(D) 열심히

해설 동의어는 단어의 원래 의미보다는 문맥상 의미를 꼭 확인해야 한다. "because they have a fairly sizable account with us"에서 fairly는 sizable(상당한 크기의)을 수식하는 부사로 '꽤'라는 뜻으로 쓰였다. 따라서 (C)가 정답이다.

어휘 equally 동등하게

6

해설 이메일에 따르면, Stark 씨는 회사가 장차 무엇을 하길 바라는가?
(A) 사무실 확장하기
(B) 새로운 서비스 제공하기
(C) 더 많은 고객 유치하기
(D) 5명의 직원 고용하기

해설 세부 사항 문제로 in the future가 문제의 키워드이다. "Let's make it our goal to get five more clients by next quarter."에서 next quarter가 미래의 의미로 "더 많은 고객을 유치하자."라고 하고 있으므로 정답은 (C)이다.

7

해설 이메일 수신자들은 무엇을 하도록 요청받았는가?
(A) 전문 세미나에 참가하기
(B) 축하 행사에 참석하기
(C) 장기자랑에 참여하기
(D) 상을 위해 동료에게 투표하기

해설 지문 마지막 부분에 감사를 표시하기 위해 "to invite you all to lunch next Thursday"라고 말하면서 점심에 초대하고 있다. 지문에서 쓰인 lunch가 선택지에서는 celebratory activity로 바꿔 쓰였다.

어휘 celebratory 축하하는

DAY 12

본문 p.324

| 1 (D) | 2 (D) | 3 (B) | 4 (C) | 5 (B) |

1-2

대체 에너지 회의

5월 5일 오전 9시에서 오후 5시
엑스포 센터 / San Francisco, CA

일정		참석 규정
오전 9:00 – 오전 9:30	아침 식사와 인사말	선택
오전 9:30 – 오전 10:00	올해의 안건들	필수
오전 10:00 – 오전 11:00	Stanford 대학의 John Chambers 교수의 연설	초대장을 받은 분들만
오전 11:00 – 오후 12:00	기후 변화에 대한 UN 대사의 연설	필수
오후 12:00 – 오후 1:00	점심 식사	선택
오후 1:00 – 오후 2:00	새로운 기술의 시연	필수
오후 2:00 – 오후 3:00	Solar-Tech의 연설과 시연	필수
오후 3:00 – 오후 4:00	덴마크의 Hydro Industries의 해일 생성의 시연	선택
오후 4:00 – 오후 5:00	모든 정부 기관 담당자와 기업 대표들의 질의 응답 시간	선택

어휘 greetings 인사 optional 선택 사항 required 필수의 agenda 토의 주제 address 연설 ambassador 대사 demonstration 시연 tidal 조수의, 해일의 generation 발생, 생성

1

해석 덴마크의 Hydro Industries가 어떤 종류의 발표를 할 것인가?
(A) 최신의 태양열 발전 현황
(B) 기후 변화
(C) 울트라 축전지
(D) 해일의 생성

해설 질문의 키워드는 Hydro Industries of Denmark이다. 이를 표에서 찾으면 연관된 정보 "tidal wave generation"을 찾을 수 있다. 따라서 정답은 (D)이다.

어휘 latest 최신의 capacitor 축전기

2

해석 오전 11시에 잡힌 일정은 무엇인가?
(A) 대표 이사의 연설
(B) 점심 휴식
(C) Solar Tech의 시연
(D) UN 대사의 연설

해설 세부 사항 문제이다. 문제의 키워드 11:00 A.M.을 지문에서 찾으면 "Address by United Nations Ambassador on Climate Change"이다. 따라서 정답은 (D)이다.

3-5

배터리 관리

새 전기 자동차의 구매를 축하드립니다. 가장 중요한 것 중 하나는 배터리를 잘 관리하시는 것입니다. 배터리를 적절하게 관리함으로써 배터리의 수명을 10년까지 늘릴 수 있습니다. 배터리들은 10년의 보증 기간을 가지고 있지만, 소유자가 이 지침에 따라서 관리할 경우에만 해당됩니다.

사용 후 매번 배터리를 충전하십시오. 자동차는 스마트 충전기를 제공받는데, 배터리가 과하게 충전되는 것을 예방해 줍니다. 이 스마트 충전기는 배터리의 전압 수준을 확인하고, 적절한 수준까지 전류의 세기를 점점 줄입니다. 이 스마트 충전기는 또한 '세류 충전'이라고 알려진 것을 제공하는데 이것은 배터리를 사용하지 않을 때 최대 충전 용량의 배터리를 유지시키는 것입니다. 비록 충전 시에 110 볼트도 사용 가능하지만, 220 볼트를 사용하기를 권유합니다. 220 볼트가 더 빠르고 효율적입니다.

어휘 proper 적절한 lifespan 수명 overcharged 과충전된 voltage 전압 taper 점점 가늘어지다 amperage 전류의 세기

3

해석 무엇에 대한 지시 사항인가?
(A) 운전하는 법
(B) 전기 배터리 충전
(C) 자동차 엔진 관리법
(D) 품질 보증이 결정되는 방식

해설 지문의 "proper maintenance of the batteries"로부터 배터리 관리법에 관한 것임을 알 수 있다.

어휘 determine 결정하다, 결심하다

4

해석 사용자가 항상 해야 하는 것은 무엇인가?
(A) 배터리에 물을 넣을 것
(B) 배터리에 산을 추가할 것
(C) 매번 사용한 후에 배터리를 충전할 것
(D) 배터리를 매일 시험해 볼 것

해설 세부 사항 문제로 "Recharge your batteries after each use."로부터 정답이 (C)임을 알 수 있다.

어휘 acid 산, 산성

5

해석 지시 사항에 따르면, 충전 시 권유되는 전압량은?
(A) 110볼트
(B) 220볼트
(C) 12볼트
(D) 명시되지 않음

해설 질문의 키워드는 recommended와 voltage이다. 지문에서 "We recommend the use of a 220-volt system"으로부터 바로 (B)가 정답임을 알 수 있다.

어휘 specify 명시하다

DAY 13

본문 p.326

| 1 (C) | 2 (A) | 3 (C) | 4 (C) | 5 (A) |
| 6 (B) | | | | |

1-3

왓슨 씨께,

귀사의 발포 고무 배달과 관련해서 미국에 있는 저희 가구 공장에서 겪고 있는 어려움 때문에 이 글을 씁니다. 아시다시피, 저희는 미국 전역에 5개의 다른 가구 생산 공장을 가지고 있고, 귀사의 발포 고무가 저희 가구 제품의 75%에 쓰이고 있습니다. 하지만 지난 30일 간, 귀사의 발포 고무 선적의 지연으로 인해 저희 공장이 생산을 멈추는 일이 발생했습니다. 이것은 용납할 수 없는 일이고 우리는 이 문제가 즉시 시정될 거라는 당신의 확답을 받아야겠습니다. 그렇지 않으면, Acme 발포 고무와 한 공급 계약을 취소하고 다른 회사로 교체할 수밖에 없습니다. 이 문제에 대해서 귀사가 이해해 주셨으면 합니다.

Tom Brokaw
물류 이사
Savannah 가구

어휘 foam rubber 발포 고무 cease 멈추다 at once 즉시 otherwise 그렇지 않다면 force 어쩔 수 없이 ~하도록 하다; ~에게 강요하다 switch 바꾸다

1
해석 이 편지의 목적은 무엇인가?
(A) 가구의 판매량을 증가시키기 위해
(B) 발포 고무의 판매량을 증가시키기 위해
(C) 발포 고무의 배송에 대해 항의하기 위해
(D) 배송 문제를 보고하기 위해

해설 편지의 주제 문제로 "I am writing to you in reference to problems we are experiencing with your company in foam rubber deliveries to our furniture plants around the United States."라는 첫 문장부터 글쓴이는 배달 지연에 대한 불평을 하고 있음을 알 수 있다. 따라서 정답은 (C)이다.

어휘 report 보고하다

2
해석 배송 지연의 결과는 무엇인가?
(A) 제품 생산의 중단이 야기되었다.
(B) 가격 상승을 야기시킨다.
(C) 모두에게 불편하다.
(D) 공장 이전을 야기시킨다.

해설 지문의 "delays of your foam rubber shipments have forced our plants to cease production"으로부터 공장 가동이 중단되었음을 알 수 있다. (A)의 stop은 지문의 cease를 다른 말로 바꿔 쓴 것이다.

어휘 relocation 이전

3
해석 만약 문제가 해결되지 않는다면, Brokaw 씨가 할 일은 무엇인가?
(A) 시간을 더 준다.
(B) 가격을 흥정한다.
(C) 다른 제조업체를 알아본다.
(D) 다른 제품을 개발한다.

해설 What, problems, not resolved가 질문의 키워드이다. "we will be forced to cancel our supply agreement with Acme Foam Rubber and switch to another company"에서 문제가 해결되지 않으면 다른 생산 업체를 찾을 것이라고 했으므로 정답은 (C)이다.

어휘 resolve 해결하다 negotiate 협상하다

4-6

일터에서 당신의 생산성을 최대화할 수 있는 조언과 비법

잠을 충분히 잔 후에도, 책상 앞에서 하루 종일 보낸다면 피곤함을 느끼고 스트레스를 받는 것은 당연한 것입니다. 다행히, 당신의 활력을 유지하고 하루 종일 스트레스 받지 않도록 하기 위해서 할 수 있는 것이 몇 가지 있습니다. 가장 좋은 점은 이러한 비법들이 대부분 전혀 돈이 들지 않는다는 점입니다.

활동성을 유지하기
신체 활동의 부족은 졸림이나 근육의 피로를 유발할 수 있습니다. 의학박사 Winnie Manson의 연구에 따르면, 낮 동안에 신체적으로 활동적인 사람들이 명철함을 유지하고 정보를 더 빠르게 처리할 수 있다고 합니다. 그래서 몇 시간 간격으로 밖으로 나가서서, 5분 정도 산책을 하십시오. 날씨나 장소의 제약이 따른다면, 실내에서 하십시오. 계단을 오르는 일이 특히 기운을 나게 해 줄 수 있습니다.

물 많이 마시기
탈수는 일상에서 피곤함을 유발하는 흔한 원인입니다. Michigan 대학의 최근 연구에서, 연구자들은 하루에 최소한 8잔의 물을 마시는 것이 학생들의 정신을 더욱 맑게 해 주고 하루 종일 집중하게 해 준다는 것을 발견했습니다. 병이나 물을 담을 수 있는 용기를 가까이에 두시고, 당신이 필요하다고 느끼기 전에 물을 드십시오.

자연과 접촉하기
당신의 일터에 나무를 심은 화분을 두십시오. 연구자들은 사무실에 신선한 꽃이나 녹색 식물을 기르는 사람들이 여러 가지 혜택을 볼 수 있다고 결론지었습니다. 그들은 더욱 창의적이고 혁신적인 생각을 하고, 긍정적으로 생각을 하며, 더 깨끗한 공기로 숨 쉴 수 있습니다. 야자나무, 담쟁이, 양치식물은 쉽게 기를 수 있는 식물입니다.

어휘 stress-free 스트레스를 받지 않는 trick 비법 physical 육체적인 drowsiness 졸림 clearheaded 두뇌가 명석한 invigorating 기운 나게 하는 dehydration 탈수, 건조 clarity 명료성 original 창의적인 palms 야자과 식물 ivy 담쟁이덩굴 ferns 양치류

4
해석 독자들에게 해 주는 조언은 무엇인가?
(A) 취미 갖기
(B) 정원에 채소 심기
(C) 낮 동안에 짧은 산책하기
(D) 오후에 건강에 좋은 간식 섭취하기

해설 질문의 키워드는 advice이다. 지문의 "take a five-minute walk

every few hours"로부터 글쓴이는 하루 중에 짧게라도 걸으라고 조언하고 있다.

어휘 take short walks 잠깐 산책하다

5
해석 물을 마시는 것에 대해 추론할 수 있는 것은?
(A) 피로를 예방해 준다.
(B) 찬 물이 따뜻한 물보다 더 좋다.
(C) 집중하는 데 도움을 주지 않는다.
(D) 목이 마를 때 물을 마셔야 한다.

해설 drinking water가 이 질문의 키워드이다. 지문 중간에 "Dehydration can be a common cause of daily tiredness."가 나오는데, 탈수(dehydration)는 몸에 물이 부족한 현상이고, 이것이 피곤을 야기한다고 했으므로 물을 많이 마시면 피곤을 예방할 수 있다는 것을 알 수 있다.

어휘 prevent 예방하다

6
해석 기사에 따르면, 창의력을 증가시킬 수 있는 것은?
(A) 더 많은 수분 섭취
(B) 가까이에 식물을 두는 것
(C) 규칙적인 운동
(D) 충분한 수면

해설 질문의 키워드인 increase와 creativity를 지문에서 찾으면 "They create more original and innovative ideas" 부분에서 지문 속의 original이 선택지에서는 creativity로 바꿔서 쓰인 것을 알 수 있다. 따라서 정답은 (B)이다.

DAY
14   본문 p.328

1 (D)   2 (D)   3 (D)   4 (D)   5 (C)
6 (A)

1-3

우리는 New York 시의 금융가에 Empire 은행이 문을 여는 것을 발표하게 되어서 기쁩니다. Empire 은행은 Bank of the West와 Great Western Bank 사이의 합병의 결과물입니다. Empire 은행의 자산은 1,000억 달러를 초과했습니다. Bank of the West와 Great Western Bank의 합병은 우리 고객들에게 전국적인 서비스를 제공할 것입니다. 이로써 저희는 미국의 모든 50개 주에 은행 지점을 가지게 되었습니다. New York 시에 Empire 은행 지점을 연 것은 우리 회사 역사에서 획기적인 일입니다. 또한 Empire 은행은 증권 거래를 담당하는 강력한 부서를 두고 있습니다. Eagle 증권이 저희 은행 고객들을 위해서 모든 옵션과 주식 거래를 제공합니다. 우리의 새로운 고객들에게 감사하는 마음으로, 평생 무료로 이용하실 수 있는 당좌 예금을 개설해 드립니다. 여러분 모두가 7월 5일 금요일 오전 9시에 개점 행사에 참석하실 수 있습니다.

어휘 exceed ~을 초과하다 symbolize 상징하다 landmark 획기적인 사건 securities 증권 trading 거래 stock 주식 checking accounts 당좌예금

1
해석 Empire 은행의 어떤 부서에서 주식 거래를 제공하는가?
(A) 미국 증권
(B) Bank of the West
(C) Empire 은행
(D) Eagle 증권

해설 세부 사항 문제로 질문의 키워드인 provides stock trading을 지문에서 찾아야 한다. "Eagle Securities will provide a full range of trading options and stock trading for our banking customers." 부분에서 Eagle 증권이 서비스를 제공함을 알 수 있다.

2
해석 Empire 은행은 몇 개의 주에 지점을 갖고 있는가?
(A) 35개 주
(B) 35개 주
(C) 49개 주
(D) 50개 주

해설 세부 사항 문제로 질문의 키워드는 In how many states, branches이다. 해당 내용을 지문에서 찾으면 "We now have bank branches in all fifty states of the United States."라고 했으므로 모든 50개의 주에 지점이 있음을 알 수 있다.

3
해석 Empire 은행이 신규 고객에게 제공하는 것은 무엇인가?
(A) 50달러 상당의 저축 채권
(B) 커피와 케이크
(C) 무료 주식 거래 계좌
(D) 무료 당좌 예금 계좌

해설 질문의 키워드는 What, offer, new customers이다. 지문에서 해당 내용을 찾으면 "we are offering free checking accounts" 부분에서 정답을 찾을 수 있다. 따라서 정답은 (D)이다.

어휘 savings bond 저축 채권

4-6

Consolidated Financial Services의 대표 이사인 John H. Hastings의 일정표

월요일 6월 21일	오전 8:00에서 오전 11:00 오후 1:00에서 오후 5:00	주주들과의 미팅 상공 회의소와의 회의
화요일 6월 22일	오전 8:00에서 오전 10:00 오후 2:00에서 오후 4:00	부회장들과 미팅 노조 계약과 관련한 노조 관계 위원장과 미팅
수요일 6월 23일	오전 8:00에서 오전 11:30 오후 1:00에서 오후 5:00	화물 운송 업체와 미팅 공급 계약서와 관련해서 Beneto 철강 대표 이사와의 회의
목요일 6월 24일	오전 8:00에서 오전 10:00 오후 2:00에서 오후 4:00	San Felipe인 Heather Jones와 미팅 Order of Masons 앞에서 프레젠테이션
금요일 6월 25일	오전 8:00에서 오전 10:00 오후 2:00에서 오후 3:00	주주들과 아침식사 Pacific 대학의 졸업생들을 위한 기조연설

어휘 consolidated 통합된 stockholder 주주 Chamber of Commerce 상공 회의소 labor 노동, 근로 freight forwarder 화물 운송업자 shareholder 주주 keynote address 기조연설

4

해석 이 일정표는 누구를 위한 것인가?
(A) Consolidated Financial Services의 영업 사원
(B) 대표 이사의 개인 수행원
(C) Consolidated Financial Services 영업 관리자
(D) Consolidated Financial Services의 대표 이사

해설 누구를 위한 일정표인지를 묻는 문제로 문서의 제목 부분에서 정답을 찾을 수 있다. 이 일정표는 대표 이사 John H. Hastings를 위한 것이다.

5

해석 San Filipe 시장과의 회의는 언제인가?
(A) 월요일
(B) 화요일
(C) 목요일
(D) 금요일

해설 질문의 키워드인 When과 Mayor of San Filipe를 보고 찾으면 되는 간단한 문제이다.

6

해석 금요일 오전 8시에 잡힌 일정은 무엇인가?
(A) 주주들과의 아침 식사
(B) 이사회 위원들과의 아침 식사
(C) 부사장들과의 아침 식사
(D) 상공 회의소와의 아침 식사

해설 질문의 키워드인 Friday at 8:00 A.M.을 지문에서 찾으면 되는 간단한 세부 사항 문제이다.

DAY 15

본문 p.330

| 1 (D) | 2 (A) | 3 (A) | 4 (A) | 5 (C) |
| 6 (D) | 7 (B) | 8 (A) | | |

1-4

Casanville 다리의 다가올 도로 보수 공사

7월 2일 – 대망의 Casanville 다리의 도로 재건 공사가 다음 달에 착수됩니다. 보수 공사는 양쪽 길에 한 차선씩을 추가하는 것을 통해서 도로를 확장하는 공사인데, 이로 인해 차량이 좀 더 빠른 속도로 이동할 수 있습니다. 건설 공사가 끝날 때까지 좀 더 심한 교통 체증이 예상됩니다. 지난 토요일, Saint Juste Transportation Agency (SJTA)는 8월 3일 월요일에 Casanville 다리의 도로 공사를 진행할 예정이라고 발표했습니다. 위에서 언급한 것처럼, 다리의 양쪽 도로가 느린 교통 흐름을 경험할 것이고, 결과적으로 운전자들이 교통 정체로 인해 일시적인 불편함을 겪게 될 것입니다.

교통 혼잡 시간을 피해서, 도로 공사가 3교대로 진행될 것입니다. (주중: 오전 11시에서 오후 5시, 오후 10시에서 오전 5시 / 주말: 오전 10시에서 오후 4시, 오후 9시에서 오전 7시)

다리 보수 공사는 3주 후에 완료될 것입니다. 상황에 따라서, SJTA는 운전자들에게 Casanville 다리를 이용하지 말아 주실 것과 대신에 Forest Avenue나 Ponoma Street를 이용해 주실 것을 권고해 드립니다. 두 도로 모두 Van Waals 다리로 연결되어 강 건너편으로 갈 수 있게 해줍니다.

어휘 anticipated 기대하던, 대망의 underway 진행 중인 widen 넓어지다, 넓히다 undertake 착수하다. shift 교대조

1

해석 기사는 주로 누구를 위한 것인가?
(A) 여행사 직원들
(B) 해외 관광객들
(C) 도로 공사 작업자들
(D) 지역 운전자들

해설 For whom으로 시작하는 문제는 글을 읽을 독자를 추론하는 전체 지문 문제이지만 초반에 힌트가 나온다. 첫 문단 전체와 drivers will have to face temporary discomfort due to traffic delays 부분에서 (D)에게 도로 공사 안내를 하고 있는 것을 알 수 있다.

2

해석 [1], [2], [3], [4]로 표시된 부분 중에서 다음 문장이 들어가기에 가장 알맞은 곳은?

"위에서 언급한 것처럼, 다리의 양쪽 도로가 느린 교통 흐름을 경험할 것이고, 결과적으로 운전자들이 교통 정체로 인해 일시적인 불편함을 겪게 될 것입니다."

(A) [1]
(B) [2]
(C) [3]
(D) [4]

해설 as stated above와 due to traffic delays가 힌트가 될 수 있다. 앞에서 언급한 내용으로 두 개의 차선에 대한 내용, 이 다음에는 '정체'와 관련된 내용이 나와야 한다. 앞에서 양쪽 차선에 대한 내용이 나오고 뒤에는 To avoid the rush hours가 나오는 (A)가 가장 적절하다.

3

해석 도로 공사에 대해서 언급한 것은?
(A) 평소보다 막히는 교통 흐름을 야기할 것이다.
(B) Casanville 다리의 통제를 야기할 것이다.
(C) 마무리까지 몇 달 이상이 걸릴 것이다.
(D) 수리 작업이 포함되어 있다.

해설 (A)는 안내문의 heavier traffic congestion is to be expected가 패러프레이징된 것이다. several months가 아닌 three weeks가 공사 기간이므로 (C)는 오답이다.

4

해석 SJTA가 추천한 방법은 무엇인가?
(A) 우회하기
(B) 러시아워 피하기
(C) 느린 속도로 운전하기
(D) Casanville 다리 이용하지 않기

해설 SJTA의 조언은 세 번째 문단의 SJTA advises motorists not to get on the Casanville Bridge, but instead take Forest Avenue or Ponoma Street이다. 다른 길을 이용하라고 했으므로 정답은 (A)이다.

5-8

상담원 [오후 2:30]
안녕하세요. 상담원입니다. 무엇을 도와 드릴까요?

Ross Dickerson [오후 2:31]
최근에 Milky Way M3 휴대폰을 구입했는데 터치스크린에 문제가 있어요. 터치스크린이 원하는 대로 작동을 하지 않아요.

상담원 [오후 2:32]
고객님. 좀 더 상세히 말씀해 주세요. 정확히 어떤 부분이 불편하셨나요?

Ross Dickerson [오후 2:34]
타이핑을 치면 아무런 반응이 없어요. 터치스크린을 밀어서 전화를 받으려고 해도 전혀 작동하지 않아요.

상담원 [오후 2:35]
아마도 터치스크린이 응답을 하지 않는 것 같아요. 다음과 같이 해보세요. 우선 고객님 휴대 전화를 컴퓨터에 연결해 주세요. 그리고 두 번째로 휴대 전화를 공장 설정으로 복원해 주세요.

Ross Dickerson [오후 2:40]
네, 이미 해봤어요. 안타깝지만 해도 아무것도 변하지 않았어요.

상담원 [오후 2:42]
만약 그렇다면 선택할 수 있는 것이 하나 있어요. 아직까지 보증 기간이 남아 있기 때문에 리퍼브 제품으로 교환할 수 있어요.

Ross Dickerson [오후 2:43]
어떻게 해야 하는지 알려 주세요.

상담원 [오후 2:45]
고객님 제품을 저희 센터로 보내 주세요. 그러면 저희가 고객님께 우편 요금이 지불된 박스를 곧바로 보내 드릴 거예요. 아니면 고객님께서 직접 휴대 전화를 가까운 저희 공인 서비스 업체에 맡겨 주세요.

어휘 have trouble with ~에 대해 문제가 있다 in detail 상세하게 turn off 끄다 it appears that ~인 것처럼 보인다 unresponsive 응답하지 않는 under warranty 보증 기간 중인 refurbished 리퍼브의 postage-paid box 우편 요금이 지불된 상자 authorized 승인된, 허가를 받은

5

해설 Dickerson 씨가 고객 서비스 센터에 연락한 이유는 무엇인가?
(A) 주문하기 위해
(B) 제품을 반송하기 위해
(C) 기술 지원을 받기 위해
(D) 배송 지연을 알리기 위해

해설 휴대 전화의 터치스크린이 제대로 작동하지 않았기 때문에 이에 대한 문제를 해결하기 위해 고객센터로 연락했다. 상담원이 이 문제를 해결하기 위한 절차를 알려 주고 있다. 따라서 정답은 (C)이다.

6

해설 채팅 내용에 따르면 Dickerson 씨의 휴대 전화에 대해서 알 수 있는 것은 무엇인가?
(A) 곧바로 고칠 수 있다.
(B) 보증 기간이 이미 지났다.
(C) 잘못된 주소로 배송되었다.
(D) 터치스크린이 손상되었다.

해설 The touchscreen is not working as expected라는 표현에서 터치스크린이 손상되었음을 알 수 있다. 따라서 정답은 (D)이다.

7

해설 상담원이 제품에 대해 추천한 해결책은 무엇인가?
(A) 가까운 서비스 업체에서 수리해라.
(B) 교환을 위해 보내라.
(C) 전액 환불을 받아라.
(D) 터치스크린을 교체해라.

해설 휴대 전화를 리퍼브 제품으로 교환해 주겠다고 했으며 이를 위해 제품을 보내 달라고 했다. 따라서 정답은 (B)이다.

8

해설 오후 2시 42분에 상담원이 "만약 그렇다면"이라고 쓸 때 그 의도는 무엇인가?
(A) 대안을 제시하려고 한다.
(B) 불편함에 대해 사과한다.
(C) 보증 기간을 연장하도록 설득하길 원한다.
(D) 할인 쿠폰을 주면서 문제에 대한 보상을 한다.

해설 터치스크린이 작동하지 않아 해결책을 제시하려고 했지만 해결이 되지 않은 상황이다. 그래서 교환해 주겠다며 말하며 또 다른 해결책을 제기하고 있다. 따라서 정답은 (A)이다.

DAY 16 본문 p.332

| 1 (A) | 2 (D) | 3 (B) | 4 (C) | 5 (B) |

1-5

연 2회 진행되는 6번째 Gerry Garcia 예술 축제
9월 10일에서 12일

Psychedelic 예술 협회에 의해 후원되는 Gerry Garcia 예술 축제 (GGAF)가 모든 사람들을 놀라게 할 것입니다. 3일 동안 이어지는 이 행사는 유명한 작가들의 작품을 보여 주고 현지 음악가와 배우들이 여는 작은 콘서트들도 포함합니다. 아이들을 위한 놀이뿐만 아니라 음식과 조각품들이 판매됩니다.

아래는 행사 목록 중 일부입니다.

▶ 8월 10일 금요일, 오후 1시 미술관 서관
Johann Strauss'의 <내 주위의 얼굴들> 첫 번째 전시입니다. 전시는 9월 15일까지 진행됩니다.

▶ 8월 11일 토요일과 12일 일요일 오전 10시에서 오후 6시, 소방서 소풍 장소, 아이들의 공예품

▶ 8월 11일 토요일 오후 6시, Balboa 야외 극장
(우천 시: Cortez 강당) 아일랜드 고아원 합창단의 공연 (대중의 열렬한 요청에 의해 재공연) 입장권을 구매해야 합니다.

▶ 8월 11일 토요일과 12일 일요일 오후 1시에서 8시, Fallen Heroes Memorial Park, 음식과 공예 시장

▶ 8월 12일 일요일 오후 2시와 8시, Savoy 극장

Mata Hari 극단이 유명한 작가인 John Lloyd의 작품 〈인과응보〉를 공연합니다. 입장권이 필요합니다.

8월 1일까지 입장권을 판매합니다. 입장권과 행사 목록에 대해 더 많은 정보를 원하시면 www.ggaf.org.phx를 방문하세요.

수신: Leah Sharpe ⟨leahsharpe224@ggaf.org.phx⟩
발신: Jasmine McIntyre ⟨jmcintyre@swt.org.za⟩
제목: 정보
날짜: 8월 15일

Sharpe 씨께,

Gerry Garcia 예술 축제에서 우리 고아원 합창단이 여러분을 즐겁게 해 드릴 기회를 주신 것에 감사를 드립니다. 날씨 때문에 외부에서 공연을 할 수 없었던 것과 적은 수의 사람들만이 행사를 관람한 점이 안타깝습니다. 하지만 참석하신 많은 분들이 저희의 앨범을 사주셨고, 유명한 웹 사이트에서 저희의 노래를 내려 받을 수 있는지를 알고 싶어 하셨습니다. 우리는 관객들로부터 받은 긍정적인 반응에 정말 감사하고 있습니다.

앞으로 이 축제에서 다시 공연하기를 희망합니다.

Jasmine McIntyre
아일랜드 고아원 합창단 운영 이사

어휘 semi-annual 연 2회의; 6개월마다의 psychedelic 환각을 일으키는 encompassing 둘러싸는, 포함하는 showcase 진열하다, 전시하다 incomplete 불완전한 choir 합창단 craft 공예품 ensemble 합주단, 극단

1
해석 예술 축제 행사 기간에 있을 행사가 아닌 것은 무엇인가?
(A) 발레 공연
(B) 예술 공예 전시
(C) 미술 전시회
(D) 먹거리 마켓

해설 세부 사항 문제이다. ballet performance는 공연 목록에서 찾을 수 없으므로 정답은 (A)이다.

2
해석 공연(연극)은 언제 관람할 수 있는가?
(A) 8월 1일
(B) 8월 10일
(C) 8월 11일
(D) 8월 12일

해설 문제의 키워드는 When, play이다. 우선 play가 공연이라는 뜻이 있는데 이 내용은 지문의 Theatre Ensemble(극단)이 나오는 곳에서 찾을 수 있다. 이 부분의 날짜를 확인하면 (D)가 정답임을 알 수 있다.

3
해석 축제에 관해 언급된 것은 무엇인가?
(A) 1주일간 시행된다.
(B) 1년에 두 번 열린다.
(C) 매일 오전 10시에 시작한다.
(D) 온라인으로만 표를 구매할 수 있다.

해설 광고의 제목 부분에서 The 6th Semi-Annual Gerry Garcia Arts Festival로부터 일 년에 두 번 열리는 행사임을 알 수 있다.

어휘 purchase 구입하다

4
해석 왜 McIntyre 씨는 Sharpe 씨에게 이메일을 보냈는가?
(A) 행사를 위한 티켓을 구매하기 위해서
(B) 공연 일정을 변경하기 위해서
(C) 감사 인사를 하기 위해서
(D) 초대를 거절하기 위해서

해설 두 번째 글의 주제 문제이다. 전형적인 주제 문제로 지문의 초반에 "My gratitude for your giving us the chance to entertain you with music of our orphanage"라고 하면서 감사를 표현하고 있으므로 정답은 (C)이다.

어휘 decline 거절하다

5
해석 아일랜드 고아 합창단에 대하여 암시된 바는 무엇인가?
(A) 처음 참여한 것이었다.
(B) Cortez 강당에서 공연했다.
(C) 현재 아일랜드에서 순회 공연 중이다.
(D) 합창단의 웹 사이트에 방문자가 많다.

해설 두 지문 연계 문제이다. 우선 두 번째 글의 "weather did not allow us to perform outdoors"에서 외부에서 공연을 못했다는 것을 알 수 있고, 첫 번째 글의 "In the event of rain: Cortez Auditorium"에서 비가 올 경우 강당에서 대신 공연을 한다는 것을 알 수 있으므로 정답은 (B)이다.

DAY 17
본문 p.334

| 1 (B) | 2 (C) | 3 (A) | 4 (A) | 5 (D) |

1-5

Milne 사무용품

8월 10일

Williams, Redman
4001 Fifth Ave, Suite 305 Toronto, Ontario M4W 1A7

계좌 번호: XXXX-3001   고객 ID: WRA4001305

Williams 씨께,

지난 5년 동안 귀하의 꾸준한 이용에 감사를 표하기 위해서, 우리는 귀하의 Milne 사무용품(MOS) 신용 카드를 즉시 적용되는 골든 리워드 특별 등급으로 상향 조정해 드렸습니다. 이 등급은 수많은 혜택을 특징으로 하는데, 그 안에는 3,000달러 한도 증액, 150달러 이상 구매 시 무료 배송, 그리고 특별 행사의 무료 참가권이 들어갑니다. 더불어, 골든 리워드 고객들은 MOS 신용 카드를 사용함으로써 매달 선택된 물품은 20퍼센트의 할인을 받게 됩니다. 이달에는 모든 전자 제품이 오직 골든 리워드 고객들에게만 할인됩니다. 할인은 구매 시 적용될 것이고 "SR 포인트"로 영수증에 표시될 것입니다.

귀하의 상향 조정된 신용 상태에 대한 더 많은 세부 사항은 첨부된

안내 책자에서 확인할 수 있습니다. 귀하의 계좌에 대해서 질문이 있으시면, 무료 전화 709-565-7710으로 월요일에서 토요일 사이에 오전 10시에서 오후 5시까지 MOS 고객 서비스로 전화하세요.

Oscar Wilde
이사, 카드 이용 고객 서비스 팀

Milne 사무용품
178 E Maple Street, Toronto, Ontario M4W 1A7
영수증

출력: 7월 17일 오전 9시 3분   고객 ID: WRA4001305

CLD974	Orocan 등받이 의자 (검정)	129달러
SNW235	Florentine 노트북 컴퓨터 (모델 2433CH)	170달러
KVN291	Grappa 컴퓨터 전시 캐비닛	430달러
SMR886	Sedgewick 표준 스테이플러 12개 각각 9.00달러	108달러
SMR810	Canon 레이저 프린터	310달러
소계		1,147달러
판매 세금		113.40달러
신용카드 XXXX-278에 의한 총 결제액		1,260.40달러

SR 포인트가 물품 번호 SNW235와 SMR810에 적용됨
할인된 제품은 교환 또는 환불이 되지 않습니다.
반품은 구매일로부터 30일 이내에 가능합니다.

어휘 gratitude 감사 patronage (고객의) 애용 privilege 특권 take effect 효력을 발휘하다 complimentary 무료의 reflect ~을 반영하다

1
해석 이 편지의 목적은 무엇인가?
(A) 노트북 컴퓨터와 사무용품을 주문하기 위해서
(B) Williams 씨에게 신용 카드가 변경됨을 알려 주기 위해서
(C) Milne 사무용품의 전 품목 할인을 홍보하기 위해서
(D) Williams 씨의 제안을 받아들이기 위해서

해설 편지의 주제 문제이다. 글의 초반에서 "we have upgraded your Milne Office Supplies (MOS) credit card"라고 언급하고 있으므로 신용 카드의 변경을 알려 주고 있다.

어휘 storewide 점포 전체의

2
해석 편지에 의하면, Williams 씨에 관해 무엇이 암시되고 있는가?
(A) 그는 MOS가 주최하는 경매에 참석했다.
(B) 그는 MOS에서 온라인 구매를 했다.
(C) 그는 장기 고객이다.
(D) 그는 이전 주문에 3천 달러를 썼다.

해설 Williams 씨에 대한 내용은 첫 번째 지문 전반에 걸쳐 나오므로 선택지를 먼저 읽고 선택지의 키워드를 지문에서 찾아 내용을 확인한다. 첫 문단 첫 줄에서 "To express our gratitude for your patronage for the past 5 years"로부터 5년 동안 MOS를 이용한 고객임을 알 수 있다. patronage는 '고객의 애용'을 뜻하는 단어이다.

어휘 auction 경매

3
해석 7월에 골든 리워드 고객들이 어떤 제품에 20% 할인을 받았는가?
(A) 컴퓨터와 주변 장치
(B) 필기도구
(C) 사무용 가구
(D) 사무용품

해설 두 번째 지문 후반에 "SR points applied to item numbers SNW235 and SMR810"라고 언급된 부분과 첫 번째 지문에 "Discounts will be applied at the time of sale and reflected as 'SR points' on the receipt."라고 언급된 부분에서 힌트를 얻어 연계 문제를 풀 수 있다. SR point가 적용되는 SNW235와 SMR810는 각각 휴대용 컴퓨터와 프린터이므로 정답은 (A)이다.

어휘 peripheral (컴퓨터) 주변 장치

4
해석 편지의 첫 문단 여덟 번째 줄에 있는 단어 "applied"와 의미가 가장 가까운 것은?
(A) 효력이 발휘되다
(B) 호소되다
(C) 연락이 닿다
(D) 열심히 하다

해설 동의어 문제는 문맥 안에서 단어가 쓰인 뜻을 확인해야 한다. "Discounts will be applied"에서 applied는 "할인이 적용된다"라는 뜻이므로 (A)가 적절한 동의어이다.

어휘 appeal 관심을 끌다, 호소하다

5
해석 영수증에 따르면, 구입에 대해서 알 수 있는 것은?
(A) 손님은 각각의 물품에 대해서 10%의 할인을 받았다.
(B) 구입 후 30일이 지나면 교환만 가능하다.
(C) 환불은 영수증 없이 이루어질 수 있다.
(D) 일부 구입 품목에만 환불이 적용된다.

해설 "No refunds or exchanges will be made on discounted products."에서 refunds는 몇몇 제품에만 환불이 적용된다고 말한 (D)가 정답이다.

DAY 18   본문 p.336

1 (A)   2 (B)   3 (C)   4 (D)   5 (C)

1-5

The Hampshire Times
Hampshire가 옷을 입다

10월 30일 - 34 Macedon Avenue에서 활기 넘치는 거래 장면을 목격하는 것은 어려운 일이 아닙니다. 10월 10일, 그곳에 전국적인 소매상점인 Harold 남성복 매장이 엄청나게 많고 대단한 대중들에게 최신 점포를 개점했기 때문입니다. 지역의 구매자들은 Harold 매장이 파는 유명한 옷들을 다른 소매업자들의 가격보다 50%까지 싸게 살 수 있는 것에 들떠 있습니다. 엄청난 일요일 할인 판매로 유명

한 이 직판장은 이전의 Rochester 금융 복합단지를 인수해서, 지금까지 가장 큰 가게 중 하나를 수용할 수 있게 개조했습니다.

Hampshire 상공 회의소의 의장인 Sigmund Taber는 "Harold 남성복 매장이 Hampshire에게는 굉장한 일입니다. 도시는 소득세 수입에 의해 굉장한 혜택을 얻게 될 것이고, 대략 30개의 새로운 일자리가 만들어졌습니다."라고 말한다. 그는 또한 "지역 주민들은 이렇게 훌륭한 매장이 마을에 있는 것이 매우 편리하다는 것을 알게 되었습니다. 우리는 좋은 옷을 찾기 위해서 더 이상 Helmsford의 쇼핑몰까지 멀리 여행할 필요가 없습니다."라고 말한다.

이 가게의 영업 시간은 아침 8시에서 저녁 10시이다. 남문은 Macedon Avenue에 있고, 서문은 Chestnut Parkway 바로 옆에 있는 Duke Street에 있습니다. 충분한 주차 공간이 있습니다. 하지만 이 지역의 교통 혼잡 시간 동안에는 주차장에서 나오거나 들어가기가 매우 힘듭니다.

편집장님께,
Hampshire에 있는 Harold 남성복 매장의 점포 설립에 대한 10월 30일자 당신의 기사를 읽었습니다. 가게가 마을에 매우 편리함을 가져다주었지만 동시에 우리 마을에 오랫동안 살아온 많은 주민들에게 불편함으로 다가오고 있습니다. Duke Street에 사는 저희 중에 몇몇은 집 앞의 교통 체증으로 인해 방해를 받고 있습니다. 가게의 운영 시간에는 대개 Duke Street에 긴 줄의 자동차들과 트럭들이 있습니다. 자동차들이 진입로 앞을 막고 있어서, 집에 들어가거나 나가는 것이 어려워졌습니다. 배달 트럭들은 대개 Macedon Avenue 입구를 이용하지 않는데 Duke Street 입구가 적재 구획에서 가장 가깝기 때문입니다.

Harold 남성복 매장이 Duke Street 입구에 대해서 할 수 있는 것이 없다는 것을 알고 있습니다. 그래서 주민 몇 사람과 저는 Hampshire 마을 위원회에 Duke Street와 Macedon Avenue 교차로에 신호등을 설치해 달라고 요청했습니다. 이것이 교통 흐름을 좀 더 효율적으로 만들어 줄 것이고, 우리에게 조금이나마 안도감을 줄 것입니다. 저희는 다른 Hampshire 거주자들께 이 문제가 논의될 11월 30일 다음 번 위원회 모임에 참석함으로써 문제가 해결될 수 있게끔 도와 주실 것을 간청 드립니다.

Leonard Nesmith
이 문제를 걱정하는 주민

어휘 inaugurate 개관을 선언하다 haberdashery 남성복 매장 townsfolk 마을 사람들 hinder 저해하다 intersection 교차로 implore 애원하다, 간청하다

1

해석 기사에 따르면, Harold 남성복 매장이 왜 쇼핑객들에게 인기 있는가?
(A) 저렴한 가격 때문에
(B) 고객 서비스 때문에
(C) 제품의 다양성 때문에
(D) 우수한 반품 정책 때문에

해설 세부 사항 문제로 질문의 키워드 why와 popular를 바탕으로 내용을 지문에서 찾으면 "Local shoppers have been excited for the popular clothing that Harold's sells for up to fifty percent off other retailer's prices."로부터 다른 상점의 절반 가격에 옷을 구입할 수 있음을 알 수 있다.

2

해석 Taber 씨가 Harold 남성복 매장에 대해 무엇이라 말하는가?
(A) 충분한 주차 공간이 없다.
(B) Hampshire가 경제적인 혜택을 보게 한다.
(C) Helmsford에 분점을 개업할 것이다.
(D) Hampshire의 다른 가게들과 경쟁하게 만든다.

해설 Taber 씨가 한 말 중에 "The town will greatly benefit from income tax revenues"라는 부분이 있는데, (B)의 financially(재정적으로)와 연관 시켜서 정답을 고를 수 있다.

어휘 adequate 적절한 competition 경쟁

3

해석 배송 트럭에 대해 알 수 있는 것은 무엇인가?
(A) 트럭들 때문에 교통사고가 증가하였다.
(B) 많은 트럭이 Macedon Avenue를 이용한다.
(C) Harold 매장의 서쪽 출입문을 주로 이용한다.
(D) 아침에는 거리가 트럭들로 붐비지 않는다.

해설 두 지문을 읽어야 풀 수 있는 연계 문제이다. 두 번째 지문에서 트럭들은 적재 구역이 가장 가까운 Duke Street를 자주 이용한다고 했고 첫 번째 지문에서 Harold 매장의 서쪽 출입구가 Duke Street와 연결되어 있다고 했으므로 정답은 (C)이다.

어휘 road accident 교통사고

4

해석 Nesmith 씨가 배송 트럭에 대해 언급한 것은 무엇인가?
(A) 적재 구역을 이용하지 않는다.
(B) Duke Street 이용을 금지해야 한다.
(C) 운영 시간을 줄여야 한다.
(D) 거주민들의 도로를 자주 막는다.

해설 두 번째 지문 첫 번째 문단에서 "Vehicles stop in front of our driveways"라는 말이 나오는데, 바로 그 앞에 "there is usually a long line of cars and trucks on Duke Street"와 같이 트럭이 언급되고 있다. 따라서 트럭이 거주민들의 도로를 자주 막음을 알 수 있다.

5

해석 Nesmith 씨는 마을 주민들에게 무엇을 요청하는가?
(A) Harold 남성복 매장을 이용하지 말기
(B) Harold 남성복 매장까지 대중교통 이용하기
(C) 교통 체증을 해소하려는 노력 지지하기
(D) 지역 의원들에게 편지 보내기

해설 두 번째 지문의 후반부를 보면 "We implore fellow Hampshire residents to help us make our case" 부분에서 지역 주민들에게 이 문제를 함께 논의하자고 요청하고 있다.

어휘 patronize 애용하다 public transportation 대중교통 cause 대의명분 ease 덜어주다 traffic congestion 교통 체증

DAY 19

본문 p.338

| 1 (A) | 2 (A) | 3 (A) | 4 (C) | 5 (C) |

어휘 renowned 유명한, 저명한 insight 통찰력 admission fee 참가비 disruption 혼란 press kit 기자 회견 자료집 first come, first served 선착순 outlook 전망 marvelous 놀라운 magnificent 엄청난 commitment 약속

1-5

아시아 태평양 비즈니스 투자 워크숍
홍콩 시립 오디토리엄
11월 11일 화요일

이 워크숍은 아시아 태평양 지역 비즈니스 투자에 관한 최신 동향을 논의하기 위해 마련된 전문 워크숍입니다. 아시아 태평양 지역은 전 세계에서 가장 빠르게 성장하는 시장 중 하나입니다. 저명한 연사들이 다양한 주제에 대해서 그들이 가진 통찰력을 공유할 것입니다. 참가자들은 워크숍에 참가하기 위해 이름을 등록해야 합니다. 참가하길 희망하는 사람들은 이메일 registration@asiapacificworkshop.com로 참가를 10월 11일 당일 혹은 그 전까지 확정해야 합니다. 참가비는 무료입니다.

워크숍 기간 동안 혼란을 피하기 위해 최소 30분 일찍 도착해 주시기 바랍니다. 참가자들은 보도 자료집과 자료를 등록 데스크에서 수령하실 수 있습니다. 각 워크숍에 좌석이 한정되어 있기 때문에 참가는 선착순으로 이루어질 것입니다.

시간	발표자	워크숍 제목
오전 9:30	Martial Graham	시장 전망과 경제 전망
오전 11:00	Coman Lee	전략적 투자
오후 12:00	오찬	
오후 1:00	Tachibana Sato	당신의 미래를 위한 오늘의 계획
오후 2:30	Antonio Griezman	강력한 투자 기초 구축
오후 4:00	Xiu Ying Wang	투자 의사 결정에서 위기 관리

발신자: w.xiuying@wanginvestment.com
수신자: rashford@asiapacificworkshop.com
제목: 11월 워크숍
일자: 10월 3일

Rashford 씨께,

이런 훌륭한 워크숍의 일원이 될 수 있게 된 점에 대해 깊은 감사의 말씀을 드립니다. 제가 알기로는 엄청난 수의 사람들이 11월에 있을 행사에 참석한다고 들었습니다. 이번 행사가 아시아 태평양 지역에 있는 사람들과 기업에게 엄청난 영향을 끼칠 것이라 확신합니다.

제가 이 글을 쓴 이유는 다음 달에 있을 연설 일정 조정 여부를 여쭤보기 위해서입니다. 제가 받은 일정에 따르면 제가 마지막 발표자입니다. 안타깝게도 제가 홍콩에서 점심 식사 이후에 중요한 약속이 있습니다. 그래서 늦어도 11시 반에는 행사장을 떠나야 합니다. 이미 주최자인 David Solanke 씨에게 해당 내용을 알려 드렸습니다. 그러나 아마도 제가 제대로 전달해 드리지 못한 것 같습니다. 그래서 만약 가능하다면 일정을 변경해 주시고 수정된 자료를 가급적 빨리 모두에게 배포 바랍니다.

Xiu Ying Wang

1
해석 참가자들에게 권고되는 것은 무엇인가?
(A) 행사장에 일찍 오기
(B) 등록비를 온라인으로 지불하기
(C) 개인 여행 보험 준비하기
(D) 워크숍 동안 휴대폰 끄기

해설 팸플릿 두 번째 문단 초반에 힌트가 나온다. 혼란을 피하기 위해 30분 전에 행사장에 오라고 했으므로 정답은 (A)이다.

2
해석 경제 전망에 대해서 연설할 사람은 누구인가?
(A) Martial Graham
(B) Coman Lee
(C) Tachibana Sato
(D) Antonio Griezman

해설 일정에서 경제와 관련된 내용을 찾아야 한다. 경제 전망을 뜻하는 economic perspective는 economic outlook, economic forecast, economic prospect와 같은 표현이다. 따라서 정답은 (A)이다.

3
해석 Wang 씨는 워크숍에서 언제 발표하기를 원하는가?
(A) 오전 9시 반
(B) 오전 11시
(C) 오후 1시
(D) 오후 2시 반

해설 연계 지문 문제이다. 원래는 4시에 예정되어 있었지만 점심 식사 이후에 약속이 있고 그 때문에 최소한 11시 반에 출발을 해야 한다. 따라서 9시 반 연설이 유일하게 할 수 있는 시간대이다. 따라서 정답은 (A)이다.

4
해석 Wang 씨에 대해 알 수 있는 것은 무엇인가?
(A) 홍콩에 거주한다.
(B) 워크숍 주최자이다.
(C) 워크숍 동안에 약속이 있다.
(D) 최근에 연설 주제를 바꿨다.

해설 (A), (B)는 없는 내용이고, 연설 주제를 바꾼 적은 없다. 이메일에서 약속이 있어 연설 순서를 바꿔 달라고 요청했으므로 정답은 (C)이다.

5
해석 Wang 씨가 Rashford 씨에게 요청한 것은 무엇인가?
(A) 참가비 확인
(B) 호텔 승인 받기
(C) 이벤트 서류 업데이트
(D) 워크숍 위치 변경

해설 이메일 제일 마지막에 일정을 변경하고 수정된 일정을 모두에게 배포해 달라고 요청했다. 따라서 (C)가 정답이다.

DAY 20

본문 p.340

| 1 (C) | 2 (C) | 3 (C) | 4 (B) | 5 (C) |

어휘 tricky 까다로운 focus on ~에 초점을 맞추다 optimize 최적화하다 be subject to ~의 대상이다 regarding ~에 관한 instructor 강사 highly-intensive 매우 강도 높은 bridge the gap 간극을 메우다 consist of ~로 구성되다 evaluation 평가 psychotherapist 심리 상담사 certificate 인증서 sign up 등록하다

1-5

Jason Madison 대학교 커뮤니케이션 센터

커뮤니케이션에 문제가 있나요? 커뮤니케이션을 얼마나 잘하고 있나요? 인간 관계라는 것은 놀랍지만 때로는 무척 복잡합니다. 타인과의 관계를 이해하고 향상시키는 창의적인 방법을 발견하세요.

이틀에 걸쳐 진행되는 이 쌍방향 프로그램은 여러분의 커뮤니케이션 능력과 사람과의 관계, 업무 관계를 최적화하는 데 초점을 둘 것입니다. 수업은 Jason Madison 대학교 커뮤니케이션 센터의 최근 새롭게 단장한 리서치 랩에서 목요일과 금요일, 오후 5시에서 7시까지 이뤄질 것입니다. 본 프로그램에 관심이 있는 분들은 하나의 과정 혹은 두 개 모두 등록할 수 있습니다. 각 과정은 참가자의 수에 따라 변경될 수 있습니다. 수강료는 Jason Madison 대학교 커뮤니케이션 센터 사무실이나 학교 홈페이지 www.jmu.edu/communicationcenter/programs/payment를 통해 지불할 수 있습니다. 프로그램과 관련한 문의 사항은 강사 Russel Wilson 씨(r.wilson@jmu.edu)에게 문의 바랍니다.

커뮤니케이션 프로그램 리스트
매우 강도 높은 2일 프로그램의 일정은 다음과 같습니다.
과정 1 – 4월 30일
대인간 차이 좁히기 & 적극적 경청 능력
과정 2 – 5월 1일
보디랭귀지 읽기 & 관리 능력 향상

일정	과정 1	과정 2	둘 다 수강
Jason Madison 대학교 학생	20달러	35달러	40달러
타 학교 학생 & 비학생	30달러	45달러	50달러
4월 5일 이후 등록	40달러	55달러	70달러

본 프로그램은 그룹 토론과 숙련된 심리 치료사의 평가 세션으로 구성되어 있습니다. 참가 인증서가 제공될 것입니다.

발신자: Adrian Monro〈amonro1212@ucla.edu〉
발신자: Russel Wilson〈r.wilson@jmu.edu〉
제목: 커뮤니케이션 프로그램 문의
일자: 4월 10일

Wilson 씨께,

4월 30일에 있을 프로그램에 관해 질문 드립니다. 등록하기에 아직 늦지 않았으면 좋겠습니다. Jason Madison 대학교에 다니는 친구에게 이 프로그램에 대해서 방금 들었습니다. 커뮤니케이션 스킬을 향상시키는 방법을 배우는 것에 관심이 있습니다. 과정 1에 빈자리가 있는지 확인 바랍니다. 과정 2에도 관심이 있지만 졸업 시험 때문에 이 프로그램에는 아쉽지만 참가를 할 수 없습니다. 다음 프로그램 일정에 대해서도 알려주시면 감사하겠습니다.

감사합니다.
Adrian Monro

1
해석 공지의 목적은 무엇인가?
(A) 프로그램 일정을 확인하기 위해
(B) 새로운 학생들을 환영하기 위해
(C) 수업을 홍보하기 위해
(D) 문제에 대한 해결책을 제시하기 위해

해설 커뮤니케이션 향상 프로그램을 알리기 위한 것이므로 (C)가 정답이다.

2
해석 Jason Madison 대학교 커뮤니케이션 센터에 대해 알 수 있는 것은?
(A) 월요일을 제외하고 매일 문을 연다.
(B) 대학교 바깥에 있다.
(C) 최근에 리모델링 되었다.
(D) 대학생들만 사용할 수 있다.

해설 공지문의 두 번째 문단에서 recently renovated라는 표현이 나온다. 따라서 정답은 (C)이다.

3
해석 Monro 씨가 프로그램에 지불할 비용은 얼마인가?
(A) 20달러
(B) 35달러
(C) 40달러
(D) 70달러

해설 연계 지문 문제이다. Monro 씨가 이메일을 보낸 일자를 보면 4월 10일, 즉, 해당 학생 여부와 상관없이 4월 5일 이후 등록에 해당한다. 이메일 내용을 보면 과정 1만 참가할 수 있다는 내용이 나온다. 따라서 정답은 (C)이다.

4
해석 Monro 씨는 이 프로그램을 어떻게 알게 되었는가?
(A) 광고를 통해
(B) 친구를 통해
(C) 게시판을 통해
(D) 심리 상담자를 통해

해설 이메일에서 Jason Madison 대학교에 다니는 친구에게 프로그램에 대해 들었다고 했으므로 정답은 (B)이다.

5
해석 Monro 씨는 무엇에 대해 묻고 있는가?
(A) 등록비
(B) 프로그램 시간 일정
(C) 참가 가능성
(D) 프로그램 변경

해설 이메일에서 과정 1에 관심이 있는데 너무 늦은 것은 아닌지 말하고 빈자리 있는지 확인해 달라고 했다. 따라서 정답은 (C)이다.

Actual Test

본문 p.344

Part 5

101 (A) 102 (D) 103 (A) 104 (A) 105 (A)
106 (C) 107 (C) 108 (B) 109 (B) 110 (B)
111 (D) 112 (C) 113 (B) 114 (D) 115 (C)
116 (B) 117 (C) 118 (D) 119 (C) 120 (B)
121 (A) 122 (D) 123 (B) 124 (D) 125 (C)
126 (B) 127 (C) 128 (D) 129 (B) 130 (D)

Part 6

131 (B) 132 (C) 133 (B) 134 (C) 135 (A)
136 (D) 137 (B) 138 (C) 139 (D) 140 (D)
141 (B) 142 (B) 143 (C) 144 (A) 145 (A)
146 (B)

Part 7

147 (B) 148 (C) 149 (A) 150 (D) 151 (C)
152 (D) 153 (A) 154 (C) 155 (C) 156 (C)
157 (C) 158 (D) 159 (D) 160 (A) 161 (C)
162 (A) 163 (C) 164 (A) 165 (B) 166 (B)
167 (B) 168 (C) 169 (B) 170 (A) 171 (D)
172 (C) 173 (A) 174 (B) 175 (A) 176 (D)
177 (C) 178 (D) 179 (A) 180 (A) 181 (D)
182 (C) 183 (B) 184 (A) 185 (B) 186 (D)
187 (D) 188 (D) 189 (D) 190 (C) 191 (B)
192 (C) 193 (D) 194 (B) 195 (A) 196 (B)
197 (C) 198 (A) 199 (C) 200 (A)

Part 5

101
해석 Kirkwood Manufacturing 사의 Carl이 전화하면 바로 저에게 알려 주세요.

해설 동사 inform 뒤에 목적어가 와야 하므로 목적격 대명사인 (A)가 정답이다.

어휘 inform 알리다 right away 당장, 바로

102
해석 Park 씨의 일정은 꽤 빡빡하지만, 여전히 새로운 직원들을 감독하고 훈련시킬 시간을 냈다.

해설 schedule을 수식하는 적절한 형용사를 찾는 문제이다. (A) '잘못된', (B) '확실한', (C) '이른'은 문맥상 어색하다.

어휘 supervise 감독하다 train 교육하다 employee 고용인 tight 빡빡한, 꽉 찬

103
해석 New York행 788편은 Los Angeles에서 예상치 못한 기계 문제로 인해 2-3시간 늦게 출발했다.

해설 (A) later는 부사로 쓰일 때 숫자(a couple of hours) 뒤에 쓰여서 '~ 뒤에, 나중에, 후에'의 뜻이므로 정답이다. 또 than을 보고 비교급 later를 정답으로 고를 수도 있다.

어휘 take off 이륙하다 expect 기대하다 due to ~때문에 mechanical 기계적인 lately 최근에

104
해석 West Munster Street와 Saint Jose Avenue는 모두 다음 주 수요일에 지방 정부가 시행하는 정기 안전 검사로 인해 폐쇄될 것이다.

해설 both A and B의 상관접속사가 되기 위해서는 (A) and가 들어가야 한다. 이때 A와 B의 품사가 같아야 하는 점에 유의한다.

어휘 avenue 거리 regular 정기적인 inspection 검사 local 지역의 government 정부

105
해석 Beeler Office Supplies는 신제품을 위한 공간을 마련하기 위해 향후 두 달 동안 다른 품목에 할인을 할 것이다.

해설 동사 will be offering 뒤에 목적어가 와야 하는데, discount는 가산 명사이기 때문에 복수 형태로 쓰인 (A)가 정답이다. 단수 형태인데 관사가 없는 (B)는 오답이다.

어휘 office supplies 사무용품 room 공간 product 제품

106
해석 지역 음식 박람회와 토론회에 참석하는 데 관심이 있는 사람들은 4월 5일까지 등록해야 한다.

해설 동사가 2개(are, register)이므로 접속사가 필요하고, 빈칸부터 symposium까지 형용사절로 묶어서 앞의 대명사 those를 수식하므로 (C)가 정답이다. Those는 뒤에서 수식하는 구 혹은 절이 있으면 "~하는 사람들"이라는 뜻으로 쓰인다.

어휘 participate 참여하다 local 지역의 fair 박람회, 축제 symposium (학술) 토론회 register 등록하다

107
해석 Steve Otis 씨는 단 2년 만에 Chicago 지점의 지점장으로 승진되었다.

해설 빈칸에 들어갈 동사로 (C)가 가장 적절하다. (A) 시도하다 (B) 지원하다 (D) 동의하다

어휘 regional 지방의 branch 지점 promote 승진시키다

108
해석 미국의 안전 기준에 따라, UBS Engineering은 기계의 오일 양을 정기적으로 확인해야 한다.

해설 조동사(should)와 동사원형(check) 사이에 부사가 와야 하므로 정답은 (B)이다.

어휘 in compliance with ~에 따라 safety standard 안전 기준 fluid 유체 machinery 기계(류) regularize 규칙화[합법화]하다

109
해석 당신이 참고하기 위해 최근에 발행된 장비 보험 증서를 설명하는 서류가 첨부되었다.

해설 빈칸은 equipment insurance policy를 수식하는 분사로 (B)가 가장 적절하다.

어휘 equipment 기구 insurance 보험 policy 정책 for one's reference 참고를 위하여

110
해석 직원들을 위해서 간단한 식사를 제공하는 구내식당과 더불어 1층에 간이식당이 있다.

해설 빈칸에 들어가기 가장 적절한 전치사는 (B)이다. 접속부사인 (C)와 접속사는 (D)는 소거하고, (A)와 (B) 중에 해석을 통해서 정답을 찾을 수 있다.

어휘 serve 제공하다 casual 간단한, 가벼운 snack stand 간이식당 ground floor 1층 just as 꼭 ~처럼 in addition to ~에 더하여

111
해석 선임 재무상담사 직책에 지원하기 위하여 지원자들은 인사과에 최소 2개의 추천서를 제출해야 한다.

해설 전치사 of 뒤에 명사가 와야 하므로 (D)가 정답이다. a letter of recommendation은 '추천서'라는 뜻이다.

어휘 senior 고위의 applicant 지원자 submit 제출하다 personnel department 인사과

112
해석 기술문서 작성 세미나에 참여하기를 원하는 사람들은 늦어도 1월 3일까지 등록해야 한다.

해설 who부터 seminar까지 빈칸을 수식하는 형용사절로 빈칸에는 주어 역할을 할 명사 또는 대명사가 와야 한다. (A) 목적격 대명사, (B) 소유대명사, (D) 접속사이기 때문에 오답이며, (C) anyone은 긍정문에서 '어떤 사람이라도'라는 뜻으로 쓰이고 단수 취급하므로 정답이다.

어휘 attend 참석하다 register 등록하다 no later than 늦어도 ~까지는

113
- 해석: 공휴일 작업 일정표가 이미 회사의 인트라넷에 게시되었으므로 서면으로는 배부되지 않을 것이다.
- 해설: 빈칸에 접속사가 와야 하는데 (A), (C)는 전치사이며 (D)는 전치사 혹은 부사이다. 두 문장 사이의 인과관계를 고려해도 (B)를 정답으로 고를 수 있다.
- 어휘: post (안내문 등을) 게시[공고]하다 distribute 나누어 주다, 배부하다 regardless of ~에 상관없이 in case of ~의 경우

114
- 해석: 직원들의 생산성을 향상시키기 위한 회사의 헌신은 성과에 유익한 영향을 미칠 것으로 예상된다.
- 해설: 품사 문제로 빈칸에는 명사 effect를 수식하는 형용사 (D)가 와야 한다.
- 어휘: commitment 헌신 productivity 생산성 workforce 노동자 effect 영향 performance 성과, 실적 benefit 혜택, 이득 beneficial 유익한, 이로운

115
- 해석: 오늘 주문된 상품들은 영업일 3일 이내에 주문서에 표기된 주소로 배달될 것이다.
- 해설: (A) toward는 '~무렵에'라는 의미의 시간의 전치사로 쓰일 수 있지만 뒤에 시점을 나타내는 명사만 올 수 있다. 빈칸에 가장 자연스러운 전치사는 (C)이다.
- 어휘: deliver 배달하다 order form 주문서 business day 영업일, 평일 apart from ~외에는, ~을 제외하고

116
- 해석: 주문 내역의 정확한 배달 날짜는 당신이 웹 사이트에서 선택한 배송 방법에 따라 달라진다.
- 해설: 빈칸은 동사 자리로 (B)가 정답이다. (A)는 주어와 수 일치가 되지 않아 답이 될 수 없고, 자동사인 depend on을 수동태로 표현한 (D)도 오답이다.
- 어휘: exact 정확한 method 방법 select 선택하다 depend on ~에 달려 있다, ~에 의해 결정되다

117
- 해석: 연간 주주 회의에서 Mellone Corporation의 대표 이사인 Rio 씨는 유럽 시장으로의 회사 확장에 대해 개요를 설명할 계획이다.
- 해설: 빈칸에는 전치사 on 뒤에 들어가는 명사이면서 동시에 뒤에 오는 명사인 expansion을 목적어로 받는 동사의 성질을 가지는 동명사 (C)가 들어가야 한다.
- 어휘: annual 매년의 stock holder 주주 expansion 확장 outline 개요를 서술하다; 윤곽을 보여주다

118
- 해석: Phil Airlines와 Air Beijing이 하나의 항공사로 점진적으로 통합되었기 때문에 비행 일정표에 약간의 변화가 있을 것이다.
- 해설: integrate A into B는 'A를 B로 통합하다'라는 표현으로 (D)가 정답이다.
- 어휘: gradually 점진적으로 integrate 통합시키다 single 단 하나의, 단일의

119
- 해석: 소프트웨어 개발자들이 대부분 독립적으로 일하기 때문에 주간 직원 회의가 그들이 서로 협력할 수 있는 유일한 방법이다.
- 해설: 전치사 with 뒤에는 명사 혹은 대명사가 와야 한다. each other (=one another)는 '서로'라는 의미를 가진 대명사로 정답은 (C)이다.
- 어휘: mostly 주로 independently 독립적으로 collaborate with ~와 협동하다

120
- 해석: 7월 5일에 British Broadcasting은 전 세계의 아마추어 공연 예술가들을 소개하기 위한 새로운 프로그램을 시작할 것이다.
- 해설: 빈칸은 명사 program을 수식하는 형용사(분사) 자리인데, 문맥상 (B)가 정답이다. dedicate A to B는 'A를 B에 바치다' 또는 'A를 B의 용도로 사용하다'라는 의미가 있다.
- 어휘: broadcasting 방송 showcase 소개하다 amateur 비전문가 perform 공연하다

121
- 해석: 전 직원은 내부 기밀 정보에 대한 회사의 새로운 정책을 따르도록 부탁받았다.
- 해설: 빈칸 뒤에 목적어가 아닌 전치사 with가 있으므로 문맥상 (A)가 가장 자연스럽다.
- 어휘: firm 회사, policy 정책, internal 내부의, classify ~로 분류하다 comply with ~에 순응하다, 따르다

122
- 해석: 상업 지구에서 멀지 않은 Amici라는 이탈리아 식당은 고객들에게 저녁을 대접하기에 훌륭한 장소이다.
- 해설: 전치사 문제로 far from은 '~로부터 멀다'이므로 (D)가 정답이다.
- 어휘: district 지역 client 고객

123
- 해석: 감독자들이 송장에 서명하기 전에 건설 현장에 도착한 자재를 철저하게 조사할 것을 권한다.
- 해설: 앞의 전치사가 at이므로 장소를 의미하는 복합명사가 와야 하는데 construction site가 건설 현장이라는 복합명사이므로 정답은 (B)이다.
- 어휘: advisable 권할 만한, 바람직한 supervisor 관리자 inspect 검사하다 thoroughly 철저하게 construction 건설 invoice 송장 site 현장 industry 산업

124
- 해석: 〈Style and Trends〉지의 여름 호에 실리기 위해서 사업 분석가들이 작성한 기사들은 마감일 전에 제출되어야 한다.
- 해설: 전치사 문제로 '여름 호에 실리기 위해서'라는 의미로 (D)가 가장 적절하다.
- 어휘: article 기사 analyst 분석가 issue (간행물) 호 inclusion 포함 submit 제출하다

125
- 해석: Simon Sea Food의 맨체스터 지점은 바쁜 여름 성수기를 준비를

도와줄 6명의 종업원을 고용하였다.

해설 six servers로 문장이 끝났으므로 빈칸에는 수식어구가 들어가야 한다. to부정사로 동사가 부사가 될 수 있으므로 정답은 (C)이다.

어휘 assist 돕다 prepare for ~를 준비하다

126

해설 TRI Airlines를 이용하는 모든 승객은 비행기를 기다리는 동안에 배터리 충전기를 사용해도 좋다.

해설 be welcome to는 '~하는 것을 기꺼이 받아들이다, 환영하다'라는 뜻이므로 정답은 (B)이다.

어휘 passenger 승객 recharger 충전기

127

해설 연례 검사 기간에 비상대피 계획에 어떤 문제도 없었으므로 이번에는 시설에 어떤 변화도 없을 것이다.

해설 빈칸에 올 적절한 접속사를 고르는 문제로 부사인 (D)는 제외하고, (A)~(C) 중에서 해석을 통해서 정답을 도출한다. 따라서 (C)가 정답이다.

어휘 establishment 시설 evacuation 대피 annual 연간 inspection 검사, 점검

128

해설 인천 세계 어린이 축제의 각 행사는 120석으로 제한되고, 선착순으로 채워진다.

해설 a first-come first-served basis은 '선착순'이라는 뜻이므로 빈칸에 올 단어는 (D)이다.

어휘 limited to ~으로 한정된 first-come first-served 선착순 custom 관습 basis 기준

129

해설 마케팅 부의 비서인 Evans 씨는 회의 일정의 변경 사항을 직원들에게 알리는 일을 담당한다.

해설 advise A of B는 'A에게 B를 알리다'라는 뜻으로 문맥상 (B)가 정답이다. 이런 형태로 많이 쓰이는 동사로는 inform, assure, convince, notify 등이 있다.

어휘 administrative 관리상의 be responsible for ~에 책임이 있는 advise 알리다

130

해설 Harada 씨의 경력이 너무 인상적이어서 Fukui 공장의 관리직으로 채택되었다.

해설 so ~ that 사이에 올 형용사를 고르는 문제로, 의미상 (D)가 가장 자연스럽다. (A)가 '자격을 갖춘'이라는 뜻일 때는 대부분 사람을 설명하는 형용사로 쓰인다.

어휘 background 배경 managerial 경영[관리]의 plant 공장 qualified 자격이 있는 knowledgeable 많이 아는 impressive 인상적인

Part 6

131-134

Vana Novak, 비품 과장
Realto Auto Store
515 S. Chamboard

Novak 씨에게,

Western Wheel & Tire의 혁신적인 사람들이 개발한 놀라운 새 타이어 모델을 소개하기 위해 편지를 쓰고 있습니다. 현재 사용하고 계신 브랜드에 상관없이 새로운 SX 250 타이어를 사용해 봐야 하는 이유를 설명해 드리고 싶습니다.
무엇보다도, 이미 긍정적인 고객 피드백을 상당히 많이 받았기 때문에 저희 Western Wheel & Tire는 SX 250가 시장에서 가장 유망한 모델이라는 것을 알고 있습니다. 게다가 SX 250는 불과 몇 달 전에 출시되었음에도 불구하고 현재 국내에서 가장 잘 팔리는 타이어입니다.
아마도 열광적인 후기가 매우 궁금하실 겁니다. 더 많은 정보는 동봉된 팸플릿에서 찾아보실 수 있습니다.

Devin Di Promo
마케팅 에이전트

어휘 remarkable 놀랄만한 the best-selling 가장 잘 팔리는 enclosed 동봉된

131
해설 문맥상 '~와 상관없이'가 가장 적절하므로 (B)가 정답이다.

132
해설 빈칸 뒤에 tire model이라는 명사가 있으므로 형용사인 (C) promising이 빈칸에 가장 적절하다.

133
해설 문맥상 타이어의 장점을 추가로 소개하고 있기 때문에 (B)가 가장 적절하다.

134
해설 (A) SX250은 현재 온라인으로 구매할 수 없습니다.
(B) Western Wheel & Tire에 300달러를 기부할 수 있습니다.
(C) 아마도 열광적인 후기가 매우 궁금하실 것입니다.
(D) 고객 서비스 센터는 월요일에서 토요일까지 운영합니다.

해설 빈칸 뒤에서 더 많은 정보는 팸플릿에서 볼 수 있다고 했으므로 어떤 정보와 관련된 내용이 와야 한다. 따라서 열광적인 후기에 대해서 언급한 (C)가 정답이다.

135-138

발신: Barry Scott 〈b.scott@huntington.com〉
수신: Huntington 전 직원
날짜: 10월 15일
제목: 시 선거

선거가 다가오면서 전 직원이 투표할 것을 독려하는 바입니다. 투표함으로써 여러분의 의견을 표출할 수 있습니다. 전 도시 및 주 선거일 때는 특히 그렇습니다. 여러분 상당수가 자녀가 있고 투표할 시간이 없다는 점을 이해합니다. 좀 더 높은 투표율을 독려하고 여가 시간을 제공하기 위한 방편으로 10월 26일인 다음 주 금요일에 전원에게 반차를 제공하려고 합니다. 여러분이 지지하는 후보를 위해 아침에 투표하고, 오후 1시 전에 출근하세요. 이 정도면 모두가 투표하고 점심을 먹을 충분한 시간이 될 것입니다.
모두 이 시간을 투표하는 데 이용하기를 바랍니다. 이미 투표를 하신 분들은 오전 휴식 시간을 즐기십시오.

Barry Scott
인사부장
Huntington International

어휘 urge 강력히 권고하다, 독려하다 vote 투표하다 citywide 전 도시의 encourage 독려하다 voter turnout 투표율 take advantage of ~을 이용하다

135
해설 주어진 빈칸에는 동사 urge의 목적 보어로 to부정사를 써야 하므로 정답은 (A)이다.

136
해설 주어진 문장의 빈칸에는 접속사가 와야 하는데 understand 뒤의 목적어절을 이끌어야 하므로 접속사인 (D) that이 가장 적절하다.

137
해설 a higher voter와 호응하는 단어로 (B)가 가장 적절하다. voter turnout은 '투표율'이라는 뜻이다.

138
해설 (A) 출구조사에서 이번 선거가 접전이 될 것이라고 예측합니다.
(B) 투표를 하지 못하는 사람들은 상관에게 보고 바랍니다.
(C) 이 정도면 모두가 투표하고 점심을 먹을 충분한 시간이 될 것입니다.
(D) 직원들이 심각한 교통 체증에 갇혀 있습니다.

해설 빈칸 앞에서 오후 1시까지 출근하라고 했으므로 시간적인 여유가 있음을 알 수 있다. 따라서 정답은 (C)이다.

139-142

주변 주거지의 강력한 반대에도 불구하고 Orange County 공항의 건설은 완공되었다. 새로운 공항은 Newport Beach 자택 소유자 협회로부터의 끈질긴 반대에도 불구하고 개항될 예정이다. 항공 운항이 시작되면, 거주민들의 반발이 더욱 거세질 것으로 예측된다.
Orange County는 Orange County 공항(SNA)의 완공에 완강한 입장을 보였는데, 이는 Los Angeles 국제공항(LAX)으로 착륙하는 불편함을 피하길 원하는 주민들에게 SNA 공항이 훌륭한 대안이기 때문이다. Orange County 행정 위원회는 항공사들이 보다 조용한 엔진과 소음 방지 기술을 탑재한 최신 비행기를 사용할 것이기 때문에 소음 증가는 상대적으로 별로 심각하지 않을 것이라는 입장이다. 위원회는 1억 달러 규모의 새로운 시설의 개항을 일반 사람들이 넓은 마음으로 이해해줄 것을 요구하고 있다. Orange County에 일자리, 상업, 관광이 창출될 것이며 모두에게 이익이 될 것이다.

어휘 construction 건설 despite ~에도 불구하고 vehement 격렬한 objection 반대 opposition 반대 predict 예측하다 resident 주민 pertinacious 완강한, 끈질긴 resolute 단호한 alternative 대안 minor 작은 facility 시설

139
해설 기사의 내용은 주민들이 공항 건설을 반대하는 것이므로 문맥상 가장 적절한 것은 (D)이다.

140
해설 반대(opposition)와 어울릴 수 있는 형용사는 (D) fierce이다.

141
해설 기술적으로 소음을 줄이려고 노력했으므로 소음 문제는 상대적으로 (relatively) 심각하지 않을 것이므로 정답은 (B)이다.

142
해설 (A) 이 시설은 자연재해로 인해 심각하게 손상을 입었다.
(B) Orange County에 일자리, 상업, 관광이 창출될 것이며 모두에게 이익이 될 것이다.
(C) 수용 능력이 지난달에 비해서 5퍼센트 증가할 것이다.
(D) 항공사가 그 건설을 이유로 파업에 돌입할 것이다.

해설 앞에서 넓은 마음으로 이해해 달라는 내용이 나오는데 빈칸에는 그 이유에 해당하는 내용이 나오는 것이 가장 적절하다. 따라서 정답은 (B)이다.

143-146

발신: 인사부
수신: Patrick Robinson, 인사부 차장
제목: 필요한 직위에 외국인 고용

아시다시피 우리 회사는 다양한 직위에 능력 있는 공학자와 과학자를 고용하는 데 어려움을 겪어 왔습니다. 국내에서 많은 지원자를 뽑을 수 있는 반면, 공학과 과학 분야에 전문화된 직위에 충원을 못하고 있습니다. 교육 프로그램이 있기는 하지만, 인력 부족이 심각합니다. 우리는 이 문제를 해결하기 위해 직원들이 제안을 해주길 원합니다. 직원들은 제 개인 이메일 주소로 아이디어를 보낼 수 있습니다. 회사가 고려하고 있는 하나의 방법은 공학자들과 과학자들의 해외 고용입니다. 최근의 비자 규정은 더 많은 미국 회사들이 높은 수준의 전문 지식을 갖춘 외국인을 고용하고 후원할 수 있도록 하고 있습니다.

어휘 recruit 모집하다 qualified 자격이 있는 various 다양한 candidate 후보 domestically 국내에서 shortage 부족 resolve 해결하다 submit 제출하다 via 통하여 regulation 규정 sponsor 후원하다

143
해설 부족한 인력난을 해결할 수 있는 방법 중 하나는 훈련 프로그램(training program)이다.

144
해설 전치사 for 뒤에 명사가 와야 하므로 빈칸에 들어갈 것은 명사형인 (A)이다.

145
해설 (A) 회사가 고려하고 있는 하나의 방법은 공학자들과 과학자들의 해외 고용입니다.
(B) 회사는 다음 달에 본사를 이전할 계획입니다.
(C) 인사과에서 더 많은 직원을 고용할 계획입니다.
(D) 우리 회사는 경쟁 회사들과 비교해 경쟁 우위를 가지기 위해 노력하고 있습니다.

해설 지문 초반에 공학자와 과학자를 고용하는 데 어려움을 겪고 있다고 했다. 제목에서도 알 수 있듯이 하나의 방법으로 외국인 고용에 대한 내용이 나와야 함을 알 수 있다. 따라서 (A)가 정답이다.

146
해설 문맥상 전문 지식을 갖춘 노동력을 구해야 하므로 소유를 나타내는 전치사 (B) with가 적절하다.

Part 7

147-148

쿠폰
Oriental Express 중식당
저녁 특별 메뉴
5.59달러+세금 (정가 6.75달러)
선택사항

| #1 브로콜리를 곁들인 소고기 옥수수, 마늘밥과 레몬 혹은 사과 파이와 함께 제공 | #2 스프링 랩 데친 줄기 콩과, 볶음밥, 레몬 혹은 사과 파이와 함께 제공 | #3 사천식 닭 요리 상추와 밥, 레몬 혹은 사과 파이와 함께 제공 |

주 중 오후 5시에서 9시까지 이용 가능
쿠폰 원본만 사용 가능
1인 1매 사용 가능
본 쿠폰에 명시된 선택 사항에만 사용 가능

어휘 serve 제공하다 blanch 데치다 indicate 나타내다 exclusively 오로지, 독점으로

147
해설 쿠폰에 대해 언급된 것은 무엇인가?
(A) 전체 메뉴에 있는 모든 요리에 사용 가능하다.
(B) 한 번만 사용할 수 있다.
(C) 유효 기간은 30일이다.
(D) 커플에게만 적용된다.

해설 Limit one per customer라고 언급되어 있는 것을 보아 1명당 1번만 사용될 수 있다는 것을 알 수 있으므로 (B)가 정답이다. 쿠폰에 제시된 요리만 선택 가능하므로 (A)는 틀렸고, (C)와 (D)는 언급되지 않았다.

148
해설 특별요리 가격에 포함되어 있는 <u>않은</u> 것은 무엇인가?
(A) 밥
(B) 디저트
(C) 음료
(D) 채소

해설 (A)에 해당되는 것은 garlic rice와 fried rice, (B)는 lemon or apple pie, (D)는 lettuce와 string beans이다. (C)에 대한 내용은 없다.

149-151

PERTH (2월 2일)
Perth의 Ocean Breeze 호텔은 3개월간 영업을 중지한 이후에 새로운 주인과 함께 다시 문을 엽니다.

한때 유명했던 호텔의 인기는 사그라졌고, 호텔이 다시 일어설 수 있을지는 불확실합니다. 그 호텔을 운영했던 예전의 주인들은 무료 아침 식사나 주차와 같은 서비스와 시설을 없애고 객실 요금을 인상하기로 결정했습니다. 숙박료는 20% 인상되었고, 동시에 호텔 직원은 줄어들었습니다. 이로 인해 애초에 Ocean Breeze 호텔

을 행락객 사이에 유명하게 했던 동급의 서비스를 받지 못하는 것에 대해 점점 많은 고객들이 실망하게 되었습니다. 6개월 전에 호텔을 인수한 새로운 소유자들은 호텔을 원래대로 돌려놓기 위해 Randolph Morehouse와 계약을 체결했습니다. "호텔의 품질을 낮추면서 더 많은 돈을 벌고자 했던 소유자들의 이전 결정은 엄청난 실수"라고 말한 Morehouse의 최근 인터뷰를 인용하자면 "지금부터 고객들은 훌륭한 커피와 차 서비스뿐만 아니라 가벼운 아침 식사를 무료로 제공받으실 겁니다. 더 중요한 것은 저희가 매우 합리적인 가격으로 대리 주차 서비스를 제공할 것이며, 물론 모든 객실에 무료 인터넷 서비스도 제공할 예정이라는 사실입니다."라고 합니다. 그는 또한 서쪽에 위치한 상당수의 오래된 객실이 완전히 재단장을 하였고, 로비도 더 훈훈하고 매력적인 모습으로 완전 개조를 했다고 말했습니다. Morehouse는 Ocean Breeze 호텔이 다시 한 번 행락객과 출장객을 위한 장소가 될 것이라는 점에 매우 자신감을 가지고 있습니다.

어휘 popularity 인기 once-famous 한때 유명한 diminish 약해지다 take over 인수하다 room rate 객실요금 amenity 소모품 및 서비스용품 in the first place 첫째로 sacrifice 희생하다 continental breakfast 빵, 잼, 버터, 커피 등으로 이루어진 가벼운 아침 식사 reasonable cost 합리적인 비용[가격] undergo 변천하다 refurbishing 재단장 facelift 개조 inviting 매력적인 renovation 개조 inauguration 개업 decline 하락

149

해석 기사의 주제는 무엇인가?
(A) **사업의 주요 개선 사항**
(B) 건물 개조에 대한 미래 계획
(C) 새로운 호텔의 개업
(D) Perth의 관광객 수 감소

해설 주제 문제로 전체적인 내용을 이해한 후 주제를 찾아야 한다. 지문의 초반을 읽고 주제가 잡히지 않으면 지문을 다 읽은 후 마지막에 주제 문제를 푸는 것도 시간을 아끼는 방법이다. 호텔이 경영진 교체와 경영진 실수로 어려움을 겪은 후에 정책 변경을 시행하는 내용이 나오므로 (A)가 정답이다.

150

해석 Morehouse는 어떤 사람인가?
(A) 식당업자
(B) 전문 여행자
(C) 인테리어 디자이너
(D) **호텔 관리자**

해설 세부 사항을 확인하는 문제로 the new owners contracted Randolph Morehouse to put the hotel back on the map라고 언급된 후에 Morehouse와의 인터뷰를 통해 호텔의 변화 내용이 나오고 있으므로 (D)가 정답이다. 객실 및 로비 개조와 서비스 개선 등이 언급되어 있으므로 (C)는 정답이 될 수 없다.

151

해석 Ocean Breeze 호텔의 서비스로 명시되지 <u>않은</u> 것은 무엇인가?
(A) 따뜻한 음료
(B) 발레 파킹
(C) **할인된 객실요금**
(D) 편안한 로비

해설 excellent coffee and tea service, offering valet parking, lobby has had a compete facelift라고 언급되어 있으므로 호텔의 서비스로 명시되지 않은 것은 (C)이다.

152-153

Renato Butland [오후 3:45]
고칠 부분이 있는지 매년 차량 점검을 해 주셔서 정말 감사드립니다.

Natalie Green [오후 3:46]
아니에요. 제가 좋아서 한 일인데요.

Renato Butland [오후 3:49]
그런데 이 차를 팔려고 해요. 새로 태어날 가족 때문에 큰 차량이 필요해서요.

Natalie Green [오후 3:52]
축하드려요! 차량 외관, 내부 모두 깨끗하고 관리가 잘 되어 있기 때문에 구매자들이 이 차를 매우 좋아할 것이라고 확신해요.

Renato Butland [오후 3:53]
하지만 움푹 들어간 부분이 있는데 차량 재판매 가치를 올리기 위해서라도 수리가 필요해요.

Natalie Green [오후 3:54]
문제 없어요. 그건 제가 할 수 있어요.

Natalie Green [오후 3:57]
제가 아는 친구 중 한 명이 중고자동차 판매상이에요. 명함을 찾아 볼게요. 연락해서 견적을 요청하실 수 있을 거예요.

Renato Butland [오후 3:59]
고마워요.

어휘 exterior 외부 not to mention ~은 말할 것도 없고 dent 움푹 들어간 곳 estimate 견적

152

해석 Butland 씨에 대해서 알 수 있는 것은?
(A) 차량 판매점에서 일한다.
(B) 엔지니어다.
(C) 움푹 파인 부분을 고칠 수 있는 사람을 알고 있다.
(D) **집안에 아기가 태어날 것이다.**

해설 3시 49분 대화에서 아기가 태어나기 때문에 큰 차가 필요하다고 했다. 따라서 (D)가 정답이다.

153

해석 오후 3시 54분에 Green 씨가 "문제 없어요"라고 쓸 때 그 의도는 무엇인가?
(A) **차에 있는 움푹 파인 부분을 없앨 수 있다.**
(B) Butland 씨에게 차 재판매 가격에 대해서 알려줄 수 있다.
(C) Butland 씨를 위해 차를 시장에 내놓을 수 있다.
(D) 차량의 상태를 고려하여 차를 파는 데 동의한다.

해설 글을 통해 Green 씨의 직업이 차량을 수리하는 엔지니어임을 알 수 있다. 바로 앞에서 차 수리가 필요하다고 했으므로 문제가 없다는 것은 이것을 수리할 수 있다는 의미이다. 따라서 정답은 (A)이다.

154-155

발신: alerts@greatwesterncred.com
수신: gladysquigley@musthaveitshop.com
날짜: 4월 13일
제목: 자동 공지 – 답신 불가

저희는 최근 귀하의 Great Western 적립 예금 계좌에서 자금 이체 요청을 처리했습니다.

거래 세부 내역
날짜 및 시간
4월 27일 2시 20분

이체 금액
900.00달러

입금 계좌 종류
자유입출금

상기 이체에 실수가 있다면 최대한 빨리 Great Western Credit Union으로 연락 주세요. 저희 고객 서비스부는 1-805-555-9807 번으로 고객님을 위해 24시간, 365일 도와 드립니다. 저희 웹 사이트 www.greatwesterncred.com/customerservice를 통해서도 연락하실 수 있습니다.

어휘 process 처리하다 request 요청 transfer 이체 fund 자금 transaction 거래 assist 돕다 around the clock 24시간 내내 procedure 절차 operation 운영 available 이용 가능한

154

해석 이메일의 목적은 무엇인가?
(A) 자금 거래에 관한 정보를 주기 위해
(B) 입출금 계좌에 대해 묻기 위해
(C) 은행 수수료 지불을 요청하기 위해
(D) 신규 절차를 설명하기 위해

해설 주제를 찾는 문제로 이메일 초반에 명시된 Transaction Details를 통해 이체 거래에 대한 내용을 자동으로 알려 주는 것이므로 (A)가 정답이다.

155

해설 Great Western Credit Union의 고객 서비스 부서에 대해 명시된 것은 무엇인가?
(A) 운영 시간을 변경했다.
(B) 이메일을 통해 연락 가능하다.
(C) 언제든지 이용 가능하다.
(D) 새로운 웹 주소가 생겼다.

해설 Our customer service department can assist you around the clock, 7 days a week라는 내용을 통해 (C)임을 알 수 있다.

156-157

여러분, 안녕하세요?

전 직원은 친환경 기술에 중심을 둔 우리의 새로운 제품에 대한 서비스 연수에 참가하기를 바랍니다. 연수는 6월 25일 Stratford 호텔에서 열릴 예정입니다. 숙박, 주차, 식사와 참가비는 전 직원에게 완전히 제공될 예정입니다.

여러분이 모임 장소에 정시에 와야 하기 때문에 아래의 일정을 꼼꼼히 읽어 주십시오. 발표에 부정적인 영향을 미칠 수 있기 때문에 행사장에 늦게 들어오지 마세요.

행사 일정: 오전 8시 – 커피를 마시기 위해 아래층의 Red 회의실에서 만나기

오전 8시 15분 – 회의 연설자들과 만나기
오전 9시 – 회사 발표를 위해 Green 회의실에서 만나기
오후 12시 – Oasis 레스토랑에서 제공되는 점심 식사를 위한 휴식
오후 2시 – 회사 발표 재개
오후 5시 – 해산

어휘 service training 서비스 연수 green technology 친환경 기술 compensation 보상금, 보수 venue 장소 impact 영향 dismissal 해산 appreciate 고마워하다 outcome 결과 participant 참가자 notify 알리다 beforehand 미리

156

해석 회의의 목적은 무엇인가?
(A) 신규 사업 파트너 소개하기
(B) 직원들의 성공적인 성과에 감사하기
(C) 새로운 기술을 소개하기
(D) 직원들을 위한 디너 파티를 주관하기

해설 초반에 '전 직원이 친환경 기술에 중심을 둔 우리의 새로운 제품에 대한 서비스 연수에 참여하기 바란다'는 내용이 언급되어 있으므로 회의의 목적으로 가장 적절한 것은 (C)이다.

157

해석 회의에 대해 사실인 것은 무엇인가?
(A) 이 행사에 참석하기를 바라는 사람은 식비를 지불해야 한다.
(B) 주차 공간이 없는 관계로 참석자들은 대중교통을 이용해야 한다.
(C) 회의는 9시간 정도 진행될 것이다.
(D) 회의에 늦는 사람은 관리부에 미리 알려야 한다.

해설 (A) 식사는 제공된다고 했으며, 주차에 대한 내용이 언급되었고, (B)에 대한 직접적인 내용은 없다. (D)와 관련된 내용도 언급되지 않는다. 연수가 오전 8시에 시작해서 오후 5시에 끝나는 것으로 보아 대략 9시간 동안 진행되는 것을 알 수 있으므로 (C)가 정답이다.

158-160

NAM
북미 원주민 박물관
122 Onondaga St, Biloxi, Mississippi 90876

3월 7일 토요일로 예정된 우리의 연간 축제와 도자기 판매 행사에 당신을 초대합니다. 지역 부족들이 기부한 다양한 도자기들 중에 선택해보세요. 모든 수익금은 박물관 유지비로 사용됩니다.

북미 원주민 박물관은 19세기 부족장인 Wes Studi의 역사적인 가치가 있는 집에 20년 전에 세워졌습니다. 박물관은 고대 토템 기둥과 북미 원주민들의 훌륭한 전시품으로 구성된 놀라운 컬렉션입니다. 산책로와 돌로 만든 정원이 멋지게 조경된 이 시설에 포함되어 있습니다.

도자기 판매 당일에는 박물관 골동품 상점에 10% 할인이 제공됩니다. 운영 시간은 화요일부터 목요일까지는 오전 10시부터 오후 7시까지이며, 주말에는 오전 11시부터 오후 4시까지입니다. Anna Crow의 삽화가 4월 6일까지 박물관 정규 운영 시간에 현재 전시 중입니다. 더 많은 세부 사항은 www.nativeamericanmuseum.org를 방문해 주세요.

어휘 ceramic 도자기 wide selection 폭 넓은 선택 tribe 부족, 부족 집단 upkeep 유지 tribal chief 부족장 showcase 보여 주다 artifact 공예품 landscaped 조경된 waive 청구되다

158
해설 무엇이 광고되고 있는가?
(A) 한 시설의 개장
(B) 모금 행사
(C) Wes Studi의 강의
(D) 북미 원주민 공예품의 판매

해설 광고문에서 광고하는 제품이나 대상은 주로 글의 초반에 나온다. ~ inviting you to participate in our yearly festival and ceramic sale이 광고 대상이며 선택지에서 ceramic이 artifacts로 패러프레이징되어 있는 것을 볼 수 있다. 따라서 정답은 (D)이다.

159
해설 북미 원주민 박물관에 관하여 명시된 것은 무엇인가?
(A) 메인 갤러리를 리모델링하고 있다.
(B) 조각품 강의를 진행한다.
(C) 최근에 조경을 했다.
(D) 과거에 사유지였다.

해설 state나 mention 관련 문제는 패러프레이징이 중요하다. The Native American Museum was founded two decades ago in the historic home of nineteenth century tribal chief Wes Studi.에서 박물관이 예전에는 historic home, 즉 private residence였다는 것을 알 수 있으므로 (D)가 정답이다.

160
해설 3월 7일에 북미 원주민 박물관에서 일어나지 않을 일은 무엇인가?
(A) 지역 부족들에 의한 기부가 있을 것이다.
(B) 할인이 제공될 것이다.
(C) 박물관은 오후 4시까지 열려 있을 것이다.
(D) 삽화가 전시될 것이다.

해설 (B)는 A 10 percent discount will be given by the museum's curio shop에서, (C)는 11:00 A.M. to 4:00 P.M. on weekends, (D)는 Illustrations by Anna Crow is the current exhibition에서 사실 여부를 확인할 수 있다.

161-163

수신: Sara Smith〈sarahsmith@aol.net〉
발신: customerservice@azureshoppe.co.au
날짜: 2월 21일, 오전 7시 3분
제목: 구매 번호 110958

Smith 씨께,

Sydney 최고의 양품점인 Azure RYW Shoppe에서 주문하신 세부 사항은 다음과 같습니다.

구매번호 110958

설명
품명: 튜브 톱   사이즈: 2   색깔: 고동색
수량: 1개   단가: 42달러   총액: 42달러

현 상태
재고가 있고, 배송 준비 중

세금을 포함한 중간 합계: 42달러
배송비: 3달러
행사 가격 적용: 우수고객 20% 할인
신용 카드 ********6793으로 결제: 21.90달러

구매하신 제품들은 3일에서 5일 이내에 배송될 것입니다. 배송 확인 번호와 선적 번호는 제품이 저희 창고를 떠날 때 당신에게 이메일로 전송될 것입니다. 주문에 변경 사항이 있다면, www.azureshoppe.co.au에 방문하셔서 고객님의 계정에 비밀번호를 입력하시고, 늦어도 오늘 오후 4시까지 변경을 완료해 주십시오.

Azure Shoppe에서 구매해 주셔서 감사하고, 고객님을 모시게 되어서 기쁩니다.

고객 서비스 팀
Azure Shoppe

어휘 maroon 고동색, 밤색 quantity 수량 unit price 단가 in stock 재고로 loyalty 충성심 warehouse 창고 allow 허용하다 merchandise 상품 confirm 확인하다 gift certificate 상품권 refund 환불 entitle 자격을 주다

161
해설 이메일을 보낸 이유는 무엇인가?
(A) 상품의 반납을 허용하려고
(B) 남성복을 소개하려고
(C) 최근에 구매한 제품을 확인하려고
(D) 새로운 지점의 개점을 알리려고

해설 지문 초반에 Listed are the details of your order라는 언급과 이하 주문 상품의 세부 사항 및 가격, 배송 관련 정보 등이 나오기 때문에 정답은 (C)이다.

162

해설 Smith 씨는 Azure Shoppe로부터 5일 이내에 무엇을 받게 될 것인가?
(A) 이메일
(B) 상품권
(C) 환불
(D) 영수증

해설 The items you bought will be shipped within three to five days.라고 하면서 A tracking and shipping number will be e-mailed to you when the item leaves our warehouse.라고 했다. 주문한 물품이 창고를 떠나는 시점이 배송 나가는 시점이라고 볼 수 있으므로 이때 이메일을 받게 될 것이다. 따라서 정답은 (A)이다.

163

해설 Smith 씨에 대해 추정되는 것은 무엇인가?
(A) 무료 배송을 받는다.
(B) 주문을 변경했다.
(C) **Azure Boutique에 계정이 있다.**
(D) Azure Boutique의 신규 고객이다.

해설 추론 문제로 type in your password for your account라고 언급된 부분이 있는 것을 보아 Smith 씨는 이미 Azure Shoppe의 계정을 가지고 있는 것으로 추론할 수 있으므로 정답은 (C)이다.

164-167

발신: Susanna Bogart
수신: Caitlyn Love
날짜: 12월 29일
제목: 여행 비용

Love 씨에게

판매부에 12월 여행 비용 상환을 신청하고 있는데, 방금 각 판매 직원의 식대를 입력하는 것이 더 이상 가능하지 않다는 점을 알게 되었습니다. 대신에 사이트에는 식사에 대한 일일 고정액이 명시되어 있습니다.

거의 모든 판매 직원이 사무실 밖으로 외근을 가고, 정기적으로 점심이나 저녁 식사를 하면서 협상을 하기 때문에 식대는 대부분 우리 직원만의 식대뿐만 아니라 고객 비용 또한 포함되어 있습니다. 이러한 상황 때문에 우리 판매 직원들은 아마도, 아니 꼭 사이트에 적힌 고정액보다 훨씬 더 많은 비용을 지불합니다.

이 식사가 우리 직원들을 위한 것이라는 점과 우리의 예산이 고객의 식대를 포함해야 한다는 점을 고려해 주십시오. 회계부에 계시니, 실제 영수증을 제출하며 좀 더 면밀한 평가를 해 주실 것을 정중하게 요청합니다.

Susanna Bogart
선임 영업 사원
영업부

어휘 file for ~을 신청[제기]하다 reimbursement 상환, 배상 accessible 접근[이용] 가능한 notably 특히 ought to ~해야 하다, ~할 의무가 있다 cover 포함하다, 다루다 cordially 다정하게, 진심으로 evaluation 평가 encounter 맞닥뜨리다, 부딪히다 negotiate 협상하다 deal 거래

164

해설 Bogart 씨가 직면한 문제는 무엇인가?
(A) **웹 사이트에서 특정 데이터를 입력할 수 없다.**
(B) 식대 변제는 없을 것이다.
(C) 고객과의 거래 협상 마감일을 맞추지 못했다.
(D) 직원들이 영수증 제출하기를 여전히 기다리고 있다.

해설 대부분 지문에서 문제를 먼저 이야기 하고 그 이후에 문제에 대한 해결책을 말하는 경우가 많다. 이 문제에서도 개별 식대를 데이터로 넣을 수 없는 것이 문제이므로 정답은 (A)이다.

165

해설 이메일에 따르면, Bogart 씨가 원하는 것은 무엇인가?
(A) 고객과의 식사 준비하기
(B) **고객과 함께 먹은 식사 비용을 되돌려 받기**
(C) 새로운 휴가 규정 제안하기
(D) 영업 회의 일정을 다시 잡기

해설 지문에서 고객과 함께 한 식사 비용이 정해진 식대를 훨씬 초과하는 경우가 많기 때문에 Bogart 씨는 식사에 든 초과 비용도 회사로부터 돌려받기를 원한다. 따라서 정답은 (B)이다.

166

해설 Love 씨는 누구일까?
(A) 컴퓨터 기술자
(B) **회계원**
(C) 영업 부장
(D) 행사 운영자

해설 Love 씨는 이메일 수신자로 이메일 마지막 부분에 회계부에 있다는 것이 언급되어 있는 것을 보아 주어진 선택지 중에 (B)일 가능성이 제일 크다.

167

해설 [1], [2], [3], [4]로 표시된 부분 중에서 다음 문장이 들어가기에 가장 알맞은 곳은?

"이러한 상황 때문에 우리 판매 직원들은 아마도, 아니 꼭 사이트에 적힌 고정액보다 훨씬 더 많은 비용을 지불합니다."

(A) [1]
(B) **[2]**
(C) [3]
(D) [4]

해설 due to this circumstance라는 표현은 앞의 내용이 원인이 되어서 뒤에 이어질 내용이 결과에 해당할 때 쓸 수 있는 표현이다. 사이트에 고정액이 명시되어 있는데 그보다 더 많은 돈을 지불하고 있는 이유에 대한 내용이 먼저 나와야 한다. 두 번째 문단에서 직원들이 외근을 하고 고객을 만나면 금액치를 초과할 수밖에 없다고 했다 따라서 (B)가 가장 적절하다.

168-171

Joshua Jamison [오후 3:30]
안녕하세요. 인사과 Joshua Jamison입니다. 도움이 좀 필요합니다.

Gabriel Sanches [오후 3:31]
안녕하세요. 물론이죠. 무엇을 도와 드릴까요?

Joshua Jamison [오후 3:32]
금요일 오후에는 문제없이 인트라넷에 접속을 했었는데요. 오늘 아침에는 제 온라인 계정으로 접속을 할 수 없었어요.

Gabriel Sanches [오후 3:34]
불편을 끼쳐 드려 죄송해요. 아마도 주말 동안 업데이트가 있어서 그럴 겁니다. 오전 5시까지 작업을 마쳤어요.

Joshua Jamison [오후 3:35]
하지만 제가 여러 번 정확하게 비밀번호를 입력을 할 때마다 항상 잘못된 비밀번호라고 해요. 왜 이렇게 되는 건가요? 이게 제 컴퓨터 만의 문제인지 아니면 전사 차원의 문제인지 모르겠어요.

Gabriel Sanches [오후 3:38]
몇몇 직원들이 얘기하기로는 "접근 거부" 메시지를 받았다고 하더라고요. 이에 대해서 제가 작업을 하고 있어요. 이 문제에 대해서 이미 검토하고 있으며 확실하게 말씀드릴 수 있는 것은 이 시스템 결함은 오늘까지는 해결이 될 거에요.

Joshua Jamison [오후 3:40]
알겠습니다. 하지만 제가 5시 전까지 중요한 프레젠테이션 준비로 인트라넷에서 서류를 다운로드 해야 하거든요.

Gabriel Sanches [오후 3:42]
확률은 50대 50이에요. 몇몇 직원들이 말하길 비밀번호를 초기화하면 계정 접속에 도움이 된다고 해요. 만약에 이게 안 되고 급한 도움이 필요하시다면 Jason Lee에게 연락 바랍니다. Jason Lee가 프리젠테이션 한 시간 전에 다운로드 할 수 있게 도와줄 거에요.

어휘 access 접속하다 get access to ~에 접속하다 company-wide 전사 차원의 examine 검토하다 glitch 결함 resolve 해결하다 reset 초기화하다

168
해석 Sanches 씨는 누구인가?
(A) 은행원
(B) 디자이너
(C) 컴퓨터 기술자
(D) 사회자

해설 사내에서 접속 문제가 생겼을 때 연락을 하게 되는 사람이다. Sanches 씨가 접속 문제를 해결할 수 있는 방법을 알려 주고 있으므로 그가 컴퓨터 기술자임을 알 수 있다. 따라서 정답은 (C)이다.

169
해석 Sanches 씨에 따르면 Jamison 씨가 언제 다시 계정에 접속할 수 있는가?
(A) 금요일
(B) 오후 4시
(C) 오후 5시
(D) 내일 아침

해설 후반부에서 오후 5시까지 프레젠테이션 때문에 자료를 다운로드 받아야 한다고 했다. 그래서 Jason Lee가 한 시간 전에 다운로드 할 수 있도록 도와 준다고 했으므로 4시에 다시 접속할 수 있음을 알 수 있다. 따라서 정답은 (B)이다.

170
해석 Sanches 씨가 Jason Lee를 언급한 이유는 무엇인가?
(A) Jamison 씨를 도와줄 수 있다.
(B) IT부서 책임자이다.
(C) 현재 프리젠테이션을 위해 외근 중이다.
(D) 인트라넷 연결 문제에 대한 책임이 있다.

해설 give a hand는 help와 같은 표현이다. 따라서 정답은 (A)이다.

171
해석 오후 3시 38분에 Sanches 씨가 "작업을 하고 있어요"라고 쓸 때 그 의도는 무엇인가?
(A) 프리젠테이션을 위해 컴퓨터를 설치한다.
(B) 비밀번호를 변경하는 방법을 배운다.
(C) 웹브라우징과 홈페이지 구축에 대한 작업을 한다.
(D) 인트라넷에 접속할 수 있는 방법을 찾고 있다.

해설 여기서 working은 access denied message에 대한 문제를 해결하고 있다는 뜻이다. 다시 인트라넷에 접속할 수 있는 방법을 찾는 것이므로 정답은 (D)이다.

172-175

Smithtown의 주요 도로 복원 공사

6월 25일 Smithtown – 내일부터 Smithtown의 주요 도로들은 공사에 들어갈 것이고, 도로 공사가 끝날 때까지 4개월 동안 차선 통제와 새로운 교통 통제 계획이 예정되어 있습니다.

전체 계획은 세 단계로 시행될 것으로 계획되었습니다. 첫 번째 단계에서 6번가와 7번가 사이의 Grimes 도로의 3킬로미터가 재포장될 것입니다. 이 포장 공사는 대략 2주 후에 끝날 것으로 예정되어 있습니다. 첫 번째 단계가 완료될 때까지, 도로의 차선 1개만 월요일부터 금요일, 오전 9시에서 오후 5시까지 이용 가능하므로 교통부는 운전자들에게 9번가를 지나서 Grimes 도로와 만나는 Victor 도로를 이용하라고 권고하는 바입니다.

두 번째 단계는 7월 말에 시작됩니다. 두 번째 단계가 진행되는 동안에 Dickenson 고속도로에 5A 출구의 확장이 진행될 것입니다. 새롭게 건축된 Vintage Five 아웃렛이 1월 이래로 수많은 쇼핑객을 끌어들이고 있기 때문에, 이 공사로 더 많은 교통량을 소화할 수 있을 겁니다. 출구로 향하는 교통 혼잡을 완화하기 위해서 5A 출구 램프에 2개의 선로가 추가 건설될 예정입니다. 더불어, 램프의 길이도 연장되고 똑바로 되어 운전자들은 더 안전한 운전을 즐길 수 있게 될 것입니다.

45세인 Leonard Cooper는 Pasadena Road에 사는 주민인데, Pasadena Road는 5A 출구에서 500미터 반경에 있습니다. Cooper 씨는 이 계획을 주시해 왔고, 도로를 개선하는 것이 현명한 계획이라는 것을 알게 되었습니다. 그는 "이 변화는 몇 달 전에 행해졌어야 해요. 램프가 확장되기 때문에, 운전자들은 이전에 램프가 자동차의 속력을 줄이거나, 끼어드는 차량에게 양보하기에 충분히 길지 않았던 때보다 고속도로를 빠져나가기가 쉬워질 거에요."라고 말했습니다. 그리고 나서 그는 "제가 듣기로는 확장 공사가 2달까지 걸릴 수 있다고 하는데 기다릴 가치가 충분하다고 생각합니다."라고 첨언했습니다.

마지막 단계는 추가적인 도로 보수 작업인데, 예를 들어 밤에 보이는 운전 표지판을 야간 운전자들을 위해서 설치하고, 손상을 입은 가드레일이나 포장도로를 복구하는 작업 등입니다. 날씨 상태에 따라서, 교통부는 전체 공사 과정이 빨라야 10월 26일에 끝날 것으로 예상합니다.

Fred Peters

어휘 lane closure 차선 폐쇄 execute 실행·수행하다 phases 단계 boulevard 도로 repave 다시 포장하다 insist 고집하다, 주장하다 alleviate 완화하다 congestion 혼잡 ramp 경사로 radius 반지름, 반경 initiative 계획 merge 합치다 maintenance 보수, 유지 luminous 어둠에서 빛나는, 야광의 outcome 결과 ease 덜해지다, 덜어주다

172
해석 계획의 의도된 결과물이 아닌 것은 무엇인가?
(A) 쇼핑센터 근처의 교통 혼잡을 완화시키기
(B) 야간에 교통 표지판의 가시성을 더 확보하기
(C) Smithtown의 통행료를 낮추기
(D) 지역 안전 문제를 해결하기

해설 (A), (B), (D)는 지문에 언급되어 있으나, (C)에 대한 내용은 찾을 수 없으므로 정답이다.

173
해석 직원들이 재포장을 어디에서 시작하는가?
(A) Grimes 도로
(B) Victor 도로
(C) Dickenson 고속도로
(D) Pasadena 도로

해설 In the first phase, three kilometers of Grimes Boulevard between Sixth Avenue and Seventh Avenue will be repaved.라고 명시되어 있으므로 정답은 (A)이다.

174
해석 두 번째 단계가 얼마 동안 진행될 것으로 예상되는가?
(A) 2주
(B) 2달
(C) 5개월
(D) 1년

해설 네 번째 문단에서 Leonard Cooper가 언급하는 단계가 두 번째 단계인데 I hear that this expansion will take up to two months라고 했으므로 정답은 (B)이다.

175
해석 [1], [2], [3], [4]로 표시된 부분 중에서 다음 문장이 들어가기에 가장 알맞은 곳은?
"이 포장 공사는 대략 2주 후에 끝날 것으로 예정되어 있습니다."
(A) [1]
(B) [2]
(C) [3]
(D) [4]

해설 pavement work 앞에 This가 있으므로 이전에 '포장 공사'에 대한 내용이 나왔음을 알 수 있다. 두 번째 문단에서 재포장 공사에 대해서 언급되어 있으므로 (A)가 정답이다.

176-180

Windy City 전기 회사
1123 E Branchville St., Chicago, IL 60605

11월 6일
Ronald Chin
237 Faraday Ave. Apt 6
Chicago, IL 60601
계좌번호 56–665–A4

Chin 씨께,

Windy City 전기 회사가 이제 모바일 고지서 지불 시스템을 가지고 있다는 것을 알고 계셨나요? 본 서비스가 6월 1일 시작된 이래로, 서비스를 사용하는 수백 명의 주요 고객들은 고지서를 관리하기 위한 이 전자 공제 시스템에 매우 만족하고 있습니다. 고객님의 은행이 계좌에서 월별 고지서 청구액을 공제할 수 있도록 허용함으로써 매달 직접 추가적인 노력을 들이지 않고서도 매달 고지서를 늦지 않게 지불할 수 있습니다.

등록은 쉽습니다. 간단히 저희의 웹 사이트 http://www.windycityelectric.com/adform에서 찾을 수 있는 서류를 작성하시고, '제출' 버튼을 누르시든지, 도움을 받기 위해 708-555-2234, 고객 서비스 상담 전화로 연락 주세요. 등록이 완료된 후에, 고객님은 고지서를 지불하고 확인할 수 있습니다. 이 기회를 사용하시기를 기대합니다.

Sandra Smith
고객 서비스 매니저

Windy City 전기 회사
월별 고지서
6월

Ronald Chin
237 Faraday Ave. apt 6
Chicago, IL 60601
계좌번호 56–665–A4

마지막 요금 지불은
5월 15일 – 73달러

현재 요금(6월 15일까지 납기)
79달러

다음 번 전기 사용량 측정 날짜
7월 1일

사용량 측정은 정해진 날짜에 되어야 하며, 그렇지 않으면 귀하의 청구 금액은 이전 사용량에 근거해서 계산될 것입니다.

어휘 deduction system 공제 시스템 deduct 공제하다 sign up 등록하다, 가입하다 submit 제출하다 additional 추가적인 charge 비용 reading date 측정 날짜 designated 지정된, 정해진 estimate 평가하다 method 방식 exist 존재하다 adjust 조정하다

176
해석 편지가 Chin 씨에게 전송된 이유는 무엇인가?
(A) 그에게 갱신된 그의 계좌번호를 알리기 위해
(B) 은행을 광고하기 위해
(C) 최근 청구서의 변경 사항을 설명하기 위해
(D) 서비스 가입을 권유하기 위해

해설 전기 회사에서 모바일 청구서 및 결제 시스템을 제공한다고 홍보하며 서비스 사용을 권유하고 있으므로 정답은 (D)이다.

177
해석 편지에서 Windy City 전기 회사에 관해 명시된 것은 무엇인가?
(A) 새 광고 기획안을 작성하고 있다.
(B) 고객서비스 부서를 개선했다.
(C) 고지서를 납부할 수 있는 다른 방법을 제공하고 있다.
(D) 최근 웹 사이트 주소를 변경했다.

해설 181번 문제와 마찬가지로 (C) 고지서를 납부할 수 있는 다른 방법을 제공하고 있다.

178
해석 Smith 씨가 권유한 서비스를 사용하기로 결정한다면, Chin 씨는 무엇을 해야 하는가?
(A) 그녀와 약속을 잡는다.
(B) 적은 진행 수수료를 지불한다.
(C) 그의 가장 최근 청구서 사본을 보낸다.
(D) 완성된 서류를 제출한다.

해설 fill out the form and click "submit"라고 명시된 부분에서 (D)의 내용을 확인할 수 있다.

179
해석 월별 계산서에 Chin 씨에 관해 언급된 것은 무엇인가?
(A) 자동 고지서 시스템이 이용 가능하기 전에 계좌를 가지고 있었다.
(B) 이전 검침일자를 조정해야 했다.
(C) 청구서 중 하나를 늦게 납부했다.
(D) 추가 설치비를 내야 한다.

해설 첫 번째 글에서 서비스 개시일이 6월 1일인 것을 확인할 수 있고, 두 번째 글에서 지난번 납기일이 5월 15일이라고 명시된 것으로 보아 (A)를 알 수 있다.

180
해석 월별 계산서에 따르면, Chin 씨의 다음 요금 납부일은 언제인가?
(A) 6월 15일
(B) 7월 15일
(C) 8월 22일
(D) 9월 1일

해설 두 번째 글에서 현재 요금(current charge)과 납기일이 명시되어 있기 때문에 (A)가 정답이다.

181-185

발신: pcornwallis@dunkirkassoc.com
수신: jdreyfus999@giuk.com
제목: 인터뷰
날짜: 10월 12일
첨부: 직원 설명서

Dreyfus 씨께,

지난주에 Liverpool 직업 박람회에서 저희 부스를 방문해 주셔서 감사합니다. 만나게 되어 반가웠고, Grosvenor International에서 귀하가 쌓은 경력에 깊은 인상을 받았습니다. 우리가 이야기했던 직책에 대해 귀하가 제출한 지원서 감사합니다.

인사부가 귀하의 지원서를 검토했고, 다음 주에 저희 사무실에게 면접을 진행하면 좋겠습니다. 아래에 저희가 면접 가능한 날짜가 나와 있고, 귀하에게 가장 편안한 시간을 선택하시면 됩니다.

10월 21일 수요일	10월 22일 목요일	10월 23일 금요일
오전 9시/오후 3시	오전 10시/오후 1시	오전 9시 반/오후 1시

직원 설명서를 읽어 보시고, 저희 정책에 대한 몇몇 질문에 대답할 준비를 하세요. 면접 후에, 고용 위원회가 상의하고 결정 사항을 귀하에게 늦어도 10월 27일 월요일 이전에 알려 드릴 것입니다. 질문 사항이 있으시면 저에게 알려 주세요.

Paris Cornwallis

수신: pcornwallis@dunkirkassoc.com
발신: jdreyfus999@giuk.com
제목: 답신: 인터뷰
날짜: 10월 13일

Cornwallis 씨께,

Dunkirk and associates에서 면접을 볼 기회를 주셔서 감사합니다. 여러 프로젝트의 컨설턴트로 오랜 세월 일하면서 팀을 운영하는 직업을 갖기를 고대했습니다. 면접 일정에 대해서는 오후 면접이 좋을 것 같아서 3시에 면접을 진행하면 합니다.

그런데 지난주에 언급했던 것처럼 면접에 대해 질문이 하나 있는데요. 저의 능력을 보증해줄 수 있는 사람들의 연락처가 적힌 추천서를 가지고 가야 할지도 모르겠습니다. 전혀 문제가 될 것 같지는 않지만 몇 부를 준비해야 하는지 알고 싶습니다.

미래에 귀하의 회사 일원이 될 수도 있는 기회를 주셔서 감사하며, 다음 주에 뵐 수 있기를 기대합니다.

Julia Dreyfus

어휘 application 지원서 look into 검토하다 policy 정책 reserve 예약하다 reference 추천서, 증빙서류 vouch 보장하다, 인정하다 update 갱신하다 scenery 배경 suitable 적합한

181
해석 Dreyfus 씨는 Dunkirk and Associates의 일자리를 어떻게 찾았는가?
(A) 동료를 통해
(B) 회사의 웹 사이트를 통해
(C) 신문 광고를 통해
(D) 취업 박람회를 통해

해설 첫 번째 메일 도입부에 지난주 직업 박람회 부스에서 만났다는 사실이 언급되어 있으므로 (D)가 정답이다.

182
해설 Dreyfus 씨는 면접 전에 하도록 요청받은 것은 무엇인가?
(A) 경력 샘플을 준비하기
(B) 이력서를 갱신하기
(C) 출판물을 읽기
(D) 신원조사를 받기

해설 직원 설명서를 읽으라고(go through the employee handbook) 명시되어 있으므로 정답은 (C)이다.

183
해설 Deyfus 씨의 면접은 언제 있을 예정인가?
(A) 화요일
(B) 수요일
(C) 목요일
(D) 금요일

해설 면접 일정은 첫 번째 이메일에 나와 있고, 두 번째 메일에서 Deyfus 씨가 오후 3시 면접이 좋을 것 같다고 이야기했다. 3시를 일정표에서 찾으면 (B)이다.

184
해설 Dreyfus 씨가 새로운 직장을 구하고 있는 이유는 무엇인가?
(A) 관리직에 관심이 있기 때문이다.
(B) 이사했기 때문이다.
(C) 환경 변화를 원하기 때문이다.
(D) 더 알맞은 스케줄이 필요하기 때문이다.

해설 두 번째 지문에서 컨설턴트로서의 수년간의 경력 이후에 팀을 운영하는 일을 하고 싶다고 했으므로 (A)가 정답이다.

185
해설 Dreyfus 씨가 문의한 정보는 무엇인가?
(A) 면접관의 이름
(B) 필요한 추천서의 부수
(C) 새 직책에서 맡게 되는 업무
(D) 면접 장소

해설 두 번째 지문에서 추천서를 몇 부 가지고 가야 하는지 묻고 있으므로 (B)가 정답이다.

186-190

Boston Hemisphere 골프 클럽
신규 주민 및 비거주민 신청서

410 Boston Post Rd #34, Sudbury, MA017776
www.bostonhemisphereregolfclub.com, www.bhgolfclub.com

신규 주민 및 비거주민 회원을 위한 신청 절차
1. 오직 Boston Hemisphere의 물리적 경계 내에 기본 거주지가 있어야 거주로 처리됩니다.
2. 필요 서류: 현 공공요금 고지서 혹은 운전 면허증만 가능. 서류는 지원자의 이름과 현 주소를 포함해야 합니다.
3. 새로운 회원은 멤버십 카드를 획득할 때까지 클럽 시설에 대한 이용이 불가합니다.
4. 지불 절차가 진행되면 환불은 불가하고 확인 이메일이 신청자의 이메일 주소로 보내질 것입니다.

월간 회원비	신규 회원 [4월 2일까지]	신규 회원 [4월 2일 이후]	
골프 클럽	600달러	650달러	비거주민에게는 계정에 75달러의 추가 요금이 부과됩니다.
가족 수영장	100달러	125달러	
피트니스 센터	75달러	100달러	

발신자: Eric Dier 〈e.dier@abase.com〉
수신자: Christian Neves 〈c.neves@bhgolfclub.com〉
일자: 4월 25일
제목: 멤버십

Neves 씨께

최근에 Boston Hemisphere 골프 클럽 웹 사이트에서 멤버십 지원 양식을 살펴보았습니다. 제가 이해한 바는 월간 회원비가 Boston Hemisphere 거주자에게는 650달러이며 비거주자는 추가로 75달러를 지불해야 한다는 것입니다. 하지만 제가 확실하지 않은 것은 제가 이 둘 중 어디에 속하는가입니다. 저는 사진작가입니다. 9월에서 1월까지는 Boston Hemisphere에서 거주합니다. 그리고 나머지 기간 동안에는 캐나다에서 거주합니다. 제가 서로 다른 두 지역에 거주하고 있기 때문에 거주자를 위한 멤버십 지원을 미루고 있습니다. 제가 거주자 멤버십 자격이 되는지를 확인 부탁드립니다. 저는 벌써 그 날을 손꼽아 기다리고 있습니다.

감사합니다.

Eric Dier

발신자: Christian Neves <c.neves@bhgolfclub.com>
수신자: Eric Dier <e.dier@abase.com>
일자: 4월 26일
제목: 회신: 멤버십

Dier 씨께,

문의 감사드립니다. 저희 정책에 따르면 Boston Hemisphere에 1년 중 6개월 이상 거주하는 사람에게 거주 회원 자격이 주어집니다. 그렇기 때문에 귀하께서는 아쉽지만 거주자 요금을 적용받으실 수 없습니다.

하지만 저희 골프 클럽의 회원으로 여러 가지 혜택을 누리실 수 있습니다. 회원이 되시면 원하시는 시간에 첫 번째로 예약하실 수 있는 기회가 주어집니다. 그리고 기존 가격에서 25퍼센트가 할인된 가격으로 수영장, 테니스장, 헬스시설 등을 이용하실 수 있습니다. 그리고 골프 레슨, 장비 수리, 식사 및 다과를 회원 분들께 할인된 요금으로 제공하고 있습니다.

저희 클럽 회원 수가 150명으로 제한이 되기 때문에 가능한 한 빨리 지원서를 작성해 주시기 바랍니다. 멤버십은 통상적으로 4월에 마감이 됩니다. 멤버십에 관한 더 많은 정보를 원하시면 저에게 연락해 주시기 바랍니다.

Christian Neves

어휘 resident 거주자 non resident 비거주자 process 절차 solely 오직, 오로지 boundary 경계 utility bill 공공요금 applicant 지원자 obtain 획득하다 confirmation 확인 surcharge 추가 요금 assess 평가하다, 부과하다 account 계정, 계좌 examine 살펴보다, 검사하다 membership dues 회원비 belong to ~에 속하다 hold off ~을 미루다 qualify for ~에 대한 자격을 얻다 inquiry 질문, 질의 be entitled to ~에 대한 자격이 주어지다 amenity 시설 refreshments 다과 fill out 작성하다 with regard to ~에 관한

186

해석 Boston Hemisphere 골프 클럽에 대해 알 수 있는 것은?
(A) 세 종류의 회원이 있다.
(B) 어떠한 정보도 요구하지 않는다.
(C) 회원이 되고 나서 시설에 대한 완전한 접근이 가능하다.
(D) 환불 불가 정책이 있다.

해설 환불이 불가능하다고 했으므로 정답은 (D)이다. 멤버십 카드를 획득하고 나서야 시설을 이용할 수 있다고 했으므로 (C)는 오답이다.

187

해석 Dier 씨가 첫 번째 이메일을 쓴 이유는?
(A) 주소를 정정하기 위해
(B) 골프 레슨을 예약하기 위해
(C) 멤버십을 갱신하기 위해
(D) 추가 정보를 요청하기 위해

해설 첫 번째 이메일에서 멤버십 가입을 미루고 있는 이유에 대해서 설명을 하고 있다. 자신이 거주자인지 비거주자인지에 대해 알려 달라고 했으므로 추가적인 정보를 요청하고 있음을 알 수 있다. 따라서 정답은 (D)이다.

188

해석 회원 혜택으로 언급되지 않은 것은?
(A) 일정 조정 우선권
(B) 장비 수리
(C) 레슨 할인
(D) 사교 모임

해설 두 번째 이메일에 회원의 혜택에 대해서 기술되어 있다. (A), (B), (C)는 다 명시되어 있지만 사교 모임에 대해서는 언급되어 있지 않다. 따라서 (D)가 정답이다.

189

해석 Dier 씨는 멤버십으로 얼마를 지불할 것인가?
(A) 600달러
(B) 650달러
(C) 675달러
(D) 725달러

해설 연계 지문 문제이다. Dier 씨가 이메일을 보낸 날짜는 4월 25일이다. 이메일을 보낸 시점에서 아직 멤버십 가입을 하지 않았기에 4월 2일이 지난 골프 클럽 요금이 적용된다. 또한 거주자가 아니기 때문에 비거주자 추가 요금인 75달러를 추가로 내야 한다. 따라서 650달러에서 75달러를 더한 (D) 725달러가 정답이다.

190

해설 두 번째 이메일에서 Neves 씨가 Dier 씨에게 제안한 것은 무엇인가?
(A) 설문조사 실시하기
(B) 온라인으로 지원서 제출하기
(C) 즉시 멤버십 가입하기
(D) 시설 구경하기

해설 두 번째 이메일 마지막 문단에서 클럽 회원 수가 제한되어 있으므로 가능한 한 빨리 가입하라고 했다. 따라서 정답은 (C)이다.

191-195

Tech Life Magazine
1월, 125호
목차

▶ 50페이지
DES[Digital Electronics Show] 표지 기사
칼럼니스트 Franklin Oliver 씨가 게임에서부터 리포트 정리까지 휴대폰에서 할 수 있는 모든 것에 관한 최고의 75개 어플리케이션에 대해 소개합니다.

▶ 73페이지
온라인 비즈니스
스페셜리스트와 패널리스트가 태블릿 PC의 장단점에 대해서 통찰력을 공유합니다.

▶ 88페이지
2017 DES 최고 제품
칼럼니스트 Henderson Lee 씨가 3,000개 이상의 업체가 DES에서 선보이는 제품에 대해서 알려 드립니다. 이번 행사에서 최고의 제품을 선정했습니다.

▶ 103페이지
패스워드를 재설정하라
오랜 기간 동안 가장 중요한 패스워드를 아직 바꾸지 않았다면 지금이 적기입니다. 올바른 패스워드를 선택하는 최고의 방법이 여기에 있습니다.

▶ 118페이지
비하인드 더 씬
칼럼니스트 David Jeffrey 씨가 내년 가장 기대되는 블루투스 키보드에 대해서 살펴봅니다.

▶ 121페이지
오래된 가전 제품 재활용
칼럼니스트 Damian Miller 씨가 오래된 PC와 전자제품을 새로운 방식 혹은 올바르게 사용할 수 있는 곳에 기부하는 방법으로 증가하는 전자폐기물을 방지하는 방법에 대해서 설명해 드립니다.

[Irish291], 3일 전

〈Tech Life Magazine〉에 대해서 언급할 때 제일 먼저 할 말은 오직 디지털 포맷으로만 가능하다는 것입니다. 이 잡지는 PC는 말할 것도 없고 매우 다양한 주제를 다룹니다. 매우 유익하며 흥미롭습니다. 〈Tech Life Magazine〉이 150페이지 남짓이라는 것을 감안하면 거의 모든 내용이 기술에 대한 정보에 치중하고 있습니다. 제가 만족했던 최고의 기사는 환경과 관련된 주제입니다. 아쉽지만 이 잡지는 구성이 탄탄하지만 링크 옵션의 장점을 이용하지 못하고 있습니다. 그래서 여러분이 클릭 한 번으로 다양한 관련 기사를 쉽게 찾기가 어렵습니다.

발신자: 구독 부서 <customerservice@techlive.com>
수신자: Jane Sinclair <j.sinclair@spx.com>
일자: 5월 2일
제목: 구독 관련

Jane Sinclair 씨께,

저희 〈Tech Life Magazine〉을 최근에 구독해 주셔서 감사드립니다. 구독료와 관련된 문제를 겪으시게 해서 죄송합니다. 비용 청구서는 월마다 보내집니다. 만약 지불하신 이후에 연속으로 청구서를 받으셨다면 저희에게 청구 명서 영수증 사본을 포함해서 우편으로 보내주시기 바랍니다.
구독과 관련된 문제 발생 시 주저 마시고 저희에게 연락해 주시기 바랍니다. 저희 〈Tech Life Magazine〉으로 즐거운 시간 보내시기 바랍니다. 감사합니다.

Alison Brie
구독 부서 매니저

어휘 issue (정기 간행물의) 호 table of contents 목차 cover story 표지 기사 share one's insight on ~에 관한 통찰력을 공유하다 pros and cons 장단점 take a look at ~을 살펴보다 on the rise 증가하는 combat 물리치다 donate 기부하다 a wide variety of 다양한 informative 유익한 be dedicated to ~에 헌신하다, 노력하다 take advantage of ~을 이용하다 navigate 항해하다, 비행하다 bill 청구서, 계산서 consecutive 연속인 encounter 만나다, 마주치다 hesitate 주저하다

191
해석 잡지 중 어떤 섹션이 다양한 전문가의 관점을 포함하고 있는가?
(A) DES 표지 기사
(B) 온라인 비즈니스
(C) 2017 DES 최고의 제품
(D) 비하인드 더 씬

해설 목차 73페이지를 보면 specialist and panelists가 의견을 공유한다는 말을 통해서 다양한 전문가의 관점을 포함하고 있음을 알 수 있다. 따라서 정답은 (B)이다.

192
해석 아직 발매되지 않은 제품에 대해서 말하고 있는 사람은 누구인가?
(A) Franklin Oliver
(B) Henderson Lee
(C) David Jeffrey
(D) Damian Miller

해설 118페이지에서 next year's most anticiapted에서 알 수 있듯이 아직 출시되지 않은 제품에 대해서 언급하고 있는 것을 알 수 있다. 따라서 정답은 (C)이다.

193
해석 리뷰에 따르면 잡지 중 리뷰어가 가장 좋아하는 페이지는 어디인가?
(A) 50페이지
(B) 88페이지
(C) 118페이지
(D) 121페이지

해설 연계 지문 문제이다. 리뷰를 보면 The best article로 시작하는 부분을 통해 정답을 유추할 수 있다. 환경과 관련된 부분에 제일 만족한다는 내용이 나오므로 목차에서 환경과 관련된 부분을 찾아야 한다. 제일

마지막 121페이지에서 증가하는 전자폐기물을 방지하는 내용에 대한 기사가 나온다. 따라서 정답은 (D)이다.

194

해석 리뷰를 보면 이 잡지의 단점은 무엇인가?
(A) 비용이 약간 비싸다.
(B) 구성이 온라인 판에 적절하지 않다.
(C) 발매일이 너무 늦다.
(D) 다양한 주제를 다루지 않는다.

해설 리뷰 제일 마지막 문장에서 이 잡지의 아쉬운 점이 나온다. 구성이 좋지만 온라인 버전의 장점을 살리지 못하고 있다는 말이 나온다. 따라서 정답은 (B)이다.

195

해석 이메일에 따르면 Sinclair 씨가 문의한 것은 무엇인가?
(A) 구독 이중 지불
(B) 배송 지연
(C) 상품 파손
(D) 구독 연장

해설 이메일의 If you receive two consecutive bills에서 볼 수 있듯이 이중 지불에 대해 문의했음을 알 수 있다. 따라서 정답은 (A)이다.

196-200

〈Fairview County Newspaper〉는 오클라호마 시티에서 가장 큰 월간 신문 중 하나입니다. 〈Fairview County Newspaper〉는 월간 판매 부수가 약 1만 2천부입니다. Fairview County Newspaper는 흑백으로 인쇄됩니다. 계절적 요소 또한 가격 책정 시에 고려됩니다. 광고 요율은 자주 변경될 수 있습니다.

저희 신문에 광고를 내기로 결정하셨다면 이미지는 제출 이후에 변경이 불가하기 때문에 보내실 때 신중을 기해 주시기 바랍니다. 정확한 견적을 원하시면 신문 광고 매니저 Susan Schmidt (s.schmidt@fairviewnewspaper.com)에게 연락 바랍니다.

〈Fairview County Newspaper〉 광고 요율 [2월]

사이즈	1호	6호	12호
1/4 페이지	300달러	1,500달러	2,800달러
1/2 페이지	500달러	2,500달러	4,500달러
전체 페이지	1,100달러	5,000달러	9,900달러

발신자: Heidi S. Kim 〈H.S.Kim@ideabox.com〉
수신자: Susan Schmidt 〈s.schmidt@fairviewnewspaper.com〉
일자: 2월 25일
제목: Fairview County Newspaper 광고
첨부 파일: Fairview_County_Newspaper_layout

Schmidt 씨께,

제 광고에 관한 첨부 파일을 확인해 주시기 바랍니다. 귀사에 광고를 하려고 생각하고 있습니다. 하지만 이 광고가 정말 효과가 있는지에 대해서는 확신이 들지 않습니다. 한정된 예산 때문에 신중을 기해야 합니다. 우선 6호에 1/2페이지로 시작하려고 합니다. 현재 가격이 2,500달러로 알고 있습니다. 소규모 사업체를 위한 지역 신문 광고 프로젝트는 정부 보조금을 받는다고 들었습니다. 혹시 할인을 받을 방법이 있을까요? 혹시 있다면 알려 주세요.

감사합니다.

Heidi S. Kim

발신자: Susan Schmidt 〈s.schmidt@fairviewnewspaper.com〉
수신자: Heidi S. Kim 〈H.S.Kim@ideabox.com〉
일자: 2월 26일
제목: 회신: 질문에 대해

Kim 씨에게,

지역 신문에 광고를 하는 것이 과연 가치가 있는지 궁금해 하실 것입니다. 그뿐만 아니라 광고가 실제로 고객에게 전달되는지에 대해서도 궁금해하실 것입니다. 〈Fairview County Newspaper〉에 광고하는 것은 수십만의 Fairview County 가정과 인근 지역사회에 한 달에 한 번씩 알릴 수 있는 가장 효과적인 방법입니다.

안타깝지만 정부에서는 저희 신문에 보조금을 지급하지 않습니다. 좋은 소식은 귀하께서는 신규 고객이시기 때문에 기본 광고 요율에서 20퍼센트 할인된 가격을 제공해 드릴 수 있습니다.

귀하와 거래할 수 있기를 기대하겠습니다.

Susan Schmidt
광고 매니저

어휘 circulation 발행 부수 frequently 자주, 종종 put an ad 광고를 싣다 submission 제출 quote 견적액 place an advertisement 광고를 하다 limited budget 한정된 예산 start out with ~로 시작하다 subsidize 보조금을 주다 worthwhile 가치가 있는 grant support to ~에게 지원금을 주다

196

해석 공지의 목적은 무엇인가?
(A) 구독을 장려하기 위해
(B) 잠정적 고객에게 정보를 제공하기 위해
(C) 신문 월 구독료를 설명하기 위해
(D) 광고를 취소하기 위해

해설 공지에서 신문에 광고를 하게 될 때 금액과 기타 세부 사항에 관한 정보를 제공하고 있다. 따라서 정답은 (B)이다. 돈에 관한 얘기는 나왔지만 월 구독료에 관한 것은 아니므로 (C)는 오답이다.

197

해석 〈Fairview County Newspaper〉에 광고하는 것에 대해 알 수 있는 것은?
(A) 다양한 종류의 색상을 사용한다.
(B) 이미지는 수정 가능하다.
(C) 계절별 요율이 있다.
(D) 전국적으로 유통된다.

해설 색상은 흑백이며, 이미지는 제출 후에는 수정이 불가능하다고 했다. 그리고 이 신문은 지역 신문이다. 계절적 요소가 가격에 영향을 미친다고 했으므로 정답은 (C)이다.

198

해석 첫 번째 이메일에서 Kim 씨가 요청한 것은 무엇인가?
(A) 할인된 광고료
(B) 구독 취소
(C) 광고 구성 변경
(D) 월간 판매 부수

해설 첫 번째 이메일 마지막에서 혹시 할인을 받을 수 있는지 물었으므로 (A)가 정답이다.

199

해석   Kim 씨는 얼마를 내야 할 거 같은가?
(A) 500달러
(B) 1,500달러
(C) 2,000달러
(D) 2,500달러

해설   연계 지문 문제이다. 6호에 1/2페이지에 대한 가격이 첫 번째 이메일에도 나와 있지만 2,500달러이다. 두 번째 이메일에서 20퍼센트 할인을 해 준다는 내용을 종합해 보면 2,000달러를 내야 한다. 따라서 정답은 (C)이다.

200

해설   두 번째 이메일, 두 번째 문단 첫 번째 줄의 "주다"와 가장 유사한 의미는
(A) 주다
(B) 인정하다
(C) 받다
(D) 알다

해설   grant는 동사로 쓸 때에 '주다'는 뜻으로 give와 동일한 의미를 가진다. '인정하다'라는 뜻도 있지만 여기에서는 support가 뒤따라 나오기 때문에 적절하지 않다. 따라서 정답은 (A)이다.

토익 한번에 끝내기 RC

신토익 개정판

20일만에 끝내는
가장 빠른 토익 솔루션

- 깔끔한 문제 풀이 전략 & **풍부한 실제 문제** 수록
- 정확하게 핵심만 콕콕 짚어 주는 **문제 해설 포인트**
- 매일매일 **섹션별·단계별 학습**으로 문법, 독해, 어휘 완성

新토익 실전 모의고사의 끝판왕!

• 나혼자 끝내는 新토익 실전서 •

신토익 LC+RC 5회분 + 해설집

신토익 LC+RC 6회분 + 해설집

나혼자 끝내는 新토익 FINAL 실전 모의고사

- ✓ 최신 출제 경향을 완벽 반영한 실전 모의고사 5회분 수록
- ✓ 해설집을 따로 구매할 필요가 없는 LC+RC 합본 실전서
- ✓ 정답/오답 이유, 패러프레이징, 문제의 키워드를 단숨에 파악하는 핵심 강의 해설집
- ✓ 실전용 · 복습용 · 고사장 버전의 3종 MP3

나혼자 끝내는 新토익 기출모의 1200제

- ✓ 한 권으로 끝내는 신토익 실전 모의고사 6회분 수록
- ✓ 해설집을 따로 구매할 필요가 없는 LC+RC 합본 실전서
- ✓ 저자의 노하우를 담아 문제의 키워드를 단숨에 파악하는 알짜 해설수록
- ✓ 실전용 · 복습용 · 고사장 버전의 3종 MP3

나혼자 끝내는 신토익 FINAL 실전 모의고사 | 제이드 김·김선희 지음 | 2018년 5월 출간 | 15,000원
나혼자 끝내는 신토익 기출모의 1200제 | 김랑·박자은·넥서스토익연구소 지음 | 2018년 12월 출간 | 16,000원

나혼자 끝내는 新 토익
파트별 실전 시리즈

PART 1~4 / 5&6 / 7

 온라인 받아쓰기 제공

 저자 직강 무료 음성 강의 제공

 저자 직강 PART 7 공략법 제공

취약한 파트만 집중적으로 공략하자! 파트별 공략 실전 시리즈!

- 최신 출제 경향 반영 파트별 실전 모의고사
- 스스로 점검하고 보완할 수 있는 나혼토 체크 리스트 제공
- 실전용·복습용·고사장 버전 MP3 무료 다운로드
- 어휘 리스트 & 테스트 제공

나혼자 끝내는 신토익 PART 1~4 | 신토익 실전 12회 수록 | 이주은 지음 | 2017년 3월 출간 | 16,000원
나혼자 끝내는 신토익 PART 5&6 | 신토익 실전 12회 수록 | 박혜원·전보람 지음 | 2017년 2월 출간 | 13,000원
나혼자 끝내는 신토익 PART 7 | 신토익 실전 10회 수록 | 이미영·박선영 지음 | 2017년 7월 출간 | 15,000원